Decision Sciences

Designed as an advanced undergraduate or graduate textbook, *Decision Sciences* provides a unified perspective of a rich and varied field. *Decision Sciences* synthesizes current research about different types of decision making, including individual, group, organizational, and societal.

Special attention is given to the linkage between problem finding and problem solving. The principal message emerging from the book is that decision making entails a complex set of processes that need to be understood in detail in order to develop sound prescriptions or policy advice.

Decision Sciences

An integrative perspective

Paul R. Kleindorfer
The Wharton School, University of Pennsylvania

Howard C. Kunreuther
The Wharton School, University of Pennsylvania

Paul J. H. Schoemaker
Decision Strategies International, Chicago

CAMBRIDGE
UNIVERSITY PRESS

Published by the Press Syndicate of the University of Cambridge
The Pitt Building, Trumpington Street, Cambridge CB2 1RP
40 West 20th Street, New York, NY 10011-4211, USA
10 Stamford Road, Oakleigh, Victoria 3166, Australia

First published 1993

Printed in the United States of America

Library of Congress Cataloging-in-Publication Data

Kleindorfer, Paul R.
Decision sciences : an integrative perspective / Paul R. Kleindorfer, Howard C. Kunreuther, Paul J. H. Schoemaker.
  p. cm.
Includes index.
ISBN 0-521-32867-5 (hc). – ISBN 0-521-33812-3 (pbk.)
1. Decision-making – United States. I. Kunreuther, Howard C.
II. Schoemaker, Paul J. H. III. Title.
HD30.23.K46   1993
658.4′03 – dc20   92-45149
                                                                        CIP

A catalog record for this book is available from the British Library.

ISBN 0-521-32867-5 hardback
ISBN 0-521-33812-3 paperback

Contents

To Stephanie, Gail, and Joyce,
and especially our children;
That they may choose wisely

Preface

This book reflects our current and evolving thinking about the field of decision sciences. It is somewhat embarrassing to admit that it has been over 10 years since we first envisioned writing what was originally intended to be a monograph. Had we ever imagined that it would take us so long to complete, it is not clear that we would have ever started on this endeavor. Now that we have finally finished, we are glad that we were not perfectly informed about the convoluted path it would take.

One of the reasons for the hiatus between start and finish has been the burgeoning literature in the field of decision sciences. Many of the recent studies have raised more new questions than they have answered old ones. The other principal factor that has caused the long gestation was the many pleasurable discussions among the three of us, which repeatedly stimulated us to reflect anew on what the field of decision sciences is really all about.

In truth, the field of decision sciences is still in its infancy compared with the many disciplines from which it draws, such as philosophy, economics, sociology, psychology, and even management science. It was only in 1974 that the Decision Sciences Group was formed at the Wharton School. Since that time a number of universities around the country and the world have formed decision sciences centers as well. Each one has its own orientation and flavor, but the basic mission is generally the same: to understand and improve decision making.

Our definition of the field of decision sciences is quite broad and has led us to cover more territory than perhaps should be encompassed in a single volume. However, since we feel it is important to focus on both the problem-finding and problem-solving aspects of decision making, we necessarily touch on many subjects. Specifically, we see an increased need for careful descriptive analyses of the institutional arrangements associated with specific problems as well as the actual decision process itself. Only by understanding this context in detail can one suggest meaningful ways of improving decision making. This descriptive–prescriptive linkage is a central focus throughout the book.

In general, the book examines decision making at multiple levels, starting with individual choice and then moving on to group, organization, and societal levels. Even though we cover each of these areas in separate chapters, we stress at the outset that important nestedness of these levels occurs within problems: For instance, an individual choice is usually embedded in a group or social context that can greatly influence the final action.

Our book can be read on several different planes. For those not familiar with the field of decision sciences, the book is designed to be a broad introduction, as the title suggests. Although not a formal textbook, the book covers many of the decision science concepts in sufficient detail to provide students with the key insights or messages of a particular theory or model. There are no formal proofs in the text itself. However, some that we feel are of critical importance are included in technical appendixes. We also have endeavored to provide a comprehensive set of references for each of the areas discussed that unfulfilled readers can turn to for more meat.

For researchers familiar with many of the concepts of decision sciences, the book presents an alternative framework for analyzing problems. Ours is only one of several ways to approach the field of decision sciences. We are quite partial to this approach, but recognize that it may constrain others. We welcome a dialogue with our colleagues on other ways one can structure and operationalize the area.

For practitioners, this book identifies a number of the pitfalls associated with decision making and suggests ways of improving the process. A variety of contexts is used to illustrate the different approaches. We look forward to gaining more insight from this sample set concerning how to apply these concepts to other problems.

Even though we are pleased to have completed this book at last, we view it as the continuation of a dialogue with our colleagues in the years to come. The field of decision sciences is in an unusually fertile stage of development. We hope our book provides a timely overview and synthesis that may direct our and others' efforts in the most promising directions.

This book owes a great deal to a number of our friends and colleagues, who have contributed their ideas and suggestions to it. In the early stages of this book, Philip Jones was instrumental in convincing us to continue the project. As our work developed, our close colleagues, Jonathan Baron, Colin Camerer, John Hershey, and James Laing, were important in providing detailed suggestions for structuring the ambitious enterprise we had in mind.

We also owe a great debt to many who have commented on various parts of this book and provided their constructive criticism and ideas unsparingly. We would like, in particular, to thank Jonathan Baron, Max Bazerman, David Bell, Gianpiero Bussolin, Colin Camerer, Douglas Easterling, Ward Edwards, Baruch Fischhoff, Bruno Frey, Kenneth Hammond, John Hershey, Robin Hogarth, Eric Johnson, Philip Jones, Daniel Kahneman, Ralph Keeney, Craig Kirkwood, Joshua Klayman, Marc Knez, James Laing, Lola Lopes, George Loewenstein, Gary McClelland, Kenneth MacCrimmon, James March, Stephanie Olen, John Payne, Howard Raiffa, J. Edward Russo, Mark Shanley, Mark Silver, Paul Slovic, Gerald Smith, Richard Thaler, Amos Tversky, W. Kip Viscusi, Donald Wehrung, and Detlof von Winterfeldt.

We are grateful for the assistance of these colleagues and many others unnamed who helped us in structuring our ideas in completing this task. While the traditional exemptions exonerating any of those named from blame apply, we hope this book will serve as a useful reflection and synthesis of the strands of decision science research represented by the work of these scholars.

We also acknowledge the institutional support provided by The Wharton School, the Wharton Center for Risk Management and Decision Processes, and the Graduate School of Business at the University of Chicago. Partial support from NSF Grant #5ES 8809299 is gratefully acknowledged. In particular, we thank Sylvia Dobray, Consuelo Prior, Linda Schaefer, and Marjorie Weiler, who provided invaluable administrative assistance. Judith Farnbach and Cambridge University Press are acknowledged for their helpful editorial advice.

Paul Kleindorfer
Howard Kunreuther
Paul Schoemaker
March 1993

Part I

Introduction

1

The scope of decision sciences

1.1 Introduction

The emerging field of decision sciences is concerned with understanding and improving decision making of individuals, groups, and organizations. At issue is not only how decision makers "solve problems," but also how they came to identify and accept such problems and learn from the results of their actions.

Decision making may be defined as intentional and reflective choice in response to perceived needs. Anthropologists such as Pierre Teilhard de Chardin (1959) consider this ability to reflect and choose as the fundamental characteristic distinguishing man from lower forms of life. While the recognition of this ability may provide the reader with a momentary feeling of superiority, history is also replete with examples of human limitations in decision making. Our purpose in this book is to provide a basis for understanding these limitations as they relate to individual, organizational, and societal decision processes and to use this basis to provide insights as to how such decision processes might be improved.

The dilemmas of choice in the face of an uncertain and complex world have long been the focus of religion, literature, and philosophy. In Western literature, classical epic poems and tragedies depict the gradual evolution of human choice from a metaphorical extension of the will of gods in Homer's epics to the realm of willful, if not always rational, choice in Euripides' tragedies. Writers such as Friedrich Nietzsche and Julian Jaynes have described this emergence during the first millennium B.C. from ritual and metaphor to willful action and reflective choice as a matter of the utmost importance in Western culture. People began to view their actions as something beyond the momentary impulses of their current existence to an evolving, connected whole of past, present, and future. The result of this was the view that people could partially affect, and be held responsible for, their choices. It was to be many centuries, however, before the process of reaching such choices was subjected to systematic analysis.

Religion and moral philosophy provided the early foundations for analyzing choice behavior by setting rules for evaluating the motives and

	DESCRIPTIVE THEORIES	PRESCRIPTIVE THEORIES
Individual	Psychology Marketing Psychiatry Literature	Decision Theory Economics Operations Research Philosophy/Logic
Group	Social Psychology Organizational Behavior Anthropology Sociology	Game Theory Organization Behavior Clinical Psych/Therapy Finance/Economics
Organization	Organization Theory Sociology Industrial Organization Political Science	Planning – Strategy Control Theory/Cybernetics Organization Design Team Theory/Economics
Society	Sociology Anthropology Macro Economics	Legal Philosophy Political Science Social Choice

Figure 1.1. The disciplinary roots of decision sciences

consequences of choice. But it was not until the triumphs of natural science in the seventeenth century that a basis was laid for the systematic investigation of natural phenomena and, much later, of human behavior.

Over the next two centuries, fundamental advances were made in philosophy, economics, biology, psychology, and sociology. Taken together, the result of these studies was a model of the human species as a complicated, evolving organism, embedded in a series of nested social and economic systems. Decision making and choice became areas of immense theoretical and applied interest in many fields. The elaboration and integration of these fields continue. Figure 1.1 lists some of the current disciplines involved in the study of decision sciences today. At the risk of oversimplification, we have divided these fields into two categories of analysis: descriptive and prescriptive. Descriptive analysis refers to how people actually make decisions. Prescriptive analysis indicates how decisions should be made according to a set of well-defined criteria. Prescriptive analysis can range from formal axiomatic theories to more informal approaches for aiding decision making. As we shall see, which prescriptive approach one selects for improving the decision process requires understanding the context and descriptive realities of the situation in question.

At the descriptive level, research in the behavioral sciences has increased our understanding of the role of organization and structure on the decision making process. In particular, significant empirical efforts have been undertaken on procedures used by organizations to resolve conflicts and generate solutions between decision makers with different goals and objectives. Political science has addressed similar issues at the level of governmental and bureaucratic decision making. Psychology provides experimental evidence on the limited ability of decision makers to process information and the systematic biases and simplifying decision procedures people employ. Finally, sociology provides a perspective on the nature of information diffusion processes and the role of social norms in the decision-making process.

At the prescriptive level, economics offers a well-developed paradigm for structuring decision making by individuals and firms. At the societal level, an extensive literature is now emerging that provides guidelines for aiding the public choice process. The fields of management science and operations research arose during World War II and thereafter, with an initial emphasis on improving decision making in military and business organizations. A wide range of optimization models has been developed for the purpose of maximizing profits or minimizing costs for part of the firm's operations. In recent years these techniques have been extended to many areas of societal decision making, such as transportation and energy system planning. Finally, the field of information systems is a product of the computer age. Its primary contribution to decision sciences is in the development of interactive computer models, sometimes referred to as decision support systems, which improve decision makers' ability to evaluate complex decision situations.

In reality, it is not so straightforward to categorize a theory as descriptive or prescriptive. Psychology has been primarily concerned with characterizing individuals' information-processing abilities and identifying systematic biases through field studies and controlled laboratory experiments (descriptive analyses). Based on this understanding of human behavior, there has been research by psychologists in trying to correct these biases (prescriptive analyses). Until recently, research in economics focused almost exclusively on the development and application of models of choice as to how individuals and firms should behave (prescriptive analysis). Today more attention is being given to understanding the impact that imperfect information and misprocessing of data have on the final choices of individuals and the performance of markets (descriptive analysis).

Utilizing concepts from these disciplines, we view the field of decision sciences as integrating descriptive analysis with prescriptive recommendations. Descriptive analysis provides insights on the values, beliefs, and choice processes actually used by decision makers. Prescriptive analysis helps to clarify values and beliefs and suggests ways of improving decision processes using criteria from rational models of choice, such as expected utility theory, as guidelines. The basic framework of this book for integrating descriptive and prescriptive analysis is described at the end of this chapter. We first consider some of the important organizational and technological factors that have affected decision making in industrial societies and then illustrate the problems of interest in this book with some examples.

1.2   Historical developments

It is instructive to consider from a historical perspective why the study of decision making has become increasingly important. The reasons are evident. During the two centuries since the industrial revolution, goods and services available in the market have grown exponentially in variety and complexity. Revolutionary changes in transportation and communication have made economies, both national and international, more tightly interconnected. The workplace has become the realm of science and electronics in place of the manual arts and crafts of two centuries ago. The buildings we live and work in are filled with a bewildering array of labor-saving innovations, which are wonderful when they function properly, and which remind us of an earlier, simpler age when they don't. When one considers all of this, it is clear that the pace of life has quickened. There has been a tremendous increase in the complexity and frequency of decisions confronting individuals and organizations as they seek to understand and cope with their social and economic environment.

Consider individual decision making. Two centuries ago, most decisions revolved around one's survival and associated daily family activities (excluding a few aristocrats who had other concerns). The situation is vastly different now. Today's teenager is already making decisions on complicated consumer items such as cars and computers that were not even invented a century ago. The price of all this is longer educational preparation for life and a much deeper division of jobs and expertise once maturity is reached. Thus, as Alvin Toffler has pointed out, our personal lives have become exceedingly more complex in terms of the choices we must make and, at the same time, our educational and professional lives have become narrower as we attempt to stay abreast of at least one of the myriad occupational specialties responsible for supporting our lives.

There have been both positive and negative consequences of these changes at the individual level. Very few would gainsay the importance of the increases in the quality of life and level of goods available to the average person today relative to his predecessors of a century ago. On the other hand, the dizzying pace of associated choice activity and the specialization in education and jobs associated with today's high technology organizations have also caused a deep feeling of loss of control and alienation among many members of modern society. The post–World War II mobile society and the liberation of women have had their impact on the family and have exacerbated the feeling of being alone in a world that one cannot control. Leaving the nuclear family and living in a society that can be wiped out in a nuclear war has created its own set of tensions.

One interesting development of this felt alienation has been a growth of interest in group choice processes as a means of sharing responsibility for these complicated decisions and partially recapturing the emotional support that the family provided in the past. The number of community, social, and economic groups supporting individual interests has grown astronomically over the past century as individuals have attempted to gain a sense of identity and control over their destinies through banding together with like-minded others. Interestingly, although these groups have provided support to individuals, the sheer number of such groups has immensely complicated the social and political processes attempting to balance individual interests in setting public policy.

The recent controversy in different states on the abortion issue stimulated by the Supreme Court decision is one of many examples of the importance of groups in rallying around certain positions and making a political impact. Mancur Olson (1965) has described the increasingly complex problem of dealing with such special interest groups as a major impediment to national economic growth and social consensus. Thus, some of the steps taken by individuals to cope with increased choice complexity have had far-reaching effects on decision making at the group and societal levels as well.

These same effects are also evident in organizational decision making. Two centuries ago, all but a few governmental organizations were small in size with only rudimentary administrative and accounting procedures. The industrial revolution, starting in England in the late eighteenth century and spreading like wildfire to Europe and the United States, changed all of this. First, factories were built to house the newly developing mass production technologies. New energy sources were developed to power these complexes. Organizational and management innovations were designed to cope with the increasing size and complexity of these factories.

The economies of scale available through these new manufacturing technologies provided incentives to develop wider markets. New transportation modes, both rail and shipping, made this possible, and brought with
them at the end of the nineteenth century the beginnings of the large
geographically dispersed firms that have grown into today's conglomer-
ates.

Alfred Chandler (1977) has called this transformation from small, fam-
ily-centered business units to multinational giants the substitution of Adam
Smith's "invisible hand" of the marketplace by the "visible hand" of internal organization. Chandler ascribes this substitution to the fact that the
complex products we have come to rely on in modern society require
much larger production and service organizations than the simpler products of former times. These large organizations also imply immense problems in coordinating and controlling organizational decision making, and
in designing the incentive and information systems that support such decision making.

At the societal level there has been a radical change in the role that
government has played in our lives in the past fifty years. Prior to that
time individuals and firms operated in a relatively laissez-faire environment with the government collecting taxes to support a relatively small
bureaucracy and military activities, and with firms occasionally prose-
cuted for violating antitrust regulations. Today there are a number of federal and state agencies that are involved in information provision and
regulation to protect us against health, safety, and environmental risks.
Financial risks are mitigated through unemployment insurance and gov-
ernment-subsidized health care. How much risk we are willing to tolerate
is a subject of considerable controversy. There is a price to pay for zero
risk. The challenge is to frame the problem so people can see what the
trade-offs are.

This brief historical sketch points out the vastly changed role of consumers, organizations, and social institutions over the past two centuries.
A primary goal of this book is to understand the implications of these
changes for decision making, both descriptively and prescriptively.

1.3   Framework of the book

The preceding discussion illustrates the broad scope and importance of
decision sciences. In this section we wish to outline briefly the framework
this book follows in addressing these issues.

1.3.1   *Key aspects of decision making*

Figure 1.2 depicts two major areas of interest with respect to the decision-
making process. The box at the top, labeled procedural and technological

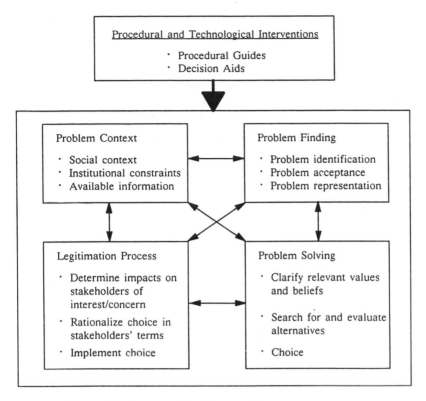

Figure 1.2. Aspects of decision making

interventions, encompasses prescriptive measures to guide and improve the decision-making process. Such interventions may be as simple as check lists and may extend to sophisticated decision support systems using advanced information technology, quantitative models, and data base management techniques.

The second and larger box in Figure 1.2 indicates the major features of decision making. Problem context refers to the social, institutional, and informational environment of the decision process. This is important in determining who may be affected, who has power, what information is available to decision makers and affected stakeholders, and, possibly, the values and beliefs evoked by the problem context in question.

Problem finding is the activity associated with identifying that a decision opportunity exists for a particular decision maker. It also involves the process by which the problem is accepted as within the decision-making purview or responsibility of the decision makers. Finally, problem finding gives rise to a representation of the problem, including some elemental notions of the source and structure of the problem identified and criteria for when the problem will have been resolved. Problem finding involves tracing the perceived source of the problem to the needs, values, and beliefs that the decision maker brings to bear in defining the problem as a decision or choice opportunity.

Problem solving is the activity associated with taking action or choice so as to resolve well-formulated problems. This involves articulating relevant values and beliefs, finding appropriate alternatives for choice, evaluating these, and choosing one that seems to resolve the perceived problem or choice situation.

The legitimation process is the final activity associated with decision making. It consists of determining the impacts of potential choice outcomes on stakeholders outside the decision-making body in question and rationalizing the decision makers' preferred choice in these stakeholders' terms. The importance of legitimation processes has been increasingly realized by political scientists and sociologists as an important ingredient of choice. Essentially, the necessity of legitimation focuses the decision makers' attention *ex ante* on constraints and values of individuals who may be affected by certain alternatives. To the extent that the decision maker cares about these stakeholders, possibly because they have the power to constrain the present or future choices if dealt with callously, the anticipation of legitimating a decision outcome can have strong effects on choice.

1.3.2   *Fundamental issues*

In addition to these categories in isolation, there are many interactive effects between each category. We have just dealt with one such interaction between legitimation and problem solving. Other interactions are easily imagined, and we shall be exploring these in some depth in this book. Without going into detail here, we can point to several issues raised by this interactive view of the several components of decision-making and problem-solving activity. We wish to highlight three fundamental issues at this point, which guide the presentation of much of the material in this book.

1. Linking descriptive and prescriptive analysis. A central theme of this book is that sound prescription must begin with good description. We take the view that all phases of the decision-making process in Figure 1.2 must be first understood before they can be improved. As an example of what we have in mind, it should be clear that different context and legitimation processes may trigger different problem-finding and problem-solving procedures for a given decision-making body. Consider the decision of whether to buy a new foreign car or an American car. The same decision may be made in very different ways depending on whether it must be legitimated to others as contrasted with being simply enacted by the decision maker with only his own conscience to bear witness to the validity of his choice. It is therefore important to describe clearly the actual nature of problem context and legitimation processes in understanding and improving choice processes.

A second reason for good descriptive analysis is to provide an operational basis for prescription. It is one thing to observe that a decision outcome is faulty. It is another to know the cause, and this is where descriptive theories are crucial. By modeling the decision process, and understanding its foibles and biases, we are often able to pinpoint the cause of faulty decision making. This may then allow a direct intervention, through procedural constraints or decision aids, in correcting the situation.

2. Recognizing abilities and limitations. Given that descriptive analysis is important, the next step is to adopt the proper perspective on how to view the fundamental actor in decision making, the decision maker. The view we adopt in this book, supported by considerable recent research in psychology and sociology, is that humans have many limitations and biases and that these provide the key to understanding what they will do in choice situations. To put it simply, people do not have immense memory, perceptual abilities, or information-processing abilities. When confronted with tasks that require such faculties, they must therefore adopt certain heuristics or shortcuts. Understanding the resulting consequences for the outcome of these tasks is then a key aspect of descriptive analysis. Such an understanding must clearly rest on a realistic assessment of the cognitive abilities of decision makers. It also provides interesting implications for the nature of appropriate prescriptive interventions in alleviating task overloads on decision makers' cognitive faculties.

Human emotions are also important in understanding decision making. Consider problem acceptance, for example. It is a widely held view that a major reason that many choice situations are resolved in favor of doing nothing (the celebrated status quo solution) is fear. Accepting a problem implies accepting responsibility for resolving the resulting choice dilemma. This can be a very threatening experience, especially if the results of the decision-making activity are publicly announced. Other emotional factors, such as love, hate, regret, and disappointment, may also be seen as very important to understanding choice processes in many problem contexts.

3. Linking nested decision structures. To this point, we have been viewing problem context and legitimation processes as given elements of the
decision-making environment. In fact, however, these elements themselves require choice. An individual may view a personal choice as having a social context encompassing his immediate family. By redefining
the problem as a group choice problem and bringing his family into the
problem-finding and problem-solving process, the context changes. The
individual, and the original choice problem, are now part of a larger decision structure including his family.

In a more general fashion, one may view many choice problems as
parts of larger social problem contexts. As either observer (analyst) or
decision maker, one must adopt a perspective on what the scope of the
problem domain is and what will remain as context. Hogarth (1981) has
likened this choice of perspective to that of a scientist adjusting his microscope to the proper resolution. With a very aggregate focus, larger
parts of the problem are subject to analysis, possibly with less resolution
or precision associated with each part. With a more refined focus, the
scope narrows with tighter problem boundaries, but concentrates then with
more precision on some aspects of the overall problem domain.

Nested decision structures play an important role in the analysis of decision making in groups, organizations, and larger social systems. As we
move to these higher levels of social aggregation, it is important to see
them as aggregations of lower levels. Of course, group decision making
is more than just the sum of its parts. At the level of the group, for
example, much can be gained from understanding the choice processes
of individuals involved in the group.

As a final point on nested decision structures, it is frequently the case
that decision problems involving several individuals or organizations require a clear delineation of controllable aspects of the decision environment from those which must be taken as given. Those which are controllable can be subjected to a prescriptive, action-oriented analysis, whereas
those that are given must be understood through a careful descriptive
analysis, but may not be readily changeable by the decision maker. For
example, corporate planners are clearly interested in how competitors will
respond to their firm's actions. In analyzing the problem of selecting an
appropriate course of action for the corporation, the planner is interested
in a sound prescriptive approach to the corporation's choice alternatives.
As a part of this problem, it is necessary to use a valid descriptive model
for competitors' responses in evaluating such alternatives. Thus, one cor-
ollary of the existence of nested decision structures is embodied in the
old maxim: Let us change those aspects of the world that should be changed;
let us be at peace with those aspects that cannot be changed; and let us
be able to distinguish those aspects over which we have some control and

those we do not. In the language of this book, this reduces to: Prescribe where change appears possible and desirable; describe where it is not; and hope for the best.

1.4   Illustrative examples

We now consider five examples of decision making, each of which illustrates a different level of social complexity (individual, group, organizational, interorganizational, and societal). In looking at each of these problems there are a set of questions that are addressed:

- What is the nature of the problem? Specifying one's goals and objectives enables one to determine what are the important features of the problem with which one needs to be concerned.
- Who are the key stakeholders? The relevant interested parties are defined by the type of problem one is considering and the specified goals and objectives.
- What type of information does one want to collect in order to structure the problem? The answer to this question depends partly on the ease with which data are available and the accuracy of the information.
- What type of choice procedures are utilized and are there ways to improve the final decision? There is a trade-off here between accuracy and effort. Complicated decision rules may require considerable data and a great deal of time to reach a final solution. Do the additional costs of utilizing such procedures justify the benefits from a better solution?
- What type of options are considered? Each problem will produce a set of different alternative ways of dealing with it. How well can these programs be specified and how can they be evaluated?
- How can you justify your solution to others who are concerned with the problem? Here one needs to consider problems of legitimacy and credibility in presenting a course of action to both those individuals who are and are not involved in the decision-making process.

1.4.1   *Example 1: selecting a student apartment (individual level)*

Students wishing to live off campus have the problem of selecting an apartment that meets their needs and satisfies their pocketbook. If there are several students who want to share the apartment, then one has to determine individual values for different features (e.g., rent, size, location) and find ways of reconciling any differences that may exist. The apartment-sharing selection problem is a good example of a nested decision structure.

The interested parties that interact with each other in the apartment selection process are shown in Figure 1.3. Landlords or real estate offices are the source of supply, setting the monthly rents and conditions under

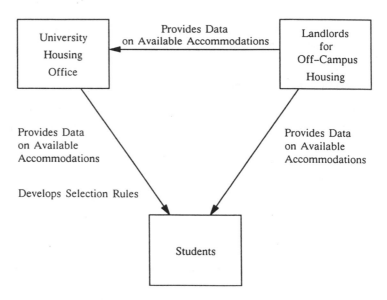

Figure 1.3. The university housing problem

which the apartment is rented. This information may also be provided to a university housing office, which may aid the student in the selection process.

Some students may begin the search by contacting the housing office to obtain a list of available options. Others may search on their own for an apartment by checking newspaper advertisements and posted "for rent" signs or by getting leads from friends in the area. The choice process can also vary among individuals. Some students may proceed sequentially by looking at apartments one at a time until a particular unit satisfies their needs. Others may prefer to look at a number of apartments and then choose the one they like the best. There will also be differences among students in the types of information they collect in order to choose between apartments. Some persons will be primarily concerned with the rent and the number of rooms without worrying too much about the precise distance from campus or the noise level. Others may be more exhaustive in their evaluation of factors upon which to base their final choice.

It is important to understand the problem-solving process (descriptive analysis) before attempting to improve decision making (prescriptive analysis). For example, the university housing office may want to provide students with guidelines on the selection of an apartment. The type of data the office assembles will depend upon what information students are interested in seeing. If most individuals learn about the characteristics of

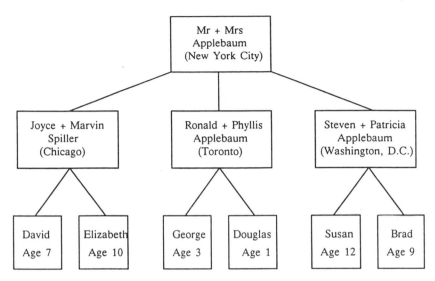

Figure 1.4. The Applebaum family tree

apartments from friends and neighbors, then it may be necessary to provide only limited data on the address and monthly rent. If, on the other hand, many people use the housing office as their chief data source and want a great deal of information readily available on apartment characteristics, then a more exhaustive description of available alternatives may be appropriate. We shall examine the descriptive–prescriptive aspects of individual decision-making problems in Chapters 3–5.

1.4.2   *Example 2: planning a family reunion (group level)*

Where should the Applebaum family hold their reunion next June? As shown by the family tree in Figure 1.4, there are four different cities and three different generations involved in making this decision. This problem involves a group decision-making process that can differ widely depending on the family structure and the interaction between members. At one extreme, the decision can be made by one of the parties (e.g., the grandparents), whereas at the other extreme a voting scheme could be introduced to determine the final choice among the proposed locations. There are also process issues to be resolved. For example, prior to making a final decision, what discussions should take place, who should be involved, and what information should be brought into these discussions? For this illustrative example, the following questions might arise:

Cost

- What are the maximum costs each family member is willing to pay?
- Who pays for the family reunion? For example, will each family pay an equal share or does one or more parties (e.g., parents, grandparents) pay a larger proportion of the cost?
- What is the maximum distance each family is willing to go?
- What modes of transportation are open for consideration (e.g., automobile, plane)?

Accommodations

- What type of accommodations do different members of the family prefer for the reunion?
- Is there general agreement on facilities that are desirable for a reunion (e.g., swimming, tennis, cottages or hotel)?

The answers to these questions are likely to suggest a set of possible candidates for a reunion site. Each of these choices may satisfy only some of the needs of each of the parties. This is what makes the problem an interesting one. The final choice will involve a trade-off between dimensions such as cost, distance, and available facilities and a compromise among the possibly conflicting preferences of Applebaum family members concerning how to evaluate such trade-offs. The final choice will then depend upon the relative power of each family member, the decision process involved in choosing among alternatives, and the criteria for evaluating different options. Prescriptively, various techniques have been proposed for improving group decision making. These involve procedures for eliciting individual preferences and group choice criteria as well as methods for evaluating alternatives in terms of these criteria and for resolving conflict among group members. These matters are dealt with in detail in Chapters 6 and 7, where we consider group decision-making methods.

1.4.3   *Example 3: production planning (organizational level)*

A typical problem facing manufacturing firms is developing production plans for the different items that are offered to consumers or wholesalers. The sales department and the production department are normally involved in this planning process. These two groups are likely to conflict because of differing performance measures. The sales department is judged on the basis of customer service, so it is concerned with the demand side of the picture. The performance of the production department is judged on how dependably and cheaply it can produce an item. Hence this department is concerned with the supply side of the picture.

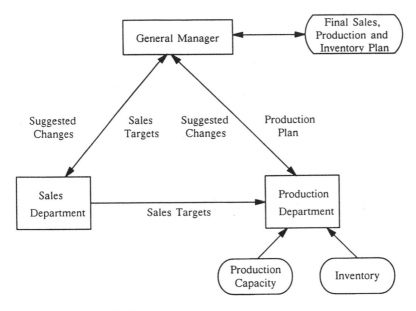

Figure 1.5. Production planning example

To be concrete, let us consider the planning problem of a ready-to-eat-cereal manufacturer, which we call Munchy Cereals Company, a division of the Crunch-Bunch Group. The ready-to-eat-cereal industry is characterized by a great deal of competition; company goals are to maintain customer loyalty to Munchy's brands and to gain shelf and promotion space from retailers while coordinating proper ordering from Munchy's production facilities. Ideally Munchy's sales department would like to have a sufficient number of units on hand of all items to satisfy retail customers without delay. This calls for either high inventory levels or quick response time in producing small lots of items to meet individual retailer orders on demand. Ideally the production department wants to produce efficient-sized runs of different items and keep inventory levels low. To run the business profitably, it is clear that the production and sales departments will have to compromise to provide reasonable delivery times to customers while incurring reasonable production costs.

The organizational decision process of Munchy Cereals determines how final decisions are made. One type of decentralized structure is shown in Figure 1.5, where there are three interested parties: The sales department sets the target for the next month; the production department attempts to set production targets that meet these sales goals, either from existing inventory or planned production, but it may be constrained from doing so by existing capacity limits; thus, planned sales and production targets must be given to the general manager (GM) whose primary role is to reconcile differences between sales targets and the ability of production to meet these targets.

In the decentralized system described in Figure 1.5, the GM simply asks the question: "Can sales targets be met by production targets plus existing inventory?" If the answer is yes, then the process is completed for the month; otherwise, the GM provides feedback to both sales and production with suggestions for ways to readjust their targets to be compatible with each other. The planning process continues until the two departments have reconciled their plans or the GM imposes his own targets. An alternative system would be a more centralized structure where the GM sets both sales targets and production plans. This would clearly entail different responsibility and authority, information, and incentive structures than the decentralized process already described. Ascertaining which of these two planning processes would provide more timely and effective decisions requires a careful evaluation.

This example illustrates organizational decision making. It combines elements of individual (e.g., the GM) and group (e.g., the sales department) decision making in a purposeful undertaking (in this case, making a profit from a coordinated production and sales effort). The key issues to be determined are the authority, incentive, and information structures to be put in place by the organization's designers (e.g., the owners of a firm) to accomplish the task of the organization. Prescriptively, organizational decision making raises two problems; first, how to support individual decision makers in the organization to increase their effectiveness; second, how to design the organization so that organizational participants solve the right problems and coordinate their actions. Clearly these two design problems must be carefully linked to each other and to the needs and limitations (as determined by a careful descriptive analysis) of organizational decision makers. We return to the first design question in Chapter 5 when we discuss how the production planning manager's decision process might be supported by mathematical programming methods and decision support systems to increase that manager's effectiveness as a decision maker within the Munchy organization. The second issue of linking and coordinating decision makers' actions is the subject of Chapter 8, where we discuss prescriptive and descriptive theories of organizational design and decision making.

1.4.4   *Example 4: managing inventory in blood banking (interorganizational)*

The problem of managing the supply of blood for patients in a hospital illustrates the role of organizational design on the operation of a system where the effectiveness is not measured strictly in monetary terms such as profits. Rather, hospitals are judged by the quality of their service and must consider the value of a human life as part of their decision process.

Blood normally has a life span of only 21 days unless it is frozen, which is a costly procedure. It is obtained at collection sites such as a mobile unit or a regional center, stored in the regional center or a local depot, and then transferred to a hospital to satisfy patient demand for blood transfusion. An important inventory question is, How much blood should be collected and shipped between each point in the network? The trade-offs relate to the costs of being short of units so that patient demand is not completely satisfied, compared with the cost of having units that are outdated (i.e., over 21 days old) so they have to be discarded. There are two elements of uncertainty in the problem: the demand for blood by different patients, and the available number of donors who normally supply blood as well as those who can be called on short notice (e.g., 1 day) to supply blood.

There is no easy answer to this inventory–distribution problem; in fact, solutions depend upon the objectives and the structures of the blood banking system. If hospitals want to be able to supply blood immediately to 99 out of 100 patients, then they will have to keep a much higher inventory level than if their desired quality of service was lowered to satisfying 95 out of 100 patients. The interorganizational structure of the blood-banking system also plays an important role in determining inventory-related costs for any given "quality of service" objective.

Two types of network configurations are illustrated in Figure 1.6. In the multi-echelon tree configuration there are four interested parties (who interact with each other): The regional center supplied blood to a local center where it is sorted and then shipped to individual hospitals for the needs of their patients. In the star network the regional center collects and sorts blood, supplying units to individual hospitals for their patients. In each system there are one or more clusters of hospitals that are supplied with blood by either a local or regional center. Comparing the merits of a multi-echelon or star network requires answers to a set of questions:

- How large should each cluster of hospitals be in the network, and which hospitals should it contain? As the cluster increases, then the cost of transporting blood also increases, but the regional or local center can operate more efficiently.
- For each type of network, should blood be allocated to hospitals in a centralized fashion through prescribed rules developed by the regional or local center, or in a decentralized manner where each hospital requests the blood it needs?
- For each network what type of charging mechanism should be imposed on a hospital for blood they receive? In practice two proposals have

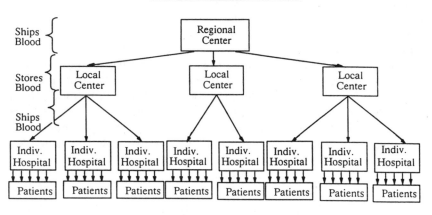

Figure 1.6. Alternative organizational structures for distribution of blood

been implemented in different hospitals. A *retention system* requires hospitals to pay for all units they receive whether or not they use them. A *rotation system* provides blood to hospitals free of charge on loan and requires them to return unused units after a fixed period of time.

We shall return to these questions in Chapter 8 when the impact of organizational and interorganizational structures on operating policies of firms will be explored further.

1.4.5 *Example 5: siting of liquefied natural gas (LNG) facilities (societal level)*

When dealing with a societal issue, there are a number of different parties, each with its own objectives, information bases, and decision rules. In contrast to the group decision-making problem associated with planning a family reunion, the interested parties may come together only infrequently, if at all, so there is no guarantee that there will be any type of consensus among them. In fact, they are likely to exhibit critical differences: Some groups may be in favor of siting a particular facility (e.g., a nuclear power plant) in a given location; others may be in favor of siting the facility elsewhere; still others may not be in favor of siting such a facility anywhere.

To illustrate these points, consider the problem of where to site LNG facilities. A potential source of energy that requires a fairly complicated technological process, LNG has the potential to create severe losses, although with very low probability. The process converts a gas into a liquid so it can be shipped by sea in specially constructed tankers. It is received at a terminal where it undergoes regasification and is then distributed. The entire system (i.e., the liquefaction facility, the LNG tanker, the receiving terminals, and regasification facility) can cost more than $1 billion (Kunreuther and Linnerooth, 1983).

Figure 1.7 depicts one view of the decision process where questions are investigated in a sequential fashion: If an LNG project is considered in the national interest (D1), then one determines if there exists a potential site (D2) safe enough to be approved (D3).

Different parties play a role in each of these three decisions. Each party has its own agenda, which may, to a large extent, be determined by constraints or mandates. For example, the Department of Energy may specify whether a proposed project is in the public interest (D1). The search for potential sites (D2) by gas companies is limited by physical constraints such as a deep-sea port. In evaluating the safety risk associated with a proposed site (D3), local groups and state agencies have to determine whether it meets certain prescribed standards.

These descriptive features of the problem indicate that there are likely to be conflicts between societal welfare and the well-being of specific groups. At a prescriptive level, we are interested in the role of negotiations in determining when and where the siting of such an LNG facility is in the public interest and how to share equitably the costs, risks, and benefits of such a facility if it is desirable to build it. These matters are discussed in more detail in Chapter 9, where we consider societal decision making.

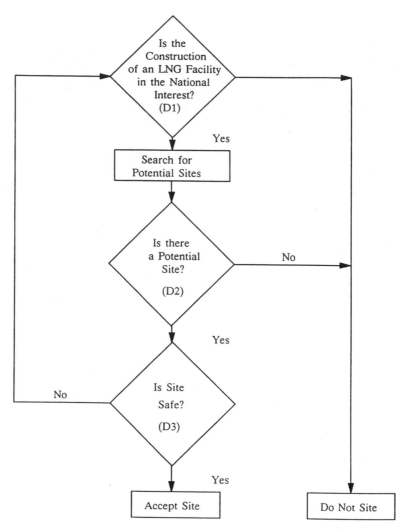

Figure 1.7. Sequential decision process for US LNG siting decision

1.5   Organization of book

The remainder of the book explores the process of decision making at each of the different levels outlined earlier from both a descriptive and prescriptive viewpoint. Chapter 2 is concerned with the problem-finding–problem-solving process. Some attention is given to the importance of goals, values, and needs in identifying and representing a problem. The next three chapters focus on individual decision making, though many of the concepts discussed here are relevant to the other levels. Chapter 3 first examines the process of generating alternatives and then turns to the prediction and inference problem. Particular attention is given to the heuristics and systematic biases of individual judgment under uncertainty and the role of feedback and learning in correcting them. Chapter 4 is devoted to valuation and choice. Axiomatic models such as expected utility theory suggest guidelines for making choices but there is considerable empirical evidence that we summarize showing that individuals violate these axioms both in their valuation process as well as in their choices. Hence a spate of descriptive models has attempted to capture actual behavior. In Chapter 5 we present five different holistic approaches for dealing with different choice problems and evaluate each of them relative to the others on a set of criteria.

Chapter 6 looks at the group decision-making process by building on our understanding of individual choice. Here special attention is given to the group problem-finding and problem-solving process and the alternative approaches for aggregating individual opinions and obtaining group estimates of probability.

Chapter 7 is a more technical treatment of group decision making through formal modeling. Game theory, negotiation and bargaining, collective choice procedures, and principal–agent models are explored in the context of specific examples.

Chapter 8 provides an overview of the literature on organizational decision making. Through the use of a set of illustrative examples, we explore decision making by a unitary actor within an organization, decisions within organizations, and the challenges in designing better organizations. Chapter 9 explores the societal decision-making level with some emphasis on low-probability, high-consequence events. After examining under what conditions the free market system is likely to perform imperfectly, attention is given to the types of public policy programs that might be utilized to deal with these risk-related issues. The Epilogue reviews the basic concepts that have motivated the book and revisits the problems presented in Chapter 1 to determine whether they could be structured and analyzed somewhat differently than at the outset. After looking at a set of global problems facing society today, we conclude by outlining open research questions that relate to the linkage of descriptive and prescriptive analysis.

2

Problem finding and alternative generation

2.1   Nature of problem finding

Most research on decision making focuses on how problems are solved. In this chapter, we consider the question of *which problems* are solved and how alternatives are generated for problem solving. These are fundamental activities underlying effective problem solving and decision making. Clearly, if we spend our time solving the wrong problems, or if we restrict attention to an inferior set of alternative solutions, then no matter how effective our problem-solving procedures may be, the outcome will be poor.

Figure 2.1 reproduces the problem context and problem-finding aspects of Figure 1.2, together with some typical examples of problem finding at various social levels. We note the following descriptive and prescriptive aspects of problem finding of interest:

1. *Problem identification*: the process by which a decision maker recognizes that a problem or decision-making opportunity exists.
2. *Problem acceptance*: the decision maker focuses attention on the problem as something worth considering further (as opposed to ignoring it).
3. *Problem representation*: the problem or decision situation is linked to potential improvements that may be achievable and perhaps some alternatives for problem solving are considered.

From a prescriptive viewpoint, we will be concerned with procedures to improve recognition and acceptance of problem situations. This leads to procedures for clarifying the objectives to be satisfied by problem-solving activity and for improving the management of time and attention so that important problems are dealt with first.

To illustrate the issues involved in problem finding, we consider the example from Figure 2.1 at the individual level. Consider the following situation. You are single and living with your parents. Although your living quarters are comfortable and convenient to your place of work, increasing frictions about your habits and social behavior have developed between you and your parents. You see many of your friends leading a more independent, and seemingly happier, existence on their own.

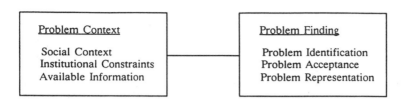

	Social Level		Problem Context		Problem Finding Activity

Social Level	Problem Context	Problem Finding Activity
Individual	Finding living quarters	Framing the problem properly
Two–Person	Doctor–Patient	Communicating and understanding the patient's illness
Group	Family	Finding a site for the family reunion
Organization	Improving quality	Diagnostic: What's the real problem
Social	Facility siting	Resolving conflicts among competing interests

Figure 2.1. Typical examples of problem-finding activity

This situation illustrates the challenge of problem finding and alternatives generation. A problem state is perceived. You have a (perhaps unreliable) model indicating that improvement is possible. Yet, what is the problem? Is it to come up with an improved living situation with your parents (e.g., move to the basement, with a separate entrance, and sound proof your quarters)? Is it to change your life-style to conform to your parents' apparent wishes (thereby avoiding any confrontation with them on this issue)? Perhaps you should consider the problem of finding an affordable and convenient apartment. Solving any of these "problems" would involve investments of time and energy. Which problem would (should) you spend time solving and what alternatives should you consider for each problem? This answer would depend on your needs and values and (based on your knowledge of your family, the housing market, and home remodeling) your initial estimates of the costs and benefits of attempting to improve your state through each of the various options. If you solve the wrong problem, you may not remove the underlying problem state.

Note also the importance of problem context in this example. Suppose you rented an apartment and you faced the same kinds of frictions, but this time from a nosy and self-righteous landlord. With this changed problem context, your problem-finding activity might change as well. You would very likely see the problem to be solved as finding another apartment.

Finally, note that we have defined this problem as an individual problem-finding situation. But the context could quite easily be elevated to the level of your family by making them aware of your own problem, bringing them into the problem-finding–problem-solving process and looking in this broader context for the right problem to solve.

The reader might wish to consider each of the other social situations in Figure 2.1.

In the case of a doctor–patient relationship, the issue is usually diagnostic, determining whether the patient has a problem and how to treat it. But the patient may be primarily looking for sympathy. The doctor may be only looking for income or professional advancement. What is the real problem here?

Consider the family reunion problem discussed in Chapter 1. The problem-finding activity here is in framing the issues correctly. What are the real objectives of the family reunion? Are there particular family members who have special problems or needs? Do there exist past issues (e.g., unresolved conflicts) that complicate the decision?

One of the greatest challenges for organizations in the private and public sector is improving quality. A typical example of a quality problem is given in the WAD Company Case (Table 2.1). Improving quality means finding the right problem(s) to solve.

At a societal level, the LNG siting problem of Chapter 1 is a good example of how different groups may see problems differently. Environmentalists may see the primary problem as protecting the environment and mitigating risks of new energy facilities, whereas energy planners may see the problem primarily as providing adequate energy supplies for a region. If you were a public policy maker with responsibilities for regulating the siting of such a facility, you would have to be very sensitive to these different representations of the same problem.

In all of these examples, additional complexities, such as institutional constraints, naturally arise as we consider more complex levels involving groups, organizations, and social contexts. Nonetheless such issues as problem identification, acceptance, and representation represent common challenges of problem finding and problem definition at every social level. As we shall see, the central issue in problem finding is that human de-

Table 2.1. *The WAD Company*

The WAD Company makes high-quality wooden-framed windows and doors. They have been having increasing complaints from one of their major customers, Homec Inc., a company that uses WAD's windows and doors in home remodeling kits. The question facing WAD is: What is the reason for its quality problems and how can it work with Homec to clear these up? Homec says: "Fix the problems or we're taking our business elsewhere."

WAD does not have a formal quality program, but its president, David Fixer, has always emphasized quality in WAD's production operations and he is confident that the current problems with Homec are not the result of actions by WAD employees, who are among the most skilled carpenters in the region. He is sure the problems lie elsewhere. In fact, Mr. Fixer followed up on the last 10 customer complaints for a single product, WD-17, a high-cost, high-quality hardwood door. All but one of these complaints involved installation by the customer, and it seems clear to Mr. Fixer that the big problem is inadequate information provided to the customer on how to install the product (which involves a number of adjustments to assure fit, sound and moisture insulation, and stability of the hinge works). Customers usually install the doors themselves because Homec's installation cost is quite high.

Homec's sales manager, Nancy Lee, is of a different opinion. WAD uses a number of different sources for its hardwood, and Ms. Lee claims that different woods have to be installed differently, even by Homec's own installation teams. Moreover, according to Ms. Lee, products like WD-17 were often chipped or damaged in shipment and customers complain about any such damage, especially for the high-priced Homec products. Some of WAD's window products warp once installed because of moisture problems. Mr. Fixer claims that this too is because of improper installation, but Ms. Lee feels that the real reason is that some of WAD's windows are not designed properly so that water collects on the bottom wood surfaces, leading to warping. Ms. Lee has advanced other arguments as well, but because Homec does not keep a separate data base on delivery defects or customer complaints on WAD's products, there appears to be no way for Mr. Fixer to sort out truth from fiction. And now with relations between Homec and WAD deterioriating, it seems even more difficult to get to the bottom of WAD's problems with Homec.

Under the circumstances, what would you do if you were in David Fixer's shoes?

cision makers have only limited information-processing capabilities so that we must allocate our attention and energies to only a few of the many problems we might address. Which of these problems we actually do address, and how we generate alternatives for these problems, are the central topics we consider in this chapter.

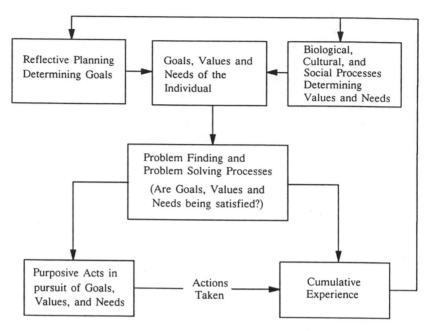

Figure 2.2. The evolutionary nature of problem finding

2.2   **Descriptive aspects of problem finding**

We first consider a general framework for problem finding. This framework begins with a simple introspective question. When do I discover I have a problem?

Problems are typically discovered in one of two ways (G. Smith, 1988a, 1988b, 1990). In *reactive or passive problem finding,* the recognition of problems is triggered by an outside influence such as another person, a reminder letter, or a personal experience that forces you to recognize a problem situation and do something about it. If you are an absent-minded professor, the outside influence could be a bounced check reminding you of the sorry state of your finances. If you are a homeowner, the outside influence could be a theft at a neighbor's house, which alerts you to the fact that your own home may be vulnerable to illegal entry.

Proactive or purposive problem finding involves thinking creatively about the goals you wish to accomplish. This process of imagination and planning may give rise to a recognition that substantial improvements to your current state are achievable. Problems are identified as specific and recognized areas where you believe such improvements may be achieved. Managers engage in such proactive activity all the time, using techniques such as planning and performance monitoring. The purpose of these activities is to look actively for the most important problems to solve to maintain the organization on an acceptable or improving path.

Both reactive and proactive problem finding are responses to differences between the perceived status quo and what an individual believes is possible, desirable, or necessary for his or her well-being. Figure 2.2 depicts this view of the problem-finding process. Goals, values, and needs underlying problem finding are determined by the biological, cultural, and social context within which the individual functions. Problem finding is the process triggered when environmental cues indicate that goals, values, and needs are not being satisfied at an adequate level. This leads to problem-solving activity and action. The evolving results of the individual's action become his or her cumulative experience. This experience then conditions the processes determining goals, values, and needs that will trigger future problem-finding and problem-solving activities.

To elaborate the model of Figure 2.2, we need to understand how problem states are perceived and attended to by individuals in various contexts. To do so, we first review relevant research on perception, memory, and attention. This research indicates that significant limitations exist in our abilities to perform these information-processing activities. As a result, individuals allocate their scarce attention and information-processing faculties to environmental cues and problems by attending to these sequentially. This leads us to a discussion of goals, values, and needs, all of which are important in determining which problems are perceived and addressed first.

2.2.1 *Perception, memory, and attention*

This section is an introduction to perception, memory, and attention. Because each of these areas is a well-developed field in its own right, our treatment will be necessarily selective. Our purpose is to sketch the nature of these processes, to illustrate their linkages, and to understand the limitations they impose on human decision making.

We begin with perception. Following Stephen Pepper (1967), we view the perceptual act as a conscious activity linking an individual through received sense data to the environment. In its simplest form, perception requires a perceived object (called the objective reference of perception) and an observer. When I say "I see a house," the "house" is the objective reference, and "I" is the observer.

Philosophers have argued for ages whether there is an objective reference independent of the sense data that we perceive. (If we turn our backs, does the "tree" we were just looking at continue to exist?) Idealist philosophers have concentrated on sense data as the main focus of concern, whereas realist philosophers attribute objective properties, independent of the observer, to the references of the perceptual act. We follow Pepper (1967) and cognitive psychologists (e.g., Rumelhart, 1980) in seeking a synthesis between the idealist and realist positions. Instead of focusing on the objective reference (e.g., the "house"), with a passive observer-assimilating sense data, we focus on the observer as an active participant in the perceptual process. This change of focus leads to interesting insights on the nature of perception and its relation to problem finding.

Characteristics of perception. To illustrate, consider the following example. You are thirsty and decide to have a drink of water. You look for and find a suitable glass, fill it, and satisfy your thirst. In this context, the perception of "a suitable glass" as you enter your kitchen is an object of such a shape as to hold water, with anticipated visual and tactile properties. The act of perceiving the glass consists of seeing such an object and, through drinking, fulfilling your expectations of the purpose of the glass. When you find the object you believe to be a glass, you fill it and reinforce the correctness of your perceptions by drinking the water in the glass.

This simple example illustrates the most important characteristics of active perception; it is done as part of some purposeful act and it is consummated by determining that the objective reference of perception fulfills our expectations. These expectations are referred to as schemata (Rumelhart, 1980). A schema refers to the conceptual model in memory of what we anticipate we shall perceive. If we find what we expected to find, then the schema (mental model) of this perception is supported. In the example given, we would have simple schemata for "glass," "kitchen," "drinking," and so on and more complex schemata integrating these simple schemata into the act of "going to the kitchen to get a drink of water." Note that each of the simple schemata in this example could be further linked to other schemata in our memory. Thus, the schema "glass" might be linked to both a schema of a "typical glass" as well as to particular examples of a glass (e.g., "your favorite glass for drinking water" or "the glass in the cupboard with a small chip in it").

From a philosophical viewpoint, this description of perception underscores Immanuel Kant's famous dictum: "There are no percepts without concepts." That is, to perceive a "glass" requires that we have a notion of what a "glass" is. The act of perception then both assimilates sense data associated with the "glass" we see and reinforces our entire cognitive schema of "glass" and its purposes. In this sense, perception links both subjective sense data and objective references in mutually reinforcing processes, providing an interesting bridge between realist and idealist positions on perception.

From a psychological viewpoint, this same approach has found acceptance and experimental support (see Simon, 1979b, and Rumelhart, 1980). It suggests that the faculties of perception, memory, and attention are linked. When we get a drink of water, we have stored in our memory a schema for how this act should proceed and the objects (glass, faucet, etc.) required to accomplish it. Our attention focuses on these objects as a part of satisfying our thirst. When we have done so, all aspects of this process are reinforced (our schemata, our sense perceptions, and the rewards from focusing attention).

Perceptual limitations. While perception, memory, and attention are linked, they are also limited resources. George Miller (1956) has summarized early research on limitations to our perceptual abilities. To illustrate the nature of this research, consider the following experiment. Suppose that a horizontal line is drawn. Next suppose that a marker (a point) is placed on the line toward either the left end or the right end of the line. In a series of trials, almost everyone will unerringly be able to discriminate whether the point placed in each trial is on the left end of the line or the right. Suppose now that additional locations for the point are possible – for example, left, middle, and right, all equally spaced along the line. When the number of possible categories for placement of the point increases, subjects will begin to make mistakes in discriminating which slot the marker occupies in a given trial. In fact, normal subjects can only discriminate roughly 10 locations accurately. Beyond that, their perceptual abilities deteriorate rapidly.

Miller reports other experiments testing the ability of subjects to discriminate unidimensional stimuli, such as musical pitches, concentrations of salt solutions, and loudness of tones. In each of these cases, the number of perfectly discriminable alternatives seems to be in the range of 7 ± 2, leading Miller to dub 7 ± 2 as a magical number reflecting the upper limit to human perceptual discrimination abilities for unidimensional stimuli.

A little thought shows that we can distinguish more than 7 objects from one another, however. For example, many individuals can distinguish the sounds of most of the instruments in an orchestra. All of us can recognize the faces of more than 7 ± 2 people. The key here is that these stimuli are not unidimensional, like loudness, pitch, and position of a point on a line, but multidimensional. For such stimuli, Miller reports results indicating that as the number of independently variable dimensions of the stimuli increases, so do our powers of discrimination. For example, if instead of locating points on a line, we attempt to judge their position in a square, then normal subjects can classify accurately some 20 to 25 positions. (The corresponding results for the line are only half that number.) Adding the second dimension of vertical position to that of horizontal position thus allows additional discrimination.

What happens when the number of independent dimensions is increased further? Experimental results show that discrimination continues to increase but at a decreasing rate. As a rough estimate, Miller suggests that when the number of independent dimensions is 6 to 7, we can discriminate some 150 alternatives. The question then arises, how many independent dimensions can we actually perceive? This appears to differ across individuals and across stimuli and is further complicated by sequential processing of stimuli – we take in certain dimensions first, then process a second set of dimensions, and so on. In this sequential way, a very large number of independently variable dimensions can be discriminated (as we do when we decode human speech or read a book). Even so, as these examples hint, immediate perceptual discrimination powers of human decision makers are quite limited.

The procedure just suggested of expanding our powers of discrimination by sequentially processing stimulus dimensions introduces memory as a key to discrimination. For we must store and recall successively discriminated dimensions if we are to integrate these into an overall judgment of what we are perceiving. The question of immediate and ultimate limitations to perceptual discrimination is therefore linked to memory limitations. These we now discuss.

Short- and long-term memory. Memory researchers such as Norman (1969) and B. Underwood (1969) describe memory as having at least two levels: short-term (primary) and long-term (secondary). Short-term memory contains items that relate to the immediate, conscious present. Long-term memory contains items that may have been absent from consciousness for some time; they belong to the past. Figure 2.3 depicts the relationship between these two memory systems. Items in short-term memory fade if not rehearsed by focusing attention on them. If items are rehearsed, they are more likely to be transferred to long-term memory, where they are integrated into various schemata. Such schemata are also subject to decay over time if not rehearsed through recall.

Memory researchers have studied the span of immediate memory intensively and have found that normal subjects can store about 7 (the magical number again!) items of information in immediate memory. A simple experiment verifies this. An experimenter reads to subjects strings of unrelated letters, digits, or words with a one-second interval between each successive stimulus. A typical string might be: "A J X R 2 Y 8 4 Z Z

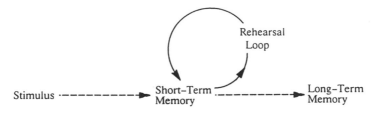

Figure 2.3. Short-term and long-term memory systems (*Source:* Waugh and Norman, 1965. Copyright 1965 by the American Psychological Association. Reprinted by permission)

E." The question is, What is the longest string that can be recalled without error? The answer is roughly 7 ± 2.

If we can rely on immediate memory for only 7 ± 2 items, how is it possible that chess masters can look for very brief intervals (5 to 10 seconds) at a game in progress and then reconstruct the entire chess board without error (de Groot 1965)? The answer seems to be that the "items" stored in immediate memory can be encoded in sophisticated ways, so that each of the 7 or so items in immediate memory can be very large "chunks" of information retrievable from long-term memory. To illustrate this simply, consider the task of remembering the sequence of digits (1 4 9 2 1 7 7 6 1 8 1 2), after only a brief exposure to these digits. If this were attempted in raw form, most people would make errors in recall. However, if this same sequence were encoded in groups of four during exposure to them, then the entire sequence becomes 1492, 1776, 1812, which can be stored in immediate memory as three salient dates in American history. Thus, the information content of immediate memory can be enhanced by clever encoding schemes as well as experience (as in the example of the chess masters' recall abilities) that use mnemonic devices to allow us to store significant amounts of information in immediate memory under a single "code name." For example, the name "Pennsylvania" may be stored as one "chunk" in short-term memory, with readily accessible facts from long-term memory then retrievable in association with this single word.

The structure of long-term memory has been the subject of considerable research in cognitive psychology (see Shiffrin and Atkinson, 1969; Simon, 1979; Rumelhart, 1980). The basic model emerging from this research attempts to answer two questions: How is information stored in long-term memory and how is it recalled? The model suggests the following structure. Memory may be viewed as a network of nodes and links. The nodes might be viewed as "labels" and the links represent associations between various labels. For example, the label "chair" might be linked to the label "table." Further, each label is viewed as being the label for a schema depicting the anticipatory set of various objects, actions, and concepts. For example, the node "chair" might have a schema depicting both the general expectations one has of chairs, as well as links to other nodes with schemata representing specific instantiations of "chair"– for example, a schema representing my favorite easy chair. Also linked to these schemata may be various "episodic schemata" that are the representations of episodes involving general schemata. For example, concerning "chair," there may be schemata representing my anticipations for what my favorite easy chair feels like when I sit in it. There may also be links to schemata representing specific episodes in my experience involving chairs (e.g., the time my favorite easy chair collapsed as I sat down in it).

We may summarize this discussion of long-term memory by likening long-term memory to an interconnected network of labels, where each label, when focused on, presents a slide or a filmstrip to the mind's eye. These slides and filmstrips are what we have called schemata.

The major limitations to the operation of long-term memory are limitations on our ability to access what is stored there (recognition and recall). Such access limitations relate to the way our "node-link" structure is set up, and the nature of context variables conditioning access. For the present, we wish only to concentrate on the latter issues. What researchers have found is that the context surrounding access to memory may strongly influence whether and what is recalled. This is because we tend to organize information coming into long-term memory so as to integrate it with our current memory structure. Thus, new information will be linked to existing information depending on the context in effect when the information is stored. This organization of the new information and the context surrounding its acquisition then affect the retrieval of the same information at a later point.

The most important control process related to retrieval is the process of attention. Kahneman (1973) defines attention as "the allocation of information processing capacity to mental activity." Just as perception and memory are limited in humans, so is our information-processing capacity. Without belaboring the point, one need only compare one's arithmetic abilities with those of a modern computer to conclude that our information-processing capacities are indeed limited. Thus, research on attention is concerned with which activities we attend to and with what intensity. The basic model of attention arising from this research can be stated as follows: We tend to pay attention to those activities that are most pressing within our perceptual field. Activities are attended to in

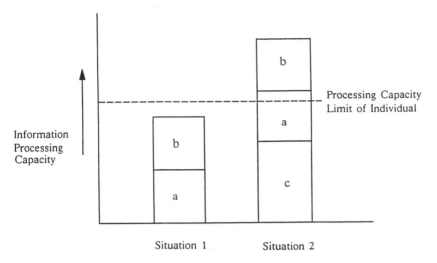

Figure 2.4. Attention and information-processing limits (Based on G. Underwood, 1976, p. 218)

the priority order indicated, until information-processing capacity is exhausted. Figure 2.4 depicts this model of attention.

In Situation 1, an individual is attending to two activities *a* and *b* (e.g., eating breakfast and reading the newspaper). In Situation 2, a third activity *c* enters the perceptual field (e.g., the telephone rings). If *c* is attended to because it is believed to be more important than *a* and *b*, then all available processing capacity is used and activities *a* and *b* must be deferred.

This example illustrates the key principles arising from attention research. First, attention is limited. Second, this implies that activities are attended to sequentially in order of perceived priority. This raises the central issue of attention management: What determines these priorities? We follow the literature in psychology in linking these priorities to our goals, values, and needs.

2.2.2   *Goals, values, and needs*

Goals, values, and needs all refer to certain desired results or preferred states. Psychologists and sociologists have argued that our "desires" are many, but our cognitive and physical makeup limits our ability to pursue them. This leads us to structure our "desires" hierarchically so that we attend to the more important ones (like staying alive) before we attend to less basic ones (like being loved). It is this argument of hierarchically structured goals, values, and needs that we shall pursue here. First, however, it will be useful to define and distinguish each of these terms.

A *goal* is a desired end-state resulting from planning activity. The same definition applies to the term *objective,* which may be thought of as more open-ended. An objective can never be fully achieved, whereas goals can. Because goals are generated by proactive planning, they are intentional and purposeful guides to what the decision maker wishes to accomplish.

A *need* represents a basic drive that arises from our biological and cultural background.[1] Tolman (1932) and others classified needs into three levels: primary needs (hunger, thirst, etc.); secondary needs (including innate sociorelational needs such as affiliation, dominance, etc.); and tertiary needs (including learned sociorelational needs such as the pursuit of cultural goals). Needs are our basic response tendencies and they are conditioned by our cumulative biological, cultural, and social experience.

Milton Rokeach (1973, p. 5) defines a *value* as "an enduring belief that a specific mode of conduct or end-state of existence is personally or socially preferable to an opposite or converse mode of conduct or existence." In other words, values represent personal or social preferences for desired end-states and appropriate means of attaining them. Values can be either personal or social and they can be either instrumental (preferable modes of conduct) or terminal (preferable end-states of existence). Instrumental values include such modes of behavior as ambition, courage, honesty, and courtesy, whereas terminal values include end-states such as a world at peace, freedom, pleasure, and wisdom.

Let us briefly distinguish now between goals, on the one hand, and values and needs, on the other. Goals are purposefully determined, whereas values and needs need not be. Values and needs may represent desires or drives below the level of our awareness. When they are consciously intended preferences, they become objectives and goals. For example, we may value a comfortable life (a personal terminal value) and purposefully pursue goals to achieve this end (e.g., earning a certain income).

The distinction between needs and values is more complex. Behaviorist psychologists, such as B. F. Skinner (1969), would see little difference between values and needs since behaviorist psychology deals only with observable response tendencies. The mental states, induced by values, needs, or whatever, leading to these response tendencies are, for the behaviorist, purely conjectural and secondary. Sociologists like Rokeach (1973), however, distinguish between "values" and "needs," seeing needs

1 As defined in the pioneering work of the psychologist Edward C. Tolman (1932, p. 335), a "need" is "a readiness or tendency to persist toward and to perform a consummatory response." Tolman thus emphasizes that needs give rise to purposeful activity to fulfill these needs.

as basic biological and behavioral drives and values as cultural and social constructs. In this framework, values are viewed as the cognitive representation of individual needs as transformed by social and institutional context.

For example, the need for shelter and clothing may be transformed into a value for a comfortable life, the need for security into values of co-operative behavior and world peace, and the need for dominance into values concerning ambition, courage, honor, or national security. Thus, values may be viewed as transformations of needs into individually and socially acceptable manifestations of these needs. As such, an individual's values reflect needs, but they also tell us something about individually and socially acceptable ways of fulfilling these needs.

Let us consider some of the examples of Figure 2.1 to illustrate goals, values, and needs.

Individual: finding suitable living quarters. The basic needs here are shelter and warmth. Beyond these, an individual might also perceive needs related to acceptance and love, both by her family, if she continues to live with her parents, and by friends who might come to visit.

Terminal values in this context would be desirable end-states associated with living quarters, including comfort and status aspects of where we live. Instrumental values would include values associated with how we interact with our family in choosing our living quarters and how we pay the costs of these quarters. These values would co-determine how well our various underlying needs will be satisfied by the process and outcome of our choice of living quarters.

Goals in this context might include the cost of our chosen living quarters, time to work, and space. These would represent specific targets that we might consider reasonable constraints to impose on ultimately acceptable living quarters. They would first arise out of our evaluation of what would fulfill our basic needs and values, and they might be further refined as we proceeded through the process of finding living quarters.

Two-person context: doctor–patient. The patient's needs are to remain healthy. The doctor's needs might be to maintain a secure income and a good professional reputation. A rich set of values surround doctor–patient relationships, however, and these can be in conflict with the basic needs. For example, the doctor may be confronted with tough financial choices in choosing a treatment, since some treatments may make the doctor more susceptible to malpractice suits or some patients may not be able to pay as readily as others. But not selecting the best treatment for a patient, regardless of financial status or possible lawsuits, may conflict with the medical code of ethics and may affect the doctor's professional reputation.

In terms of goals, the patient may have a specific time-frame in mind for getting back on the golf course or to some other normal routine. The doctor may also have a similar temporal goal for treatment effects. Both may have financial goals associated with any treatment.

Organizational level: improving quality. At the organizational level, goals are very much a part of daily life. These pertain to specific targets for cost, time, and quality improvements, as measured by internal measurement systems, by external customer satisfaction surveys, and by the bottom-line results of the business over time. But accomplishing organizational goals requires linking these to action programs, and one of the most important action programs in recent years has been the area of quality improvement. Here goals might be targets for reducing product defects, for reducing delivery time to customers, and for improving other attributes of the organization's products and services.

Whereas identifying goals in organizations is easy, defining needs for an organizational problem context like improving quality is difficult, because needs, as we use the term, apply only to individuals. In fact, one of the greatest problems in launching a quality program at the organizational level is ensuring "buy-in" by organizational participants.[2] In other words, individuals in the organization must want to cooperate in achieving improvements. And they will only want to cooperate if they see their needs and values being satisfied by participating in the quality improvement process. In many organizations, accomplishing this has required very significant changes from traditional hierarchical management styles to a bottom-level, participatory management style, which encourages all employees to look proactively for problems to solve and to find solutions that will benefit the organization. We shall have more to say about organizational and group processes in Chapters 6–8.

2.2.3   *Needs and value hierarchies*

These examples illustrate our basic points. Needs are primary; values are derived from these as individually and socially acceptable modes of behavior and end-states; goals and objectives are more specific states or targets determined through purposeful planning to fulfill needs and values. From the perspective of problem finding, it is important to note that our goals, values, and needs are rarely in a tranquil equilibrium with our environment or with our inner selves (Elster, 1986). Indeed, the objec-

2 For a discussion of this problem in the quality context, see Pall (1987).

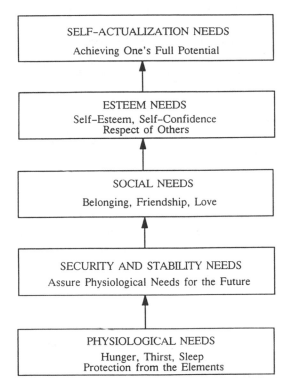

Figure 2.5. Maslow's hierarchy of needs (Based on "Hierarchy of Needs" from *Motivation and Personality* by Abraham Maslow. Copyright 1954, by Harper & Row, Publishers, Inc. Copyright © 1970 by Abraham H. Maslow. Used by permission of HarperCollins Publishers)

tives we end up pursuing in problem-solving behavior are the result of a complex interaction between our instinctive drives (or needs), the interest of self vis-à-vis others (balancing personal and social values), and short- versus long-term perspectives in planning (goals). For instance, your desire to learn may conflict with many other objectives, such as earning money, having a good time now, or helping out one's family. Thus, the objectives we ultimately pursue reflect trade-offs between goals, values, and needs that cannot be attained simultaneously. It is important to understand how these trade-offs are resolved in determining an individual's priorities for problem finding.

Maslow's hierarchy. Consider needs. According to Maslow (1954), needs can be ordered hierarchically, as in Figure 2.5. Our most basic concern is with physiological needs such as hunger, thirst, sleep, and protection from cold or heat. Once these basic life-support needs are reasonably well satisfied, our concerns will shift to security needs. For instance, if stranded on an island, we would construct some type of shelter, stockpile food, and secure a water supply. These actions are not aimed at the immediate present, but rather safeguard the satisfaction of our physiological needs in the future, especially as many of these are recurring. After security and stability needs are satisfied, social needs become predominant. These include the need for belonging, for friendship, and for love. They concern the human rather than physical environment that surrounds us. When these social needs are adequately satisfied, a fourth level of need manifests itself, self-esteem and the esteem of others. Many people in the economically developed countries of the West are in the fortunate position of having their physiological, security, and social needs satisfied. Yet they may not be fully happy, as their objectives and needs are focused on achievement and recognition thereof. Finally, for those who seemingly have it all – health, money, friends, prestige, power – a last need may manifest itself, the need to self-actualize, to realize one's potential fully in whatever ways one wishes to feel special as a complete person.

Value systems. Just as needs may be prioritized in hierarchies, so also are the values derived from them. For example, Rokeach (1973) reports extensive empirical evidence on "value systems" for various cultural and social groups. These value systems are rankings of the various instrumental and terminal values held by different groups. It should come as no surprise that different groups have different values and rankings thereof. For example, comparing low-income and high-income groups in the United States, Rokeach reports significant differences. The rich rank "a comfortable life" considerably lower relative to other terminal values than do the poor, perhaps because the rich already possess it. Similarly, the rich rank the instrumental value "clean" much lower relative to other instrumental values than the poor, again because cleanliness is likely taken for granted by the rich. Looking across age groups, educational backgrounds, or cultures presents similar stark differences in value systems. It is clear from these differences in value trade-offs that individuals from these different groups would see problem finding in very different lights. What would be a problem for an individual from one group in not attaining a specific level of some instrumental or terminal value might not even be noticed by someone from another group.

It can be argued, based on Maslow's need hierarchy, that differences in value systems between groups (e.g., between the rich and the poor) are simply the result of different levels of need fulfillment possible to members of these groups. One individual may be pursuing basic needs of food and shelter while another, having satisfied these needs, is pursuing higher-level needs. But understanding an individual's values goes deeper than this and requires, at the least, an understanding of the social and cultural forces shaping these values. For example, suppose someone is pursuing a need for "esteem." How will the person operationalize this objective? First, one would identify the reference groups, if any, that are important to this individual as the basis of the esteem he or she seeks. As Douglas and Wildavsky (1982) point out, however, the definition of reference groups raises essential cultural issues. In some cultures, there may be no such reference groups; esteem in such cultures is purely self-esteem. In other cultures, such reference groups may be socially defined (as in the caste system) and in still others there may be a naturally defined reference group (one's local village). Thus, to understand the operationalization of "esteem," more than just a needs hierarchy is required, although the concept of a structuring of goals, needs, and values into a hierarchy of relative importance is useful in understanding the order in which cues and problems are attended to.

In summary, goals, values, and needs are the conscious and subconscious ends toward which individuals strive. They may be thought of as being organized in a system or hierarchy of objectives, allowing trade-offs between conflicting objectives. From the point of view of problem finding, this hierarchy of objectives presents the basic reference data for triggering the recognition that a problem exists due to perceived unacceptable levels of achievement of one or another of these objectives.

Aspiration levels. One model of the process through which the indicated hierarchy of objectives operates in selective attention is called the *aspiration level* model. According to this model, operational specifications of goals, values, and needs may be viewed as reference points to which the individual aspires. Achieving a comfortable life-style, for example, is specified through an aspiration level of a certain income level, together with levels of other related goal indicators. When these aspiration levels are not met, or are threatened by perceived events, they trigger the recognition of impending problem states. Such problem states are then attended to in order of the value trade-offs incorporated in the individual's hierarchy of goals and objectives.[3] This model, pioneered by March and

3 As Bettman (1979) has argued, there is an important distinction to keep clear between strict hierarchies, such as that of Maslow (1954), and the hierarchy of goals that trigger problem finding. In the latter, the hierarchy need not be strict in the sense that one goal always takes precedence over some other goal. Rather, the goal hierarchies associated with aspiration level models of problem-finding activity may be viewed as having considerable parallelism and nonuniqueness or situational characteristics to them, so that they are not always processed in the same manner and so that no absolute or unique ordering of goals need be present. We use hierarchy in this chapter in the Bettman sense of an ordering of nested goals and associated aspiration levels, but an ordering that may change with time or may be triggered in different ways in different problem contexts.

Simon (1958), goes further in suggesting that aspiration levels are adjusted upward as the objectives in question are easily met, and are adjusted downward when these aspirations levels are difficult to meet. In this manner, one can see how cumulative experience also affects problem-finding activity, to the extent that such activity is triggered by impending violations of aspiration levels. The aspiration level model has received wide support and application in psychology (Siegel, 1957) and consumer behavior (Bettman, 1979; Bettman, Johnson, and Payne, 1991). It is intuitively appealing because it relates to our everyday experience in using reference points, based on our experience, to indicate what we can normally expect from the world. From the point of view of problem finding, the aspiration level view may be viewed as a model of how problem recognition is triggered.

2.3   Acceptance and representation of problems

Suppose a potential problem is perceived. What will determine whether a decision maker confronted by this perceived problem will "accept" the problem as important enough to devote problem-solving energy to it? The preceding discussion suggests the following theory (Simon, 1957b, Pounds, 1969) of problem acceptance. Decision makers construct or obtain from their cumulative experience a conceptual representation (which we call a model or a schema), against which they judge the existing situation and potential improvements to it. Such a model could be characterized by a set of aspiration levels for a hierarchy of objectives, together with a reasoned basis for believing each aspiration level is desirable and obtainable. These models or views of the world represent reference points or expectations of normalcy. When these expectations are not fulfilled, a problem state is recognized (which may or may not be attended to).

The key to problem acceptance is therefore the models used by the decision maker to represent and define normalcy. At the level of elemental survival needs, such models are the result of biological and social evolution, which determine levels of need satisfaction below which problems (or cold, hunger, etc.) are triggered. For goals and values that are more socially and cognitively conditioned, we can identify several types of models to define normalcy. We classify these under the headings of historical models, communicated models, and planning models.

Historical models. These are models based on extrapolations of the past. According to such models, a problem state is recognized when the unfolding present looks very dissimilar from the recent past. For example, suppose that during the period from 1986–1989 a hospital was able to supply blood immediately to over 99 out of 100 patients, whereas in 1990 this figure dropped to 96 out of 100. The hospital's blood bank administrator may see this drop in service level as a problem. In effect, historical models take the past as a reference point to form expectations about acceptable performance in the future and to define problem states when these reference points are violated. Historical models are the most common benchmarks of expectations, both for individuals as well as organizations. We are conditioned by our experience, both in the way we perceive the world and in our conceptions of how the world should operate.

Communicated models. Of course, we learn not only from our own limited experience, but also from that of others. This other experience, passed on through books, the media, and word of mouth, we call communicated models. Such communicated models indicate what others have and have not been able to accomplish, providing inspiration and realism for what we may hope to accomplish. For example, in the marketplace, organizations keep a sharp eye on their competitors to understand best industry practice. The resulting process of imitating positive moves by competitors has been described by Schumpeter (1934) and Nelson and Winter (1982) as a determining factor in technological innovation and market structure.

Communicated models come in many forms, from friends and neighbors, from scientific journals, from the media, and so on. What distinguishes these various models is the degree to which decision makers understand and trust them as being relevant to their own situation. Thus, a parent may see in her child's actions great potential harm, perhaps because she has learned from her own experience and from Dr. Freud or Dr. Spock how children should develop. Her child does not share these same models and thus sees no problem in his or her actions. This example also illustrates why problem-finding activity may be quite different from individual to individual, since the models used to define a problem state may be very different.

Planning models. Historical models and communicated models are reactive. Environmental cues are perceived and processed on the basis of a model of how the environment should look under normal (i.e., nonproblematical) conditions. Churchman (1961), Ansoff (1965), Ackoff and Emery (1972), and G. Smith (1988b) have emphasized the importance of another class of models in defining problem states. These might be called planning models, and they have a proactive or purposeful character. They are carefully thought out conceptions of what is achievable with measurable control indicators and goals to enable the "planner" to understand whether things are going "according to plan." Such models are frequently used in organizations to monitor and coordinate activities and can be as simple as a budget projection. When deviations from the plan are detected (e.g., a positive variance on an expense item in a budget), a problem is defined. The essence of planning models is that they embody intentional triggers, defined by the planner, to define problem states.

Summarizing this discussion, we view problem representation and acceptance as the process of setting reference points of acceptability and monitoring environmental cues for deviations from these. The determination of such reference points results from our models of the world based on historically based expectations, information from others, and purposeful planning.

Figure 2.6 summarizes the descriptive aspects of problem finding we have discussed to this point. The major activities involved are labeled the *Scanning Process,* the *Interrupt Process,* and the *Acceptance Process* (Simon, 1979a). Scanning refers to the manner in which data are collected and processed from the environment. Interrupts occur when the decision maker perceives a sufficiently troublesome state to trigger attention and problem identification activity. Acceptance occurs when the decision maker believes sufficient improvement is possible to warrant the costs of problem solving. From a descriptive point of view, one might expect the following shortcomings for each of these problem-finding activities.

Scanning: Scanning is based on our models, expectations, and plans and is constrained by the basic limits on our perception and memory.

Interrupts: Interrupts are based on trigger levels or thresholds determined by our models of normalcy and on the manner in which we prioritize violations of these thresholds. In particular, a hierarchy of interrupts based on objectives determined by our goals, values, and needs determines the sequence in which perceived problems are attended to. The constraints on this process are those implied by limits to our scarce attention (or information-processing) resources.

Acceptance: We accept problems that we perceive and that we believe to be important enough to warrant investing our time and energy further in solving. Problem acceptance is therefore constrained by the accuracy of our evaluation of the importance of perceived problem states.

The pitfalls of problem finding have been summarized pithily by Mitroff and Kilman (1978a) who suggest the following errors in problem finding:

> Type I Error: Detecting a problem when there isn't one.
> Type II Error: Not detecting a problem when there is one.
> Type III Error: Solving the wrong problem.

As should be clear from our discussion, Type III errors may result in

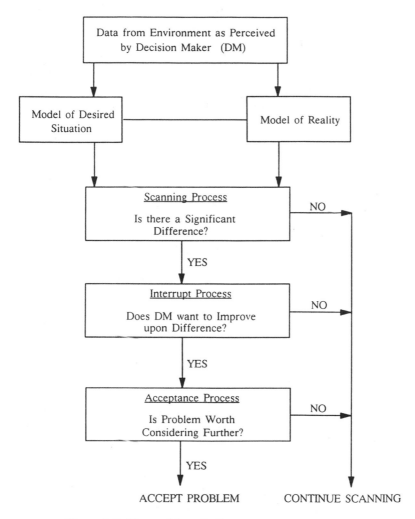

Figure 2.6. The problem-finding process

particular from limitations to our scarce resource of attention, since another phrasing of Type III error might be, "Solving an unimportant problem when an important one is waiting."

Perhaps one final point should be made on the descriptive side concerning acceptance. A major reason cited for lack of acceptance of perceived problem states is frequently not that we have evaluated them improperly, but that we fear the responsibility of accepting the problem perceived and then not being able to solve it. We have ignored these affective (or emotion-based) features of acceptance here. In part, these are accounted for by referring to the values and needs that they represent. That is, many of our fears and reasons for responsibility avoidance arise because of conflicting values of accomplishing something personal, but not risking the disapproval of others. To this extent, problem avoidance may be viewed as not compromising the value of the esteem of those whose disapproval we fear. But, as Freud and Pogo have pointed out, frequently those whose disapproval we fear most are none other than ourselves. Thus, the issue of problem avoidance is more complicated than this short description bears out.[4]

2.4   Prescriptive aspects of problem finding

The previous section characterized the problem-finding process as being subject to information-processing limitations, which lead to various short-comings. We now propose a set of prescriptive guidelines for improving the process. These guidelines are concerned with ensuring that the steps in the problem-finding process depicted in Figure 2.6 are implemented properly and in line with the interests of the decision maker or decision-making group. Thus, we structure our discussion of prescriptive approaches to problem finding into guidelines for clarifying goals, values, and needs; for managing attention more efficiently; and for validating the models and beliefs that underlie problem finding.[5]

2.4.1   *Clarifying goals, values, and needs*

It would be a pity if we were to solve problems in pursuit of the wrong goals. The first question that naturally arises in prescriptive problem finding is therefore to clarify what our values and needs are, and what goals and objectives these imply. We shall discuss systematic ways of evaluating value structures in Chapter 4. But in the end, these amount to the rather simple dictum of spending some scarce resources of energy and attention to determine whom we are trying to please and in what ways. In somewhat more detail, this amounts to specifying the stakeholders in a given problem context and role-playing their objectives as well as our own. By making a table of the involved parties (the stakeholders) and what we believe they care about, we clarify two important issues: first, the relevant objectives from their viewpoint and from ours; second, our

---

4 See Corbin (1980) for a further discussion of research on problem acceptance.
5 Deep normative questions about what set of values to hold will not be addressed here, as these belong mostly to the domains of religion, moral philosophy, and humanities. Recent concerns about the need for more ethics courses in business programs, however, highlight their relevance to daily problem solving. The Wall Street scandals of the 1980s revealed serious moral deficiencies in otherwise talented and effective decision makers. They remind us of the fundamental framing roles values play in problem definition.

relationship to these stakeholders from our viewpoint. This table of stake-holders' values (including our own) separates and clarifies our personal values and goals in relationship to our social needs of justifying ourselves to others.

One way of visualizing the resulting trade-offs between our social and personal values is through the different roles we play in our lives. A student devotes time to four or five different courses, extracurricular activities at the university, social life with friends, as well as hobbies and interests. Within an organizational setting, a manager assumes many different roles as well. Mintzberg (1973), in his study of managerial work, characterized many different roles for the typical manager, from figurehead and leader to disturbance handler to resource allocator. By recognizing the complexity of our lives through the roles we play, we may be able to understand better the very different objectives that these roles imply and which we embody.

For example, in her role as figurehead, a manager may perceive the importance of attending a particular meeting with a good customer because she perceives that her company's well-being demands her presence for prestige purposes to maintain a high volume of sales in the future. In her role as disturbance handler, the manager may perceive that a particular conflict between two departments should be handled in one way, even though her role as resource allocator might dictate another approach. The point is that the roles we play may be viewed as potentially conflicting value systems, each of which may be justified in certain contexts. By viewing a given context from the vantage point of different roles we believe are justifiable, we help to clarify which values we believe are foremost for the given context.

Ashby (1956) has characterized the reasons for our different roles as resulting from our attempt to provide "requisite variety" in our response to a complex world. We cannot deal with all potential problems that emerge in our lives, so we develop responses to important subsets of these problems in a consistent fashion. The roles we play may be viewed as our attempts to provide a livable and consistent response to certain classes of problem contexts. The fact that these responses may not be mutually consistent is just a reflection of our inability, in the face of a complex world, to design a consistent response to every conceivable problem situation. By analyzing what we would do in our different roles, we nonetheless shed light on both the conflicts between these roles and the underlying needs and values that gave rise to them.

2.4.2 *Attention management*

Limitations in our information-processing abilities lead us to attend to problems and potential problems sequentially. To ensure that the right problems are perceived and dealt with, two issues arise. First, to avoid spending time on nonproblems (Type I errors), one needs appropriate filters so that unimportant cues from the environment are filtered out and not attended to at all. Next, to avoid not spending time on real problems (Type II errors), one needs alerting systems to recognize when such problems are likely to be present. Both filters and alerting systems are referred to as processes for managing attention (Bettman, 1979; Simon 1979).

Let us consider filters first. In this age of information overload, we cannot attend to every cue that might be relevant. In organizations and in our personal lives, the scarce resource today is not information; it is time and attention. By designing proper filters, we can avoid a great deal of irrelevant information (and perhaps some relevant information as well, alas). In this regard, we should recognize that the most natural filters are what we read and whom we talk to. These determine in great part the sources of information for our problem-finding activity. By carefully selecting these two filters, we make choices about not only what we will perceive, but what we will not perceive.

In an organizational setting, Mintzberg (1973) has discussed the importance of filters in making the top manager's various roles manageable. Ackoff (1967) provides a similar perspective in arguing that many managers are overloaded with irrelevant information (Ackoff calls the systems providing such information "mis-information systems"). To avoid irrelevancies, we need to ask what aspects of the environment do I *not* wish to see or hear about except in unusual circumstances.

Keen and Scott-Morton (1978) describe a successful application of filter design in the form of a computer-based decision support system for the production planning department of a large corporation, similar to the problem discussed in Chapter 1 (Figure 1.5). The department's difficulty stemmed from the overwhelming amount of information produced by reports on past sales and inventory records generated by routine computer runs. The reports were three inches thick and so detailed that it was extremely difficult to determine potential problems in the production plans. Therefore, the firm developed an interactive computer model as an important decision aid for the production-planning process. The three key managers (production planning, sales, and marketing planning) could easily check past sales records of selected items by interactive queries, with the results presented in easily digested graphical format. Not only could all the decision makers view the same data profiles, but they could systematically evaluate potential problems and devote their attention to these cases. Models were embedded in the system to determine automatically whether sales and inventory positions for each item were within bounds projected on the basis of past data for the same items. In this way, most items could be controlled automatically and filtered away from the attention processes of managers. The result of this new decision support system was a reduction in managers' time devoted to production planning from 6 days spread over a 20-day period to a half day spread over 2 working days.

The second major tool for managing attention is an alerting system. In an organizational setting, the quality control department has an important role to play in alerting the manufacturing division to when it is making defective units. Samples of produced items are taken periodically and specific characteristics are compared with performance standards. If sufficient numbers of the sample items are unsatisfactory, a problem is signaled.

Clearly, the basic philosophy of alerting systems is no different from the normal triggers we have been referring to in problem finding. Alerting systems simply systematically design these triggers to indicate a problem when there is one (and otherwise not). The importance of alerting systems has grown as the computer technology that is frequently used to implement them has improved. For example, credit card companies use them to note a sudden excessive use of a credit card. Typically firms use systems based on a model of expected performance (e.g., a historical or planning model) that alerts responsible decision makers when current performance is quite different from what history or the plan would lead one to expect. In so doing, decision makers can set the alerting system so that they will not miss important cues indicating potential problems.

2.4.3 *Validating beliefs and premises*

A final important matter for prescriptive problem finding is validating the models, beliefs, and premises that are the basis for representing and evaluating potential problems. The more accurately our models reflect what is achievable and what the status quo is, the more likely we are to accept real problems (and avoid Type III errors). We shall have more to say on this topic in Chapter 3 when we discuss inference and prediction. For the present, however, let us note that there is frequently a trade-off between postponing judgment on a problem until more information is at hand and acting now. Thaler and Shefrin (1981) have proposed a model of individual choice that reflects this conflict. They postulate that an individual is both a farsighted planner and a myopic doer. In the context of the problem-finding process, the farsighted planner would like to collect more information, whereas the myopic doer prefers to look at the world directly and classify a situation as "a problem" or "not a problem."

Frequently, individuals and organizations invoke simplistic rules that enable them to be myopic doers without being fully aware of the consequences of their proposed actions. For example, in our blood bank example in Chapter 1, a hospital may claim that it should always have enough units of blood in stock to satisfy demand. It may have no idea of the implications this policy has for inventory ordering or costs.

Scientific models provide examples of well-validated models. These provide our farsighted planning side with better data on the implications of our otherwise myopic actions. In the blood bank example, data could be assembled on the expected number of shortages as well as inventory storage costs for different ordering policies by the hospital. By formulating and validating a precise model of the inflows and outflows of blood from the blood bank, a more rational choice of stocking policies could be determined. In many cases, of course, there may be no accurate scientific model to base decisions on. For example, in the liquefied natural gas (LNG) siting problem described in Chapter 1, it is only possible to specify very crudely the probability of a catastrophic accident because experts diagree widely on these figures. In these cases, it is wise to recognize the limits of analysis and human knowledge in the problem-finding process.

2.5   Linking problem finding and problem solving

By way of summary, we present the various elements of the problem-finding process, both descriptive and prescriptive, in Figure 2.7. These elements are interesting in their own right, but they also condition the problem-solving process, as we now discuss.

First, the goals, values, and needs that trigger problem finding are likely to provide the basic definition of when we will say that a problem has been solved. From a descriptive viewpoint, therefore, one may expect the problem context that triggered dissatisfaction on one or another dimension of our hierarchy of objectives to influence problem solving strongly. Thus, if the problem perceived in problem finding is based on violating some reference point of normalcy, then one may expect problem-solving activity to be concerned primarily with restoring the condition of the reference point. From a prescriptive viewpoint, we have argued that this conditioning of problem finding by problem context and objectives makes it imperative that the needs, values, and goals to be satisfied by problem solving be clearly understood.

The second key aspect of problem finding influencing problem solving is the representation of the problem in terms of the context, models, and data that were used to determine that it was a problem in the first place. As Newell and Simon (1972) and Lindblom (1977) have pointed out, problem representations determined during problem finding have a strong

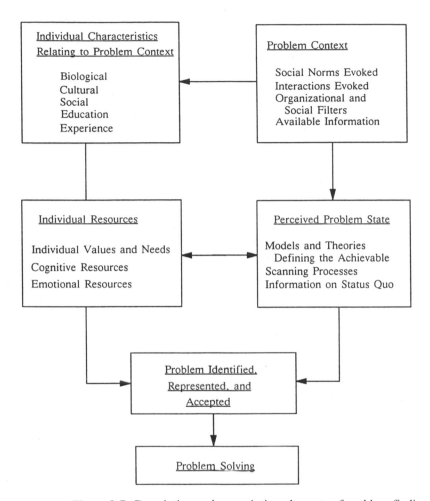

Figure 2.7. Descriptive and prescriptive elements of problem finding

influence on problem-solving activities.[6] Thus, generating an appropriate representation of the problem is an important element of the overall problem-solving process.

The third link between problem finding and problem solving concerns the set of alteratives that are generated in problem analysis and solution. How a problem is framed in the problem-finding/structuring phase of decision making can strongly affect the alternatives one considers for

---

6 See also G. Smith (1989) and the review article by Evans (1989) which summarize recent research on problem finding and problem solving, and which discuss the interaction of problem representation on Type III errors.

problem solution because such alternatives will be generated to restore reference conditions or otherwise remove the problem as recognized. We now consider the alternative generation process in more detail.

2.6   Alternative generation: descriptive aspects

Alternatives are usually generated with particular problems, objectives, and goals in mind. As noted already, objectives tend to be open-ended whereas goals are more specific. Let us return to an earlier example: If a student is searching for an apartment off campus, then one objective may be to "pay a low rent." This can be translated into a specific goal such as "pay less than $400 per month." This goal will eliminate numerous apartments from consideration, thus reducing the information-processing load on the individual.

2.6.1   *Learning about alternatives*

One easy way of reducing the collection of data is to examine only options that are close to the current solution. Individuals who automatically trade in their old Ford every two years for a new Ford follow this strategy to the extreme. If people limit their search for alternatives to the immediate neighborhood of their current position, then their present position will be the primary determinant of the set of feasible alternatives generated. Consider the process of job selection by new college graduates. Of the approximately three thousand occupations that exist today, only a small subset is usually examined by any single individual. These tend to be the jobs with which students have personal knowledge, either through others who have worked in this field or from their own experience.

New alternatives are often examined only after becoming dissatisfied with the current situation. For example, if one suffers a burglary this may trigger consideration of the alternative "install a burglar alarm." Much empirical evidence suggests that people take protective action only *after* an unfortunate experience rather than before. We usually avoid generating alternatives unless stimulated by a disaster or significant departure from satisfactory performance.

We also learn about alternatives from friends and acquaintances. If a friend raves about her new car, we may be influenced by her positive experience. Similarly we may reject other alternatives from consideration because of specific complaints by someone we know. This process of reducing the number of alternatives may not be defensible on statistical grounds but it does reduce the time and energy expended on the problem analysis phase. Not only do friends and acquaintances reduce the cognitive strain of generating alternatives, they also provide a social context in which decisions can be made.

A classic example of the latter is Whyte's (1954) study on the adoption of air conditioners on two blocks in a neighborhood. One side of the street had no air conditioners whereas practically all apartments on the other side had the units displayed in their windows. Whyte learned that there had been considerable discussion among those neighbors who had purchased air conditioners because their children played together in an adjoining alleyway. Families on the other side of the street did not have such a common play area for their children. The informal conversations and social interaction in one block led over time to widespread adoption of air conditioners, demonstrating a classic pattern in the diffusion of an innovation or alternative.

2.6.2 Isolating alternatives

The search for alternatives is often influenced by the choice process itself. For example, an investor may consider his investment alternatives to consist of individual securities. Alternatively, his decisions might be looked at as choosing among different portfolios (i.e., combinations of securities). To illustrate, consider the following problem posed by Tversky and Kahneman (1981):

Imagine that you face the following pair of *concurrent* decisions. First examine both carefully and then circle the options you prefer.

Decision I: (Choose either A or B)
        A. A sure gain of $240
        B.[7]   .25 $1000
               .75 $0

Decision II: (Choose either C or D)
        C. A sure loss of $750
        D.   .75   −$1000
               .25 $0

Most people look at these choices *in isolation,* preferring A in Decision 1 and D in Decision 2. However, if all four alternative pairs, AC, AD, BC, BD, are considered simultaneously, it becomes apparent that the majority preference AD is inferior to BC. This is easily seen by combining the lotteries (if one assumes they are independent of each other), yielding

7 Option B is diagrammed as a lottery offering a 25% chance of getting $1,000 and a 75% chance of getting $0.

the following net results:

AD	.25	$240
	.75	−$760
BC	.25	$250
	.75	−$750

In case a single choice must be made from many mutually exclusive options, individuals will often examine alternatives sequentially rather than making complete comparisons between them. In a "satisficing" decision rule, this process continues until an acceptable alternative is found. For example, in searching for housing, a particular apartment might be examined. If unsatisfactory, another apartment will be looked at. Once an apartment has been found that is acceptable, the decision process is terminated. The other end of the spectrum (from "satisficing" rules) would be to consider first *all* feasible alternatives and then make a final choice. Most decisions lie in between the sequential satisficing rule and an exhaustive evaluation of all alternatives. Chapter 4 will examine in further detail the links between searching for alternatives and settling on a final choice.

At a descriptive level, individuals frequently generate alternatives by engaging in local search and identifying options in isolation of others. Local search is associated with such terms as incrementalism, anchoring, uncomprehensive analysis, business as usual, not changing a winning horse, narrow problem focus, and noncreative decision making. The isolation effect refers to our tendency to simplify problems by breaking them into smaller ones of manageable size. There is no guarantee, however, that the sum of the optimal solutions to the subproblems constitutes the global optimum, or even comes close to it.

2.6.3   *Rigidity in problem solving*

Closely related to local search is the broader phenomenon of "rigidity in problem solving" (Adams, 1974), a field of research originating with the Gestalt psychologists that shows that learned habits and past history can cause problem finding and problem solving to be so anchored in the past that creativity is stifled. As an example, consider the following puzzle (we'll give you an answer to this puzzle later, but try to solve it now).

Bird and train puzzle: Two trains are 50 miles apart. At exactly 2 p.m. the two trains start toward each other on parallel tracks, each traveling 25 mph. Simultaneously, a bird starts at one train and flies until it meets the other train, turns around and heads back to the first train until it meets it, reverses direction again and continues flying back and forth between the two trains until the trains pass each other. If the bird is flying at 100 mph, how far will it travel in its back and forth journeys until the trains pass each other?

Another example of rigidity is Bartlett's (1958) famous cryptoarithmetic problem, which also stimulated considerable interest in the artificial intelligence literature (Newell and Simon, 1972).

Cryptoarithmetic problem: The following problem is to be considered a simple problem in arithmetic. To each letter of the names DONALD, GERALD and ROBERT is associated a unique digit from 0 through 9. Your task is to figure out the digits which correspond to each of the letters in the given names so that the following addition is correct DONALD + GERALD = ROBERT, i.e.,

DONALD
GERALD
ROBERT

All that is known is that D has the value 5.

Now what happens in practice when experimental subjects try to solve these two puzzles? In the bird and train puzzle, people who have been exposed to algebra word problems tend to pose quite complicated procedures and mathematical formulations for determining the length of the arc describing the bird's flight path. In reality, this is not necessary. The trains will meet one another one hour after they start since they are 50 miles apart, heading directly toward one another and traveling 25 mph. Thus, the bird will be in the air for one hour and must therefore travel 100 miles, since its speed is 100 mph. What prevents some people from getting this answer quickly (or at all) is that their past experience leads them to represent the problem in too complicated a manner. Similarly, the cryptoarithmetic problem tends to be solved from right to left, as in ordinary arithmetic. Many subjects solving this problem substitute D = 5, deduce that T must equal 0, but then get no further since no direct clue is provided for L or R as they are working from right to left. Starting from the left, however, makes it clear that E = 9, which thus provides further clues.[8]

In business, such rigidity is sometimes referred to as "functional blindness" (or *betriebsblind* in German). Marketing managers may only see marketing solutions whereas manufacturing people will favor product improvements (we return to this in Chapter 8). The paradox of creativity is that it requires both great familiarity with a subject matter *and* the ability to approach it from a fresh angle. For example, workers in a plant making sparkplugs were less able to generate alternative uses for them than workers outside the plant (see D. Johnson, 1972). Nonexperts often envision many more innovative applications. In science, breakthroughs frequently come from the fringes or interfaces of fields. Hence, seeking outside views

8 The entire solution is T = 0, G = 1, O = 2, B = 3, A = 4, D = 5, N = 6, R = 7, L = 8, E = 9. Readers may also wish to try CROSS + ROADS = DANGER, which is a more difficult cryptogram since no clue is provided at all.

1.	2.	3.
4.	5.	6.
7.	8.	9.

Figure 2.8. Self-imposed constraints: Draw four lines through all dots without lifting your pencil.

and challenging one's own assumptions are key to richer alternative generation.

Several other studies exist that illustrate how human decision makers often get locked in by their experience to perceiving and/or solving new problems the way they have solved previous problems (see Kaufman, 1991). As in the preceding examples, this prior experience is used as a starting point for either problem representation, the problem-solving process, or the alternatives to be considered for a given problem. Thus, although prior experience is critical to our overall cognitive abilities, it can also be a barrier to effective decision making.

2.6.4   *Self-imposed constraints*

A further characteristic of how people generate alternatives is that they frequently impose constraints on these alternatives that are simply not necessary. To illustrate the pervasiveness of such constraints, consider the nine-dot puzzle shown in Figure 2.8. The task is to draw four straight lines that pass through all nine dots without lifting one's pen from the paper. (For those who know this example, try to solve it with just three lines.)

Self-imposed constraints often operate as well in those many instances where people fail to do something because they think it will not work or cannot be done, otherwise known as self-discouragement and timidity. An important characteristic of the creative person is that he or she is willing to be ridiculed or declared insane for trying the unusual or "impossible."

Other creativity barriers include social norms and cultural taboos. Going against established norms may well be the key to solving a complex problem. As an example, consider the following puzzle. You are in a barren room. In the middle is a steel pipe sticking out from the concrete floor four inches high. Its diameter is just a bit larger than a ping-pong ball that rests at the bottom of this pipe. In addition, the room has the following supplies: a hammer, thread, safety pin, matches, and a newspaper. Your task is to get the ping-pong ball out of the steel pipe (without damaging either). Try both problems (due to Adams, 1974) before reading further.

In the nine-dot puzzle, the key to the four-line solution is to go outside the nine dot area. For example, first draw a horizontal line through the top row and continue to the right. Then angle back sharply and go through Dots 6 and 8, and shoot up vertically through the first column. Finally, continue with the diagonal through Dots 1, 5, and 9, which completes the puzzle. The three-line solution centers on the recognition that the points are dots rather than dimensionless algebraic points. Thus vertical lines may be drawn through each of the columns, with slight angles so that the lines touch at some very high and low point. In a related vein, the line to be drawn might be considered to be so thick that just one line covers nine points. The puzzle with the ping-pong ball can be solved by urinating into the steel pipe, which violates a social norm. Such creativity, however, saved at least one bomber crew in World War II. Upon approach to landing, they discovered that the landing gear was stuck because all hydraulic fluid had leaked out. The flight engineer then hit upon the idea of urinating into the hydraulic system, thus temporarily restoring pressure. It worked; they landed safely.

The challenge of breaking out of traditional frames of mind is the hallmark of creativity. Perkins (1981) developed an interesting "snowflake" model of creativity, based on laboratory evidence and biographical study. Six traits or characteristics make up the corners of Perkins's snowflake. The first is a strong personal commitment to aesthetic solutions. For example, Albert Einstein was obsessed with simplicity in physics, searching in vain for the unified theory of nature's basic forces. To mathematicians and physicists, a theory or proof has to be elegant, as in Fermat's principle of least time (later generalized to Hamilton's principle of least action). The second trait concerns good taste in what questions to ask. The 1991 Nobel Prize in economics went to Ronald Coase for asking some very basic (yet penetrating) questions, such as, Why do firms exist? His insightful questions spawned entirely new research fields and journals (e.g., institutional economics and economic views of law). Mental agility is the third trait: the ability to think in opposites, also known as Janus thinking (after the Roman God Janus who has two faces looking in opposite directions). Tolerance for ambiguity, thinking in images or metaphors, and the desire to connect seemingly unrelated ideas all belong to this corner.

These three traits are largely cognitive, although the first one is driven by deeply held values. The remaining two traits address more dispositional characteristics. The fourth corner is about risk taking and not being afraid of failure. Excellence usually requires many attempts. Pablo Picasso is renowned for perhaps 10 or 20 masterpieces. However, these outliers were drawn from a lifelong creative effort amounting to about 20,000 pieces of art, much of it mediocre. This overall output translates into 400 pieces per year for 50 years, or an average of more than one creation per day (weekends and holidays included)! The fifth trait concerns objectivity: the courage to seek criticism and outside views. In science, this means openness to new evidence; in the arts, a willingness to listen to and be judged by peers. Lastly, Perkins identifies inner motivation as a key driving force in creative people. Without love or passion for your subject, it is difficult to spend the many hours necessary to create a great book, composition, or scientific work. When Gauss was congratulated on his brilliant proof of a key theorem in mathematics, he replied that there had not been a day in the last 15 years or so that he did not think about that problem. Intense commitment and obsession are common traits in uncommonly creative people.

The snowflake theory has both descriptive and prescriptive elements. It is hard to generate passion for a subject where none exists to begin with, or to be brilliant in science without a certain genetic endowment. However, being open to criticism is a skill most of us can learn to improve. Likewise, seeking simple solutions, tolerating ambiguity, and taking risks are traits we have the power to change (within limits). The next section examines the proactive dimensions of creativity in more detail.

2.7   Alternative generation: prescriptive aspects

The challenge in improving the process of generating alternatives lies in overcoming the problems associated with bounded rationality, learning and complexity. In order to generate a wider or better set of alternatives, individuals must free themselves from the constraining influences of learned habits, self-discouragement and timidity, and premature problem closure.[9] Essentially, the question boils down to being more vigilant and creative in the generation of options. How is this to be done?

2.7.1   *Phases of creativity*

Various stages have been distinguished in the process of creativity. The first is *preparation* and concerns the collection of data and other supporting material. When searching for a job, this might mean utilizing the services of central information sources such as a university placement office or employment agency. When undertaking scientific research, this implies immersing oneself in the literature to study theories and evidence relevant to the problem at hand.

9 See Osborn (1963), Evans (1989), and Evans and Lindsay (1989) for an extended discussion of blocks to problem solving, and the entertaining book by Adams (1974) for a review of experimental evidence on problem-solving performance. On the prescriptive side, see Russo and Schoemaker (1989) for ways of avoiding various "decision traps."

Next the *production phase* involves the actual generation of ideas. This phase is not well understood psychologically and constitutes the essence of creativity. It entails conscious as well subconscious processes and is only partly under rational control. Various techniques exist to enhance idea generation ranging from brainstorming to *synectics* (see Hogarth, 1987). This latter technique emphasizes the power of metaphorical or analogical thought processes. For example, when Kukule discovered the closed structure of the benzine ring in chemistry, he credited this breakthrough to a dream in which a snake was biting its own tail. This vision resembled the hexagonal structure of benzine.

The third phase is the *evaluation of ideas*. Recognizing it as a distinct phase highlights that it is often useful to separate the generation of ideas (i.e., ideation) from their evaluation. Brainstorming techniques often emphasize the importance of not evaluating ideas, so that people can freely propose alternatives without having to simultaneously judge them. Importantly, the people who can best generate ideas may not be best in evaluating them, and vice-versa.

The ability to generate different alternatives depends of course on the *complexity of the task*. Apartment selection is normally considerably easier than choosing a job. The preparation phase in either case, however, requires an individual to consider carefully the main objectives and determine how well specific alternatives are likely to meet them. Such coupling of the evaluation phase with the ideation phase may be necessary to narrow down a set of alternatives.

2.7.2 Widening the set of alternatives

As part of the creativity process, there may be considerable learning from others. One person's ideas on a set of alternatives may trigger suggestions from others. The more formal process of *brainstorming,* to be discussed in Chapter 6, enables individuals in a group setting to suggest a set of alternatives for consideration by others without being criticized as to their feasibility. At the simplest level, one can begin generating a list of alternatives by envisioning best and worst outcomes and determining alternatives that lead to them. For example, Van Gundy (1987) suggests beginning this process by asking two questions: Wouldn't it be nice if? and Wouldn't it be awful if? This type of exercise and other "broadening" procedures are intended to break the bonds that anchor us to our present, limited sets of alternatives.

Sometimes the set of alternatives can be enlarged by combining features of existing alternatives to obtain new ones. For instance, when the National Aeronautical and Space Administration (NASA) had to decide what research activities to engage in, they distinguished between actions,

Table 2.2. *Generating scientific objectives for a space program*

Action phase	Target feature	Target subject
Characteristic circulation patterns in	The photosphere of	The sun
Measure tidal deformation of	The surface of	The moon
Establish the structure of	The interior of	Jupiter
Measure relativistic time dilations in	———	The space environment

Source: Keeney and Raiffa (1976).

objects, and target features. A long list was created under each heading, and combinations of actions, objects, and features were systematically generated. Table 2.2 demonstrates this approach using *four* action phases, *three* target features, and *four* objects. An exhaustive combination of these yields 48 different research tasks (i.e., $4 \times 3 \times 4$). Some of these are nonsensical, such as "measuring tidal deformation in the interior of the space environment." After eliminating the infeasible combinations, NASA still had more than one thousand meaningful lower-level research tasks left. Also, they had the assurance that few aspects were overlooked.

Metaphors may also be used to highlight unexpected aspects or implications. As noted earlier, this technique goes under the name of synectics (Gordon, 1961) and uses analogies to join seemingly unconnected elements. The analogies may be personal, biological, or symbolic. For example, an engineer might imagine himself to be a bridge. In so doing, he envisions water splashing against the bottom of the bridge (e.g., his feet or face), and thereby may suddenly think of corrosion problems. As for biological analogies, birds have provided inspiration for the design of aircraft, beehives for architectural designs, and so on.

Symbolic analogies may also be useful for more abstract tasks, such as teaching a course. Suppose the instructor views his role in the course as a mother. This analogy directs attention to the importance of birth (i.e., teaching and nurturing of ideas) and caring (i.e., the importance of establishing a trusting relationship with students). The role of metaphor is particularly important in science. For example, in physics Fermat anthropomorphized light as seeking the path of least travel time. In doing so, he provided an explanation for the refraction law in optics and proposed various novel hypotheses (e.g., concerning converging lenses) that subsequently were found to be correct.

We have already alluded to institutional ways of widening the alternative generation process. University placement offices and housing offices often provide comprehensive listing of different jobs and apartments so that students have a centralized data base at their fingertips. In a broader vein, advertising can play a key role in generating information on options.

Unfortunately, people will encounter the problem of information overload in coping with data from these different sources. Here new computer technology may play an important role as a decision aid. For instance, a computer could store a great deal of information related to the characteristics of different apartments so that students can easily retrieve the data in the form they need. Furthermore, the computer might enable individuals to select a subset of alternatives having specific features. It is an open question today how much impact microcomputer technology will have on the alternative generation process. If people are reluctant to consider more than a few options because of memory and other mental limitations, computers may be a useful tool for freeing them from these constraints.

2.7.3 *Relaxing self-imposed constraints*

The bird and train problem, the nine-dot problem and the cryptoarithmetic problem all illustrate how rigidity, learned habits, and self-imposed constraints can be significant blocks to creativity. How can we avoid or remove such self-imposed constraints? Several techniques exist (beyond brainstorming and synectics) to unfreeze people from myopic perspectives. We briefly review some well-known ones here.

Lateral thinking (de Bono, 1973) can often be used to expand the range of alternative solutions. Consider, for instance, the problem of how to solve complaints about slow elevators in an office building. Convergent thinkers would accept the diagnosis of "slow elevators" and start to work on ways to speed them up. Divergent thinkers would mentally walk around the problem and note that we are dealing here, in part, with perceptions about time spent waiting. One solution is to change the time perceptions by giving people something to do, from adding bulletin boards to installing mirrors beside the elevators. In the same spirit, restaurants commonly use entertainment to make the waiting time seem less long.

Dialectic reasoning (Mitroff and Emshoff, 1979) is another important mind-expanding technique. It includes "devil's advocacy" as well as systematic attempts to construct two plausible but opposite interpretations of a case. Our judicial system follows this approach directly by constructing a thesis (of guilt) and antithesis (of innocence) from the same body of evidence, in the hope that a synthesis of these two views (by an impartial judge or jury) will lead to an improved judgment. Royal Dutch/Shell, the Anglo-Dutch oil giant, uses this approach in its strategic planning process (see Wack, 1985a, 1985b). Every two or three years, the company constructs two to four widely divergent views of the future, ranging from say an economic boom scenario to a world in which environmentalists enact increasingly strict legislation, with a huge price tag. Importantly, the company leaves it up to senior managers to debate the merits of these alternative scenarios. They often spark new ideas for innovations or a better appreciation of the risk–return ratio of the current plans. The creative tension inherent in dialectical thinking can be a valuable impetus to new thoughts or perspectives.

A host of indirect approaches exists as well for improving creativity. Henry (1991) devotes entire chapters to such activities as networking, imaging, mental mapping, as well as the honing of intuition and judgment. One company advises newcomers to schedule a lunch with a person from outside their department every week to stay abreast of larger issues. Others train people in the art of remapping (see McCaskey, 1982), recognizing that changing your world views is a little bit like dying. We can think of a mental map here as a limited set of interwoven assumptions (e.g., the importance of hard work or honesty), a domain-specific theory (e.g., the efficiency of a free-market system), or an entire life-shaping paradigm (e.g., Islamic fundamentalism). First, there may be shock or anger when discovering that one's view is not as complete or generally accepted as once thought. The stark realization that one's map is in fact not the territory may instill grief or depression, similar to the loss of a friend or relative. Trusted and familiar maps provide security and their loss (such as the earth not being flat or the sun not rotating around the earth) can be highly upsetting. Finally, acceptance of a new map (e.g., the Copernican view) may slowly set in.

McCaskey (1982) describes the personal pain Charles Darwin experienced over several decades in developing his new biological map of natural selection (especially concerning its conflict with church and existing theory). Few of us will ever personally experience new maps on the order of Newton, Darwin, or Einstein. Yet, our own intellectual and emotional growth requires the destruction of old maps and creation of new maps for the various complexities we encounter throughout life, from developing a career to creating a family and the ultimate acceptance (religious or otherwise) of our own mortality. How well we network, map, imagine, and judge will much affect the problems we encounter in life and the extent to which we shall accept and resolve them.

2.8   Concluding comments

John Dewey, the famous American pragmatist philosopher, said: "A problem well stated is a problem half solved!" The objective of this chapter has been to pose a framework to help understand why certain problems and decision situations are identified and accepted for problem-solving activity while others may go unnoticed. The framework we have described is based on the fundamental premise, which enjoys support in both biological and social science, that humans are purposeful in their problem-finding and problem-solving activity and that they strive to satisfy a nested hierarchy of needs through this activity. But in so doing they are limited in their information-processing abilities – including their abilities to perceive, remember, and process information. Thus, in Simon's famous phrase, these human decision makers enjoy only bounded rationality (see Simon, 1957b).

The implications of this boundedness are severalfold. Most important, bounded rationality implies a significant gap between what a perfectly rational decision maker would wish to accomplish in problem finding and problem solving and what normal people can accomplish. Second, different decision makers are likely to perceive and accept problems to different degrees. Third, tools to aid decision makers need to fit the limitations of both decision makers and the problem context. We have explored these issues in this chapter for the interrelated areas of problem finding and alternatives generation. But these will be recurrent themes in the remainder of the book as well.

Part II

Individual decision making

3

Prediction and inference

3.1   Understanding decision making

It is not clear that we can ever fully understand the processes of judgment, evaluation, and choice. As John F. Kennedy once remarked:

The essence of ultimate decisions remains impenetrable to the observer – often, indeed to the decider himself. . . . There will always be the dark and tangled stretches in the decision making process – mysterious even to those who may be most intimately involved. (From Sorensen, 1963)

Indeed, being a good decision maker does not imply that a person necessarily understands his or her decision process. For example, most of us know how to ride a bicycle; however, it may be difficult to verbalize or teach this skill (which entails automated behavior) to others. With decision making and judgment, matters may be yet more complicated as we are trying to think about thinking itself.[1] In the next three chapters we shall examine different phases of the problem-solving process as depicted in Figure 3.1. By imposing this framework, we will be able to gain considerable insight into the decision process itself, although some of its tangled stretches may continue to elude us.

The prediction and inference phase, to be discussed in this chapter, deals with the description of alternatives, in particular the formation of judgments and beliefs with respect to possible outcomes. Our concern in both this chapter and the next is with the descriptive and prescriptive aspects of problem analysis. Chapter 5 thereafter explicitly links the descriptive and prescriptive aspects by highlighting legitimation as a key element in selecting and implementing a decision procedure. For ease of exposition we shall treat each of the different phases, that is, prediction and inference, valuation, and implementation, separately. However, we should recognize that the actual decision-making process is seldom conducted in such a sequential manner. Typically, there is much interaction and feedback among these three phases. Our discussion of problem anal-

---

1 However, since part of our decision making is conscious or "controlled" cognition, some of it may actually be easier to introspect about. The next chapter will examine the reliability of people's personal insights into their own decision making.

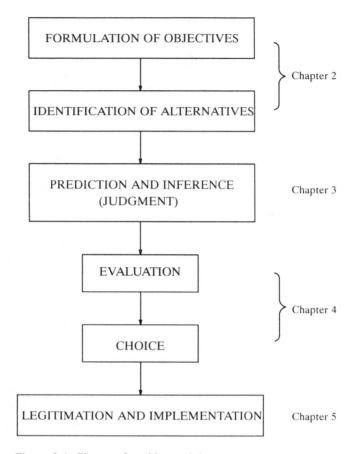

Figure 3.1. Phases of problem-solving process

ysis will continually explore the implications of information-processing limitations and bounded rationality for decision making. We shall see that the limitations on memory, judgment, and attention discussed in Chapters 1 and 2 are central to understanding how individuals characterize alternatives, form beliefs, and predict consequences.

3.2   Prediction and inference: descriptive aspects

Once an appropriate set of alternatives has been generated, the decision maker typically examines the possible consequences of each option and their likelihoods of occurring. This section is concerned with two complementary aspects of this phase: predicting outcomes (y) from a given data set (x) and inferring the structure of data from a given set of out-

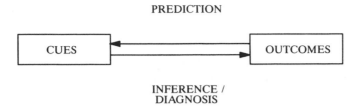

Figure 3.2. Prediction and inference

comes (see Figure 3.2). The first aspect is usually called *prediction* and
the second *diagnosis* or *inference*.[2] Either type can be based on causal or
correlational reasoning. In the latter instance, we predict or infer *x* from
y because we know that they are strongly correlated, without necessarily
knowing why.

To illustrate these concepts, consider the problem of predicting the annual salary a student might receive from a job upon graduation. To make
this prediction, we can collect salary information on past offers made to
other students, as well as any data regarding students' current experience
with the job market. Either data set would enable us to draw some inferences regarding the salary distribution. We might further decompose
the salaries into different majors to look for systematic differences or we
could undertake some type of causal analysis by investigating the impact
of economic conditions on the demand for different jobs. For example,
computer analysts may currently be in high demand but in short supply,
thus yielding higher salaries.

The prediction you make can either be a point estimate or a probability
distribution. Saying "I expect the job offer to be about $35,000" is a
point estimate. Alternatively, you might provide a probability statement
such as, "There is a 60% chance that one of the job offers will have a
salary greater than $35,000," or, "I am 90% confident that the student's

2 There is, however, no agreed-upon theory that clearly distinguishes among such concepts as inference, induction, diagnosis, prediction, deduction, causation, correlation,
  implication, etc.

starting salary will be between $25,000 and $50,000." The next subsection examines different approaches to providing point estimates. Thereafter, we discuss how people estimate and express uncertainty.

In predicting the outcomes of possible decision alternatives, the set of relevant dimensions or attributes must first be identified, say $y_1, \ldots y_n$. For example, suppose the alternatives are different graduate schools from which to obtain a Masters of Business Administration (MBA). In this case, y_1 might represent a school's tuition cost, y_2 the grade point average (GPA) the student might earn, y_3 the prospect of getting a good job afterward, y_4 the quality of the education, and so on. For each possible school, we could try to estimate its score along each of these outcome dimensions. Of course, each y_i is itself determined by multiple factors, some of which the student can control and some she cannot. Let us focus on just one dimension, say y_2. Future GPA in graduate school depends on such factors as the type of MBA program (x_1), the person's quantitative background (x_2), her GMAT score (x_3), the amount of time spent studying (x_4), the quality of her fellow students (x_5), and so on. Hence, the prediction of just y_2 entails a complex multivariate function $f_2(x_1, \ldots, x_n)$ of other factors.

3.2.1   *Development of the Lens model*

To assess how well humans can infer such relationships (in order to predict outcomes), decision scientists starting with Hammond (1955) have conceptualized this task as follows. A set of independent variables $x_1, \ldots, x_n$ determines the value of some dependent variable y_e and a human's predictions thereof, denoted y_s. Figure 3.3 shows this diagrammatically. The independent variables x_i are information cues that the human uses to predict the true outcome y_e. The subscript e here refers to the environmental (i.e., the objective) outcome, whereas the subscript s refers to the subject's prediction of this outcome (i.e., it is subjective). Because the diagram resembles light rays in a convergent lens, the conceptualization in Figure 3.3 is known as the Lens model.

Usually, the relationship $y_e = f_e(x_1, \ldots, x_n)$ is probabilistic, due to the incompleteness of the set of cues, the difficulty of precisely specifying the true function relating y_e to the cues, and instabilities in the environment. Thus, the relationship between future grade point average and its determinants is hard to know with certainty. When you have to predict outcomes repeatedly, a logical first step is to try to uncover the nature of f_e. This is, for example, attempted in econometric modeling, sales prediction, and weather forecasting. However, for more idiosyncratic decisions people often make their predictions intuitively. They may not possess the know-how to construct explicit models; they may be unwilling

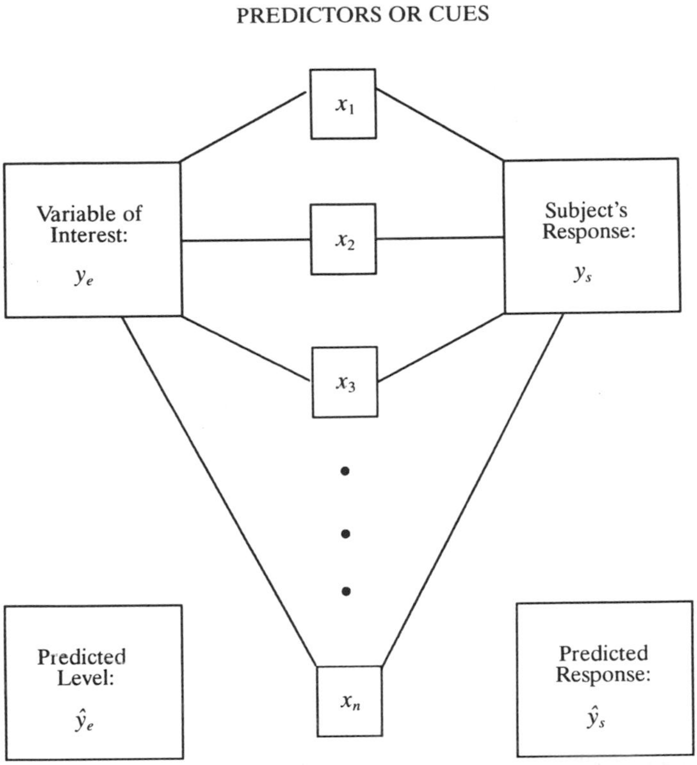

PREDICTORS OR CUES

Figure 3.3. Diagram of the Lens model. *Note:* $\hat{y}_e$ and $\hat{y}_s$ are prediction models.

or unable to invest the time and cost required; or they may be unable to collect the necessary data. Hence, in our individual daily decisions, we commonly predict outcomes intuitively, using various informational cues x_i.

The Lens model is the central framework of social judgment theory, a research approach initially developed by Hammond (1955) and Hoffman (1960), and formalized by Hursch, Hammond, and Hursch (1964). Its intellectual roots trace back to the pioneering work of Egon Brunswik (1943 and 1955), a psychologist interested in visual perception. Brunswik emphasized that our recognition of objects is based on imperfect cues that may be partly overlapping. For example, the identification of a person's face relies on multiple cues (e.g., nose, eyes, hair, mouth) that contain enough redundancy so that one can recognize the person from multiple angles. Brunswik termed this capacity "vicarious functioning," which permits you to recognize a face when it is partially covered or has aged.

Table 3.1. *Numerical data for Lens model example*

	Predictor variables					Dependent variables	
Case	x_1	x_2	x_3	x_4	x_5	y_e	y_s
1	55	28	1	49	35	588	341
2	86	12	29	81	16	929	741
3	95	48	16	64	44	936	985
4	16	50	74	24	78	837	593
5	92	1	10	1	41	673	380
6	63	26	0	81	20	499	665
.	.	.	.	.	.	.	.
.	.	.	.	.	.	.	.
.	.	.	.	.	.	.	.
45	40	31	97	8	84	798	640
46	59	52	20	83	40	889	752
47	53	19	78	26	56	930	796
48	86	27	26	53	66	985	797
49	39	35	95	17	69	875	693
50	98	49	7	52	41	834	808

His overall philosophy is known as "probabilistic functionalism," since it views humans as functioning in a world that is mostly indirectly observable and only partly predictable. Individual cues (e.g., a nose or chin) bear an imperfect relationship to the object to be judged (e.g., it could be someone else's nose as well). And different observers may put different weights on any given cue.

Hammond, Hursch, and Todd (1964) extended Brunswik's viewpoint to social judgments, especially concerning people's behavior and predictive performance. The research agenda that ensued from social judgment theory is quite broad, and focuses on such general questions as:

- How do people, in their natural environment, combine multiple cues in arriving at judgments. Are there any general strategies or processes they use?
- What are the actual characteristics of the tasks people encounter (in terms of kind of cues, their structure, relationships to outcomes, feedback, etc.)?
- How much do people (especially experts) differ in their reliance on various cues or factors when confronted with the same prediction task?
- How close do people come to an optimal weighing and integration of cues (when compared say against a statistical prediction model)?

- To what extent can and do people improve their judgments when they receive various kinds of feedback about their performance?
- Can social conflict be mediated by better understanding the information-processing models of the conflicting parties?

Social judgment theory has seen a wide range of applications. It has been used to study various kinds of medical judgments, audit reports by accountants, graduate school admission judgments, psychological diagnoses, financial predictions of stock prices, and recommendation by social workers (see Brehmer and Joyce, 1988). A well-known study by Hammond, Rohrbaugh, Mumpower, and Adelman (1977), to be discussed in Chapter 6, used the theory to reconcile the police, the minority community, and the city's mayor who were in an emotional stalemate concerning which new bullet to adopt for the Denver police department.

The Lens model has enabled researchers to assess the accuracy of people's intuitive predictions and inferences. Before reviewing the main findings of this extensive line of research, we shall discuss a numerical example to introduce key concepts and terminology of the Lens model.

Numerical example. Table 3.1 shows a data set consisting of five independent predictors, x_1 through x_5, and two dependent variables y_e and y_s. Think of y_e as the variable to be predicted (e.g., interest rates or future sales) and of y_s as someone's estimates or best guess thereof. In our example the correlation between y_e and y_s turns out to be .52. Although by no means perfect, this correlation is significantly better than chance prediction and indicates that the person is somewhat knowledgeable about y_e. In actuality, this example is entirely simulated so as to illustrate both the psychological and statistical questions of interest in the Lens model.

The variables x_1 through x_5 were each filled in at random in Table 3.1 by drawing random numbers from the interval 0–100, using a procedure that assumes uniformity and statistical independence. Next, the following equations were defined to calculate the two dependent variables:

$$y_e = 3x_1 + \sqrt[3]{2x_2^2} + 8\sqrt{x_3 x_4} + 100 \log_e(x_5)$$
$$y_s = 50 \sqrt{x_1} + 6x_2 + .1x_3 x_4 + \bar{\epsilon}$$

Note that y_e, which represents the true environment, is a nonlinear deterministic function of x_1 through x_5. In contrast, y_s is incomplete and stochastic, since it represents fallible human prediction. It is incomplete in that x_5 is missing from the y_s equation. It is stochastic in that a random error term $\bar{\epsilon}$ is included, which was assumed to be normally distributed with mean 0 and a standard deviation of 80. Thus, the human model would not generally make the same prediction for identical cases. Also, note that the y_s model is somewhat simpler than y_e, containing only one nonlinearity $\sqrt{x_1}$ and one interaction effect ($x_3 * x_4$). Assuming these y_e

and y_s were to represent values from an actual case, such as stock prices or future grade point averages, decision researchers might proceed stepwise as follows.

Steps in constructing a model. First, they would wish to construct a table such as Table 3.1, without any knowledge of the true y_e and y_s equations. Second, they would likely examine this table using linear regression models first, to see how important the various predictors actually are. Third, if behaviorally oriented, they might examine how closely y_s predicts y_e and *why*. This could entail a comparison of the regression models $\hat{y}_s$ and $\hat{y}_e$. Fourth, they might be interested in helping the human (y_s) predict better. Let us examine each step in turn, assuming that y_e represents students' grade point averages in their first MBA program year.

The first step is to identify and measure suitable x_i variables. Presumably the students' GMAT scores will matter as well as their undergraduate education. Beyond that, however, it is less obvious what predictors will be important, such as age, gender, income, or nationality. It will pay to consult with experts (e.g., admissions officers) to set up the right table. Nonetheless, some variables will be left out since grade points entail a host of observable but also unobservable factors.

The next step is to subject whatever incomplete data structure you have garnered to regression analyses, with y_e and y_s as the dependent variables. When linear regression was applied to the full data set underlying Table 3.1, the following equations emerged:

$$\hat{y}_e = 414 + 2.69x_1 - .81x_2 + 3.92x_3 + 3.04x_4$$
$$\hat{y}_s = -160 + 3.88x_1 + 6.94x_2 + 5.82x_3 + 4.4x_4$$

Note that x_5 is left out of this analysis, as it is supposed to be a missing variable (i.e., one that does matter but is unrecognized by the human expert). In addition to these two regression equations, the following relevant statistics are noteworthy (the column labeled R^2 – the coefficient of determination – refers to how much of the variation in a set of data is explained by a linear regression model):

	R^2	*Correlation with* y_e
$\hat{y}_e$	.689	.830
$\hat{y}_s$	.858	.542
y_s	—	.521

In words, the table shows that the expert is more linear than the environment (since .858 > .689) and that $\hat{y}_e$ is a better predictor than either $\hat{y}_s$ or y_s. This is not surprising because objective models often (although not always) outperform intuitive predictions. What is surprising, however, is that $\hat{y}_s$ predicts y_e better than y_s (i.e., .542 > .521). In other words, a linear regression model of the human expert does a better job of predicting y_e than the human does. How can that be?

The answers relate to the third and fourth steps (analysis and improvement). The high R^2 of the $\hat{y}_s$ model (namely .858) suggests that the human is highly linear in processing the predictor variables x_1 through x_4. However, because the R^2 is also less than one, we know that either random noise (in the human's judgment process) or unrecognized expertise (e.g., nonlinearities or additional cues not modeled for) is present. One way to test which of these two possibilities applies is to examine the unexplained variance or so-called regression residuals. If the residuals are truly random, noise is the explanation. If, however, significant correlations exist among the residuals or with the x_i, the model may be misspecified. (Since we can look behind the curtain in this simulated example, we know that both explanations are true, with the noise term being the dominant explanation.)

The relative importance of noise versus misspecification primarily determines whether substituting $\hat{y}_s$ for y_s is likely to improve predictive performance. In our example, $\hat{y}_s$ does somewhat better than y_s. Thus, it must be that the expert's intuitive predictions (y_s) contain some degree of random noise. The $\hat{y}_s$ model eliminates this noise and for that reason can outperform the expert, provided no significant cues or nonlinearities are overlooked. Note that noise can also be eliminated or reduced by averaging the opinions of *multiple* experts. Such "consensus forecasting" enjoys a strong performance record when compared with the results of individual experts (Armstrong, 1985).

In general, however, the best approach to prediction is to build a good y_e model. If that is impossible (e.g., because no past data exist or y_e is subjective or the future has changed), it boils down to a choice between y_s (an expert) or $\hat{y}_s$ (the expert's model). For example, when deciding what city to relocate to, no objective y_e exists that reflects your particular preferences. However, you might be able to specify what attributes matter to you – such as climate, schooling, jobs, culture, housing costs – and use a places rated almanac (which contains rankings of cities by various attributes) to develop an intuitive rank order. Alternatively, you could build a linear model of your own preferences – either by choosing appropriate weights for each attribute or by carefully scoring 30 or so cities and performing a regression on these subjective scores – and then apply this model to all cities. Chances are that this linear model of your own trade-offs will give you a ranking different from your intuitive list. Moreover, the ranking based on a linear model of your judgments is likely to predict your true preferences better than your initial intuitive scores.

In sum, building a model, even a totally subjective one such as $\hat{y}_s$, is usually a better approach to prediction than unaided intuition. In the next

Table 3.2. *Summary of Lens model variables*

y_e	Target variable to be predicted (e.g., interest rates)
y_s	Subjective prediction by human expert of y_e
$\hat{y}_e$	Statistical prediction of y_e using a (linear) regression model derived from past y_e observations
$\hat{y}_s$	Statistical prediction of y_s using a (linear) regression model derived from past y_s observations
R_a	Correlation between y_e and y_s (to measure how well the expert predicts y_e)
R_e	Correlation between y_e and $\hat{y}_e$ (to measure how well the objective regression model predicts y_e)
R_s	Correlation between y_s and $\hat{y}_s$ (to measure how well the subjective regression model predicts y_s)
R_m	Correlation between y_e and $\hat{y}_s$ (to measure how well the subjective regression, or so-called bootstrap model, predicts y_e)
C	Correlation between residuals of the $\hat{y}_e$ and $\hat{y}_s$ models (if C is near 0, the bootstrap model captures most of the human expertise)

chapter, we shall make the same point about determining final choices (rather than predictions) and discuss more complex procedures for building subjective models. Table 3.2 summarizes the various Lens model variables discussed so far (with their notation) and defines some new ones to be discussed next.

3.2.2   *Empirical findings using the Lens model*

Several conclusions emerge from the many empirical studies conducted with the Lens model (for reviews, see Slovic and Lichtenstein, 1971; Ebert and Mitchell, 1975; Brehmer, 1976; and Brehmer and Joyce, 1988). We can draw some of these conclusions from Table 3.3, which shows results from representative Lens model studies. The studies involve a number of prediction tasks from a variety of arenas, including the stock market, medicine, and student GPAs. We will discuss each of the measures cited in the table in detail below. N_1 and N_2 refer to the number of experts used in each study and the number of predictions each expert made, respectively.

Achievement indexes. These are measured by R_a, the correlations between y_e and y_s. In general, these correlations are found to be relatively low. In the sample of studies examined by Camerer (1981) they range from $-.01$ to $.84$, with an average value of $.33$. So, on average, intuitive

Table 3.3. *Summary of major Lens model studies*

Type of prediction task	R_a	R_e	R_s	R_m	C	N_1	N_2
Future return on common stock	.01	.78	.82	.01	.04	21	18
Faculty evaluations of graduate students	.19	.54	.78	.25	−.01	1	111
Life-expectancy of cancer patients	−.01	.35	.41	.13	−.06	3	186
Changes in stock prices	.23	.80	.85	.29	−.02	5	35
Mental illness using personality tests	.28	.46	.77	.31	.07	29	861
Grades and attitudes in psychology course	.48	.62	.90	.56	−.01	8	50
IQ scores on basis of psychograms	.51	.64	.91	.51	.13	15	100
Business failures using financial ratios	.50	.67	.79	.53	.13	43	70
Student ratings of teaching effectiveness	.35	.91	.71	.56	−.02	1	16
Performance of life insurance salesmen	.13	.43	.60	.14	.06	16	200
IQ scores using Rorschach tests	.47	.54	.85	.51	.05	10	78
GPA of graduate students	.33	.69	.65	.50	.01	98	90
GPA of average students	.37	.69	—	.43	—	40	90
Changes in security prices	.23	.59	.55	.28	.06	47	50
Value of ellipses in experimental task	.84	.97	—	.89	—	6	180
Means	.33	.64	.74	.39	.03		

Source: Adapted from Camerer (1981). Used by permission.

prediction yields modest results. This also holds true if other performance measures are used besides correlation.

Linear human thinking. Lens model research suggests that humans tend to think about the environment linearly, whether the environment is linear or not (see Brehmer and Brehmer, 1988). As noted earlier, this means that the linear regression of y_s on the x_i typically yields a higher R^2 (i.e., coefficient of determination) than a regression of y_e on x_i. Table 3.3 shows for each study the mean R_s and R_e values, where R_s is the correlation between $\hat{y}_s$ and y_s and R_e the correlation between $\hat{y}_e$ and y_e (see definitions in Table 3.2). As before, the variables $\hat{y}_s$ and $\hat{y}_e$ refer to the predictions of the two linear regression models. The $\hat{y}_s$ model makes predictions using a linear regression equation derived from the subject's intuitive guesses (hence its subscript s); the $\hat{y}_e$ model is a linear regression equation derived from the true outcomes or environment (hence its subscript e). Table 3.3 suggests that the mind of the human expert is typically simpler (i.e., more linear) than the environment he or she is trying to predict, since R_s is higher than R_e in 10 out of the 13 studies where both of these correlations were computed.

Internal noise. The preceding conclusion again raises the question about the unexplained variance in the human's model: Is it systematic or random? If it is systematic, the linear model is incorrect; that is, the human knows more than the linear model tells us. And if this in fact is true, we should find some correlation between the residuals of the $\hat{y}_s$ model and the residuals of the $\hat{y}_e$ model. (For example, if the human correctly predicts a high y_e value, while $\hat{y}_s$ and $\hat{y}_e$ don't, the residuals of $\hat{y}_s$ and $\hat{y}_e$ will have the same bias for that case.) Table 3.3 reveals, however, that the correlation between the $\hat{y}_e$ and $\hat{y}_s$ residual terms (called C) is generally negligible (see also Ullman and Doherty, 1984). Empirically, the unexplained variance (or residual) in the $\hat{y}_s$ model is mostly random error. This explains in part why R_a is usually low.

Other evidence suggests more directly that intraperson reliability is often quite low. In a study of nine x-ray specialists, Hoffman, Slovic, and Rorer (1968) found that the *intra*expert correlations between a set of 96 cases judged one week and then repeated a week later were as low as .6, indicating considerable judgmental inconsistency. The *inter*person reliabilities among these nine radiologists were lower yet, ranging from $-.11$ to .83, with a median of .38. Apparently, the way these x-ray specialists used the available information differed significantly from one expert to the next and even for the same expert from one week to the next. Moreover, it was found that they used the available cues in a highly linear fashion and usually focused on just a few of the relevant cues.

Cue utilization. This brings us to the third major lens model finding, concerning cue utilization (Brehmer, 1969; Castellan, 1972). Comparing the equations of the $\hat{y}_e$ and $\hat{y}_s$ regression models allows us to judge whether humans give proper weight to the various cues. Of course, this comparison is only legitimate if the true environmental model is indeed known. Because this is seldom the case in real-world prediction tasks, researchers use experimental tasks where they determine and control the true environmental relationship (as in our numerical example). Subjects first gain experience in these hypothetical environments (via trial and error), and then researchers check how well they inferred the relationship between y_e and x_i.

In such experiments (see Brehmer and Brehmer, 1988, for a review), subjects typically exhibit poor insights into how much weight they actually place on different cues. Subjects believe they place more weight on minor cues than they really do and think they place less weight on major cues than is actually the case (Slovic and Lichtenstein, 1971). Thus, subjects engage much more in "differential dimension focus" (i.e., looking at just a few variables) than they are aware of themselves. In essence, they believe in their own complexity whereas in reality their judgments depend on just a few major variables. Practically, this means subjects may ask for information they hardly use.

Insensitivity to nonlinearities. Subjects do not easily uncover nonlinearities and interaction effects (apart from overlooking minor or secondary variables). For example, suppose the true model is

$$y_e = w_1 x_1 + w_2 \sqrt{x_2}$$

where y_e could be salary, x_1 years of experience, and x_2 level of education. The nonlinearity in x_2 is typically underestimated; instead of recognizing the diminishing marginal value of x_2 (education), less weight is given to the term x_2 in general (Summers and Hammond, 1966).

Suppose now the true model is

$$y_e = w_1 x_1 + w_2 x_2 + w_3 x_1 x_2$$

so that the effect of x_1 and x_2 on y_e also depends on the particular combination of x_1 and x_2. Such interaction between x_1 and x_2 seems hard for us to learn even though interactions commonly occur (Brehmer, 1969). For example, the prediction of someone's salary on the basis of experience (x_1) and gender (x_2) probably entails an interaction between these two variables. Graphically, this means that the plot of salary (y) against experience (x_1) has a different slope for men than women. In such cases, the effect of x_1 and x_2 on y cannot be represented with just an additive model.

External noise. The ability of subjects to infer a multivariate relationship between y_e and $x_1, \ldots, x_n$ often deteriorates when random noise is introduced (Hammond and Summers, 1965). For instance, let the true model be

$$y_e = w_1 x_1 + w_2 x_2 + \bar{\epsilon}$$

where $\bar{\epsilon}$ denotes a random disturbance term, with a mean of zero and a symmetrical distribution. Such random noise masks the connection between y_e and x_1 and x_2, and greatly impairs learning as the variance of the error term increases. It may also encourage the inclusion of irrelevant cues (Castellan, 1973). Unfortunately, in the real world such noise is almost always present, making it truly difficult to learn and predict outcomes accurately on the basis of unaided experience.

Cue learning. It has also been found that subjects find it more difficult to learn new relationships after already having acquired knowledge of an existing one than when little or no such prior knowledge exists (see Peterson, Hammond, and Summers, 1965; Castellan, 1974; Klayman, 1988). In other words, if the world suddenly changes in underlying structure, for example, due to new regulation, new technology, or new competitors, the new $\hat{y}_e$ model will be more quickly learned by newcomers than by oldtimers who are still anchored to the original $\hat{y}_e$ model. Also, when correlations are introduced among the x_i variables, subjects often fail to recognize the redundancies among such correlated cues, thereby overestimating the importance of correlated cues.

Feedback about performance can be given at multiple levels, such as (1) *outcome feedback* about what actually happened, (2) *relationship feedback* about which cues matter most or least in the particular task environment, and (3) *policy feedback* about how much weight the person is actually placing on various kinds of cues and how they are subjectively combined. Feedback at level two seems most productive, even if people don't know their own subjective model. Learning from outcomes alone, in contrast, seems quite difficult for people (see Doherty and Balzer, 1988). Also, instructions about what to emphasize or deemphasize may help, especially since people often have a hard time ignoring cues that they deem important but are in fact irrelevant. Telling them that certain kinds of information is irrelevant usually does not do the trick, but teaching them when and how to ignore irrelevant cues can work, as Gaeth and Shanteau (1984) demonstrated with experienced decision makers.

The preceding sections on Lens model results reflect merely a subset of the many studies conducted within the social judgment theory framework. Their distinguishing feature is that they seek to study human prediction and inference in psychological terms, with an in-depth understanding of the task environment, using natural settings as much as possible. This poses, however, a research dilemma in answering key questions about cue utilization and learning. Whenever cues are highly correlated and hard to observe (as they commonly are in real versus laboratory settings), inferences about relative weights become increasingly difficult to make within the multiple regression paradigm. As Brehmer and Joyce (1988) point out, many of the social judgment theory studies conducted fail to employ truly representative designs and/or real experts. In addition, Klayman (1988) notes that Lens model studies on multiple-cue learning often fail to address the interesting question of how humans discover cues in the first place (that is, how do they formulate and test hypotheses?).

Hammond, Hamm, Grassia, and Pearson (1987) further emphasized that humans may perform well along a cognitive continuum that ranges from purely analytic to highly intuitive. When prediction tasks are restructured by experimenters to permit statistical analysis, such as a numerical coding of cues, focusing on a subset of cases, or requesting responses on artificial scales, distortions may be introduced that do not put experts in the best light. For example, Phelps and Shanteau (1978) found that livestock experts rating the breeding quality of pigs evaluated cues differently when looking at actual photographs of the pigs than when rating numerical profiles scores along the key dimensions that mattered to the experts. When presented with photographs, the experts used fewer cues, exploiting the presence of highly intercorrelated cues (see also Ebbesen and Koneci, 1975). As such, the earlier stylized findings regarding the Lens model must be viewed with some of these caveats in mind. Nevertheless, the basic image of people as linear information processors prone to random as well as systematic bias seems well supported by the data.

Bootstrapping. Given these findings on the fallibility of human prediction, it would clearly be better to rely on objectively validated y_e models. In stable worlds, this would indeed be the preferred policy (as Table 3.3 shows). But what if this is not possible (because no past data exist or things have changed)? In that case human experts are the only source, and as noted before the choice boils down to y_s versus $\hat{y}_s$. Interestingly, the empirical evidence in Table 3.3 shows that $R_m \geq R_a$ for all cases listed. Recall that R_a refers to how well the expert predicts intuitively: R_m, in contrast, measures how well the expert's own regression model predicts the criterion y_e. The somewhat surprising conclusion is that a linear model of the decision maker ($\hat{y}_s$) will almost always outperform the intuitive predictions (y_s) of the expert himself (see Dawes and Corrigan, 1974; Dawes, Faust, and Meehl, 1989). The use of this model $\hat{y}_s$ is called bootstrapping, as though a person were pulled up by his or her own bootstraps. Of course, the $\hat{y}_s$ model only uses y_s and x_i information (not y_e). However, by estimating the implicit weights used by the human forecaster and eliminating any noise or inconsistency, the model usually outperforms its source (i.e., typically $R_m \geq R_a$).

The ideal solution, it might be argued, is to use *both* model and human. Blattberg and Hoch (1990) constructed precisely such a metamodel, in which human intuition (y_s) and bootstrapped regression estimates ($\hat{y}_s$) were combined into a man–machine model $\hat{y}_{mm} = w_1 y_s + w_2 \hat{y}_s$. Using experienced managers in the fashion industry, they found that the combined model ($\hat{y}_{mm}$) outperformed either of its components y_s or $\hat{y}_s$. The optimal weighting was about equal: 50% for the human and 50% for the model (i.e., $w_1 = w_2$). However, this result may only apply when dealing with truly experienced experts who operate in a complex, nonlinear environment and who appreciate when certain exceptions to a linear rule come into play. Many earlier studies, with often less experienced subjects, suggest that humans have usually little to contribute beyond a linear combination of the cues.

Apart from predictive improvement, there may be other reasons to keep humans involved (see Dawes, 1979). First, someone has to ensure that the model is still applicable or legitimate overall. Second, it may be deemed unethical or undesirable to make decisions exclusively with a model. For example, would you personally like to be evaluated solely by a computer model when applying for credit or when trying to get into graduate school, or, yet more personally, when receiving a medical diagnosis concerning a potentially serious illness? Few people would say yes, even if statistical evidence exists to prove the predictive superiority of the model. For example, you may not consider correlation the appropriate measure of performance when it involves you personally; or, you may want some human assurance that you are not somehow an exception to the rule.

In many applied settings, officials use a mixture of statistical and intuitive prediction. For instance, in MBA admissions, the computer may determine the clear accepts and rejects, whereas a human committee deliberates the gray area and unusual cases. Indeed, in both undergraduate and graduate admissions, the trend is to move away from only computerized or standardized approaches. Many schools rely less on SAT or graduate admissions test scores. In part this reflects dissatisfaction with test distortions due to coaching or training, and unfairness with respect to certain minorities (e.g. socially disadvantaged or foreign students). However, educators are also concerned about the tests' inability to measure such intangible dimensions as creativity, leadership potential, or the ability to function productively in teams.

So far we have only focused on single-point estimation, such as providing a best estimate of someone's future salary or grade point average in graduate school (as opposed to an entire probability distribution). The general conclusion is that the reliability of intuitive judgments, even for experts, is usually low. People can often be outperformed by their own models provided we can identify the cues underlying their predictions. However, in many situations it may be desirable to obtain more than just a best estimate, particularly since the world is uncertain. In the extreme, we may want an entire probability distribution for each y_i dimension and each decision alternative. People seldom do this in daily decision making. It is more likely that only selected consequences will be estimated probabilistically. For these dimensions, uncertainties are usually viewed as a discrete rather than a continuous random variable, with just a few outcome levels. For instance, in the apartment selection problem described in Chapter 1, a dimension of interest might be future rent increases. Suppose this increase depends on some unknown event, for example, whether a rent control law is passed. How might people assess the likelihoods of such unknown events? How would you?

In the next section we introduce the *theory of argument* to help us understand how people commonly reason about uncertainty, and to integrate this theory with the Lens model discussed previously. That is, we shall compare how individuals estimate the probability of some target event ($\hat{y}_s$) with the probability estimates derived from statistically based models ($\hat{y}_e$).

3.2.3   *The theory of arguments*

In recent years psychologists have undertaken considerable research on judgment under uncertainty. They have concluded that individuals exhibit systematic biases when estimating the probability of outcomes. These findings raise disturbing questions regarding the rules and strategies that individuals use in making inferences. However, they have also raised questions about the legitimacy of the experiments (L. Cohen, 1981), both in terms of subjects used and the artificiality of the tasks.

The framework we propose here for discussing people's reasoning processes under uncertainty is based on a theory of arguments developed by Toulmin (1958). After outlining the elements of this framework in the next section, we will relate this framework directly to the Lens model discussed in the previous section. Thereafter, we use the framework to discuss important features that summarize the kind of biases and heuristics observed in laboratory experiments.

General concepts. The basic elements of the theory of arguments are depicted in Figure 3.4. When making judgments, an individual usually collects or receives a set of data (*D*), which can take many forms. The information can be of an idiosyncratic or historical, statistical nature. For example, an individual may have "inside information" about rents paid for certain apartments or salary offers for particular jobs. In the case of assessing potential flood damage to one's house, the data could be in the form of historical records of flooding in that particular area.

The *source* of the data may also be important in making judgments. Information could have been obtained from others, such as the rents other students are now paying, published job offers others have received, or official flood damage statistics to nearby houses. Personal experience with a particular situation is another form of data. The monthly rent from a

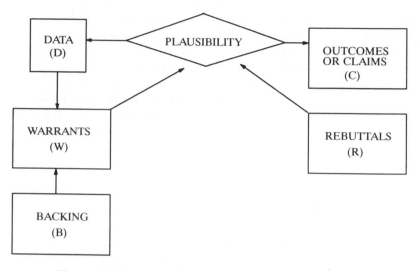

Figure 3.4. Elements of a theory of arguments (Adapted by permission from Toulmin, 1958)

previous apartment or a current salary may unduly influence an individual's judgment. Similarly, previous flood damage either to one's current house or a previously owned one may strongly affect the estimate of future damage.

As shown in Figure 3.4, an individual will make certain claims (*C*) regarding outcomes on the basis of data that have been collected. These claims may be in the form of a frequency distribution on a particular attribute (e.g., the range of apartment rent) or a specific probability estimate (e.g., the probability that a person will find an apartment with monthly rent below $300 or that a salary will be offered that is greater than $25,000). With respect to probability estimates, such as the chance of a flood, the claim could be of the form "there is a 10% chance that the flood will cause damage of $10,000 or more to this house in the coming year."

How are the data sources and claims related? According to the theory of arguments, individuals use warrants (*W*) or premises to connect *D* with *C*. Warrants and premises provide the rationale or plausibility for arguing that *D* implies *C*. For example, a student may claim that he will not be able to find an apartment with rent less than $250 since all the information received from the university housing office shows rents higher than that amount. Support for any warrant comes in the form of backings (*B*), which represent some evident truths or assumptions. The backing, in essence, legitimates or certifies the assumptions inherent in the warrant. For example, the student can legitimate his warrant regarding the rents by certifying that the university housing office has a comprehensive list of all available apartments in the area.

As a counterforce to the backing there is always an opportunity for rebuttal (*R*), highlighting the conditions under which the warrant or claim may not be true. A rebuttal to the preceding argument regarding rents might be that the university housing office only receives a list of available apartments from a limited set of tenants. For instance, landlords who prefer not to use the university office may charge monthly rents below $250. Note that many arguments, predictions, or inferences fit the general structure shown in Figure 3.4. This structure in turn may help pinpoint weaknesses or biases in subjective predictions.

Relationship to information imperfections. Much evidence suggests that a person's reasoning process connecting *D* and *C* relies on various mental shortcuts that often cause biases. The reasons for this include:

Information-processing limitations. Because most individuals have a difficult time dealing with large amounts of data, they tend to be selective in the types of information they use in making a claim.

Complexity. Individuals *simplify* problems because of their difficulty in dealing with complexity. The context in which the problem is presented and the nature of the task play a key role in the types of warrants used to go from *D* to *C*.

Coherence. Underlying the entire reasoning process is the individual's desire to paint a coherent picture of the world. People want to provide a plausible set of arguments to justify what they are doing and want to be able to explain why they took certain steps or drew certain conclusions. One aspect of coherence seeking is the tendency to provide causal explanations where in fact they might not exist, or to make uncertain situations more certain through the use of deterministic rules or heuristics.

This theory of arguments can be mapped onto a variation of the Lens model, as shown in Figure 3.5. The data set $x_1 \ldots x_n$ represents information available to the subject in making a decision. Two types of claims are being made: the subject's response y_s and some criterion value y_e. The subject's response results (implicitly) from a set of warrants (*W*) and backings (*B*) that operate on the data and yield some conclusion. Similarly, the criterion value is based upon some reference process that stipulates how the data *should* be processed according to some prescriptive or normative model. Frequently, this reference process uses statistical analyses, which reflect a formal theory (e.g., Bayesian analysis) concerning how the data should be analyzed. This reference process may

DATA

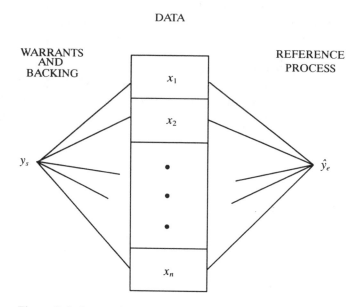

Figure 3.5. Integrating the theory of arguments with the Lens model

yield values $(\hat{y}_e)$ that differ from the subject's response (y_s) for two related reasons: Different data sets were used or a different functional form was assumed. In the next section we examine differences between subjects' responses and reference criteria by looking at five general features or alleged biases concerning individual judgment under uncertainty.

3.3   Judgment under uncertainty: key features

In this section we examine important characteristics of judgment under uncertainty, as distilled from a large and growing literature in experimental psychology. This research has its beginnings in the 1950s as the infant study of cognitive processes began to uncover interesting characteristics of choice and judgment under uncertainty. Early work characterizing information-processing limitations is summarized in Edwards (1954), Miller (1956), and Newell and Simon (1972). This work highlights the limitations of people's information-processing, memory, and perceptual abilities. These limitations in turn give rise to a variety of heuristics that individuals use to make judgments under uncertainty. Although these heuristics economize on people's bounded rationality, they also give rise to systematic biases. Many of these biases can be classified into three general areas:

- Violations of elementary as well as more complex statistical principles.
- The use of incomplete or biased data in grounding judgment.
- Incomplete or improper processing of available data.

The recent literature on expert systems and artificial intelligence grew out of an attempt to understand as well as improve on these heuristics and biases by using computer-based decision support systems (to aid in judgmental tasks). These decision support systems use the power of computers and mathematical models to provide support for statistical computations, fast and easy access to available data, and correct – or at least consistent – processing of available data. These systems especially offer a coherent and systematized foundation for choice and judgment in well-defined problem areas, such as medicine and oil drilling. The continuing use of such decision support systems allows for empirical validation of the rules embodied in the system and the gradual refinement and correction of judgmental errors.

We shall consider the topic of decision support systems in more detail in Chapter 5. Our present aim is to review the heuristics and biases that characterize judgment under uncertainty. It is these biases that more prescriptive approaches, such as decision analysis and expert systems, are designed to rectify.

3.3.1 *Feature 1: ignoring base rates (statistical error)*

People's intuitive approaches to inferences deviate in systematic ways from the Bayesian framework[3] as illustrated by the following problem.

A particular city of 100,000 inhabitants is afflicted with AIDS, which presently occurs in only 1 out of 100 cases. Recently, a test for the presence of AIDS has been developed. Although the test is quite reliable, it is not perfect, as shown by comparing the true state of the patient with the diagnosis.

True state	Diagnosis		
	Positive	Negative	
Yes	95%	5%	100%
No	10%	90%	100%

"Yes" means the patient has AIDS. "Positive" means the test says the patient has AIDS. Thus of all the cases where the patient really had AIDS, the test gave a correct diagnosis in 95% of the instances.

3 This framework derives from Bayes' law, a statistical theorem that tells us how to make inferences on the basis of base rates (i.e., prior odds) and conditional probabilities. This section will apply Bayes' theorem numerically to a numerical example (see Figure 3.6). For an actual (medical) application, see de Dombal (1988).

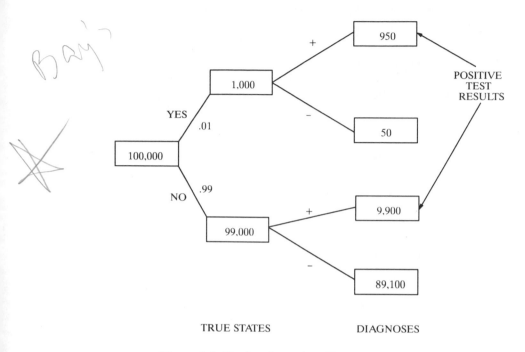

Figure 3.6. Testing the entire village. *Note:* Of the 100,000 villagers, exactly 10,850 will have positive diagnoses. Of these, only 950 will actually have the disease, or less than 9%.

Suppose a randomly selected citizen from this community is now given this test. The outcome is positive. According to your best intuitive judgment, what do you feel is the probability that this person, in fact, has AIDS?

Most people will answer 95%, ignoring the claim that AIDS occurs only in 1 out of 100 cases in this city. To demonstrate that this prior probability should indeed be considered, assume the extreme cases of either nobody having AIDS or everybody having it. In those cases, these prior probabilities of either 0% or 100% simply dominate whatever the test says. Similarly, when the prior probability is between these extreme values it should be factored into the judgment.

In Figure 3.6 we derive the proper answer using Bayesian analysis by simply testing the entire city. Thus, of the 100,000 inhabitants, 1,000 have the illness and 99,000 do not. Of the former group, 950 will be properly diagnosed as positive, however, 9,900 of the healthy group will have a false positive. Thus, in total, the test will yield 10,850 positive results, of which only 950 in fact have the illness. Hence, the probability that a randomly selected person whose test is positive will indeed have AIDS is only 8.76%.

Why do individuals ignore the base rate associated with the chances of a disease and base their judgment entirely on the test itself? According to the theory of arguments, these individuals may reason that we are dealing with a specific person who is presumed to have a disease. This is why the test was given in the first place. Or they may doubt how up-to-date the 1 in 100 prior probability is, given that the disease is spreading or that significant regional variations exist. Further, the problem as presented does not indicate what role (if any) a physician played in ordering the test. Those who ignored the prior probability may have assumed that a physician had intervened in the process and knew something about the patient. (Even though the problem does state that the person was randomly selected, this may not be believed given the controversy surrounding AIDS testing.) The importance of the *source* of information in people's responses is illustrated in the following example suggested by Cohen (1981):

Consider two diseases. Disease *A* is 19 times more prevalent in the population than *B*. A doctor claims you have disease *B*, and you know the doctor is correct in his diagnosis 80 percent of the time. He prescribes medicine for *B*. Do you take this medicine or ask him for medicine related to *A*?

If you decide to accept the doctor's recommendation then you should ask why. Bayesian analysis of this problem suggests that you have a higher probability of contracting disease *A*. However, you may feel that the doctor has special knowledge about your own condition, in which case the base rate is viewed by you as irrelevant.

The latter problem also illustrates the nestedness feature of decision making. Contradicting a doctor by asking for medicine related to *A* introduces some social conflict that most patients would prefer to avoid. The importance of the source of data, be it a test or a doctor, suggests that individuals may create scripts or scenarios in their own minds that go beyond the data presented in the specific problem. Much research is needed to understand what types of warrants and backings are invoked by subjects for different problem representations (to provide meaning, coherence, and consistency to subjects).

The underweighting or outright ignorance of prior probabilities is a well-documented empirical result in Bayesian inference, although Edwards (1968) encountered the opposite phenomenon in book-bag poker chip experiments. To explain base rate ignorance, Tversky and Kahneman (1980) highlighted the role of causal schemes in information utilization. When revising the probability of some hypothesis H_1 on the basis of some piece of information or datum D, three cases can be distinguished as follows:

Causal (Case 1): D is viewed as a cause of H_1, for example, estimating the probability that a randomly selected daughter will have blue eyes given (*D*) that her mother has blue eyes.

Diagnostic (Case 2): D is viewed as a result or outcome of H_1, for example, estimating the probability that a randomly selected mother will have blue eyes (*D*) given that her daughter has blue eyes.

Incidental (Case 3): D is viewed as having no particular relationship to H_1. This was the case in the preceding medical example, where most people consider the .01 probability simply irrelevant.

In all three cases, the effect of *D* on the probability of H_1 is fully determined by Bayes' theorem. Psychologically, however, the status of the datum seems to matter. For example, most people judge Case 1 to have a higher probability than Case 2, whereas they are in fact equal. This equality follows directly from elementary probability theory, given an assumption that the incidence of blue eyes is stable across generations. The example demonstrates the psychological dominance of causal over diagnostic reasoning.

To illustrate the psychological impact of a datum being viewed as incidental versus causal, consider the following two formulations of a similar statistical inference problem suggested by Bar-Hillel (1980).

a.   A cab was involved in a hit-and-run accident at night. Two cab companies, the Green and the Blue, operate in the city. You are given the following data:
  • 85% of the cabs in the city are Green and 15% are Blue.
  • A witness identified the cab as a Blue one. The court tested his ability to identify cabs under the appropriate visibility conditions. When presented with a sample of cabs (half of which were Blue and half of which were Green), the witness made correct identifications in 80% of the cases and erred in 20% of the cases.

b.   A cab was involved in a hit-and-run accident at night. Two cab companies, the Green and the Blue, operate in the city. You are given the following data:
  • Although the two companies are roughly equal in size, 85% of cab accidents in the city involve Green cabs, and 15% involve Blue cabs.
  • Same as in Problem 1.

In each problem subjects were asked, What is the probability that the cab involved in the accident was Blue rather than Green? In Situation *a*, the median response of subjects was 80%, compared with 55% for Situation *b*. Statistically, the prior probability of a blue taxi being involved in an accident is 15% for both cases. Nevertheless, this prior probability or base rate is generally ignored in Situation *a* because it is viewed as incidental to the problem. In Situation *b*, however, the cover story provides a *causal* link between the base rate and the hypothesis, thereby increasing its impact. The Bayesian answer to the cab problem is 41%.

In the context of the theory of arguments, an individual might use the following reasoning in Situation *a*: Because we are looking at a specific cab identified by a witness, the historical or base rate data are quite irrelevant or uninformative to the situation; only the witness matters. In Situation *b*, the event "accident" is connected to both the population of taxicabs and the witness, so the base rate should influence judgments. Scholz (1987) has analyzed the cab problem in detail and found that subjects use a *large* set of reasoning strategies for this problem. These range from analytic to intuitive and numerical to episodic. To some subjects it is an algebra problem into which they plug the right (or wrong) numbers, whereas others construct miniature stories to give the problem more meaning and structure. Without a better understanding of the "tool box" or repertoire of mental strategies available, it is hard to know whether, when, and why base rate ignorance is a bias.

3.3.2   *Feature 2: overweighing of concrete data (statistical error)*

Individuals are often unduly influenced by salient or concrete data in estimating the probability of a particular outcome. To illustrate this phenomenon, consider the following personality sketch provided by Tversky and Kahneman (1973) of an individual who was chosen at random from a sample consisting of 70 lawyers (*L*) and 30 engineers (*E*):

Jack is 45 years old. He is married and has four children. He is generally conservative, careful, and ambitious. He shows no interest in political and social issues and spends most of his free time on his many hobbies which include home carpentry, sailing, and mathematical puzzles.

What is the probability that Jack is one of the 30 engineers in the sample of 100? Now suppose that the sample consisted of 30 lawyers and 70 engineers (i.e., the reverse case). Would you change your estimate of the probability?

Kahneman and Tversky (1972) showed that individuals tend to ignore the base rate in estimating these probabilities. They call the heuristic underlying this error *representativeness*. Whether Jack is from the low or high engineer group makes little difference to people. They draw conclusions about the probability that an individual is an engineer or lawyer based on the salient information in the story. If a person's personality description fits that of an engineer, then they assume he is likely to be one. Suppose a neutral story such as the following one is given:

Dick is 30 years old. He is married with no children. A man of high ability and high motivation, he promises to be quite successful in his field. He is well liked by his colleagues.

Subjects felt there was an even chance that the individual was a lawyer or engineer independent of the base rate. The warrants and backing used in their arguments apparently ignored the parent population.

A Bayesian analysis of this problem requires two pieces of data: the base rate data (X_1) and the ability of the sketch to predict a profession (X_2). With respect to X_1, let $P(L)$ and $P(E)$ be the respective probabilities associated with drawing an engineer or lawyer at random from the population. Regarding X_2, let $P(S \mid L)$ represent the conditional probability of drawing such a personality sketch from the population of lawyers and $P(S \mid E)$ the conditional probabilities that it is drawn from engineers. Because we know that the person is either a lawyer or engineer, $P(S \mid L) + P(S \mid E) = 1$. Thus, if $P(S \mid E) = 1$, it is certain that the individual is an engineer and the base rate is irrelevant. However, if $P(S \mid E) < 1$ then the desired Bayesian estimate is derived as follows:

$$P(E \mid S) = \frac{P(S \mid E)P(E)}{P(S \mid L)P(L) + P(S \mid E)P(E)}$$

In case no sketch is provided at all, subjects correctly provide a response of 30% for the probability that Jack in the example is an engineer. Once a somewhat detailed sketch is provided, however, individuals tend to ignore the base rates.

3.3.3   Feature 3: misconceptions of chance (statistical error)

Although Bayes' theorem is admittedly counterintuitive, people violate much more basic laws of probability. We shall discuss three examples (of increasing complexity) that clearly demonstrate misconceptions about chance and randomness. They concern statistical runs, sample sizes, and regression effects.

Statistical runs. Consider the following two questions:

1. Suppose a family has had three boys (B). What are the chances that the next child will be a girl (G)?
2. Suppose a coin has been tossed three times and heads (H) have emerged on each flip. What are the chances that the next toss will be a tail (T)?

The base rate data (X_1) for each of these problems are the same: In Problem 1, $X_1 = (B, B, B)$, and Problem 2, $X_1 = (H, H, H)$. Let $P(G)$ be the probability that the next child is a girl and $P(T)$ the chance that the next flip is a tail. An individual who feels that $P(G) > 1/2$ or $P(T) > 1/2$

may be reasoning that there is a long-run self-correcting mechanism to compensate for the run of boys or heads. This person does not believe that either of these events is solely determined by a random process.

What troubles statisticians are comments of the sort "A tail is due now." If an individual feels comfortable with this type of reasoning process, it may be difficult to combat his backing with a statistical rebuttal. A different type of reasoning process might be used if the person feels $P(G)$ or $P(T)$ to be less than $1/2$. In this case the backing may be that "the coin is unbalanced given that there were three heads in a row" or that "boys run in the family." The reverse phenomenon seems to occur in sports, where players often believe they are on a hot streak. Surprisingly the "hot hand" phenomenon in basketball seems largely a statistical illusion (Gilovich, Vallone, and Tversky, 1985). It is not, however, an illusion that is easily demonstrated and thus has received extensive rebuttal (see Camerer, 1989a).

Sample size insensitivity. People often use sample data incorrectly in making statistical judgments, as the following example illustrates.

Suppose two divisions of a company produce a certain product using the same technology. One division is large and produces 10,000 items a day. In the past year, it counted five days on which the number of defective items exceeded 5%. The other division is small, producing just 1,000 items per day. It counted 15 days last year on which more than 5% of the daily production was defective. Which is the more effective division?

Since the larger division is more representative of an "effective division," there is a tendency to pick that one. However, a large sample is less likely to deviate from its long-run probability than a small sample. In this example, it is, in fact, more likely that the small division is the more effective one, using binomial sampling theory.

Kahneman and Tversky (1972) have explained this insensitivity to sample size as due to the representativeness heuristic. Ask yourself when you have a better chance of beating a stronger opponent in tennis: when playing just one set or when playing the best out of three sets? If you think it makes no difference, you consider either match to be equally representative of your true levels. However, because chance plays a role as well, the longer you play the more likely it is that the stronger player wins. You can be lucky on a few points, but not an entire set (let alone three sets).

Regression toward the mean. Consider the following problem.

Suppose a randomly selected person is given an IQ test and scores 140. Will a retest be more likely to yield a higher or lower score than 140?

Many individuals say that both are equally likely, since the observed score of 140 is viewed as representative of the person's true IQ level. In reality the measured IQ is the sum of some true IQ (or average) plus a random error term associated with it. An extremely high score is more likely to have a positive than negative error term. Thus, when retesting a person with a very high score, it is more likely that you observe a score below than above the previous one; i.e., the second score will tend to regress back toward the presumed population mean of 100.

This phenomenon was empirically discovered by Sir Francis Galton, who plotted the heights of fathers against sons. Although tall (short) fathers tended to have tall (short) sons, the latter were usually not quite as tall (or short). Regression toward the mean also occurs in professional sports, where it is misdiagnosed as sophomore jinx. Athletes often do not perform as well in their second professional year as in their first. A statistical explanation for this decline is that only those who did well the first year are invited to play the second year. For this subgroup the uncontrollable factors were probably positive, a condition that cannot generally be counted on for the next year. Thus, although the selected subgroup is probably considerably better than those not asked to stay, their second-year performance levels will tend to average somewhat below their first-year levels (if one assumes away any possible learning or motivational effects).

3.3.4   *Feature 4: familiarity and availability (data collection issue)*

Considerable evidence suggests that individuals estimate the chances of various events happening on the basis of their familiarity with these events. Their knowledge may come directly from personal experience or indirectly through the media. The most common example of this is embodied in the availability heuristic.

Availability. To illustrate the availability heuristic, consider this question: Which of the following do you think caused more deaths in the United States last year: emphysema or homicide? In making this judgment, most people assess how common either mode of death is using instances they can recall. Again, this is a reasonable estimation approach provided various biasing factors are corrected for. The most important one is recognizing that the news media give much more (about 250 times more!) coverage to homicides than to emphysema fatalities, making it much easier to recall cases of homicide. Not surprisingly, on average people judge homicide to be twice as common as emphysema. However, objective estimates of death frequencies suggest that one is about 15% more likely to die from emphysema than from homicide (see Lichtenstein, Fischhoff, and Phillips, 1982).

A bias related to the availability heuristic concerns the ease of mental search for examples that satisfy a given question. For example, do you think that the English language has more words that start with *k* or ones that have *k* in the third position? Because it is easier to think of words starting with *k* than of words whose third letter is *k*, most people judge that *k* in the first position is more common. In fact, it occurs more frequently in the third position (Tversky and Kahneman, 1973 and 1974). Thus, differences in the salience, extent of reporting, ease of search, or imaginability may cause systematic biases due to the availability heuristic.

Also, we may be unduly influenced by a recent or dramatic event whose instance provides little information about probabilities of other similar events. Evidence from field studies suggests that individuals who have been in accidents or suffered damage from natural disasters estimate the future probability of these events to be higher than those who have not experienced a loss (Kunreuther et al., 1978). For flood, fire, or other random disasters, however, statistical evidence indicates that the "experienced" and "nonexperienced" groups have the same chances of suffering a future loss. One reason for this bias may be that people want to provide a justification for their probability estimates. By recalling certain features or experiences they can more easily provide a rationale for their estimate than by referring to historical data, which often are difficult to recall or abstract. Mass media coverage or personal experience provides easy rationales for overestimating the probability; historical or statistical data are difficult to assimilate, so they are not used as readily.

Hindsight. After experiencing certain events or looking back on historical records, individuals tend to feel that some occurrences should have been easier to predict than may in fact have been the case. In order to assess how much we have learned, we must make a comparison between what we know now and what we knew then. This is often difficult, however, as the old state of knowledge may be irretrievable.

Experimental studies demonstrate clearly that subjects commonly believe they knew more than they really did. For example, prior to President Nixon's trip to China and Russia in 1972, Fischhoff and Beyth (1975) asked subjects to assign subjective probabilities to various possible outcomes, such as the establishment of diplomatic relations, meetings with Chairman Mao, and demonstrations by Soviet Jews. After the visits were completed and extensively reported on by the news media, these same subjects were asked to recall or reconstruct their earlier predictions. The tendency was to overestimate in hindsight the probabilities that had been given to events that did occur, and to underestimate the probabilities of events that did not happen.

Fischhoff (1975) suggests that the reason for this hindsight bias is cognitive, related to how the mind works, rather than motivational.[4] Just as adding water to wine makes the latter irretrievable in its old form, so will new information become quickly integrated with old information. The implications are that we systematically underestimate how much we have learned, and generally undervalue the informativeness of new information or experiences. The *unavailability* of previous knowledge states appears to be one important cause of hindsight biases (see Hawkins and Hastie, 1990).

3.3.5   *Feature 5: anchoring and adjustment (processing issue)*

Estimate the probability of getting at least one red ball in seven independent draws (one at a time, with replacement) from an urn containing only 10% red balls.

In making this judgment many people focus on the stated probability of .1 and adjust upward in view of having seven draws (Bar-Hillel, 1973). This anchoring and adjustment heuristic, however, usually leads to an insufficient adjustment. Typically people give responses below the correct probability, which is .52. This answer is found by subtracting from one the probability of not getting any red balls in seven trials, which is $(.9)^7$ or .48.

Another striking example of the anchoring bias was reported by Tversky and Kahneman (1974). They asked one group of high school students to estimate within five seconds the following product $1 \times 2 \times 3 \times \ldots \times 7 \times 8$. Another group was asked to estimate the product $8 \times 7 \times 6 \times \ldots \times 1$. The mean guess was 5,412 for the ascending sequence and 2,250 for the descending one, showing clearly a bias of anchoring and insufficient adjustment. The correct answer is 40,320.

Anchoring and adjustment also has a qualitative version, known as incrementalism (Lindblom, 1959). It refers to subjects or managers, considering only options not too different from the current solution or practice. Cyert and March (1963) referred to this as "local search." Anchoring may also underlie the often-noted conservatism bias in forecasting and prediction (Armstrong, 1985).

---

4 Motivational biases (e.g., wishful thinking, sloppy arithmetic, or rationalizing) will generally diminish as incentives are provided for people to try harder. Cognitive biases, in contrast, are largely unaffected by payoffs, since they reflect people's mental limitations.

3.3.6 *Feature 6: overconfidence (processing issue)*

Both experts and nonexperts may have difficulty calibrating what they know and do not know. Consider the following almanac-type question:

Give a range of values so that you are 90% certain that the 1980 population of Philadelphia falls between your stated upper and lower limits.

A series of such questions asking for 90% confidence intervals enables the experimenter to determine the proportion of time (p) the individual is correct. If $p = .9$, then the individual is well calibrated. If $p < .9$, then the person is overconfident, placing too narrow a range on the estimate. If $p > .9$, then the individual is too cautious since she is correct more often than the stated confidence intervals imply. (The population of Philadelphia was 2.8 million in 1980.) Yates (1990) provides an especially clear discussion of how to construct and decompose calibration scores.

Studies of calibration suggest that people are generally too confident in their ability to predict uncertain outcomes. Consider, for example, weather forecasters who are in the business of quantifying uncertainty. In Figure 3.7 five calibration curves are shown, dealing with such predictions as next day's temperature, precipitation, wind direction, and wind velocities. The curves are based on 241 to 12,635 predictions and reveal a strong tendency toward overconfidence. For instance, of all the predictions assigned a confidence level of .9, the forecasters were correct only between 70% and 80% of the time (on average). Conversely, when assigning low probabilities (say, below .2), they were more often correct than they should have been (except for the data collected by Root). Apparently, the forecasters were too confident a particular weather condition would not occur.[5]

This pattern of being too often correct for low probabilities and too little for high probabilities is yet more pronounced in Figure 3.8, where a different prediction task was used. The subjects here were college students who had to assign probabilities to possible answers to almanac-type questions. For example, they would be asked to assign a subjective probability to the potato being indigenous to Ireland. The issue of interest was not how much general knowledge the students had, but rather how well the students recognized the limits of their knowledge. Again, in both directions there is a very strong overconfidence bias for both easy and more difficult questions.

---

5 More recent data on 24-hour precipitation forecasts, however, show weather predictors to be almost perfectly calibrated (Murphy and Winkler, 1984). Much of this is due to timely, numerically precise feedback, as well as calibration training.

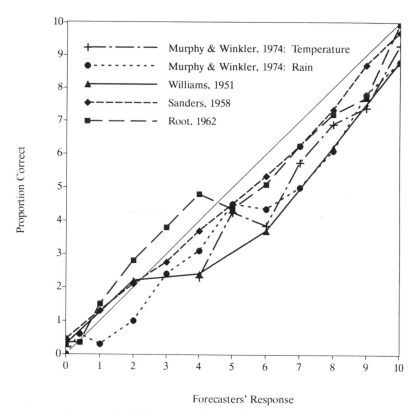

Figure 3.7. Calibration with weather forecasters (*Source:* Lichtenstein, Fischhoff, and Phillips, 1977. Reprinted by permission of Kluwer Academic Publishers)

A similar overconfidence bias is found when asking students whether they will be in the top or bottom half of their class on some upcoming midterm. In our experience, the vast majority (around 90%) truly believe they will be in the top 50%. In a similar fashion, Svenson (1981) found that 80% of all drivers feel they are better than the average driver. Part of this overconfidence seems motivational (Taylor and Brown, 1988) and part cognitive (Oskamp, 1965; Lichtenstein et al., 1982).

In addition, there may be cultural differences in probabilistic thinking. Wright and Phillips (1980) found that one group of Asians, for example, had a strong tendency to say that they were 100% sure when assessing unknown quantities. A corresponding group of British subjects used 100% assessments relatively infrequently. Indeed, across the full spectrum of probabilities, the Asian group was more extreme and less well calibrated than the British.

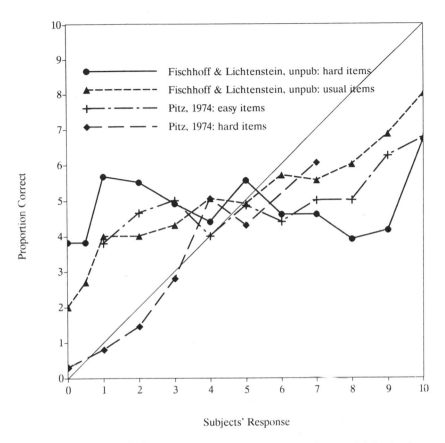

Figure 3.8. Calibration with almanac questions (*Source:* Lichtenstein et al., 1977. Reprinted by permission of Kluwer Academic Publishers)

The general lessons to be learned from the calibration literature are that (1) people do not usually realize how overconfident they are, (2) calibration tends to be worse on more difficult tasks,[6] and (3) feedback and training can lead to considerable improvements in calibration (see Lichtenstein et al., 1982; Fong, Krantz, and Nisbett, 1986). Most important, because of the information-processing heuristics described earlier, intuitive probabilities are likely to be poorly calibrated, which thereby causes systematic biases in people's estimates of probabilistic consequences.

6 Although this may seem obvious, task difficulty per se need not worsen calibration. All it should do, ideally, is reduce the incidence of extreme probabilities and increase the judgment frequency around the middle of the scale (near the base rate). Such a shift in frequencies along the horizontal axis should in itself not result in poorer calibration.

3.3.7   *Summary*

We have only begun to scratch the surface as to when and why individuals use particular heuristics and exhibit certain biases. The reference points in the laboratory experiments have been statistical models such as Bayesian inference or probabilistic calculations. People have been asked to make estimates without decision aids such as the calculator or computer. Even with such devices, however, it is not clear that greater accuracy would be forthcoming. The theory of arguments introduced at the beginning of this section suggests that the warrants and backing in proceeding from data (*D*) to claims (*C*) are different from those provided by statistical reasoning. It is fair to conclude from the cited studies that people are poor intuitive statisticians.[7] They have a difficult time thinking about the world in probabilistic terms. Instead there appears to be a strong tendency to reduce or disregard uncertainty, leading to insufficient use of prior information and a tendency to be overconfident. Given these limitations we now turn to prescriptive analysis, that is, how to improve prediction and inference.

3.4   Prediction and inference: prescriptive analysis

Improving the prediction and inference process under conditions of uncertainty is a challenging task. We ignore here the extensive literature on forecasting and econometrics (see Makridakis, Wheelwright, and McGee, 1983, or Wilson and Keating, 1990), which offers numerous formal models and techniques for both inference and extrapolation. Our focus instead will be more conceptual and judgment oriented. One important conceptual issue concerns the meaning of probability. People view this concept from a variety of perspectives, which in turn gives rise to multiple meanings. We discuss different types of probability in the first part of this section. We then consider how one might judge or legitimate the validity of a causal model. This discussion focuses on the validity of the arguments that people use to draw inferences from data. The section concludes by proposing a set of procedures for improving the ability of individuals to refine their arguments and improve their estimates.

3.4.1   *The multiple meanings of probability*

In discussing ways of improving causal inference under uncertainty, it is important to recognize that the concept of probability is relatively recent.

---

7 Scientists are arguably better at this, but only to the extent that they avoid the simplifying heuristics discussed here through careful calculations and tested methodologies.

Even though games of chance are ancient, the earliest written evidence that people knew the basic properties of probability as currently defined is 1654 (see Hacking, 1975).

The systematic study of probability started with Pascal's solutions to some long-standing card game problems, and from there onward it has been the subject of a fierce debate. This debate has focused on two fundamental views of probability. On the one hand, there are statistical and empirically observable issues regarding stochastic laws of chance. On the other hand, there are epistemological issues, concerning reasonable degrees of beliefs in propositions devoid of statistical or even empirical content. The various issues are still debated today, and alternative conceptions as to the meaning of probability exist (see Kyburg and Smokler, 1980). To simplify matters we shall distinguish three types of probability. The following three statements are examples of each.

1. The probability of getting exactly two heads upon three independent flips of a fair coin is 3/8.
2. The probability of dying in a car accident on a random day, trip, and road in the United States is 1 out of 4,000,000.
3. The probability that the United States is still a democracy in the year 2060 is .7.

The first statement belongs to the *classical view,* where probability is defined as the number of outcomes favorable to the event of interest divided by the total number of possible outcomes (J. Bernoulli, 1713; de La Place, 1951). The outcomes referred to here must all have equal probabilities. For example, three flips of a fair coin may result in eight equiprobable outcomes, namely HHH, HHT, HTH, HTT, THH, THT, TTH, and TTT. Since three of these (i.e., HHT, HTH, and THH) are favorable to the event considered (i.e., exactly two heads), its probability is 3/8.

Some limitations (and criticisms) of the classical view are that the concept of equiprobability is ill-defined (i.e., it begs the question as to what probability is) and that it does not apply to cases where there are infinitely many outcomes. It is beyond our scope to discuss the merits of these criticisms. However, it is obviously difficult to assign a classical probability to the event that a third world war will occur within the next three decades. First, it would not be clear what the equally likely elementary events are and, second, all the many pathways to war are too complex to be calculated.

The second statement above belongs to the *frequency view* of probability (von Mises, 1964). It proposes to characterize regularly occurring phenomena by their long-run frequencies. The probability of a person dying in a car accident is determined by looking at statistical data over a very large sample of car trips in the United States. This concept of probability finds much usage in actuarial work (e.g., insurance), quality control, forecasting, or wherever regularly occurring, stable, repetitive processes are observed. The difficulties with this definition of probability are (1) that it is never exact, as this would require an infinite sample; (2) that it only applies to cases where replication is possible (i.e., unique events cannot be handled); and (3) that replication under identical conditions is problematic.

For these reasons, plus philosophical arguments as to whether randomness really exists in nature (other than as a result of our limited knowledge), a third view exists. This *subjective view* holds that no probability can be objective (DeFinetti, 1937; Savage, 1954; Pratt, Raiffa, and Schlaifer, 1964). The source of uncertainty is our limited knowledge about an otherwise deterministic universe. Probability is one way to measure or quantify this uncertainty. This so-called subjective probability is a degree of belief measure, conditional on a given state of knowledge at a given point in time, for a particular person. Subjective probabilities can be measured by asking people for odds on an event or by using a known reference lottery. For example, which would you rather bet on: obtaining heads on the toss of a fair coin or Bucharest being the capital of Hungary? If you prefer the second bet, your subjective probability that Bucharest is the capital is at least .5 (if we assume you are reasonably rational).

By repeating such questions and changing the known probability, you can bound someone's subjective probability for any unknown event. Of course, in order for a set of subjective probabilities to be meaningful, certain consistency conditions must be satisfied. For example, if you believe that Bucharest is the capital of Hungary with probability of .5, then you must also believe that Bucharest is not the capital of Hungary with probability .5, since it either is or is not the capital of Hungary.[8] A more detailed discussion of the consistency conditions necessary for subjective probabilities to satisfy is presented in DeFinetti (1974).

It is important to note that all three views of probability impose conditions such that the resulting measure obeys the properties of mathematical probability. For instance, the subjectivists require coherence (among other things). This view stipulates that whatever subjective probabilities you hold, it must not be possible for a clever bookmaker to lay multiple fair bets against you such that the bookmaker wins no matter what happens. For example, suppose you felt the probability of rain (for some day and place) is .7, and the probability of no rain .6. A clever bookie could now give you $7 to $3 odds on rain in one bet (which is a fair bet), and $6 to $4 odds on no rain in another bet. If you play both, you lose $3

---

8 Budapest is actually the capital of Hungary, and Bucharest that of Romania.

Table 3.4. *Three major schools of probability*

1. Classical	Requires no empirical data as it is mostly analytical
	Cannot handle infinite sets easily
	Is very objective (in the sense of consensus)
	Requires knowledge of elementary events
	Is strongly model bound
2. Frequency	Requires historical data (i.e., is empirical)
	Presumes stable world
	Probability is never exact
	Presupposes possibility of exact replication
	Does not apply to unique events
3. Subjective	Requires neither data nor formal analysis
	May differ from person to person
	Applies to all conceivable uncertainties
	Coherence is a key requirement
	Denies possibility of objective probabilities
	Claims to subsume the other schools philosophically

in case of rain, and $1 in case of no rain. By assuring that subjective probabilities for exhaustive and mutually exclusive events sum to one, this exploitation possibility is ruled out.

By way of summary, Table 3.4 lists some of the major distinguishing features for each of the three schools. To stimulate and challenge your thinking, let us briefly consider two questions that test your own conceptions of probability.

1. If 9 out of 10 in a class feel they will score in the top half of the class, will at least some be irrational in their belief? None of the three schools would consider this statement to be irrational per se. For example, if all students flipped fair coins (to generate a prediction) there would be some chance of getting 90% heads. However, the probability of some degree of miscalibration or overconfidence on the part of some students would be very high, especially if it were a large class.

2. The second question is more difficult and involves the following prisoner's paradox. Three people *A*, *B*, and *C* are in prison. They know that one of them has been selected by random lottery to be hanged. The guard knows who it is, but is not allowed to tell. Being clever, *A* asks the guard to name one of the other two who will not be hanged. The guard says *C*. What is now the probability that *A* is the one to be hanged, 1/2 or 1/3? Remember that *A* knew all along that at least one of the other two would not be hanged!

If we assume the guard randomly chooses one name, *B* or *C*, knowing that neither will be hanged, no new information was obtained regarding *A*. His probability is still 1/3. However, *B*'s probability is now 2/3. To show this from a frequency viewpoint, imagine three shells *A*, *B*, and *C*, one of which contains a pea. Suppose the experimenter, who knows that in this case the pea is under *A*, turns over either *B* or *C*, in the knowledge that neither contains the pea. If you now believe that *A*'s probability is higher than 1/3, and bet accordingly, you will lose money in the long run. Only 1/3 of the time will the pea actually be under *A*. This teaser highlights that the process by which information is generated is important in assessing its value.

3.4.2   *Developing good subjective models*

Any measurement of the likelihood of an event is based upon the assumption that some meaningful relationship exists between subjective uncertainty and an encoded probability (Wallsten, 1990). Several concepts are useful in determining the nature of this relationship, including whether there are causal linkages.[9] We shall start with techniques for improving subjective probabilities and then examine causal models.

Subjective probabilities. Many practical techniques exist to improve subjective probability judgments (see Russo and Schoemaker, 1989). We shall briefly discuss three: reason generation, scenario construction, and prospective hindsight.

A simple technique to improve probability estimates about some uncertain event is to list the various reasons why it may turn out one way versus another. Koriat, Lichtenstein, and Fischhoff (1980) reported much improved calibration when subjects were asked to generate both reasons pro and con a particular outcome. A related approach is to construct a so-called *fault tree,* which details by category why a complex system might fail. This is commonly used in high technology areas (e.g., nuclear power plants, computers, airplanes) but may also apply to "low tech" cases such as why a new restaurant may fail. Figure 3.9 shows a restaurant fault tree (from Dube-Rioux and Russo, 1988). When hotel school managers (from Cornell University) were asked to construct their own

---

9 Philosophers have debated for ages the precise meaning of causality (Mackie, 1980). For a penetrating psychological analysis, see Einhorn and Hogarth (1986), who identify the kind of cues people respond to when making causal attributions (such as spatial or temporal contiguity, event sequence, or past conditions).

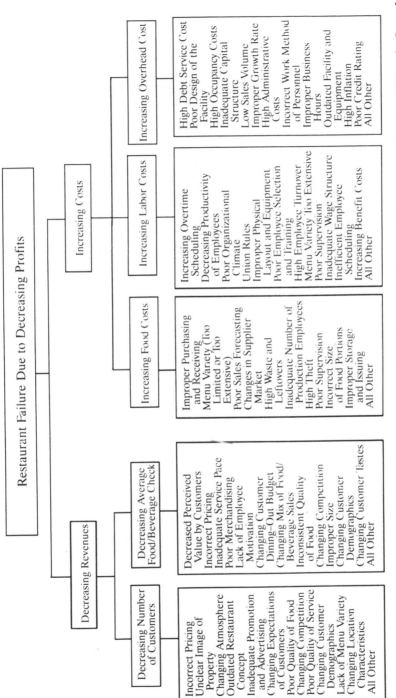

Figure 3.9. Fault tree for a restaurant (*Source:* Dube-Rioux and Russo, 1988. Copyright John Wiley & Sons Ltd. 1988. Reprinted by permission of John Wiley & Sons Ltd.)

tree or extend ones given to them, their subjective probabilities typically improved.

A natural next step beyond reason generation is to examine reasons or events in combination. By constructing detailed scenarios of optimistic or pessimistic worlds, subjects are more likely to stretch their confidence ranges. Scenarios remind people in vivid ways that the world can turn out very differently from what was expected. If the scenarios are causally coherent and internally consistent (see Schoemaker, 1993), they may overcome the availability bias or the "out of sight, out of mind" effect. Companies such as Royal Dutch/Shell put extensive resources in providing managers with challenging industry scenarios against which to test their strategies or to prompt more innovative planning (see Wack, 1985a, 1985b). Contrary to statistical principles, people often find detailed, concrete scenarios more believable than abstract, skeleton scenarios. Tversky and Kahneman (1983) examined this phenomenon and called it the conjunction fallacy. They found that people often judge the probability P of the conjunction $A \cap B$ to be larger than either $P(A)$ or $P(B)$. For instance, the combination of a recession and high unemployment may seem more likely than either of these alone. Ironically, such statistical fallacies may end up strengthening the credibility of an unusual scenario, which in turn may help overcome biases due to overconfidence, anchoring, or availability. (Note that it may take a bias to beat a bias.)

Scenario impact can be further enhanced if we manipulate the temporal setting. Several studies have reported greater ability of subjects to imagine causes for events that already happened than for those that are still in the future (for a review, see Mitchell, Russo, and Pennington, 1989). For example, one group of subjects might be asked to explain in hindsight why a wedding or party turned out to be a fiasco, whereas another group is asked to do so in foresight. The only difference is the temporal setting: In one case the party already has flopped, in the other it may. Usually subjects generate more and richer reasons in the hindsight than foresight condition. According to Mitchell et al. (1989) the reason is not the temporal setting per se, but the certainty inherent in the hindsight condition. When we know for sure that something has happened, we may be more motivated and use different cognitive strategies to explain it. Thus, by imagining future outcomes as already having happened, we can increase our insight and calibration. This technique is called *prospective hindsight* and relies in large measure on our great facility to generate causal explanations in hindsight. The next section examines causal models in more prescriptive terms.

Causal models. Suppose that in your evaluation of different apartments you are concerned with the potential noise from your new neighbors. You cannot use the apartment on a trial basis, so you have to judge the probability of different levels of noise at specific times of the day and night by some indirect measures and some type of causal model. You might visit the area, observe the type of people who frequent it, and perhaps ask some questions of the current residents of the apartment. You will have an implicit causal model associated with noise generation into which you assimilate the data collected and derive a probability estimate of different levels of noise. How can you judge the accuracy of your prediction? We shall consider three concepts in evaluating causal models:

Reliability. This refers to how reliable the predictions are that you make under a given set of circumstances. If you visit the apartment at 2 p.m. and hear no noise, then how confident can you be that the apartment is generally quiet in the afternoon?

Robustness. This refers to the degree to which you can generalize from one circumstance to another. For example, can your causal model say anything about noise in the evening given that it is quiet at 2 p.m.?

Validity. This refers to how accurate your causal model is in terms of characterizing a range of situations. Validity is thus a function of reliability and robustness. The more reliable and robust a model is, the more valid it is under a wide range of conditions.

Some causal models are designed to predict general phenomena under a wide variety of conditions but they will not be very reliable. The economic model of supply and demand is in this spirit. As the price decreases, the model predicts that demand will normally increase. It may be difficult, however, to say how large the increase will be. This causal model is very robust but not very precise or reliable concerning magnitudes. It thus has validity for only certain types of prediction. It would be inappropriate, for example, to use this model (without refinement) to determine the probability that demand for Product X will be over 10,000 units per month if the price were decreased from $1.00 to $.90.

The three concepts of reliability, robustness, and validity are all related to the theory of arguments that has guided our discussion of prediction and inference. An individual constructs a model of behavior to provide backing for the outcomes in which he or she is interested. For example, if you observe well-dressed individuals on the street near an apartment you are considering, you may conclude that the people are in the higher-income bracket and that they lead relatively quiet lives. In using these data to reach your claims or belief about outcomes, there is an implied model that relates "dress" to "income" and "income" to "style" of living. A rebuttal argument could be constructed through a model that contends that good dressers have more money, more money leads to more parties, and parties create noise.

Models that have high internal validity (for a particular individual) may have limited external validity. It is thus important to confirm your causal reasoning with some data from outside sources. These data can be in the form of additional inputs from those who have had personal experience with the phenomenon. For example, discussions with other tenants in the block where your potential apartment is located may provide you with detailed data on how much noise you can expect. You may also want to rely on theories developed by the scientific community as a basis for your predictions. For example, sociologists who have studied the relationship between income and life-style could provide insight into the particular problem under consideration. By modifying your internal perceptions of the world through external sources you may arrive at a more valid estimate of the probabilities.

This discussion of judging causal models through the theory of arguments provides a basis for dialogue between scientists and practitioners. The biases and heuristics that have been discussed in the previous section may be due to a particular model that individuals use, which in turn may be supported by a set of arguments. People generalize from small samples they feel are reliable or representative of a larger body of knowledge. They are overconfident and anchor on recent information. By having them examine the reliability, robustness, and validity of their models they may be more receptive to changing their views.

3.4.3   *Procedures for refining a given argument*

Throughout our discussion of prediction and inference we have assumed that individuals use a set of arguments to support their reasoning process. The arguments may not be explicitly articulated, which could be one reason that individuals are not aware that they are making statistical errors. Even if people can state a position clearly, it does not mean that they have thought through the rationale for their claim. The procedures outlined in this section are designed to refine a given set of arguments and perhaps force a rethinking of the situation. The biases revealed in laboratory experiments suggest that individuals tend not to follow statistical reasoning when providing answers to structured questions. We do not know what arguments individuals are actually using to provide backing for their answers. By providing additional evidence to individuals in different forms they may be able to articulate their positions better.

Feedback. In some situations it may be possible to provide rapid feedback by comparing the actual outcome with the predicted one. A classic example is weather forecasting, where the meteorologist learns each day about the accuracy of his prediction. These data may help him analyze the causal model that guided the prediction. In a similar fashion, doctors may learn from past experiences about their accuracy in diagnosing diseases.

For certain problems it may not be possible to obtain feedback until after a decision is made. Apartment selection, job choice, and marriage are good examples of cases where people may have to rely on limited past experiences or those of others to refine their arguments.

Incentive systems. Feedback alone may not force an individual to take stock of the arguments used and the causal model guiding actions. Investment-counseling services are rewarded for good performance by maintaining their customers and by being recommended to others. Hence, they have an incentive to monitor their own predictions and examine the models they use to forecast company performance. Meteorologists who provide special forecasts to certain groups (e.g., farmers) are in demand to the extent that their predictions are reasonably accurate. Doctors become viewed as expert diagnosticians in their field by virtue of their past records. To the extent that good performance is translated into higher rewards, there should be considerable interest in using better causal models.

Expanding and improving the data base. Because of limits in our computational abilities and our memory, we need decision aids to help make predictions. Historical data on weather patterns have enabled meteorologists to develop computer programs for improving forecasts. The use of computer-based decision support may aid all of us in making better decisions. If people recognize that statistical analysis can aid their reasoning process and that the computer is a useful tool for facilitating computation, then they may be interested in using this innovation as part of their decision process.

Strengthening the rebuttal. One way to force an individual to refine an argument is to ask her to engage in a dialectical process. By providing rebuttals or counterarguments to the supporting model we can see how well it stands up to attack. Fischhoff (1982) and Nisbett and Ross (1980) have suggested this approach as a way of debiasing or improving one's inference ability.

Consider the case where an individual does not buckle his seat belt because he assumes the probability of a car accident is negligible. A useful exercise might be to analyze the assumptions on which this estimate is based. Specifically one would have to determine the number of car miles driven in the United States (or his region of the country if such data exist) and divide this figure into the relevant number of accidents.

The result would be the chance of an accident per car mile driven. If this figure is higher than the person's original estimate, he may not accept that these figures have any personal meaning. For example, he may argue that he is much better than the average driver so that probabilities based on aggregate data are inappropriate for analyzing his problem.

Education and training. In a more general vein, it is an open question how well we can teach individuals to think probabilistically about problems and to improve their reasoning process. People may want to construct arguments that enable them to deal with a world that is more certain than the data may indicate. Textbooks on probability are now being written to teach probability in grade school so that young children will become more aware of the importance of dealing with uncertainty when encountering real problems. How well this process will actually work remains to be seen.

Probability encoding. Finally, various techniques exist for encoding the probabilities of uncertain outcomes. A person's response may either be direct, requiring a number, or indirect, as when choosing between two gambles. In the latter case, the reference point may be external, such as a wheel of chance, or internal, as when assessing whether it is more likely that sales will or will not exceed a given level. Alternatively, the person may be asked for confidence levels of varying probability, or asked to draw a cumulative probability function. All these methods should yield the same probability distribution if the person is consistent.

In reality, however, the different methods serve as consistency checks, as often the person will find one method much more natural than another. It is thus particularly important to know what level of precision is required for a given variable, within a certain range. Encoding is as much art as science. As such, it underscores the need for good decision psychology as part of prescriptive analysis.

3.5   Feedback and learning

Lastly, the prediction and inference phase provides an opportunity to link the present decision to previous ones, so as to reap the benefits of past experience. For example, if a manager has been too optimistic on many past occasions in projecting sales, it would behoove him or her to adjust the current estimates downward. The Bayesian model is the most complete and formal prescriptive system for updating and learning. Furthermore, decision analysis (especially decision trees) can provide valuable guidance on the value of obtaining additional information. At the individual level, however, these techniques are little used. In part this reflects lack of training, but also the complexity of these techniques when used in practice. Instead, most people prefer to approach the learning task intuitively. Unfortunately, this causes problems. Numerous studies have highlighted the difficulties of learning from experience (Fischhoff and Beyth, 1975; Einhorn and Hogarth, 1978; Klayman and Ha, 1989). We shall recount here some of the major obstacles, following Russo and Schoemaker (1989).

3.5.1 *External obstacles*

Even if we were very eager and capable learners, the normal decision environment makes learning difficult. Here are, in brief, the major external obstacles.

Missing feedback. For a large class of decisions (e.g., marriage, career, surgery), we may never find out what the other option(s) would have yielded. We seldom keep track of rejected alternatives (be they job applications, academic majors, or potential mates). Thus, it may be difficult to apply the lessons from similar past decisions (e.g., college admissions) to the current one, unless we consciously try to find out what happened (or would have happened) to the options we did not choose (Einhorn and Hogarth, 1978).

Confounded feedback. Suppose, however, that you had kept track of those candidates you rejected, say, in your capacity as a sales manager. And suppose further that 80% of the people you hired turned out to be successful in their jobs, whereas only 50% of the ones you rejected did well in other (similar) jobs (as far as you can tell). Does this confirm the quality of your decision rule? No, not necessarily. Your feedback is confounded by the fact that after you hired some and rejected others, different things happened to them. For example, just having been turned down may have demotivated some of the rejected people, resulting in lower performance. But had they been accepted they might have done just as well. Or, perhaps you gave those you hired a dynamite training program or an excellent incentives package and that's why they did better.

The point is that feedback is often highly confounded with what are called *treatment effects:* actions taken after the decision (consciously or unconsciously) that affect the outcome. Self-fulfilling prophecies are a prime example of this (Jussim, 1986). For example, tests of the efficacy of drugs often use placebos and double-blind procedures to control for unconscious treatment effects.

Noisy feedback. Third, your feedback may not be informative because it contains random noise along with signal. How much can you really learn from, say, a few stock market decisions that turned out well or poorly? Whenever chance plays a significant role in determining outcomes, we either need large samples to sort out who is the better portfolio manager or we need to focus on process instead of outcomes. Thus, for unique and uncertain decisions (such as whom to marry, or where to start your career), examining the outcome (i.e., success or failure) is likely to be less informative than an examination of the reasons and thinking process underlying the decision. The latter, however, are more ambiguous and subjective, causing many to focus, perhaps unduly so, on the proverbial bottom line (i.e., outcomes).

Thus, the natural environment in which our decisions get played out is by no means an easy one for learning from past outcomes. Indeed, we might accumulate many years of decision-making experience and yet fail to get any better (which also happens in sports). To turn feedback into learning requires study and experimentation, so as to overcome the problems of missing, confounded, and noisy feedback. Just as professional athletes dissect and analyze their game (via videos, statistics, extensive practice of component parts, coaching, etc.), the lessons from past decisions may only become apparent under disciplined examination. Much of this examination should occur in the analysis phase, where we ought to ask to what extent past experiences are relevant to the present problem.

3.5.2   *Internal blocks*

Not only does nature fail to hand us on a gold platter the feedback we need to learn from our decisions, but our psychological makeup also hinders learning. Even if the feedback is relatively clear, we may fail to extract its key lesson because of ego problems and cognitive biases. Let's briefly examine each type.

Ego defenses. Most of us have a positive self-image and like to view ourselves as being in control of our lives. Although healthy at one level (Taylor and Brown, 1988), this attitude may lead us to systematic distortions of feedback. When negative feedback is received, we are prone to rationalize it in such a way that it does not reflect too badly on our skills. As Festinger (1964) and others have shown, we can be quite ingenious in coming up with self-serving attributions, ranging from "I did not say or mean that" and "unforeseeable factors arose" to "it is Johnny's fault" or "it does not matter that much to me." To some extent such ego defenses are necessary to remain positive and motivated about our life and capabilities. However, they may also cause us to be slow learners or no learners at all.

On the flip side of the coin, we are usually quite eager to take credit for good outcomes. As Langer (1975) has shown in various experiments, most of us harbor an illusion of control. We believe we can influence affairs more than the objective evidence justifies. This illusion seems rooted in a deep-seated need to have mastery over our destiny and environment, and indeed to most of us the perception of no control would be highly debilitating. Several studies have shown that giving workers (the perception of) more control leads to greater productivity and happiness (Perlmuter and Monty, 1977). When dental patients were given the option to switch off the power drill, they exhibited less sweating and anxiety (even though they never touched the power switch). However, our need for control also leads us into superstitious behaviors (e.g., rain dances, students having favorite pens or sweaters for examination taking) and erroneous beliefs about chance. For example, people who were allowed to pick their own lucky number in state lotteries (as in Massachusetts) gambled more than those who were simply assigned a number (by computer).

Cognitive biases. Much learning occurs in hindsight, after we have found out what happened. To appreciate fully what an outcome tells us, we must compare what we thought at the time (i.e., what we expected) with what actually transpired. This, as noted earlier, is very difficult psychologically. Our mind does not easily engage in such time travel, since it does not keep verbatim records of what we thought at an earlier point in time. Cognitive economy dictates that we continually update our memories, integrating the new information with the old. One price we pay for this is that the old becomes altered, as when pouring water into wine.

Studies by Fischhoff and others (see Fischhoff and Beyth, 1975; Hawkins and Hastie, 1990) have demonstrated that we suffer from biased recall of our earlier thoughts and predictions. In hindsight, we believe that we assigned a greater subjective probability to things that happened (than we really did), or a lower probability to those that did not. In short, we suffer from a "knew-it-all-along" bias, which makes the past appear more obvious or clear than it was at the time. Unfortunately, this cognitive illusion leads us to underestimate uncertainty in prediction tasks (when calibrated on past events) and to underestimate the value of new information (believing we already knew most of it). Both of these (underestimating uncertainty and undervaluing new information) can cause havoc in the analysis phase, resulting in overconfidence and premature decision making.

The tendency not to appreciate fully the value of new information is further exacerbated by the confirmation bias, the inclination to search for evidence that confirms rather than refutes our favorite hypotheses (Klayman and Ha, 1987). In structuring and analyzing problems, it especially pays to entertain *multiple* hypotheses concerning options, estimates, and consequences – in the spirit of the theory of arguments. Likewise, when developing causal models for better prediction or inference, the ability to think disconfirmingly is crucial. In the philosophy of science, the importance of falsification has been well appreciated since the work of Sir Karl Popper (1968). Similarly, in management – especially when elaborate decision support systems exist – the temptation must be resisted to use evidence selectively to bolster favorite hypotheses.

In sum, the problem-structuring phase entails challenging questions concerning the description of alternatives and the estimation of outcomes, both of which require inference and prediction, including learning from related past experiences. In addition, the feedback obstacles discussed here come into play when implementing our decisions (as discussed in Chapter 5), at which point opportunities arise for monitoring, intervention, and control. Such postdecision activities will only bear fruit, however, if we can obtain the right feedback and honestly assess what it says about our assumptions, reasoning process, and decision frames.

4

Valuation and choice

4.1   Introduction

This chapter is concerned with individual values and preferences, as well as the process of choice. Perhaps no other subject in decision sciences has attracted so much attention because of its theoretical and practical importance. In economics, both the theoretical and econometric analyses of consumer and firm behavior, which form the very foundations of micro- and macro-economics, are firmly grounded in the utility theory paradigm, one of the major theories of valuation and choice to be discussed in this chapter. Similarly, in management science and business, theories of valuation and choice pervade nearly every functional area. In finance, the theory of capital markets, portfolio selection, investments, and savings functions are all analyzed in terms of the utility theory paradigm, generalized to include risk. Similarly, marketing, insurance, and operations rely heavily on this theory.

In the public sector as well, major decisions regarding both public goods (e.g., the location of a park) and public "bads" (e.g., the location of a noxious facility such as a hazardous waste incinerator) require an analysis of the values of individuals affected by these goods and bads. Indeed, values matter for all social choice problems in which regulators and politicians act in the name of the public. Increasingly, the public policy and management literatures dealing with problems of this sort have relied on explicit models of valuation to represent the preferences of the public.

We will utilize a framework that characterizes problems along three dimensions: alternatives, states of nature, and outcomes. Any choice problem involves a set of alternatives $A_1 \ldots A_m$ and states of nature $S_1 \ldots S_n$ that reflect the degree of uncertainty about different events occurring. The intersection of a given alternative j with a particular state of nature k yields the vector of outcomes $\bar{X}(A_j, S_k)$ where $\bar{X}(A_j, S_k) = [X_1(A_j, S_k) \ldots X_r(A_j, S_k)]$, with r representing the number of different attributes that are valued by the decision maker. The valuation challenge is how to assign utilities to the different alternatives that reflect an individual's basic preferences. This choice problem requires the decision maker to rank the set of possible outcomes and find some criterion func-

States of Nature

Alternatives	S_1	S_2			S_n
A_1	$\bar{x}_{11}$	$\bar{x}_{12}$	.	.	$\bar{x}_{1n}$
.	.				.
.	.	.			.
.	.				.
A_m	$\bar{x}_{m1}$	$\bar{x}_{m2}$		.	$\bar{x}_{mn}$

Figure 4.1. General representation for choice problems

tion for combining the different states of nature with the resulting outcomes. Figure 4.1 depicts the relevant matrix for combining alternatives, states of nature, and outcomes so that choices can be made or predicted.

Frank Knight as early as 1921 distinguished between three classes of problems: decision making under certainty, risk, and uncertainty. By certainty he meant that each alternative could yield only one set of outcomes. This implies that Figure 4.1 collapses to an mx1 matrix since there will only be one state of nature, S_1. The other extreme of uncertainty concerns cases in which no likelihoods can be assigned to the states of nature. Figure 4.1 would then just contain different states of nature and outcomes that might occur without assigning any probability to particular states of nature. Decision making under risk implies that there is some probability (which may be ambiguous) associated with each state of nature.

We feel that most if not all real-world problems involve decision making under risk. Some situations come close to the case of certainty, such as selecting an apartment from a set of alternative housing options. Even here, however, some uncertainty is associated with some outcomes such as noise level from other apartments or from the street. In the case of a highly uncertain problem, such as investing in a revolutionary new technology (e.g., superconductivity), corporate executives may be able to determine the possible outcomes that could emerge, but they may be unwilling or unable to assign any kind of probabilities to these outcomes. However, such complete absence of any feel for relative likelihoods is quite rare.

For this reason, we shall focus most of our attention in this chapter on examining the valuation and choice process for the intermediate case of decision making under risk. Nonetheless, we shall begin the discussion with a treatment of the certainty case for two reasons. By initially restricting the analysis to a single state of nature, we can focus more clearly

Multiple Dimensions or Attributes

Alternatives	X_1	.	.	.	.	.	.	.	X_r
A1	x_{11}	.	.	.	.	.	.	.	x_{1r}
.	.								.
.	.								.
.	.								.
.	.								.
A_m	x_{m1}	.	.	.	.	.	.	.	x_{mr}

Figure 4.2. The case of certainty with multiple attributes

on the valuation process. In addition, we can see more easily why valuation and choice are often intertwined or nested within each other.

4.1.1 *Motivating example (apartment selection)*

Jim House is a graduate student looking for an apartment and he is aware of nine possibilities. He is focusing on five different attributes – rent, time to campus, noise level, number of bedrooms, and quality of the kitchen – in making this decision. To simplify his choice process, he assumes that each attribute is known with certainty. How should he value the different features of each apartment and their relative importance? What types of decision rules might he use to make his selection?

Given that there is only a single state of nature, we can construct a simple submatrix for this type of problem in which the columns represent the different attributes X_1 through X_r as shown in Figure 4.2. In this figure, the row A_m is equivalent to the outcome vector $\bar{X}(A_m, S_1)$ in Figure 4.1 with S_1 being the only state of nature. We assume that Jim House has contacted the university housing office and visited the nine apartments, after which he was able to construct the matrix displayed in Table 4.1.

Let us now examine four rather different choice procedures Jim might use in determining which apartment to select:

Decision Rule 1: Choose the apartment with the lowest rent.

In this case Jim focuses only on a single attribute in making his choice. He doesn't need to evaluate the other attributes. By this rule he chooses Apartment 2.

Decision Rule 2: Choose the apartment that is closest to the university subject to the constraint that the rent doesn't exceed $500 a month.

Table 4.1. *Apartment selection problem*

Alternative apartments	Rent per month (\$) X_1	Minutes to campus X_2	Noise level X_3	Number of bedrooms X_4	Quality of kitchen X_5
1	400	5	Low	2	Old
2	320	30	Medium	1	Average
3	600	20	Low	3	Modern
4	450	15	Medium	3	Old
5	380	20	High	1	Average
6	500	10	Medium	3	Modern
7	460	20	High	2	Old
8	475	35	Medium	2	Modern
9	460	40	Low	2	Modern

Here two attributes are considered important but the evaluation process is still very crude. Rents have only two values: acceptable ($\leq$\$500) or unacceptable ($>$\$500). There is no need to trade off travel time for rent. This rule selects Apartment 1.

Decision Rule 3: Balance travel time against rent in some fashion and choose the apartment with the highest overall value.

Here Jim is being less specific because he does not say exactly what trade-off he is prepared to make between rent and travel time. Initially he may be able to eliminate some apartments because they are worse than others on both rent and distance. Specifically, Apartments 3, 4, and 6–9 are inferior to Apartment 1, which has both lower rent and less travel time than any of these six apartments.

Jim's final choice will depend on two factors: (1) how he values different rent amounts and travel times, and (2) the relative weights he assigns to the two attributes considered important. One way to capture this valuation process is to define and scale a value function v that reflects Jim House's preferences for different points in the rent–travel time space. There exists a large literature in economics and management science that provides guidance on how to construct multi-attribute value functions (for an overview see Keeney and Raiffa, 1976).

The weights in the models reflect the relative importance of each of the attributes when making trade-offs and thus co-determine the overall value of a particular alternative. Apartment 2 becomes more attractive as the relative weight given to rent increases; as travel time becomes more important then Apartment 1 will be more desirable. Appendix A provides a more detailed discussion on how to determine weights of additive value functions.

Decision Rule 4: Set cutoff levels for rent (e.g., $400) and distance (e.g., 20 minutes), so that only apartments satisfying both constraints remain in contention and then balance off all attributes for those remaining apartments. In this case, two apartments remain in contention (1 and 5). To choose one, Jim must make value trade-offs among five attributes.

Each of these four decision rules reflects a different set of valuation and choice processes regarding different attributes. For example, Decision Rule 1 specifies that only rent is important, whereas Decision Rule 4 regards all of the attributes to be relevant but, because of difficulties in processing information, it considers only two features at the outset to simplify the decision process. These four decision rules sometimes lead to the same choice of apartment. But, if Jim chooses Apartment 1 using Decision Rule 4, he will have done so for reasons different from those implied by Decision Rule 2. Moreover, for other problems these two strategies may produce quite different choices. Thus, we cannot necessarily infer the rule a person is using from his final choices. Later in this chapter, we examine further how to make inferences about individual decision processes and values on the basis of observed choices.

4.1.2 *Choice heuristics*

These four decision rules describe the steps through which information is collected and processed in evaluating alternatives and making choices. Each rule reflects a specific heuristic or rule of thumb for simplifying the decision process. This section identifies more general rules or choice procedures for well-specified alternatives, such as selecting between available apartments.

Domination procedures. When many alternatives are present, it is common to reduce the choice set to a more manageable size by first eliminating "inferior" alternatives. One approach is domination. It entails the identification of alternatives that are equal to or worse than some other alternative on every single dimension. For example, Apartment 7 is dominated by Apartment 4.

The domination principle, however, could lead to a suboptimal elimination if not all relevant attributes are considered. For example, Apartment 1 dominates Apartment 8 on the first four attributes in Table 4.1. If it were eliminated based on these comparisons and later the person decided that the "quality of kitchen" is an important attribute, then Apartment 8 might in fact be a desirable alternative.

Also, if certain alternatives turn out to be infeasible, earlier dominated alternatives may become worthwhile candidates again. For example, if it turns out that Apartment 7 is rented to another person, Apartment 4 could again become a viable option for Jim House. Similarly, introducing a new alternative can increase the set of dominated ones. Domination is thus a relative property, critically dependent on the particular attributes and alternatives being considered.

Conjunctive or disjunctive procedures. A second approach for screening out undesirable alternatives is to use conjunctive or disjunctive decision rules. Under the conjunctive rule an alternative is accepted if each dimension meets a set of preset standards or thresholds. For example, in the apartment selection problem, one might require rent to be less than $500, distance less than 40 minutes, no more than a medium noise level, at least two bedrooms, and at least an average kitchen. The only apartment that meets the conjunction of all these five conditions is Apartment 8. If more alternatives had been shown, several apartments might have passed this conjunctive test, which essentially partitions the alternatives into accept–reject categories. "Accept" in this initial screening round means "examine further."

Conjunctive rules are of the form "A_i is acceptable if x_{i1} is acceptable *and* x_{i2} is acceptable *and* . . . *and* x_{ik} is acceptable" for the k attributes in question. A major drawback of the conjunctive rule is that it is noncompensatory. If an alternative fails barely on a given dimension, surplus or slack elsewhere cannot compensate for this. For example, Apartment 9 was ruled out because it was 40 minutes from campus even though it is at least as good as Apartment 8 on all other dimensions.

Closely related to the conjunctive rule is the disjunctive strategy. Here an alternative is accepted if it scores sufficiently high on at least one dimension. For example, an apartment might be selected (for further evaluation) if its rent is not more than $400. Disjunctive rules are of the form "A_i is acceptable if attribute x_{i1} is sufficiently high *or* x_{i2} is sufficiently high *or* . . . *or* x_{ik} is sufficiently high" for the k attributes examined. Disjunctive strategies are also noncompensatory since trade-offs between attributes are not permitted. To simplify the choice process further, alternatives may be evaluated using only a subset of the attributes the person values. Such simplifying rules are frequently encountered in daily decision making. For example, in selecting a meal in a restaurant someone might use a disjunctive rule by focusing only on fish meals or dishes whose prices are below a specific level.

Elimination by aspects. A third type of choice rule is the elimination-by-aspects (EBA) approach. It focuses on intradimensional comparisons among the particular set of alternatives using preset standards or aspiration levels. The following television commercial (cited in Tversky, 1972) illustrates how it works:

"There are more than two dozen companies in the San Francisco area which offer training in computer programming." The announcer puts some two dozen eggs and one walnut on the table to represent the alternatives, and continues: "Let us examine the facts. How many of these companies have on-line computer facilities for training?" The announcer removes several eggs. "How many of these companies have placement services that would help you find a job?" The announcer removes some more eggs. "How many of these companies are approved for veterans' benefits?" This continues until the walnut alone remains. The announcer cracks the nutshell, which reveals the name of the company and concludes: "This is all you need to know in a nutshell."

Each of the questions posed by the announcer in this example represents a particular attribute or aspect with a preassigned criterion value. The selection of a particular question enabled the announcer to eliminate some of the schools (eggs) because they did not meet the relevant criterion value. After several attributes have been examined only one school remains and the process ends. That is the essence of the elimination-by-aspects technique.

The use of EBA requires the decision maker to assign some type of weight or priority to the importance of each of the different attributes associated with a particular problem. The order in which the attributes will be reviewed depends on their relative importance, although the ordering may vary over time. For instance, in selecting meals the attribute ordering may differ from day to day, according to some probabilistic rules. We can, for example, think of the "importance weights" as the numbers on a roulette wheel, such that a particular attribute with more numbers assigned to it will have a greater chance of being looked at first. Thus the EBA can be thought of deterministically (for one specific case) or probabilistically (across cases over time).

In the stochastic EBA rule, the roulette wheel is spun so that the pointer determines which attribute is examined first and all alternatives that do not satisfy the preset standards are eliminated. The wheel is spun again to determine the second attribute to be examined. The process continues until only one alternative remains or all attributes are examined. If there are several alternatives remaining at the end of the process, then the individual has to use some tie-breaking rule (e.g., selecting the alternative that has the highest value on the most important dimension).

Consider the stochastic use of EBA for the apartment selection example. Suppose that the roulette wheel was spun three times and landed respectively on monthly rent, noise level, and travel time. Figure 4.3 depicts the final choice process for this problem. Note that according to

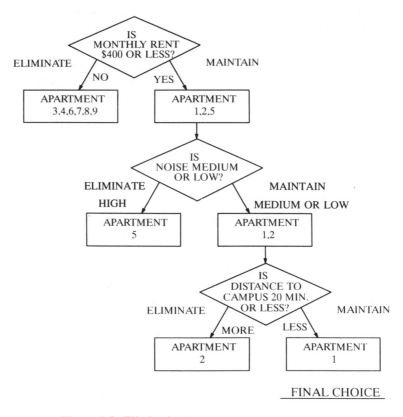

Figure 4.3. Elimination-by-aspects procedure

this choice model the number of bedrooms and the quality of the kitchen do not enter into the decision process because all of the alternatives except Apartment 1 were eliminated after the attribute "noise level" was considered. Had the quality of kitchen been more important than distance, then Apartment 2 would have been chosen instead of Apartment 1.

The advantage of the EBA rule is that it reduces cognitive strain by simplifying information-processing requirements. It has the drawback of being noncompensatory. For example, Apartment 2 was eliminated because it is too far from campus. Had Jim compared Apartments 1 and 2 on all dimensions he might have decided it was worth being further from campus in order to pay less rent and have a better kitchen.

Lexicographic rules. A heuristic related to elimination by aspects is a lexicographic ordering whereby all alternatives are ranked in a manner analogous to the way words are arranged in a lexicon (or dictionary). The most important dimension is examined first, and alternatives are ordered just on the basis of that first dimension (e.g., the first letter of a word). If one alternative is preferred over all the others on the basis of this single attribute, then it is chosen. If there are ties on the first attribute, then the second most important attribute is considered, and so on, consulting each attribute in order of its importance to break ties until a single alternative remains (see Fishburn, 1974).

If one were using a quantitative scale for judging alternatives, then ties would be less likely, so that the first attribute (e.g., rent) would usually determine the ranking of different options. Only if there were two apartments, for example, that had exactly the same rent would one turn to the second attribute. A more plausible use of a lexicographic model in such situations divides the attribute into qualitative characteristics (e.g., high, medium, and low rents). In that case only alternatives with a desirable characteristic (e.g., low rents) would be candidates for the second stage.[1] New attributes would continue to be introduced until all apartments were completely ranked. The lexicographic model has the advantage that if one's first choice is not available (e.g., someone has already taken the apartment), then one can automatically turn to the second choice. Other methods described in this section, such as EBA, would have to start the process over again, since they do not provide a complete ranking of alternatives but just divide them into "accept" or "reject."

Additive (difference) models. Another heuristic that requires considerably more computation on the part of an individual is the additive or linear rule. In this approach the individual evaluates each relevant attribute j through a value function v_j and indicates its relative importance value by a weight w_j. Let x_{ij} denote the level of alternative A_i for attribute j. The overall value for an alternative i is given by

$$V_i = \sum_j w_j v(x_{ij})$$

The alternative with the largest overall value (i.e., $\max(V_i)$) is the most desirable one under this rule.

In the case of apartment selection, this model would require each individual to determine the value function and the relative importance of the five different attributes (see Appendix A). The decision rule used is compensatory since decreases in the value of one attribute may be compensated, in part, by increases in the value of another. The additivity assumption implies that there are no interaction effects between attributes.

---

1 Even this modification, however, can be overly sensitive to how the cutoffs are set separating say "low" from "medium."

For example, the valuation process associated with noise level would be independent of the number of bedrooms in the apartment. Even with this simplifying assumption the process of computing optimal choices with this model may be time-consuming. But who said it's easy to choose among multi-attributed alternatives?

A variation on the linear model is the additive difference rule, which involves binary comparisons between two alternatives on each attribute (Tversky, 1969). For example, say that in the apartment selection problem the final choice is between Apartments 3 and 4. A common procedure for such pairwise choices is first to examine differences in rent, then differences in time to campus, and so on, and keep a running total as to how much one apartment is better than the other. In other words, for Apartments 3 and 4, the additive difference model posits that people examine the following vector of differences:

$$[v_1(x_{31}) - v_1(x_{41})], [v_2(x_{32}) - v_2(x_{42})], \ldots ,[v_5(x_{35}) - v_5(x_{45})]$$

Differences in values for the attribute "rent" may not be directly comparable with differences in the values of "time to campus." Hence, we need a transformation function ϕ_j to make the dimensions comparable, and to reflect differences in importance attached to the various attributes with respect to overall preference. The additive difference model predicts that alternative A_3 is preferred to A_4 if:

$$\sum_{j=1}^{5} \phi_j[v_j(x_{3j}) - v_j(x_{4j})] > 0$$

The advantage of this rule is that it focuses only on attributes where the two alternatives differ. Further, utilities have to be added only once across attributes (in the form of differences) rather than twice (as when evaluating each alternative separately). Still, this approach requires estimation of values, weights, and a transformation function. Also, it is limited to pairwise comparisons, although the model could be used repeatedly once the choices have been narrowed down to a few alternatives.[2]

Experimental evidence. The particular rule a person uses depends much on the complexity of the task. This was experimentally demonstrated by Payne (1976) who examined subjects' information search strategies in a hypothetical apartment selection task. The choice was varied in complexity by changing both the number of alternatives (2, 4, 8, or 12) and

---

2 If, for instance, three apartments are left, three pairwise comparisons could be conducted. Unfortunately, unless all ϕ_j are linear, this method does not guarantee transitive rankings (for $r > 2$).

the number of attributes provided (4, 8, or 12). The information for a given level of task complexity was provided in a form similar to Table 4.1 except that the values of attributes for different apartments were placed in envelopes posted on a large board. Subjects were given as much time as they wished, and Payne recorded which envelopes they opened.

Four strategies were examined, namely, conjunctive, EBA, additive, and additive difference. When faced with just two alternatives, subjects favored compensatory rules, such as the additive and additive difference rules. When presented with more complex tasks (i.e., more attributes and alternatives) the decision strategies changed in favor of quick elimination rules such as the conjunctive and EBA approaches. These conclusions were based on objective measures of information search (such as the number of envelopes examined by subjects) as well as more subjective analyses of protocols (i.e., subjects' verbal accounts of what they did).

Russo and Dosher (1983) similarly used process-tracing techniques to determine what strategies individuals used for choosing between two multidimensional alternatives. In one experiment they asked subjects to determine which one of a pair of college applicants was most deserving of a scholarship based on two to five attributes (e.g., family income, test scores, grade point average). Most subjects used an additive difference model as a way to reduce cognitive effort. Their experiments involved tracing eye fixations as well as verbal protocols.

The use of verbal protocols by researchers brings us back to the quote from John F. Kennedy with which we began Chapter 3: How much can a person really know and verbalize about his or her own decision process? Two types of protocols are usually distinguished: concurrent or "think aloud" protocols and retrospective protocols in which the subject explains afterward how the decision was made. Whereas the latter may seem less intrusive – in the sense of not interfering with or possibly altering the decision process itself – the retrospective protocol has proved to be especially untrustworthy (Nisbett and Wilson, 1977; Ericsson and Simon, 1980, 1984).

Subjects may give explanations after the fact that clearly contradict other evidence. For instance, they may say that price was examined before nutrient information when choosing among soup cans, while eye-fixation records show the opposite. Such ex post fabrications or distortions may reflect (a) subjects' desires to appear rational or at least knowledgeable about how their own decision was made, (b) limited insight into the underlying cognitive process (such as what was and was not in short-term memory at a given point), or (c) ordinary forgetting or distortions of recall. For these reasons, many researchers trust concurrent protocols more, even if they do run the risk of actually changing the underlying decision process (due to being asked to think aloud). Hence even concurrent protocols would need collaborative evidence, as suspicions remain about subjects' ability to tell the "truth" (see Russo, Johnson, and Stephens, 1989).

The debate about the value of verbal protocols touches on an even deeper issue, namely, what it means to explain or understand a decision process. Some of the decision rules discussed earlier in this section (e.g., the domination or conjunction rule) are clearly intended as *process* models; they seek to describe how people might actually work their way through a decision. Others (e.g., the additive rule) are meant more as *paramorphic* rules;[3] they try to mimic or predict outcomes of the underlying decision process without claiming to capture the sequence and manner in which information is processed. In particular, the additive difference model requires rather complex nonlinear mathematical transformations of value differences, and as such is more paramorphic.

Some rules, such as elimination by aspects, exhibit both process and paramorphic characteristics. The deterministic part of EBA, in which options are eliminated as soon as they fail to meet any one of the preordered sets of attribute levels, is very much a process model. However, its stochastic part, according to which the ordering of attributes or aspects is drawn at random from a stable and complete probability distribution is much more paramorphic. It captures the reasonable notion that people may vary from day to day as to which criteria matter most in deciding what to have for lunch or which TV program to watch. But the idea that they draw these attributes at random from some well-defined density function is more a researcher's way of modeling this process than actually describing what happens psychologically. In general, true process models will only entail mental operations that are within a subject's cognitive capabilities (without resort to "as if" arguments).

E. Johnson and Payne (1985) have developed an interesting "cognitive algebra" to measure how many basic mental operations (such as addition, multiplication, and binary comparison) a particular rule entails for a typical task. Their premise is that subjects tend to adopt those rules that strike a good (some would say optimal!) balance between a rule's mental effort and its expected decision quality. The issue arises, however, how subjects can make such metadecisions (i.e., decisions about how to decide) well if they have serious information-processing limitations and are averse to mental effort in general. After all, this metadecision requires either an extensive simulation as to how different rules are likely to perform in the given task environment (and how effortful they are) or extensive experience with the task (and an ability to store, retrieve, and use this accu-

---

3 Paramorphic here means "above the form." Paramorphic models do not describe the actual process but serve as "as if" models.

mulated wisdom). Thus, we run again into some ambiguity as to what is real and what is paramorphic in the descriptive models proposed by decision researchers.

Although the issue of process versus paramorphic rules is important, Einhorn, Kleinmuntz, and Kleinmuntz (1979) have argued that the two are complementary rather than competing ways of modeling decision processes (also see Hogarth, 1974). Each approach highlights (or obscures) different aspects and in that sense complements the other. For example, linear models (which tend to be paramorphic) reveal clearly what tradeoffs are being made between competing attributes. Process models, in contrast, highlight the order in which information is processed as well as how much information is likely to be used. Which kind of representation is better depends on what the objectives are. For prediction tasks, paramorphic models may be fine. But if you wish to compare, say, two medical experts or to improve their decision process, a black box model will not do and process representations are needed. The next section further examines process models that provide finer detail than the representations discussed so far. These micromodels, it turns out, are often needed for a full understanding of how complex decisions get made as well as how to improve these decisions.

4.1.3 *Microprocess models*

Micromodeling got its start with attempts to understand expert problem solving in well-delineated task domains. Newell and Simon (1972) set out to describe in considerable detail how humans perform a variety of semistructured problem-solving tasks such as playing chess and checkers, proving theorems in logic and geometry, scheduling jobs in a job shop, and selecting a portfolio of stocks to satisfy an investor's needs. They believed that by providing detailed micromodels of problem-solving behavior in each of these contexts we could learn much more about the underlying decision processes and, perhaps, build a more precise and general theory of cognitive processes.

This approach to understanding cognitive processes is called the *information-processing model* of problem solving. In essence, this model views the problem solver as a computer, with a built-in logic or "program" that indicates at each step of the problem-solving process what the person does next. A descriptive theory of problem-solving behavior based on this approach indeed is often in the form of a computer program that simulates the person's thought process.

We could use this approach to examine exactly how Jim House goes about selecting different apartments from the time that he checks a list at the university housing office to the time he makes a final selection. We

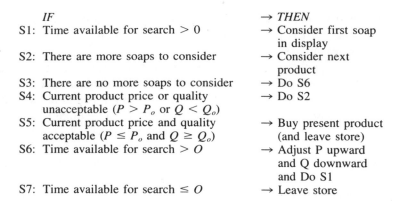

Figure 4.4. Production system for soap purchase decision

will illustrate this approach with an even simpler problem: choosing a bar of soap at the supermarket. We will assume that the shopper starts the search for an appropriate product with some initial expectation of acceptable price (P_o) and quality (Q_o). Suppose the search is terminated when a product has been found satisfying these initial expectations. If no such product is found, these expectations are adjusted (P_o upward and Q_o downward) and the search is begun afresh until either the consumer finds an acceptable product or runs out of time. Figure 4.4 presents a simple model of this process. This model is called a production system since it produces decisions step by step. It is essentially a sequence of "if–then" statements. If the condition to the left of the arrow is true, then the action to the right of the arrow is performed. If the statement to the left of the arrow is false, proceed to the next statement just as in a computer program.

This model could be expanded considerably (e.g., by defining how the consumer measures and adjusts quality and price). We omit these matters here. The example does illustrate, however, the more detailed nature of information-processing models of choice. The resulting micromodel is a detailed step-by-step process description of the problem-solving context of interest. It is usually precise enough (for modeling purposes) to write a computer program to mimic the choice process in question.

How are models of this type constructed? The answer is simple: through concurrent and retrospective protocols. The problem solver is asked to verbalize what he or she is doing while solving the problem and thereafter. These protocols are then analyzed and the elementary information-processing steps (S1–S7 in the example) are identified on the basis of this protocol under the assumption that the subject's description of her actions reasonably characterizes her behavior. A model is then formulated to conform to these steps. The model can be further validated to determine its predictive accuracy (e.g., whether it predicts which brand of soap is actually purchased) as well as its structural or process accuracy (how well the actual problem-solving process represented in protocols conforms to the details of the model).[4]

Beyond their value as descriptive theories, information-processing models have also given rise to the prescriptive fields of artificial intelligence and expert systems (Shortliffe, 1976). Artificial intelligence systems are computer-based programs designed to solve certain tasks, such as medical diagnosis or pattern recognition, faster or more efficiently than do un-aided humans. Information-processing models of human problem solving often provided the logic and motivation for such artificial intelligence systems. And some perform very well.

For example, an artificial intelligence (AI) backgammon program beat the world champion in 1979 (Berliner, 1980). AI systems for playing chess now exist that compete at the grand master's level of play. The structure of these systems was motivated by intensive study of the methods and heuristics used by grandmasters (i.e., by information-processing models of grandmasters playing chess). Similarly, AI systems in such diverse fields as medical diagnostics (Shortliffe, 1976) and corporate planning (Dhar, 1983) have been motivated by micromodels of expert practitioners in the relevant fields. Thus, such micromodels appear to provide a very solid basis for prescriptive efforts.

Micromodels of human problem-solving behavior have the distinct advantage of yielding detailed knowledge about a given problem solver's approach. This also is their major drawback. They tend to be quite specific to the problem solver and the problem context. The reader may wish to verify this by constructing an information-processing model similar to Figure 4.3 for some everyday decision like selecting what to eat at break-fast. Then ask a friend to model the same decision and compare the two models. There will likely be some similarities but also many differences. The models themselves may be so complex that the similarities and differences are hard to see at first glance. The end result of this exercise is likely to be that you understand your own choice process for the decision in question much better, even though you may find it difficult to compare it with someone else's process for the same decision.

4.2   Decision making under risk

Much recent research on valuation and choice has focused on decision making under risk. The impetus for most of this research has stemmed

---

4 Process criteria for model validation include predictions about how much time the person will need for various tasks or how much information he or she utilizes (plus the sequence in which the information is processed).

Table 4.2. *Payoff matrix for insurance decision*

	Stolen	Not stolen
Insure	$W - 150$	$W - 150$
Do not insure	$W - 10{,}000$	W

from failures of expected utility theory, a formal model of choice developed by von Neumann and Morgenstern (1947) for dealing with problems of risk. This model consists of a set of formal axioms characterizing rational behavior and a strategy for choosing among alternatives.[5] An excellent behavioral discussion of these important axioms is provided in Dawes (1988). For highly formal treatments of the utility axioms and the theoretical foundations of measurement, see Krantz, Luce, Suppes, and Tversky (1971), or Fishburn (1970, 1982).

Recently this approach has come under close scrutiny as a descriptive theory of choice and several alternative models have been proposed. This section examines the expected utility model and then turns to recent tests of the theory. Thereafter alternative descriptive and prescriptive models of choice are examined.

4.2.1   Motivating example (insuring against theft)

Roberta Glover has moderate assets including a coin collection valued at $10,000. She is considering whether to insure this collection against theft. She has estimated the chances of the collection being stolen and her insurance agent has quoted the lowest premium he could find. Roberta must now decide whether she should insure her collection.

This choice problem is the simplest possible example of decision making under risk. There are only two alternatives (insure versus do not insure), two states of nature (theft versus no theft), and a single attribute (dollar value). Table 4.2 summarizes the relevant data to help Roberta make her final choice assuming that her wealth level is W and the insurance cost $c = \$150$. We assume that she can obtain an identical coin collection for exactly $10,000 and that she will be indifferent between receiving $10,000 and not having her collection stolen at all.

The more general version of the insurance problem with multiple at-

---

5 These axioms, which were the foundation of von Neumann and Morgenstern's (1947) theory, have been modified by Savage (1954), Raiffa (1968), and others. They normally include the axioms of Completeness, Transitivity, Continuity, Independence, and Reduction of Compound Lotteries.

tributes, multiple alternatives, and more than two states of nature was already depicted in Figure 4.1. Recall that the outcome vector $\bar{X}_{mn}$ represents all consequences for alternative A_m assuming state of nature S_n occurs. Besides money, the consequence vector in this example might include inconvenience, anger, sentimental value, and other concerns associated with theft and insurance. Roberta reflected these concerns in the $10,000 figure. The various alternatives could include partial insurance and varying deductible levels.

4.2.2 Expected utility theory

Expected utility theory has been the dominant outcome-based approach for dealing with risk ever since von Neumann and Morgenstern (1947) proposed a set of formal axioms to define rational behavior (as inspired by De Bernoulli, 1738). They assumed that an individual chooses that alternative A_1 from a set of possible alternatives A_i ($i = 1 \ldots m$), which maximizes the expected value of his or her utility function (U). A person's utility function is defined over a set of outcomes for the relevant attributes in the problem. There are two key questions that need to be addressed if one is to apply this theory:

- How does one measure (or what does the analyst assume about) this utility function over the outcome space? This requires a *descriptive* analysis.
- Can an individual improve final choices by maximizing expected utility? This requires a *prescriptive* analysis.

We now address both of these questions.

Axioms of utility theory. In utility theory, a person's decision problem is solved through the evaluation of a set of outcomes (O_{ij}) that result jointly from a choice of alternative i and the occurrence of some state of nature j with given probability (p_{ij}). Figure 4.5 depicts these elements diagrammatically for the case of a single attribute. A utility function can now be constructed if the following axioms are satisfied. This function will reflect attitudes toward risk as well as the person's values for the outcomes under certainty.

The encoding process for measuring utilities (to be discussed later) assumes that the person's risk preferences satisfy these five axioms.

1. *Completeness.* For any choice between outcomes O_1 and O_2, either O_1 is preferred to O_2 (denoted $O_1 > O_2$), $O_2 > O_1$, or both are equally attractive (denoted $O_1 \sim O_2$).
2. *Transitivity.* If $O_1 > O_2$ and $O_2 > O_3$, then $O_1 > O_3$.
   (Also if $O_1 \sim O_2$ and $O_2 \sim O_3$, then $O_1 \sim O_3$).

ALTERNATIVES   OUTCOMES

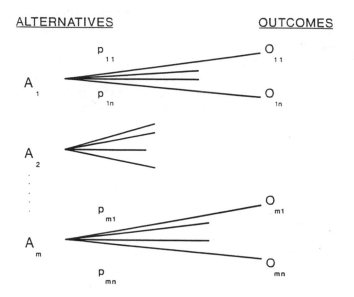

Figure 4.5. Lottery representation of risky options

3. *Continuity.* If $O_1 > O_2 > O_3$, then there exists some probability p between zero and one such that the lottery

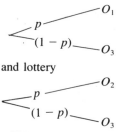

is as attractive as receiving outcome O_2 for certain.

4. *Independence.* If outcome O_1 is as attractive as outcome O_2 under conditions of certainty then lottery

and lottery

will be equally attractive (for any values of O_3 and p). <u>In other words, outcome O_3 and p are irrelevant to the final choice, provided $O_1 \sim O_2$. This is also known as the substitution axiom.</u>

5. *Reduction of Compound Lotteries.* A compound lottery (i.e., one whose initial outcomes are themselves lotteries) is equally attractive as the simple lottery that is obtained when multiplying through probabilities. For example:

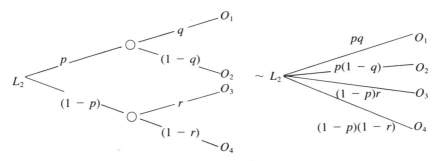

These axioms imply the following key EU theorem (as proved in Appendix A):

EU Theorem. A utility function U can be defined on the outcomes with the property that an alternative with a higher *expected utility* is always preferred to one with a lower level of expected utility.

Constructing a utility function. To construct a utility function a person must make indifference judgments between a sure option and a two-outcome lottery. To illustrate, suppose that the analyst wants to derive a utility function for apartment rents and presents the person with the following choice:

Rent known with certainty to be O_2
      versus
Rent is uncertain but will result in O_1 or O_3 from the lottery with probabilities p and $(1 - p)$ respectively

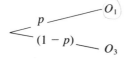

where $O_1 > O_2 > O_3$. The analyst can elicit preferences by specifying three of the above four parameters (p, O_1, O_2, O_3) and asking the person to indicate the value of the fourth variable so that he is indifferent between the two apartments. Two of the most common methods for eliciting such indifference values are

- The *certainty equivalence (CE) method*: Where an indifference level for O_2 is elicited for given values of p, O_1, and O_3.
- The *probability equivalence (PE) method* where an indifference level for p is elicited for given values of O_1, O_2, and O_3.

In constructing the utility function, U, one arbitrarily sets the utilities of two reference points of the particular attribute and derives the other utility levels in relation to these benchmark values. Normally these points are chosen as two extremes (e.g., lowest and highest rents). This function U will be unique up to a positive linear transformation, which means that if $U(A) > U(B)$ then also $U*(A) > U*(B)$ whenever $U*(x) = aU(x) + b$ with $a > O$.

In this sense expected utility is similar to a temperature scale (e.g., centigrade vs. Fahrenheit); that is, it is not a ratio scale but an interval one. For example, if City A is twice as warm in Fahrenheit than City B, this would not be true in Celsius (in general). But if the difference in temperature between Cities A and B is greater than the temperature difference between Cities C and D in one scale, this will also be true in any other scale that is a positive linear transformation of the first one. Thus, expected utility preserves an ordering on differences (but not on ratios) when linearly transformed.

Roberta's utility function. To construct this special kind of utility function, Roberta has to supply indifference judgments between a sure option and a simple two-outcome lottery expressed on final wealth levels. Let's assume Roberta's assets are currently worth $100,000 (including the coin collection of $10,000). Her utility function for wealth can now be assessed over a range appropriate for this particular insurance problem, namely $90,000 (in case theft occurs without insurance) to $100,000 (in case of full claim reimbursement). In constructing the utility function, U, we may arbitrarily set the utilities of two reference points of the particular attribute and then measure other utilities in relation to these benchmark utilities (as in the case of temperature scales). As noted, these points are often chosen to be the two extremes (e.g., lowest and highest wealth) that might be encountered in the problem. Thus, we could set $U(90,000) = 0$ and $U(100,000) = 100$ for Roberta's decision.

One way to construct Roberta's utility function now is to ask her for a certain wealth level W_1, such that she is indifferent between W_1 for sure and the following lottery

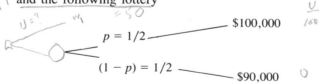

Suppose her answer is $94,000. If the axioms referred to above hold, then $U(W_1) = .5U(0) + .5U(100)$ or $U(94,000) = 50$. This utility point (derived from the above lottery) can now be plotted in Figure 4.6.

By constructing new lotteries, using outcomes whose utilities are known, we can obtain the utility of other wealth levels between $90,000 and $100,000. For example, at this point we can construct two new choices

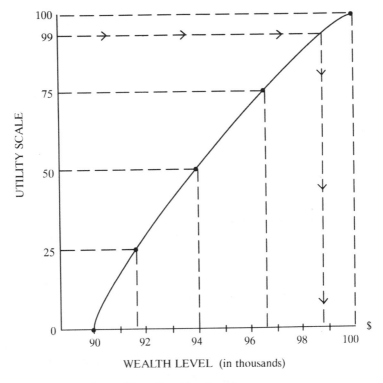

Figure 4.6. Roberta Glover's utility function

that will determine the values of W_2 and W_3 for which Roberta Glover is indifferent between the following two lotteries respectively:

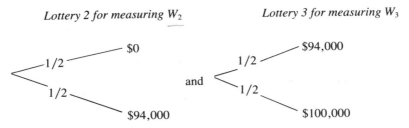

Lottery 2 for measuring W_2   *Lottery 3 for measuring W_3*

Suppose the indifference point for the second lottery is $W_2 = 91,700$ and for the third lottery $W_3 = 96,600$. Using the same kind of calculation as above we can determine that $U(91,700) = 25$ and $U(96,600) = 75$. Continuing in this manner, we can obtain as many points as necessary to plot a utility function for wealth between $90,000 and $100,000 such as the one depicted in Figure 4.6. (Appendix A formally proves this procedure.)

If the person's preferences are consistent with the axioms of utility theory, we should obtain the same function if instead of $p = 1/2$, we arbitrarily chose any other level of p for comparing the lotteries. Moreover, the axioms imply that if one used the PE method, the utility function would not change either. In the preceding example, if one arbitrarily specified the following comparison:

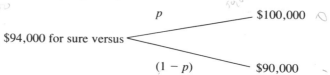

p ———— $100,000

$94,000 for sure versus

$(1 - p)$ ———— $90,000

then the indifference probability (p^*) should be $p^* = 1/2$, thus yielding $U(94,000) = 50$ (as we found before in the first CE question posed to Roberta).

The optimal choice A^* is the alternative that maximizes expected utility. Thus, if we accept the axioms postulated by von Neumann and Morgenstern (NM), the criterion for choosing among alternatives becomes simple and elegant. The shape of the utility function implicitly informs us about someone's attitude toward risk (Friedman and Savage, 1948). For example, a concave function implies that the person is risk averse, preferring a sure thing to a gamble with the same expected value. If Roberta were indifferent between a certain wealth level of $40,000 and a 50–50 chance of either $0 wealth or $100,000, then her preference would imply risk aversion with respect to this choice. We can thus determine locally as well as globally how someone's attitude toward risk changes with the level of a particular attribute (e.g., wealth, health). A large literature discusses how utility theory can be used to measure a person's attitude toward risk in a more formal manner. The interested reader is referred to this literature (e.g., Keeney and Raiffa, 1976) for more details.

Lastly, note that there exists a close link between valuation and choice in the measurement of utility. As Dyer and Sarin (1982) and others have shown formally, the shape of an individual's utility function is determined by two factors: the strength of preferences for outcomes under certainty and the person's attitude toward risk taking. This confounding has led some researchers to talk about *intrinsic* risk aversion (Bell and Raiffa, 1982). The latter refers to the concavity of $U(.)$ when defined on $v(x)$, so as to control for the effect of nonlinear value functions under certainty.

Choosing alternatives. Choosing between two alternatives requires the person to estimate the probabilities (p_j) of different states of nature (S_j) occurring. For any alternative A_i, the expected utility $E[U_i]$ is then given by

$$E[U(A_i)] = \sum_j p_j U(x_{ij}) \tag{4.1}$$

where $U(x_{ij})$ is the utility of the outcome x given alternative A_i and the occurrence of state of nature S_j. The optimal choice $A*$ is the alternative that maximizes expected utility. Thus, if we accept the axioms postulated by von Neumann and Morgenstern, the criterion for choosing among risky alternatives becomes simple and elegant.

Suppose that Roberta estimates the probability of her coin collection being stolen as being $p_1 = .01$ (and thus the likelihood of no theft taking place as $p_2 = .99$). Given her utility function for wealth over the relevant range, the expected utility of *not* purchasing theft insurance for her coin collection is:

$$EU(\text{do not insure}) = .01 \ U(\$90,000) + .99 \ U(\$100,000) = 99$$

The 99 utile level follows from the function plotted in Figure 4.6. We can also use this graph to find the highest premium that Roberta would still find attractive. We can see that $U(98,800) = 99$, which implies that Roberta should be willing (according to EU theory) to pay up to $200 for an insurance policy against coin theft even though her expected loss is only $100 (i.e., .01 times $10,000). In other words, she should be willing to pay an extra $100 over the expected loss for protection either because of having a concave value function for wealth and/or intrinsic risk aversion with respect to the uncertainty associated with remaining uninsured. Note that Roberta's utility function could also be used to assess policies with different upper limits on coverage below $10,000 as well as policies entailing varying levels of personal deductibles. Appendix A provides more technical demonstrations of EU's analytic power in solving complex decision problems under risk.

4.2.3 *Multi-attribute utility functions*

So far the discussion has focused on utility for outcomes measured along just one attribute. Usually, however, multiple attributes must be considered explicitly. For example, human lives have to be traded off against dollars in making highways safer. The cost of energy is weighed against environmental concerns when siting nuclear power plants. Apartment rents are weighed against location and space. Insurance premiums may be weighed against peace of mind in determining whether to buy coverage. People are often reluctant to make such trade-offs explicitly, either for political or personal reasons. If so, they make them implicitly as in the example where Roberta lumped all nonmonetary aspects together and then priced them out. If these other aspects are small, this procedure may be fine. However, if the nonmonetary issues are major in magnitude and concern, an explicit trade-off may be needed.

One procedure for determining multi-attribute choices is to *explicate* the relationship among the different (often hidden) attributes in the utility function. Returning to Figure 4.1, which depicts a general matrix for evaluating alternatives under uncertainty with n states of nature, consider the outcome vector for alternative m under state of nature j: $\bar{X}(A_m, S_j)$. Suppose we write the utility function for this outcome as $U[(x_1, \ldots, x_r)_{m,j}]$, where the x_i represents the levels of the various attributes given A_m and S_j. The key problem is to uncover the nature of the U function in terms of the x_i. For example, there may exist a utility function on each attribute separately $U_i(x_i)$. This is the case when U has an additive form, that is,

$$U(x_1, \ldots, x_r) = w_1 U_1(x_1) + w_2 U_2(x_2) \ldots + \ldots w_r U_r(x_r) \qquad (4.2)$$

where the scalar coefficients w_i reflect the relative weights given to each attribute. In general, however, there is no reason why $U(x_1, \ldots, x_r)$ should be an additive function of the different attributes. For example, there may be an interaction between noise tolerance and location in determining the utility of an apartment. If a person can tolerate a given noise level less well after a long rather than a short amount of commuting time, negative synergy exists between these two attributes.

The normative procedure for determining multi-attribute choices is the same as that for the one-attribute problem. To simplify the analysis, however, it can help to determine the relationship among attributes in the utility function. The following section introduces three properties that, whenever they apply, greatly simplify multi-attribute utility analyses.

Key tests. The first property is known as *preferential independence*. Under this condition, the trade-offs one is willing to make between any pair of attributes are independent of a third attribute. For example, if x_1 and x_2 are preferentially independent (PI) of x_3, then the trade-offs the decision maker is willing to make between x_1 and x_2 do not depend on the level t at which x_3 is fixed. If every pair of attributes is PI of all other attributes, a condition referred to as *mutual* PI, then the utility function must be additive. This means that each attribute x_i has its own utility function $U_i(x_i)$, which can be constructed independently of the other attributes and

$$U_i = \sum_i w_i U_i(X_i)$$

This brings us to a second independence concept called *utility independence*. If this condition holds, the utility function over a single attribute, say $U_2(X_2)$, does not depend on other attributes. Suppose you were offered a gamble involving attribute x_2 and asked to provide a certainty equivalent for this gamble. In the context of our earlier example, for instance, what level of monthly rent for sure would be as acceptable as a 50–50 chance at either \$200 or \$600 rent per month? If your answer does not depend on the levels of the other attributes x_1 and x_3 (e.g., location and space) then x_2 is utility independent (UI) of x_1 and x_3. To be sure, you should check other lotteries along the x_2 dimension as well. UI for x_2 essentially means that your willingness to gamble along the X_2 dimension does not depend on the levels at which $x_1, x_3, \ldots x_r$ are fixed. In general, if every X_i is UI of the others, the utility function is either additive or multiplicative. If it is multiplicative, its general form is:

$$U(x_1, \ldots, x_r) = \sum_i w_i U_i(x_i) + \text{all possible cross-product terms}$$

③ A third useful independence condition is *additive independence*. If it holds, $U(x_1 \ldots, x_r)$ must be additive. It is tested for by comparing the following type of lotteries (assuming the two-dimensional case).

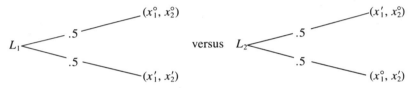

If L_1 is as attractive as L_2 for any given values of x_1° and x_1', it follows that the decision maker does not care how the outcomes from different attributes are combined (if one assumes equal probabilities). The person only looks at the marginal probability distributions and not the particular mixtures (i.e., joint distributions). This implies that there does not exist any interaction between the attributes, which is only true (in general) for an additive utility function.

Most of the theoretical and empirical research on multi-attribute utility functions has investigated these and other conditions under which the function $U(x_1, \ldots, x_r)$ can be separated into components, so that it may be written as

$$U(x_1, \ldots, x_r) = F[U_1(x_1), U_2(x_2), \ldots, U_r(x_r)]$$

A detailed but excellent discussion of various independence conditions and how to test for them empirically appears in Keeney and Raiffa (1976). A simple example (with only three dimensions) is discussed in Appendix C. Of course, it may turn out that none of the independence conditions holds. Four strategies can be followed in that case. The most common one is to restructure or redefine the attributes to avoid interaction effects. For example, if there were an interaction between noise and travel time, one could create a new attribute "quality of living," which includes both the quietness of the apartment as well as the commute to and from work.

A second strategy is to explore various subranges of the x_i to see if certain limited independence conditions apply. For instance, tolerance for noise levels might start to interact with commuting times that are over 30 minutes. If so, an additive form could be used for times below 30 minutes. A third approach is to examine *subsets* of attributes that might be additive. Lastly, if all else fails, one might seek holistic modeling (e.g., using regression methods) to find the best $U(x_1, \ldots, x_r)$ to fit some interval ranking of a set of $\bar{x} = (x_1, \ldots, x_r)$ vectors.

Determining choices. Once the form of $U(x_1, \ldots, x_r)$ has been determined, the problem is solved in the same manner as with just one attribute. To illustrate this, consider a simplified apartment problem, entailing the following two attributes:

x_1 = travel time (say, on a scale from 0 to 100)
x_2 = noise (say, on a scale from 0 to 10)

Suppose now that we know $U(x_1, x_2)$ and we have to compare a sure apartment offer $A_1 = (90, 6)$ with one where the noise level is uncertain, as follows:

$$A_2 = \begin{bmatrix} 80, \begin{smallmatrix} \overset{.5}{\diagup} 9 \\ \underset{.5}{\diagdown} 4 \end{smallmatrix} \end{bmatrix}$$

The utility of the certain apartment will simply be $U(90, 6)$. The risky option, A_2, on the other hand, entails two distinct alternatives with the following probabilities:

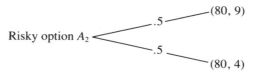

Risky option A_2 — .5 — (80, 9); .5 — (80, 4)

Once we have formulated this vector lottery we can calculate its expected utility, that is,

$$E[U(A_2)] = .5U(80, 9) + .5U(80, 4)$$

If the utility function can be expressed in an additive form, then one assigns weights to each of the two attributes and uses equation (4.2) to compute the utilities of each of the outcomes. If nonadditive, more complex calculations will be needed (as shown in Appendix C).

Our discussion of utility theory has so far ignored some additional complicating features, such as the presence of multiple time periods (which would require some type of discounting) and so-called state-dependent utilities (Karni, 1985). For instance, when you are in a telephone booth, a quarter may have more utility to you than a dollar (if we assume you cannot change money). Thus, utilities may depend on the prevailing state of nature, or on the decision act chosen. Although such considerations require further refinements of the utility model (see section 4.6), they do not alter its basic structure. Once problems have been laid out in terms of alternatives, states of nature, and outcomes, the decision boils down to estimating probabilities and utilities, and multiplying them through. Unfortunately, this is not as simple in practice as it might seem in theory, as we discuss next.

4.3   Biases in assessment procedures

The elicitation procedure for determining a person's utility function requires *indifference judgments* between two basic options, at least one of which must be a lottery. An extensive literature (see Einhorn and Hogarth, 1981, or Schoemaker, 1982) suggests that even these basic elicitation choices often differ from or are more complex than the utility theory axioms imply or assume (see also von Winterfeldt and Edwards, 1986). Consider, for instance, the problem of choosing a response mode after an individual has been presented with the following choice:

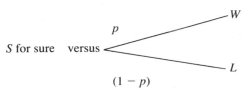

where S is the sure amount, p is the probability of winning, W is the gain, and L is the loss (or lower amount of the lottery). We assume that $L < S < W$ but that these values are relative rather than absolute amounts so they are not constrained by sign. Thus, the outcomes could be all positive, negative, or a combination of wins and losses.

Two of the most common methods for eliciting indifference values are:

- The certainty equivalence (CE) method where an indifference level for S is elicited for given values of p, W, and L.
- The probability equivalence (PE) method where an indifference level for p is elicited for given values of S, W, and L.

According to EU theory, the same utility function should be elicited for any individual whether one uses the CE, PE, or other proper methods. Yet, considerable empirical evidence suggests that systematic differences emerge when one changes the mode of presentation from CE to PE or vice versa (see Hershey and Schoemaker, 1985, or E. Johnson and Schkade, 1989).[6]

Illustrative example. The following example illustrates differences that were observed in an experimental context. (More details on these and other experiments can be found in Hershey, Kunreuther, and Schoemaker 1982; see also MacCrimmon and Wehrung, 1986.)

In an experiment, 64 students were divided into two equal groups. Each group was asked a different question.

Group 1   You face a situation where you have a 50% chance of losing $200 and a 50% chance of losing nothing. Would you be willing to pay $100 to avoid this situation?
                    YES   NO   INDIFFERENT
Group 2   You can pay $100 to avoid a situation where you may lose $200 or nothing. Would you pay if there were a 50% chance of losing?
                    YES   NO   INDIFFERENT

In the first group, only 6% were willing to pay $100 to protect themselves against the loss (i.e., they were risk averse). Therefore, 94% were either risk neutral, (i.e., willing to pay exactly $100) or risk prone (i.e., unwilling to pay $100).

In contrast, in the second group, 32% were willing to pay $100 if $p = 50\%$ (i.e., they were risk averse). The remaining portion of the group was either risk neutral or risk prone. Note, however, that these two problems are identical within EU theory. They only differ in what is emphasized: dollars versus percent. These discrepancies are even more pronounced when asking for CE and PE judgments, rather than ordinal choices (see Schoemaker and Hershey, 1992b).

Other biases. As Figure 4.7 illustrates, analysts constructing utility functions face other potential biases. Not only must they decide on a response mode when eliciting indifference judgments (such as CE vs. PE), they must also select appropriate stimuli (levels for probabilities and payoffs). Although it should not matter according to NM theory whether 50–50 gambles or 30–70 gambles are used, in practice it does matter. With lower probabilities, utility functions are typically less concave (i.e., less risk averse). Also, it matters considerably whether gain, mixed, or loss gambles are used, although rational subjects should adopt a final wealth perspective. That is, losses and gains are defined relative to a reference

6 For this reason, McCord and Neufville (1986) propose an elicitation procedure involving only lotteries. Although this may get around the certainty effect inherent in the Certainty Equivalence (CE) method, it is more complex and may fail to capture legitimate attitudes concerning sure amounts.

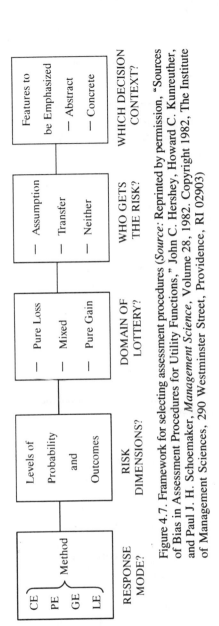

Figure 4.7. Framework for selecting assessment procedures (*Source*: Reprinted by permission, "Sources of Bias in Assessment Procedures for Utility Functions," John C. Hershey, Howard C. Kunreuther, and Paul J. H. Schoemaker, *Management Science*, Volume 28, 1982. Copyright 1982, The Institute of Management Sciences, 290 Westminster Street, Providence, RI 02903)

point (such as the status quo) and risk attitudes should ideally be defined relative to final wealth levels. If not, preferences could be manipulated or become inconsistent (as shown later when discussing the "isolation effect").

Likewise, it shouldn't matter within EU theory whether the risk you are evaluating is one you are assuming or transferring away. For example, if you are indifferent between receiving $80 for sure and a 50–50 chance at $200 or 0, you should be equally willing to exchange $80 for the gamble as the gamble for $80. However, often people overvalue what they already own, which is known as the status quo bias or endowment effect (Samuelson and Zeckhauser, 1988; Kahneman, Knetsch, and Thaler, 1990). Lastly, it should not matter, according to EU, what cover story or context is used to describe the choices. Whether a sure loss of $50 is described as being an insurance premium or a negative payoff of $50 should not matter when weighed against a given probabilistic loss. Yet, people are typically more risk averse when the choice is put in an insurance framework (Hershey and Schoemaker, 1980).

Biases versus measurement errors. What might explain such elicitation discrepancies? One analytical approach assumes that though there does exist a true utility function $U^*(x)$, it is estimated through a "noisy" elicitation procedure. For any given method, the estimated utility function $\hat{U}(x)$ is related to the true function in the following manner:

$$\hat{U}(x) = U^*(x) + \bar{\epsilon}$$

where $\bar{\epsilon}$ represents some kind of random error.

There will be a systematic bias whenever $E[\bar{\epsilon}] \neq 0$. Eliashberg and Hauser (1985) conjecture that differences in utility functions from alternative elicitation procedures are due primarily to measurement errors. They claim that each time individuals are given a choice between a certain outcome and a reference lottery there is a random component that affects their indifference level. The nature of the random error might be different for CE and PE elicitation procedures. Alternatively, random response errors may propagate nonlinearly when using a subject's answer to one lottery to set up a subsequent one, as in the case of Roberta's utility function (see Schoemaker and Hershey, 1991).

The random noise viewpoint results in probabilistic statements regarding the preference of one lottery over another, such as Lottery A being preferred to Lottery B with some probability p. A specialized formal literature exists on stochastic preferences and random utility (see Luce, 1959, or Hauser, 1978), although it has also been used more informally. For example, Lichtenstein and Slovic (1971) tried to explain certain preference reversals (to be discussed later) by assuming that subjects exhibited less random error in binary choice tasks than in rating or pricing tasks (where each option is considered in isolation). Berg and Dickhaut (1990) present intriguing evidence that response errors decline when subjects play for bigger prizes with real money.

An alternative hypothesis (to that of random noise) is to question whether people really follow EU theory. This raises more fundamental questions. What does it mean to specify a person's utility function? Do utility functions really exist or are they artificially constructed? Do people feel comfortable thinking probabilistically? Are their responses reliable indicators of their attitudes toward money (or whatever other attributes are involved) and uncertainty? To what extent is a person's utility function influenced by how the information is presented to him or her? These questions have descriptive significance for understanding how valuation is integrated into choice. They hold prescriptive importance to the extent that we want to reflect people's basic values in the advice we give them on more complex choices. To examine whether the EU violations are deep and fundamental versus contrived or minor, we now turn to more specific experimental evidence.

4.4   Violations of axioms of choice

Experimental evidence over the past 30 years has challenged the axioms that form the basis of the expected utility model. We shall briefly summarize some of the important findings that emerge from these studies.

4.4.1   Intransitivity of preferences

Suppose you were asked to make pairwise comparisons between five lotteries with the following probabilities of winning (P_w) and amounts to win $(\$_w)$:

Lottery	P_w	$\$_w$
A	7/24	5.00
B	8/24	4.75
C	9/24	4.50
D	10/24	4.25
E	11/24	4.00

Transitivity requires that if a person prefers A to B and B to C then he should prefer A to C (see Axiom 2 in previous section 4.2.2). Tversky (1969) found that a number of people preferred A to B, B to C, C to D, and D to E but preferred E to A. (Note that in his experiment all probabilities were displayed visually, as a fraction of a circular disk.) Individuals tended to view the probability of winning between adjacent gambles as approximately the same, and hence in these cases preferred the lottery with the higher payoff. However, once the probability differential exceeded a certain level, they focused primarily on P_w and chose the lottery with the greater chance of winning. Thus, the intransitivity was due to the use of a different processing rule for pairwise comparisons of adjacent versus far apart lotteries.

The data of this experiment cannot be accounted for via noise or random utility. Tversky (1969) explicitly tested for a probabilistic version of the transitivity axiom, called weak stochastic transitivity. It requires that if A is preferred to B at least 50% of the time by a given subject, and B is preferred to C at least 50% of the time as well, then A should be preferred to C at least 50% of the time. Subjects systematically violated weak stochastic transitivity, which argues against the random noise view.[7]

4.4.2   *The Allais paradox*

The French economist and Nobel Laureate Maurice Allais (1953) devised a clever set of choices that has led many people, including those who were instrumental in developing utility theory, to violate the third EU axiom discussed earlier, which is known as the independence principle. The choices are as follows:

Situation I

Choice *A*   100% chance of winning $1 million (i.e., 1 million for certain)

Choice *B*   10% chance of winning $5 million
89% chance of winning $1 million
1% chance of winning nothing

Now consider the next two choices ignoring the previous choice situation.

Situation II

Choice *C*   11% chance of winning $1 million
89% chance of winning nothing

Choice *D*   10% chance of winning $5 million
90% chance of winning nothing

Most people prefer *A* in Situation I and *D* in Situation II. It is easy to see why this violates the independence principle. Suppose we represent these situations as lotteries. Assume we have 100 numbered tickets in an urn, 1 of which will be selected at random. The four choices can now be represented as follows:

7 Schoemaker and Waid (1982), however, proved that for choice alternatives with more than two attributes a random weights model might violate weak stochastic transitivity. Much depends on how the stochastic model is formulated.

	Lottery Ticket Numbers (1–100)		
	1	2–11	12–100
Choice *A*	$1 million	$1 million	$1 million
Choice *B*	$0 million	$5 million	$1 million
Choice *C*	$1 million	$1 million	$0 million
Choice *D*	$0 million	$5 million	$0 million

Thus, if *A* is preferred to *B*, then *C* should be preferred to *D*, since the preference order ought to be independent of the value of the common outcome in the last column (according to EU's independence axiom).

The Allais problem is paradoxical in that people both want to obey the axiom as well as have *A* in Situation I, and *D* in Situation II. However, these two wants are inconsistent. This becomes particularly clear when writing out the expected utility implications. Say the utility function is defined in millions of dollars, then the preference of *A* over *B* in Situation I implies that:

$$U(1) > .1\ U(5) + .89\ U(1) + .01\ U(0)$$

or

$$.11\ U(1) > .1\ U(5) + .01\ U(0)$$

On the other hand, *D* being preferred to *C* implies:

$$.1\ U(5) + .9\ U(0) > .11\ U(1) + .89\ U(0)$$
$$.1\ U(5) + .01\ U(0) > .11\ U(1)$$

Note that the Allais paradox is not as robust against the random noise argument as the transitivity violation. A small epsilon of noise could cause Allais type violations. Also, the Allais paradox works less well with small amounts of money.

The Allais paradox, however, does raise fundamental questions about EU's linear treatment of probabilities as depicted graphically in Figure 4.8. This so-called Marschak-Machina triangle can be used to plot gambles with three or fewer outcomes. The vertical axis represents the probability (P_H) of getting the highest possible outcome *H*; the horizontal axis, the probability (P_L) of getting the lowest outcome. The third probability (P_M) of getting the middle amount (M) is left implicit in the graph, since $P_M = 1 - P_L - P_H$. This constraint also forces the figure to be triangular.

Figure 4.8 illustrates how the Allais choices are plotted. The *A* option, entailing a sure gain of $1 million, is treated as a certain gamble with $P_M = 1$ (and thus $P_L = P_H = 0$). Throughout, $H = \$5$ million, $M = \$1$ million, and $L = \$0$. Choice *B* is uniquely identified, in Figure 4.8, by the coordinates $P_H = .1$ and $P_L = .01$ (and thus $P_M = .89$). Likewise,

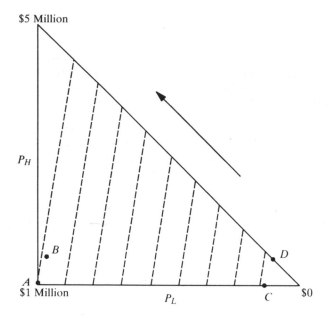

Figure 4.8. Marschak-Machina triangle. *Note:* Dashed lines are iso-utility contours. (*Source:* Machina, 1987. Reprinted by permission)

C and D correspond uniquely to two sets of coordinates, namely $P_H = 0$ and $P_L = .89$, and $P_H = .1$ and $P_L = .9$ respectively.

Note the symmetry among the choice pairs: A is in relation to B as C is in relation to D (i.e., they form a parallelogram). The EU violation implicit in preferring A to B but D to C becomes graphically apparent when introducing indifference curves. It follows from EU that the indifference curves in this triangle must be straight, parallel lines with preference increasing as one moves upward to the left (see arrow). That is, if

$$P_H U(H) + P_M U(M) + P_L U(L) = C \text{ (constant)}$$

then upon substituting $P_M = 1 - P_L - P_H$ we get

$$P_H = \frac{C - U(M)}{U(H) - U(M)} + P_L \left(\frac{U(M) - U(L)}{U(H) - U(M)} \right)$$

or

$$\frac{dP_H}{dP_L} = \frac{U(M) - U(L)}{U(H) - U(M)} = K \text{ (constant)}$$

The steeper the slope, the more risk averse the person is. If the slope is such that A is preferred to B – meaning A is on a higher indifference line than B – then also C must be on a higher indifference line than D. As such, preferring D to C (while preferring A to B) violates the linearity assumption built into EU's treatment of probability.

We shall later revisit this diagram to illustrate graphically how recent models have relaxed some of the EU axioms to account for Allais-type behavior and other EU violations to be discussed next.

4.4.3   *The Ellsberg paradox*

Another classic EU anomaly was posed by Ellsberg (1961) who felt that individuals may violate the independence axiom for different reasons. The choices revolve around an urn that contains 30 red balls and 60 black or yellow balls, with the proportion of these last two colors being unknown. Subjects in the experiment are told that the number of black or yellow balls was determined by a random process. With this background information, they are asked to express their preferences in each of the following two situations. Each choice is followed by drawing only one ball from the urn, with the following payoffs.

Situation I	
Choice A	Win \$100 if a red ball is pulled
	Win \$0 if a black or yellow ball is pulled
Choice B	Win \$100 if a black ball is pulled
	Win \$0 if a red or yellow ball is pulled
Situation II	
Choice C	Win \$100 if a red or yellow ball is pulled
	Win \$0 if a black ball is pulled
Choice D	Win \$100 if a black or yellow ball is pulled
	Win \$0 if a red ball is pulled

If you are like most people, you will prefer A to B in Situation I and D to C in Situation II. The reason most often stated is that because the number of black and yellow balls is ambiguous, one is unsure of the probability of winning in B and C. Most people have a preference for known probabilities.

Yet a little reflection reveals that these two preferences are inconsistent with the independence axiom. To see this let us define:

p_1 = probability of a red ball
p_2 = probability of a black ball
p_3 = probability of a yellow ball

Then the four choices are represented as follows

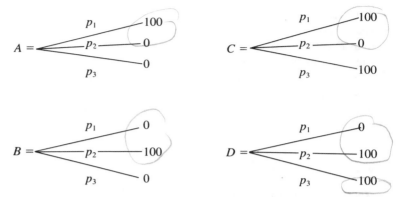

If $A > B$, then the independence axiom implies that $C > D$ since the only difference between the two pairs of lotteries is the outcome associated with a yellow ball. Since this outcome is identical for A and B, it should be irrelevant in the choice between these two alternatives. A similar argument holds for the comparison between C and D, as writing out the EU equations will show. Apparently, however, other factors influence the choice process, such as aversion to ambiguity.

Slovic and Tversky (1974) explicitly tested the robustness of the EU violations underlying the Allais and Ellsberg examples. They presented subjects with a set of arguments designed to indicate "errors in thinking" and then gave individuals the option to change their preferences (if they wished). However, they found a general persistence of behavior in favor of violating the independence axiom. People used various arguments to defend their choices, which underscores the controversial nature of EU's substitution or independence axiom.[8] As we shall see later, recent descriptive models have relaxed or abandoned this contentious axiom.

4.4.4 *Framing and response mode effects*

In making their choices, many individuals focus on the gains and losses associated with a given lottery rather than examining its impact on final wealth, as in the Roberta Glover insurance example. This can lead to inconsistent choices. Consider the following example suggested by Kahneman and Tversky (1979). Please state your preference in each of the following situations.

8 MacCrimmon and Larsson (1979) in contrast found that their executive subjects often "corrected" their choices once it was explained that they violated certain axioms. However, Slovic and Tversky (1974) noted that normative pressure or conformity needs might have caused these reversals rather than a true belief in the axioms.

Situation I

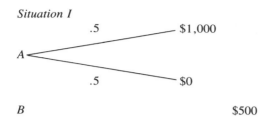

B $500

Situation II
Imagine that you have received $1,000 and must choose between the following two options:

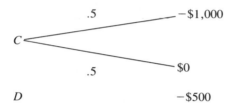

D   −$500

Kahneman and Tversky (1979) found that most people choose *B* and *C*. They prefer a certain gain in Situation I, but want to gamble on *not* losing in Situation II. Note, however, that these are identical choice situations once the $1,000 gift received up front in Situation II is added back into the outcomes.

The apparent reason for this violation is that individuals tend toward risk aversion on the gain side, preferring certainty (*B*) over an uncertain amount that has the same or slightly larger expected value (*A*). However, people are risk prone when there is some chance that they may *not* lose, even if the expected value of the uncertain losses is the same or larger in magnitude than the certain loss. Kahneman and Tversky (1979) termed this asymmetry in risk attitude the "reflection effect." Thus, if we can reframe the reference point such that gains become losses or vice versa, we can influence people's risk taking. Additional framing examples exist (such as the isolation effect discussed in section 2.6.2) that indicate systematic violations of EU's implicit principle of asset integration (see Thaler, 1985 and 1990). Asset integration means expressing consequences in terms of final wealth levels, by aggregating all gains and losses of a given alternative and looking at the *net* payoff (see also Tversky and Kahneman, 1986).

Preference reversals. Suppose that you had the option to play either of the following two gambles:

Gamble	Probability of winning (P_w)	Amount to win ($\$_w$)	Probability of losing (P_L)	Amount to lose ($\$L$)
L-Bet	.33	$16	.67	$2
H-Bet	.99	$4	.01	$1

Which one of these gambles would you prefer to play? *L* or *H*?

Most subjects who are given this choice respond that *H* (standing for high probability) is more attractive to them, even though the expected values of the two choices are nearly identical. However, when asked for how much they would at a minimum be willing to sell *L* or *H* to another person, they normally require a higher dollar amount for *L* than *H*.

This preference reversal phenomenon is highly robust. The first experiments suggesting the possibility of preference reversals were conducted by Slovic and Lichtenstein (1968) and Lindman (1971) in a laboratory setting. They found that the response mode used (choice versus ratings) affected people's evaluation of the gambles. This led Lichtenstein and Slovic (1971) to design experiments showing preference reversals of the preceding kind. Lichtenstein and Slovic (1973) further demonstrated preference reversals using real money wagers on the floor of a casino in Las Vegas. Since that time, numerous psychologists and economists have tried to make the preference reversal phenomenon disappear, by controlling for income or wealth effects, order effects, or strategic misrepresentation or bargaining features of these choices. None of them have been successful in their efforts, as reviewed by Grether and Plott (1979) and Slovic and Lichtenstein (1983).

The preference reversal phenomenon is disturbing from the viewpoint of expected utility theory and other preference models because it seems to violate very basic notions of rationality. Which axioms it exactly violates and why, however, are less clear. Initially people argued it violated the transitivity axiom (Grether and Plott, 1979). However, Holt (1986), Karni and Safra (1987), and others pointed out that it fundamentally violates the independence axiom (given the way the experiments and incentives are typically set up). In addition, psychological models were developed to explain this bias. One focused on expression effects entailing an anchoring and adjustment process (Goldstein and Einhorn, 1987); another focused on differential weighting of stimuli as a function of their compatibility with the response mode (Tversky, Sattah, and Slovic, 1988). We shall review more recent findings and explanations of preference reversals in section 4.5.4, when discussing response mode models.

4.5   Alternative descriptive models

The violations of expected utility theory discussed in the preceding section have stimulated much interest in understanding the factors that influence the valuation and choice process. In this section several approaches will be discussed for dealing with these problems. One approach has focused on the role of anticipation in decision making, by incorporating attributes into the utility function to reflect possible regret, elation, or disappointment associated with certain outcomes (Bell 1982, 1985; Loomes and Sugden 1982). Kahneman and Tversky (1979) have taken another tack by developing an alternative outcome-based approach called "prospect theory," designed to explain many of the EU anomalies discussed in the previous sections. It is part of a larger class of generalized utility models, some of which will be discussed as well. Also, there have been statistical modeling approaches that use the decision maker's actual choices or preferences as the dependent variable in order to determine the relative weights being placed on statistical moments or risk dimensions. Finally, models have been developed that directly address ambiguity effects. We shall discuss each of these five approaches in turn.

4.5.1 *Regret models*

People often remark, "If only I had done this instead of that, things would have worked out better." This reaction to outcomes after the fact may actually be a part of the valuation and choice process prior to making a decision. If so, it may be necessary to introduce attributes into a person's utility function to reflect her feelings concerning one alternative over another should certain outcomes occur. We can illustrate this approach with the earlier insurance example:

Suppose Roberta Glover can purchase insurance against the theft of her coin collection for $150. If the collection is stolen she will receive $10,000. She estimates the chances of the collection being stolen in the next year to be $p = .01$.

Table 4.2 depicted the set of monetary outcomes that could occur under both states of nature: "stolen" and "not stolen."

As shown before, this problem is evaluated within traditional utility theory by comparing the expected utilities of the two alternatives for a given level of wealth W:

$$E[U(\text{insure})] = U(W - 150)$$
$$E[U(\text{do not insure})] = .01U(W - 1000) + .99U(W)$$

The alternative yielding the higher expected utility is chosen.

By introducing anticipation into the picture the situation is changed, since Roberta may now ask the question, How would I feel if my coin collection were stolen and I were uninsured? Alternatively she could ask, How would I feel if I purchased theft insurance for next year and nothing happened to my coin collection? Both of these questions involve the con-

Table 4.3. *Regret matrix for insurance decision*

	Stolen	Not stolen
Insure	0	$150
Do not insure	$9,850	0

cept of regret associated with choosing one alternative versus another. In this example, we can determine the dollar level of regret for each of the four outcomes listed in Table 4.2 by constructing a regret matrix: Table 4.3.

Roberta could have saved $150 by not insuring if the state "not stolen" occurred, resulting in the value of $150 in the *cell*, "Insure—Not Stolen." Conversely, her regret level would be $9,850 (i.e., $10,000 minus the $150 premium she would otherwise have paid) in case her collection were stolen and she were uninsured. In the remaining two cases there will be no regret at all (for most people).

To determine the preferred choice, the person could now use a two-attribute utility function $U(X_1, X_2)$. X_1 represents the impact of a given alternative on final wealth (as in Table 4.2) and X_2 the impact of a given alternative on ex-post feelings of regret (as in Table 4.3). The exact form of this two-attribute function, especially the weight given to regret, varies from one person to another and possibly across circumstances. The final choice thus depends on the probabilities of each state of nature, the utilities associated with each potential outcome as well as the person's anticipation about regret feelings for each choice under each state of nature.[9]

The use of regret or rejoice anticipations as an additional attribute in a utility function may help explain some of the violations of standard utility theory. For example, the violation of the independence condition in the Allais problem might have been due to an anticipation effect. When asked why they prefer A to B, people often respond by saying "I would feel horrible if I had chosen B and learned that I had won nothing. By choosing A, I know that there is a guaranteed $1 million." When confronted with the choice between C and D, the .01 difference between .89 and .90 associated with not winning anything does not loom as significant, and does not so easily lend itself to feelings of regret.

Regret models highlight the importance of the context in which choices

9 It is a complex question as to whether regret considerations are normative. One negative is that regret models of the multi-attribute utililty (MAU) variety can violate transitivity and independence of irrelevant alternatives. The positive side is that regret is a genuine emotion, which therefore should be part of any utilitarian analysis.

are presented. For instance, if problems are presented in payoff matrix form (Figure 4.1) versus independent lotteries (as in Figure 4.5), the role of regret or elation may be different. Regret is highly dependent on mental accounting and imagination. As such, we need more than just a second attribute but also a psychological theory of problem representation. Two examples (the first from Tversky and Kahneman, 1981; the second from Savage, 1954, and Thaler, 1980) illustrate this point.

Example 1. *An Unanticipated Loss*

Situation A   Imagine you have decided to see a play where the admission is $10 per ticket. As you enter the theater you discover you have lost a $10 bill. Would you still pay $10 for a ticket for the play?

Situation B   Imagine that you have decided to see a play and paid the admission price of $10 per ticket. As you enter the theater you discover that you have lost the ticket. The seat was not marked and the ticket cannot be recovered. Would you pay $10 for another ticket?

In Situation *A*, 88% of 183 subjects responded that they would buy another ticket, while in Situation *B* only 46% of 200 subjects were willing to purchase a ticket. Why do people behave differently, in violation of the sunk-cost principle? (According to this principle, past or sunk expenses should be irrelevant to the new decision because these sunk costs will be incurred no matter what is decided. Thus, they should cancel out of the comparison but often don't. See Arkes and Blumer, 1985.)

We conjecture that in cases where there is a link to past actions, regret or self-incrimination influences the decision as to whether to buy another ticket. Situation *B* forces the individual to reflect more directly on the $10 loss: Buying another ticket is framed by many as paying $20 to see the play. Although the play may be worth this to some, others find this $20 too high or feel they don't deserve to see the play given their "stupidity." In Situation *A*, in contrast, the $10 loss is less directly linked to the ticket purchase.

Example 2. *An Unanticipated Gain*

You bought a case of wine for $5 a bottle in the 1950s and are now offered $100 a bottle for the wine. Would you sell it? (Note: You have never paid more than $35 for a bottle of wine.)

If you answer no, the underlying reason may be an anticipation or rejoicing effect associated with enjoying the unexpected fruits of your good investment. There may be other values associated with this choice besides monetary returns. Individuals frequently refuse to sell a painting they have purchased at a very low price, even though they would never buy the object at its current market value. Another possible factor influencing the wine decision could be the anticipation that the object will command an even higher price in the future. But in that case, the person should buy even more bottles (assuming some investment or borrowing capability exists).

4.5.2   *Prospect theory*

Kahneman and Tversky (1979) proposed an alternative outcome-based model called "prospect theory" to account for violations of the axioms of utility theory.[10] Prior to evaluating alternatives, this theory postulates a set of "editing operations" that include *coding* (i.e., what reference point to use), *combining* amounts that are guaranteed in a given gamble, *canceling* of terms that are common to both options, *simplifying* by rounding probabilities and outcomes, and *eliminating* dominated options. In its second phase, the theory proposes that such edited alternatives are evaluated using an expectation-type model of the following form:

$$V = \Sigma \; \pi(p_i)v(x_i)$$

where p_i represents the probability of outcome x_i occurring for $i = 1, \ldots n$; $\pi(p_i)$ is a probability weighing function and $v(x_i)$ a value function.

The π function concerns decision weights that are applied to the given probabilities. It is assumed that $\pi(0) = 0$ and $\pi(1) = 1$. However, $\Sigma\pi(p_i)$ need not equal 1, and as such the decision weights are different from subjective probability transformations. The π function is shaped as shown in Figure 4.9, and is assumed to exhibit the following properties: subadditivity for small p, meaning that $\pi(rp) > r\pi(p)$ for $0 < p < 1$; overweighing of small probabilities and underweighing of high ones; subcertainty, meaning that $\Sigma\pi(p_i) < 1$; subproportionality, meaning that $\pi(pq)/\pi(p) < \pi(pqr)/\pi(pr)$, where p, q, and r are between 0 and 1; and finally discontinuous end points, which partly explains the type of certainty effect observed in the Allais paradox.

In prospect theory the value function $v(x)$ refers to *changes* in financial position, as opposed to *final* wealth levels for a utility function. As shown in Figure 4.9, $v(x)$ is presumed to be concave for gains (implying risk aversion), and convex for losses (implying risk proneness), whereas traditional utility models assume risk aversion throughout. The changes in financial position are defined relative to a variable *reference point*, which depends on the framing of the decision. The value function is applied differently for strict prospect than regular (or mixed) ones. A prospect is

---

10 We consider prospect theory outcome-based because it seeks to model in a parsimonious way well-known expected utility (EU) violations, without getting into process details. However, the shape of the value function and the emphasis on reference points has much psychological support. The π function, in contrast, seems less well motivated psychologically (although see Hogarth and Einhorn, 1990, or J. Baron, 1988).

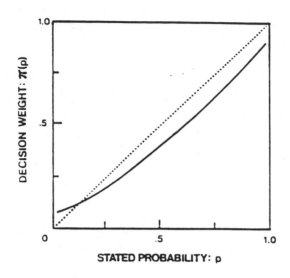

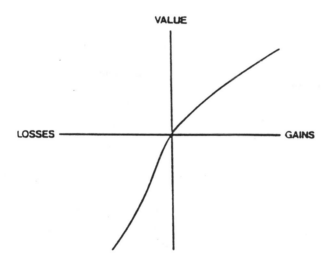

Figure 4.9. Prospect theory's probability and value functions (*Source:* Kahneman and Tversky, 1979. Reprinted by permission)

considered strict if all of its possible outcomes have the same sign: either all positive or negative. If this is the case, prospect theory predicts that the smallest magnitude (which is guaranteed) is factored out first before applying the expectation rule. Thus, a lottery offering a .5 chance at $10, a .25 chance at $5, and a .25 chance at $3 would be evaluated as follows:

$$V = v(3) + \pi(.5)[v(10) - v(3)] + \pi(.25)[v(5) - v(3)]$$

For prospects with both positive and negative outcomes, the evaluation rule is similar to the EU model, except for the $\pi(p)$ function.

Unlike EU theory, prospect theory emphasizes the importance of decision framing in understanding choice behavior. A powerful example of such framing effects is the following set of choices adapted from Tversky and Kahneman (1981).

A rare plague has just been identified in a small village, endangering the lives of 600 people. Public health officials have two programs with which to combat this plague. According to the best available scientific evidence, the consequences will be as follows.

Program *A*   Exactly 200 lives will be saved
Program *B*   A 1/3 chance of saving all 600 lives, and a 2/3 chance of saving none.

Program *A* concerns a serum that is foolproof; however, there is only enough for 200 people. Program *B* involves an experimental dilution of the serum to treat all 600 villagers; however, there is a 2/3 chance that the dilution will be too great, making the serum totally ineffective. Assuming these are your only options, and that you are the senior public health official, which program would you choose?

Now imagine the same scenario, but assume that the options are as follows:

Program *C*   Exactly 400 lives will be lost.
Program *D*   A 1/3 chance that nobody will die, and 2/3 chance that 600 people will die.

Note that these two situations are identical, except that the first one expresses the alternatives in terms of lives saved, whereas the second formulation emphasizes lives lost. Due to such framing differences the percentages of subjects who selected the sure alternative dropped from 72% to 22% ($N = 155$) in going from the lives saved to lives lost version. Tversky and Kahneman (1992) offer a generalization of prospect theory to many outcomes and cases of uncertainty as well as risk.

4.5.3   *Generalized utility theories*

Prospect theory belongs to a class of models that comes under the heading of generalized utility (GU) theory. These models retain the expectation

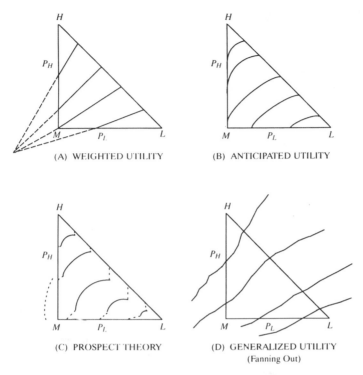

Figure 4.10. Indifference curves for selected generalized utility models (*Source:* Camerer, 1989b. Reprinted by permission)

operator of EU, but permit nonlinear weightings of probability. Each of these models offers different treatments of the probability dimension, and thus permits nonlinear indifference curves in the Marschak-Machina triangle discussed earlier. Figure 4.10 shows the kind of indifference curves permitted by some of these generalized models (for discussion, see Camerer, 1989b, 1992).

It is beyond the scope of this book to review these various models in detail, especially since many are quite technical and focus on establishing alternative axiomatization of risky choice. A key notion, however, is that many exhibit *rank dependence*: The expected utility associated with one branch of a lottery depends on how it ranks (in outcome and/or probability) relative to other branches. Unlike EU, where each branch contributes additively to the overall expected utility, GU models permit branches to interact. In a sense, one branch can overshadow or "intimidate" another branch of the same lottery. Weber and Camerer (1987) and Camerer (1992) provide excellent reviews of various GU models. Camerer (1989b)

Table 4.4. *Some generalized utility models*

Model type	Equations for $(x, p; y, 1 - p)$	EU axioms relaxed
Weighted utility (Chew and MacCrimmon, 1979)	$\dfrac{pw(x)U(x) + (1 - p)w(y)U(y)}{pw(x) + (1 - p)w(y)}$	Independence, reduction
Anticipated utility (Quiggin, 1982; 1985)	$g(p)U(x) + [1 - g(p)]U(y)$ with $g(0) = 0$ and $g(1) = 1$	Independence, reduction
Prospect theory (Kahneman and Tversky, 1979)	$\pi(p)v(x) + (1 - p)v(y)$ or $v(x) + (1 - p)[v(y) - v(x)]$ in case $y > x > 0$	Transitivity, independence, reduction
Fanning out (Machina, 1982)	No specific form; just requires fanning out of indifference curves	Independence

and Schoemaker (1991b) conducted experimental comparisons among these models and found none to be clearly superior.

Table 4.4 identifies some of the main competing generalized utility (GU) theories. The equations indicate how the prospect $(p_1, x_1; p_2, x_2; \ldots; p_n, x_n)$ would be evaluated under the various models. More complex models exist as well, such as those of Luce (1988) and Fishburn (1984). The defining characteristic of these various nonexpected utility models is that they permit nonlinear weighting of probability. In addition, some allow confounding of utility and probability (e.g., Hey, 1984) or violations of transitivity (e.g., Kahneman and Tversky, 1979; Loomes and Sugden, 1982).

As Machina (1982 and 1987) emphasized, we can think of these generalized utility models as obeying EU theory locally but not globally. For instance, once we fix the probabilities p_H and p_L in Figure 4.10, the shapes of the indifference curves can be considered linear and parallel in the neighborhood of p_H and p_L. The curvature and nonparallelism only become significant when comparing gambles that lie in different regions of the triangle. Machina (1982) rescued the EU model somewhat from the onslaught of behavioral criticism by showing that most standard economic results do not depend on the independence axiom. For example, we can still assume that a particular individual is risk averse and examine what his optimal portfolio should be without having to assume that he maximizes expected utility.

However, we and others believe the problem is deeper and more fundamental than one of degrees of local and global approximations. Much empirical evidence suggests that EU theory is structurally flawed in its treatment of *both* probability and value (see Schoemaker, 1982). It misses important context and process effects that cannot be easily approximated using "as-if" utility models. We sympathize, nonetheless, with the plight of economists who desire models that permit abstraction from specifics and aggregation across individual actors and firms. The generalized utility route is one way to go, although it may get ensnarled in its own complexity and intractibility. An alternative is to consider process models (in specific applications) that sacrifice on elegance and generality, but get closer to how people really think. However, we then face the problem of how to aggregate the individual process models to determine the impact of behavior in markets or across situations.

4.5.4 *Response mode models*

To understand the evolution of response mode models, we must place them in their historical context. Prior to generalized utility, various mean-risk models had been proposed as approximate outcome models. In finance, for example, it is commonly assumed that choices are made on the basis of expected return and variance (Markowitz, 1952). The definition of an individual's perception of risk, however, may vary. For example, Fishburn (1977) suggested measuring risk as a probability-weighted power function of the below-target outcomes. Lichtenstein (1965) had earlier proposed additional moments besides variance, such as skewness and kurtosis. In general, such *statistical moment models* were viewed as approximations to expected utility theory. By expanding the utility function as a Taylor series around the lottery's mean, it follows directly that the expected utility of the lottery can be approximated as a function of its statistical moments (see Hirshleifer, 1970, for details).

It was, of course, an empirical question as to how well moment models predicted people's choices. Payne (1973) reviewed various moment studies and contrasted these with so-called *risk-dimension models*. The latter assume that subjects' evaluations of gambles are a direct function of the stated or primary risk dimensions, that is, probabilities and outcomes. For statistically untrained subjects, additive risk-dimension models generally yielded much higher (adjusted) R-squares than did moment models (Schoemaker, 1979).

To illustrate, suppose a subject is given a set of 30 gambles of the type shown in Figure 4.11. These so-called duplex gambles are uniquely characterized by their probability of winning (P_W), the amount to be won ($\$_w$), the probability of losing (P_L), and the amount to be lost ($\$_L$). The gamble is played as a package deal, with the actual payoff depending on the

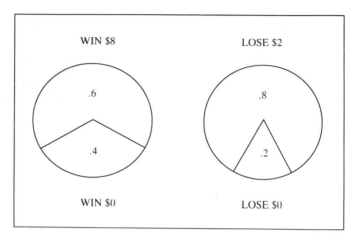

WIN $8   LOSE $2

.6   .8

.4   .2

WIN $0   LOSE $0

Figure 4.11. Example of a duplex gamble (*Source:* Slovic and Lichtenstein, 1968. Copyright 1968 by the American Psychological Association. Reprinted by permission)

outcomes of the two disks whose pointers are spun independently. If we let Y equal the subject's evaluation of these gambles, the following two regression models might be contrasted:

Risk-dimension model: $Y = w_0 + w_1 P_w + w_2 \$_w + w_3 P_L + w_4 \$_L$

Statistical moment model: $Y = b_0 + b_1 \text{EV} + b_2 \text{Variance}$

where

$$\text{EV} = P_w \$_w - P_L \$_L$$
$$\text{Var} = P_w(1 - P_w)\$_w^2 + P_L(1 - P_L)\$_L^2$$

Schoemaker (1979) found a significantly higher adjusted R-square for the additive than the moment model when tested with statistically untrained subjects. In contrast, for subjects who knew the concept of expected value or expected utility, the moment model did better. Because the majority of people are blissfully ignorant of either concept, it is useful to explore why the risk-dimension model did so much better. The answer lies partly in Figure 4.12, which depicts an information-processing model of people's choice process when selecting one of two given duplex gambles. It was derived by Payne and Braunstein (1971) using process-tracing analysis. According to their model, subjects first consider the probability dimension in both gambles. If $P_w < P_L$, the gamble with the lower P_L value tends to be chosen. If $P_w > P_L$, subjects will select the one with the highest $\$_w$. The Payne and Braunstein (1971) study clearly demon-

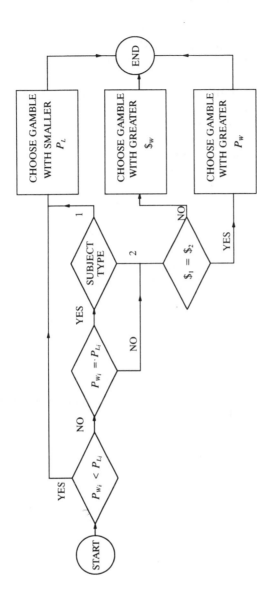

Figure 4.12. Flowchart of a choice process (*Source:* Payne and Braunstein, 1971. Copyright 1971 by the American Psychological Association. Reprinted by permission)

strated that most people focus on the primary risk dimensions (such as P_L, P_w, $\$_L$ and $\$_w$) rather than statistical moments.

In addition, it was found that the weight a particular dimension receives depends on the task. In the case of binary choices, intradimensional comparisons are probable, resulting in more even weighting of risk dimensions (Payne and Braunstein, 1971; Payne, 1982; Russo and Dosher, 1983). In case of isolated evaluations, anchoring and adjustment models are more likely, often resulting in lopsided weighting of risk dimensions (Goldstein and Einhorn, 1987; Schkade and Johnson, 1989). Further, the particular dimension that will serve as the anchor depends on the problem's context, the response mode used, and the subject's risk attitude.

For instance, it was found that the regression weights associated with the risk dimensions discussed earlier varied as a function of the response mode used – that is, whether subjects had to rank the gambles or bid on them. Slovic and Lichtenstein (1968) interpreted such changes in weights as adaptations of the subject's information-processing strategy to the particular response mode, with the aim of reducing the information load. They further suggested that differences among the four weights (for a given response mode) might reflect a subject's belief that some of the risk dimensions are more important than others for the task at hand. These findings gave rise to the preference reversal research discussed earlier in this chapter. They also hold the key to their explanation.

In a set of careful experiments, Tversky, Slovic, and Kahneman (1990) tried explicitly to compare and eliminate various proposed explanations for the preference reversal phenomenon. These included (1) intransitivity as in regret models, (2) violations of the independence axiom as in generalized utility models, and (3) response mode models as described earlier. Each of these predicts a different set of responses when applied to choice and bid tasks involving H and L bets. Based on 620 response patterns, these researchers rejected both the intransitivity (which includes regret) models as well as the generalized utility ones. The phenomenon seems largely due to the overpricing of the L bet (as also found by Bostic, Herrnstein, and Luce, 1990).

This overpricing explanation is part of the compatibility hypothesis referred to earlier: Dimensions that are more compatible with the requested response mode get more weight (Tversky et al., 1988). Such response mode effects imply violations of *procedure invariance*, the notion that logically equivalent elicitation procedures should yield equivalent responses. This applies not just to risk preferences but to any kind of judgments entailing scale differences and comparability, and as such poses formidable problems for those interested in developing general rational choice models. As Tversky et al. (1990) concluded: "because invariance – unlike independence or even transitivity – is normatively unassailable

Table 4.5. *Possible origins of response mode biases*

I. Encoding/framing
PE reframing (Hershey and Schoemaker, 1985)
II. Evaluation
Contingent weighting (Tversky et al., 1988)
III. Expression
Proportionate matching (Goldstein and Einhorn, 1987).

Note: The studies listed are representative but by no means exhaustive of each class of explanation.

and descriptively incorrect, it does not seem possible to construct a theory of choice that is both normatively acceptable and descriptively adequate."

The last word has certainly not been written about response mode effects. Several causes may underlie them, as suggested in Table 4.5. The discrepancies between CE and PE elicitation modes were in part attributed in Hershey and Schoemaker (1985) to framing. The presumption was that some subjects when faced with a PE judgment for a 50–50 gamble offering $0 or $200 versus $100 for sure would frame it as a choice between $0 for sure versus even chances of gaining $100 or losing $100. In other words, they recode the gamble's outcomes relative to the sure amount, making it a mixed domain rather than pure gain gamble. Such reframing is unlikely in the CE mode where the sure amount itself needs to be adjusted (i.e., there is no fixed reference point). As discussed already, other response mode biases, such as preference reversals, may be due to overweighting dimensions that are compatible with the response mode. Lastly, it could be that subjects have fairly consistent valuations of gambles but use simple heuristics (such as anchoring and adjustment) to come up with the sometimes unusual indifference judgments requested by researchers. This is the basic idea behind Goldstein and Einhorn's (1987) proportionate matching concept (as part of their expression theory).

4.5.5 *Ambiguity effects*

The question of how risk dimensions, especially probabilities, are weighted also arises in recent work on the role of ambiguity. Ellsberg's (1961) paradox highlighted the fact that people may treat ambiguous or uncertain probabilities differently from known ones, in violation of the independence and reduction axioms of EU theory. To illustrate this, suppose two equally credible experts provide probability point estimates of .01 and .03 respectively that a given dam will collapse. According to EU, this should be treated the same as if both had provided an estimate of .02. Most people, however, would not consider these two cases equivalent. The former, in which the experts disagree, entails uncertainty or ambiguity, which is usually disliked. The latter, in contrast, is a standard case of decision making under risk.[11]

Sometimes a further distinction is made between uncertainty and ambiguity. If you know for sure that a coin to be flipped was selected with equal probability from two coins offering a .3 and .7 chance of getting heads respectively, the case is one of uncertainty. Although you do not know the probability of heads for sure for the coin selected, you do know that it is either .3 or .7 with equal chances. Thus, you know the second-order probability distribution, that is, a probability distribution defined on an uncertain probability. In the case of ambiguity, the second-order probability distribution, as well as any higher-order ones, is unknown.[12]

A number of experiments have confirmed Ellsberg's original "ambiguity aversion" hypothesis (Becker and Brownson, 1964; Slovic and Tversky, 1974; MacCrimmon and Larsson, 1979). In the domain of potential losses, where underwriters operate, experimental and field studies imply that subjects are averse to ambiguity when probabilities are small but not when they are large (Einhorn and Hogarth, 1985, 1986; Hogarth and Einhorn, 1990).

Theorists recently have incorporated ambiguity formally into subjective expected utility models either by employing nonadditive probabilities (Fishburn, 1988; Hazen and Lee, 1989; Schmeidler, 1989) or factoring ambiguity into the utility function (Sarin and Winkler, 1992). Fishburn (1992) has developed a theory that treats ambiguity as a primitive concept without direct reference to likelihood, subjective probability, preference, or decision. For a comprehensive survey of recent developments in modeling preferences under uncertainty and ambiguity, see Camerer and Weber (1992).

Psychologists, too, are attempting to understand ambiguity aversion. Einhorn and Hogarth (1985, 1986a) developed and tested a behavioral

11 One could ask each expert to provide a second-order probability distribution associated with the chances of a dam collapsing and average these two distributions. According to expected utility theory, however, one only needs a point estimate of the probability in order to evaluate different alternatives due to the linearity assumption regarding probability.

12 The distinctions between risk, uncertainty, and ambiguity are not fundamental within a Bayesian view. Uncertainty, as defined here, simply reduces to risk once second-order probabilities are multiplied through. Ambiguity, in turn, just requires coherent subjective probabilities (Savage, 1954). Psychologically, however, the cases are clearly different. Moreover, philosophers would not all accept the Bayesian view (see Kyburg and Smokler, 1964).

theory that characterizes choice under ambiguity as the output of an anchoring and adjustment process. Heath and Tversky (1991) contend that individuals' attitudes toward ambiguous situations depend upon their feelings of competence as measured by their general knowledge or understanding of the relevant context. Frisch and Baron (1988) provided a similar explanation of behavior when there is ambiguity about the probability. Other psychological hypotheses include anticipation of how others might judge you if a bad outcome occurs (Curley, Yates, and Abrams, 1986) and the presumption that ambiguity is more likely to be resolved against you than in your favor (Ellsberg, 1961).

Although models such as these are in an early state of development, they can provide insight into Ellsberg-type preferences, behavioral anomalies in warranty pricing (Einhorn and Hogarth, 1986a), and differences in insurance pricing by actuaries and underwriters for ambiguous versus nonambiguous events (Hogarth and Kunreuther, 1989, 1992; Kunreuther, Hogarth, and Meszaros, 1993). More critical tests are needed, however, to determine which of several approaches to modeling ambiguity is most appropriate. As before, this comparison will entail trade-offs between model parsimony and psychological realism. Nonetheless, it is evident that ambiguity needs to be factored into descriptive and possibly normative models of choice.

This concludes our summary of alternative descriptive models of risky choice. Note that three of the five approaches discussed (prospect theory, generalized utility, and ambiguity models) have targeted the probability dimension as the weak link in EU theory. The remaining approaches (regret theory and response mode models) especially question the value or utility side of the EU equation, as does prospect theory (see also Lopes, 1987).

The alternative descriptive models we have reviewed provide interesting additional perspectives on prescriptive choice as well. On the one hand, the axioms of EU theory are reasonably compelling. On the other hand, the results reviewed here on the descriptive side suggest that human decision makers exhibit a rich set of behavior when facing choice under risk and ambiguity. And this behavior is frequently at odds with EU theory and its generalizations. Perhaps the best approach to the prescriptive side of choice is to use the theoretical benchmarks of EU to stimulate reflection by confronting decision makers with their rationale in specific decision situations. In doing so, one should not be surprised if these benchmarks are at odds with the choices that decision makers would and do make on their own. At the least, however, these benchmarks provide a perspective against which decision makers can begin to judge the why and wherefore of their actual choices under risk.

4.6   **Intertemporal preferences**

So far, our discussion has been restricted to choices among options whose outcomes all occur within the immediate time frame. When time is introduced explicitly into the valuation and choice process, it is often done via the discounted utility model. We shall discuss this model first as a useful benchmark. Thereafter, we shall examine some important behavioral deviations from this benchmark.

4.6.1   *Discounted utility (DU)*

Suppose you could choose between one fine dinner this week (with a companion at a time and restaurant of your choosing) or two such dinners about a year from now. How should you choose, assuming you cannot sell or transfer your dinner vouchers? As simple as this question seems, the normative answer is by no means clear. Although we make intertemporal trade-offs all the time (e.g., deciding to delay or postpone activities), the proper yardstick to use for such choices is less obvious. One answer that has been proposed is discounted utility (Koopmans, 1960). Simply transfer the utility of any future outcomes into the present by applying an appropriate discount factor, just as one would with future money amounts. However, what should this discount rate be and must it be the same across circumstances? For example, should future pains be discounted the same as future pleasures?

Various axioms have been identified that justify the discounted utility (DU) model (Koopmans, 1960; Meyer, 1976). Like the EU model, the DU representation rests on a crucial independence axiom. This axiom postulates that a person's preference between two consumption streams (i.e., profiles of consumption indexed by time period) should be *independent* of consumption items that are identical (both in time and pleasure or pain) between the two options. To illustrate, consider the following choice situations (adapted from Loewenstein, 1987).

Situation I. Which alternative would you prefer?

Alternative	This weekend	Next weekend	Two weekends from now
A	French restaurant	Eat at home	Eat at home
B	Eat at home	French restaurant	Eat at home

Situation II. Which alternative would you prefer?

Alternative	This weekend	Next weekend	Two weekends from now
C	French restaurant	Eat at home	Lobster dinner
D	Eat at home	French restaurant	Lobster dinner

According to DU, your choice between the first and second options should be the same in both situations, and independent of what happens two weekends from now. Algebraically, for Situation I, the discounted utilities for *A* and *B* are, respectively,

$$DU(A) = U(\text{French}) + \frac{U(\text{eat home})}{(1 + k_1)} + \frac{U(\text{eat home})}{(1 + k_2)}$$

$$DU(B) = U(\text{eat home}) + \frac{U(\text{French})}{(1 + k_1)} + \frac{U(\text{eat home})}{(1 + k_2)}$$

The equations are identical for Situation II, with "lobster dinner" replacing "eat home" as the third term. Note, the third term cancels out under DU in both Situation I and Situation II (entailing *C* versus *D*). However, is this a reasonable property? In Loewenstein's (1987) study, 84% of subjects preferred *B* over *A*. But 57% preferred *C* over *D*. This reversal of preference violates DU's core independence axiom.

A related axiom (and implication) of DU is Koopman's (1960) assumption that preferences should be stable over time if telescoped forward or backward. To illustrate, suppose someone is indifferent between the following two consumption streams (indexed by time period):

$$[8, 9, 3, 5, 7, 2] \sim [8, 4, 6, 6, 3, 9]$$

Stationarity implies that $[9, 3, 5, 7, 2] \sim [4, 6, 6, 3, 9]$. Moving everything up by one time period should not affect preferences, since the first time period has the same outcome (of eight units) for both options. Although this assumption is reasonable for monetary income streams, it would be unreasonable for many other attributes. For example, if you prefer [steak, hot fudge] over [steak, cheese], it does not follow that you would necessarily prefer [hot fudge] to [cheese] in case the main course [steak] is dropped or skipped.

Specifically, DU does not permit consumption synergies across time periods. It does not address problems associated with habit formation. The savoring or anticipation associated with the lobster dinner two weekends from now is not allowed to interfere (either positively or negatively) with the pleasures derived from eating at home or eating out at the French restaurant. However, such intertemporal portfolio effects do occur and seem entirely reasonable in such cases. For this reason alone, the DU model does not enjoy the same normative standing as does EU.

An issue closely related to the normative aspects of intertemporal preferences and discounted utility is that of dynamic consistency. Dynamic choices are ones in which nested decisions occur, usually across different time periods. For instance, the decision to invest in a research and development process now in order to see later if a commercial development phase is desirable is a dynamic rather than static (or one-shot) choice.[13] Similarly, the decision about what undergraduate major to pursue hinges on subsequent options (e.g., regarding graduate school or jobs) and as such is a dynamic one.

The standard normative way to solve dynamic decisions is via decision trees (Raiffa, 1968), using a procedure called "folding back." You essentially start backward, at the end of each branch, and ask how you would make the nested choice in that branch if you ended up there. You substitute the expected utility of the preferred nested option for that choice node and tackle the next one. This way you prune the tree of all down-the-line decisions, so that the current or up-front choice can be expressed purely in terms of expected utilities or values, without having to consider any subsequent decisions. This approach, however, only focuses on consequences and is generally inconsistent with generalized utility models that permit the process by which uncertainties get resolved to influence valuation. The issue debated in the literature (e.g., Wakker, 1988, vs. Machina, 1989) is whether this inconsistency casts a normative doubt over folding back and discounting, or over generalized utility theory.

To illustrate this issue, let us revisit the Allais paradox restated as follows:

	States of nature	
Alternatives	I (.11 chance)	II (.89 chance)
A	$1 million	$1 million
B	Lottery L	$1 million
C	$1 milllion	$0
D	Lottery L	$0

where Lottery L offers a 10/11 chance at $5 million and a 1/11 chance at $0. Note that these alternatives correspond exactly to the Allais options discussed in section 4.4.2 (to see this just multiply out the probabilities). Suppose further that the decision maker exhibits the Allais-type prefer-

---

13 When expressed in terms of decision trees (Raiffa, 1968), static choices are ones with just one choice node followed by chance nodes. Dynamic choices have decision nodes followed by chance nodes followed by decision nodes, etc. The latter kind is most common in multiperiod decisions, although intertemporality per se does not imply dynamic choice or vice versa.

ences of $A > B$ and $D > C$, and also assume that $L > \$1$ million by this person. Such preferences violate EU theory (as discussed before) but are permitted under GU. However, now the following GU paradox emerges (due to Wakker, 1988). If this person were informed that State I were to occur with certainty, he would clearly choose B over A (since $L > \$1$ million). If told that State II were to emerge, he would be indifferent between A and B (as both offer \$1 million). Yet, when not told which state will emerge, this person prefers A to B. Can this be rational, given that B is at least as preferred as A *no matter* which state emerges? Further, if the person truly prefers B to A, should he then prefer not to know which state is to emerge (when offered the opportunity to find out), since this might propel him to choose A (the "less" preferred option)? In other words, should this person reject useful and valid information so as to avoid dynamic inconsistency in his actions?

Machina (1989) countered this apparent criticism of GU theory by noting that, if properly applied, GU models would avoid such dynamic inconsistency. Also, he emphasized that GU models may indeed violate *consequentialism*: the view (implicit in the preceding analysis) that dynamic choice should only be governed by consequences, independent of history or process. Since GU models, unlike EU ones, entail nonseparability of preference, it is inappropriate to ignore other branches (even resolved ones) in the risk basket. To use a consumer goods analogy, EU assumes additivity of the expected utilities associated with each branch. GU assumes nonadditivity, such that the utility of one lottery branch may be enhanced or reduced by what happens in the other branches (discussed earlier as rank dependence). Similar nonseparability occurs intertemporally, if my ranking of options today depends on what consumption profiles I face tomorrow.

The normative issues underlying the consequentialist versus nonseparability views are quite complex when applied to uncertainty and intertemporal cases. Few theorists would insist on separability (or additivity) when faced with a basket of commodities, because they may truly interact (i.e., a fruit salad can easily generate more utility than the sum of its components). In contrast, the nonadditivity of a lottery's outcomes – which after all are mutually exclusive – is more difficult to accept normatively, unless regret or other psychological factors are introduced. The case of intertemporal preferences appears to be in between. Although outcomes across periods are longitudinally mutually exclusive, the notion that utilities can interact over time seems nonetheless reasonable (due to satiation, memory effects, need for variety, etc.). Unfortunately, discounted utility models (which assume separability or additivity) cannot capture such intertemporal interactions.

4.6.2   *Behavioral aspects*

Leaving aside the rather complex question as to how normative the DU model is under different circumstances, we now turn our attention to behavioral issues with DU serving as a descriptive benchmark. Our discussion will focus first on some field data and then turn to experimental evidence on framing (in particular, reference point) effects and the role of anticipation. For additional intertemporal anomalies, see Loewenstein and Thaler (1989).

Consumer buying behavior. In a study on consumer preference involving energy savings, Kempton and Neiman (1987) collected evidence of systematic violations of rational choice principles and indeed common sense. Suppose you must choose between one of two refrigerators, which differ only in price and energy efficiency. Brand *A* costs $800 new with an annual operating cost of $25 whereas *B* sells for $700 but has an operating cost of $85 per year. Discounted at 15% per year, over a 10-year time period, *A* costs $925.50 and *B* costs $1,126.60. Yet, people commonly prefer the option with the lower initial cost even if it proves overall to be more expensive. This does not just apply to appliances but to tax payments, education, and other domains of life. The Department of Energy estimated that the average consumer implicitly *undervalues* the worth of the energy savings offered by more efficient refrigerators by about 65%. In the context of this example, this means that *B* is valued at roughly $838, slightly above *A* at $830 (as psychologically perceived). Part of the explanation seems to be that people are reluctant to lay out big sums. However, other factors – ranging from reference points to regret or anticipation – are likely to play a role as well.

Reference points. Just as risk preferences are often different for gains than losses (Kahneman and Tversky, 1979; Tversky and Kahneman, 1981, 1986), intertemporal preferences seem sensitive to reference points as well. For example, subjects usually require a considerably greater compensation to postpone receiving a desired item than the difference between their reservation prices for an immediate versus delayed receipt of that same item.

To illustrate, consider the following three choices based on Loewenstein (1988).

Problem 1.   What is the most you would pay today for a Sony VCR with remote control (list price $300)? If you pay this amount, you will receive the VCR *later today*. You should be willing to pay the amount you specify but not a penny more.

Amount you would pay $_____ (V_0)

Table 4.6. *Responses to delay questions*

	Immediate consumption price (v_0)	Delayed consumption price (v_1)	Difference immediate– delayed ($v_0 - v_1$)	Delay premium ($v_{0 \rightarrow 1}$)
Mean	$272	$226	$46	$126
(S.D.)	(13.9)	(13.5)	(14.3)	(16.0)

Problem 2. Suppose you had bought the above VCR for the amount you specified on the line above. What is the smallest payment you would be willing to accept today to delay receiving the VCR for one year. You should be willing to delay receiving the VCR for the amount you specify but not for one penny less.

Amount you require to delay receiving VCR ($v_{0 \rightarrow 1}$)

Problem 3. (Posed at a later point.) What is the most you would pay today to obtain a Sony VCR with remote control *in one year* (list price $300)? If you pay this amount you will receive the VCR on this date in one year. You should be willing to pay the amount you specify but not a penny more.

Amount you would pay $_____ ($v_1$)

Subjects' mean responses ($N = 34$) are shown in Table 4.6. The mean of $46 in column 3 is simply the difference between a VCR's perceived value today (column 1) and its value if received one year from today (column 2). However, as shown in the last column, subjects require as much as $126 on average to accept a one-year delay in delivery of the VCR once purchased. This asymmetry is reminiscent of the gain–loss asymmetries discussed under prospect theory and appears to entail a temporal reference point.

A second anomaly, presumably related to this framing effect, concerns DU's fundamental postulate of *positive* discounting of time. The further removed an event is (in time), the less it should be valued (in theory). Psychologically, however, other things matter besides end-state consumption. Our mind is a highly complex consumption organ (see Schelling, 1988), which derives considerable satisfaction from anticipation. Often some delay in consumption will actually be preferred over immediate consumption. However, our mind is also prone to derive negative consumption when contemplating undesirable events. Consequently, we often wish to speed up punishment or dreaded events (such as examinations, tax audits, or dental appointments), so as to "get it over with."

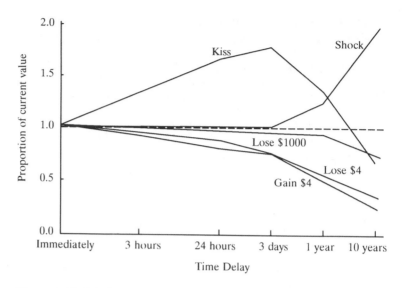

Figure 4.13. Maximum payment to obtain/avoid outcomes at selected times (*Source:* Loewenstein, 1987. Reprinted by permission)

Figure 4.13 illustrates these tendencies. Thirty undergraduates were asked to indicate the most they would be willing to pay now to experience or avoid five events at six different time intervals (ranging from immediate to 10 years from now). The five events were: (1) receiving $4; (2) avoid losing $4; (3) avoid losing $1,000; (4) avoid receiving a (nonlethal) shock of 110 volts; and (5) obtain a kiss from your favorite movie star. The vertical axis of Figure 4.14 indicates how much each event was valued as it was moved further into the future. All future valuations are relative to the immediate valuation, such that all five curves start at a ratio of 1. Under DU and positive discounting in general, all events (both positive and negative) should lose absolute value as they are placed further into the future. That is, positive events lose value when delayed and negative events (e.g., punishment) should be postponed as long as possible.

As Figure 4.13 shows, however, only for monetary events did the predicted change in value materialize. Concerning the electric shock, delay was actually deemed undesirable (within the 10-year time frame); that is, subjects were willing to pay substantially more to *avoid* a delay in a shock to be received 10 years from now than to avoid one to be received 1 year from now. Rationally, however, a shock 10 years from now is less onerous than one a year from now, and hence subjects should pay less (not more) to avoid it (under positive time discounting). Regarding the kiss, time preferences were nonmonotonic. In the short term, delaying the kiss was preferred, but when postponed beyond three days it steadily declined in value (as if becoming stale or losing salience).

This pattern is highly consistent with a model that adds utility from anticipation (a kind of process utility) to utility from outcomes or end-state consumption. It recognizes, as Jevons (1905) highlighted, that utility can be derived from at least three sources:

1. Memory of past events.
2. Pleasure of present events.
3. The anticipation of future events.

We are a long way from understanding the psychological bases of these and other sources of pleasure, although memory, framing and mental simulation are likely to play key roles therein. As such, the intertemporal domain remains largely terra incognita, both descriptively and prescriptively. It includes such perplexing issues as how much to weight past, present, and future utility (Thaler, 1981), how much to plan versus to operate incrementally or myopically (Stoltz, 1956), to what extent to restrict future options via actions now (Elster, 1979; Thaler and Shefrin, 1981), and how well we can know, shape, or anticipate our future preferences (March, 1978). On the positive side, however, since many of our intertemporal choices involve money or equivalents thereof, the discounted utility or value model does provide much practical guidance.

4.7   Summary and conclusions

The principal conclusion from our discussion of valuation and choice is that no *simple and general* model exists for describing how preferences of individuals are determined and how choices are or indeed should be arrived at. Process models can capture the sequence of steps that individuals may follow in dealing with a particular problem, but these models pay little attention to why one alternative or attribute is intrinsically valued more than another. Outcome-based models assume that individuals are guided by personal utilities in valuing choice, but, as we have seen, people systematically violate axioms that appear to be quite reasonable on the surface. Alternative approaches have attempted to patch up these violations but are only partly successful in this regard. Indeed, one is left with the feeling that any general, formal model will quickly evoke counterexamples.

Rather than try to construct a general purpose model for capturing the valuation and choice process, we deem it important to recognize that individuals will exhibit significant differences across preference tasks for the following reasons:

- Each problem has a unique set of characteristics and associated institutional arrangements and constraints. *Complexity matters.*
- Each individual has his or her own set of constraints and perceived links with other problems. *Nestedness matters.*
- Small changes in a problem's wording may lead to different reference points, different information-processing strategies, and different allocations of attention to specific dimensions of the problem. *Context matters.*

Pervading our discussion in Chapters 3 and 4 is the realization that people use different types of reasoning processes to construct plausible, credible, and coherent arguments for their behavior. These arguments will be a function of the complexity of the problem, nestedness features of the situation, and the context in which the data are presented. These conditions matter not just descriptively, but also come into play when advising people how to choose.

In the next chapter we shall examine these aspects in more detail by explicitly developing a set of criteria for evaluating alternative solution approaches concerning the inference, evaluation, and choice phases. This discussion will highlight the importance of legitimation and implementation, and indicate how the field of decision sciences can take steps toward better integrating descriptive analysis with prescriptive guidelines.

5

Evaluating prescriptive approaches

5.1   Introduction

The previous three chapters have described how problems are identified and evaluated. We have discussed several different types of theories concerned with how decision makers perform these activities:

Descriptive theories: These are theories and associated experimental evidence and field studies concerned with how actual decision makers actually perform these activities.

Normative theories: These are theories like expected utility theory based on abstract models and axioms that serve as theoretical benchmarks for how decision makers *should ideally perform* these activities.

Prescriptive theories: These are theories and associated experimental evidence and field studies concerned with *helping decision makers improve* their performance in problem finding and problem solving, given the complexities and constraints of real life.

The dominant features of the descriptive theory we have presented are the limitations in cognitive abilities of decision makers, leading to systematic biases in choice behavior when compared with normative benchmarks such as expected utility theory and statistically based inference and prediction procedures. We have also indicated some prescriptive approaches, such as bootstrapping, to improve (although not necessarily optimize) decision making.

In discussing these descriptive, normative, and prescriptive theories, we have considered problem finding and problem solving as an ordered, interconnected set of phases: identification, representation, acceptance, alternative generation, evaluation, and choice. We now consider several holistic approaches to problem solving, with a view to providing a synthesis of the descriptive, normative, and prescriptive theories previously discussed. These holistic approaches may be viewed as competing prescriptive theories for accomplishing and piecing together the problem-solving phases mentioned previously.

Table 5.1. *Some common approaches to solutions*

Problem	Solution approach
Whether to donate a kidney	Intuitive
Which students to admit to an MBA program	Bootstrapping
What stocks to invest in a portfolio	Decision support system
How to meet production targets	Mathematical programming
Whether to drill for oil at a specific site	Decision analysis

What distinguishes these prescriptive approaches is not just their degree of formalism, but also the data and other resources (e.g., time and information technology) required for their implementation, as well as properties such as ease of use and understandability. This raises the essential question addressed in this chapter: How does one choose an appropriate prescriptive approach for a given problem or decision situation?

Table 5.1 summarizes the five procedures, or prescriptive approaches, to be discussed in the context of specific problems. In thinking about solution approaches, a typical reaction is that a solution approach must surely depend on the problem structure, problem context, and the decision maker's criteria for solving the problem in question and legitimating the solution. Figure 5.1 presents this view of the (meta-) choice of solution approaches to problem solving (see also Figure 1.2 for a more detailed view). Concerning this figure, one would expect the choice of solution approach to be conditioned by the following examples.

Problem context and available resources: A problem in an organizational or group context may require a different approach than when set in an individual context. For example, even if the solution to the problem is well understood by the decision maker in advance, a formal and complete analysis may be required to legitimate this solution in an organizational context (see March and Feldman 1981). Similarly, the availability of resources, such as computers, historical data bases, or time may condition which prescriptive approach one selects.

Problem type: Problems differ in many ways, according to their complexity, data requirements, values evoked, and structure. For example, a woman's decision whether to have an abortion is clearly qualitatively different from choosing a cost-minimizing production plan. These differences have implications for the type of solution procedure appropriate for the problem in question.

Decision maker characteristics: The skills and experience of the decision maker affect the solution procedure chosen. Solution approaches

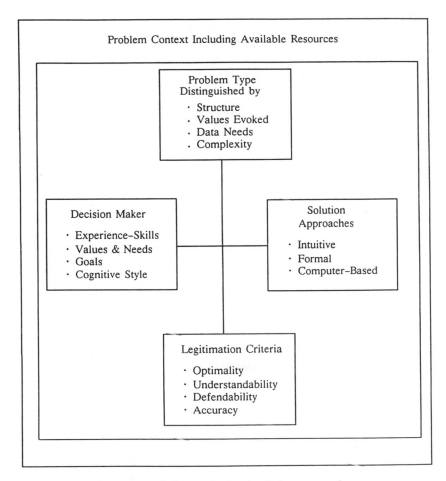

Figure 5.1. Prescriptive analysis of solution approaches

such as mathematical programming systems require technical expertise. The values and cognitive style of the decision maker may also enter the selection of a solution approach. Some decision makers have an aversion to formal models and data analysis; others are strongly inclined to use them. As we shall see, these differences may be related to the personality characteristics and cognitive style of decision makers.

Legitimation criteria: Finally, the nature of the legitimation process associated with problem solving will affect the choice of solution approaches. As discussed in Chapter 1, legitimation is the process by which the results of problem solving are represented as plausible solutions to the relevant problem. This involves identifying the stakeholders to whom the decision maker wishes (or is required) to make such a representation. (This may just be the decision maker herself, or it may involve others, say, her supervisor in an organization.) Legitimation involves both outcome legitimation (e.g., a structured argument that the chosen outcome is optimal) as well as process legitimation (e.g., the outcome was derived using "state-of-the-art" solution methods).

Both these forms of legitimation can affect the solution approach chosen. For example, the chief executive officer of a firm may wish to use expected utility theory in evaluating an investment decision. However, she may legitimate her choice of preferred investment alternatives to stockholders in other terms, such as expected profit and expected dividends, because of the difficulty of explicating and defending her utility function to stockholders as the basis of investment choice. The point here is that the requirements of an anticipated legitimation process may affect which solution procedure she uses.

Based on the above characterization of prescriptive analysis, two principles guide selection of solution approaches.

1. *Trade-offs and balance*: Proper choice of a prescriptive solution approach must balance what is desirable from the perspective of each of the four conditioning elements of a problem: problem context, problem type, decision maker characteristics, and legitimation processes. A desirable approach from one of these perspectives may conflict with that of another. The challenge is to recognize potential differences between approaches and then choose a procedure that comes closest to meeting the needs of the individual or group involved with the problem.

2. *Descriptive–prescriptive synthesis*: In evaluating alternative solution approaches, one first describes the process and consequences of implementing the solution approach. Then one applies the principle of balance in selecting among alternative approaches. Thus, prescriptive choice among solution approaches integrates descriptive theory (what will likely happen using a certain approach) with prescriptive theory (what one would like to have happen, given the constraints and context of the problem).

In the next section we describe five commonly used holistic prescriptive approaches for structuring and solving the problems described in Table 5.1. We then develop a framework for the (metachoice) problem of choosing between such approaches for a given problem. Thereafter, we discuss in more detail problem context, problem type, decision-maker characteristics, and legitimation processes conditioning this choice. Finally, we consider issues of implementation and feedback, which allow us to learn from experience and refine our knowledge of solution procedures.

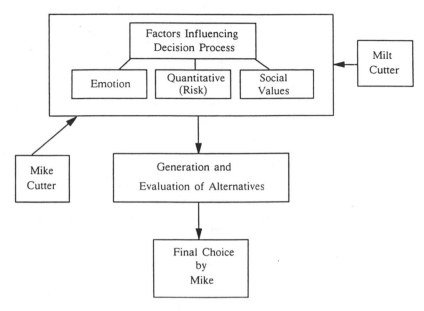

Figure 5.2. Mike Cutter's kidney transplant decision

5.2   Some common prescriptive approaches

Several of the approaches described in this section enjoy a large literature, so we shall only be scratching the surface in our brief review. There are also many other possible solution approaches and problem types than those represented in the following discussion. Our aim is not to survey this rich domain but rather to provide a sense of the diversity of holistic approaches available and the resulting complexity in choosing among these techniques on the basis of problem type, context, and decision maker.

5.2.1   *Intuitive approach*

Mike Cutter has a twin brother, Milt (55 years old), who has lost one kidney and now has another one seriously infected, which may have to be removed. The doctor has suggested that Mike donate one of his kidneys to Milt as a transplant. Mike has 10 days to make a decision. He received a checkup from the doctor who informs him that both his kidneys are in excellent condition. Should Mike donate his kidney?

  Figure 5.2 depicts Mike Cutter's choice concerning the kidney transplant. The problem is hard for him to structure because it involves difficult emotional aspects and social value questions as well as quantifiable risk factors. On the emotional side Mike has deep concerns for the survival of his brother, which makes it difficult for him to analyze this problem through purely quantitative methods. Also, the issue of donating a kidney raises larger questions about the value of human life. At what point does one reduce the chances of surviving oneself to improve the probability that another person is able to live?

There may be some benefit in looking at the problem more systematically by specifying the set of alternatives open to the Cutter brothers. If Mike decides to donate the kidney, can the doctors estimate the chances that Milt will survive and for how long? What are the probabilities that Mike will need another kidney in the future? If Mike requires a transplant himself, it will be almost impossible to turn to his one-kidney brother for help since this would lead to certain death for Milt. Are there other options for Milt aside from turning to his brother? Are other kidneys available? What about dialysis and a kidney machine?

Even though it is possible to raise a set of broader questions associated with the risk of different options, the final decision by Mike and Milt is likely to be based on intuition rather than formal analysis. There is a long history associated with making decisions on the basis of feeling rather than systematic analysis. Managers operate this way whenever they say, "I know this is the right step to take even though I cannot prove it on quantitative grounds." Frequently these comments are heard for unprogrammed or nonroutine decisions where there is not a large amount of experience on which to base one's judgment (Simon, 1981). In this case both Mike and Milt need to legitimize their final choice to themselves as well as to the outside world. Quantitative analysis may help to structure the problem, but in the final analysis it is likely to be Mike's intuition about "what is the right thing to do" that will determine his final choice. Moreover, many outsiders would implicitly accept that this is as much an "emotional" as a "rational" decision.

5.2.2   *Linear rules and bootstrapping*

Jane Officer has to make final choices for the entering MBA class of 1988, knowing that she can only admit 200 students from 1,000 who have applied. She has assembled the following information from the submitted application forms on the characteristics of each student: Graduate Record Examination (GRE) results, undergraduate grade point average (GPA), quality of undergraduate institution (QUAL), and letters of recommendation (LET). Based on these data she must determine which students to accept. How should she proceed?

Figure 5.3 depicts the system under which Officer is operating. She has a data base on each application with information of both a quantitative

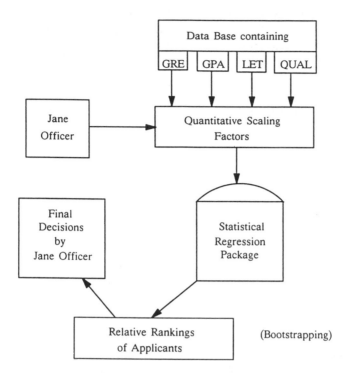

Figure 5.3. Jane Officer's admission system

nature (GRE and GPA) and qualitative nature (QUAL and LET). She decides to scale each of the latter two items on a 1–5 scale with 1 being the highest and 5 the lowest value. In this way Officer is able to use a statistical regression package to determine the relative rankings of each of the applicants using a linear decision rule based on past outcomes. After examining these results, she then makes a final decision on which students to admit, put on a waiting list, or reject.

The Lens model discussed in Chapter 3 provides the conceptual basis for undertaking the statistical regression analysis. The admissions officer's objective is to diagnose the potential success of prospective students in much the same way that a doctor diagnoses the condition of a patient. The set of cues from the application form, such as GRE and GPA, provide a measure of how well a student is likely to do if accepted. Let these cues be represented by X_1, X_2, X_3, . . . , X_n. The officer's response to previous student applicants on the basis of these factors is given by Y_j, which represents some type of performance measure for applicant j. The scaling of Y_j depends upon the objectives used by the admission officer.

If applicant *j* is judged in terms of how well he or she will perform academically, the values of Y_j might be based on a 1–10 scale where 1 would be outstanding and 10 poor. On the other hand, if she were only concerned with whether the student should be admitted, then the scale might take only 3 values: 1, accept; 2, unsure; 3, reject.

By using the statistical regression package shown in Figure 5.3, Officer can obtain a linear decision rule that weights each of the cues, [X_i i = 1 . . . m], on the basis of actual past decisions made (i.e., Y_j for each applicant *j*). The resulting rule will be of the form:

$$Y_j = b_1 X_{1j} + b_2 X_{2j} + \ldots + b_m X_{mj}, \qquad j = 1 \ldots n \qquad (5.1)$$

where b_i represents Officer's implied weights associated with each variable of interest X_i, i = 1 . . . m, and X_{ij} = value of attribute *i* for student *j*, *j* = 1 . . . . *n*. These weights are based on the assumption that the expert combines data in a linear fashion when judging potential outcomes.

Judging the performance of the actual decisions Y_j requires comparing these against some overall measure of success (Y_{ej}) for each student *j*. One possible criterion would be the grade point average of each student at the end of the two-year MBA program. Another measure would be the type of job or starting salary of each graduating student. As indicated in Chapter 3, there is considerable evidence from a number of different studies that a linear decision rule such as equation (5.1) will outperform the expert's own judgment based on some criterion Y_{ej}. In other words the linear rule helps pull the expert up by his or her own bootstraps, since the weights are determined by a regression equation based on past outcomes and variables that the expert considers to be important.

In the context of the admissions decision, Jane Officer may want to rely on a decision rule, such as equation (5.1), based on her past behavior to determine the relative ranking of different individuals. She then may want to triage students on the basis of a rule such as: Group 1 will definitely be admitted; Group 3 will definitely be rejected. Group 2 will require more careful scrutiny by Jane Officer and her staff. In this way the decision rule helps to provide initial screening for admissions, but the officer can still rely on her own intuition and special knowledge for judging borderline cases.

There are other advantages of this two-stage holistic approach. The use of a linear rule enables Officer to convey to the applicants and their parents that the semiautomatic procedure judges everyone with the same criteria. If there is a committee rather than a single individual making these decisions then the rule serves as a starting or reference point for further discussion as to who should and should not be admitted. People still have the final decision and can use their expertise to overrule a computer-based approach if special circumstances dictate this, or if the rule suggests that the situation is too close to call by computer alone.

5.2.3 *Decision support systems*

Mr. Fidelity is a senior trust officer in the Seashore Bank. He invests money for his clients in stocks and bonds and maintains careful records of each of his clients' holdings and earnings. Mr. Fidelity manages over a hundred accounts ranging in value from $50,000 to $1 million. Seashore Bank receives commission and brokerage fees for managing these accounts. Mr. Fidelity's accounts represent both individuals as well as estates in trust, and his clients are very diverse in the goals for their investment portfolios. Some, in high tax brackets, are looking primarily for capital gains through growth in the value of their stock holdings; others are primarily interested in short-term earnings through stocks that pay high dividends. There are also significant differences among his clients as to their willingness to accept risk for potentially higher earnings. Many of his clients have special wishes that must be respected, such as investing a given proportion of their assets in a specific company, avoiding particular companies (e.g., those producing or marketing alcoholic beverages or doing business in certain countries of the world), or only investing in tax-exempt bonds. Mr. Fidelity spends much of his time advising his clients on prospective changes in their portfolios.

In order to provide better service to his clients and to keep pace with several competitor banks and brokerage houses, Mr. Fidelity has recommended that the Seashore Bank install a computer-based Portfolio Decision Support System (PDSS) to assist portfolio managers in the bank's trust division. Pursuant to this recommendation, bank management commissioned an external software development firm, which had installed similar systems in other banks, to undertake a feasibility study of such a system. Their proposal looks exciting, but it is rather expensive and entails many changes in operating policy for the trust division. Bank management's question to Mr. Fidelity is simple: How can we justify such a system?

Before considering the proposed PDSS in more detail, a very brief review of portfolio theory is in order. Modern portfolio theory originated with Markowitz (1959) and Sharpe (1963). Their model assumes that the investor (one of Mr. Fidelity's typical clients) wishes to invest B in a set of stocks $1, \ldots, N$, so as to maximize his expected utility of wealth. If the investor's initial wealth is W, she invests $X_1, X_2, \ldots, X_N$, in the respective stocks in question (where $X_i = 0$ if no money is invested in stock i). If the earnings per dollar invested in stock i are R_i (a random variable), then the earnings of the entire portfolio are just

$$R = R_1X_1 + R_2X_2 + \ldots + R_NX_N \tag{5.2}$$

If the investor's utility function for wealth is $U(W)$, then she will want to select a portfolio $X_1, X_2, \ldots, X_N$, so as to

$$\text{Maximize } E[U(W - B + R)] \tag{5.3}$$

subject to:

$$X_1 + X_2 + \ldots + X_N = B \tag{5.4}$$

The key to understanding problem (5.2)–(5.4) is how to obtain the portfolio return R easily from the variables $X_1, X_2, \ldots, X_N$. This is precisely what the theory of Markowitz and Sharpe allows one to do for many variables (see Appendix A for the complexities of just two stocks). They assume that the investor has a utility function that depends on the mean and variance of returns $(W - B + R)$. They provide computational methods for obtaining this overall mean and variance from the means, variances, and covariances of the individual stock returns $R_1, R_2, \ldots, R_N$. Using these procedures, one can in theory derive an optimal portfolio for any given utility function U which depends only on the mean and variance of portfolio returns. Such an optimal portfolio will have the property that it minimizes the variance (i.e., risk) of portfolio returns among all those portfolios with the same or larger expected returns, and that it maximizes expected returns among all those portfolios with the same or smaller variance as the given portfolio. To use this theory, one needs only to estimate the means, variances, and covariances of all prospective stocks of interest. This estimation is usually based on historical data on the returns generated by the stocks in question.

In theory, one could replace Mr. Fidelity entirely by using a model based on the Markowitz–Sharpe theory. The reason this has not happened in practice is that clients frequently have complexities associated with their portfolio decisions not captured by the risk and return of a portfolio (some of these have already been indicated). Moreover, many of the clients also wish to discuss their accounts with a competent professional. Finally, the assumptions of the Markowitz–Sharpe theory are complicated and may or may not be relevant to the typical investor. For all of these reasons, Mr. Fidelity feels reasonably secure in his job as trust officer.

An important aspect of portfolio theory and practice is the use of historical data to predict future returns. Thus, if Mr. Fidelity is asked whether investing in a given stock is a good idea, he would typically undertake a review of the historical returns and risks associated with the stock, supplemented by his knowledge of the industry in question and market trends.

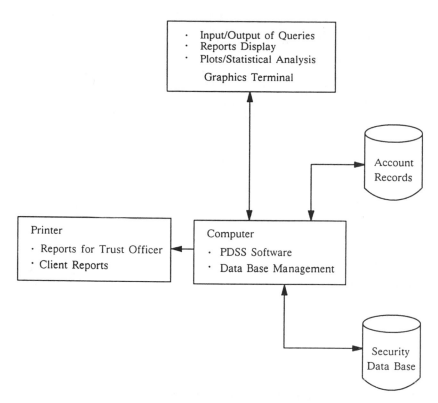

Figure 5.4. Outlines of portfolio DSS (Based on Keen and Scott-Morton, 1978)

To do so in a more precise fashion requires a large data base on past performance of the stock in question (and others in the investor's portfolio). If Mr. Fidelity believes that the earnings of some stock are in trouble or show particular promise, he would like to be able to determine quickly which of his accounts show holdings in that stock. It is these types of questions for which a PDSS can provide quick and useful assistance to him.

The outlines of an on-line portfolio management system (called PDSS) presented to Seashore Bank by their external consultants are given in Figure 5.4. The basic capabilities of the system include the following:

1. Queries on a particular stock. The PDSS allows the trust officer to determine quick summaries of the past performance of the stock in question (expected value and variance of returns, yearly highs and lows, etc.).
2. Queries on industry performance. Similar information on past performance can be provided for industry aggregates (e.g., the steel industry).

3. Queries concerning accounts. The PDSS allows the holdings of a particular account to be displayed, along with earnings and other pertinent information. The PDSS also allows quick determination of which accounts have holdings in a particular stock.
4. Changes in portfolios. The system facilitates placing buy and sell orders and updating accounts.
5. Routine reports. A feature of the proposed PDSS of great attraction to clients is the ability to provide computer analyses of their accounts and prospective changes to them.
6. Management control. More advanced versions of the PDSS allow assessment of the performance of individual trust officers.

In its simplest form, the proposed PDSS would help the trust officer to provide quick and reliable information to clients. From the trust officer's point of view, this could be a tremendous benefit. On the negative side, the introduction of a PDSS for portfolio management has not been an easy task for trust officers and security analysts (see Keen and Scott-Morton, 1978, and Alter, 1980), because it entails the use of sophisticated computer technology. On balance, however, the pressures of competition and the perceived and actual increase in service provided by such systems to clients have outweighed these costs. The use of PDSS for portfolio management has been steadily introduced in major banks throughout the United States. Given the size of Mr. Fidelity's account base, he therefore seems on firm ground in recommending the gradual introduction of the proposed PDSS. (See Eom and Lee, 1990, for a survey of specific DSS applications in a number of different areas including portfolio management.)

5.2.4   *Mathematical programming*

Bernie Munch, manager of operations of Munchy Cereals, is confronted by a serious problem in meeting production targets. Munchy Cereals has grown rapidly over the past decade, both in its standard hot-cereal line as well as its newer product line of dry cereals. The key issue confronting Bernie is how to provide sufficient production capacity for Munchy's fast-growing new dry-cereal line for the coming year. Munch's existing dry-cereal plants are located at Andover (Massachusetts), Harrisburg (Pennsylvania), Houston (Texas), and San Francisco (California). They have four market areas: North, South, East, and West. The basic alternatives open to Bernie in meeting the increased demand are to add an additional shift at either Andover or at Harrisburg. (San Francisco is already operating at two shifts in satisfying the West Market, and Houston is a new plant which is just getting underway and for which two-shift operations are not feasible.) Bernie must decide which of these two alternatives to pursue within the near future, since otherwise significant sales loss will occur, undermining Munchy's developing market growth in its new product line. Table 5.2 presents the relevant cost and demand data for these two alternatives.

Bernie Munch's capacity planning problem is typical of many short- and medium-run business problems. The objective (of profit maximization or cost minimization) is clearly understood. Moreover, the alternatives to the problem are clear. However, analyzing these alternatives is difficult because of the volume of data and the complexity of the analysis involved. In the present case, let us suppose (as would be typical) that Bernie wishes to determine the least cost alternative for adding new capacity, subject to meeting demand forecasts for the next year.

A heuristic solution to this problem would be the following. Consider first Alternative 1. Suppose that, if possible, the plant to supply each market is the one that has the lowest combined per unit transportation and production costs. Table 5.3 presents these costs for Alternative 1. The cost of supplying a unit (say 1,000 boxes of cereal) of product from Andover to the North Market is 16 = 3 + 13, the sum of the cost of making the unit of product at Andover (13) plus the cost of shipping it to the North Market (3). Following the strategy, one would like to supply the North Market from Harrisburg, the South Market from Houston, the East Market from Harrisburg, and the West Market from Houston or San Francisco. Clearly, this is not feasible since, for example, the Houston plant can only supply 300 units and the South Market requires 400.

One feasible solution in the spirit of this approach is Table 5.4 (for Alternative 1). For example, this solution shows Andover using its entire capacity (of 500) to supply the East Market. The cost of this solution is easily computed from Table 5.3 to be 37,900.

Bernie's problem is now clear. He must first compute the cost of the best shipping and production policies for each of the two alternatives. He then simply compares the costs of these "optimal" production and shipping schedules and chooses the alternative with the lowest total cost. For this simple problem (with only four markets and four production facilities), Bernie could probably obtain a pretty good solution intuitively. However, if Bernie wanted to do a more detailed analysis of shipping patterns to submarkets within each of the four market regions, then a much larger problem would result. To see how such a larger problem would be solved, let us state Bernie's simpler problem in more formal terms.

Let the cost of making a unit of dry cereal at Location i (Andover, Harrisburg, Houston, San Francisco, or Des Moines) be denoted C_i and the cost of shipping each unit of product from Location i to Market j be T_{ij}; then the total annual cost of a given production and distribution plan

Table 5.2. *Bernie's problem data*

Unit transportation cost				Annual capacity alternative			Unit production cost
N	S	E	W	1	2	Plants	
3	6	2	10	500	1,000	Andover	13
5	5	3	9	1,000	500	Harrisburg	10
8	2	6	5	300	300	Houston	9
5	8	11	2	1,000	1,000	San Francisco	12
600	400	700	1,000	Annual demand			
North	South	East	West	Market			

Table 5.3. *Total per unit costs, demands and capacity – alternative 1*

Total unit costs				Annual capacity Alternative 1	Plants
16	19	15	23	500	Andover
15	15	13	19	1,000	Harrisburg
17	11	15	14	300	Houston
17	20	23	14	1,000	San Francisco
600	400	700	1,000	Annual demand	
North	South	East	West	Market	

Table 5.4. *Feasible solution for Bernie's problem*

From–to	North	South	East	West	Total
Andover	0	0	500	0	500
Harrisburg	600	100	200	0	900
Houston	0	300	0	0	300
San Francisco	0	0	0	1,000	1,000
Cost	9,000	4,800	9,100	1,400	37,900

is just the cost of production plus the cost of transportation, that is $C_i + T_{ij}$ per unit for cereal produced at Location i and shipped to Market j. Thus, we can summarize Bernie's production and distribution planning problem as the solution to the following mathematical program.

$$\text{Minimize} \quad \sum_{i=1}^{4} \sum_{j=1}^{4} (C_i + T_{ij}) X_{ij} \tag{5.5}$$

subject to:

$$\sum_{i=1}^{4} X_{ij} = D_j, \quad j = 1, \ldots, 4 \tag{5.6}$$

$$\sum_{j=1}^{4} X_{ij} \leq S_i, \quad i = 1, \ldots, 4 \tag{5.7}$$

where

> X_{ij} = amount shipped annually from Plant i to Market j
> D_j = annual demand in Market j
> S_i = annual capacity of Plant i (which may depend on which alternative Bernie chooses)

The mathematical programming problem (5.5)–(5.7) is known as a transportation problem. Very efficient procedures have been available for some time for solving such problems (see, e.g., Hillier and Lieberman, 1974). Using this approach, one finds that the optimal production and shipping patterns for the two options under consideration are as in Table 5.5. On the basis of these figures Bernie would clearly prefer Alternative 1 since its overall cost is 37,400 compared to 38,300 for Alternative 2.

A computer-based system for this problem is shown in Figure 5.5. The box "Capacity Planning" refers to the generation of alternative locations and shift options. The box "Production/Distribution Planning" refers to the transportation algorithm just described. Finally, the "Evaluation" box could be a graphics terminal to display and compare the various alternatives at their respective optimal production and distribution planning solutions. In Bernie's case, we have only two alternatives, so the comparison of total costs is simple. In a more complicated setting, a decision support system framework (as in the portfolio example) would be useful to assist the decision maker in both the evaluation and the capacity planning aspects of the system shown. In fact, one might view the system displayed in Figure 5.5 as a decision support system for capacity and production/distribution planning. The reason we refer to it as a mathematical programming system is simply that the heart of the evaluation process embodied in this system is the optimization model (5.5)–(5.7).

Table 5.5. *Optimal shipping patterns and cost (Alternatives 1 and 2)
for Bernie's problem*

From–to	North	South	East	West	Total
Alternative 1					
Andover	500	0	0	0	500
Harrisburg	100	100	700	0	900
Houston	0	300	0	0	300
San Francisco	0	0	0	1,000	1,000
Cost	9,500	4,800	9,100	14,000	37,400
Alternative 2					
Andover	600	0	400	0	1,000
Harrisburg	0	100	300	0	400
Houston	0	300	0	0	300
San Francisco	0	0	0	1,000	1,000
Cost	9,600	4,800	9,900	14,000	38,300

5.2.5   Decision analysis approach

Oliver Slick (Oli to his friends) is an oil driller who is deciding whether
to drill a field that has had mixed success in the past. He decides to
consult his good friend Bill Branch who recently has received an MBA
degree in decision sciences and is well schooled in quantitative approaches to analyzing problems. Oli informs Bill that there is a seismic
test he can use that will provide additional information about the likelihood that he will strike oil in a particular field. The two sets of interrelated questions that Oli must answer are:

1. Should he use a test?
2. Should he drill for oil?

Figure 5.6 provides a broad overview of Oliver Slick's problem, which
will enable him to address these questions. Data are required on the costs
of the test as well as the profits or loss associated with drilling or not
drilling for oil. These payoffs will have to be weighted by the probabilities associated with different outcomes (e.g., favorable or unfavorable
tests, striking or not striking oil). Branch recommends the use of decision
analysis as a technique for systematically evaluating Oli's options.

An individual who has a problem under uncertainty such as Oli Slick's
must choose between alternatives on the basis of probabilistic events that
lead to a set of outcomes. Figure 5.7 depicts a decision tree that captures

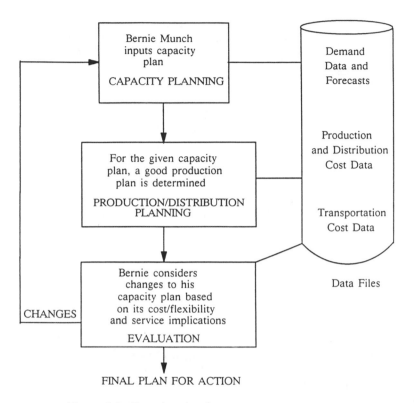

Figure 5.5. Capacity planning system

these features of the oil drilling problem. The two alternatives facing Slick are: Test or don't test and drill or don't drill. These are depicted by squares in the figure. The probabilistic events are given by circles. The drilling problem is sequential in nature because the outcome of a test (if Oli chooses that route) will determine whether he should drill for oil. The final outcome at the end of each branch of the tree is designated by the heading "Profits or (Loss)."

Once this type of tree is drawn, it is necessary to collect detailed information on the relevant costs, payoffs, and probabilities of different outcomes in order to determine which alternative path to follow. We have labeled the probabilities of the relevant events on the decision tree. Thus $P(O) = .31$ and $P(D) = .69$ are respectively the chances that Oli will strike oil or that the well will be dry if he drills at a particular site without first using a test. Similarly $P(F) = 3$ represents the chance that the test will be favorable. Some of the probabilities are conditional on other events occurring given the sequential nature of the problem. In particular, the

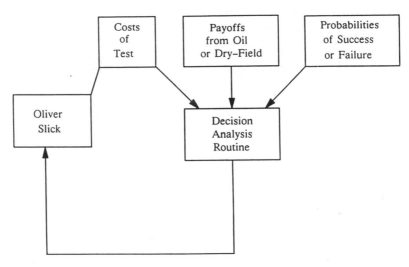

Figure 5.6. Oliver Slick's problem

top portion of the tree indicates that Oli has to estimate the chances of
striking oil if the test is favorable (i.e., $P(O \mid F)$) or being dry if the test
is favorable ($P(D \mid F)$). Similar probabilities are obtained for an unfavorable test $P(O \mid U)$ and $P(D \mid U)$. In this case the only information
available is prior probabilities associated with the test given that there is
oil or the site is dry. For example, it is possible to estimate $P(F \mid O)$
based on past seismic test experiences with specific sites.

The final element associated with the decision tree involves the payoffs
associated with each branch. These include the costs of the test, the drilling expenses, and the returns to Oli should oil be found. If Oli is a risk-
neutral entrepreneur, because either he has sufficient wealth or he views
this potential investment as a small drop in a large bucket, then the potential benefits of the seismic test can be determined through the use of
expected-value techniques with the relevant probabilities serving as weights.
If, on the other hand, Oli is either risk averse or a risk taker, then it is
necessary to use his utility function with respect to evaluating the payoffs.
The decision on whether to undertake a test would be based on expected
utility maximization, as discussed in detail in Chapter 4.

Finally, note the sequential nature of the decision process. An analysis
is undertaken to determine whether to use the seismic test. If Oli decides
not to test, then he can immediately specify whether to drill for oil by
comparing expected values or expected utilities at the appropriate square
node on the tree. On the other hand, if a test is approved, then Oli must
wait until its outcome before deciding whether to drill. If he would have

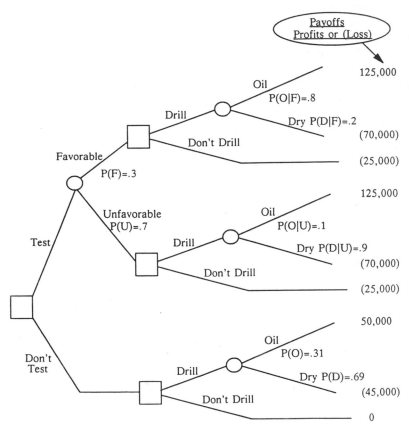

Figure 5.7. Decision tree for Oliver Slick

drilled for oil independent of the test's outcome, then it would never have been profitable to use a seismic analysis in the first place.

Oli agrees to use decision analysis on this problem because Bill convinces him that it will provide insight into the relative importance of seismic testing in terms of final payoffs. He is convinced that the technique has value because it forces him to estimate probabilities and outcomes from different alternative actions. On the other hand, he finds the process of specifying these figures extremely difficult. For example, it is not easy for him to estimate the probability of striking oil independent of a test or conditional on its results. Bill Branch points out that one can undertake sensitivity analysis to determine whether a particular decision will be changed as probability and payoff estimates are varied. Furthermore, Branch points out that a number of his clients have successfully used decision analysis to structure and solve problems similar to the oil-drilling case.

Oli undertakes the analysis and on the basis of his estimates agrees to a seismic test. The result is favorable so he drills for oil and strikes it rich. He is overjoyed and feels that decision analysis should be used to structure all his problems. Bill Branch urges great caution in using this technique indiscriminately. He indicates to Oli that had he drilled and not found oil he might have had the opposite reaction to this approach; yet there was a positive probability of a dry well even after a favorable test. On a general note, certain types of problems more easily lend themselves to decision analysis than others. In particular, those problems where there is a large data base from past studies from which to estimate probabilities and outcomes tend to be more amenable to this approach because of greater confidence in the estimates upon which final decisions are made.

Oli decides that he will want to use decision analysis as an important input in choosing between sites because Bill and he agree that there is a large data base on which to build. Bill recommends that he build an interactive computer-based model that will probe for estimates of relevant probabilities and payoffs as well as determine Oli's utility function. This approach has features of the portfolio problem discussed previously and enables the individual manager to become an integral part of the decision process. On that final note, Oli sails into the sunset to inspect another site, confident that he has found a useful friend in decision analysis. Is he right? Does this apply to you and your problems?

5.3   Prescriptive analysis of solution approaches

The preceding examples indicate the scope of solution approaches available for analyzing various decision contexts. They also hint at the issues involved in choosing a solution approach based on problem features, available resources, and legitimation criteria. In this section we present a more detailed discussion of these aspects of choosing a solution approach. The following section then relates choice of solution approach to the personal and philosophical perspective of the decision maker. Our intention throughout is prescriptive. We wish to highlight how a particular decision maker might select a particular holistic solution approach to assist that specific decision maker in improving the decision process and legitimating this process and its outcome to other stakeholders whom the decision maker considers important.

To begin with, let us present the results of a simple introspective experiment performed by the authors themselves. We asked ourselves how well we thought each of the five solution approaches examined in the previous section would deal with each of the example problems considered. Averaging and rounding our three responses resulted in Table 5.6. The entries are on a 1–10 scale, where 1 indicates that the approach was

Table 5.6. *Authors' comparison of solution approaches for examples*

Problem approach	Kidney	Admission	Portfolio	Production	Drilling
Intuitive	10	5	3	1	5
Bootstrapping	1	10	3	1	4
DSS	2	8	10	8	3
Math program	1	3	6	10	2
Decision analysis	3	1	5	3	10

felt to be very difficult to apply to the problem indicated and 10 indicates that we felt that the approach was just right for the problem.

Table 5.6 indicates in an informal manner the fact that some problem-solving approaches may be more appropriate than others for particular problems. The introduction to this chapter has already pointed out several reasons for this. These include (see Figure 5.1) the following.

Problem context and available resources. Different problem contexts may make one or another solution approach more appropriate. The availability of computers, for example, is necessary for decision support systems and mathematical programming. Moreover, the problem context may dictate which stakeholders will have to be satisfied with the process and outcome of the decision in question. In particular, organizational contexts may call for legitimating the problem solution (and its approach) to a broader diversity of other stakeholders than would an individual problem context. Comparing Bernie Munch's problem with that of Oli Slick, for example, we see immediately that Bernie must be able to legitimate his solution to his superiors (and ultimately to the stockholders) at Munchy Cereals, whereas Oli Slick operates independently and has only himself to answer to in legitimating his solution. This may well lead Bernie to adopt a defensible objective of minimizing costs in a formal manner, while Oli can adopt a decision analysis approach to his problem. The reader may wish to consider the problems Bernie would have in explaining his recommendations to his management or Munchy's stockholders if these recommendations were derived using a decision analysis approach.

Problem type. The examples illustrate problem types that vary from "messy problems" (see McCaskey, 1982, and Simon, 1963) to well-structured problems (see Keen and Scott-Morton, 1978). Some involve large data manipulations, and others don't. Some problems must be resolved quickly (e.g., the Cutters' problem), whereas others are ongoing (the Seashore

Bank problem). These differences are clearly related to the choice of solution approach. For example, mathematical programming requires that the problem be precisely structured and that all parameters of interest be estimated or identified. When these prerequisites are at hand and the objective is clear (as in Bernie Munch's problem), this solution approach has much to recommend it. In other instances (e.g., Jane Officer's problem), the required structure and data would be very difficult to determine.

Legitimation criteria. The criteria appropriate for judging the process and outcome of problem solving can be quite different in different contexts for different individuals. Some may be in a position to apply only their own criteria (e.g., Oli Slick), whereas others must contend with organizational and social legitimation issues (e.g., Jane Officer and Mike Cutter). Different solution approaches may therefore be more or less appropriate depending on the ability of the decision maker to legitimate his or her choice after using the solution approach.

Considering the three issues together, we may view the problem of choosing a solution approach as that of matching the requirements of the problem context, available resources, problem type, and legitimation criteria against the characteristics and requirements of each solution approach. This matching process gives rise to the principles of *balance* and *descriptive–prescriptive synthesis* stated in the introduction to this chapter. Namely, the decision maker (DM) must first describe the likely outcomes of using each solution approach, and then choose a solution approach that, from the perspective of that DM's own value system, best balances the dictates of the problem with these characteristics and requirements. Figure 5.8 provides a partial list of the dimensions of concern under each of the three headings described, together with the five solution approaches we have illustrated (and which are only a very small subset of all solution approaches).

Figure 5.8 illustrates the problem dictates of concern here. For each given problem, one must analyze these characteristics in understanding the nature of the problem and its context. Similarly, one must describe and predict the major attributes of competing solution approaches that might be applied to this problem. The resulting choice problem is analogous to lining up a series of filmstrips of a given situation, each photographed from a different angle. The angles (or filmstrips) of interest here are problem context, problem type, and legitimation criteria, as seen in Figure 5.8.

These problem filmstrips must be aligned (or balanced) with corresponding filmstrips representing the requirements and predicted performance of alternative solution approaches under consideration. The requirements of a given solution approach (e.g., the use of a computer)

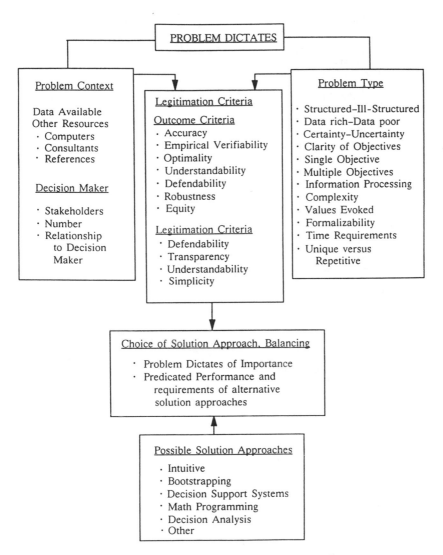

Figure 5.8. Problem dictates and solution approaches

determine which solution approaches are feasible, whereas the predicted performance of solution approaches determines how well legitimation criteria of interest will be served by using each of the alternative solution approaches. Given a feasible set of solution approaches, and predicted performance on each legitimation dimension, the decision maker must then use his or her preferences for the attributes and performance of solution approaches in determining which to use in a given problem context.

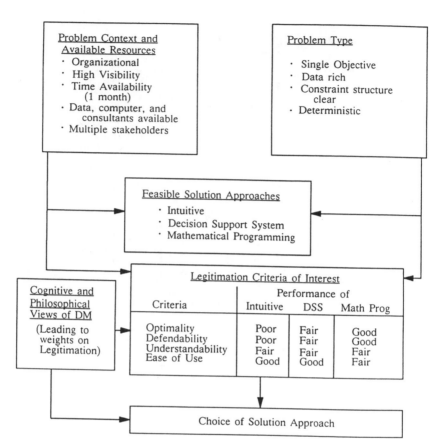

Figure 5.9. Assessing the performance of alternative solution approach for Bernie Munch's problem

This final or metachoice problem is discussed in more detail in the next section.

Let us illustrate these concepts for Bernie Munch's capacity expansion problem of section 5.2.4. Figure 5.9 specifies the details of Figure 5.8 for Bernie's problem. The problem context and available resources indicate an organizational problem of high visibility, with computers and data for detailed analysis available. The time frame for the decision is short, within the next month. The problem type is a deterministic, data-rich planning problem, with a well-specified objective (cost minimization) and a clear constraint structure (that of meeting market demands from available production capacity). From these problem dictates, three competing solution approaches are feasible.

In an *intuitive* approach, Bernie would size up the situation on the back of an envelope, do some preliminary calculations to ensure feasibility, and go with his best guess. In this analysis, he could, of course, consider not just cost and demand issues, but also qualitative issues (e.g., the ability of a particular plant manager to move quickly in installing a second shift). .

A *decision support system* might be appropriate, given that the data are available for doing comparative cost and demand analyses. Bernie could set up a rudimentary DSS to answer specific inquiries, such as how much a particular production and shipping pattern would cost, or what the transportation delays of such a plan would be. This DSS would then be a query answering system, perhaps with some additional facilities to display results in an understandable fashion.

Mathematical programming would be the system analyzed in section 5.2.4 and displayed in Figure 5.5. The next step in this choice problem is the determination of the legitimation criteria of interest and a prediction of the performance of each of the competing solution approaches on these criteria. We show in Figure 5.9 the legitimation criteria of interest. Obviously, many other criteria might be listed, but let us suppose these are the major ones of interest to Bernie.

Optimality: How close is the solution to the lowest cost solution, subject to the feasibility constraints (on meeting demand)?

Defendability: Can the solution approach be defended to the stakeholders of interest to Bernie (i.e., his managers and possibly Munchy's shareholders)? Similarly, can the outcome be defended (e.g., to Munchy's plant managers) as reasonable?

Understandability: In a related vein, are the solution approach and its outcome likely to be understandable to Bernie and other stakeholders?

Ease of use: How easy is each solution approach to implement?

The final step is to predict the characteristics and performance of alternative solution approaches on each of the legitimation criteria of interest. We provide our assessments of this in Figure 5.9 for the three solution approaches under consideration. If Bernie sees his problem and the performance of the indicated solution approaches as we do, he would probably choose mathematical programming as his solution approach. Clearly, however, this will depend on how he approaches the problem. His final choice will therefore turn not only on his views of which approaches are feasible (given the problem context and available resources), but also on his own values in judging the relative importance of each of the legitimation criteria of interest. We now consider this latter problem in more detail.

5.4   Cognitive and philosophical orientations

The issue of how to choose a solution approach ultimately becomes a matter of personal and philosophical preference. To see this we must first appreciate the importance of cognitive style. The way people define problems, think about them, and resolve them reflects their basic preferences for perception and judgment. It is hard to argue that a particular mode of cognitive functioning is generally superior to another. Each will have its strengths and weaknesses, which in part explains why different schools of thought exist in decision making and the philosophy of rationality. Although many conceptual frameworks are available to differentiate cognitive styles, we find the typology of Carl Jung the most useful for our purposes.

The essential premise is that seemingly random variations in (decision) behavior stem from basic differences in the way people use and prefer to use their mental faculties. We shall examine two important dimensions along which people differ in this regard. The underlying theory is due to Jung (1971), although most of the empirical research and measurement was developed by Isabel Myers (1962).[1] First let us distinguish between perception and judgment.

"Perception" is understood to include the processes of becoming-aware, – of things, people, occurrences or ideas. "Judgment" is understood to include the processes of coming-to-conclusions about what has been perceived. If people differ systematically in what they perceive and the conclusions they come to, they may as a result show corresponding differences in their reactions, in their interests, values, needs and motivations, in what they do best and what they like to do most. (Myers, 1962, p. 1)

With respect to perception, two opposite orientations might be distinguished, namely *receptive* versus *preceptive* information processing.[2] The receptive type is open to information and has a good eye for detail. He or she appreciates facts in their own right rather than for their relationship to theories or hypotheses. The preceptive type, on the other hand, mostly looks for patterns and goes quickly beyond the data. To this person facts are only important and relevant to the extent that they support or reject preconceptions about the world. Neither orientation is generally superior to the other, as we shall see later.

---

1 For more recent descriptions of this test, see Myers and McCaulley (1985) as well as Myers (1988).

2 See also our discussion of perception in Chapter 2. Note that our labels of "receptive" and "preceptive" correspond to "sensing" (S) and "intuition" (N) in the Myers-Briggs test; similarly, our labels "systematic" and "intuitive" correspond most closely to "thinking" (T) and "feeling" (F).

The second dimension of interest is judgment. Does the person prefer a *systematic* or an *intuitive* approach to judgment? Of course, both are used, but often people have a preferred or dominant style in which they feel most comfortable. The intuitive type ultimately trusts intuition, feeling, and hunches more than analysis. The systematic type is just the opposite, preferring reasoned or analytical decision making. To characterize these different orientations in the context of managerial decision making, Table 5.7 lists some key features of each (see also Rowe and Mason, 1987). The important point is that each orientation has its strengths and weaknesses, depending on the nature of the task. Consequently, different types are better suited for different occupations, as shown in Table 5.8. Here the two dimensions of perception and judgment are cross-classified, resulting in four basic psychological types. The table briefly characterizes each type in a general sense, and indicates which occupations go well with which psychological orientations.

So far our discussion has been descriptive, focusing on basic cognitive orientations. These orientations, however, strongly influence to what extent different prescriptive theories appeal to us. Thus, the ultimate acceptance of a theoretical approach depends critically on one's cognitive orientation. Before discussing the various prescriptive approaches in this context, we shall identify a set of philosophical orientations that closely relate to cognitive style (see Mason and Mitroff, 1973). Indeed, the different philosophical orientations to be discussed might be viewed as archetypal approaches of various psychological types to the acquisition of knowledge and the assessment of truth. To illustrate, imagine how you would approach the task of marketing a new product in a foreign country. How will you obtain information or evidence, and how will you ascertain what sort of reality exists out there?

One approach is to develop careful data banks of facts, where there is general agreement about their importance. This so-called Lockean approach is consensual, is strongly empirical, and follows an inductive representation. Elementary facts are expanded and extended into increasingly more general facts, which ultimately define reality. Importantly, it is assumed that only one reality exists, namely the one everybody agrees on. Due to its emphasis on facts, this approach accords well with the receptive type.

A second approach, called Leibnizian, is to obtain knowledge from axioms and proofs. The emphasis is on formal reasoning. A set of elementary or formal truths are postulated, and their logical consequences are explored with deductive rigor. Two good examples of this approach are mathematical programming and formal expected utility analysis. The guarantor of truth, in both these cases, is internal consistency or logical deduction. The focus is theoretical rather than empirical. Its emphasis on

Table 5.7. *Decision-making characteristics of different cognitive styles*

Receptive	Suspend judgment and avoid preconceptions. Be attentive to detail and to the exact attributes data. Insist on a complete examination of a data set before deriving conclusions.
Preceptive	Look for cues in a data set. Focus on relationships. Jump from one section of a data set to another. Build a set of explanatory precepts.
Systematic	Look for a method and make a plan for solving a problem. Be very conscious of one's approach. Defend the quality of a solution largely in terms of the method. Define the specific constraints of the problem systematically early in the process. Discard alternatives quickly. Move through a process of increasing refinement of analysis. Conduct an ordered search for additional information. Complete any discrete step in analysis that one begins.
Intuitive	Keep the overall problem continuously in mind. Redefine the problem frequently as one proceeds. Rely on unverbalized cues, even hunches. Defend a solution in terms of fit. Consider a number of alternatives and options simultaneously. Jump from one step in analysis or search to another and back again. Explore and abandon alternatives very quickly.

Table 5.8. *Cognitive style and occupational choice*

	Receptive and systematic	Receptive and intuitive	Preceptive and systematic	Preceptive and intuitive
Focus their attention on	Facts	Facts	Possibilities	Possibilities
and handle these with	Impersonal analysis	Personal warmth	Impersonal analysis	Personal warmth
Thus they tend to be	Practical and matter-of-fact	Sociable and friendly	Enthusiastic and insightful	Intellectual, ingenious
and find scope for their abilities in	Production Construction Accounting Business Economics Law Surgery	Sales Service Customer relations Welfare work Nursing General practice	Research Teaching Preaching Counseling Writing Psychology Psychiatry	Research Science Invention Securities analysis Management Cardiology

Source: Adapted from Myers (1962, p. 56).

relationships and model building is especially appealing to the preceptive type. Again only one reality is presumed, although this time it is not readily shared since it is highly formalized and abstract.

A third approach combines the empirical and theoretical to develop multiple representations. This so-called Kantian approach emphasizes the interaction between theory (i.e., the a priori assumptions about the world) and facts.) What is considered relevant data depends on one's implicit theories, whereas one's theories in turn depend on what facts are used. The guarantor of truth in this system is the extent of agreement between the various models. Thus, if the same marketing decision is recommended by two different models, then the Kantian inquirer will be quite confident as to the appropriate course of action.

Finally, an approach may be followed that is purposely internally conflicted. This so-called Hegelian or dialectical system is Kantian in its reliance on multiple representations, but differs in its emphasis on the use of opposing or contrary models. Consequently, the guarantor of truth is not the degree of agreement among the various models, but rather whatever synthesis emerges. A prime example is the U.S. justice system. In determining the truth, two mutually inconsistent models are constructed, namely one of guilt and one of innocence. Each of these presumptions is fully developed and tested on the admissible data by the prosecution and defense, respectively. Finally, both the thesis and antithesis are presented to a jury who then arrives at a synthesis. Note that the focus in the dialectical system is on decision making, which occurs in the synthesis phase. Because of its conflicting premises, its courtship of ambiguity, and the intuitive resolution of the opposing models, this approach may appeal more to the intuitive than the analytic type.

Now let us return to the original question in deciding how to choose. As a first point we noted that this decision cannot be made with the tools of prescriptive decision theory itself as it concerns an evaluation of those tools. Thus, the issue is truly a metaquestion external to decision theory as such. Second, we suggested that problem perception and judgment are essentially subjective matters, anchored strongly in the cognitive structure of the decision maker.

If we apply these typologies of cognitive style and inquiring modes to the various decision methodologies, the following conclusions suggest themselves. The expected utility approach is Leibnizian insofar as it emphasizes axioms and theorems. It is preceptive to the extent that it views the decision reality as consisting of acts and their associated probability distributions. The systematic framework of expected utility theory or decision analysis will of course appeal to the analytic or systematic judgment type. However, the level of abstraction and theoretical orientation of the system will appeal more to the intuitive type, leaving it somewhere in the middle with regard to this dimension.

Mathematical programming is an interesting case in itself. At one level the technique, as embodied in linear programming, can be used as a theoretical approach, so that it is highly preceptive and Leibnizian. In this context it is interesting to note that some students after learning linear programming go through a phase where they deem almost all problems to be reducible to mathematical programming ones. The receptive-analytic type would be particularly prone to such a view of the world.

Simulation, as another variant of the mathematical systems approach, is a more flexible approach than linear programming and is grounded in empirical data. To the extent that simulation is used to explore different representations of the world (i.e., to conduct "what if" analyses using different assumptions), it is more Kantian. Depending on how this very flexible method is used, it could appeal to almost any psychological type.

The various nonoptimization approaches, such as intuition and bootstrapping, should be viewed as non-Leibnizian. They implicitly question reliance on theoretical superstructures and criticize their imposition on the world without much regard for its actual nature. The use of decision support systems may reflect a Hegelian design approach, in that multiple models can be developed from different premises. Moreover, since the user is allowed to explore various hypotheses in a nonsystematic manner, it has a strong intuitive orientation. Of course, constructing extensive data banks in such a system would suggest a receptive or Lockean basis.

In summary, the various methods can seldom be purely classified as falling exactly in one of our cognitive or philosophical cells. Much depends on how the method is used and with what intention. Just as a screwdriver can be used for a routine task as well as a creative one, the decision methodologies discussed must similarly be viewed as flexible in application. However, inherent limitations do exist, as with the screwdriver. In general, the question of truth might be viewed as consisting of two components, namely internal validity, which concerns logic, reasoning, and analysis, and external validity, which asks whether the premises and assumptions accord with the empirical reality. Of course, the more realistic the model is made, the more difficult it becomes to assess the internal validity of various solutions. Since any model by definition entails a simplification and thus distortion of reality, its degree of truth will always be open to debate. Moreover, how much weight one places on internal versus external validity is ultimately a matter of psychological and philosophical preference.

5.5   Conclusions

The approaches compared in this chapter can be viewed from the perspective of decision making by individuals as well as from the broader context of group, organizational, and societal aspects. At the individual level we have been concerned with the relationship between how alternative approaches perform in relation to specific problem and person types. We have also considered how resource constraints, in the form of data, computer facilities, and other personnel, may restrict the solution domain. Finally, we have discussed the need to legitimate the final decision as well as the solution approach used to reach the decision. Thus, not only outcome legitimation may be required but also decision process legitimation.

Each of the five problems also illustrated the interaction of the individual decision maker to a larger set of stakeholders. Mike Cutter was concerned not only about his brother Milt's reaction to his decision on whether to donate a kidney but also to friends' and neighbors' feelings. Society sanctions certain actions and disapproves of others. Most physicians reflect some of these norms in their recommended courses of action. Hence Mike faced a dilemma as to what he should do.

Jane Officer has to defend her position to all rejected applicants, and perhaps their parents, as well as to the admissions committee to whom she reports. If there were disagreements about particular applicants, she could turn to her formal decision rule to help legitimate her position. On the other hand, if the decision process involved group discussions then a different legitimation process would have to be followed.

Mr. Fidelity is concerned about his reputation both with his clients as well as with his fellow employees at the Seashore Bank. For this reason he may not only use the Portfolio Decision Support System, but may also share ideas with other managers in the bank and study their decisions. Final choices may thus be a function of clients' needs, an existing data base, and others' actions.

Bernie Munch must concern himself not only with the operations of Munchy Cereals but also with the reaction of the Andover and Harrisburg plants to his final decision. The chances are that the managers of both these plants will have some problems if Munch recommends a second shift, because it will require recruiting new employees for the production line. Hence organizational considerations influence the final choice with respect to meeting production targets. In fact, after investigating the situation in more detail Munch may conclude that he will not be able to install a second shift in either city immediately. This may lead to a reduction of production plans or the use of overtime in one of the four cities where Munchy operates.

At first blush, it appears that the decision facing Oli Slick is an individual one since he is an entrepreneur rather than a manager for a large organization. On the other hand, if Slick required venture capital to finance his oil drilling operation, then his investors may be interested in the basis for his decision on whether to drill a particular well. If Slick is successful, as in the example given, then his use of decision analysis will probably not be questioned. Should he hit a few dry wells, then there may be some concern with the type of analyses he is using. Under these latter circumstances a different decision process may emerge that involves interaction between Slick and his investors before final action is taken. This scenario is typical of the interaction between problem context, legitimation, and the prescriptive analysis of alternative solution approaches to problem finding and problem solving.

The topics of this chapter are central to the book. Looking backward, we see that the descriptive features of individual decision making come into play when discussing prescriptive analysis of solution approaches. The way in which a problem is identified and framed, for example, will determine its context and its legitimation requirements. Alternative approaches to problem analysis, valuation, and choice will be required depending on the dictates of the problem. Looking ahead, we shall see in the chapters that follow that groups and organizations can be used to improve problem solving and decision making. Groups and organizations also serve as major contexts for legitimation of individual problem finding and solving.

We see in the previous examples of holistic solution approaches the outlines of a metatheory of prescriptive choice. We depict this in summary form in Figure 5.10. This figure is intended only as a rough guide to summarizing our discussion. Figures 5.8 and 5.9 provide the detailed and more complete framework. But some additional insight may be garnered by comparing the solution approaches we have considered on two dimensions of interest, as shown in Figure 5.10.

On one axis, we show legitimation/value complexity, which refers to the complexity of the values reflected in the decision problem. For example, Mike Cutter's problem is considerably more difficult in this regard than the cost minimization problem Bernie Munch faces. Many ethical problems have the same kind of value complexity as Mike Cutter's problem, including abortion rights, euthanasia, hand-gun control, and so on. Intermediate between Mike Cutter's problem and that of Bernie Munch we have a problem like that of Mr. Fidelity, which has some complexity in meeting the needs of different clients, but not all of the value complexity of Mike Cutter's problem.

The other axis in Figure 5.10 is labeled information-processing complexity. This might refer to the amount of data and manipulation required. It reflects the degree of difficulty that an unaided human decision maker would face in dealing with the information-processing issues associated with the problem in question. For example, Jane Officer's problem has a lot more data than that associated with Mike Cutter's problem.

Considering these two dimensions simultaneously, we see in Figure

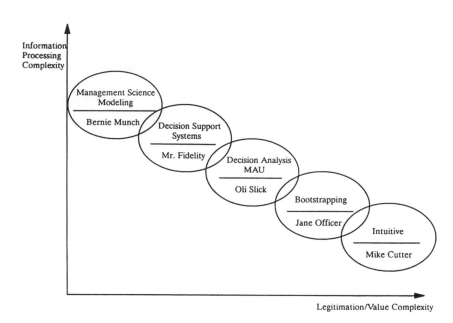

Figure 5.10. Information-processing and legitimation/value complexity. *Note*: Each circle represents a class of solution approaches and one of the examples discussed in Chapter 5.

5.10 that various problems and solution approaches can be plotted in various parts of this two-dimensional grid, depicting again in summary form the basic principle we have been considering throughout this chapter: Different problems require different solution approaches. We have attempted in this chapter to develop both a sensitivity to this basic principle and a framework, embodied in Figures 5.8 and 5.9, for prescriptive analysis of alternative solution approaches to fit various problems and problem contexts.

Part III

Multiperson decision making

6

Group decision making

6.1   Individuals, groups, and organizations

The importance of groups in decision making and social interaction is apparent. In addition to the compelling social reasons for group cooperation and coordinated action, it is also clear that information-processing and physical limitations of individuals imply the desirability, indeed necessity, that certain problems be solved by groups. For example, typical business planning problems require the specialized skills of experts in marketing, finance, operations, and human resources. Few individuals possess all of these skills and knowledge, making a group of experts unavoidable. Similarly, scientific problems as well as sociopolitical decision making usually require the expertise of more than one individual. Finally, social and family support groups are important to most of us in coping with complexity and uncertainty.

Our aim in this chapter and the next is to introduce important concepts for the descriptive and prescriptive analysis of groups, and to illustrate these with applications to some classic group decision-making problems. In doing so, we shall be following two different streams of research on groups. The first stream, based on theoretical and experimental work in social and industrial psychology, has been concerned with the decision processes used in groups. This first stream of research will be covered in this chapter. The second stream, based on economics and modern game theory, is normative, formal, and abstract in character, and will be the subject of the next chapter. As with our discussion of individual decision making, we are interested here in descriptive theories not just for their own sake but also as the foundation for prescriptive approaches to improving the outcome and process of group decision making.

The chapter proceeds as follows. First, we relate briefly group problem solving to the framework for individual decision making examined in previous chapters. We then consider several topics in the area of group process, including concepts such as polarization and conformity which are particular to groups. This discussion provides a basis for considering the classic problems of group choice and group judgment. We then briefly consider two examples of group choice in task-oriented groups, the first being that of group judgment and forecasting (e.g., the Delphi method) and the second "group planning," based on Ackoff (1978) and Saaty (1980).

6.2   Group problem finding and problem solving

Theories of group process have deep roots in philosophy, sociology, and psychology. In philosophy, especially since Hegel and Kierkegaard, it has been recognized that social interactions and institutions are central to our knowledge of the external world. Similarly, in sociology and psychology, the study of groups has been a foundation for understanding conflict and social interaction (as in Georg Simmel's work), the individual's relation to society (as in Emil Durkheim's pathbreaking work), and for understanding and developing emotional well-being (as in Kurt Lewin's research on group dynamics and therapy). Our own concern is with just a small subset of this broad literature, namely with group problem solving.[1]

We imagine a group of, say, 5 to 20 individuals concerned with identifying a problem, generating alternatives, and choosing among them. The problem might be one of group choice (e.g., the board of directors of a corporation deciding on whether to invest in a new technology) or group judgment (forecasting the sales that might be expected for a particular product line for the next five years). The phases of group problem solving are similar to those we have already examined at the individual level:

1. Problem finding and representation (as in Chapter 2).
2. Problem analysis (as in Chapter 3).
3. Evaluation and choice (as in Chapter 4).
4. Implementation, legitimation, and learning (as in Chapter 5).

It should be apparent from these phases of group problem solving that individual and group decision making have much in common. Indeed, groups can be studied from the perspective of the values, beliefs, and limitations of their individual members. However, groups also have integrative, existential characteristics, such as trust and cohesion, that go beyond simple extrapolations of values and beliefs of individual members in the group. It is these group-specific characteristics that will occupy our attention for much of this chapter. The interaction of individual characteristics and group processes is shown in Figure 6.1.

Figure 6.1 illustrates several important points. First, the performance of a group on a particular task depends on many interacting factors:

1 For an introduction to the history of group problem solving, see Cooper (1975).

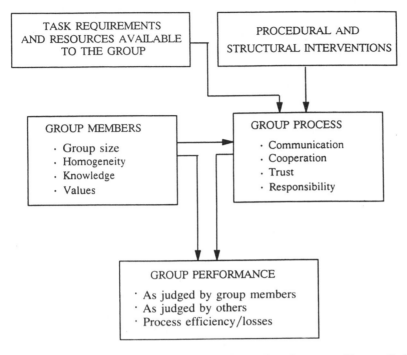

Figure 6.1. Group problem solving and performance (*Source*: Steiner, 1972)

- The nature of the task itself.
- The composition of the group in terms of heterogeneity/similarity of personal characteristics and backgrounds.
- The agenda the group follows.
- The interrelationships among the group members.
- The degree of power held by each individual.
- The behavior of the group leader.
- The time pressure and incentive structure under which the group operates.
- The resources available to the group (e.g., group members' knowledge, availability of data, computers, etc.) for its task.

We have categorized these aspects in the figure into factors depending on the task, the group, and the procedures imposed on (or voluntarily followed by) the group. Group performance, as an outcome of all of these interacting factors, must itself be understood in terms of several indicators: first, how group members themselves feel about what they have done; second, how others (perhaps the group's employer) judge the group's performance; and, finally, the efficiency in time and resources used by the group in its activity.

As noted by Bottger and Yetton (1988), following the pathbreaking work of Steiner (1972) and Davis (1973), group performance on a particular task is a function of both the resources available to the group and the strategies the group uses in employing these resources. In particular, the group process itself is central in predicting performance, as shown in Figure 6.1. For instance, performance depends on process issues such as communication and participative goal setting. Also what Steiner (1972) calls process losses, namely the transactions costs of group problem solving, depend directly on group process. For example, for certain problems, a participative process may yield higher subjective satisfaction among group members than an analytical process, but it may take much longer and be less effective in generating a good solution.[2] Finally, prescriptive recommendations to improve group decision making are best understood at the level of process, as most interventions are aimed at changing the group's procedures, information, or resources (see Figure 6.1).

In understanding group processes, let us first note that key features of individual problem finding and problem solving continue to manifest themselves at the group level. Information-processing limitations afflict groups as well as individuals (e.g., Driver and Streufert, 1969; Miller and Simons, 1974). Groups are also subject to framing effects and probability assessment biases, arising from effects similar to those that apply to individuals (e.g., Nisbett and Ross, 1980; Hogarth, 1987). In addition to properties inherited from their individual members, however, groups also have biases and characteristics of their own. It is these essentially group characteristics that we wish to concentrate on here. We begin with some examples of famous group blunders to illustrate the kinds of decision biases one may find in groups.[3]

6.2.1   *Groupthink, conformity, and polarization*

"How could we have been so stupid?" This was John F. Kennedy's reaction after the Bay of Pigs fiasco, which saw a CIA-financed group of Cuban expatriates attempt to invade and "take over" Cuba in 1962. The ragtag invasion troup was quickly wiped out by Cuba's alert armed forces. The United States stood humiliated as the rest of the world watched, incredulous at the impropriety and stupidity of the whole operation. The group who made this decision consisted of the best and brightest in the American government, including Dean Rusk, Robert McNamara, and the

2 See Vroom and Yettin (1973) for a map of the effects of participation on process losses and group effectiveness for various types of task. Nutt (1989) examines related results in a corporate planning context.

3 For entertaining reading on the very fallible nature of group decision making, see also Janis (1972) and Huxham and Dando (1981).

Kennedy brothers, John and Robert. This group did not fail because these people were intellectually inferior. What happened is that the group followed a poor process, arrived at a poor solution, and then spent its energies warding off challenges to the group consensus. This phenomenon was termed "groupthink" by Irving Janis (1972).

There are numerous political and military blunders that exhibit the same inexplicably foolish character: Pearl Harbor in 1941, the U.S. invasion of North Korea in 1951, the Vietnam War in the 1960s, the Watergate scandal leading to President Nixon's resignation in 1974, and the more recent Iran–Contra scandal toward the end of the Reagan administration. These are well-documented public sector blunders, but there are plenty in the private sector as well.

A well-known corporate example concerns the Corvair story at General Motors. The intent had been to develop a sporty and innovative car to compete with the Ford Mustang in the mid 1960s. This project turned out to be a disaster, mainly because of the Corvair's poor safety record. Even though GM employees had objected to safety issues, somehow these were not sufficiently taken into account. And although clearly no one in GM's top management would purposely build an unsafe car, efforts of the management team to push for increased sales and profits resulted in this ill-fated new automobile.

A similar process seems to have occurred within NASA and Morton Thokiol (an engineering firm), leading to the much-publicized explosion of the shuttle *Challenger* in January 1986. In this case, there was some evidence before the fact that low temperatures could lead to the failure of O-rings (the failure of one or more of these was the acknowledged cause of the *Challenger*'s midair explosion). Yet, after some last-minute discussion and teleconferencing among responsible executives before the planned launch, these problems were discounted and the *Challenger* launch was undertaken when the outside temperature was near freezing at the launch site. Another group decision-making disaster! We see from these examples that, too often, smart groups of people end up making very unwise decisions. Why?

Upon analyzing the circumstances under which these groups function, researchers discovered some common elements. Often groups that failed to make wise decisions were highly cohesive, in which people knew each other well and liked each other. Insulation of the group due to the secrecy of the issue or for other reasons also seemed to be a common factor. Strong directive leadership, with the chairperson saying clearly what he or she favored, seemed also present. Finally, high stress in terms of deadlines, the importance of the decision, and its complexity all seemed to be contributing factors to the resulting "groupthink." As Janis (1972) explains, groupthink is a characteristic of group decision making that causes otherwise capable individuals to make manifestly poor decisions in a group setting. Groupthink has distinct symptoms such as an illusion of invulnerability, stereotyping of people outside the group, and putting pressures on people inside the group who disagree with the majority opinion to remain silent. Self-censorship – that is, not speaking up against the majority opinion for fear of ridicule or the desire to keep harmony – is an important symptom as well. The end result of groupthink is that too few alternatives are examined and too few objectives are taken into account. Information search is usually poor, with few counterarguments to the preferred alternative being discussed. In general, groupthink seems to occur when the desire to be efficient or not to rock the boat becomes more important than the quality of the decision itself.

Fortunately, there are some useful remedies for groupthink.[4] They entail trying to delay consensus, spreading power, seeking additional inputs, and encouraging conflict among ideas (as opposed to among people). For example, it is useful if the leader remains impartial and does not reveal his or her own ideas too quickly or too strongly. Also, the "devil's advocate" position should be elevated to an important role and rotated so that the same person does not always end up being the devil's advocate (with the danger of being discounted or ignored). Breaking a group up into subgroups and asking the subgroups to report back to the main group is also an effective way to encourage diversity of views. Likewise, inviting outside experts, especially those who are known to disagree with the initial leaning of the group, is a good way to introduce new considerations. Finally, role-playing adversaries and other stakeholders is an excellent technique to assure a multiplicity of viewpoints. The key, as Janis (1972), Mason and Mitroff (1981), and Nutt (1989) have argued, is to encourage diversity and to challenge assumptions before a convergence and choice are attempted. If we recall Toulmin's theory of argument in Chapter 3, fleshing out good rebuttals is central to avoiding groupthink.

Groupthink illustrates the negative consequences of group conformity and self-censorship. The classic experiment on conformity was conducted by Asch (1956). He showed people three lines of the type shown in Figure 6.2. The lines are labeled *A*, *B*, and *C*, and the subject is asked which of these three lines is equal in length to the test line, shown on the left. When subjects are asked to do this alone, 99% get it right. Only those with poor vision, or perhaps those under the influence of drugs, could miss this very simple straightforward judgment. However, what happens

---

4 See Park (1990) for a recent review of the literature on groupthink and remedies for it. Esser and Lindoerfer (1989) examine groupthink in the context of the *Challenger* explosion.

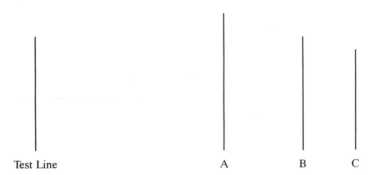

Test Line   A   B   C

Is the Test Line equal in length to A, B, or C?

Condition	Error Rate
Subject is alone	1%
With 1 person who says "A"	3%
With 2 who say "A"	13%
With 3 who say "A"	33%
With 6 who say "A" and 1 who says "B"	6%
Group Reward	47%

Figure 6.2. The Asch experiment (*Source*: Asch, 1956)

if you are in a lineup with one other person who answers before you do? In the Asch experiment, the people preceding the subject were actually part of the experiment and were instructed to say the wrong line, namely Line *A*. When one person before the subject says *A*, the error rate jumps from 1% to 3%. If two people in front of the subject both say *A*, 13% of the subjects also say *A*. When three or more persons before the subject say *A*, this error rate becomes as high as 33% for a judgment as obvious as Figure 6.2. Moreover, if the people in the lineup are told that a group reward will be given depending on how many in the group get it right, then 47% of the subjects give the wrong answer. Note, however, that if one other person says Line *B*, even with six others voting for Line *A*, the error rate of the final respondent drops to only 6%. Thus, a little bit of support goes a long way to reinforcing truth.

It is not always clear whether subjects say what they don't believe, or whether hearing other people's opinions first actually causes them to change their own minds. Evidence has been reported for both of these explanations (see Moscovici, 1985). As a practical issue, however, what matters is that people can be influenced in group settings to go against their better judgment. If such social influence exists with these rather simple judgments, imagine how much hearing other people speak might influence what you have to say on a complex issue, such as whether to invade a country, or what new car to build. Hence, one of the dilemmas in group decision making is that even though two people should know more than one, they start to influence each other so that the full benefit of their independent opinions is not always realized. One solution is to keep the opinions independent by simply polling people beforehand and not having them exchange views. This is the essence of the Delphi technique which we discuss further below. However, for certain kinds of problems, interaction and open dialectical processes are important to arrive at a better overall judgment.

The problem of social influence in groups is also manifested in a phenomenon called the "polarization effect." This finding was originally published under the label of "the risky shift." Stoner (1968) found that after a group had debated whether to invest in a particular project, the group often ended up being more likely to take risks than the individual opinions prior to the group meeting would have predicted. This was surprising in that most people believe groups to moderate extreme views, rather than accentuate them. However, under many conditions there is a tendency for groups to polarize the majority opinion, if one exists to begin with (Moscovici and Zavalloni, 1969, and Doise, 1969). In case there are two powerful factions, one arguing pro and one arguing con, the group will usually moderate. That is, the group judgment will be in between the means of those two factions. However, if there is an initial leaning in the group toward Alternative X over Y, then there is a significant probability that the group opinion will shift even further in the direction of X.

One reason is that the arguments in favor of X may get much more "air time" than those in favor of Y. A second is that people in groups take diluted responsibility for the group action (in the extreme, leading to crowd madness such as lynching). A third is that people who desire to be more risk taking than average realize that they are not that extreme at all, leading to greater individual extremity. A fourth reason, related to the groupthink literature, may be the group's tendency to imbue Alternative X with greater value than it may have on a priori grounds of individual preferences, in order for the group to legitimate the choice of X over Y as obvious.[5]

An alternative explanation of choice shift in groups has been offered by Neale, Bazerman, Northcraft, and Alperson (1986) who have argued that the choice shift or polarization effect may be due to framing factors.

---

5 At the individual level, such rationalizations directed toward making chosen alternatives appear "superior" are often seen and have been documented thoroughly by Leon Festinger (1964) in his work on "cognitive dissonance."

We know from our discussion of Chapter 4 that individuals tend to be risk averse in positively framed choice situations and risk prone in negatively framed situations. Neale et al. argue that groups may find it easier to communicate risk-neutral preferences than risk-averse preferences. Thus, group discussion may attenuate both risk-averse and risk-prone dispositions of individual group members, moving the group's "effective preferences" in the direction of risk neutrality. The result of this is that groups tend to make more risky choices than their individual members in positively framed choice situations (e.g., an investment decision that is framed in terms of the potential earnings resulting from the investment) and more cautious choices than their individual members in negatively framed choice situations (e.g., the same investment decision framed in terms of the potential losses that might result in negative states of the world). Neale et al. find some experimental support for this framing explanation of group choice shift effects.

Whatever the specific reasons, these interesting experimental results suggest that groups do not simply average individual choices and opinions, but tend to add or detract something from them. Whether this change is positive or negative depends on many variables that are difficult to generalize about.

Conformity and polarization are but two characteristics of decision processes particular to groups. The most important other interpersonal issues in the groups are trust, communication, and cooperation, as well as related performance and learning effects. As we shall see in our discussion of experimental results later in the chapter, a central finding of the social psychology literature on groups is that communication, trust, and cooperation are mutually reinforcing (see Golembiewski and McConkie, 1975). Communication tends to reinforce both cooperation and the ability to design creative compromise solutions (see Steinfatt and Miller, 1974, and Dawes, 1980), whereas lack of trust undermines both communication and cooperation. Argyris and Schon (1974) point out, for example, that lack of trust leads to defensive behavior, such as relying on easily defensible and accepted theories, with a consequent lack of openness to creative problem solving and learning from the environment and fellow group members. This research highlights the fragile nature of trust and communication in creative problem solving. It is quite easy to fall into the closed and sterile mode of groupthink rather than to promote openness, dialectical testing of arguments, counterarguments, and learning.

6.2.2   *Group decision support systems*

The most important implication of these considerations for group problem solving is that openness and learning must be actively pursued. One common obstacle to effective group problem solving is, of course, bounded rationality – that is, the group's inability to evaluate possible compromise solutions. As a result, group members may choose whichever alternative appears initially "safest" and begin marching down the path of groupthink to shore up their position. Referring to Figure 6.1, if the demands of the task and the available resources are mismatched, an obvious solution would be to use computers or other decision aids to support the group's decision process. Such support can facilitate communication, as well as the generation and evaluation of alternatives. Group decision support systems are growing in number and scope (see, e.g., Adelman, 1984, 1988; Rao and Jarvenpaa, 1991). Typical group decision support systems (GDSS) entail a meeting room with enough computer terminals to accommodate a group of 10–15 individuals. The group terminals are networked and serviced by a master work station (MWS), controlled by a facilitator (see Figure 6.3). The input of any group member, as well as summaries of the group's inputs and decisions, are shared visually through an overhead projection controlled by the facilitator, which is visible to each group member (see also Phillips, 1982, regarding requisite decision modeling).

A typical session using such a GDSS would proceed as follows (see Nunamaker, Dennis, Valacich, and Vogel, 1991, for a discussion of this type of GDSS session and supporting hardware and software).

Step 1: Statement of the group task

The group would discuss its task and agree to a succinct verbal summary of this task. A typical task for a quality improvement team might be the following:

> "Understand and improve the speed and accuracy of sales order fulfillment to our industrial customers."

Step 2: Electronic brainstorming

Each group member would input into his/her terminal as many ideas as possible related to the task at hand. In the case of the task of improving sales order fulfillment, the group members would probably type in what they believe the sources of current problems with deliveries to be. As these are typed in by individual group members, they would also be projected on the screen visible to all group members (and remain available for further classification and discussion).

Step 3: Idea classification

Ideas generated in Step 2 would be grouped together and redundant ideas would be consolidated.

Step 4: Prioritization of alternatives

The group would prioritize the most important approaches to the problem at hand. In the case of the sales order fulfillment task, the most important problems would first be highlighted. Then possibly each of these problems would be subjected to Steps 1–3 to determine possible approaches to this problem. This prior-

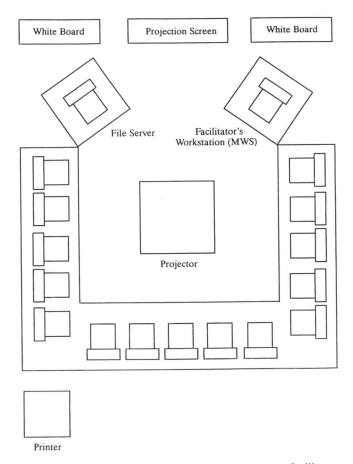

| White Board | Projection Screen | White Board |

File Server

Facilitator's
Workstation (MWS)

Projector

Printer

Figure 6.3. Typical group decision support system facility

itization might be accomplished using various voting methods to be described in Chapter 7. But the prioritization could be just on the basis of group discussion and consensus.

Step 5: Assignment of follow-up responsibilities

Responsibilities would be assigned to group members to implement the group's decisions.

This GDSS may look simple, but it is actually a very powerful intervention. Note that the group has a record of its activities in machine-readable form after it has finished a session of the described type. This facilitates implementation and follow-up. Perhaps most important, the above process considerably improves the efficiency of group interactions and thus decreases process losses in group problem solving. Moreover, by

IDEA

implementing anonymous voting and information gathering in Steps 2 and 4, the GDSS process can reduce the problems caused by conformity and groupthink.

A recent application of GDSS to strategic technology planning by Kleindorfer and Partovi (1989) used the analytical hierarchy process (AHP) of Saaty (1980, 1991). Such planning typically involves top managers from manufacturing, engineering, finance, and marketing, who must decide which of several alternative technologies to adopt for the firm's manufacturing operations. Just as in the production planning example of Chapter 1, each of the firm's experts may hold very different views and skills, which he brings to this discussion. Because technology choice can have important strategic consequences for the firm, it is critical that the technology planning group engage in a thorough and open discussion. To avoid falling prey to defensiveness and groupthink, Kleindorfer and Partovi developed a planning process, based on a group decision support system, to surface technological priorities from the widely varying perspectives of the stakeholders involved. By summarizing these priorities and related financial information in easily understood form, communication was greatly facilitated. Moreover, when there are disagreements, group members are able to examine their source in terms of underlying assumptions and valuations of available options. Thus, the rationale for and against various alternatives becomes more transparent, challengeable, and ultimately defensible. This emphasizes the main point of group decision support systems, namely to enhance the information-processing resources available to the group through the intelligent use of information technology.

6.2.3   *Dialectics, conflict resolution, and legitimation*

We introduced the concept of dialectics in Chapter 5. The foundations of dialectics were first developed by the great philosopher Hegel (1770–1831), who explored in his writings the benefits of conflict. He noted that a dialectical process that actively weighs both the pros and cons of a given theory or course of action can yield a better sense of what is right than a process that only seeks consensus. (Of course, the process losses from such a dialectical process may be higher than for a consensual process.) Hegel argued that a dialectical process provides a sense not just of what is right but also how right or plausible a theory or course of action is. This same idea has been advanced by several decision scientists as a means of increasing the effectiveness of group planning (e.g., Churchman, 1971; Mason and Mitroff, 1973). The dialectical approach, in which one side advances its arguments and the other side does likewise, while a third party tries to reconcile the conflicting viewpoints, has a long tradition in European philosophy and Western law. It reflects Hegel's view that on complex issues a thesis needs to be developed as well as a counterthesis (called the antithesis), so that the best of both views can be combined in a synthesis that is superior to either of its antagonistic components. The synthesis developed enjoys a legitimacy that is colored and strengthened by its relationship to the opposing points of view leading to it as synthesis, just as the truth claim in the theory of argument (see Chapter 3) is enhanced by exploration of rebuttals as well as warrants and backings.

The dialectical approach has been especially embraced in legal disputes, where it is very difficult to determine by scientific or objective means where the truth lies. Hence, the courts and the public at large put their faith in a particular process for deciding the truth, rather than in a particular body of knowledge or any particular individual. (In Anglo-Saxon law, a professional judge may decide, however.) Through public and adversarial (read dialectical) hearings, following a carefully developed code of conduct, the judicial courts try to distill from the conflicting pieces of evidence presented on which side the truth lies. A similar process, less formal but no less dialectical, is followed in many corporations when subgroups within the planning department are given the task of advocating differing, conflicting courses of action (e.g., Mason and Mitroff, 1981). If such a process is to succeed, a mechanism must exist to achieve a synthesis or consensus after the conflicting points of view have been explored. In the corporate planning context this may be straightforward – top management has the power to make a decision as to which course of action is the most appropriate. In other instances, however, resolving conflicting points of view is not so easy, especially in the public sector. When conflict resolution cannot be anticipated by amicable compromise or by means of someone in power enforcing consensus, legitimation of decision quality must be pursued by other means. One approach is the social judgment theory advanced by Kenneth Hammond and his associates (see Hammond, Rohrbaugh, Mumpower, and Adelman, 1977).

6.2.4 *Social judgment theory*

We illustrate the ideas of social judgment theory by describing its application to the very controversial decision of the city of Denver about a new bullet that the police department wished to introduce to better "immobilize" suspects. The police department maintained that they needed a new bullet because bullets used by the department had been ineffective in stopping escaping suspects. The minority community in Denver was especially angered by the prospect of a new, heavier bullet; they wanted to ensure that no injury would occur to innocent suspects or possibly

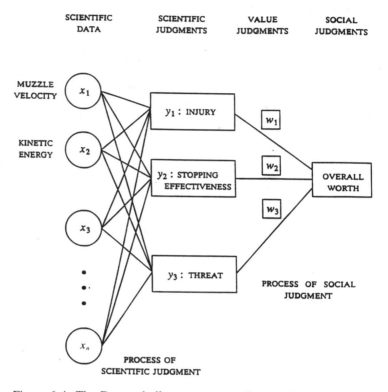

Figure 6.4. The Denver bullet controversy (*Source*: Hammond, Rohr-baugh, Mumpower, and Adelman, 1977. Reprinted by permission)

innocent bystanders. The issue quickly assumed great emotional impor-tance and led to a stalemate situation, in which each side had its own ballistics experts testify in favor of its proposed bullet. It became clear that this dialectic process, in which experts were essentially hired guns, was not leading to a satisfactory resolution of this important public policy issue. Hence, it was decided to hire a decision consultant, Hammond and his associates, who introduced a rather different framework for resolving this conflict.

The decision consultant recognized that there was a confusion of facts and values in the debate. His proposal was to separate clearly the value judgments from the factual ones, by using a framework of the type shown in Figure 6.4. The left side contains the specific features across which the various candidate bullets differed, defined in a scientific and objective manner – for example, bullets differ in their kinetic energy, muzzle ve-locity, weight, shape and penetration ability. However, these microattributes of the bullets are not very meaningful to politicians or the public in general. These latter groups think more in terms of the variables shown in the middle of the diagram, namely how the bullets differ with respect to injury potential, stopping effectiveness, threat to bystanders, and so on. To provide a mapping from the scientific attributes (denoted x_i) to the socially relevant attributes (denoted y_i), scientific judgments are needed from ballistic experts. Politicians and the public at large should have no substantive input into these judgments. Their role is to select the right variables y_i and the right experts and to ensure the integrity of the process.

Once all the x_i variables have been linked or mapped into y_i variables, the question arises, which combination of the feasible y_i levels is most desirable from a public policy viewpoint? This is denoted in Figure 6.4 by the box on the right side, labeled "overall worth." Defining the ideal bullet, in terms of y_i variables, depends on the trade-offs one is willing to make between, for example, increased injury potential versus increased stopping effectiveness. This trade-off is essentially a political or public judgment, not to be made by the police department only. It can be thought of as determining a set of policy weights (denoted w_1 through w_n) which indicate the priorities that the community in Denver gives to the various desiderata. By decomposing the problem into a set of scientific judgments and a separate set of value judgments, Hammond and his associates were able to identify a bullet that was acceptable in the view of all parties concerned.

One benefit of social judgment theory, seen in this example, is that the people making the scientific judgments need not be informed about the policy or value weights w_i, whereas policy makers need not really know how a given bullet scores in terms of its y_i values. In ascertaining the policy weights, Hammond et al. asked the policy makers to choose among hypothetical as well as real bullets, defined only in terms of their y_i variables, so as to disguise the particulars of the bullets that had earlier given rise to controversy. (In essence, they built a bootstrap model of the policy makers' judgments.) By imposing a veil of partial ignorance, the problem was stripped of its emotional context. It also reduced distorting the facts to fit one's precommitments (i.e., gaming). The separation of facts and values, as in this one application of social judgment theory, is often a good technique in dealing with complex and emotionally charged issues.

To summarize, we have discussed two rather different approaches to group problem solving and conflict resolution. One might be labeled the holistic approach, in which different factions (possibly appointed by the group itself) argue things out, subject to certain rules of evidence and procedure. The other method, followed by social judgment theory, imposes a priori a clear framework that limits people's roles to either those of value experts or fact (scientific) experts.

6.3   Aggregation of opinions and probabilities

If we follow the social judgment theory approach and recognize separate roles for fact and value estimation, then a natural question arises as to what to do when group members disagree about either facts or values. To take the preceding example, what happens if several experts estimate the x_i values in Figure 6.4 and they disagree on their estimates, for example, of muzzle velocity of one of the bullets? What estimate should then be used? Similarly, what should the city council do in the same context when its members, representing different citizen constituencies, have different value trade-offs as embodied in the value weights w_i? We provide some answers in this section to the first question, aggregating expert opinions to obtain a group judgment. We analyze the second question later in the chapter under the topics of negotiation and collective choice. We note right away that neither the group judgment nor the group choice problem has a unique and compelling answer, even when these topics are taken separately.[6] Different contexts may require different procedures. Moreover, when there is severe disagreement about facts or values in a given group, a collective opinion or consensus choice may simply not be possible. Indeed, a major purpose of research on group decision making is to recognize both the possibilities for achieving group consensus as well as the inherent limitations involved in group choice.

6.3.1   *Group estimation of probabilities*

So what can be done to achieve a "group judgment" when group members disagree. The question is relevant to oil companies predicting the oil price based on internal surveys as well as ballistic experts trying to estimate the muzzle velocity of a bullet. The simple answer seems to be just to average the experts' opinions. However, this is neither as simple nor as desirable as it initially sounds. Let's use two prediction problems to illustrate the underlying issues.

Consider just two experts, equally qualified, who have rendered independent opinions on the success or failure of two investments, called A and B. Also, they have indicated the joint probabilities of these investments, recognizing the importance of taking a portfolio perspective. Their views are as given in Table 6.1. In this example (due to Raiffa, 1968), Expert I believes Project A to have a 30% chance of success, and Project B an 80% chance. Expert II on the other hand believes these probabilities to be 70% and 20% respectively (almost reversed!). As for

---

6 When both fact and value estimation must be accomplished simultaneously, of course, even greater problems exist (see Bacharach, 1975).

Table 6.1. *Data for prediction example for Projects A and B (%)*

	Expert I			Expert II		
	Success (A)	Failure (A)	Tot.	Success (A)	Failure (A)	Tot.
Success (B)	24	56	80	14	6	20
Failure (B)	6	14	20	56	24	80
Totals	30	70	100	70	30	100

Table 6.2. *Illustrating expert opinion aggregation for Projects A and B (%)*

	Averaging joint probabilities			Average marginal probabilities		
	Success (A)	Failure (A)	Tot.	Success (A)	Failure (A)	Tot.
Success (B)	19	31	50	25	25	50
Failure (B)	31	19	50	25	25	50
Totals	50	50	50	50	50	100

the joint probabilities, Expert I assumes there is a 24% chance that both projects will succeed, versus 14% according to Expert II. Note, however, that these experts do agree on one thing: Both believe that the outcome of Project *A* is unrelated to that of Project *B*. This statistical independence follows because all joint probabilities are simply the product of their corresponding marginal probabilities (i.e., the associated row and column probabilities).

Suppose we now wish to somehow "average" the views of these equally competent experts. Should we average the joint probabilities (i.e., the entries inside the matrix) or the marginal probabilities (i.e., those at the border). And does it matter? To find out, let's do both (see Table 6.2).

In the left matrix, each cell entry is the average of the two experts' opinions (e.g., 31% = (6% + 56%)/2). The border numbers were obtained (via addition) after averaging the margins. In the right matrix, the marginal probabilities were first obtained by averaging the experts (e.g., 50% in the first row is the average of 80% and 20%). Thereafter, the joint probabilities were obtained by multiplying the marginals. Note that both methods result in the same marginal probabilities. This is generally true if Projects *A* and *B* are statistically independent (but not otherwise). However, the *joint* probabilities will almost always differ between the two methods, even under high symmetry and statistical independence.

Because both methods agree on the marginals, one might argue for the one that averages the joint probabilities, (i.e., the left one). Note, however, that in the left matrix Projects *A* and *B* are no longer statistically independent. Success in both projects is now 19%, rather than the 25% the independent marginals imply. Because both experts agree on the statistical independence of the projects, should that not be preserved in whatever aggregation method one uses? As we shall see shortly, there is no simple answer here.

However, first we should emphasize that this problem not only arises in multivariate cases. Consider the following additional example. Two experts both agree that the future oil price (e.g., one year from now) is approximately a normal distribution (truncated at $0 and say $100). They even agree on the standard deviation. Only their means are different: $20 versus $30. If we assume the experts are equally competent, should the average of these opinions be a normal distribution with mean $25, or a bimodal distribution obtained when adding the two distributions and normalizing? The case for the normal can be made by arguing that one should preserve what the experts agree on, that is, a Gaussian distribution of fixed variance. The case for the bimodal can be made via simulation. Suppose you randomly (with 50–50 chances) listened to one or the other expert, and selected a price at random from his distribution. What frequency distribution would you end up with after repeating this process a million times? Answer: a bimodal distribution with a peak around $20 and one around $30. The bimodal highlights the experts' *dis*agreement, rather than what they agree on.

The dilemma is that you cannot have it both ways. Each method has both desirable and undesirable features. In fact, there are many ways to average out distributions, and there simply is no one best method for all cases. The first step is to recognize that one must choose among incompatible criteria. We shall encounter similar impossibility dilemmas in the next chapter on group choice. The following are some a priori properties one may or may not wish an averaging method to satisfy.

P1. *Preservation of distributional form*

If all experts agree on the distributional form (e.g., normals), then the aggregate distribution should also have this form.

P2. *Sample size independence*

Polling more experts (randomly) should not lead to a systematic change in the shape (e.g., variance) of the aggregate distribution, if we assume experts' distributions are randomly drawn from some population of experts.

P3. *Sensitivity to expert opinion*

If some experts change their views in one direction (without any changes in the views of other experts), the aggregate distribution should change in that direction as well.

P4. *Expert intercorrelation*

The method should be able to reflect the dependence among experts. For example, if an expert were polled twice (being perfectly correlated with herself), this should not affect the distribution. Adding a highly correlated expert should have less impact than adding one less correlated with the others.

P5. *Consensus reflection*

If all experts agree that Event A is more probable than Event B, so should the aggregate distribution. For example, if all experts agree that the possibility that next year's price of oil will be less than \$20 a barrel is more likely than the possibility that it will be greater than \$30 a barrel, then the aggregate distribution should reflect this consensus. Also, if all agree on statistical independence among variables, so should the aggregate distributions.

These properties are just to illustrate possible desiderata. They are not stated formally (see Genest and Zidek, 1986, for a review of formal models), and there are many other conditions one might wish to impose. The key point is that many of these conditions are likely to be *mutually incompatible*. Several impossibility theorems exist (see Bacharach, 1975) that prove this incompatibility formally. These theorems underscore that our intuitive conceptions about group rationality are often naive and unattainable. They reflect a fallacy of composition in which we view groups as though they were a single individual.

From a practical standpoint, the best approach would be first to identify the desirable properties one strives for (e.g., P1 through P5). Then, consider the various methods for taking averages, and score for each method what properties it satisfies. A metadecision can then be made on how to average based on how important each of the desired properties is. To illustrate, consider just two averaging methods:

M1. Add distributions and renormalize (e.g., as in the bimodal example). In the case of two normal distributions $f_i(x; \mu_i, \sigma_i, \rho)$, $i = 1, 2$, with mean μ_i, standard deviation σ_i, and correlation ρ, the group aggregate distribution would be given by $f_{12}(x) = [f_1(x) + f_2(x)]/2$, assuming equal weighting.

M2. Average selected moments (e.g., means and variances, as in the normal example). In the case of two normal distributions, as above, this would yield $f_{12}(x) = f_{12}(x; \mu_{12}, \sigma_{12})$, a normal distribution, with mean $\mu_{12} = (\mu_1 + \mu_2)/2$ and standard deviation $\sigma_{12} = (\sigma_1 + \sigma_2)/2$.

Table 6.3 indicates the properties M1 and M2 each satisfies, with room for other methods to be added. We note that P5 here refers only to consensus reflection on events (that is, if both experts deem Event A more

Table 6.3. *Properties of two judgment aggregation methods*

	Properties				
	P1	P2	P3	P4	P5[a]
Methods					
M1	−	+	+	−	+
M2	+	+	+	−	−

[a] P5 here refers only to consensus reflection on events.

probable than B, then their aggregate opinion should also reflect this), but not on such other properties as statistical independence.[7]

As in Chapter 5, one would have to evaluate the relative importance of the properties P1–P5 and other process variables (such as the transactions cost of performing the aggregation, storing, communicating, and defending the results) in deciding whether M1 or M2 were the superior method for a particular problem.

A property that neither of these two methods satisfies is P4, reflecting correlation among experts. A practical and theoretically sound (i.e., internally consistent) method for dealing with P4 is the Bayesian approach developed by Winkler (1981). It assumes that you (the analyst) know for each expert what her best guess is and how much confidence she has in this estimate (based either on a standard deviation estimate or a confidence range such as the [5%, 95%] interval). Moreover, it assumes that each expert's subjective probability distribution is normal. The analyst must then estimate for each pair of experts to what extent their predictions are correlated, perhaps using historical data if available. With this information, a Bayesian procedure is used to arrive at a "consensus distribution," which will be normal as well. Its mean is a weighted average of the individual experts' means, with the weights reflecting differences in both confidence and intercorrelations.

To illustrate the method with a numerical example, assume that three experts have estimated some future commodity price. Their best guesses

7 The properties in this table are relatively intuitive. Concerning P5, note that by definition of M1 as the average of the density functions (i.e., of elementary event probabilities), M1 satisfies P5. But M2 does not, as the reader may verify by taking two distributions with the same standard deviation but with means that are far apart. Then, for some $\mu > 0$, consider the events $A = \{x \in \Re \mid \mu_1 - \Delta \le x \le \mu_1 + \Delta \text{ or } \mu_2 - x \le \mu_2 + \Delta\}$ and $B = \{x \in \Re \mid \mu - \Delta \le x \le \mu + \Delta\}$, with $\mu = (\mu_1 + \mu_2)/2$. If, say, $\mu_2 - \mu_1 > 10\sigma$ (σ being the common standard deviation), then it is easily seen that A is more probable than B according to both distributions f_i, $i = 1, 2$, but that B is more probable than A according to the aggregate distribution resulting from M2.

Table 6.4. *Calculations for Winkler's Bayesian method*

Inputs	k = number of experts
	μ_i = mean estimate of Expert i
	σ_i = standard deviation of Expert i
	r_{ij} = correlation between Expert i and j
	(All distributions are assumed to be normal)
Transformations	C = covariance matrix where $c_{ij} = r_{ij}\sigma_i\sigma_j$
	$A = C^{-1}$ (inverse of matrix C) with elements a_{ij}
	$$w_i = \left(\sum_{j=1}^{k} a_{ij}\right) \Big/ \left(\sum_{m=1}^{k}\sum_{j=1}^{k} a_{mj}\right)$$
Outputs	μ = mean estimate for the group of experts
	σ = standard deviation of group estimate
where	$$\mu = \sum_{i=1}^{k} w_i\mu_i \qquad \sigma = \sqrt{1/(eAe')}$$
	with $\mathbf{e} = (1, \ldots, 1)$ and $\mathbf{e}'$ the transpose of $\mathbf{e}$

and standard deviations (in parentheses) are $60 (6), $62 (5), and $70 (7) respectively. Moreover, let their intercorrelations be $r_{12} = .6$, $r_{13} = .5$, and $r_{23} = .6$. If we assume normality, Winkler's proposed averaging procedure (see Table 6.4) gives 26% weight to Expert 1, 67% to Expert 2, and only 7% to Expert 3. Expert 3 counts little because of his relatively low confidence and high correlation with the other two experts. The weighted average of the consensus distribution is calculated as being 62. The consensus standard deviation is calculated in a more complicated manner (as shown in Table 6.4) and is lower than those of the individual experts, namely 4.8 due to diversification effects. This estimate reflects the positive correlations among the experts' opinions. If there were no such correlation (i.e., $r_{ij} = 0$), then the consensus standard deviation would be even smaller, namely 3.36. It would yet be lower if the experts were negatively correlated, due to the "portfolio effect" of independent or off-setting information sources in reducing risk. In the case of zero correlation, the weights would be 32%, 45%, and 23%, with a new consensus mean of 63.

6.3.2 Feedback, learning, and the Delphi method

We know from our discussion of individual decision making that individuals tend to exhibit various biases, as examined in Chapter 3. Can

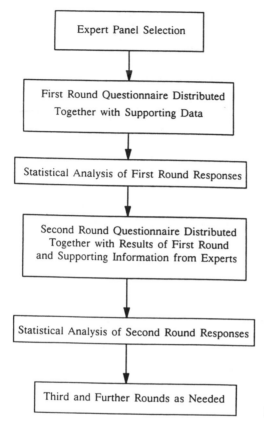

Figure 6.5. The Delphi method

group judgments correct such biases? The answer seems to be yes, to some extent. From both a theoretical point of view (Einhorn, Hogarth, and Klempner, 1977) as well as from experimental results (Dawes and Corrigan, 1974), group judgments appear to be more accurate than the judgments of the typical (i.e., randomly chosen) group member. As discussed in Chapter 3 under bootstrapping, averaging multiple opinions usually yields the benefit of canceling errors. One might conjecture that the benefits of group judgment can be further enhanced by allowing group members to interact in some fashion. And this indeed is borne out in some experimental research (Linstone and Turoff, 1975). On the other hand, our discussion of groupthink and other group biases provides a caution that group interaction should be controlled to assure that diverse opinions and minority views are not suppressed.

In general, we can imagine several levels of social interaction for ar-

Table 6.5. *Illustrative first-round questionnaire*

Widget industry sales estimates 1992–1996

The following figures and graph show historical sales figures for widgets for the last five years. Please indicate your estimate for each of the next five years for total industry sales (in $000s) and for the Wacky Widget Company's sales.

Year	% Increase industry sales	Industry sales	Wacky Widget sales
1985	8.2	1,100	340
1986	9.1	1,200	370
1987	12.5	1,350	410
1988	3.7	1,400	505
1989	1.8	1,425	515
1990	—	—	—
1991	—	—	—
1992	—	—	—
1993	—	—	—
1994	—	—	—

Please return this questionnaire to the Delphi facilitator with any supporting information you wish distributed to the panel.

Source: Based on the Delphi process used at the American Hoise & Derrick Company (see Basu and Schroeder, 1977).

riving at a group judgment, ranging from open committee meetings and conference calls on the telephone to more anonymous and statistical methods. When there is reason to believe that some group members may be "gaming" the facts or that social interaction may lead to polarization and conformity rather than learning and open discussion, then a more anonymous aggregation procedure is preferred. The best known method for controlled, anonymous group interaction is the Delphi method (see Linstone and Turoff, 1975), which we shall briefly describe by means of a forecasting example using the Wacky Widget Company.

Imagine a panel of 15 to 20 "experts" from Wacky who are interested in forecasting the company's sales for the next five years. The Delphi process proceeds as shown in Figure 6.5. After the panel is selected (for size, balance, and expertise), data on the past sales of the company and various external estimates of the future business climate are distributed to all, together with the requested estimates. Table 6.5 illustrates a typical first-round questionnaire of the Delphi method.

After all panel members have responded anonymously to the first-round questionnaire, results are statistically summarized (means, standard deviations, ranges, etc.) and distributed to the panel members in a second-round questionnaire. This second-round questionnaire is entirely similar to the first-round questionnaire except that a statistical summary of first-round responses from the panel is also enclosed. This second-round questionnaire may also be accompanied by supporting material (reports from the literature on business activity or other pertinent data) that panel members feel appropriate to share with one another. The Delphi process continues in this way until an equilibrium is achieved (i.e., until little change in the distribution of responses from the panel is experienced any more), which usually takes only three or four rounds.

Some of the salient characteristics of the Delphi method are the following. First, the questionnaires and responses are anonymous to avoid polarization and conformity, and to promote thoughtful responses and learning, without defensiveness. In spite of this anonymity, participants are involved and can provide information to their fellow panelists (anonymously) throughout the process (although the Delphi facilitator may have to "neutralize" supporting information to maintain anonymity). Finally, note that the Delphi method can in principle use any of the statistical aggregation methods (such as Winkler's) in providing feedback to panelists after each round of responses. Delphi's intent is to add to the benefits of statistical aggregation, discussed previously, some controlled feedback and learning. Judgmental methods such as Delphi have continued to be important and practical methods for forecasting and expert opinion aggregation since they were first introduced in the 1950s by Norman Dalkey and Olaf Helmer at the Rand Corporation to forecast trends related to military systems and strategies.

6.4   Group decision processes and planning

In this section we consider the important application area of strategic planning. Because of the many skills required to develop any complex plan, this is by its very nature a group decision. For concreteness, we shall be considering an organizational planning context such as the production planning problem or the blood bank problem of Chapter 1. Imagine a group of 5 to 15 people with the responsibility to develop a strategic plan for their organization that will spell out what they expect to happen in the next 1–5 years and what goals they believe their organization should strive to accomplish.

We view strategic planning here as the evaluation and choice processes that determine how the world will be viewed, and the goals that the organization will pursue given this world view. It is the interaction between the planning group's representation of the environment and the specification of goals in terms of this representation that provides the challenge of strategic planning. As a result, representing the environment and spec-

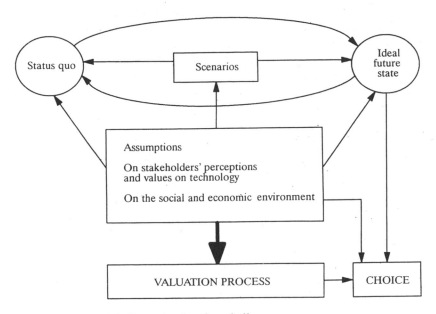

Figure 6.6. Strategic planning challenges

ifying goals of the planning process must be solved jointly. Ackoff (1978) synthesized a powerful planning framework for approaching this joint problem, and his framework has since been operationalized by Mitroff and Kilmann (1978a) based in part on Churchman's (1971) views on inquiring systems. In this approach (see Figure 6.6) planning is considered a future-oriented activity that requires two essential steps: (1) specifying an ideal future state (or target) that will serve as a reference point for planning; and (2) determining scenarios that describe the environment and the organization as it moves from the "status quo" to the desired state.

Performing these two steps requires an explicit analysis of assumptions, namely, (3) under what assumptions (regarding stakeholders, technology, the world at large, etc.) are various possible "ideals" actually desirable, and under what conditions will these various ideals be achievable?

Ackoff attaches particular importance to the process by which the above steps are carried out. He argues that most planning methods, especially those rooted in the positivistic analytical tradition, are "reactive" in the sense that they begin with the "status quo" and simply extrapolate this in a locally desirable direction (in essence, "reacting" to local problems and using only local search). He contrasts this with teleological or purposeful planning,[8] which he refers to as "proactive," which first deter-

8 Also known as "ideal point" planning.

mines an "ideal state" in a fairly unconstrained way and then determines scenarios for approaching this ideal state as closely as possible (thus "acting" to attain a "prospective" good). Ackoff's normative assertion is that planning groups are best served by proceeding in the order of steps (1) to (3), determining alternatives and feasibility restrictions only *after* a delineation of possible "ideal states" have clarified what possible directions planning might take.

Of course, going through the process of designing ideal states may not bring any improvement over, say, standard decision analysis when (as is usually assumed in normative theories of problem solving) all feasible alternatives are known to begin with and stakeholders' preferences over consequences of policy actions are stable. However, when they are not, as is frequently the case in strategic planning, the presence of an ideal state can strongly affect search, evaluation, and choice of alternative planning futures.

As noted in Chapters 2 and 3, individual and organizational searches tend to be local and problematic, that is, there is a strong tendency for decision makers to consider only a limited number of alternatives. And these usually originate as an extrapolation of history and the "status quo" rather than as the result of a comprehensive analysis of all possibilities. Ackoff's teleological approach to planning is directed explicitly at alleviating this temporal and technical myopia of the planning processes by projecting the perceptions and values of the planners against an idealized perspective. The key here is to have the planning group analyze first their ideal state and then to have this drive their analysis of alternative actions for moving closer to this ideal.

Concerning evaluation and choice, research on cognitive dissonance (e.g., Festinger, 1964) indicates that the presence of an ideal point may strongly influence choice and "ex post" felicity (even when the ideal is not achievable). In commenting on this work, Zeleny (1981) pointed out that ideal states may also be useful reference points for discussion and compromise among conflicting stakeholders.

Ideal points may also serve as a useful reference for understanding the values and decision processes of stakeholders and relating these to external reference groups (as in M. Thompson, 1983). In particular, the process of defining various ideals as functions of alternative assumptions on stakeholder values is responsive to objections raised by Marcuse (1964) that modern technological planning should cool its one-sided ardor for determining the "facts" associated with various policy alternatives and expend some effort in defining the alternative futures within which individual values and technical data become socially meaningful.

Pursuing this approach requires multiple skills in defining the ideal point and analyzing scenarios and assumptions. The required skills (e.g., in finance, economics, technology) will determine who should participate in the planning group. We can delineate two classes of problems that our planning group may address.

Establishing the planning framework
• Problem identification.
• Design of ideal states.
• Identification of stakeholders.
• Scenario generation.

Evaluation and choice
• Forecasting: behavioral, factual, and political.
• Impact and value analysis.
• Responsibility and accountability analysis.

Concerning these problems, Ackoff's approach has made its most important contributions to the first category: setting the stage for planning. Detailed evaluation and choice have been the province of more analytical traditions of decision science, such as multi-attribute choice models (including social judgment theory), Delphi techniques, and group decision support approaches, as described previously. One may argue that this division of labor is, in fact, appropriate. That is, the broad sweep of human imagination and desire should be unleashed in setting the stage for planning, but scenarios and value conflicts generated by this creative process are best evaluated in a detailed and analytical form.[9]

However, both forecasting and value analysis require a state within which these analyses take place (i.e., they are nested within some context). In Delphi forecasting, for example, one must begin with a well-formulated question. Similarly, for trade-off analysis among conflicting attributes or stakeholder values, solutions can only be interpreted against the history, the political and social processes, and the assumptions underlying the impact analysis in question. From this perspective, then, the development of scenarios, testing of assumptions, and contrasting of possible ideals is a necessary precondition for applying the more analytic techniques that traditional decision science has provided.

Regarding the group's planning process, it is worth noting that some of the philosophical approaches discussed in Chapter 5 can be used to obtain better scenarios and ideal states. For example, following Mason and Mitroff (1981), one can imagine a dialectical (or Hegelian) method for analyzing assumptions. By generating two antithetical sets of assumptions (e.g., low versus high demand for a product or a price), one

9 For a more detailed discussion of scenario planning in the context of strategic planning, see Schoemaker (1991c, 1993).

might generate contrasting scenarios. These, in turn, can be used to elucidate both the scope of feasible scenarios and the implications of the antithetical assumptions at issue. In a similar manner, a model-based, analytical (Leibnitzian) approach could properly be used to explore the implications of an interrelated set of technical assumptions. When coupled with group decision support methods for brainstorming, idea classification, and prioritization, both qualitative assumptional analysis as well as quantitative modeling can be focused on the same planning problem. Such strategic planning problems clearly represent a fertile and important area for group problem solving.

6.5   Summary and conclusions

This chapter has introduced group decision making using several illustrative problems of group planning and judgment. We have emphasized the importance of group process and the effects of social interaction on group performance. In particular, we have noted that while groups can bring additional problem-solving resources to a given situation, they may also exhibit distinct liabilities, such as those related to groupthink. Avoiding these group biases is essential if the full power of group decision making is to be harnessed. This debiasing may involve anonymous feedback, as in the Delphi process, or dialectical reasoning, as in the planning examples given, or group decision support systems to increase the information-processing capacity of the group. In the following chapter we build on these descriptive theories as we consider formal models of group choice and their relationship to the group process issues examined in this chapter.

7

Formal models of group decision making

7.1 Introduction

In this chapter, we approach groups from the perspective of "methodological individualism," in which groups are viewed primarily from the point of view of the individuals who make up the group. We begin our study with a brief overview of the elements of game theory as a formal representation of certain group choice problems, based on the preferences and beliefs of individuals in the group. We then apply the game theory representation of group choice problems to the problems of cooperation and bargaining. We shall also review the experimental literature on cooperation to explore when cooperation is likely to occur under conditions of conflict.

We use this same formal and individualistic methodology to consider certain collective choice problems such as choosing a president for a country or a location for a hazardous facility that must serve several communities in a region. Finally, we introduce the principal–agent paradigm, which has become important in economics and finance for understanding contractual relations between two or more parties.

7.2 Introduction to game theory

The theory of games is concerned with formal models of groups of self-interest-seeking individuals engaged in a common endeavor, but whose members may have different preferences and beliefs about what the group should do. As such, game theory is a formal framework for understanding conflict and conflict resolution. As we shall discuss, game theory can be viewed as either a normative or as a descriptive theory, and it enjoys a rich literature in both theory as well as experimental and field studies. Game theory is immensely important to many branches of the social and natural sciences, including economics (J. Friedman, 1990), political science (Ordeshook, 1986), management science (Shubik, 1982), decision sciences (Luce and Raiffa, 1957), sociology and psychology (Steinfatt and Miller, 1974), and biology (Axelrod, 1984). The formal theory of games dates only to von Neumann and Morgenstern's famous 1944 trea-

Table 7.1. *Examples of two-person games*

	Player 2		Player 2	
	A_2	B_2	A_2	B_2
Player 1				
A_1	4, −4	−3, 3	10, 10	9, 20
B_1	2, −2	0, 0	20, 9	−20, −20
	1. Zero-sum Game		2. Crossing Game	

tise, but the conceptual framework provided by game theory has had a fundamental impact on the social sciences.

7.2.1   *Game forms and solution concepts*

Table 7.1 shows two examples of two-person games. Each person (1 and 2) has two strategies, which we have labeled (A_1, B_1) and (A_2, B_2). The entries in the cells indicate the respective payoffs to Players 1 and 2 for each of the four strategy combinations. Game 1 is called a "zero-sum" game because the payoffs to Player 1 are always the negative of those to Player 2 – what one player wins, the other loses. Game 2 is the so-called crossing game (Moulin, 1986). One may think of the strategies in the crossing game as being those of two drivers approaching an intersection simultaneously. Each player may either stop (the *A* strategy) and let the other player go through the intersection first, or go (the *B* strategy). If both go, there is an accident with payoffs (−20, −20). If both stop, and then proceed, the payoffs are (10, 10). Otherwise the player who stops loses 1 unit of payoff for injured pride (resulting in a payoff of 9) and the other player receives a payoff of 20. Game theory attempts to provide reasonable predictions about what players in games such as these might do. The reader might wish to consider what the outcome of the games in Table 7.1 might be.

There are several ways of describing games, only two of which will concern us in this chapter (see Shubik, 1982, for a full discussion of game representations):

1. The *normal form* (also called the strategic form) of games is illustrated in Table 7.1. A normal form game *G* is specified by indicating the players in the game, their strategies, and the joint payoffs to each player from each strategy combination. In addition, the specification of *G* in normal form requires a statement about information – for example, in the preceding examples, whether both players know the other player's pay-

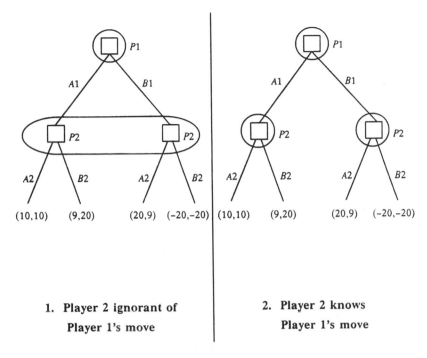

1. Player 2 ignorant of Player 1's move

2. Player 2 knows Player 1's move

Figure 7.1. Extensive form of crossing game

offs as well as their own. We shall be concerned here almost entirely with games of complete information in which the payoff structure is common knowledge to all group members. The usual assumption in normal form games is that players choose their strategies simultaneously and we shall adopt this assumption here. If one of the players (usually called the "leader") gets to move first, this can profoundly affect the logical outcome of a game. Detailed description of sequencing of moves requires a different representation of the games, called the extensive form representation.

2. The *extensive form* (or game tree form) of a game spells out in a decision tree the exact sequence of feasible moves for each player and the information available to each player at each node of the decision tree. Figure 7.1 indicates an extensive form representation of Game 2 of Table 7.1. In this representation of the game, Player 1 is first called upon to make his choice between A_1 and B_1 (the two branches at the top node in the tree). Then Player 2 has to choose a branch corresponding to his two choices (A_2 and B_2). Thereafter, the players receive the indicated payoffs at the bottom of the tree. The additional features captured by extensive

form games are sequencing of moves and more detailed representation of available information.

In Figure 7.1, we indicate the "information set" available to each player at each move by drawing a circle around what they can distinguish. In the case of Game 2 of Table 7.1 (and Figure 7.1.1), we have drawn the information set around both of the nodes marked P_2 to indicate that Player 2, when called upon to move, cannot distinguish between these two nodes – that is, he does not know which strategy Player 1 has selected. This is equivalent to saying that Players 1 and 2 choose their strategies (or moves) simultaneously. If Player 1 actually moved first and Player 2 knew what strategy Player 1 had selected before making his move, then this would be indicated by drawing a separate information set about each of the nodes P_2 (as in Figure 7.1.2). As the reader can readily see for the games in Figure 7.1, sequencing of moves and information available can have a significant effect on the outcome of a game. Sequencing of moves and available information have very interesting consequences in the crossing game, since either player would be very happy to convince the other player (and be certain that it was understood) that she had "precommitted" to the A strategy (i.e., she couldn't stop at the intersection), forcing the other player to the rational "follower" B strategy.

Our interest in this chapter will be primarily with normal form games, with no uncertainty and under perfect information. Thus, the games of interest here can be represented in "matrix form" as in Table 7.1, where every player knows the game matrix. Any such normal form game can be specified through three parameters: N, X, and U, where $N = \{1, 2, \ldots, n\}$ are the players in the game, $X = \{X_i \mid i \in N\}$ is the collective strategy space, of which X_i is player i's space of feasible strategies, and $U = \{U_i \mid i \in N\}$ is a set of utility or payoff functions, with U_i being player i's utility function so that player i prefers (the outcome of) strategy $x \in X$ over strategy $y \in X$ if and only if $U_i(x) > U_i(y)$.

As an example, the parameters N, X, U of Game 1 in Table 7.1 are $N = \{1, 2\}$, $X_i = \{A_i, B_i\}$, $i = 1, 2$, and utility functions $U_i(x)$ as given in the table for every $x \in X$, that is, for every strategy combination of the two players.

Game theory is primarily concerned with predicting "rational" outcomes to games such as those of Table 7.1. By rationality is meant here that each player $i \in N$ attempts to maximize his own utility without regard for other players' ultimate payoffs. Naturally, in some games it may be beneficial for two or more players to coordinate strategies so as to yield an improvement for everyone. But the baseline assumption of game theory is that such coordination will only take place if it does not reduce the utility of the players involved. In particular, altruism is not considered rational unless it leads to a better outcome for the player(s) exhibiting such altruism, in which case the behavior involved might be better thought of as only apparently altruistic.

Given the just indicated narrow view of rationality, the two concepts of greatest importance in describing outcomes of games are the Nash equilibrium and Pareto efficient solutions, which we now define.

Definition: Consider any normal form game $G = [N, X, U]$. A *Nash (or non-cooperative) equilibrium* for G is any strategy $\bar{x} \in X$ which, for every $i \in N$, satisfies

$$U_i(\bar{x}_i, \bar{x}_{-i}) \geq U_i(x_i, \bar{x}_{-i}), \qquad \text{for all } x_i \in X_i, \tag{7.1}$$

where $x_{-i} = (x_1, \ldots, x_{i-1}, x_{i+1}, \ldots, x_n)$ is the vector x minus its ith component. Thus, a Nash equilibrium of G is a collective strategy $\bar{x} = (\bar{x}_1, \bar{x}_2, \ldots, \bar{x}_n)$ of the n players such that no individual player, acting on his own, can improve his situation. Nash equilibriums are strategies that cannot be improved by unilateral changes in behavior. The set of all Nash equilibriums of a game G (which may be empty) is denoted $\sigma_o(G)$.

A *Pareto efficient solution* for G is any strategy $x^* \in X$ for which there is no strategy $x \in X$ for which $U_i(x^*) \leq U_i(x)$ for every $i \in N$ and there is some $j \in N$ for which $U_i(x^*) < U_i(x)$. Thus, a Pareto efficient strategy x^* is any strategy for which there is no other strategy x at which every player can be at least as well off as at x^* and some player can be strictly better off at x than at x^*. The set of all Pareto efficient solutions of a game G is denoted $\sigma_p(G)$.

Examples show that Nash and Pareto solutions for a given game may either be identical, overlap, or not intersect at all. Let us illustrate these solution concepts for the games in Table 7.1. For Game 1 (G_1), the reader can verify that $\sigma_o(G_1) = \{(B_1, B_2)\}$ and $\sigma_p(G_1) = X$ (the whole strategy space). That (B_1, B_2) is a Nash equilibrium is verified by checking that neither player has an incentive to depart from this strategy if the other player is playing his component of it. For example, if Player 1 selects B_1, then Player 2 surely prefers to select B_2 (and get 0) rather than A_2 (and get -2). In the same vein, if Player 2 selects B_2, then Player 1 prefers to select B_1 (and get 0) rather than A_1 (and get -3). We see that neither player has an incentive to depart from the Nash equilibrium strategy by himself. The reader can check directly that no strategy other than (B_1, B_2) is a Nash equilibrium. Concerning Pareto solutions, since this is a zero-sum game, every strategy is Pareto efficient. If one player were made better off by moving to another strategy, the other player must, by the zero-sum nature of the game, be made worse off.

The reader may verify in a similar fashion for Game 2 (G_2) in Table 7.1 that $\sigma_o(G_2) = \{(A_1, B_2), (B_1, A_2)\}$ and $\sigma_p(G_2) = X \backslash \{(B_1, B_2)\}$, that is, every solution other than (B_1, B_2) is Pareto efficient in G_2. The strategy (B_1, B_2) is not Pareto efficient since it is dominated by all three of the

Table 7.2. *Prisoner's dilemma game*

	Player 2	
	C_2	D_2
Player 1		
C_1	4, 4	−2, 6
D_1	6, −2	0, 0

other strategy combinations (dominated in the sense that any of the other strategies make both players better off).

7.2.2   Cooperation and social dilemma games

The Nash solution concept σ_o is a noncooperative or individualistic solution concept. The Nash solution would be a reasonable prediction of the outcome of a game or conflict situation in which participants could not make binding agreements beforehand or where noncooperation might otherwise be reasonably expected. The Nash solution concept embodies the notion "every man for himself."

The Pareto solution concept, on the other hand, embodies group rationality, at least of a weak sort. The Pareto concept suggests that any strategy move that makes at least one person better off without making anyone else worse off should be selected by the group. One might think that such a weak restriction on group rationality would always be satisfied. The essence of the social dilemmas literature (Dawes, 1980), however, is that there are a variety of reasonable situations under which the outcome of group choice is not Pareto efficient, neither in theory nor in practice. We begin with the most famous example of such a social dilemma, the prisoner's dilemma (Rapoport, 1966).

Table 7.2 presents the classic prisoner's dilemma game. Either player can either cooperate (Strategy C) or defect (Strategy D). This game has the following story associated with it. Two thieves are caught, but without the incriminating evidence of their booty, which has been stashed away. They are held in different cells and cannot communicate with one another. They each have two strategies: remain silent (the C strategy) or turn state's evidence and incriminate the other thief (the D strategy). If both remain silent, they are soon released, split their booty and live the high life (with utility payoffs 4, 4). If both incriminate each other, they both receive light sentences (with utility payoffs 0, 0). If only one defects, then that prisoner makes off with the booty while his fellow thief is sent to prison for a longer term (the payoff entries −2, 6 or 6, −2).

The reader can verify that the unique Nash solution for the prisoner's dilemma (PD) game in Table 7.2 is for both players to defect (strategy D_1, D_2) whereas the Pareto solution set is every strategy pair except D_1, D_2. This example exhibits the essential characteristic of the PD game; the intersection of the Nash and Pareto solution concepts is empty – that is, every Nash solution is Pareto inefficient. If players pursue only their own goals, they will end up with an inferior solution. In this case, if Player 1 remains silent, then it pays for Player 2 to turn state's evidence. If Player 1 turns state's evidence, then it pays for Player 2 to do the same. Thus, the dominant strategy for Player 2 is D_2, whatever Player 1 does. Similarly, Player 1's dominant strategy is D_1. But the combined result of this Nash strategy D_1, D_2 is clearly inferior to the payoffs of the Pareto solution C_1, C_2.

When might one expect a noncooperative (i.e., Nash) solution to obtain rather than a cooperative (Pareto) solution? This has been the object of considerable and continuing experimental work.[1] The typical experiment would proceed as follows. Subjects are paired, but remain separated from one another during the play of the game. They are presented with a series of games of the form given in Table 7.2 and asked to indicate their choice of strategy for each. Their choices are recorded and they are informed immediately of the choice of the other player and their resulting payoffs. In some experiments, subjects know they are playing against the same player for the series of games; in others, they know they are playing against different players each game; and for some experiments subjects do not know whether their opponent is changing over the series of games. For each fixed knowledge condition, at the end of a series of such games, subjects are given a monetary reward based on the payoffs they have accumulated. The basic question of interest in these experiments is: When subjects play a series of PD games, what determines how frequently the cooperative solution C_1, C_2 is played, relative to one of the other three strategy combinations. Recalling Figure 6.1, a number of procedural interventions in the group choice process might affect this outcome. We consider only the major findings here.

Communication. The possibility of communication has a very substantial impact on the degree of cooperative solutions. When subjects are able to speak or write to one another, they quickly determine agreements supporting the cooperative, Pareto outcome. This occurs even if subjects only meet in between plays of the game and are not allowed to discuss the game itself. Thus, face-to-face contact itself promotes cooperative be-

1 See, for example, Rapoport (1966), Marwell and Schmidt (1973), Steinfatt and Miller (1974), Dawes (1980), and Axelrod (1984).

Table 7.3. *Equity effects in the prisoner's dilemma game*

	Player 2	
	C_2	D_2
Player 1		
C_1	$4 + x, 4 - x$	$-2, 6$
D_1	$6, -2$	$0, 0$

havior in these experiments. Steinfatt and Miller (1974) report results typical of the effect of communication on PD outcomes. They conducted an experiment involving 600 subjects. Each subject was paired up with a single "opponent" and played 50 trials of the PD game in Table 7.3. Some of the pairs were allowed to communicate with one another in writing about their planned strategies during the first 13 trials of play (but not during the final 37 trials of play). Others were prevented from communicating during the entire experiment. When averaged over the 50 trials, Steinfatt and Miller found that the frequency of cooperative solutions played rose from 30% for the noncommunicating pairs to over 80% for those subject pairs allowed to communicate with each other during the first 13 trials. These results and many others in the experimental literature demonstrate the power of communication in promoting cooperation.

Equity. Consider the slightly altered PD Game in Table 7.3, from Marwell and Schmidt (1973). This game still has the PD property (that σ_o and σ_p have no intersection) as long as x is between 0 and 2. The larger x is, the more "inequitable" is the cooperative solution C_1, C_2, even though it clearly remains preferable to the Nash solution D_1, D_2. What Marwell and Schmidt found was that the more inequitable the game was (i.e., the larger x was), the fewer the number of cooperative solutions found experimentally. Thus, perceived equity seems to be an important underlying factor in promoting cooperative behavior.

Interpersonal Risk. Consider the game in Table 7.3 again, but now under the following scenario. Suppose that subjects are in separate rooms (they do not communicate) and they play the normal PD game given in Table 7.2. However, if both players select the C strategy, then Player 1 may push a "take" button and receive an additional x units of payoff (from player 2), giving rise to the payoffs in Table 7.3.[2] This is a situation that Marwell and Schmidt characterize as exhibiting interpersonal risk. If Player 2 cooperates, he becomes vulnerable to exploitation by Player 1. The larger the degree of interpersonal risk (i.e., the larger x) is, the less likely subjects are to play cooperatively. Interpersonal risk thus also seems an important determinant of cooperative behavior. This is supported by both the experimental results just noted, but also by the presence of surety bonds and other financial instruments in practice for assuring that co-operative endeavors do not lead to opportunism (Klein, Crawford, and Alchian, 1978; Williamson, 1981). Before firms are willing to commit large funds to joint projects, they may insist on performance bonds or other assurances that their partners will not exploit them after they have incurred (sunk) investment costs. Williamson (1985) refers to these financial assurances as "hostages," a very old solution to the problem of assuring "cooperation."

Reputation and repeated games. Suppose the same two players are engaged in playing the PD game in Table 7.2 over and over, and suppose that they cannot communicate or make any binding agreements. Knowing that they are likely to play a long series of trials against one another, players would have considerable incentive to play cooperatively, at least in the early plays of the game. The losses from noncooperative behavior would otherwise be substantial. This simple intuition has been verified both theoretically and experimentally (Axelrod, 1984; Radner, 1985; J. Friedman, 1990). Knowing that someone has cooperated in past plays of the game has a positive effect on subsequent cooperation. Conversely, if you know you are playing against a ruthless opponent, you will clearly tend to play the D strategy to protect yourself.

We have concentrated until now on two-person PD games. But the same cooperation–noncooperation dilemma can be studied for larger groups. Indeed, many problems in economics and political science have the same character as two-person PD games. Dawes (1980) has called these multiparty PD games "social dilemmas." All of these games share the following two properties:

    a. The payoff to each individual for defecting (noncooperative) behavior is higher than the payoff for cooperative behavior, regardless of what the other group members do.

2 The reader might find it interesting to represent the interpersonal risk game as a one-period extensive form game (see Figure 7.1), in which players first choose whether to cooperate and then Player 1 gets a final move, in which she decides whether to press the "take button."

Table 7.4. *Payoffs for five-person social dilemma game*

Number of cooperators	Payoffs to defectors	Payoffs to cooperators
5	—	$12.00
4	$20.00	$ 9.00
3	$17.00	$ 6.00
2	$14.00	$ 3.00
1	$11.00	$ 0.00
0	$ 8.00	

  b. All individuals in the group receive a lower payoff if all defect than if all cooperate.

These two properties together ensure that the essential PD property holds, namely, that the Nash solutions and the Pareto solutions of the resulting game do not intersect.

The payoffs for a five-person social dilemma game from Dawes (1980, p. 180) are shown in Table 7.4. The only strategies for each player are to cooperate (Strategy C) or defect (Strategy D). The payoffs to each player depend only on the number who cooperate. Thus, the normal form of this social dilemma game is completely specified as in Table 7.4 by giving the payoffs for each player as a function of the total number of cooperators. It is easily verified that properties labeled a and b hold, because no matter how many group members are currently cooperating, it always pays the individual to defect (since he will receive more than by playing a cooperative strategy). Yet the total social payoff if everyone cooperates (which is a Pareto solution) is $5 \times 12 = \$60.00$, whereas the total social payoff at the (unique) Nash solution where everyone defects is $5 \times 8 = \$40.00$, and everyone is worse off. Thus, if individuals myopically pursue their own self-interest and defect, the group will be overall worse off.

Dawes (1980) reports various results for games like that in Table 7.4. Besides supporting the results on communication and reputation reported for two-person games, he further finds that as group size increases, cooperation is less likely. Apparently, difficulties in establishing communication and group discipline undermine the incentives for cooperation in larger groups.

It should be apparent from this brief review of cooperation that social interaction variables, such as communication, equity, and interpersonal

Table 7.5. *Entry deterrence game*

	Incumbent	
	Collude	Fight
Entrant		
Enter	40, 50	-10, 0
Stay out	0, 100	0, 100

risk, are important in predicting the outcome of group choice processes. Interestingly, formal game theory typically *assumes* that either noncooperative or cooperative behavior obtains prior to making predictions about group choice. However, the predictions resulting from these opposing assumptions are quite different, as we have seen here. In particular, for many problems, cooperative behavior results in a more efficient solution to the group choice problem. It is therefore important to understand under what conditions cooperative behavior can be expected. The preceding results highlight the complexity of cooperation, as it depends on perceived equity, interpersonal risk, communication, trust, and so on. These results also show the nature of group design interventions required to assure cooperation (e.g., improving group communication). More generally, we see again the importance of linking descriptive and prescriptive theories. In this instance, improving group outcomes means promoting cooperation, which in turn requires a deep understanding of the descriptive, social psychological foundations of group processes.

7.2.3 *Refinements of the Nash equilibrium concept*

Game theory has remained one of the most active areas of research in theoretical and experimental decision sciences. The recent texts of J. Friedman (1990), Kreps (1990), Laffont (1989), Myerson (1991), and Rasmusen (1989) summarize much of this recent work. We wish to examine briefly one of these areas here, that of refinements to the Nash concept.

To motivate the discussion, consider the following "Entry Deterrence Game," due to Rasmusen (1989) and shown in Table 7.5.

This game concerns two firms, an entrant, and an incumbent. If the entrant decides to compete in the incumbent's market, then competition drives prices down, with total annual industry profits decreasing from 100 (in the case where the entrant stays out) to 90 (40 + 50), providing the incumbent does not fight. If the entrant enters the market and the incumbent does fight, then the entrant's profits are negative (-10) and the in-

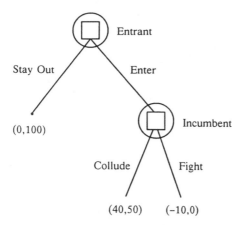

Figure 7.2. Extensive form of entry deterrence game

cumbent's profits are 0. The reader can easily see from Table 7.5 that the Nash equilibria are $\sigma_o(G) = \{(\text{enter, collude}), (\text{stay out, fight})\}$ and the Pareto set is everything except the strategy (enter, fight).

But the normal form of the game in Table 7.5 does not express the fact that the entrant first chooses whether to enter or not and then the incumbent chooses whether or not to collude.[3] To capture this, consider Figure 7.2, the extensive form of the entry deterrence game. Now it should be clear that the threat to fight is not credible. For if the entrant does enter, then the best strategy by the incumbent is to collude. And if the entrant does not enter, then the incumbent need not fight in any case.

This game illustrates the idea of "subgame perfection" first formalized by Selten (1975). For an equilibrium to be "perfect" it must make sense as an equilibrium in every subgame that can be elaborated using this strategy. In the present example, the strategy (enter, fight) is not perfect since the strategy (enter, collude) leads to strictly higher profits than the fight strategy, in the face of entry. When a game has multiple stages to it, the idea of subgame perfection can rule out, or refine, many strategy vectors that are apparently Nash equilibria. To apply the concept of subgame perfection, one begins at the end of the horizon and works backward, eliminating any dominated or nonequilibrium strategies that, given the conditions in the extensive form of the game at a particular node, could not be expected to be selected at that node by a rational player. In the present context, for example, at the node in Figure 7.2 representing that

---

3 If the incumbent has to precommit to some strategy in order to fight, then simultaneous moves are possible. For example, if the incumbent has to devote resources to new product development in order to fight the entrant, should he enter, and if these development activities must be undertaken by the incumbent before it is known whether the entrant will enter, then Table 7.5 captures the essence of the game as a simultaneous move game.

the entrant has entered, collude is the only rational strategy for the incumbent.

The concept of a trembling hand equilibrium can also be mentioned in the context of this example. In contrast to the preceding example, suppose that the entrant and incumbent must now both choose their strategies simultaneously and precommit to them. Then, as long as the incumbent believes that the entrant will stay out, the incumbent is indifferent between colluding and fighting. But suppose that there is some probability that the entrant will enter (which is a mistake from the entrant's point of view if he believes fully that the incumbent's announced fight strategy will occur upon entry). Even a small perceived probability of entry will cause a rational incumbent to play the collude strategy in the simultaneous play game. And the reader can easily reckon that if this game were played a number of times, sequentially, then this kind of reasoning would push the incumbent to the collude strategy. This is called a trembling hand equilibrium because its logic is based on one of the players choosing a strategy with a certain, though small, element of randomness. In this example, and many others, this is enough to rule out certain equilibria (here we ruled out the equilibrium [stay out, fight]).[4]

Both subgame perfect and trembling hand equilibria are "refinements" of the broader notion of Nash equilibrium. These refinements are introduced in order to pare down the set of Nash equilibria in predicting outcomes of games. Other refinements of Nash equilibria have been investigated in the same spirit.[5]

7.3   Negotiation and bargaining

To motivate the topic of negotiation and bargaining, let us consider a few examples from the public and private sectors. Background literature for these examples is provided in the excellent book by Raiffa (1982).

7.3.1   *Applications of bargaining*

Public facility location decisions. Consider the problem of locating a public facility like a trash incinerator or a waste disposal facility that the public perceives to be unpleasant, noxious, or hazardous. Several communities may need such a facility but may have trouble finding a host community because of the NIMBY (not in my backyard) and NIMTOOF (not in my term of office) syndromes. How might such communities ne-

---

4 The fact that the trembling hand equilibrium here is also subgame perfect is no accident. Selten (1975) has shown for a broad class of finite-strategy games that any trembling hand equilibrium is also subgame perfect, though the converse does not hold (see also J. Friedman, 1990).

5 See Rasmusen (1989) for an accessible discussion of such refinements.

gotiate a suitable siting location for a needed facility and appropriate payments to the host community for accepting the facility? We consider one approach to this problem in section 7.7.

Acid rain. Environmentalists have been increasingly concerned with the impact of pollutants generated by power plants and automobiles. These interact in complex ways with the environment to produce acid rain, with consequent acidification of rivers and lakes as well as damage to vegetation, fauna, and public health. Several bargaining and negotiation problems are involved here. How should the government negotiate standards for power plant emissions with the electric utility industry? How should design changes to automobiles be determined or regulated to reduce automobile emissions? Internationally, how should representatives of various countries negotiate and bargain about such standards and designs, especially if one country's emissions continually fall on another's territory because of meteorological conditions? Problems such as acid rain, ozone depletion, and global warming are especially difficult because of their broad reach and because of the difficulty of quantifying the costs and benefits of various alternatives and tracing these to the actions of individual countries or firms. In addition, the costs of programs to deal with acid rain and other global environmental problems can be enormous and many countries and firms cannot pay these costs on their own; only international cooperation and technology transfer from rich countries to poorer countries can hope to achieve lasting progress. These problems give rise to very difficult negotiation and bargaining situations in achieving cooperation and spreading the costs of various solutions.

Introduction of new technology. New technologies for manufacturing (e.g., robotics) may affect employment, skills to use these technologies, and job safety. Employees and managers may face tough bargaining problems in determining what the costs and benefits of a new technology are and who will share in these costs and benefits. External competition may make the adoption of new technology necessary for competitive viability, but if the labor force views itself as bearing an inequitable portion of the transition risks or costs, a strike or other disruptive activity can result. Bargaining problems about the timing and nature of new technologies also exist within management as finance, marketing, sales, and production specialists may see the costs and benefits of investing in new technologies from rather different perspectives.

7.3.2   *Research on bargaining*

The modern theory of bargaining dates to the early work of Zeuthen (1933). This theory was advanced considerably through its formalization by John

Nash (1950). In the Nash bargaining model as it has evolved (see, e.g., Roth, 1979), participants (negotiators) in the bargaining process choose unanimously some alternative from a given set X. The elements of X may be thought of as complete descriptions of outcomes for all bargaining participants. Each participant $i \in N$ has preferences describable by a von Neumann–Morgenstern utility function $U_i(x, \theta)$ on X and possible states of the world θ. If participants cannot agree unanimously on some $x \in X$, then a status quo or default alternative $x_o \in X$ obtains. If they do agree, their expected utilities are $\{U_i(x, \theta) \mid i \in N\}$, which depend also on the state of the world θ that obtains after x is chosen.

Different bargaining procedures may give rise to various outcomes $x \in X$ and associated payoffs as determined by the participant's preferences. We could model alternative procedures in terms of the process of making offers and counteroffers by participants (Raiffa, 1982; Rubinstein, 1982; Binmore and Dasgupta, 1987). Alternatively, we could take an outcome-oriented approach and specifiy characteristics of the outcome of bargaining that appear desirable. In this brief introduction to bargaining theory, we shall only consider outcome models. For this class of theories, Nash proposed a set of axioms as desirable properties that any bargaining procedure should satisfy. Let us consider the Nash axioms in detail. First we need to formalize our definition of bargaining problems.

Bargaining problems and bargaining solutions. A bargaining problem P is specified by three parameters: X, x_o, and U, where X is the set of available alternatives, $x_o \in X$ is the default alternative, and $U = \{U_i(x, \theta) \mid i \in N\}$ is the set of utility functions representing preferences of the participants. A bargaining solution is any procedure $\alpha(P)$ that selects an $x(P)$ X – that is, a bargaining solution is a mapping that selects an $x \in X$, given the preferences of bargaining participants and the default outcome x_o. We shall use the shorthand $U_i(x) = E\{U_i(x, \theta)\}$ to represent the expected utility to player i if bargaining alternative $x \in X$ is selected. Because players are assumed to have preferences represented by von Neumann–Morgenstern utility functions, they only care about their own expected utility of bargaining alternatives.

Nash abstracted somewhat from the structure of the underlying alternatives and considered in his axioms only the achievable "payoffs" (in expected utility terms) resulting from bargaining. In keeping with our "normal form" orientation to games, we shall emphasize the underlying bargaining alternatives. The achievable utility payoffs are, of course, determined by the bargaining alternatives X since the achievable utility payoffs, given X and N, are just the set of expected utility vectors $U = \{(U_1(x), U_2(x), \ldots, U_n(x)) \in \mathcal{R}^n \mid x \in X\}$.

The Nash axioms (see Roth, 1979). Given any bargaining problem

$P = <X, x_o, U>$, what would be a reasonable procedure for an arbitrator (or for the bargaining participants themselves) to use in choosing a particular alternative as their bargaining solution? Nash proposed the following five axioms (N1–N5) as reasonable in defining a solution procedure $\alpha(P)$ for any bargaining problem P.

N1: *Independence of equivalent utility representations*. If the von Neumann–Morgenstern (NM) utility functions U_i are transformed linearly to $V_i = a_i U_i + b_i$, where $a_i > 0$, then the bargaining problem $P' = <X, x_o, V>$ has the same solution as P, that is, $\alpha(P) = \alpha(P')$. Thus, changing utility function representations in nonessential ways does (should) not affect the solution.

N2: *Symmetry*. If a bargaining problem P is symmetric, meaning that whenever a given utility vector $U = (U_1, \ldots, U_n)$ is achievable, so is every permutation of U achievable *and* $U_1(x_o) = \ldots = U_n(x_o)$ (every player has the same expected utility at the default outcome), then every player should receive the same utility at the bargaining solution $\alpha(P)$.

N3: *Independence of irrelevant alternatives*. Suppose that $P = <X, x_o, U>$ and $P' = <Y, x_o, U>$ are two bargaining games such that Y contains X and $\alpha(P')$ is an element of X. Then $\alpha(P) = \alpha(P')$. (Thus, if the bargaining set is enlarged and an outcome is chosen that was feasible in the smaller bargaining set, then this same outcome should be chosen when only the smaller bargaining set is feasible.)

N4: *Pareto optimality*. For any bargaining game $P = <X, x_o, U>$, $\alpha(P)$ is Pareto efficient.

N5: *Individual rationality*. If the bargaining solution $\alpha(P) = x$, then the expected utility for each player at x should satisfy $U_i(x) > U_i(x_o)$, so that each player is assured at least the expected utility he would obtain at the default outcome x_o.

Nash (1950) showed that when the set of achievable utility vectors is convex,[6] these axioms imply that there is a unique bargaining solution that satisfies these axioms. This so-called Nash bargaining solution solves the following maximization problem

$$\underset{x \in X^+}{\text{Max}} \; [U_1(x) - U_1(x_o)] \cdot [U_2(x) - U_2(x_o)] \cdot \; \ldots \; \cdot [U_n(x) - U_n(x_o)] \quad \text{(NBS)}$$

where X^+ is the set of alternatives that guarantee every player a utility at least as large as the default utility, and $U(x) = EU(x, \theta)$, the expected utility of U over the possible states of the world θ. The solution to (NBS) is straightforward in principle. Interestingly, this solution can also be shown to be Pareto efficient (i.e., rational from the group's perspective).

6 This is the case, for example, when the underlying set X is convex and all players are risk averse. The set of achievable utility vectors is also convex when "mixed strategies" (lotteries among the available alternatives X) are allowed.

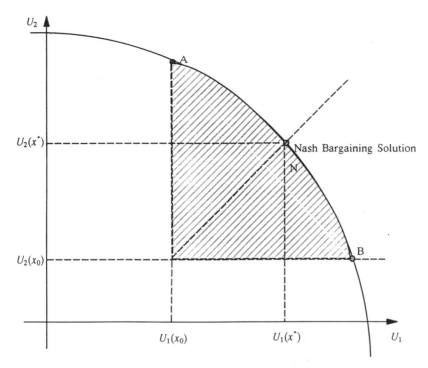

Figure 7.3. The Nash bargaining problem

In two dimensions the Nash bargaining solution can be illustrated graphically (see Figure 7.3). The problem NBS reduces simply to maximizing the product $[U_1(x) - U_1(x_o)] \cdot [U_2(x) - U_2(x_o)]$ over those x that yield a payoff at least equal to the default payoff $(U_1(x_o), U_2(x_o))$. Thus, the feasible bargaining set of expected utility payoffs is assumed to be the hatched region in Figure 7.3, in keeping with the axiom of individual rationality. Moreover, because we know the NBS solution is also Pareto optimal, we know that it must be located along the curve AB. In fact, the NBS solution for the NBS maximization problem can be shown to be the point where the 45-degree line emanating from the point $(U_1(x_o), U_2(x_o))$ cuts the Pareto frontier in achievable utility space. As shown in Figure 7.3, $[u_1(x^*) - u_1(x_o)][u_2(x^*) - u_1(x_o)]$ is the maximum possible multiplicative gain (relative to the default) from among the possible solutions along AB. From this graphical analysis, it also is intuitive that as one player's default utility $U_i(x_o)$ increases, so also will that player's utility at the resulting NBS.

As an example of a bargaining problem, consider the two-person bargaining games shown in Table 7.6. These payoffs are expressed in mon-

Table 7.6. *Payoffs for two bargaining problems*

Bargaining context R⁻			Bargaining context R⁺		
Alternative	Party 1	Party 2	Alternative	Party 1	Party 2
A	14	−5	A	2	−5
B	13	−3	B	3	−3
C	12	−1	C	4	−1
D	11	1	D	5	1
E	10	3	E	6	3
F	9	5	F	7	5
G	8	7	G	8	7
H	7	9	H	9	9
I	6	11	I	10	11
J	5	13	J	11	13
K	4	15	K	12	15
L	3	17	L	13	17
M	2	19	M	14	19

Source: Based on Rabbie, Visser, and van Oostrum (1982, p. 332).

etary terms assuming risk-neutral agents; that is, they also represent the NM utilities associated with each alternative.

Several of the alternatives in Table 7.6 deserve comment. First, the maximum joint payoff (MJP) alternative is that alternative which maximizes the sum of payoffs to the two parties. From Table 7.6, MJP = M for both R^- and R^+. The payoffs that maximize individual payoffs (the MIP alternative) are the same for both parties in R^+, whereas they are quite different for the parties in the game R^-. Indeed, the essential difference between these two bargaining games is that payoffs are negatively correlated in R^- and positively correlated in R^+. A further alternative that might be defined is the MF alternative, which maximizes "fairness" in the sense of minimizing the difference in the payoff between the two parties. From Table 7.6, we find that $MF(R^-) = G$ and $MF(R^+) = H$.

The Nash bargaining solution for these problems is easily obtained. Assume that the default payoffs are (0, 0). In an experimental setting, subjects would be told they have five minutes to come to an agreement as to which alternative they collectively agree on for a given context (e.g., R^- or R^+). If they do not agree, they receive payoffs (0, 0). If they agree, they receive the indicated payoffs. No side payments are allowed. The reader can compute from Table 7.6 that the alternatives maximizing the product of the payoffs of Parties 1 and 2 (while providing payoffs no smaller than the respective default payments) are the solutions NBS(R^-) = I and NBS(R^+) = M.

In terms of predicting the outcomes of bargaining, the Nash theory is useful as a benchmark, but experimental results also show that bargaining outcomes depend on factors other than those captured in the Nash theory. For example, for the game R^+ in Table 7.6, the NBS solution is transparently the best alternative and typically achieved by experimental subjects (Rabbie, Visser, and van Oostrum, 1982). It is an obvious win–win situation. In more complex situations where the payoff structure is less obvious but payoffs are still correlated, Bazerman, Magliozzi, and Neale (1985) found that subjects did considerably better in finding a "good solution" when given some hints, in the form of aspiration levels. For instance, they might be told beforehand how much they should expect to win at a minimum. Such aspiration levels provide a basis for a search heuristic and help subjects not to get trapped at an inferior solution.

For the game R^-, even though rather transparent, the Nash solution does not predict well (alternatives G and H tend to be chosen most frequently by experimental subjects). Moreover, even between the alternatives G and H, which outcome occurs depends on other conditions besides those treated in the Nash theory. For example, outcomes like H tend to occur more frequently when parties only know their own payoffs (private information) while outcomes like the fair outcome G tend to occur more frequently when both parties know how much the other party is receiving for each alternative. The MF (fair) solution tends to be a better predictor when everyone knows the entire payoff matrix given in Table 7.6, whereas under private information something closer to the Nash solution (namely alternative H) tends to obtain. Apparently, under shared information, parties to bargaining feel compelled to consider fairness as well as efficiency in their choice (Roth, Malouf, and Murnigham, 1979; Kleindorfer, Netschera, and Seethaler, 1992).

Many extensions of Nash's basic approach have been provided. These include a reinterpretation of Zeuthen's original model to represent the process by which a Nash bargaining solution might be obtained (Roth, 1979; Rubinstein, 1982; Wierzbicki, 1984); extensions to include lack of information on the part of the negotiator or group on the utility functions of other participants (Harsanyi and Selten, 1971; Myerson, 1979; 1981); and extensions to include multiple objectives (Raiffa, 1982; Wierzbicki, 1984). In addition, recent research has been concerned with improving negotiation in practice (Sebenius, 1981; Raiffa, 1982; Neale and Bazerman, 1991) through the use of decision support systems and interventions motivated by experimental results on the Nash theory and its offshoots (see Chatterjee, Kersten, and Shakun, 1991).

In parallel with theory development, there has also been a strong interest in experimental testing of bargaining theory. Descriptively, researchers have been interested in determining to what extent the negotiated solution arrived at by experimental subjects coincides with the efficient bargaining solutions such as the Nash solution (see Brandstätter, Davis, Stocker-Kreichgauer, 1982; Roth, 1983; Tietz, 1983; and Bazerman et al., 1985). Prescriptively, research has been concerned with applications (such as siting, acid rain, and technology choice) and in providing procedural and informational interventions that help to improve the outcome of bargaining processes. As indicated in our discussion of the R^+ and R^- bargaining games, this research corroborates that the Nash bargaining solution is generally not predictive of bargaining outcomes in experimental settings.[7] Many matters not considered in the Nash theory play an important role, including information available to participants, aspiration levels, constraints imposed on participants, and perceived equity payoffs. Given the richness of bargaining as a decision context, bargaining theory and practice will surely remain an important area of research for experimental work as well as descriptive and prescriptive modeling aimed at improving bargaining outcomes.

7.4   Collective choice and committee decision making

Game theory is concerned with predicting and evaluating the outcome of group choice problems for which the group choice $x = (x_1, x_2, \ldots, x_n)$ is the aggregate of individual choices x_i of group members. Collective choice theory, on the other hand, is concerned with group choice problems for which the group must collectively decide on a single alternative x from some set of feasible alternatives $\{a, b, c, \ldots\}$. The emphasis thus shifts from predicting reactions of group members to other members' strategies in game theory to coordinating a common choice in collective choice theory. Bargaining situations, as described previously, are themselves an important class of collective choice problems since the bargaining participants must typically decide on a group alternative to which they all agree.

Other examples of collective choice problems include choosing a president, choosing a site for a school or hospital by a community, and choosing a fare price for a mass transit system. In each of these cases, we encounter a group, using some procedure, choosing not always from a list of feasible alternatives (see Table 7.7).

The fundamental issue addressed by collective choice theory is what procedure should be used by the group in making its choice. A typical

7 See, e.g., the work of Roth (1983), and Neale and Bazerman (1991).

Table 7.7. *Typical collective choice problems*

Problem	Group	Alternatives
Choose a president	Society	List of candidates
Site a school	City council	Feasible sites
Set transit fares	Mass transit governing board	Various fare schedules

procedure might be to use majority rule or some weighting scheme to determine which alternative the group feels is best.

7.4.1 Collective choice theory

To formalize this discussion of collective choice theory,[8] suppose a group consists of individuals $N = \{1, \ldots, n\}$. The alternatives facing the group are denoted $X = \{x, y, z, \ldots\}$. Each individual $i \in N$ is assumed to have preferences over the alternatives X defined by the preference relation $\geq_i$, where $x \geq_i y$ is to be interpreted "individual i likes x at least as much as y." One way of specifying $\geq_i$ is through a utility function u_i, assigning a numerical utility $u_i(x)$ to each $x \in X$. In this case, $x \geq_i y$ if and only if $u_i(x) \geq u_i(y)$. The preferences relations $\geq_i$ are assumed to satisfy the following "rationality" properties:

P1. $\geq_i$ is *complete:* For all $x, y \in X$, either $x \geq_i y$ or $y \geq_i x$.
P2. $\geq_i$ is *reflexive:* For all $x \in X$, $x \succ_i x$.
P3. $\geq_i$ is *transitive:* For all $x, y, z \in X$, $[x \geq_i y$ and $y \succ_i z]$ implies $[x \geq_i z]$.

A relation $\geq_i$ that satisfies P1–P3 is called a weak preference order. The basic idea of collective choice theory is to determine "good" procedures for selecting an alternative for the group N if the preferences of the individuals in N are represented by the preference orders $\geq_1, \geq_2, \ldots, \geq_n$. If good procedures could be specified for determining collective choices, no matter what the preferences of the group N are, then such procedures could form the foundation of a constitution for group decision making. As the reader has probably already guessed, however, there are no ideal procedures for collective choice. We first discuss in more detail what characteristics an "ideal procedure" might possess, and indicate why no such procedures exist. The impossibility of finding an ideal procedure in

---

8 The early work in this field is reviewed in Arrow (1963a), who was largely responsible for creating the field of collective choice. Recent work is reviewed in Peleg (1984). For an interpretive discussion of the import of the theory and experimental evidence related to collective choice theory, see Hardin (1982).

general then leads us to examine special cases where "good" procedures have been found.

Suppose that $[N, X]$ and $\{\geq_i \mid i \in N\}$ are given. We seek a procedure $F(\geq_1, \ldots, \geq_n)$, depending on the preferences $\{\geq_i \mid i \in N\}$, which orders the alternatives in X according to the wishes of N. We will call $\geq_N = F(\geq_1, \ldots, \geq_n)$ the group preference order induced by F when individual preferences are $\geq_1, \ldots, \geq_n$. When $x \geq_N y$, we say "the group likes x at least as much as y." A procedure F that yields a preference of X for any constellation of preferences $\{\geq_i \mid i \in N\}$ will be called a *group choice procedure*. We shall impose various restrictions on the preference in our analysis. These might typically include that it be complete, reflexive, and transitive, but other restrictions might also be imposed. The challenge then will be to determine a group choice procedure that yields a preference having the desired properties. Let us now consider several well-known instances of group choice procedures.

Simple majority rule (SMR). Let $\{N, X\}$ and $\{\geq_1, \ldots \geq_n\}$ be given. Let $\#(x \geq_i y)$ denote the number of individuals in N for whom $x \geq_i y$. Define $\geq_N = F(\geq_1, \ldots, \geq_n)$ as follows: for all $x, y \in X$

$$x \geq_N y \quad \text{iff} \quad \#(x \geq_i y) \geq \#(y \geq_i x)$$

That is, the number of group members who like x at least as much as y is greater than or equal to the number of group members who like y at least as much as x.

To illustrate SMR, consider the following example due to Condorcet (1785). Suppose there are three individuals $N = \{1, 2, 3\}$ and three alternatives $\{x, y, z\}$ and the following preference orders obtain:

$$x \geq_1 y \geq_1 z; \qquad y \geq_2 z \geq_2 x; \qquad z \geq_3 x \geq_3 y \qquad (7.2)$$

Thus, Individual 1 prefers x to y to z. Now if $\geq_N = F(\geq_1, \geq_2, \geq_3) = \text{SMR}$, we have $x \geq_N y$ since two out of three members of N prefer x to y. Similarly, $y \geq_N z$ and zRx so that, according to SMR, the group N prefers x to y, y to z, and z to x.

Two things should be noted about SMR. First, no matter what preferences $\geq_1, \geq_2, \ldots, \geq_n$ are held by group members, SMR is complete and reflexive. In particular, for any pair $s, y \in X$, SMR induces a group ordering R of x and y such that either $x \geq_N y$ and/or $y \geq_N x$. Second, as this example illustrates, SMR is *not* transitive in general, a fact that has interesting consequences (to be discussed). Thus, whether SMR is considered an acceptable group choice procedure or not depends on whether one requires that its induced group ordering of the alternatives X be transitive or not.

Borda rule (BR). Let $[N, X]$ and $\{\geq_1, \ldots, \geq_n\}$ be given. Define the rank function

$$r(x \mid X, \geq_i) = \#(y \in X \mid y \geq_i x)$$

That is, $r(x \mid X, \geq_i)$ is the number of alternatives that Individual i finds at least as good as x. Now define the Borda rule BR $= F(\geq_1, \ldots, \geq_n) = \geq_N$ as follows: for all $x, y \in X$

$$x \geq_N y \text{ if and only if } \sum_{i \in N} r(x \mid X, \geq_i) \geq \sum_{i \in N} r(x \mid X, \geq_i) \qquad (7.3)$$

To illustrate BR, consider the following example due to Fishburn (1971). There are five individuals and $X = \{x, y, a, b, c\}$. We abbreviate $x \geq_i y \geq_i z \geq_i \ldots$ to $xyz \ldots$ in the problem data.

Person	Preference order $\geq_i$				
1	x	y	a	b	c
2	y	a	c	b	x
3	c	x	y	a	b
4	x	y	b	c	a
5	y	b	a	x	c

(7.4)

The Borda marks for x, y, a, b, c are 17, 21, 13, 12, 12. For example, x has two first place votes, one second, one fourth, and one fifth, yielding $\Sigma r(x \mid X, \geq_i) = 5 + 5 + 4 + 2 + 1 = 17$. Thus, according to BR, y is the group's preferred choice in X since it has the highest sum of ranks, namely 21. Suppose now that the least preferred alternatives $\{a, b, c\}$ are eliminated from further consideration. The preferences of group members for the remaining alternatives $Y = \{x, y\}$ are as follows:

Person	Preference order $\geq_i$
1	$x \geq_i y$
2	$y \geq_i x$
3	$x \geq_i y$
4	$x \geq_i y$
5	$y \geq_i x$

The Borda marks for this restricted set $Y = \{x, y\}$ are now 8 and 7, so that applying BR to the set Y yields the group choice x, that is:

$$\sum_{i \in N} r(x \mid Y, \geq_i) = 8 > 7 = \sum_{i \in N} r(y \mid Y, \geq_i)$$

We can now see several features of BR. First, since BR assigns a numerical value to each alternative, it induces a group order that is complete, reflexive, and transitive. However, BR violates the following property.

P4. Independence of irrelevant alternatives (IIA). Let $[N, X]$ and $\{\geq_i, \ldots, \geq_n\}$ be given. Let $\geq_N(X) = F(\geq_1, \ldots, \geq_n) \mid X)$ be the group ordering induced by the group choice procedure F when X is the set of alternatives. Similarly, let $\geq_N(Y) = F(\geq_1, \ldots, \geq_n \mid Y)$ be the group ordering induced by F when Y is the set of alternatives. Then F satisfies IIA and only if for all $x, y \in X \cap Y$.

$$x \geq_N(Y)\, y \quad \text{implies} \quad x \geq_N(X)\, y \quad \text{whenever} \quad Y \subseteq X$$

Thus, if IIA holds, elimination of some infeasible alternatives does not change the group's choice over feasible alternatives. As this example illustrates, the Borda rule does not satisfy IIA since the alternative y was feasible for both alternative sets $X = \{x, y, a, b, c\}$ and $Y = \{x, y\}$, yet the Borda rule yields y as the best choice over X and x as the best choice over Y.

Pareto rule (PR). Let $[N, X]$ and $\{\geq_1, \ldots, \geq_n\}$ be given. Define the Pareto rule group choice procedure $\text{PR} = F(\geq_1, \ldots, \geq_n) = \geq_N$ as follows: for all $x, y \in X$, $x \geq_N Y$ if and only if $[x \geq_i y$ for all $i \in N]$. Thus, under PR $x \geq_N y$ if and only if every member of the group finds x at least as good as y.

The Pareto rule is one rule satisfying the following property (SMR and BR also satisfy P5).

P5. Pareto principle. Let $[N, X]$ and $\{\geq_1, \ldots \geq_n\}$ be given and let $F(\geq_1, \ldots, \geq_n)$ be a group choice procedure. Then F satisfies the Pareto principle if and only if for all $x, y \in X$, $x \geq_N y$ only if $[x \geq_i y$ for all $i \in N]$.

To illustrate PR, consider the problem data (7.4) given earlier. For these data, $F = \text{PR}$ yields (besides $z \geq_N z$ for all $z \in X$) only $y \geq_N a$, $y \in_N b$. Thus the Pareto rule is not complete (see P1). Another way of saying the same thing is that under PR, the group may be unable to state a *decisive* preference between every two alternatives $x, y \in \text{X}$.

The P1–P5 are only a few of the properties one might wish to impose on group choice procedures. A natural question is whether there are any group choice procedures that satisfy all of these properties. The following theorem, from Arrow (1963a), provides the definitive answer to this question.[9]

Theorem (Arrow). Let $[N, X]$ be given with $\#(X) \geq 3$ and let $F(\geq_1, \ldots, \geq_n)$ be a group choice procedure that, for every set of weak

9 Arrow's theorem only applies when the number of alternatives in X exceeds two (i.e., $\#(X) \geq 3$). The reader can verify that both SMR (or BR) satisfy P1–P5 if there are only two fixed alternatives since, in this case, P3 and P4 have no force.

preference orders $\geq_1, \ldots, \geq_n$, yields a group ordering $R = F(\geq_1, \ldots, \geq_n)$. Then F must be of the form $F(\geq_1, \ldots, \geq_n) = \geq_i$ for some i – that is, F is dictatorial.

From this theorem we see that it is no accident that neither SMR, BR, nor PR satisfy all the properties P1–P5. The only group choice procedure (GCP) that does is a *dictatorial rule* (DR) that identifies group preferences with the preferences of some fixed member (say Individual 1, the "king") of the group. The reader may easily verify that any DR does, in fact, satisfy P1–P5, but clearly DRs are objectionable as GCPs on equity grounds. Although many researchers have investigated other conditions than P1–P5 that might allow for the existence of nondictatorial GCPs (e.g., Black, 1958; and Blair and Pollak, 1982), we now realize that the impossibility result embodied in this theorem is very robust. In general, no fixed procedure satisfying reasonable conditions like P1–P5 can be found to resolve differences in preferences among group or society members in all situations. Two important issues arising from this theorem are agenda control and strategic behavior.

7.4.2 Agenda control

Consider the SMR example (7.2) again, where preferences for the three group members are: (1) *xyz*; (2) *yzx*; (3) *zxy*. As noted, these give rise under SMR to group preferences $x \geq_N y$, $y \geq_N z$, and $z \geq_N x$. Now suppose that the group uses SMR to make its choice and that it does so by pairwise elimination using an agenda. The agenda specifies the order in which pairwise comparisons (and eliminations) will be done. If the agenda is (*x* versus *y*) versus *z*, then the choice between *x* and *y* leads to *x*, which when compared with *z* under SMR leads to *z* as the group choice. On the other hand, if the agenda were (*y* versus *z*) versus *x* (respectively, (*x* vs. *z*) vs. *y*), pairwise elimination voting would result in *x* (respectively, *y*). Thus, the person who controls the agenda can completely determine the outcome in this example.

Interestingly, agenda setting has no effect on the outcome under SMR with the problem data (7.4). The outcome is always *x* no matter what agenda is set, since *x* always defeats any other alternative under SMR–pairwise comparison. Such an alternative is called a *Condorcet point*. When a Condorcet point does not exist (which is quite often), McKelvey (1976) has shown that a rich class of collective choice problems has the property of this example so that the agenda setter can completely determine the outcome. Why is this? As the astute reader may have noted, this results because the group order $\geq_N$ induced by SMR is not transitive. If $\geq_N$ were, then it is easy to see that the group will always choose the same alternative from any subset $Y \subseteq X$ using pairwise elimination. For example, suppose contrary to the previous example, that $x \geq_N y$, $y \geq_N z$, and $x \geq_N z$ (not $z \geq_N x$). Then each of the three agendas [(x versus y) versus z], [(y versus z) versus x], and [(z versus x) versus y] leads to the same choice x under SMR.

Similarly, violation of P4 (IIA) also gives rise to agenda control or path dependence. For example, suppose the committee uses the Borda rule BR, which violates P4. Then the agenda setter can influence the outcome by determining what alternatives are considered. As we saw in the example (7.4), if the committee uses BR on the set $X = \{x, y, a, b, c\}$, it will come to a different conclusion than if it considers only the alternatives $Y = \{x, y\}$. If Person 2 were setting the agenda, she would prefer that BR be used over the entire set X (which yields her first choice y) rather than first eliminating the dominated alternatives $\{a, b, c\}$ and then using BR on the remaining set Y (which yields her last choice x).

The issue of agenda setting is not just of theoretical interest, but arises in many practical problems of committee and group decision making (see, e.g., Plott and Levine, 1978). The point to be noted concerning agenda setting is that, given Arrow's theorem, no GCP exists that satisfies P1–P5. But if we look for a GCP like SMR or BR that satisfies only some of the properties P1–P5, the problem of agenda setting arises.

7.4.3   *Strategic behavior*

A related problem of interest concerns strategic manipulation of GCP by voting insincerely – that is, by deliberately misrepresenting one's preferences. To illustrate, consider the problem data (7.2) and suppose under pairwise SMR that the agenda is (x versus z) versus y. As we saw, this yields y when individuals vote sincerely (i.e., according to their true preferences). Suppose, however, that Person 3 states that his preferences are zyx (instead of zxy). If Persons 1 and 2 state their preferences sincerely, then the group choice under the agenda [(x versus z) versus y] will be x instead of y, yielding an improvement for Person 3 who prefers x to y.

One may wonder whether there are GCPs that do not induce this kind of strategic behavior. As Pattanaik (1978) shows, however, in a result similar to that of Arrow's theorem, there are no procedures that are immune to such strategic misrepresentation in general, at least if one wishes other reasonable properties (like P1–P5) to be true for the GCP. Of course, rules like the dictatorial rule DR are not subject to strategic misrepresentation. There would be nothing to gain for the dictator (or anyone else) to misrepresent preferences under DR, since the dictator will determine the outcome in any case.

Given these results, we see that collective choice problems are not "mechanically" solvable. One cannot simply collect preference information and expect some rational procedure to crank out a reasonable choice for the group. One of the interesting prescriptive consequences of these results is that those taking part in or designing collective decision processes should be aware of the opportunities (their own and others') for manipulating group choice procedures by agenda setting and strategic misrepresentation of preferences.

The results discussed here may be considered negative in character. And they seem to suggest that there are no general solutions to collective choice problems. Nonetheless, we do see committees and groups making decisions all the time, and some of them appear to be quite effective. The message here is that the general results outlined in this section do not preclude that good solution procedures may be designed for particular problem types. We illustrate this in the next two sections by considering two applications of collective choice where reasonable procedures can be designed.

7.5   Collective choice for discrete public goods

Ferejohn, Forsythe, and Noll (1981) have investigated the design of procedures for solving certain collective choice problems illustrated by the following two examples.

Programming for the Public Broadcasting Network. The network of public television stations (about 150 nationwide) must decide annually on what programs it will purchase and/or produce. Each station has a program budget. The collective choice to be determined is the particular set of programs the entire network will purchase or produce and how much each station will pay for this programming.

Purchasing health equipment for a condominium. The residents of a condominium wish to purchase certain equipment for their exercise room. Residents have budgets they are prepared to use for this purpose. The collective choice to be determined is what equipment to purchase and how much each resident should pay.

Both of these problems illustrate collective choices involving what are called discrete public goods. The whole group must decide (and pay for) a particular collective choice. No single group member can afford to buy his or her own best choice without contributions from other group members. So the key here is to determine the best (or at least a good) collective choice that the group can afford. Clearly many corporate, community, and public planning problems of practical importance have this character.

One might imagine that groups facing problems like this would attempt to determine a group preference order over the feasible alternatives, perhaps using a decision support system. From the results of the previous section, however, we know that in general there may not exist a group preference order over the feasible alternatives (at least not one satisfying properties P1–P5). Moreover, Groves (1979) shows that even when monetary side payments among group members are allowed, it is not possible in general to design a satisfactory procedure for this class of problems. Specifically, they show that any procedure that is guaranteed to determine a feasible collective choice (one that the group can afford) and that satisfies the Pareto principle (P5 of section 4) will provide incentives for strategic misrepresentation of true preferences. Put differently, there are no procedures for the general class of problems illustrated by these examples that are guaranteed to be both efficient in the Pareto sense and nonstrategic. Although this seems to end the matter of finding "optimal solutions" to these collective choice problems, it does not mean that there are no "good procedures" for solving such problems. However, the design of good procedures may depend on the particular characteristics of each problem type.

7.5.1   *The programming cooperative*

To illustrate the design of a workable solution for a particular problem, let us consider the Public Broadcasting System program planning problem in more detail. For this problem, Ferejohn et al. (1978) devised a very interesting approach.

Figure 7.4 illustrates the operation of the procedure. Every station is connected to the headquarters by an interactive computer system. The procedure consists of several rounds of bidding in which stations indicate to the Headquarters their willingness to pay certain posted prices for each possible program. The prices are determined in such a way that the costs of purchasing or producing each program are covered. The idea is to use the indicated willingness to pay to update the posted prices until an equilibrium is reached at which no station wants to change its indicated program choices.

Each round takes place as follows:

1. Headquarters announces to each Station i the price q_{ij} which that station will have to pay for Program j if Station i wishes to purchase Program j. The cost of Program j is denoted by C_j. The prices q_{ij} are determined as follows:

$$q_{ij} = a_{ij}C_j \tag{7.5}$$

where a_{ij} is the share of Program j's cost C_j that Station i must pay if it

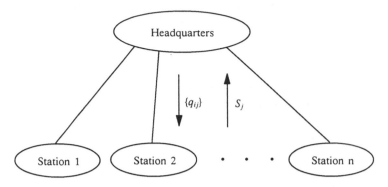

Figure 7.4. Illustrating the network programming cooperative. Stations send Headquarters messages on whether they want to purchase a program, given the current prices, where

q_{ij} = the price station i must pay for program j if it wants the program; and

S_j = the set of stations which indicate that they wish to purchase program j at the listed prices q_{ij}.

wishes to bid on Program j (it pays nothing if it doesn't want Program j). The a_{ij} are determined by

$$a_{ij} = \sum_{r=1}^{R} \frac{b_r V_{ri}}{\sum_{k \in S_j} V_{rk}} \tag{7.6}$$

where S_j is the set of stations that indicate they want to purchase Program j, and V_{ri} is welfare measure r for Station i, with b_r the weight associated with welfare measure r (the b_r are positive numbers that sum to one). In the first round, S_j is fixed by headquarters to include 80% of all the stations. After the first round, S_j includes Station i and all the stations that bid on Program j in the previous round. Welfare measures V_{ri} might include the average income of households served by Station i, the population served by Station i, or other indicators of the fair share that Station i should bear of costs for programs it purchases.

To illustrate (7.6), suppose that in the previous round Stations 1 and 2 bid on a particular Program j. And suppose that program costs are allocated only on the basis of viewing population in the region served by a station. Then if the viewing populations for Stations 1, 2, and 3 were, respectively, 100, 200, and 300, the share a_{3j} that Station 3 would have to pay for Program j, if it wants it, is $300/(100 + 200 + 300) = .5$. Thus, in this example, Station 3 would pay half the costs C_j of Program *j* if Stations 1 and 2 were the only other stations bidding on this program. The reader should note that in equilibrium

$$\sum_{i \in S_j} a_{ij} = 1 \qquad\qquad (7.7)$$

for all *j*, as long as S_j is nonempty (at least one station wants Program *j*) by the definition (7.6), so that costs C_j are exactly covered whenever equilibrium is reached.

This simple procedure allows for learning and adaptation. At the beginning of the procedure, the cost q_{ij} for Station *i* to bid on Program *j* is rather low since, for every Program *j*, S_j is set at the initial round of bidding to contain 80% of the stations. Stations can experiment a bit in the early rounds to determine whether there are enough other stations around to co-pay for particular programs to enable the total network to afford their costs. In practice, after a few rounds, stations settle on their desired programs, maintain stable bids for these, and the process converges. At equilibrium (where there are no changes in station bids for two rounds in a row), the final prices q_{ij} become the official payments from Station *i* to headquarters. It is up to Station *i* to ensure that it can afford its bid, of course.

What are the general properties of this procedure? Ferejohn et al. (1978) show that efficiency, stability, and reachability are not guaranteed by this procedure. However, in both experimental runs as well as in actual implementation of this procedure for the Public Broadcasting System, the following properties were observed empirically:

1. Outcome efficiency: Participants were pleased with the outcome of the procedure and did not see any apparent alternative that was better.
2. Transactions cost efficiency: Participants spent considerably less time in program planning after the implementation of this procedure than previously. Typically after 10 or fewer rounds the procedure converged to equilibrium.
3. Equity or fairness: Participants believed that the outcomes in terms of programs produced and prices paid for these were fair.

In summary, the Public Broadcasting System's programming cooperative, as implemented by the Ferejohn et al. procedure, appears to be a practical and efficient solution to a theoretically demanding collective choice problem.

7.5.2   *Auctions and siting problems*

In this section, we consider a very important practical mechanism for collective choice, namely auctions. Auctions have been used for centuries to determine who of a set of potential buyers will receive an indivisible good, such as a painting or a house, and what the chosen buyer will pay for the good. More recently, auctions have been proposed for such diverse problems as selling offshore oil leases, determining the cheapest source of bulk electric power, and siting noxious facilities. After a brief review of various kinds of auctions, we consider the last-named application, using auctions to deal with the collective choice problem of determining where to site a noxious facility, such as a prison, a power plant, or a waste disposal facility. The idea of using an auction in this context is to let communities bid on the minimum compensation they would require to locate the noxious facility in question in their backyard. The winner of this siting auction will be the lowest compensation bid submitted, and must house the facility in question.

Credit for drawing attention to the importance of auctions is usually given in modern times to William Vickrey (1961), who defined and analyzed several different kinds of auctions. These included the following.

The English oral auction: In this auction, bidders respond to an auctioneer and make bids in increasing order until no further increases in bid are forthcoming. The buyer making the highest bid wins the object and pays her bid. Stated more formally, assume that there are n potential buyers for some indivisible object and denote by v_i the value Buyer i assigns to the object. Let us also label buyers in order of the value they attach to the object, so that $v_1 = v_2 \geq \ldots v_n$. Clearly, with rational individuals, Buyer 1 should win this auction since she has the highest valuation v_1 unless $v_1 = v_2$, and no one else would have any incentive to bid higher than what she thinks the object is worth.

The Dutch oral auction: In this auction, the auctioneer starts counting backward from a price he knows to be larger than the value any of the buyers attaches to the object (i.e., larger than v_1). The first buyer to stop the auctioneer in his backward counting wins the auction and pays a price equal to the price at which the auctioneer stops. Note that here Buyer 1 may not win this auction, especially if she is very risk seeking, since she may be inclined to wait out the other bidders in hopes of getting the object at a bargain price. This would not happen in an English oral auction, since the highest current bid is there for all to see.

The sealed-bid auction: Bidders submit sealed bids to the auctioneer, and the bidder with the highest bid submitted wins. This method is frequently used for contract bidding in the public sector, when it is too cumbersome to gather all bidders in one room. A variant of this procedure, called the second-price auction, is that the highest bidder wins, but pays only the price of the second-highest bidder.

The key questions of interest in designing and understanding auctions are who will end up with the object, what will be paid by participants in the auction to the seller, and, of course, the usual transactions cost efficiency considerations. In the above auctions, these questions appear at first blush to be straightforward. One would expect the buyer with the highest value (v_1 in our notation) to be the "winner" and to pay the seller either the highest bid or the second-highest bid, depending on the rules of the auction. The auction scenario becomes more complicated if buyers must pay entry fees or if they have only uncertain information about the value of the object being auctioned (as in the case of oil leases, which may or may not lead to oil discoveries) and to the value that other buyers attach to the object. For example, if I am Buyer 1 and I know for certain that no other buyer values an object at more than $100, then I would not normally submit or make a bid for more than, say, $101, even if my own valuation of the object were $200. However, I might bid higher than $101 (at least in a sealed-bid auction) if I was not so sure about the values that other buyers have. The interested reader may consult Riley and Samuelson (1981), Myerson (1981), and Rothkopf, Teisberg, and Kahn (1989) for more detailed theoretical analyses of auctions under various informational assumptions. There is also a rich experimental literature on auctions in decision sciences and economics, designed to test these theories (e.g., V. L. Smith, 1982). We have a narrower focus here.

Our concern will be to describe the application of the auction framework to the problem of siting hazardous or noxious facilities such as prisons, power plants, and waste disposal plants. Siting of such facilities has been an area of continuing conflict in many countries. The accidents at Bhopal and Chernobyl have made the health and safety risks of hazardous facilities very visible. The continuing debate in this country on nuclear power and hazardous waste has further sensitized people to this problem. The central issue in this debate is that industries like chemical and nuclear power provide recognized economic benefits for society as a whole, but no one wants their toxic waste by-products in their "backyard." One approach to this problem is to engage in benefit sharing, that is, transferring wealth from those who gain from the primary activities in question to the community that hosts the hazardous facilities necessary for these activities. The question is who should share how much with whom? We now describe an auction mechanism that provides one operational answer to this question.

The idea is to have potential host communities for the facility engage in a bidding process to learn which community would incur the least "total cost." This total cost would include the costs of building the facility and related infrastructure, together with any additional compensation that the community requires for accepting the facility. Those communities or organizations not selected would pay some share of the selected community's declared cost. Let us see how such a procedure might be structured as a "low-bid auction," where the bid submitted by a community is its minimum compensation or willingness-to-accept (WTA) payment for hosting the facility.

We assume that a set of N "communities" has agreed to participate[10] in a process to determine which of these communities will be the eventual site of a hazardous facility (such as a trash-to-steam plant). The communities may be thought of as organizations that profit from the use of such a facility and therefore want to see it sited somewhere.[11] We suppose that each community has evaluated all siting options within its boundaries and knows its best option and the associated social costs (which it minimally needs to recoup to beat the status quo). We shall need the following notation to describe the low-bid auction mechanism.

V_i	Community i's value of having the facility in its own backyard ($V_i < 0$). Thus Community i's true WTA is $-V_i$.
t_i	Possible transfer payment to Community i for hosting the facility.
$V_i + t_i$	Total value to Community i if the facility is sited there.
V_{ij}	The value to Community i of having the facility sited in Community j. We assume $V_{ij} > 0$ so Community i is willing to pay up to V_{ij} to have the facility sited at Community j.
t_{ij}	Community i's transfer payment (a tax if $t_{ij} < 0$) to Community j if the facility is located in Community j.
X_i	Community i's stated WTA (its bid) for agreeing to host the facility.

Suppose that some regional siting agency has the task of determining which one of the communities will be chosen and of enforcing necessary transfer payments. To do so, it asks for an acceptance bid X_i from each Community $i = 1, 2, \ldots, N$. This (WTA) bid represents the minimum compensation required by Community i to site the facility within its jurisdiction. If the facility is eventually sited in Community j, then Community i must pay an amount $t_{ij} = X_i/(N - 1)$ to compensate the "winning" Community j, which receives total compensation $t_j = X_j$ equal to its bid.

We assume that the agency selects the lowest bid as the winning site. If $X_i = \text{Min} \{X_j \,|\, j = 1, 2, \ldots, N\}$ is the lowest bid, then total transfer payments paid by or to everyone will be

$$t_i - \sum_{j \neq i} t_{ji} = X_i - \sum_{j \neq i} \frac{X_j}{(N - 1)} \leq 0 \qquad (7.8)$$

10 We shall discuss more fully appropriate procedures for obtaining the participation of communities as potential hosts for hazardous facilities.

11 If a community does not have a feasible site itself, it can still participate in the bidding process, but its only role will be to help pay for the eventual facility.

Table 7.8. *Data for low-bid auction example*

| Site | Community | | | B_j Net benefit of each site |
	1	2	3	
Community 1	−8	4	7	3
Community 2	4	−5	7	6
Community 3	4	4	−8	0
X_i^*	8	6	10	—

where the inequality follows since, by assumption, $X_j \geq X_i$ for all $j \neq i$. Thus, the low-bid auction does not give rise to deficits.

Now let us consider bidding strategies for communities participating in the low-bid auction procedure. To do so, consider the example given in Table 7.8 involving three communities, $N = \{1, 2, 3\}$. The table gives the monetary values of the V_i and V_{ij} for each of the communities. Just looking at these data, what should Community 2 bid? If Community 2 bids $X_2 = 5$ (its true WTA) and wins, then it will end up with a total value of $V_i + t_i = -5 + 5 = 0$, since it would receive its bid in compensation if it were the winner. On the other hand, if Community 2 bids 5 and Community 1, say, is selected as the site of the facility, then Community 2 must pay $X_2/(N - 1) = 5/2 = 2.5$ to the regional authority. Because the total value to Community 2 of having the facility located in Community 1 is 4, the total value of bidding $X_2 = 5$ and "losing" the auction is therefore $4 - 2.5 = 1.5$. So, clearly, Community 2 would like to make a high bid and win or make a low bid and lose. However, Community 2 may not know what the values are for the other communities.

When each community knows its own preferences but has no information on others, then a maxi–min bidding strategy is a prudent one to follow. The maxi–min strategy, just as in the 2 × 2 games we studied, consists of maximizing the minimum payoff achievable. Formally, the maxi–min bid for Community i is the solution X_i^* to

$$V_i + X_i^* = \operatorname{Min}_j \{V_{ij} + t_{ij} \mid j \neq i\} = [\operatorname{Min}_j \{V_{ij} \mid j \neq i\}] - X_i^*/(N - 1) \quad (7.9)$$

It is easy to verify that the solution to (7.9) is a maxi–min strategy. The first expression on the left-hand side of (7.9) represents the payoff to Community i if Site i is selected, while $V_{ij} + t_{ij}$ is the payoff if some other site $j \neq i$ is selected. As X_i is increased, $X_i + V_i$ increases and $V_{ij} + t_{ij} = V_{ij} - X_i/(N - 1)$ decreases. The maxi–min payoff occurs when equality is achieved between the Site i payoff $X_i + V_i$ and the worst possible alternative site $j \neq i$ payoff, $\operatorname{Min} \{V_{ij} \mid j \neq i\} - X_i/(N - 1)$. We can solve (7.9) to obtain the following explicit expression for the maxi–min bid:

$$X_i^* = \frac{N-1}{N} \left([\underset{j}{\text{Min}} \{V_{ij} \mid j \neq i\}] \right) - V_i \qquad (7.10)$$

The maxi–min bids for the data in Table 7.8 are given in the final row, labeled X_i^*. We note that Community 2 finds it in its interest to bid slightly higher than its true WTA; it is then guaranteed a positive benefit of at least 1 (if it has the lowest bid) and more if some other community submits a lower bid than 7. If every community bids its maxi–min bid, then Community 2 would be selected as the host community (i.e., Site 2 would be selected) and Communities 1 and 3 would pay, respectively, 4 and 5 (namely one-half their respective bids). Of this 9 total, 6 would go to Community 2 and the rest to the regional authority, possibly to defray its own costs, pay for planning grants, or be returned to the general treasury.[12]

Note that the net benefits to all communities from locating the facility at Community i are

$$B_i = V_i + \sum_{j \neq i} V_{ji} \qquad (7.11)$$

We tabulate these total net benefits also in Table 7.8 in the final column. Note from Table 7.8 that Community 2 is the site that maximizes total net benefits. It is, in other words, the Pareto-efficient choice. The fact that the low-bid auction mechanism yields a Pareto-efficient choice under maxi–min bidding, as in this example, is not accidental. As shown by Kunreuther, Kleindorfer, Knez, and Yaksick (1987), this will always be the case when each community is indifferent about alternate site location, provided it is not in its backyard (i.e., as long as $V_{ij} = V_{ik}$ for all j, $k \neq i$ and for all i).

In sum, the low-bid auction mechanism has various desirable properties for helping to solve the noxious facility siting problem. It yields a Pareto-efficient site under mild restrictions. Also, while the procedure does not guarantee honest revelation of a community's true total costs, communities are dissuaded from greatly exaggerating their compensation requirements since they may be required to pay $1/(N-1)$ of their stated

---

12 An alternative form of the low-bid auction is to have each nonwinning community pay only $1/(N-1)$ times the bid of the winning community. In this case, Communities 1 and 3 would each pay 3 directly to Community 2. This form of the low-bid auction has many of the same properties of the low-bid auction presented here, but it provides less of an incentive to bid honestly, since losing communities only end up paying a portion of the low-bidder's cost. On the other hand, this modified procedure does not collect excess revenues.

requirements if they are not the low bid. The procedure generates a tax surplus (net of compensation), and it discourages coalitional strategizing since each community's required payments and transfers depend only on its own bid.

The low-bid auction mechanism has also been tested experimentally and in a field experiment (see Kunreuther et al., 1987, for details). The experimental results suggest that subjects tend to bid their maxi–min strategies and that Pareto-efficient outcomes do result. Although much remains to be done in clarifying and refining such a procedure for actual use in siting noxious facilities, the low-bid auction procedure appears to provide a reasonable approach for structuring this type of collective choice problem. However, as Arrow's theorem makes clear, the general class of all collective choice problems has no perfect solutions.

7.6   The principal–agent problem

Principal–agent problems are examples of group choice having the characteristic that one of the group's members, called the principal, has the power to set certain design parameters for the group.[13] These design parameters then influence the rewards and information available to the group and thereby also the process and outcome of the group. The principal is naturally interested in choosing the design parameters in such a way as to maximize his own well-being. Of course, the other members of the group will act as independent "agents" once the principal has set the stage by choosing a group design. In its simplest form, the principal "hires" a single agent and specifies a payment schedule that the agent will receive for performing a task that the principal either does not wish to or cannot undertake himself. A host of problems can be modeled in this fashion, including client–lawyer and employer–employee relationships. Our purpose here will be to introduce this important paradigm and provide a few examples to illustrate its wide scope of applicability.

7.6.1   A sharecropping example

Sharecropping is an age-old institution in which a principal (landowner) obtains the services of an agent (sharecropper-tenant) by paying the tenant a share of the (market value of the) crop that the agent is able to grow on the principal's lands. By paying in this way, the landowner can go on about his business and only has to show up at harvest time to measure

---

13 This section contains somewhat technical material, which may be skipped by the reader if desired.

how large the crop is. Because with a larger harvest the sharecropper earns more, he has an incentive to be diligent in his duties even though the principal-landowner may only visit the farm once a year at harvest-time. The issue of interest in this context is the sharing rule used by the principal to remunerate the tenant. The principal is interested, of course, in setting this share optimally, that is, so as to maximize the principal's residual after paying the tenant his share and accounting for his own time and monitoring efforts.

Let us consider more formally a simple version of the sharecropping problem in which the agent must decide how much effort to expend on farming the principal's lands versus doing other things with his time (e.g., leisure or working at other jobs). We shall use the following notation:

λ	The tenant's share of the harvest, λ, $\in [0, 1]$.
x	The effort (or time) expended by the tenant in farming the principal's lands – we assume that x is chosen from some interval, that is, $x \in X = [0, \bar{x}]$.
$F(x)$	The market value of the harvest resulting when the tenant expends x units of effort farming.
$V(x)$	The disutility of effort (the "opportunity cost" to the tenant) of expending x units of effort on farming rather than on leisure or in working at other jobs.
$U(x, r)$	The tenant's utility of expending x units of effort and being paid r dollars – we assume $U(x, r) = r - V(x)$, with $r = F(x)$.
$U_o(F - r)$	$F - r$, the principal's utility, which is assumed to depend only on money – the principal receives the residual of the harvest's value after paying the agent, so that $U_o(F - r) = (1 - \lambda)F(x)$.

The essence of the sharecropping problem is the rule for dividing the harvest between the principal and the agent. When the agent expends x units of effort, the harvest is of size $F(x)$, of which the agent receives $\lambda F(x)$ and the principal $(1 - \lambda)F(x)$. We assume in this model that once the principal has set the tenant's share at λ, the tenant will choose x so as to maximize the difference between his reward $\lambda F(x)$ and his cost of effort $V(x)$, that is, the tenant will choose x solving

$$\text{Maximize } U(x, r) = \text{Maximize } [\lambda F(x) - V(x)] \qquad (7.12)$$
$$\quad\; x \in X \qquad\qquad\qquad x \in X$$

If F and V are concave increasing and convex increasing, respectively, then the agent's problem can be depicted graphically as in Figure 7.5. In the figure, we show that the optimal solutions x_1 and x_2 to (7.12) correspond to two different shares λ_1 and λ_2, with $\lambda_1 < \lambda_2$. As expected, the

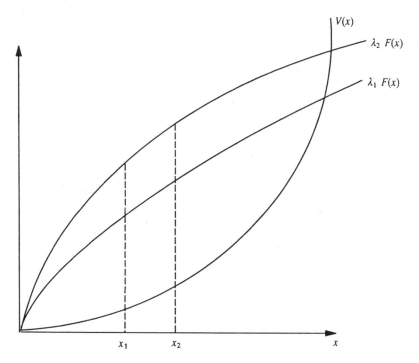

Figure 7.5. illustrating sharecropping. *Note*: x_i maximizes the difference between $\lambda_i F(x)$ and $V(x)$.

higher the share, the more the agent will work. As an example, suppose that

$$F(x) = Ax^{\alpha}, \quad V(x) = Bx^{\beta}, \quad \text{with } A, B > 0; \quad 0 < \alpha < 1 \quad \text{and} \quad \beta > 1 \quad (7.13)$$

Then F is concave increasing and V is convex increasing. If we assume an interior solution to (7.12), the first-order condition (FOC) for the optimal effort level for the agent given any λ is $\lambda F'(x) = V'(x)$, where $'$ indicates derivative. For the example (7.13), the FOC can easily be solved to yield the agent's optimal effort level

$$x^*(\lambda) = \left(\frac{\lambda \alpha A}{\beta B}\right)^{[1/(\beta - \alpha)]} \quad (7.14)$$

which is an increasing function of λ since $\beta > \alpha > 0$. From the definition of F in (7.13), the resulting market value of output $F(x^*(\lambda))$ is given by

$$F(x^*(\lambda)) = A \cdot \left(\frac{\lambda \alpha A}{\beta B}\right)^{[\alpha/(\beta - \alpha)]} \quad (7.15)$$

which is also increasing in λ. The principal is interested is choosing λ so as to maximize his residual after paying the agent, that is, the principal wishes to choose λ ∈ [0, 1] so as to

$$\underset{\lambda \in [0,1]}{\text{Maximize}}\ [(1 - \lambda) \cdot F(x^*(\lambda))] \tag{7.16}$$

Note that the principal is assumed to affect the agent's actions only through the choice of the sharing system; he cannot simply tell the agent what x to choose. Regarding (7.14)–(7.16), it is clear that the principal will choose strictly between 0 and 1. For if the principal gives the agent no share of the output (λ = 0), then the agent's effort will be zero and so will output. On the other hand, if λ = 1, then output and effort will be maximal, but the residual $(1 - \lambda)F(x)$ will be zero. Thus, some intermediate λ value must be optimal. Indeed, the FOC for the optimal solution λ* solving (7.16) is obtained from the chain rule to be

$$(1 - \lambda)F'(x^*(\lambda)) \cdot \frac{dx^*(\lambda)}{d\lambda} = F(x^*(\lambda)) \tag{7.17}$$

For the illustrative functions (7.13), the reader may verify that (7.17) yields the principal's unique optimal solution $\lambda^* = \alpha/\beta$ (which is strictly between 0 and 1 by our assumptions on α and β). This ratio can next be substituted into (7.15) to obtain the equilibrium size of the harvest. Note that the principal must know how the agent's effort will affect output (via α) as well as the form of the agent's preferences (as captured by β) in order to determine the optimal solution λ*. However, one can also imagine converging to λ* through a process of experimentation and learning.

This example illustrates the principal–agent paradigm and the principal's problem of choosing an optimal incentive system of a particular (sharecropping) type. The sharecropping problem can be extended in many ways (see Sertel, 1982), including uncertainty and risk preferences for the agent, having several factors of production (not just the agent's effort but also some capital input supplied by the principal or the agent), and having multiple agents. The sharecropping problem has also served as a model for designing task-oriented group processes, as we discuss further.

7.6.2 Principal–agent problems under risk

A second class of principal–agent problems of considerable importance in finance and economics (see, e.g. Barnea, Hangen, and Senbet, 1985; Laffont, 1989) extends the deterministic framework to include risk.[14] We

---

14 The statement of the principal–agent problem is usually credited to Ross (1973) but it has earlier roots in the literature of economic design, as seen, e.g., in Hurwicz (1973).

Table 7.9. *Probability of various output levels as a function of* x

	$F(x \mid \theta) = 0$	$F(x \mid \theta) = 5$	$B(x)$
$x = 0$	.8	.2	1.0
$x = 1$	.2	.8	4.0

first illustrate this framework with a numerical example and then formulate the more general version.

Suppose an agent can undertake two actions denoted $x \in \{0, 1\}$. Output $F(x \mid \theta)$ can be either 0 or 5, depending on an uncertain state of the world . The probability distribution of output is given in the following table. We also tabulate there the expected output $B(x)$ (the gross benefits to the principal) when the agent chooses action x (e.g., $B(1) = .2 \cdot 0 + .8 \cdot 5 = 4.0$).

Suppose the principal and the agent have von Neumann–Morgenstern preferences $U_o(r)$ and $U(r, x)$ respectively, given by

$$U_o(r) = r, \qquad U(r, x) = r - x \tag{7.18}$$

where r is money. For the agent, r is the monetary reward or incentive that the agent receives from the principal, who keeps the ouput minus whatever incentive payments he promised the agent.

The principal wishes to design an incentive system $s : Y \rightarrow I$, with $Y = \{0,5\}$ and $I = \{0, 1, 2, \ldots\}$, where $s(y)$ represents the payment the principal promises the agent if output is $y \in Y = \{0, 5\}$. We can think of $s(y)$ as a wage (which must be a nonnegative integer) depending on the level of output observed. Since there are only two output levels (0 and 5), an incentive system is entirely determined by the two numbers, s_0 and s_5, which are the promised wages (or incentive payments) that the principal announces he will pay the agent if output level 0, respectively 5, is observed. Given any incentive system $s = \{s_0, s_5\}$, we can compute the agent's expected utility from (7.18) and Table 7.9 for each $x \in X$:

$$U(r(s), 0) = .8s_0 + .2s_5 \qquad U(r(s), 1) = .2s_0 + .8s_5 - 1 \tag{7.19}$$

For example, suppose the agent chooses $x = 0$. Then from Table 7.9, output 0 (respectively 5) will result with probability .8 (respectively .2) and the agent will be paid s_0 or s_5 depending on which output obtains. The expected payoff to the agent is therefore $.8s_0 + .2s_5$ and the agent's expected utility is given by $U(r(s), 0)$ in (7.19) since choosing $x = 0$ costs the agent nothing. $U(r(s), 1)$ is computed similarly, but this time the agent's action $x = 1$ costs 1, as indicated in (7.19).

Table 7.10. *A principal–agent example*

		$U(r(s), x)^a$			
s_0	s_5	$x = 0$	$x = 1$	$c(x^*(s),s)^b$	$U_o(r(s))^c$
0	0	0.0*	−1.0	0.0 ← (x = 0)	1.0
0	1	0.2*	−0.2	0.2	0.8
0	2	0.4	0.6*	1.6 ← (x = 1)	2.4
1	0	0.8*	−0.8	0.8	0.2
1	1	1.0*	0.0	1.0	0.0
1	2	1.2*	0.8	1.2	−0.2
1	3	1.4	1.6*	2.6	1.4
2	1	1.8*	0.2	1.8	−0.8
2	2	2.0*	1.0	2.0	−1.0
2	3	2.2*	1.8	2.2	−1.2
•	•	•	•	•	•
•	•	•	•	•	•
•	•	•	•	•	•

^{a}The agent's optimal action $x^*(s)$ is indicated by *.
^{b}The incentive system implementing x at minimum expected cost is marked by a ←.
^{c}This is the principal's expected utility for the given incentive system s, evaluated at the agent's optimal action $x^*(s)$.

The principal's payoff for any incentive system s is just the output minus the incentive payments to the agent. In deciding which incentive system to choose, the principal must predict what the agent will do given the incentive system. A reasonable assumption is that, given any incentive system s, the agent will choose that action $x \in X$ which maximizes his expected utility. An important insight, elaborated by Grossman and Hart (1983), is that among all incentive systems that induce the agent to choose x (as the agent's expected utility maximizing choice), the principal will prefer the incentive system that entails the smallest expected payout.

Formally, define $C(x)$ as the minimum expected cost of inducing the agent to choose $x \in X$. Table 7.10 shows how to compute $C(x)$ for our problem. For any incentive system $s =\{s_0, s_5\}$, we first compute the agent's expected utility from choosing either $x = 0$ or $x = 1$. The agent will pick the better of these two actions, denoted $x^*(s)$ (e.g., the best action for the agent when $s = \{0, 1\}$ is $x = 0$). Then we compute the expected cost $c(x^*(s), s)$ to the principal arising from the given incentive system s, evaluated at the action $x^*(s)$ that the agent can be expected to choose, given

s (e.g., since for $s = 0, 1$} $x^*(s) = 0$, we use the first row of Table 7.9 to compute $c(x^*(s), s) = .8s_0 + .2s_5 = .2$). Finally, we compute $C(x)$ as the minimum expected cost of inducing the agent to choose x, that is,

$$C(x) = \text{Minimum } \{c(x^*(s), s) \mid s = \{s_0, s_5\}, s_0 \in I, s_5 \in I\} \quad (7.20)$$

For example, it should be clear that the cheapest way of getting the agent to choose $x = 0$ is to declare the incentive system $s = \{s_0, s_5\} = 0, 0\}$ with expected cost $C(x) = c(x^*(s), s) = c(0, s) = 0$. The reader may check from Table 7.9 that $C(1) = 0.6$, which is implemented by the incentive system $s = \{0, 2\}$. The problem of determining C(1) may be expressed as:

$$C(1) = \underset{s_0, s_5}{\text{Minimize }} [.2s_0 + .8s_5] \quad (7.21)$$

subject to:

$$.2s_0 + .8s_5 - 1 \geq .8s_0 + .2s_5, \quad (s_0 \in I, s_5 \in I) \quad (7.22)$$

The term [ ] in (7.21) represents the expected value of incentive payments to the agent if he chooses $x = 1$ (see Table 7.9). The constraint (7.22) simply states that the incentive system $\{s_0, s_5\}$ should be such that the agent will prefer $x = 1$ to $x = 0$, since the left side of the inequality is just the agent's expected utility if he chooses $x = 1$ and the right side is his expected utility if he chooses $x = 0$ (again using Table 7.9). Thus, (7.21)–(7.22) is the program that the principal must solve in order to select the cheapest way (in expected incentive payments) to induce the agent to choose $x = 1$.

Given this information, we can solve the principal's overall problem of determining a best incentive system, in the sense of maximizing his expected benefits minus the incentive payments. This can be done directly from the final column of Table 7.10, which gives the principal's expected utility U_o for each incentive scheme. Thus, the principal's optimal incentive system is $s^* = \{0, 2\}$, which leads the agent to choose $x^*(s^*) = 1$, with expected output $= .2 \cdot 0 + .8 \cdot 5 = 4$, expected incentive payments of $.2 \cdot 0 + .8 \cdot 2 = 1.6$ and expected utilities for the agent and the principal of 0.6 and 2.4.

Alternatively, we can use the function $C(x)$ defined previously to solve the principal's problem. We first solve

$$\underset{x \in X}{\text{Minimize }} [B(\text{x}) - C(x)] \quad (7.23)$$

for the best $x^* \in X$, where $B(x)$ is given in Table 7.9 and $C(x)$ is determined as previously. Then the optimal incentive system s^* is that which implements x^* at minimum expected cost $C(x^*)$. This has the interpretation that the principal selects the best $x \in X$ to implement as evaluated by his expected benefits in output produced minus the minimum expected cost of the incentive system required to induce the agent to choose x. Noting that $C(0) = 0$, $C(1) = 1.6$, we see from Table 7.9 that the optimal x from the principal's point of view is $x = 1$, where $B(x) - C(x) = 4 - 1.6 = 2.4$. Clearly either the direct approach or that based on the logic of (7.23) yields the same outcome.

This example illustrates the important elements of the principal–agent problem under risk. First, there is some underlying uncertainty, about which both principal and agent have probabilistic beliefs. Just as in the case of sharecropping, the principal cannot force the agent to choose a particular action x, but can only influence this choice through an incentive system. We have seen two (equivalent) ways of formulating the principal's design problem, one in terms of choosing the best incentive system s^* directly, and the other in terms of implementing the best action $x^* \in X$ by defining the minimum expected cost $C(x)$ of inducing the agent to choose x and then maximizing the difference between the expected benefits $B(x)$ and $C(x)$. Let us now consider a more general framework for understanding the principal–agent paradigm and its relationship to the design of group decision processes.

7.6.3   *Multi-agent principal–agent problems and design*

To apply this approach to organizations, we must consider more than one agent and see how the principal–agent paradigm might be used.[15] We shall model a task-oriented group as a collection of economic agents whose joint contribution to a productive process yields a certain output that each of them considers a good, but whose individual contributions to the group have opportunity costs (see Figure 7.6).

The principal, or group "designer," chooses a design $\delta \in \Delta$, for example, an incentive system, that influences the production decisions (or input choices) $x_i \in X_i$ of group members $i \in N$. Each agent has preferences represented by the utility function $U_i(x, r_i)$ defined on $x \in X = \Pi_N X_i$ and on their remuneration $r_i(x, \delta) \in \Re$ ($\Re$ is the real line), where $x = \{x_i \ i \in N\} \in X$ is the vector of inputs of agents $i \in N$. Given δ, the agents adjust their decisions, resulting in a collective decision $\mathbf{x}(\delta)$ and output $F(\mathbf{x}(\delta), \delta)$. The external context provides the basis for agents to determine their opportunity costs, and final product markets determine the price of output, which we will take to be unity here. Agents $i \in N$ are assumed to choose $x_i(\delta)$ so as to maximize their utility $U_i(x, r_i)$, $i \in N$. The outcome $x_i(\delta)$ in response to a given design $\delta \in \Delta$ may be thought of as the

---

15 This section is analytical and abstract in its approach to multi-agent incentive problems. The nontechnical reader may skip it without loss of continuity.

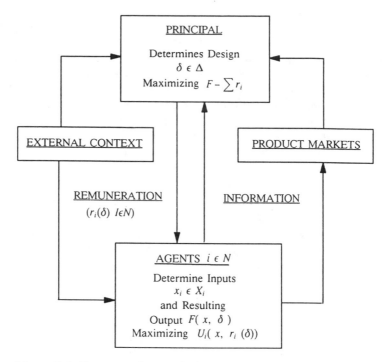

Figure 7.6. Elements of group design

equilibrium of a normal-form game among agents N, given δ. Various (cooperative and noncooperative) solution concepts are of interest in modeling this equilibrium. The principal is assumed to be a risk-neutral agent interested in choosing δ so as to maximize his residual $F(\mathbf{x}(\delta), \delta) - \Sigma_N r_i(\mathbf{x}(\delta), \delta)$. We neglect uncertainty in this example.

Although the design $\delta \in \Delta$ could involve such issues as choosing the members of the group (N) and the technology (F), we concentrate here on the design of incentives and compatible information systems from the point of view of the principal, assuming fixed (N, F). We begin with a formal statement of the principal's design problem:

$$\underset{\delta \in \Delta}{\text{Maximize}}\, F(\mathbf{x}(\delta), \delta) - \sum_{i \in N} r_i(\mathbf{x}(\delta), \delta) \qquad (7.25)$$

subject to:

$$U_i(\mathbf{x}(\delta), r_i(\mathbf{x}(\delta), \delta)) \geq U_{io}, \qquad i \in N \qquad (7.26)$$

where $\mathbf{x}(\delta)$ is the predicted outcome in response to δ and U_{io} is the reservation utility level for $i \in N$, as determined by opportunities outside the group in question (if U_{io} is not guaranteed, Individual i will simply not participate in the group).

As to the form of $r_i(\delta)$, two polar extremes have been of primary interest in the literature, sharing and wage incentives. In the former, $r_i(\mathbf{x}(\delta), \delta) = r_i(F(\mathbf{x}(\delta), \delta), \delta)$ depends on $\mathbf{x}(\delta)$ only through F, as in our sharecropping example earlier. Under wage incentives, $r_i(\mathbf{x}(\delta), \delta) = r_i(\mathbf{x}_i(\delta), \delta)$ depends only on the input of Agent i. Concerning information systems, these must be compatible with the incentive structure chosen. For example, under sharing rules the principal must only observe the output F, whereas under wage incentives he must observe individual inputs $\{x_i \mid i \in N\}$ in order to pay out the agreed-upon remuneration r_i to each agent.[16]

In this section we consider results for the problem (7.25)–(7.26) under perfect information and for various solution concepts. To begin with, we make the following regularity assumptions.

Assumptions: The production function $F(x, \delta) = F(x)$ is increasing, continuously differentiable and concave in x, with $F(0) = 0$. Utility functions are of the separable form

$$U_i(x, r_i) = r_i - V_i(x_i), \qquad i \in N, \qquad x_i \in X_i \subseteq \mathfrak{R}_+ \tag{7.27}$$

where $\mathfrak{R}_+$ is the nonnegative reals, and V_i is a continuously differentiable real-valued function.

Let us begin with a restatement of Holmstrom's (1982) interesting result that sharing incentives that exclude any payments to the principal-designer are inefficient. To this end, let the design set be the set of all sharing incentives:

$$\Delta := \{S : X - \to \mathfrak{R}^N \mid S(x) = \{S_i(x) = S_i(F(x)) \mid i \in N\}, \tag{7.28}$$
$$\Sigma_N S_i(F) = F, F \in \mathfrak{R}_+\}$$

so that each S_i depends only on the output F and the total output value is distributed among the agents N. Associated with each $\delta \in \Delta$, there is a normal-form game $\Gamma(\delta) = [N, X, W_i, \delta]$, where, substituting $r_i = S_i$ in (7.27), the "effective utility functions" W_i induced by $\delta = \{S_i \mid i \in N\}$ are

$$W_i(x, \delta) = S_i(F(x)) - V_i(x_i), \qquad i \in N, \qquad x \in X \tag{7.29}$$

We are interested in comparing the efficiency of various outcomes to the game $\Gamma(\delta)$ with first-best or efficient solutions as determined by:

$$\underset{x \in X}{\text{Maximize}} \left[F(x) - \sum_{i \in N} V_i(x_i) \right] \tag{7.30}$$

---

16 For a more detailed discussion of the compatibility of incentive and information structures, see Kleindorfer and Sertel (1979).

Any solution x^* to (7.30) is Pareto-efficient in the sense that any such solution, coupled with appropriate income transfers among agents N, weakly dominates any other $x \in X$ and feasible transfer payment scheme among N (Kleindorfer and Sertel, 1982). Equation (7.30) represents the maximum of output value minus opportunity costs of factor inputs x_i.

Theorem 1 (Holmstrom, 1982): Let $\delta \in \Delta$ be arbitrary and let $\mathbf{x}(\delta)$ be any Nash (noncooperative) equilibrium of $\Gamma(\delta)$, then $\mathbf{x}(\delta)$ is not Pareto-efficient in the sense of (7.30). In particular, sharing systems that leave no residual for the principal are not efficient in the sense of (7.30).

Proof: We merely give Holmstrom's short proof for the case where the S_i are differentiable. In this case, if we assume interior solutions, any Nash solution $\mathbf{x}(\delta)$ to $\Gamma(\delta)$ must satisfy

$$S_i' F_i' - V_i' = 0, \qquad i \in N \tag{7.31}$$

where $F_i' = \partial F / \partial x_i$, whereas any Pareto solution to (7.30) must satisfy

$$F_i' - V_i' = 0, \qquad i \in N \tag{7.32}$$

Since any feasible δ must satisfy $\Sigma_N S_i(F(x)) = F(x)$, $x \in X$, we also have that $\Sigma_N F_i' = 1$, for all $x \in X$. This last requirement is not compatible with (7.31)–(7.32) jointly, yielding the desired conclusion.

Holmstrom shows that if budget balancing is relaxed, so that $\Sigma_N S_i(F) \leq F$ is allowed, then sharing incentives can be designed that yield Pareto outcomes as Nash equilibria to $\Gamma(\delta)$. One such Pareto sharing system is of the "forcing function" form described by Harris and Raviv (1978). Namely, $S_i(F) = b_i$ if $F(x) \geq F(x^*)$ and $S_i(F) = 0$ otherwise, where x^* is any solution to (7.30). Such a sharing system imposes penalties, collected by the principal, for output performance below first-best. As Holmstrom shows, a suitable set of $\{b_i \mid i \in N\}$ can be determined[17] which will make each $i \in N$ better off than his best available other alternative and will achieve x^*.

The importance of the principal in avoiding inefficiency in this problem derives entirely from his design expertise; he contributes no other productive input. The need for the principal as residual owner and "penalty collector" disappears, however, when cooperative behavior on the part of N can be costlessly assured. To demonstrate this formally, we need an appropriate cooperative solution concept for the game $\Gamma(\delta)$. Given the form of the preferences (7.27), the Nash bargaining solution introduced earlier seems appropriate, allowing for lump-sum transfers among group members N. In this case, it is easily shown that group members will choose $\mathbf{x}^*(\delta)$ solving (7.30). That is, they will choose a first-best solu-

---

17 Namely, a set of b_i's such that $\Sigma_N b_i = F(x^*)$ and $b_i > V_i(x_i^*) > 0$, so that each $i \in N$ is at least as well off taking part in the group's activities as not.

tion, assuming that *no* unproductive principal appropriates any of the usufruct $F(x)$ of production. We summarize this in the following proposition.

Theorem 2: Let δ, $\mathbf{x}(\delta)$, and $\Gamma(\delta)$ be as in Theorem 1. Consider the Nash bargaining solution $\mathbf{x}^*(\delta)$ to $\Gamma(\delta)$ specified by

$$\mathbf{x}^*(\delta) \in \arg\max \{\Pi_N[W_i(x, \delta) + t_i - U_i] \mid x \in X_{\ddagger}^*(\mathbf{t}), t \in T\} \tag{7.33}$$

where W_i is given in (7.29), $T = \{t_i \in \Re \mid \Sigma_N t_i = 0\}$ and $X_{\ddagger}^*$ is the feasible bargaining set

$$X_{\ddagger}^* = \{x \in X \mid W_i(x, \delta) + t_i \geq U_i, \qquad i \in N\} \tag{7.34}$$

Then (as long as [7.30] has any solution), $\mathbf{x}^* = \mathbf{x}^*(\delta)$ solves (7.30), that is, it is first-best, and there exist lump-sum transfers $\mathbf{t}^* = \{t_i^* \mid i \in N\}$ such that $(\mathbf{x}^*, \mathbf{t}^*)$ Pareto dominates the noncooperative solution $\mathbf{x}(\delta)$.

Proof: The Nash bargaining solution x^* characterized by (7.33) is easily shown to maximize $\Sigma_N W_i(x, \delta)$ over X, which from (7.28)–(7.29) implies that x^* maximizes (7.30). Moreover, $\mathbf{x}^* \in X_{\ddagger}^*(\mathbf{t})$ and $\mathbf{t} \in T$, so that $\mathbf{x}^*$ certainly weakly dominates $\mathbf{x}(\delta)$ from (7.33). Finally, $\mathbf{x}(\delta)$ does *not* solve (7.30) by Holmstrom's Theorem 1. Thus, some subset of N receives the surplus $\Sigma_N W_i(\mathbf{x}^*, \delta) - \Sigma_N W_i(x(\delta), \delta) > 0$, and strict dominance obtains.[18]

From these two theorems, we see that an unproductive principal is required only when noncooperative behavior is anticipated. From our earlier discussion, however, we know that cooperation is more likely to obtain when communication and trust are present among agents N, and further enhanced under repeated game situations. More formally, as discussed in Friedman (1990), when discount factors are sufficiently small (or when gains from cooperation over noncooperation are large), the cooperative solution x^* to $\Gamma(\delta)$ can be implemented as a Nash equilibrium to the infinitely repeated game $\Gamma(\delta) \times \ldots \times \Gamma(\delta) \times \ldots$, with payoffs

$$W_i^{\gamma}(x, \delta) = \Sigma (\alpha_i)^k W_i(x^k, \delta) \tag{7.35}$$

where $x^k \in X$ is the collective input chosen by N in period (or subgame) k and $\alpha_i = 1/(1 + d_i) \in (0, 1)$, where d_i is Agent i's discount factor. In this sense, the prospect of a "long" association with an organization can be expected to promote cooperative behavior, a result that we also noted has been supported in experimental studies of bargaining.[19]

18 The reader interested in a more detailed analysis of cooperative solutions with lump-sum transfers is referred to Kleindorfer and Sertel (1982), on which this theorem is based.

19 This very point has also been argued to be the crux of the Japanese productivity miracle, based on long-term employment and cooperation- and communication-inducing incentives and organizational processes. See Tomer (1985).

This discussion is, of course, only intended as a brief introduction to the complex issue of organizational and group incentives. In particular, we have neglected the potentially productive role of principals in contributing other productive factors such as managerial expertise or capital. Also, our analysis has abstracted from a host of issues in monitoring and control inherent in group design. Even with these caveats, however, it is clear that the issues raised here on cooperative versus noncooperative internal adjustment by group or organizational agents are central to any analysis of incentival design.

7.7   Conclusions

In Chapters 6 and 7 we have discussed group decision-making research. These chapters may be contrasted in several ways. First, we noted the difference between holistic approaches to groups and the approaches followed in this chapter based on individual decision making. One may understand this contrast as related to the general concept of nested decision structures introduced in Chapter 1. Groups have existential properties of their own (such as coherence, cooperation), but many of these can be fruitfully related to the preferences, beliefs, and choice processes of the members in the group, relying, for example, on the powerful formal framework of game theory.

At the same time, we see in the research on cooperation that there must be a strong linking between descriptive and prescriptive elements of group decision making in order to understand many elements of group decision making. And these links are frequently best understood by studying group process in relation to group outcomes, as illustrated by our examples of group and committee choice. These examples provided practical insights into solution procedures for specific domains such as siting decisions. Perhaps the most interesting feature of group decision-making research is how variable group efficiency can be in task-oriented or resource allocation contexts. If groups possess the right resources, and when informational as well as incentive alignments of group members have been assured through appropriate communication and reward systems, group output and efficiency can be formidable.

Last, this chapter has shown how complex group decisions can be. Even highly abstracted and simplified representations of group conflict often defy optimization. Instead, heuristic solutions have to be found and tested, with possibly only limited generalizability to other domains (e.g., as with siting decisions). The challenge for decision scientists is to balance realism and solvability in improving the quality of group choice. As with individual decision making, this will require understanding problem context and legitimation requirements as a prelude to group problem-finding and problem-solving activities.

8

Organizational decision making

8.1   Introduction

In examining organizational decision making, we shall draw heavily on the earlier chapters dealing with individual and group decisions. After all, organizations do not make decisions, people do. Indeed, it might be argued that understanding how people make decisions and how groups function is sufficient to understand and improve organizational decision making. We take a different view. Although individual and group decision making is *nested* within organizational decision making, and is indeed important to its understanding, it is *not sufficient* to describe how organizations arrive at decisions. As foreshadowed in Chapters 1 and 2, an additional set of concepts, principles, and frameworks is needed to understand and improve organizational decisions.

Our focus in this chapter is on decision making *by* organizations (taking a global and distant perspective), as well as decision making *within* organizations.[1] The latter perspective examines how the larger organizational context affects people's perceptions of and approaches to decision problems. To address these issues we need to have some understanding of organizations in general. However, the literature on organizations is vast and cannot possibly be reviewed in a few pages. For this reason, we identify in this chapter only the most important concepts and terms needed for our decision process perspective. Multiple perspectives will be offered, including contributions from economics, organization theory, and political science. As before, both descriptive and prescriptive aspects will be addressed.

8.1.1   *Historical background*

Organizations have existed since the beginning of human civilization, in the form of hunting tribes, clans, village councils, governments, religious groups, and of course military units. This proclivity suggests that organizations serve many purposes, ranging from solving highly structured tasks

---

1 This chapter draws and builds on Schoemaker (1991a).

Table 8.1. *Historical perspective*

Time markers	External developments (technological/societal)	Organizational responses/innovations
1850	Mass production (industrial revolution)	Functional design
1900	Mass distribution (railroads)	Divisionalization (GM–DuPont–Standard Oil)
1940	Faster transportation (jet airplanes)	Conglomeration/ multinationals
1960	Faster communication (mainframe computer)	Matrix designs/consensus management (in Japan)
1980	Information revolution (personal computers/ satellites)	Decentralization/heterarchies
1990	Customization/quality (deregulation/competition/ globalization)	Invisible assets/ reconfigural capabilities

(e.g., building a car) to more enduring and abstract concerns such as city governance or spiritual enlightenment (e.g., religions). Sometimes the boundary between groups and organizations is fuzzy. Distinguishing features of organizations include the use of hierarchy, systematization of procedures, interrelated activities, specialization of tasks, and overall complexity. Organizations are typically larger than groups (often consisting of multiple, hierarchically arranged units), and their structures and scopes may vary over time depending on the efficacy of conducting activities outside versus within the organization. An additional characteristic of many current organizations is their *limited liability*, as with the modern corporation.

The evolution of corporations can be best understood in the context of larger societal changes (see Table 8.1). Complex trading organizations (such as the East India Company) arose in the sixteenth and seventeenth centuries when Italy, Portugal, Spain, England, Holland, and other nations expanded their merchant activities worldwide. Only in the early nineteenth century, however, do we see the emergence of the modern corporation, prompted by the development of railroads, telecommunication, and the industrial revolution (see Chandler, 1977). Three characteristics stand out in this development: (1) forward integration by manufacturers into distribution (due to lower transportation costs and telephone and telegraph communication), (2) the use of multidivisional structures (led by DuPont and General Motors), and (3) conglomeration (i.e., combining disparate businesses under one umbrella cutting across industries and national boundaries). The last two characteristics are primarily twentieth-century phenomena (see Williamson, 1981), especially the rise of complex multinationals.

These developments have much altered the nature of decision processes in firms, from face-to-face and informal to electronic and systematic. Authors such as Williamson (1981) and Galbraith (1973) and others have tried to understand the scope and design of organizations by treating the decision or transaction as the crucial unit of analysis. For instance, better computing technology permits better information and standardization of decision making (e.g., as in airline reservations). Also, the costs of transacting business – that is, the cost of designing agreements (or contracts), monitoring performance, and enforcing of contracts – change as information technologies, legal systems, and product markets become more complex. Indeed, the emergence of pervasive and powerful financial markets that monitor and control corporate affairs owes much to inventions in communications and computing.

The historical evolution of business firms highlights how technology and external complexity were major driving forces.[2] Both were in turn fueled by competition and such human constants as greed, fear, and hope. Economies of scale and scope especially contributed to the increased complexity of economic activities, as did the emergence of mass distribution systems such as railroads, the telephone and telegraph, and, later, jet airplanes and computers. As society grew more complex, firms needed to mirror this complexity to keep pace. Increased organizational complexity, however, comes at a price. Complex firms tend to be less flexible, more difficult to manage, and slower to change. Consequently, we see the emergence of *strategic* planning as a central activity in large firms, as well as a concern with information management (Emery, 1986) so as to better control the increased complexity. Toward the end of this chapter we shall discuss developments and challenges of the 1990s (as indicated in the last row of the table).

The remainder of this chapter seeks to understand (in light of this thumbnail sketch) how decisions get made within and by companies, and how they might be improved. Thus we study organizational decision making against the backdrop of a society that evolved from (1) the *industrial* revolution through (2) a *scientific management* phase (Frederick Taylor) to (3) an *organizational* revolution (Sloan, 1963) to (4) an *information* revolution. In the current information age, we believe that organizations

---

2 A well-known law in systems theory posits that one can only control complex external processes by possessing matching internal complexity (i.e., Ashby's, 1956, law of requisite variety).

Table 8.2. *Payoff table for ALCO's pricing decision: advertising success (probabilities and outcomes)*

Price	30% Excellent	50% Good	20% Poor
3.00	140	120	80
3.50	200	150	40
4.00	340	140	−20

Note: Expected profits (in $000) for different price levels.

can best be viewed as information-processing systems. Unlike individuals, who largely process information serially (see Chapters 2–4), organizations engage in extensive parallel and distributed processing. Not surprisingly, much emphasis is placed on information management. However, more and more, we see the key problem in organizations to be that of proper *attention* management.

8.1.2   *The ALCO Electronics Case*

To focus on decision making in organizations, let us look in on a representative meeting, at a middle-management level, in the life of a modern company.[3] This case helps set the stage for the type of questions we wish to address more systematically later in the chapter.

The ALCO Electronics Company recently developed a new type of integrated circuit (IC) for use in a variety of commercial and consumer products. The new IC is more sophisticated than one competitive product selling at $2.00 per unit but somewhat simpler than another competitive product selling at a unit price of $5.00.

Because of traditional industry price structures, top management has decided to limit its pricing alternatives to $3.00, $3.50, or $4.00 per unit. The director of marketing research, working closely with the manufacturing division, prepared the following one-year projection of profit and sales based upon different assumptions of price, promotion expenses, competition, and advertising success. For simplicity, they consider just three scenarios (see Table 8.2).

The pricing decision is to be made by a management committee. The committee members and a capsule summary of comments made at a meeting held to consider the decision are as follows:

---

3 This is a teaching case used at the Wharton School. It is discussed here in abbreviated form.

Nancy Daniels (director of marketing): I've always been an optimist. We should choose the price that offers the best profit opportunity. I believe that we should plan and work for the highest possible profit. After all we're an up-and-coming company that must take chances if we are to succeed.

Don Brown (director of research): My position is simple: Although it's fine to strive for the highest possible profits, we would be better off to plan for the worst possible conditions. That way we'll be protected against disaster. As a growing company, we cannot afford major setbacks.

Martin Roberts (assistant to the president): I have some serious doubts about Nancy's optimistic view as well as Don's pessimistic view of our problem. My own position is somewhere in between. I guess I'd have to label myself somewhat more optimistic though – about a 60% optimist, I guess.

Jane Seymour (advertising manager): Quite frankly, I'm concerned about the overemphasis on advertising in the success or failure of our new product. Sure, advertising is a factor, but you all know that product design, quality, flexibility, and other technical aspects are also extremely important. It seems to me that we would be wise to select a price that will minimize our reliance on the advertising program. Of course, I have every confidence in our advertising but let's try to avoid serious regrets later about the huge profits we *could* have made if we had only known in advance how successful the promotion would be.

Ed Glick (controller): You all seem to have an oversimplified view of profits and losses. While I certainly agree that high profits are desirable, we have to be realistic about our current financial position. Money is tight, and we're in no position with our stockholders to incur even a slight loss. In fact, in view of the poor year we're having with other product lines, we really need at least seventy-five thousand dollars of profit from the new IC if we are to meet our projections and avoid a drop in the price of ALCO stock. With this in mind, I place a higher value on the first seventy-five thousand dollars than on the next seventy-five, one hundred, or even two hundred thousand dollars.

Al Westlake (plant manager): It seems to me that we have overlooked some important information thus far. A good bit of effort has already been devoted to developing probabilities of success for our advertising campaign, and yet we are not making much use of these estimates. I play the odds whenever I bet my own money and see no reason why we shouldn't do the same thing here. The odds of a poor campaign should be weighed against those of an excellent or good campaign in making a decision.

Each of these organizational members proposes different criteria to judge the potential outcomes. With whom would you most agree? Although they all work for the same company, they prefer different courses of action. *Nancy Daniels* is interested in the best profit opportunity. If we translate her objective into a "maximize the highest possible gain" criterion, then she will favor a price of $4.00 since this has a chance of yielding the highest possible profit, namely $340,000. *Don Brown* fo-

Table 8.3. *Regret matrix for ALCO*

Price	Excellent	Good	Poor
3.00	200	30	0
3.50	140	0	40
4.00	0	10	100

Note: Expected regret levels (in $1,000) for different prices.

cuses on the worst possible condition (i.e., poor advertising success) so that his criterion is likely to be to maximize the minimum profit. This suggests a price of $3.00. *Martin Roberts* favors a compromise solution with 60% weight to Nancy and 40% to Don. This approach means calculating a weighted average, such as .6(200) + .4(40) = $136 for a price level of $3.50 compared to .6(340) + .4(−20) = $196 for a price level of $4.

Jane Seymour is worried about the regret ALCO would feel depending on how successful the advertising promotion turns out to be. For example, suppose that ALCO chooses a price of $3.00 and that the advertising success is excellent. In this case ALCO could have made $200,000 more in profits had the price been set at $4.00. Table 8.3 presents the regret matrix for each price and degree of advertising success. If Seymour used the criterion "choose the price that minimizes the maximum regret," then $4.00 would be the optimal one to choose.

Ed Glick is concerned with a safety-first type of criterion by maximizing the probability that the firm will earn at least $75,000 in profits. Given the analysis presented in Table 8.2, this implies that the price should be $3.00 since according to ALCO's calculations the firm is then certain to make $80,000.[4] Finally, *Al Westlake*'s comments imply that he would like to choose the price that maximizes expected value. A price of $4.00 maximizes the monetary expected value of the payoffs shown in Table 8.2 ($168 versus $118 or $143 thousand for prices of $3.00 and $3.50 respectively.)

The problem facing ALCO helps illustrate how people use different calculations to determine their recommended course of action. The case highlights systematic differences among individuals in valuing specific outcomes and approaching complex decisions, even if they agree on the problem's definition. Although some may reach the same conclusion about

---

4 Of course a firm is never certain to obtain a guaranteed minimum of profits. The profit matrix in Table 8.2 is a simplification of the real world and the preceding analysis must be interpreted with this in mind.

what price to choose, their *decision processes* may be quite different. For example Bob Daniels, John Seymour, and Al Westlake all believe that $4.00 is the optimal price. However, this does not mean these three individuals would necessarily agree on what strategy to follow for another problem with a different payoff matrix.

Another important set of organizational questions that affect decision processes concerns the scope and timing of the decision. Why was it structured as broadly or narrowly as it was? Who proposed the alternatives? Why is the pricing problem addressed now, as opposed to later or earlier? What decision tools, information bases, and resources are available to solve this problem? How is feedback obtained, coded, filtered, transmitted, and acted upon? What constraints exist, especially time limits?

For example, people's formal positions (or roles) in the organization are likely to affect their decision criteria. Is it surprising that the director of research (Don Brown) wants to play it safe? If the IC is a commercial failure, his research budget might be cut back. Likewise, Jane Seymour does not want a decision that reflects poorly on the role of advertising. In short, organizational members typically "stand where they sit"!

Finally, a host of normative or prescriptive questions arise, such as: What should ALCO do (ideally)? Is Don Brown acting rationally in terms of his personal perspective? Would the firm's CEO act differently? Why? What advice can be offered in terms of with whom and when to hold the meeting; with what agenda items and procedures? What data bases or decision support might be useful? Can the incentives be improved for managers to work more closely together (if this is desirable)? What formal models exist to improve these pricing decisions? How can other decisions be linked in, to get a more comprehensive portfolio perspective?

Such questions surface time and again in actual organizational decision making and should be addressed to understand how individual behavior affects organizational choice. By introducing a set of concepts, language, and frameworks from a decision process perspective, we may be able to provide guidance for improving the way organizations make decisions.

8.1.3   *Conceptual schema*

Our framework is inspired by Graham Allison's (1971) analysis of the Cuban missile crisis.[5] It can most easily be explained using a chess analogy. Suppose you are playing a game of chess against an unknown op-

---

5 However, only the unitary actor and political model correspond directly to Allison's views. For related conceptualizations see Steinbruner (1974) and MacCrimmon (1985).

Table 8.4. *A conceptual schema*

	Coordinative efficiency	
	Low	High
Goal congruency		
High	Organizational model	Unitary actor model
Low	Contextual view	Political model

ponent, whose moves are made from behind a curtain. As the game unfolds you start to develop some ideas as to the type of decision entity that resides behind the curtain. Four conceptually different organizational models might be distinguished here, reflecting different assumptions about goal congruency and coordinative efficiency. Table 8.4 shows how crossing these two axes yields four distinct quadrants, corresponding to the following four models.

Unitary actor model. This view assumes that only one person is behind the curtain, who acts from a clear set of organizational objectives and pursues a rational strategy to meet these objectives (within his or her skill level). This is a common view taken of organizations. We often think of organizations, other nations, and even our own government (Uncle Sam) as though they were rational individuals, who match means and ends so as to bring about the best decision for themselves. We treat them as monolithic entities that can be understood in terms of individual rationality.

Organizational model. This view presumes multiple decision makers, who practice division of labor (also called task differentiation), and thus must coordinate and integrate their various activities. For example, there might be a department of the rooks, a department of the queen, and so on, whose limited attentions are focused on the opportunities and threats relevant to their particular piece(s). Each of these departments has its own agenda, constraints and limitations. Nonetheless, all departments are assumed to share a common goal – winning the game – and work toward that end.

Political model. In this view, individual or departmental goals can supersede the organizational ones. For instance, the department of the rooks might knowingly reduce the probability of winning the game by some small degree so as to stay on the board or enhance its relative power position.

Of course, the probability of winning cannot be reduced too much, lest everybody is wiped out. The political model explicitly acknowledges the existence of a fine balance between individual and organizational goals, and focuses on "partisan behavior" in understanding organizational decision making.

Contextual view. Lastly, we add a contextual or residual perspective according to which much unresolved conflict exists (among goals), with low degrees of coordinative efficiency across functions and problems. For instance, the department of the rooks may be highly risk averse, whereas the bishops take big chances. Or, one of them has carefully studied past games against this particular opponent but fails to share any insights with the other departments. The contextual view holds that organizational environments are so complex and human desires so varied that each decision context becomes its own reality, with limited consistency across situations and goals (e.g., see March and Olson, 1976). The particulars of the context or environment thus become the driving force for the decision, rather than superordinate goals or comprehensive planning. This view embodies elements of Nelson and Winter's (1982) myopic routines, as well as Lindblom's (1959), Quinn's (1978), and Mintzberg's (1990) emphasis on local or micro determinants, and MacCrimmon and Wehrung's (1986) views on risk taking (see also March and Shapira, 1987). It also captures aspects of organizational ecology (Hannan and Freeman, 1989) insofar as it concerns the uncontrollable external environment and its impact on organizational form, adaptation, and survival.

Which view one adopts (for one's own organization or competitors) influences in important ways the sort of questions asked, the type of information gathered, and the decision outcomes predicted (as shown in Table 8.5). For the rational-unitary actor model, the questions closely resemble those that a single person might ask who is trying to choose systematically among the available alternatives. The other models, in contrast, focus more on relationships between people as well as the larger organizational and political setting. In his insightful book *Essence of Decision*, Allison (1971) applies each of the above frameworks to the Cuban missile crises of October 1962. At that time President John F. Kennedy faced a sudden, dangerous move on the chess board of international politics. His response depended critically on which view would be taken of the USSR. Given the secretive, dictatorial, and bureaucratic nature of the USSR, Allison shows that strong cases could be made for multiple views.

The evidence about organizational decision making is often ambiguous. Recall the downing of a Korean airliner by the Soviet Union in 1983. Some initial press accounts considered it a deliberate provocation (unitary actor), others a lower-level mistake (organizational). Yet others consid-

Table 8.5. *Four approaches to understanding organizations*

Rational unitary actor model
  What is the main problem?
  What are the alternatives?
  What are their costs and benefits?
  What are the underlying values and beliefs?

Organizational model
  How is the organization designed? How are tasks divided?
  What are the main organizational domains and powers?
  How is information processed?
  What repertoires, programs, and standard operating procedures exist?
  How are alternatives (e.g., policy options) generated?
  How are decisions actually implemented?

Political model
  Who are the key players? What are they after?
  What job pressures exist? What are the constraints?
  What coalitions exist? Who are the personalities involved?
  Where do individual and organizational goals diverge?

Contextual view
  How much is uncontrollable or random?
  What is the range of possible outcomes?
  Where are the key intersections around which things might happen?
  What outside forces exert selection pressure?
  How can we influence the larger decision context?

---

 ered it an attempt by the military to destabilize the Soviet politburo (political), or simply an unfortunate confluence of accidental circumstances (contextual). We often tend to view other parties' actions in the unitary frame, while quickly recognizing the validity of the organizational or political model for ourselves. For instance, when the United States shot down an Iranian airliner in the Persian Gulf (in 1988), no Western papers seriously considered the unitary actor model (although Iran did).

The second part of our conceptual framework concerns the *type* of decision examined. Within each of the views just considered, it is useful to distinguish among strategic, tactical, and routine decisions.

Strategic decisions directly affect the well-being and nature of the firm. They include choices about new products or markets, as well as decisions about organization design and the adoption of new technologies. Such decisions are typically novel, and occupy the thinking of senior management. However, they can be greatly influenced by people lower down in the organization (Bower, 1970).

Table 8.6. *Approaches and decision types*

Decision type	Unitary actor model	Organizational model	Political model	Contextual view
Strategic				
Tactical				
Routine				

Tactical decisions, in contrast, are primarily the domain of middle management. They include pricing decisions (as in the ALCO case), personnel choices, marketing strategy, customer interaction, procurement of raw materials and other supplies, manufacturing decisions, and operations scheduling. Of course, each of these decisions might contain strategic elements (e.g., when using inventory to guard against critical shortages or oversupply), but largely such decisions do not in and of themselves impact the bottom line or change the direction of the firm. Thus, the impact of a tactical decision on the organization tends to be secondary compared with that of strategic ones, although it can greatly affect individuals, groups, or entire departments. However, since many more tactical decisions are made than strategic ones (within a given time period), their *cumulative* impact can be as great or greater.

Lastly, we distinguish *routine* decisions, which are repetitive in nature, local in scope, minor in consequence (per occasion) and guided by organizational rules, guidelines, or policies. Typical examples include machine maintenance, supply ordering, invoicing, payroll, placing advertisements, mailings, office maintenance, and building security. Routine decisions tend to be made by clerks, secretaries, first-line managers, sales representatives, plant supervisors, and unskilled laborers.

So far we have distinguished four approaches to organizational decision making (unitary-rational, organizational, political, and contextual) and three types of decision (strategic, tactical, and routine). Table 8.6 shows a matrix crossing these four approaches (as columns) and three decision types (as rows) to suggest that different approaches may be more or less appropriate depending on the type of decision considered. It would be difficult to characterize this dependence in general, as much will depend on specific circumstances, issues, and time frames considered. Conceptually, however, we can think of the four approaches as *independent* variables in a stepwise regression model and ask how much of the variance each explains for various types of decisions (the dependent variable) across firms or over time. We shall comment in general terms on the applicability of each model or approach for different decision types.

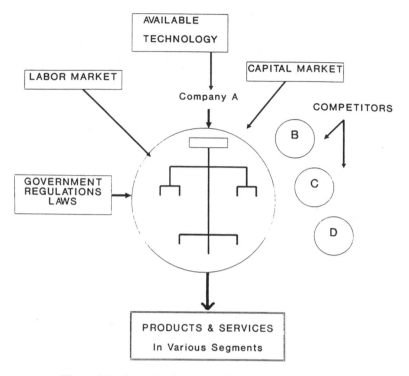

Figure 8.1. Organizational stakeholders

The unitary actor model seems most appropriate for important strategic decisions, as well as for decisions that are routine and recurrent. For the latter, the organization is likely to devise a standard set of operating procedures that are optimal, or nearly optimal, from a stockholder viewpoint. In the former, the organization is likely to rise above partisan concerns, since economic survival is at stake. However, not always.

Organizations do fail because of internal conflict and stalemates. The organizational model introduces more complexity and detail into the picture than does the rational actor model, as illustrated by the diagram in Figure 8.1. The middle circle shows the organization as a complex hierarchy surrounded by competitors and other stakeholders (such as consumers, suppliers, regulators, and unions). Whether this additional detail is needed or desirable in understanding decision making depends on the type of decisions considered. For tactical decisions, which are typically made by middle managers, the way the organization is structured can exert great influence. One reason is that such decisions usually require inputs from multiple managers (inside and outside the firm), all with their own agendas, constraints, and time frames.

In the political model the organization's reward system is foremost, especially divergences between organizational and individual goals. The political model recognizes that it is almost impossible to design an incentive system such that people act in complete harmony with the goals of the organization. It emphasizes the divergence between individual and organizational goals, as well as the fact that actions are part of a portfolio of decisions, the outcomes of which influence the relative power positions of the organizational participants.

The political model especially highlights that in addition to their formal positions people are part of informal networks and coalitions, and that organizational rationality may not always prevail because of hidden agendas. This realization is especially crucial in understanding decision making in government or other large bureaucracies. For example, although the U.S. president has enormous power in theory, in practice this power can only be exercised at a price. Forcing an issue may come at the expense of resistance, leaks, and even outright sabotage of subsequent ones. As Henry Kissinger noted: "The outsider believes a Presidential order is consistently followed out. Nonsense" (Halperin, 1974, p. 245). John F. Kennedy, for instance, was furious when he found out that the State Department had ignored his order to remove missiles from Turkey. Similarly, President Johnson's orders not to bomb certain areas of North Vietnam were outright violated. Or as President Truman remarked about president-elect Eisenhower: "He'll sit there and he'll say, 'Do this! Do that!' *And nothing will happen.* Poor Ike – it won't be a bit like the Army" (Neustadt, 1960, p. 9).

The three conceptual models combined still have limits as to how much detail they can capture. Certain processes and outcomes will remain beyond the scope or resolution of any of the three models. Many things happen in organizations that are essentially unpredictable. This view comes closest to what is called the *garbage can theory* of decision making (March and Olson, 1976). It models organizations as systems in which people, problem perceptions, and solution approaches meet in largely random ways. This view highlights the highly textured, changing nature of organizational environments. Each participant is involved in numerous decision processes, pursues multiple agendas, and is developing his or her own theories of what is going on. To quote March (1988):

From this perspective, decision processes are cross-sections of the lives of individual participants, and cannot easily be understood without embedding them within those lives. The context is a shifting intermeshing of the vagaries of demands on the lives of the whole array of actors.

In this mosaic view, two aspects are critical: (1) the cross-sectional detail of a decision and (2) the larger context that dictates how much attention a participant gives to that decision process at that time in his or her life. Cross-sectional detail here refers to how important the decision is to other people in the organization at that point in time, and how ready they are (given their own agendas) to commit. These factors, however, require such detailed knowledge and microlevel observation that they severely limit what is practically predictable. We shall later return to this viewpoint in more detail.

For now it suffices to recognize that a multitude of perspectives on organizational decision making exists. These perspectives differ in terms of empirical observations, prior assumptions, and the level of analysis. As noted earlier, one way to view alternative perspectives is as independent variables in a stepwise regression model. Each variable adds more detail and explains more (at a price). How much each perspective explains, and what remains unexplainable, depend on the type of decision, plus such factors as the type of organization, the particular industry, and its culture (as discussed later).

Road map to chapter. The next section examines decision making *by* organizations, taking a unitary actor perspective. Economic, management science, and strategic planning viewpoints will be discussed here. Section 8.3 addresses internal organizational aspects, and examines how the organizational, political, and contextual models view decision processes. Behavioral research on how large companies are actually run will be addressed here, as well as important insights from transaction cost economics. This section offers a microview of how managers typically operate, and what factors influence their decision behavior. Section 8.4 examines important macro-questions involving organizational design, including decision support systems, and is more prescriptive in orientation. Last, Section 8.5 offers an integrative perspective and highlights areas of research for further exploration.

It will be clear by now that the topic of organizational decision making is truly a complex one, having been studied from different perspectives across various disciplines. Our aim in this chapter is to select from these extensive literatures those elements that help understand and improve organizational decision making.

8.2   Unitary actor perspectives

As a first approximation, we might view organizations in the idealized form implicit in the unitary rational actor model, an approach most explicitly followed in economics.

8.2.1   *Economic approaches*

In this approach, the firm is treated as a black box, in which inputs are transformed optimally into outputs. A key concept of this approach is the production function. It specifies for a particular organization how such inputs as capital (x_1), labor (x_2), management (x_3), patents (x_4), and available technology (x_5) can be transformed into some output vector $y = (y_1, \ldots, y_m)$. This output vector includes units of physical products (y_1), services and intangibles such as goodwill (y_2), pollution (y_3), or ideological influence (y_4).

If one assumes a production function f_i for Firm i, what does it mean to behave rationally under various environmental conditions? Consider the well-known case of perfect competition, where the firm is a pure price taker. Let the revenue be $\bar{p} \cdot \bar{y} = \Sigma p_i y_i$ and the costs $\bar{c} \cdot \bar{x} = \Sigma c_i x_i$, where p is a price vector, y the output bundle, c the cost of inputs, and x the resource vector (with the dot $\cdot$ refering to vector multiplication). In that case, profit maximization simply amounts to solving the following constrained optimization problem:

$$\max \pi(x_1, \ldots, x_n) = \bar{p} \cdot \bar{y} - \bar{c} \cdot \bar{x}$$
$$\text{subject to: } y = f(x)$$
$$\text{and: } \bar{x} \geq 0$$

Under this standard maximization problem, optimal production is determined where the marginal revenue of the last output unit equals its marginal cost. It also follows, from perfect competition, that only normal returns to a factor of production are possible. Otherwise, another firm would enter the industry to take advantage of the abnormal profits. Thus, the unitary actor model, as operationalized earlier, leads to clear and testable predictions about firm behavior. It tells us what output levels should be, what profit level to expect, and so on, but provides no insights into actual decision processes.

Much of microeconomics consists of elaborations on this basic model. For instance, uncertainty might be introduced in any or all of the variables. The effect of other firms' behavior on the function f has been examined, leading to more complicated models of imperfect competition (e.g., Chamberlin, 1962; Baumol, Panzar, and Willig, 1982). Also, special cases of the production function have been studied in detail. For example, economies of scale have been examined by seeing what happens to the outputs $y_1, \ldots, y_m$ if all inputs $x_1, \ldots, x_n$ are increased by some constant factor, as shown in standard microeconomics texts (see Henderson and Quandt, 1971). The case of perfect competition, which forms the cornerstone of economists' theories, of course, seldom holds in reality. Companies' strategic decisions are typically aimed at the creation or exploitation of market imperfections and transactions costs (see Schoemaker, 1990a). In such cases, the determination of what the optimal profit of a firm is becomes much more difficult, with the game theoretic elements discussed in the previous chapter playing a pivotal role. Much depends on the type of decision problems examined, as well as the degree of approximation desired, to determine whether the unitary actor model as operationalized in economics is an appropriate model of organizational decision making at either a descriptive or prescriptive level.

ALCO revisited. In the ALCO case described earlier, the pricing decision as viewed from the rational unitary actor model would be intertwined with the production decision. The overall objective would be to maximize profits from the viewpoint of the stockholders, who are presumed to be interested only in dividends and stock appreciation. The capital asset pricing model of finance can be used to measure the return stockholders would expect for the systematic risk the firm would incur with a given price and output level for the integrated circuit. Systematic risk is defined as the business or financial risk that shareholders cannot eliminate by holding a well-diversified portfolio of securities and other assets.[6] Most of this risk is due to general economic conditions and industry effects beyond management's control.

Within this framework, ALCO's decision would be modeled as determining the price p^* and output x^* that would maximize the following after-tax quantity:

$$\text{NPV}(p, x) = \sum_{i=1}^{n} \frac{E(\tilde{c}_i)}{(1 + r_p)^i}$$

where $\tilde{c}_i$ is the net cash flow projected for Period i for a given Price p and Output Quantity x. The tilde indicates that this cash flow may be a random variable, in which case its expected value is substituted in the net present value (NPV) formula (Fama, 1976). The cash-flow projections would extend over the life of the project and are discounted by a factor r_p. This discount rate would differ for different price and output levels, because their associated income streams might entail varying degrees of systematic risk.

It is explained in detail in standard finance texts how r_p is set. It is usually less explicitly addressed how the cash-flow projections should be made. Such projections may either entail statistical extrapolations (which use regression or more sophisticated econometric techniques) as well as judgmental forecasting. Economic, financial, and marketing models could also be used. The point is that the economic approach would model the firm as optimally solving a complex pricing and production problem. It would not be assumed that firms actually do this, but rather that they act

6 The level of systematic risk dictates the discount rate to be used in calculating the net present values of various projected income streams (as shown in standard finance texts).

as if they do so. The basic rationale is that firms that fail to make optimal (i.e., profit-maximizing) decisions will lose out in the long run.

Within the economic unitary actor view, the key to understanding and predicting organizational decision making is to know the overall objective and the available alternatives. The rest follows logically and can be simulated by envisioning in each position of the organization a perfectly rational decision maker, who operates exactly according to policy, standard procedures, and specified rules. Thus, the term unitary has two meanings in the economic model: shared values of organizational members, and perfect coordination so that the firm acts as if it were a single person.

8.2.2 *Management science*

The rational unitary actor view also underlies much of management science and operations research, disciplines aimed at improving performance. Management science is unitary in only the *first* sense; that all members share the firm's overall objectives (such as cost minimization or profit maximization). It does not assume perfect coordination but instead recognizes the internal complexity of organizations that give rise to subsystems such as production versus inventory and the associated organizational constraints. Management science models have been developed to coordinate across subsystems such that local optima indeed add up to a global optimum. Thus, it shares with economics the desire to view organizations as optimizing entities, acting from a central, shared set of values, but recognizes the internal complexity and bounded rationality of firms.

The origins of management science go back to World War II, when large-scale logistical problems needed to be solved. The advent of computers also provided an important impetus, permitting large-scale simulations and calculations. Particularly relevant for many organizations was the linear programming revolution of the 1950s, which provided the technical machinery to explicitly maximize Leontief production functions, in which outputs are assumed to be proportional to inputs (Dorfman, Samuelson, and Solow, 1958).[7] Numerous industries (notably oil refining and airlines) applied mathematical programming with great vigor to such varied problems as production scheduling, chemical blending, warehouse location, and sales force deployment.

These days, many complex organizations use management science tools, either to maximize explicit objective functions or to enhance their un-

7 Management science has traditionally been focused on cost minimization, and economics on profit maximization. As such, their integration has not been as complete as it could be.

Table 8.7. *Use of management science tools in large companies*

Technique	Information on uncontrollable inputs	Typical problem area	Percentage of firms using technique
Statistical analysis	Stochastic	Forecasting and experimentation	93
Simulation	Deterministic and stochastic	Studying ill-structured, complex decision problems	84
Linear programming	Deterministic	Allocating scarce resources	79
PERT CPM	Deterministic and stochastic	Planning, scheduling, and controlling projects	70
Inventory theory	Deterministic and stochastic	Maintaining and controlling inventories	57
Queuing theory	Stochastic	Analyzing service systems	45
Nonlinear programming	Deterministic	Interdependent activities	36
Heuristic programming	Deterministic and stochastic	Planning large-scale, complex systems	34
Bayesian decision analysis	Stochastic	Risky decisions	32
Dynamic programming	Deterministic and stochastic	Sequential decisions	27
Integer programming	Deterministic	Indivisible activities	2

Source: Forgionne (1986, p. 36). Reprinted by permission.

derstanding of complex interactions (e.g., in inventory-production systems). Table 8.7 provides a summary of the extent to which various management science tools are used in large companies. Further advances in the use of these quantitative techniques rest, in our view, on three important factors:

1. Improvements in the techniques themselves through better algorithms and faster computations.
2. Greater descriptive realism in building the models (at the risk of reduced solvability).
3. Increased user sophistication and *involvement* in the application and development of the models.

Often, analysts (especially academics) prefer to trade off realism for solvability. Consequently, the models are often deemed too unrealistic or mathematically obtuse by managers. As noted in Chapter 5, legitimation and transparency are important criteria in selecting decision tools and should be weighted from both managerial and technical perspectives. This is one reason why management science has only partly delivered on its great promise (as envisaged in the 1950s). In practice, its application has been most successful with tactical and routine (or programmed) decisions but less so with strategic ones.

ALCO revisited. Applying the management science perspective to ALCO, various improvements suggest themselves. First, how well founded are the profit and sales projections? Management science offers sophisticated forecasting tools, ranging from linear extrapolation to exponential smoothing and dynamic modeling. Second, the pricing decision might be formulated as an optimization problem that maximizes profit subject to cost or output constraints associated with production. It might be modeled as a linear programming problem reflecting constraints imposed by marketing, manufacturing, and research and development, or as a more general optimization problem.[8] Third, simulation and sensitivity analysis could provide insight into the robustness of the solution. For instance, would the optimal price vary much if certain parameters, such as cost of production or demand elasticity, were changed, or different estimates were assumed?

Although standard management science does not address the pricing problem per se, several of its tools are applicable, as shown more fully in quantitative marketing texts. The main point is that management science can offer prescriptive advice on how to make an organization choose rationally, as though it were managed by a unitary actor.

8.2.3   *Strategic planning*

The unitary actor perspective is also recognizable in some (but not all) of the strategic planning literature, where the challenge is often viewed as positioning business units optimally. Traditional strategic planning and policy frameworks (e.g., the Harvard model developed in the 1960s) focused on the firm's need to adapt and reposition continually in view of external changes. The basic idea is to match the firm's comparative advantages and distinctive competencies with environmental opportunities, so as to better meet the overall objectives (such as profit, survival, employment). Specifically, this entails the following key steps:

---

8 For examples of such models see Devinney (1988, esp. chap. 11).

1. Examination of environmental threats and opportunities.
2. Assessment of one's competitive strengths and weaknesses.
3. A conceptual match of (1) and (2) to identify areas of high profit potential.
4. The design of policies, plans, incentives, and information systems to move the firm in the desired direction.

General environment. Let's start with the external environment, which can range from being very placid and predictable to being highly turbulent and complex (Emery and Trist, 1965). If the firm is in a stable industry, with predictable sales trends, forecasting and other formal planning models can be profitably used in predicting the future. However, if the industry is undergoing structural changes, or if the general economic and political environments are unstable, then extrapolations from the past can be very misleading. In such cases, it will be critical to understand better the forces underlying the environmental change. The multiple scenario method, as pioneered by Royal Dutch/Shell, is one useful technique for this (Wack, 1985a, 1985b). Table 8.8 provides some guiding steps for constructing scenarios in an organizational setting.

Good scenarios provide a balance between current trends and the unpredictable uncertainties that lie ahead. By conducting a cluster analysis of the many combinations of current trends and key uncertainties, a limited set of structurally different, internally consistent scenarios may be constructed. These scenarios should stretch the minds of the key decision takers at the top of the organization, and provide a useful background against which to assess important strategic options. For instance, they could be used to assess how robust (i.e., acceptable) a particular strategy is across various futures for a given set of objectives, goals, and constraints. Importantly, the scenario approach may overcome or mitigate some of the judgmental biases discussed in Chapters 3 and 4, such as overconfidence, myopic framing, undue anchoring on the past, and availability biases (see Schoemaker, 1993).

Competitors. In addition to analyzing the general economic and political environment in which the firm operates, it is also critical to develop a deep understanding of the firm's position relative to its competitors. This requires, first of all, a strategic analysis of the various businesses in which the firm competes. Such strategic segmentation may start with standard product or market segmentation, such as recognizing that Apple Computer competes in the home, school, and office markets. These three segments are different because they entail different customers, needs, and desired product features. For example, the purchasing decision in the home market involves small quantities and at most two decision makers. Schools, in contrast, buy in bulk using careful committee processes to structure,

Table 8.8. *Steps in scenario construction*

1. Define the issues you wish to understand better in terms of time frame, scope, and decision variables (e.g., prices of natural gas over the next five years in the Far East). Review the past to get a feel for degrees of uncertainty and volatility.

2. Identify the major stakeholders or actors who would have an interest in these issues, both those who may be affected by it and those who could influence matters appreciably. Identify their current roles, interests, and power positions.

3. Make a list of current trends, or predetermined elements, that will affect the variable(s) of interest. Constructing a diagram may be helpful to show interlinkages and causal relationships.

4. Identify key uncertainties, whose resolution will significantly affect the variables of interest to you. Briefly explain why and how these uncertain events matter, and examine as well how they interrelate.

5. Construct two forced scenarios by placing all positive outcomes of key uncertainties in one scenario and all negative outcomes in the other. Add selected trends and predetermined elements to these extreme scenarios.

6. Assess the internal consistency and plausibility of these artificial scenarios. Identify where and why these forced scenarios may be internally inconsistent (in terms of trends and outcome combinations).

7. Eliminate combinations that are not credible or impossible, and create new scenarios (two or more) until you have achieved internal consistency. Make sure these new scenarios cover a reasonable range of uncertainty.

8. Assess the revised scenarios in terms of how the key stakeholders would behave in them. Where appropriate, identify topics for further study that might provide stronger support for your scenarios, or might lead to revisions of these *learning* scenarios.

9. After completing additional research, reexamine the internal consistencies of the learning scenarios and assess whether certain interactions should be formalized via a quantitative model. If so, use this model to run some Monte Carlo simulations after obtaining subjective uncertainty ranges (or entire distributions) for key independent variables.

10. Finally, reassess the ranges of uncertainty of the dependent (i.e., target) variables of interest, and retrace Steps 1 through 9 to arrive at *decision* scenarios that might be given to others to enhance their decision making.

Source: Paul J. H. Schoemaker, "When and How to Use Scenario Planning: A Heuristic Approach with Illustration," Copyright © 1991 by John Wiley & Sons, Ltd. Reprinted by permission of John Wiley & Sons, Ltd.

evaluate, and implement the decision. In the office market, in contrast, such product features as compatibility, connectivity, and service are probably key. Apart from product or customer criteria, the focus of segmentation could be on the technology used (e.g., open vs. closed architecture), the mode and channels of sale (direct, via mail, computer stores, etc.), or the geographic region (e.g., Eastern Europe vs. the United States).

The overall challenge is to simplify the complex business reality into a limited number of key battlefields, so as to understand better on what basis to compete. Industry analysis is crucial here because in some environments (e.g., commodity habitats) there is no real basis for competitive advantage. If the consumer buys mostly on price, (e.g., in private air travel) and there are low switching costs (i.e., changing airlines is easy), it is hard to obtain a price premium. Thus, the competition shifts toward low-cost strategies, stemming from either lean and efficient operations (recall Freddie Laker's no frills airline) or economies of scale (such as having several hubs with many routes).

It is also important to understand evolutionary changes in the industry as it moves from an expansionary phase to a mature phase or possibly a declining phase. For instance, if the industry is declining but players face major exit barriers (due to high fixed costs, sunk costs, and lack of other options), a battle for market share may ensue, usually with disastrous collective consequences. Such industry analysis has recently received much attention in the strategic planning literature (see Porter, 1980). A large number of other tools are available as well to aid decision makers and consultants in their search for surplus profit or economic rent (Alchian, 1988). Many of these tools attempt to portray in relatively simple ways how individual business units are positioned on simple maps. Indeed they may treat complex business units as unitary points on a strategy graph, such that the decision process can be greatly simplified and focused (see Hax and Majluf, 1983).

A case in point is the celebrated, and now somewhat outdated, bubble chart popularized by the BCG (Boston Consulting Group, 1968). It addressed the need of CEOs running multidivisional businesses (such as General Electric, Litton, ITT) to have a simple overview of how various strategic business units (SBU) were positioned. An SBU is defined as the smallest distinct business to be analyzed strategically. It would be much smaller than an industry or even division, but larger than a single product line or market segments. For an organizational unit to qualify as an SBU it must have a definable product or service, a clear customer group, distinct competitors, and production, as well as profit autonomy. In the case of GE, turbines or electrical appliances would be an entire division. The units within electrical appliances making toasters or refrigerators would be SBUs. Within the refrigerator SBU, several product lines and market segments could be identified, but they might not be stand-alone businesses or independent profit centers.

Figure 8.2 presents a simple example of a strategy map. Each bubble

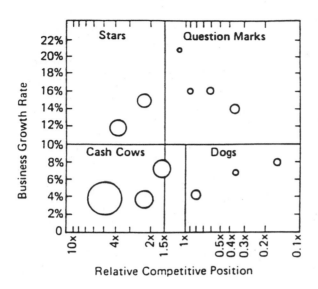

Figure 8.2. Product portfolio matrices (*Source*: Reprinted from *Long Range Planning*, Feb. 1977, B. Hedley, "Strategy and the 'Business Portfolio,'" p. 12, copyright 1977, with permission from Pergamon Press Ltd., Headington Hill Hall, Oxford OX3 OBW, U.K.)

(or circle) represents a different SBU within a company such as GE. The vertical axis represents the past growth of the business the SBU is in. The business unit's competitive position is plotted horizontally relative to other firms in the same business segment. In this figure, each SBU's market share is expressed as the ratio of its own market share (in units or dollars) with that of the nearest competitor. If an SBU is the market leader in its particular business, this ratio is greater than one; otherwise it is a fraction. Thus, the bubbles in Figure 8.2 represent the 12 SBUs of one company, in terms of their strategic positions in the relevant markets. Note that different bubbles might reflect totally different industries, all within the portfolio of this one conglomerate or diversified firm. The size of the bubble usually reflects absolute annual sales for that SBU.

As shown in Figure 8.2, market share is often a key variable in such strategy grids. One reason is the so-called *learning* or *experience curve effect*. For many (though certainly not all) products, there is a strong relationship between how many units already have been produced by an SBU, and the per-unit cost of production for that unit. The intuition behind the experience curve is quite simple: The more experience you have accumulated in producing, say, widgets, the more ingenious, efficient, and reliable your production process will be (due to numerous small improvements). If this knowledge is proprietary (i.e., not easily imitated by others), having more cumulative experience means lower average cost than your competitors have, resulting in lower prices and more market share.

Of course, these analyses greatly simplify what are in fact very complicated, interdependent decisions. This simplicity is both a strength and weakness of the unitary actor approach. It served the need of CEOs who faced unwieldy corporate portfolios amassed during the takeover wave of the 1960s (and subsequently divested in the 1980s). Simplified analyses of this type have found wide acceptance (via consultants) in industry but have met with considerable skepticism in the academic world. As with all simplifying tools, these strategy maps offer only a first approximation and should be used carefully, with a full realization of their limitations. For example, experience curves do not exist in all industries or for all products. And, if they exist, they are not necessarily proprietary. In addition, market share and market growth are not always the most important variables to focus on. The BCG has since modified and extended its framework to reflect the new realities of stagnant markets and moves away from just low-cost strategies (see Clarkeson, 1984; Hax and Majluf, 1991).

Perhaps the greatest weakness of product portfolio maps is that they do not sufficiently highlight the dynamic, competitive nature of business. Suppose your competitors also look at the world using these same tools. Would (should) that affect your decisions? Competitive counterresponses can hardly be ignored in strategic decision making, which means some type of game theoretic analysis (along the lines of the previous chapter) is called for. Of course, this requires first of all a clear identification of the competition, in all of its relevant dimensions. Often a simplistic view is adopted, such as the bubble charts or the narrow view of competition, in understanding and determining strategy.

In his well-known book *Competitive Strategy,* Michael Porter (1980) argues that firms should take a broad rather than narrow view of who their real competition is. Instead of considering only other firms producing the same product or service to be competitors, anyone who makes a claim on profits should be viewed as a competitor. As Figure 8.3 indicates, suppliers (who like to sell at a higher price) are competitors; and these include not just component suppliers but also banks (who supply money) and employees (who supply labor). Of course, customers (who want to buy at lower prices) are competitors, especially if they are powerful and demand special treatment (i.e., discounts, special services, etc.). In addition, government can be a force of competition (through taxes, regulation, etc.), as well as potential entrants and substitute products.

In spite of this pluralistic view of competition, the industrial organization approach to strategy (of which Porter is an exponent) is still much

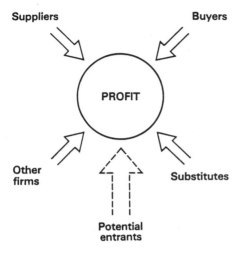

Suppliers

Buyers

PROFIT

Other firms

Substitutes

Potential entrants

What barriers protect you from each?

Figure 8.3. Forces of competition (*Source:* Adapted with permission of The Free Press, a Division of Macmillan, Inc. from *Competitive Strategy: Techniques for Analyzing Industries and Competitors* by Michael E. Porter. Copyright © 1980 by The Free Press)

wedded to the unitary actor view. Firms or strategic business units are viewed as stuck in industries or strategic groups, with limited mobility and degrees of freedom. Industry structure is presumed to dictate optimal strategies and hence the distribution of profits. Indeed, in his book on the competitive advantage of nations, Porter (1990) further emphasizes the role of environmental determinism in corporate success. No doubt the external factors surrounding firms will greatly influence their fortunes. However, as Rumelt (1991) and others have shown, much variation in profit exists among firms in the same nation, industry, strategic group, or business segment. To explain this, we must adopt more of an "inside" view of the firm, as we shall do later.

ALCO Revisited. If we link the above strategy prescriptions to the ALCO case, the following issues arise. Where does the IC fit on a matrix like Figure 8.2? In other words, will this new IC place ALCO in a market segment that is attractive (as defined in Figure 8.2), and how does it fit with the firm's core competencies? Are the sales projections and growth expectations a simple extrapolation of the past? If so, are there reasons why such an extrapolation might be wrong? Should multiple scenarios be considered instead of single-line forecasts? For example, do the projections take into account competitive responses, such as price cuts? Is ALCO's cost of production higher or lower than its competitors and if so why? If experience curve effects exist in this industry, pricing low to gain market share may be best. What other competitive barriers exist? Are patents possible? How much profit will ALCO's suppliers be making from the new IC product? What about ALCO's labor costs and operating efficiency – are they above or below average? Why?

The above issues are meant to illustrate that the strategic perspective raises a host of questions about the general environment and competitors that place the pricing decision in a larger context or frame. Oster (1990), for instance, discusses retaliatory price cuts, effects on new entrants, reputation building, and signaling, as well as antitrust concerns. Also, the strategic perspective raises portfolio questions about whether this new product fits well with the others (in terms of cash required, management skills needed, growth expectations, etc.), since a core concept in strategy is that of synergy. Firms should take on activities that in some way capitalize on existing activities (e.g., better use of equipment or people skills) so that competitive advantages are created. The strategy perspective tries to assure that the many thousands of decisions that are typically made in an organization are all focused and aligned in the direction called for by the firm's strategic vision.

In conclusion, economics, management science, and parts of strategic planning operate within the rational unitary actor view of organizations. It is often a powerful simplification that yields high returns for a small set of assumptions. However, it is only a starting point for addressing organizational decision-making issues. To gain additional insight, we need to come to terms with the firm's internal complexities, messiness, and coordinative imperfections.

8.3   Decisions *within* organizations

In the unitary actor view little attention is paid to sources of suboptimal behavior, such as misspecified incentives, poor communication, bounded rationality, hidden agendas, inconsistent information sets, or limited response capabilities. These issues are at the heart of the organizational, political, and contextual views discussed in section 8.1, where the rational elements are placed in the background. We shall start with a more economic view of internal organization, and then become more behavioral. This section adopts a descriptive microview of organizations, focusing on transactions, individual managers, power, and context. Section 8.4 adopts a more prescriptive perspective, and examines macrofeatures of organizations dealing with structure, processes, technology, and incentive systems.

8.3.1   *Transactions cost economics*

Within the transactions cost view, what happens and should happen in organizations can only be understood if we understand why organizations exist in the first place (Coase, 1937). Imagine a world consisting of only entrepreneurs (i.e., suppliers of risky capital and managerial talent) and self-employed people who sell goods and services to each other via contracts. Would organizations ever emerge in such a world and if so, why and to what extent?

The key lies in understanding that economic transactions, if mediated via contracts, are not without cost. If *A* and *B* exchange services (e.g., lawn maintenance), they attempt to engage in cooperative behavior within an atmosphere of conflicting objectives and some degree of distrust. Consequently, most such deals require contracts (oral or written) to assure that a fair exchange occurs. However, if the service to be delivered occurs over an extended time period, under conditions of uncertainty, and is moreover hard to monitor, measure, or value, then the market mechanism requires complex long-term contracts. At some point this contract mode of exchange becomes less efficient than the so-called internal organization solution.

The organizational approach is to structure economic transactions via very *general* employment arrangements, according to which one party receives a mutually agreed upon compensation per year (salary, bonus, and possibly commissions) in return for conducting a broad set of activities. This hierarchical approach (in which *A* works for *B*) eliminates the need to place a monetary value on each and every contribution by an employee, and hence reduces the need to monitor, measure, and write contracts that anticipate all contingencies. Of course, some valuation of this general employment arrangement is still necessary, but on a much broader scale, using an incomplete and open-ended employment contract.

The transactions cost view essentially argues that organizations engage in those activities that are more efficiently conducted within a hierarchical mode than a market mode. Whenever decisions get to be complex, or involve considerable uncertainty, the hierarchical model works better than the open market or contracting mode. In this sense, organizations can be viewed as market failures.

Williamson's model. What factors favor hierarchies over markets in the conduct of economic transactions? Williamson (1975, 1989) developed an important framework that distinguishes human factors from environmental ones (see also Arrow, 1974). On the human side, he lists "bounded rationality" and "opportunism." In dealing with very complex tasks that are too difficult to specify completely via contracts the organizational model wins out. Examples are building airplanes, computers, or even houses. Imagine how complex this would be for an individual entrepreneur who subcontracts all jobs to other single entrepreneurs and self-employed people (assuming away any type of formal organization). Opportunism refers to exploiting weaknesses in contracts or agreements. The more opportunistic the agents/parties are, the more costly the contracting approach becomes, because it needs to guard against every contingency and loophole. Organizations, on the other hand, reward loyalty or trust and try to structure incentives such that myopic or local opportunism does not really pay.

On the environmental side, Williamson identifies "uncertainty" and "small numbers" as favoring the organizational mode. Greater uncertainty implies more contingencies and complexity, and hence increases the cost of market transactions (i.e., designing contracts). Small numbers refer to the absence of many buyers and sellers, so that no reliable market price exists to value the exchange. For instance, if *A* invests in special equipment to service *B*, a small numbers condition is created due to "asset specificity." Without easy reference points for comparison, each party can claim higher cost or poor quality (in an opportunistic manner). This in turn drives up monitoring expenses and thus the transaction costs of a free-market exchange. Small numbers also reduce reputational considerations in exploiting vague or incomplete contracts. Often in such cases, vertical integration provides the best solution (see Klein et al., 1978).

In sum, the transaction cost view focuses on the costs of activities aimed at verifying to each party's satisfaction that a fair and mutually advantageous exchange occurs. It combines in this sense economic, behavioral, and legal disciplines. Organizations thrive when transaction costs are high relative to the value of what is being exchanged. The transaction costs perspective as such helps explain what activities firms engage in and which decisions they should subcontract out. It represents one of the more elegant and wide-ranging parsimonious models of the firm from within. However, it still misses important aspects and dimensions of organizational life, both in its treatment of bounded rationality and organizational complexity. For instance, costs are emphasized rather than benefits, in comparing competing modes of organizing. Also, the transaction is the unit of analysis rather than culture, structure, relationships, or decision processes.

8.3.2   *Behavioral perspectives*

Apart from transactions cost models, various other attempts have been made by economists to incorporate other behavioral elements in their models. For instance, Baumol (1959) and Marris (1964) assumed organizations were primarily concerned with market share and hence focused on sales maximization, subject to certain minimal profit constraints. Leibenstein (1976) instead emphasized so-called *X*-efficiency, referring to the firm's inability to operate at or even near the efficient frontier. Nelson and Winter (1981) developed an evolutionary view of firms in an industry context, with bounded rationality explicitly built into their model (in the spirit of Williamson). They assumed that firms (1) have limited routines for coping with new situations, (2) develop new routines *slowly* through incremental search, and (3) react with considerable inertia (like biological organisms) to environmental changes.[9]

Cyert and March (1963) in their book *The Behavioral Theory of the Firm* drew a sharp contrast between economic and behavioral approaches to understanding firm behavior. They questioned whether organizations could engage in the type of rationality presumed in economic theory and proposed an alternative set of behavioral concepts. To start with, they argued that most organizations "exist and thrive with considerable latent conflict of goals" (p. 117). For example, a marketing department may have as one specific subgoal the maximization of market share. However, in the extreme such a subgoal would lead to selling products at zero profit or even at a loss. This is why Baumol (1959) and Marris (1964) imposed a minimal profit constrained in their models. Due to sequential goal attention, and so-called local rationality, the implicit goal inconsistencies are seldom very visible to the organizational members themselves.

As for the decision-making process itself, Cyert and March suggest that it is often simplistic, reactive, and local. Only after a problem has clearly been viewed as serious by key people in the organization might solutions be sought (i.e., reactive decision making). Moreover, the search for solutions is typically based on rather simple models of how the environment works. Lindblom (1959) arrived at a similar view of governmental decision making, suggesting that administrators make "successive limited comparisons" as depicted in Table 8.9. Usually the search for solutions is incremental and stimulated by specific problems or crises. Searching in the immediate neighborhood of existing solutions avoids having to look at all the aspects of a problem in a comprehensive fashion. This "muddling through" approach falls far short of the classical economic view of a maximizing entity that anticipates the future with great rationality.

Other key notions in Cyert and March's behavioral theory of the firm are "uncertainty avoidance" and "environmental negotiation." Both reflect managers' limited ability to deal with uncertainty and complexity. Uncertainty avoidance manifests itself through suboptimization, the use of slack (to decouple interrelated systems such as production and inventory), reliance on routines (e.g., always using the same supplier), and not sticking out one's neck. Negotiating the environment takes the form of long-term contracts (with customers or suppliers), lobbying for protective legislation, tacit or implicit collusion with competitors on pricing or output decisions, the use of subcontractors to simplify the production

9 For further discussion on the merits of such behavioral–economic models, see Machlup (1967) and Marris and Mueller (1980).

Table 8.9. *The incrementalist approach*

---

1. Rather than attempting a comprehensive survey and evaluation of all alternatives, the decision maker focuses only on those policies which differ incrementally from existing policies.
2. Only a relatively small number of policy alternatives are considered.
3. For each policy alternative, only a restricted number of "important" consequences are evaluated.
4. The problem confronting the decision maker is continually redefined: Incrementalism allows for countless ends–means and means–ends adjustments, which, in effect, make the problem more manageable.
5. Thus, there is no one decision or "right" solution but a "never-ending series of attacks" on the issues at hand through serial analyses and evaluation.
6. As such, incremental decision making is described as remedial, geared more to the alleviation of present, concrete social imperfections than to the promotion of future social goals.

Source: Lindblom (1959). Reprinted with permission from *Public Administration Review,* © by the American Society for Public Administration (ASPA), 1120 G Street NW, Suite 700, Washington, DC 20005. All rights reserved.

task, and the myriad of insurance contracts and hedges that shift some of the risk or burden of decision making to third parties.

Rewards, power, and politics. In recent years there has been an increased interest in the internal politics of organizations. However, as Pfeffer (1981) notes, organization theory has largely ignored this component in contrast to the popular business press, where personality conflicts, palace revolts, and other power plays receive much attention. The emphasis on power highlights the role of noneconomic needs, especially if pursued as an end in itself. The focus on power, however, can also stem from an implicit assumption of self-interest seeking, combined with firms' limited ability to design incentive systems where personal goals fully coincide with organizational ones (Downs, 1967).

In organizations managers are given certain coercive, reward, and legitimate powers. Power is defined here as the potential to influence people or events in a direction one desires. Expert and leadership power, however, can only be acquired by the manager over time (French and Raven, 1968). In this sense, power is not just a vertical dimension, operating from top to bottom, but it operates laterally as well. Chester Barnard (1938) was one of the first management writers to emphasize that subordinates have considerable power as well, namely whether and how to carry out directives. He envisioned "zones of indifference" within which orders were considered legitimate, but outside of which compliance could not be expected. Indeed, he viewed organizations as complex, partly co-operative systems, with power flowing from the top down, laterally, and from the bottom up (see Williamson, 1990).

For example, an assistant may become "indispensable" because he or she is the only one who understands a complex filing system or a computer program. As specialization increases, such expert power will become more dominant. Alternatively, some people may become indispensable because of their willingness to work unusual hours or to perform activities others would not want to. In a related vein, someone's personality may lead to increased power, for example, because he or she is listened to and confided in, providing this person with increased access. The latter is often influenced by location and position. Even in these days of telephones and computer networks, physical proximity still strongly affects frequency of contact.

Additional sources of power are coalitions and rules (Mechanic, 1962). Coalitions may be formal (i.e., related to one's ability to swing a vote) or informal (e.g., ordering supplies from a trusted source rather than putting out bids). Rule power derives from discretion about when, how, and to whom to apply certain rules. For instance, the moment a physician asks a nurse to perform part of the physician's duties, the nurse gains in power. He or she obtains some degree of leverage over that physician by possibly refusing such participation on later occasions. Moreover, if the task performed by the nurse is one he or she is not supposed or licensed to perform, the nurse gains power by being an "accomplice" to some type of rule infringement. Finally, subordinates may derive power from detailed knowledge of the rules of the organization, for example, by throwing the book at higher-placed persons.

Power, as noted earlier, concerns the ability to influence affairs, that is, the capacity to mobilize resources toward a desired end. Seldom, however, is power exercised to its fullest extent, and indeed a large portion may never be directly used. Hence its major effects may be indirect (e.g., as when possessing nuclear weapons) and result from *perceptions* about power. Not surprisingly, symbols of power therefore become important in and of themselves. In organizations, these entail title, salary, office size and location, privileges (e.g., flying first class), membership in committees, dress, language. Ceremony and ritual are commonly used to solidify power, and decisions may be made or information sought primarily to enhance or solidify power (Miles, 1980; Pfeffer, 1981; Feldman and March, 1981).

8.3.3 *Contextual views*

The contextual view is interested in how decision makers really operate and what kinds of contexts they function in. Of the hundreds of books on managers, few have actually studied their behavior systematically. Those that have done so have destroyed the myth that managers are highly reflective, strategic, rational, top-down planners. More likely, they are action-oriented firefighters, whose lives are primarily controlled by the never-ending stream of demands placed on them from above, below, left, and right. Of course, they think and plan, but usually on the run. Tight work schedules, heavy travel, and long work days are typical. One classic study (Mintzberg, 1973) suggests that during an average office day a typical executive attends about eight meetings, responds to 36 pieces of mail, initiates fewer than half of all phone calls he or she has, has no real breaks, and functions very much in an open system. The nature of managerial work is characterized by variety, brevity, and fragmentation.

People who thrive in managerial jobs tend to have a preference for nonroutine tasks. Such activities as reading reports and handling mail tend to be low on the priority and interest list; seeking new information, holding unscheduled meetings, solving new problems as they arise, and taking action are high on the agenda. Most managers prefer informal oral communication and face-to-face contact over written communiqués or formal meetings. Good managers tend to be at the center of several communication networks. They function as nodes or hubs in a continually changing information field. They are parallel processors, who relish playing numerous roles (as leader, team player, arbitrator, expert, evaluator, initiator, etc.). Peter Drucker (1954) views a manager as someone who creates order out of chaos. In the metaphor of a symphony or orchestra, the manager is both composer and conductor. This contextual view applies both to small and large decisions. The following case illustrates how small, seemingly unrelated events can intersect to create truly large-scale consequences.

Berlin Wall. When thousands of East Germans crossed the Berlin Wall on the night of November 9, 1989, it was not so much by design as by happenstance and confusion on the part of East Germany's leadership. Although none of the government officials wanted the wall opened, the Czechoslovakian escape route had become a growing concern and embarrassment to them, with thousands of East Germans crossing the border southeastward by car and train. The government's plan was to permit more liberal, but still highly controlled, travel to the west through Berlin. This was meant as a relief valve for mounting pressure and unrest among the populace. Instead, the following happened (as reported in the *Chicago Tribune* of October 28, 1990).

On October 24, 1989, Egon Krenz (the new head of state after ousted potentate Erich Honecker) announced a highly restrictive law that fueled rather than quieted public anger. On November 9, amid mounting confusion and fear in the Communist Party, Prime Minister Willi Stoph handed Krentz a draft decree at 3:30 p.m., just before a Central Committee meeting. It liberalized the travel policy and emphasized the need for prompt visa decisions. Krentz introduced the decree as a temporary measure. The intent was to keep the party in power, buy time, and gain more concessions from West Germany. Upon discussing the draft in committee, amendments were made to drop the term temporary and adopt it as law. Most committee members assumed the draft had been carefully prepared in consultation with security agencies (which controlled the border), the Soviet Union, and other foreign governments. Each of these assumptions proved false.

During a press conference following the meeting, an ill-prepared government spokesman accidentally revealed the new decree. The intent had been to announce it publicly two days later, to give the border police and visa agencies time to prepare. The spokesman had inadvertently pulled out the decree when shuffling through his papers, in response to a last-minute, unplanned question. Upon reading the decree, he failed to appreciate its historic significance. When asked if this meant the wall was open, he simply reread the statement, hesitantly concluded that it apparently meant so, and hastily departed.

The ambiguity in the official's statement set the stage for further fortuitous events. At first reporters were unsure what to report since police stations (which had to approve the visas) were already closed. Nonetheless, reports leaked out via radio and television, and by 8:00 p.m. citizens believed the wall was open (ignoring the visa stipulation). Elated crowds approached the border and by 10:00 p.m. thousands had gathered at well-known checkpoints. Confused guards, who had received no warning, were unsure what to do. Although sworn to shoot unauthorized crossers, they were paralyzed by the lack of direction, the conflicting news items, and the excited masses. Many simply opened the gates.

Later that evening, Krenz officially approved the opening of the gates in an emergency meeting of the Politburo. Moscow was notified and Gorbachev quickly endorsed the action. Although the Soviets were deeply astonished that such a monumental decision, affecting the entire East–West balance, had been made without their approval and consultation, they were left with little choice. The face-saving Soviet response was that this was a matter for East Germans to decide.

As noted earlier, the contextual view comprises at least three research strands. Organizational ecology (Hannan and Freeman, 1989) emphasizes the external or environmental effects in relation to firm longevity. Organizational models (e.g., the garbage can model of choice) highlight internal complexity, in particular random interactions among people, circumstances, and decisions. Behavioral decision theory emphasizes the importance of process and context in choice (as discussed in Chapters 3 and 4). All three of these research perspectives appear relevant to the German case. External forces (involving the United States, Soviet Union, Czechoslovakia, Rumania, etc.) set the stage. Organizational mishaps caused ill-fated committee decisions and press releases. Cognitive simplification (as well as affective factors) influenced crowd reaction and guard behavior.

8.3.4   *Prescriptive issues*

Faced with so many demands on their time, how should managers decide what to focus on? Ideally they should be guided by a vision that indicates how and in what direction the organization should change. Without a vision, they become reactive and focus too much on problems that seem most pressing at the time. Such managers will fall victim to a type of availability bias, where issues that are frequently forced into their attention field are addressed before less vocal but perhaps more important ones. They might first return the call of the person who phoned already several times, instead of the more important single call. Of course, managers have to be responsive to changes in the environment. However, they are also the means by which strategies are linked to operations so some consistency over time is required. Managers must assure that the many thousands of decisions that occur in organizations all add up to a coherent whole.

As noted earlier, various writers have criticized the incremental nature of managerial decision making as though it were no more than "muddling through." Another view, however, is that good managers do this because it is the only practical way to change policy in organizations (see Braybrooke and Lindblom, 1970). The overnight U-turn usually fails; instead organizations adapt through a process of "logical incrementalism" (Quinn, 1978). This is a compromise between the purely reactive stance, where life controls you, and the utopian view of a rational manager who foresees all possibilities and fully controls life by being proactive and interactive (Ackoff, 1978).

Even organizations that are run in a top-down manner must recognize that managers are limited as information processors. For instance, it may take *many* years to implement new strategies (as General Motors found out). Not appreciating the lags, mental inertia, personal agendas, and indeed organizational power of middle managers has derailed numerous "sound" strategies. It is not enough to think rationally; strategists must also think organizationally and politically in order to *implement* new courses of direction. To a large extent, managers influence decisions *indirectly*, through the structure and processes they have put in place. We turn now to these more macro-issues.

8.4   **Organizational design**

The rational actor approach has been especially central to early theories
of organization design, such as Max Weber's (1947) theory of bureaucracy. His main concern was how to construct a perfectly rational, ma-
chinelike, organization that would outperform the patriarchal and often
arbitrary structures found around the turn of the century. The following
are the main prescriptions of this so-called bureaucratic model.

- A well-defined hierarchy should exist for reporting and for the assign-
  ment of responsibilities.
- Subobjectives should be unambiguously assigned to departments.
- Explicit rules and procedures should exist for performing work.
- Relationships between organizational members must remain formal and
  impersonal.
- Promotion and compensation should solely be based on merit, that is,
  on performance and competence.
- The rights and duties of each employee should be clearly defined and
  known to others.

By following these precepts, Weber felt that an organization could act
in a completely rational fashion, with predictable results, and high degrees of reliability. The bureaucratic model has been used successfully
in the military, certain government agencies, and assembly lines such as
General Motors, McDonald's, or car washes. Under conditions of high
certainty, with routine tasks performed on a large scale, and a social climate that does not object to task standardization, fragmentation of work,
and obedience to orders, this model can be a very efficient mode of organization. Indeed, universities often follow the bureaucratic model explicitly when registering thousands of students in just a few days at the
start of a term, or in completing other administrative tasks (e.g., payroll,
personnel benefits).

This rationalistic approach to organizational design was recommended
as well by other classical writers, such as Henri Fayol (1949) and Frederick Taylor (1947). Their ideas are discussed in detail in management
texts and will not be summarized here. The important point is that these
classicists believed in the possibility (as well as the desirability) of developing *universal* design principles, devoid of conflict and dysfunction-
ality. Through proper incentive systems, clear rules, and standard operating procedures and policies, the classicists strove for and envisioned
frictionless, unitary, mechanistic organizations. Undoubtedly, the success
of the industrial revolution and applied physics around the turn of the
century provided a powerful *machine metaphor* for the design of social
systems. However, organizations are not totally closed systems. Conse-

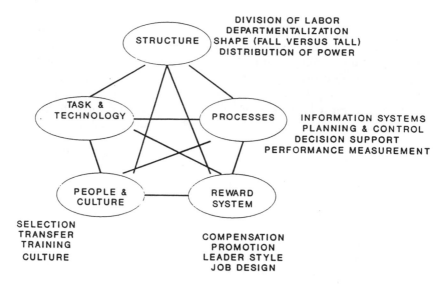

Figure 8.4. Organizational design variables (*Source:* J. R. Galbraith, *Organization Design*, ©1977 by Addison-Wesley Publishing Co. Reprinted by permission of Addison-Wesley Publishing Co., Inc., Reading, MA)

quently, many of the classical ideas had to be modified and adapted to changing circumstances.

8.4.1   *Contingency views*

What determines how and why organizations differ in their designs? By design we shall generally mean the organization's (1) structure, (2) processes, (3) reward system, (4) people and culture, as well as (5) the type of technologies employed in different tasks. Figure 8.4 provides further detail about how these various subsystems might be examined. The figure portrays the organization as consisting of five key subsystems.

Structure refers to the more static features of the organization, such as its departments, reporting hierarchy, and decision making power. *Processes* include all dynamic features that determine how the organization functions over time, such as its budgeting and planning system, performance reviews, and the nature of its information and decision support system. The *reward system* concerns both extrinsic compensation (salary, bonuses, benefits, etc.) as well as intrinsic (freedom to decide, respect, challenge, fairness, etc.). *People and culture* refers to the social climate of the firm, in terms of its norms, attitudes, shared values, degrees of trust or cooperation, as well as continuing education, career growth, hiring practices, and promotion. Last, *task and technology* denotes the kind of work the organization performs (e.g., continuous flow processing in an oil refinery vs. batch jobs in a tool shop), and how it does so (e.g., automation vs. manual).

The figure further highlights that the subsystems interact. For instance, changing from a hierarchical to decentralized structure may require a different planning process, better-educated managers, more reliance on bonus than fixed salary, and perhaps training in the independent use of computing technology. Our interest here is which of the many variables shown in Figure 8.4 are the most important under what conditions. Much literature suggests that *size* is one key variable (Khandwalla, 1977). It affects both structure and process, typically resulting in more formalized or standardized organizations.

Apart from size and standardization, it has been argued that technology, that is, the type of work flow, is a very important factor in the design of organizations. In a classic book on organization, J. Thompson (1967) identified three types of interdependence that may exist as a result of the type of technology used. As shown in Figure 8.5, the first of these is called pooled interdependence, which occurs if each organizational part contributes to the whole and vice versa (as in a commercial bank). This is the case in most traditionally designed organizations. The second type is sequential interdependence, which occurs if Department *A* can only function after having received inputs from some other Department *B*. An example would be Detroit's assembly lines. Finally, there may exist so-called reciprocal interdependence where the departments feed each other back and forth (e.g., as in a general hospital). Thompson argued that these three types of interdependence will lead to different types of coordination and decision problems. Technologies that are characterized by pooled interdependence may be best coordinated by standardization. Sequential dependence requires some decentralization and extensive planning. Reciprocal interdependence may require mutual adjustment and lower level joint decision making, as in matrix organizations.

Another organization theorist, Perrow (1967), has similarly argued the importance of technology on grounds that it affects (1) the number of exceptional cases or problems the organization must handle, and (2) the nature of the problem-solving process that will take place in the organization. For example, in industries involving well-understood technologies, problem solving is often highly routine. In industries based on innovation, the problem-solving procedures are usually less structured. Consider, as illustration, highway construction versus aerospace industry. In constructing a highway, problems are easier to predict and solve using

Technology Type	Dominant Form of Task Interdependence	MANAGEMENT AND DESIGN REQUIREMENTS			Organizational Example
		Demands Placed on Decision Making and Communications	Extent of Organizational Complexity	Type of Coordination Required	
Mediating	Pooled 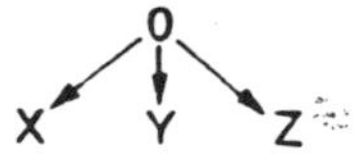 $0 \rightarrow X, 0 \rightarrow Y, 0 \rightarrow Z$	Low	Low	Standardization and Categorization	Commercial bank
Long-linked	Sequential $X \rightarrow Y \rightarrow Z$	Medium	Medium	Plan	Assembly Line
Intensive	Reciprocal 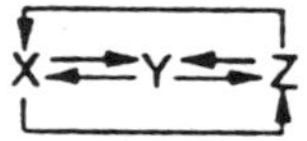 $X \rightleftarrows Y \rightleftarrows Z$	High	High	Mutual adjustment	General hospital

Figure 8.5. Types of interdependence (*Sources*: James D. Thompson, *Organizations in Action*, copyright 1967 by McGraw-Hill, reprinted by permission; Miles, 1980, reprinted by permission)

fairly standard methods and solutions. In contrast, the problems in developing a new airplane are hard to anticipate and may require extensive joint problem solving, using new concepts and methodologies.[10]

Empirical evidence. The idea that technology strongly determines the best organizational design is well supported empirically. A classic study by Burns and Stalker (1961) of various Scottish firms entering the field of electronics showed that their success depended on whether they followed a decentralized or a centralized style of decision making. These authors classified the firms into two groups, mechanistic and organic. They found that the unsuccessful firms exhibited mostly mechanistic structures that emphasize formal, hierarchical relationships, whereas firms that successfully entered the electronics field exhibited much more organic structures. Apparently this new technology required considerable lateral communication, high flexibility, and substantial decision-making power at lower levels.

Another classic study, also conducted in Great Britain, highlights further the importance of technology. Joan Woodward (1958 and 1965) studied over 100 manufacturing firms in England. She collected information on such aspects as the history of the organization, the objectives of the firm, the manufacturing processes used, the methods, forms, and routines of operation, the organization chart, the labor practices, cost structures of the companies, management's qualifications, and the firms' economic success in its industry. After obtaining these measures, the research team attempted to determine empirically the best organizational form. However, no single form emerged as being best across all industries. The optimal design was contingent upon the type of technology in which the firms were engaged.

Woodward used three major classifications for technology, namely (1) unit or small-batch firms that engage in the manufacturing of one or a few products for special order (e.g., scientific instruments), (2) large-batch or mass production firms (e.g., automobile companies), and (3) process production firms that are engaged in continuous or automated manufacturing (such as oil and chemical companies). These three gradations represent increasing degrees of technological complexity. It was found that the successful firms in the low- and high-technology classes, that is, groups (1) and (3) respectively, tended to follow more behavioral or organic forms of design. They permitted greater delegation of authority, more permissive management, and more lateral decision making.

---

10 In a related vein, Perrow (1984) has linked complexity and coupling in organizations to the potential for catastrophic accidents, such as Three Mile Island's nuclear power fiasco.

However, the successful firms engaged in mass production, performed best if they followed the mechanistic design in which responsibilities are clearly defined, the unity of command principle is strictly adhered to, and rigid departmentalization is practiced.

Many of Woodward's major findings were later replicated using more sophisticated research methodologies. One group, the so-called Aston researchers at the University of Aston in England, emphasized that some of the effects of technology as found by Woodward were due to differences in the *size* of the companies (Pugh, Hickson, Hinnings, and Turner, 1968, 1969). Indeed, size or scale will in general exert as much influence on how companies are structured as the type of technology they are engaged in (Child and Mansfield, 1972). Nonetheless, there exists strong empirical evidence that technology matters independently, because it directly determines the type of decision problems and unexpected events an organization must cope with. For a review and critique of the Aston and related studies, see Van de Ven and Joyce (1981).

8.4.2   *An information-processing view*

Given the limited guidance from the empirical literature on how to design organizations, it is especially important to have a sound conceptual basis. An excellent framework for linking decision making to the many organizational variables we have discussed is the *information-processing perspective* developed by Jay Galbraith (1973). Galbraith argues that organizations must process *more* information as their tasks increase in either complexity or uncertainty. He views the hierarchy of an organization as an information-processing network.

Typically rules, plans, and policies are the first guides on how to specify a course of action. In a sense, they represent the preplanning that the organization pursued in anticipation of possible future problems. However, seldom do the existing rules, plans, and policy guidelines cover all problem situations that may arise. Thus, a worker must occasionally seek advice from people higher up. Galbraith calls this hierarchical referral. If an organization expands, for example, into new products or markets, the number of exceptions that are not covered by standard operating procedures will increase, and the hierarchy that is supposed to deal with these exceptions may become overloaded. The question then is how the organization copes with this overload.

As shown at the bottom of Figure 8.6, two generic strategies can be pursued. The first one *reduces* the need to process information vertically within the organization. The second aims to *increase* the organization's capacity to process information vertically. Within each of these generic

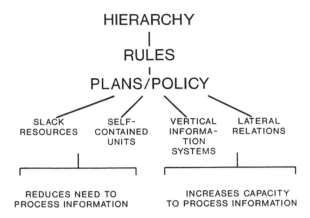

Figure 8.6. Organizational design strategies (*Source:* J. R. Galbraith, *Designing Complex Organizations,* ©1973 by Addison-Wesley Publishing Co. Reprinted by permission of Addison-Wesley Publishing Co., Inc., Reading, MA)

strategies, two substrategies can be identified. Each of these four substrategies will be briefly explained.

Slack resources. Imagine a family of five people that owns only one car. Even though the total driving needs in that family might easily be met by one car, it will require a great deal of coordination (i.e., information processing) in order to satisfy everyone's need for transportation. At some point, especially if people's schedules change from day to day, it may become worthwhile to buy a second car. This is essentially the solution of *increasing slack.* From a pure resource utilization viewpoint, the second car may not be needed. However, it makes people less dependent on each other by reducing the need for individual family members to coordinate their schedules.

Organizations operate in a similar manner. Usually there are more secretaries, photocopiers, or manufacturing machines than would be strictly needed if everybody were to coordinate carefully the use of these resources. However, scheduling and prioritizing activities have their own costs, and it is therefore suboptimal to reduce resource slack to zero.[11] The question is one of balance, that is, what amount and type of slack is optimal? Galbraith argues that as the organization faces more uncer-

11 For certain resources, like machines, it may be impossible to reduce slack time to zero even if one wanted to, because of *indivisibilities.* Subcontracting and part-time usage are options that can be utilized to reduce slack if the firm wanted to do so.

tainty, for example, due to changes in the technology it uses to produce its goods and services, it should increase the amount of organizational slack. A common example is buffer inventory, which makes linked divisions less dependent on each other. The more uncertain demand becomes, the larger the optimal buffer stock will normally be. In other words, slack inventory is a way of handling reciprocal interdependence.

Self-contained units. The second strategy for *reducing* the need to process information within a company is to *reorganize* the entire company from an input basis to an *output design*. The classical design shows as its first division in the organization chart the major inputs to its end products, namely, marketing, manufacturing, personnel, research and development, engineering, and so on. Somehow, the management of such a company must apportion these shared resources to the various products it makes. As products become more complex, this allocation problem may not be solvable in an economically efficient way. At some point it becomes worthwhile to reorganize on the basis of product categories as shown in Figure 8.7, which contrasts an input and output organizational design. General Motors made this shift in the early part of the century when it created a Cadillac division, an Oldsmobile division, a Chevrolet division, and so on. Consequently, each of these divisions duplicates the resources that were formerly shared by everyone. However, in doing so, these divisions could operate much more independently and efficiently.

In his classic book *Strategy and Structure*, Chandler (1962) chronicles the change from the input design (called the U form) to the output design (called the M form). This change started in the United States in the 1920s with such firms as General Motors, Sears Roebuck, DuPont, and Standard Oil of New Jersey. Today the multidivisional (M) form is as common as the unitary (U) form. Of course, one seldom finds a pure M-form organization, since it always pays to keep a few resources centralized, notably computing services, personnel, and finance. Nonetheless, reorganizing around self-contained units, with some sacrifices in economies of scale due to duplication of resources, can be an effective way of balancing the organization's need to process information with its capacity to do so.

Vertical information systems. In terms of *increasing its capacity* to process information, the organization can either invest in formal information systems, or permit more lateral or horizontal contact. With respect to the former, an organization may decide that all the exceptions it has to deal with can best be handled by one large computer system, which keeps an up-to-date record of various circumstances. For example, the airline industry was one of the first to move to global on-line data bases in order to schedule passengers on airplanes. Airlines could never have processed

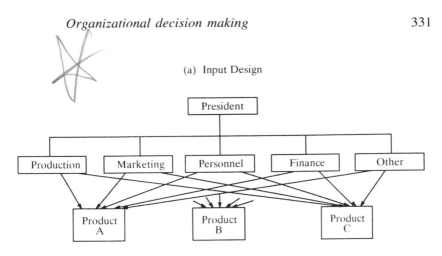

(a) Input Design

CREATION OF SELF-CONTAINED UNITS

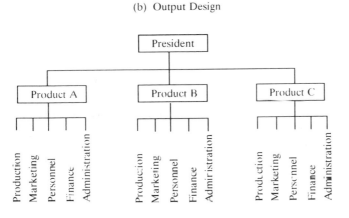

(b) Output Design

Figure 8.7. Input versus output designs

the number of reservations they handle now under the old system of checking via telephones with some central office regarding seat availability. The accounting system is another good example of an investment in a formal information system. By clearly defining such important variables as profit, gross margin, and variable costs, an enormous amount of information can be communicated using this formalized language. Thus, formalization increases vertical information-processing capacity by increasing the informational value per symbol transmitted.

Lateral relations. Finally, Galbraith argues that sometimes an organization gets overloaded because in order for two people lower down to communicate with each other, they have to go through their respective bosses. Such vertical information overload could simply be avoided if these people were permitted to talk directly with each other, even if they are in different departments. It is possible to institutionalize such lateral communication through the creation of special task forces, teams, or project groups. If lateral information flows become as important as vertical, the company can be structured in a matrix design. In this form, as shown in Figure 8.8, subordinates may have two bosses, one functional and the other product-related. For example, those working on the electrical components of Product *A* (say a new airplane) will have to report both to a project vice-president and the engineering vice-president. Who has ultimate say depends on the company and issues involved. The matrix design is especially popular in high-technology industries where frequent exchange of information is critical.

Which particular strategy an organization should pursue in matching its need to process information with its capacity to do so depends on the particular costs and benefits of the various strategies outlined in Figure 8.6. Somehow, a balance must be established between the degree of uncertainty in the environment and the organization's ability to accommodate or cope with such uncertainty. If this balancing decision is not made deliberately, the option of slack will automatically be forced upon the organization. It will take the form of suboptimal inventory levels, long lead times in delivering products, and, in general, lower performance.

Using Galbraith's framework, we can understand the enormous variety of organizational forms found in the real world. For each company, there are unique costs and benefits to each strategy, and hence a company-specific balance will be struck contingent on time and circumstance. As soon as either the technology or the outside environment changes, this balance will have to be reassessed. Hence, both the internal as well as the external environments play major roles in determining how companies should organize themselves to arrive at decisions in an efficient and effective manner.

8.4.3   *Prescriptive analysis: decision support*

We shall define a decision support system (DSS) as a computer-oriented resource aimed at aiding decision makers, either by providing better data, quicker access, better models, or more powerful solutions (in the form of software or consulting). Unlike decision analysis or traditional management science, DSS does not seek to replace the decision maker or take over large chunks of the problem, but instead to supplement or aid. How much aid to offer, and in what form, depend on (1) the problem's

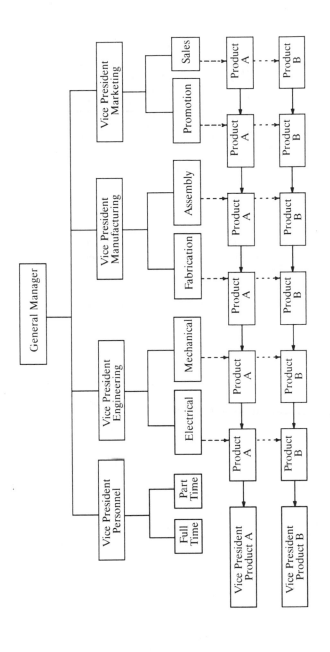

- - - - → = Technical authority over the product

———→ = Formal authority over the product

Figure 8.8. The matrix design: a compromise

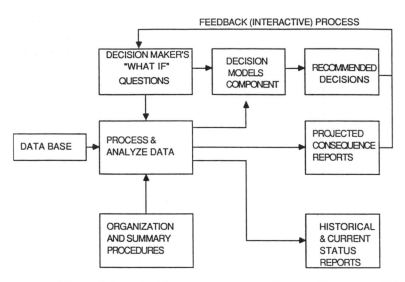

Figure 8.9. A decision support system (*Source:* Forgionne, 1986, p. 33. Reprinted by permission)

complexity, (2) the decision maker's skill, (3) the power of the DSS solution kit, and (4) the organizational context.

Regarding degree of complexity, routine problems can often be supported in numerous ways – for example, by providing up-to-date information on customers, products, prices (as in airline reservation systems), or by solving problems formally (e.g., in job scheduling or inventory ordering). Figure 8.9 shows a generic structure for a decision support system. First, it must possess a data base that can be accessed by managers for either up-to-date information (e.g., on inventory levels) or routine reports (e.g., sales trends of product X for last ten quarters). In more sophisticated systems, "what if" questions might be asked such as "What will demand for X be if we increase our price 10% and competitors keep their prices at current levels?" Also, the system may contain standard models (concerning pricing, scheduling, financial evaluation) that managers can use for their particular problems by just typing in some key information. The model can thus make specific recommendations (top row in Figure 8.9) based on the information provided.

For tactical decisions, those mostly made by middle managers, accurate data, easy spreadsheets, and good graphics are often all that is needed. Most tactical problems are too fluid and unique to benefit much from high-powered optimization; often they involve people problems, multiple objectives, negotiable constraints, and ambiguous estimates. Of course, exceptions exist. In the petroleum industry, many tactical decisions on "how to cut the barrel" (i.e., how to distill crude oil into refined products) are based on linear programming (LP) solutions. However, even here the recent price volatility of crude oil often caused optimal LP solutions to be outdated by the time the programs were run.[12]

DSS in strategic decisions requires a blend of versatility and modesty. One problem is that technical analysts often do not fully appreciate the multiple issues involved. In addition, strategic problems interconnect with others, making it hard to draw clear boundaries. And there is a political dimension, namely, whose judgments will weigh most heavily. Decision making is very much the essence and prerogative of executives. They will not lightly give this up or pass it on to models and analysts. Consequently, DSS in top decisions should be viewed as one of several inputs to aid the executive in making a final choice.

Only if we understand the organizational context are we ready to develop a DSS. Its effectiveness will, in general, depend on:

- Its ability to develop new models and problem representations quickly.
- The ability to call upon relevant data easily (by having good data-base access).
- The breadth of decision tools available (from spreadsheets and graphics to simulation and optimization).
- Ease of use by individuals, and especially *teams*.
- The ability to link, integrate, decompose, and revise problems (across functions and organizational boundaries).

ALCO revisited. Think back to the ALCO electronics case. What pricing decision would a highly rational (and slightly arrogant) analyst recommend; what suggestions would a team player concerned with finding the best solution make; and how would an astute political player pursuing his self-interest proceed? Using DSS to improve decision making requires that one be able to wear all three hats (rational, organizational, and political) and to know which one to feature at which time. Prescriptive analysis in ALCO is *impossible* without careful descriptive analysis of the organizational context. These questions suggest the following observations for ALCO. Which people participate in the IC's pricing decision is a direct function of the organization's structure. In a traditional functional structure, it is likely that marketing would be responsible. Presumably they would consult with production, research and development, and other

---

12 Although sensitivity analyses could have been conducted, large price changes cause so many other variables or parameters to change that the traditional *ceteris paribus* assumption would not hold.

functions, but at their discretion and terms. If ALCO had a product organizational design, the IC's product manager would have the primary
responsibility. Finally, if ALCO followed a matrix structure, there would
be shared responsibility, for example, between marketing and the IC's
product division. Hence, organizational structure directly influences who
will sit around the table on a particular issue, and what formal power
each party possesses.

Other important decision aspects are timing and information availability. Both are influenced by process dimension of the organization's design. For instance, if the research and development department is just
going through its annual review process, or its budget cycle, its managers
may not devote much attention or brain power to the IC pricing decision.
Similarly, if they lack good information because of the way the organizational data base is structured, their involvement may likewise diminish.
In sum, the timing and participation in key organizational decisions is
greatly influenced by the organization design. Often the outcome of a
decision (especially a complex one) depends critically on who participates
in the decision process and when, and on what information set is used
and what circumstances prevail.

8.5   Conclusions

Having traversed much ground in various disciplines the time has come
to summarize what we do and don't know regarding organizational decision making. We first address possible syntheses or reconciliations of
the various views discussed. Thereafter, we highlight what challenges
remain and the important issues that deserve more research attention.

8.5.1   *Syntheses and reconciliations*

Juxtaposing the rational and behavioral perspectives raises the question
of the extent to which organizations can and should strive to be unitary
actors.[13] After all, it is impossible and often undesirable to control fully
the decisions and thoughts of every person in the firm. Further, one won-
ders whether the four perspectives offer primarily competing versus complementary perspectives. This section examines five potential modes of
synthesis, focusing on (1) assumptional fit, (2) level of analysis, (3) design costs of collective rationality, (4) information-processing constraints,
and (5) disequilibrium.

Assumptional fit. Perhaps the simplest approach in deciding what model

---

13 This section is based on Schoemaker (1992).

to adopt, when trying to understand or predict a given organizational decision, is to examine how well the underlying assumptions fit the facts. Such unitary actor assumptions as high rationality and efficient coordination can often be tested or rated empirically. For instance, does ALCO management use analytic tools and an appropriate process in arriving at a price for its integrated circuit? Or is the organization paralyzed by top-level infighting and minimal investment in information or planning systems. Moreover, if the external environments are highly turbulent and complex, the unitary actor view is unlikely to fit well. On the other hand, in more stable environments, entailing entrepreneurial companies or military outfits, the unitary view may fit closely, since a single commander or visionary leader can rationally call the shots.

Of course, assumptional fit will in part depend on the issues or decisions examined. And conversely, different models tend to focus or define issues differently. For instance, ALCO may be quite unitary in its pricing decision but overtly political in its budgeting or promotion decisions. Also, if the prediction we are interested in is just ordinal (e.g., a higher or lower price) the unitary model may do better than when trying to predict degree or type of change (e.g., the exact price level). As such, an overall characterization of organizations or even just one decision in terms of a single model may not be feasible.

Unit of analysis. A related mode of reconciliation is to view the conceptual models as representing different degrees of resolution of the investigator's microscope. The unitary model seeks the wide angle so as to bring external forces (e.g., competitors) into the picture. The organizational and political models provide more focus on intraorganizational issues, but at the expense of environmental scope (in terms of competitors, time frame, etc.). Last, the contextual view offers fine-grained detail, but at the risk of obscuring the larger picture.

Just as physics and chemistry, or cell and molecular biology, are complementary sciences, rational and behavioral models could be viewed as operating at different levels of analysis. Unlike the natural sciences, however, the links between these different levels are often missing. Moreover, the models do not share the same underlying assumptions about people, but instead rest on different premises. As such, their complementarity is at best partial. (See Schoemaker [1991a] for an analysis of optimality models in the physical and social sciences.)

Cost of creating collective unity. An alternative mode of synthesis is to recognize that it will seldom be optimal for firms to be perfectly unitary, even if all actors are hyperrational. Note that unitary does not imply rational (e.g., a lynching mob) or vice versa. Some degree of slack or inefficiency is optimal when taking account of the design, planning, coordinating, and monitoring costs associated with perfect collective rationality. Several literature streams have emphasized such costs.

Team theory (Marschak and Radner, 1972) focuses on problems caused by uncertainty, such as (1) what information to track externally, (2) how to communicate it internally, and (3) how to act on the information. It assumes zero conflict of interest among team members, with "a complete sharing of goals and information" (MacCrimmon, 1985, p. 1323). Transactions cost economics explicitly considers conflicts of interest, specifically how to structure, monitor, and control economic exchange using contracts or hierarchy (Coase, 1937; Klein et al., 1978; Williamson, 1989). Agency theory, in turn, explores possible mechanisms to align incentives for subordinates or agents when faced with uncertainty, risk-attitude differences, and information asymmetry (Robert Wilson, 1968; Ross, 1973; Holmstrom, 1982).

The last two views directly address our two axes of goal congruency and coordinative rationality. Transactions costs influence the scope and structure of organizational activity; agency costs dictate the design of incentives and information flow (see Barney and Ouchi, 1986). Both approaches have spawned much research on the role of information asymmetry among parties, the impact of signaling, and the separation of ownership and control (see Holmstrom and Tirole, 1989). Agency models typically focus on incentive alignment assuming high individual rationality, whereas transactions costs models more generally address economizing (as opposed to strategizing) behavior under bounded rationality.

Information-processing constraints. An alternative, less rational route to arrive at a similar conclusion is via information-processing models of organization design discussed earlier. The uniqueness and variety of organizational forms reflect managers' limited coping capability (Simon, 1955), comparable with the local adaptation of species in biology. Numerous variables appear to influence organizational design, ranging from size and other organizational demographics, work flow, and technology, to environmental uncertainty.

Galbraith's (1973) model provides an interesting cognitive synthesis of behavioral and rational elements, focusing on individual information-processing limitations. He emphasizes that organizations must process *more* information as their tasks increase in either complexity or uncertainty. To survive, the organization must effectively cope with this overload, either by (1) *reducing* the need to process information vertically or (2) *increasing* its capacity to do so (as discussed earlier).

Disequilibrium. This perspective suggests yet a fourth mode of synthesis, involving lags and disequilibrium. Under high environmental change, even organizations with the best planning systems are forced to react to external events. In addition, their own reactions to external change may induce further complexity and change for other firms. Such enacted complexity perpetuates a state of disequilibrium, and may prevent optimal adaptation to the environment from ever being realized. The ensuing disequilibrium may last only short periods or may span decades as noted at the start of the chapter when we briefly discussed the evolution of organizational forms.

Table 8.1 briefly summarized the historical development of business organizations over centuries. This thumbnail sketch highlights the roles of technology and external complexity as often the driving forces behind organizational change. Economies of scale and scope especially contributed to the growing complexity of economic activities (see Chandler, 1990), as did the emergence of mass distribution systems such as railroads, the telephone and telegraph, and later jet airplanes and computers. During periods of relative stability, firms may have had time to approximate the unitary actor model. For instance, in the early part of this century Henry Ford nearly perfected the production of the Model T car, until challenged by Sloan's (1963) strategy at General Motors of model differentiation and M-form organizational design (Chandler, 1962; Armour and Teece, 1978). Depending on whether one views organizational evolution as a process of continual adaptation (Chakravarthy, 1982) or punctuated equilibriums (such as the sudden collapse of communism), the rational model may appeal less or more.

Thus we come full circle to our original questions, namely how to think about the various models and when to use them. Much, it seems, depends on the turbulence and texture of the environment (Emery and Trist, 1965). In relatively stable times (such as the 1950s in the United States), the rational or organizational models may closely describe what transpires. In accelerating periods (such as the 1970s and 1980s), the political and contextual models are likely to do better due to lags and the difficulties of arriving at optimal solutions. For instance, the deregulations in financial services, airlines, trucking, and so on, coupled with oil shocks, globalization, and takeovers, made the past two decades very difficult for U.S. corporations. More challenging yet for global firms was the crumbling of Communism. Hence, the capacity to examine strategic decisions through all four perspectives depending on time and circumstances, becomes a crucial skill. This mixed mode in turn permits sensitivity analyses and tests of robustness of predictions, prescriptions, and strategies.

Although theoretical pluralism seems highly laudable, it often leads to conflicting predictions or recommendations. Different outcomes or actions will seem plausible within different perspectives. Strategic planning, for instance, is likely to be more top-down (Chandler, 1962) and deliberative (Lorange and Vancil, 1977; Chakravarthy and Lorange, 1991) in the rational model, whereas the contextual view would favor a more incremental (Quinn, 1978), tacit, and experiential approach (see Mintzberg, 1990). To mediate between these conflicting models, the transactions cost or information-processing view might be adopted. The former tilts toward the rational side and thus may be better suited for stable worlds. The cognitive view highlights the coping (and often groping) nature of managerial decisions and as such favors more dynamic circumstances.

Having examined various perspectives, what we need next is a better developed metatheory that can guide us in the selection of the most appropriate model(s) for each circumstance. Key variables in such a metatheory are likely to be degree of goal congruency and coordinative rationality. The latter, in turn, will depend on external turbulence or instability, level of analysis, and decision type, as well as other factors.

8.5.2   *Remaining challenges*

Throughout this book we have been concerned with interactions between normative and descriptive issues. This concern is especially pertinent for organizations, which to a great extent owe their existence to bounded rationality. Several themes stand out.

Themes. First, organizational structure or design matters as it reflects a firm's adaptation to its *unique* environment. This contextualism is especially emphasized in Galbraith's framework, which permits numerous, idiosyncratic solutions to the organizational design problem.

Second, transactions matter, both as a process and unit of analysis. Transactions involve judgments and choices by boundedly rational individuals, who often need to cope with complexities. The overall organizational design greatly influences how economic and social transactions are conducted – that is, by whom, over what time period, in what manner, and with what controls. Conversely, however, transactions costs influence macrodesign issues, such as where to draw organization boundaries and how to organize internally.

Third, organizations need to be effective as well as efficient. Relatively little work (and insight) exists on how structure and process map into efficacy. Indeed, how to measure organizational effectiveness remains an important issue, to which we shall return. The interrelationships among structure, process, and outcome are key in this regard. Figure 8.10 portrays how the organization's design combines with process and context to create output. These outputs are multiple, ranging from traditional profit criteria to morale, fairness (or equity), and an ability to survive via adaptation. Whereas Figure 8.4 highlighted the interaction among five or-

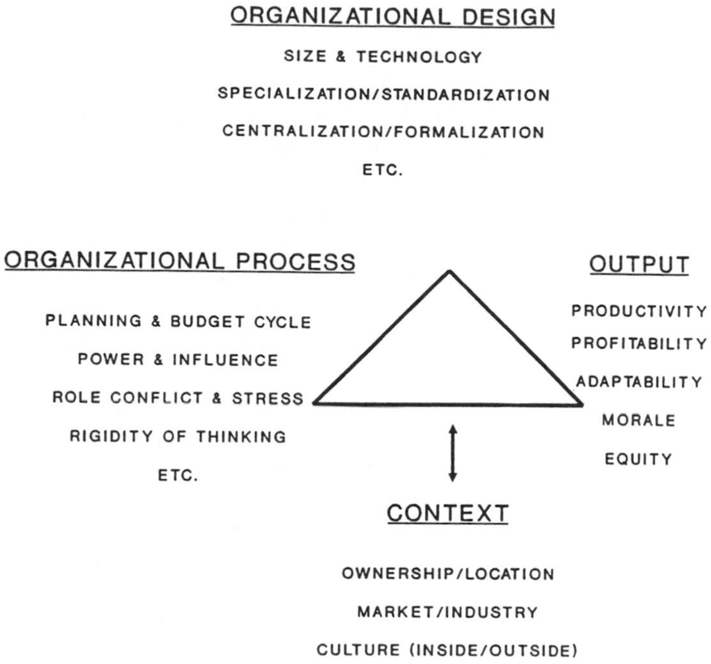

ORGANIZATIONAL DESIGN

SIZE & TECHNOLOGY

SPECIALIZATION/STANDARDIZATION

CENTRALIZATION/FORMALIZATION

ETC.

ORGANIZATIONAL PROCESS   OUTPUT

PLANNING & BUDGET CYCLE   PRODUCTIVITY

                                 PROFITABILITY

POWER & INFLUENCE

                                 ADAPTABILITY

ROLE CONFLICT & STRESS

                                 MORALE

RIGIDITY OF THINKING

                                 EQUITY

ETC.

CONTEXT

OWNERSHIP/LOCATION

MARKET/INDUSTRY

CULTURE (INSIDE/OUTSIDE)

Figure 8.10. Design–process–output triangle

ganizational subsystems, the present figure links two of these to the organization's output. This link to performance has often been absent from organizational studies (e.g., the Aston research) or poorly conceptualized. For instance, how does changing a firm's planning system to incorporate, say, scenario analysis impact both its profitability as well as adaptability, given its size, technology, structure, and particular context (e.g., for a privately held firm, operating in a fragmented industry within a united Europe)?

From a decision sciences perspective, we have a reasonable handle on process issues, thanks to the individual and group decision literatures, as well as behavioral theories of the firm. Nonetheless, decision processes will also be influenced by microconditions that escape these models, leaving a significant residual effect (as emphasized by Lindblom 1964; Cohen, March, and Olsen, 1972; Quinn 1978, 1980; and others). Also regarding structure, a considerable vocabulary and empirical base exists (in the organization theory literature). What seems lacking, however, is much decision insight into structure–process interactions and their links to performance. This realization is especially critical in designing decision support systems (DSS).

Key questions. There is still much we do not know about organizational decision making (March, 1988). The following are some key issues that, in our view, deserve much more attention.

First, we do not really know how much the four perspectives in Table 8.4 explain with respect to design, process, and outcomes. We seem to understand the rational and organizational perspectives best, and the political and contextual least well. The last two, however, strike us as very important, especially given our emphasis on process, bounded rationality, and complexity.

Second, we do not understand well how organizations deal with uncertainty, and ambiguity, both within their confines and externally. Uncertainty and ambiguity are often shunned, since people desire control and are fundamentally risk averse. Yet, ambiguity is an almost inescapable concomitant of innovation and self-renewal. Most innovation occurs in small companies, as if large ones undermine those things necessary for change or feel it is not their comparative advantage to innovate (due to size, structure, culture, downside risk, etc.).[14]

A related question is that of resilience versus rigidity (Wildavsky, 1979; Perrow, 1984). The natural tendency toward more structure (and control) often leads organizations to become very good at routines and very poor at dealing with deviations. An extreme example is a well-oiled bureaucracy that processes expense reimbursement requests with lightning speed, provided all procedures are followed to the letter, but that grinds to a halt if, say, the third carbon copy is omitted. Many organizations, especially larger and older ones, fail to be robust in dealing with variance. Instead of having flat maxima, they are highly brittle, falling apart (in the sense of nonperformance) when faced with deviation. They don't know how to learn and self-renew anymore (see Argyris and Schon, 1981; Argyris, 1985).

Third, organizations continue to struggle with how to improve their strategic positions. The choice of model will greatly affect the approach taken. Rational models will probably continue to place the locus of profit at the industry or strategic group level (Caves, 1980; Porter, 1980). Organizational and political models will likely focus on firm-specific competencies and capabilities (Amit and Schoemaker, 1993) as the primary source of variance in economic rent. They would emphasize the importance of invisible assets (Itami, 1987), core competencies (Prahalad and Hamel, 1990), and a managerial culture that blends a long-term resource focus with short-term exploitation of market opportunities (see last row

14 For example, IBM had much more at stake in entering the personal computer business than upstart Apple Computer. Apart from IBM's reputational risk, it faced the problem of product cannibalization, and of not having an organizational culture geared toward creating, manufacturing, or marketing personal computers.

in Table 8.1).[15] The contextual view, in contrast, suggests a planning mode that is more experiential and process-oriented (Mintzberg, 1990). It would focus on managing contexts and creating conditions from which good strategies might emanate, without directly forging them.

Fourth, we do not really understand the nature and impact of multiple objectives in firms. Narrow measures of efficiency or success in the short run must often be balanced with larger questions about ethics, social concerns, and equity, all of which may impact long-run success. How firms, in their constrained quest for success, introduce these multiple goals into their structures and processes remains unclear. Also, the ways in which people import these multiple objectives into their professional work and decision making merit further research.

Last, and much related to the preceding concerns, there is the crucial question of what determines good performance by managers and by the organization (see Dalton, Tudor, Spendolini, Fielding, and Porter, 1990). Each decade we see new issues and approaches on the managerial agenda. Recent concerns have included Japanese management techniques, how to build long-term commitments and far-sighted companies, and the role of takeovers, buyouts, and other forms of rationalization. The competitive nature of industry will continually shift the grounds and dimensions on which firms compete. Yet, there must exist enduring insights into how to be effective. Today these insights are largely lacking.

In part, our collective ignorance reflects the complexity of the phenomenon. However, it may also reflect having been anchored too much on rational models and concepts derived from the individual decision-making literature. Organizational decision processes are often a gloss on more complex and less visible social and political processes (see March, 1988). To understand these deeper levels, we need a different vocabulary that goes beyond unitary actor conceptions. Too few such concepts exist at the moment in our organizational vocabulary.

15 Indeed, we view the challenge of strategic management in the 1990s to lie in the merging of such 1950s and 1960s concepts of distinctive competencies and fit (Selznick, 1957; Andrews, 1971) with the 1970s and 1980s product market focuses (Porter, 1980, 1985) into a resource-based view of the firm (Penrose, 1959; Teece, 1982; Rumelt, 1984; Wernerfelt, 1984; Barney, 1989; Dierickx and Cool, 1989) that emphasizes *robust* and *dynamic* organizational capabilities (see Amit and Schoemaker, 1993; Teece, Pisano, and Shuen, 1990). This view blends long- and short-term perspectives, as well as static and dynamic. In practical terms, it addresses how to (1) compete in time, (2) assure quality throughout, and (3) reconfigure assets continually to meet ever-changing demands in highly customized product/market segments.

9

Societal decision making

9.1   Introduction

This chapter investigates alternative approaches for dealing with problems that not only affect individuals but also have important societal consequences. Such problems typically involve a broad spectrum of interests, from consumers and businesses to special interest groups and government agencies. Our particular focus is on low-probability, high-consequence events, as these bring out clearly the importance of understanding decision processes for prescribing public policy. More specifically, biases are known to exist regarding the way different interested parties deal with risks. Society is now struggling with many of these issues, and they will assume even more prominence as technology advances. The problems include such diverse areas as automobile safety, energy, environment, natural and technological hazards, consumer product safety, and occupational risks.

Based on an understanding of the decision processes of the different actors, what type of policy tools should be utilized in allocating resources? Frey and Eichenberger (1989) suggest that private markets may be inefficient when there is uncertainty because of individual limitations in collecting and processing information on the risk. For example, motorists know that their chances of being involved in an accident are low, but few can specify the probabilities of being injured, or whether driving to work is more or less dangerous than a trip on the open highway which takes twice as long. There is a general awareness that protective mechanisms, such as seat belts or air bags, will reduce the impact of an accident, but little thought is generally given to the specific benefits of using these devices.

A related factor that limits the use of markets in allocating resources is that the rules of thumb for evaluating protective measures often do not involve benefit–cost trade-offs. Many individuals in hazard-prone areas fail to engage in loss-prevention activities such as purchasing insurance because they use a simple rule like "It won't happen to me" or "I don't have to worry about this." Hence, they do not compare the cost of the protective measure with the reduction in expected loss from adopting it.

The inverse of the "It won't happen to me" rule is often invoked for projects that involve technological risks such as the construction of a nuclear power plant or the siting of a hazardous waste incinerator. The public often assumes that "if it can go wrong it will" (Murphy's Law). In essence, people focus only on the potential consequences of an accident at such facilities rather than on the chances of its occurrence. This concern with consequences may explain the difficulty in finding homes for facilities that the public considers hazardous, even though scientific experts feel they are safe. Both of these heuristics focus only on a single dimension – in the first case, "probability," and in the second case, "outcome."

A third issue that has important public policy implications concerns the aggregate impact of a systematic underreaction or overreaction to low-probability events. The relationship between micromotives and macrobehavior has been explored in detail by Thomas Schelling (1978) using a variety of social contexts. It has particular relevance to situations in which individuals utilize simplified rules of thumb such as those described previously.

For example, if few individuals purchase flood insurance even though it is highly subsidized by the federal government, then many unprotected homeowners are subject to a large personal loss if a flood severely damages their residence. Each individual in a flood-prone area should find subsidized flood insurance attractive, assuming he or she is risk averse (or even slightly risk seeking) and wishes to maximize expected utility. By not purchasing coverage an individual appears to be behaving irrationally. Should a homeowner be the only one uninsured, then she undoubtedly would have to shoulder the consequences personally. However, if most of the victims are unprotected, then the political consequences of not providing relicf may be so severe that Congress will put together a generous relief package.[1]

Homeowners are likely to assume that after the next catastrophic earthquake, flood, or hurricane, Congress will respond generously again. In fact, the decision not to take protective action, which appears to be irrational if the individual believes he is personally responsible for the loss, may be justified ex post if there is an unexpected generous response by other parties.

A fundamental issue in public policy is how much to rely on the private market to allocate resources and to what extent, if at all, government

---

1 For example, Tropical Storm Agnes in 1972 caused approximately $2 billion in damage and less than $100 million of this was covered by insurance. As a result, the Small Business Administration offered $5,000 forgiveness grants to all victims, whether insured or uninsured, and 1% loans for the remaining portion of the damage (Kunreuther, 1973).

should be involved in protective decisions prior to the occurrence of a low-probability event. In part this hinges on past experience, societal expectations, and the nature of the events. We shall illustrate some instances in which private markets operate especially poorly. From a policy perspective, such market failures are important because they involve not only *private risks* to the affected individuals but also *social risks* to others beyond those actually making the decisions.

9.1.1   *Automobile safety*

Wearing a seat belt reduces the personal risk of injury in a car accident whether or not air bags are installed. Prior to 1985, less than 20% of motorists wore seat belts voluntarily, even though it was widely known that seat belts save lives (Williams and Lund, 1986). It appears that many people do not wear seat belts because their personal probability estimates have an optimistic bias (cf. Weinstein, 1987).

In a survey of motorists, Svenson (1981) found that 90% of drivers felt that they were better drivers than average. Those drivers often justify their optimism by saying "it hasn't happened to me." Others admit a self-control problem, finding it too cumbersome to buckle up (see Schelling, 1983). We, as a society, bear some of the costs of these injuries through subsidized medical payments and lost productivity, not to mention the financial and emotional impact that a serious injury poses to the victim's immediate family. For these reasons, it may be appropriate to mandate the use of seat belts.

9.1.2   *Natural hazard protection*

There is considerable evidence that many individuals do *not* voluntarily protect themselves against a host of low-probability natural hazards. Few homeowners adopt inexpensive loss reduction measures even though this would mitigate losses should a disaster occur. For this reason, earthquake-resistant design requirements were incorporated in California building codes following the extensive damage to structures from the 1933 Long Beach earthquake (Petak and Atkisson, 1982).

What role should benefit–cost analysis play in determining the relative merits of mitigation measures for hazards such as earthquakes? What role should the federal government play in providing insurance protection when the private sector finds it unprofitable to market such coverage? In addressing these questions, one has to take into account issues of resource allocation (efficiency) as well as distributional concerns across stakeholders (equity).

9.1.3 *Siting technological facilities*

Technological facilities, like nuclear power plants and storage facilities for radioactive waste, may benefit society but concentrate risk in the regions where these facilities are located. Although scientists and experts emphasize that the health, safety, and environmental risks are very low, people who live near a proposed facility are usually strongly opposed to them. Their fears are caused by factors such as the unknowability and uncontrollability of the hazard and its catastrophic potential. These risk perceptions are not normally considered by experts (Fischhoff, Watson, and Hope, 1984; Slovic, 1987).

Compensation given to the host communities is an obvious policy tool suggested by economists for locating facilities. However, if the affected public feels that the risk to health and safety exceeds some critical level, it may view monetary payments as a bribe and refuse to accept the facility (Kunreuther, Fitzgerald, and Aarts, 1993).

These three examples illustrate that effective policies must consider psychological and sociological factors as well as economic ones. In many cases, market-based solutions may be inappropriate for dealing with these issues.

Kenneth Arrow (1963b) has suggested that "when the market fails to achieve an optimal state, society will, to some extent at least, recognize the gap, and nonmarket social institutions will arise attempting to bridge it" (p. 247). A set of policies ranging from providing better information to strict government regulation may fill this gap and improve social welfare. Before evaluating these programs we shall examine the conditions required for a private market to function for choices involving well-specified risks.

9.2   **The performance of the economic market under risk**

For most situations involving the trading of goods and services, private market mechanisms generally perform very well without the need for government interference. For problems involving risk and uncertainty, the assumptions required for a market system to allocate goods and services efficiently may not be satisfied by either buyers or sellers. Furthermore there may be other social objectives, such as equity and distributional considerations, that may conflict with the efficient resource allocation process under a free-market system.

A free-market system leads to an *efficient outcome* if the allocation of resources between parties cannot be rearranged to improve at least one person's situation while not worsening the position of others. This condition, known as Pareto optimality, was discussed in Chapter 7. The following example will be used to illustrate the types of assumptions that are sufficient for a Pareto-optimal resource allocation under conditions of uncertainty:

Assume a large number of consumers with identical wealth and the same utility function, each of whom faces an identical loss of L dollars (e.g., a fire destroying their home) which can occur with a known probability, denoted by p, that is independent of any steps taken by the consumer. Each potential loss is uncorrelated with any other loss. Many identical firms offer insurance policies to protect the consumer against this potential loss. What price and amount of insurance coverage will firms offer? How much protection will consumers want to purchase?

This paradigm describes an important class of problems facing those who demand and supply protection against risk. The following assumptions regarding the knowledge and behavior of the consumers and firms are necessary and sufficient for an efficient solution to emerge.

- Consumers and firms agree on the values of p and L.
- Consumers will purchase that amount of insurance which maximizes their expected utility.
- Each firm sets a price for insurance that maximizes its expected profit.
- Each firm is so small that its particular transaction volume with consumers has no noticeable effect on the price of insurance.
- There is no cost of entry or exit by firms.
- There is no collusion between either consumers or firms in their transactions.
- The actions of any one consumer or firm do not influence the welfare of others.

To determine the nature of the equilibrium price and quantity, there is a need to be more specific about the behavior of firms and consumers. Consider a representative insurance company – Gibraltar. It offers a price (r) per dollar of insurance that maximizes its expected profits. Since the probability of a loss is given by p, the firm will make zero expected profits if $r = p$. The total amount of coverage $D(r)$ that consumers purchase will be a function of r, so that the expected profit [$E(\pi)$] for each firm is given by

$$E(\pi) = D(r)[r - p] \tag{9.1}$$

Now, given these assumptions, it can be shown that insurance firms like Gibraltar Company will all end up charging the same price $r = p$. If $r > p$, then positive expected profits would result;[2] other firms would

---

2 We are assuming for this highly simplified example that insurance was costless to market. In reality, r will lie above p by the amount required to provide fair returns to managers and shareholders.

enter the market with a lower price to share in these profits. Eventually price would be driven to p, where each firm would just cover its costs. Clearly a price $r < p$ is not feasible since negative expected profits would result.

Consumers determine the amount of coverage to purchase that maximizes their expected utility given a selling price of r. Consider a representative homeowner, Jane. She has initial assets (A) and a von Neumann–Morgenstern utility function that displays risk aversion. Jane knows that if there is a fire she will lose L dollars unless she purchases insurance to cover all or part of this loss. On the other hand, if a fire does not occur then she will be out-of-pocket by the amount of money spent on insurance. These two events occur with probabilities p and $(1 - p)$ respectively. The expected utility $E(U)$ associated with an amount $D(r)$ of coverage is thus given by:

$$E[U(D(r))] = pU[A - L + (1 - r)D(r)] + (1 - p)U[A - rD(r)] \qquad (9.2)$$

Expected utility in equation (9.2) is maximized by setting $dE[U(D(r)]/dD(r) = 0$. This yields the following equilibrium condition for the consumer:

$$\frac{(1 - p)r}{p(1 - r)} = \frac{U'[A - L + (1 - r)D(r)]}{U'[A - rD(r)]} \qquad (9.3)$$

where U' represents the marginal utility of a particular wealth level. The left-hand side of (9.3) is a contingency price ratio, which reflects the expected cost of insurance should no disaster occur (i.e., $((1 - p)r)$ to the expected net gain in assets from insurance should a disaster occur (i.e., $p(1 - r)$). The right-hand side of (9.3) represents the ratio of marginal utility of wealth in a "disaster state" to marginal utility of wealth in a "nondisaster state" if $D(r)$ dollars of insurance were purchased.

If insurance is offered at a price that reflects the risk (i.e., $r = p$), then the right-hand side of (9.3) equals 1.[3] Jane will then want to purchase full coverage (i.e., $D(r) = L$) in order for the right-hand side of (9.3) to be 1. She will now be indifferent between having a fire or not having a fire, since the utility in both these states of the world is identical (due to full coverage). Here again we have simplified the example by assuming there are no costs associated with replacing the goods and that the damaged property and contents do not have any sentimental value.

The equilibrium for this simple problem is characterized as follows. Firms like the Gibraltar Company are willing to trade contingent claims

3 If insurance is subsidized so that $r < p$, then homeowners would want to purchase more than full coverage, since the price is so attractive. Insurance firms normally restrict coverage to the maximum value of the loss to avoid moral hazard problems.

at a price $r = p$ to consumers. The claim is contingent upon the insured's house being damaged or destroyed by fire (excepting fraud). Consumers like Jane are willing to purchase full coverage at the market price.

9.3   Examining the assumptions

Economists have used the performance of the free-market system as a benchmark to evaluate policy options for dealing with the more complicated problems that arise in the real world. It is for this reason that we explicated the set of simplifying assumptions about consumer and firm behavior. When these conditions are satisfied, a free market will produce solutions that are Pareto optimal without any interference by the public sector or the presence of special institutional arrangements within the private sector.

The free-market model resembles the no-friction model of the physicist. It does not normally provide a picture of the world as we know it, but is a valuable tool for shedding light on a complicated reality. Most of the assumptions for the preceding insurance problem are not satisfied in practice. For one thing, there are problems associated with information collection and processing by consumers and firms. Furthermore, there are factors such as market power, externalities, and public goods that produce market inefficiencies and may call for the government to formulate policies for improving social welfare. This chapter will not dwell at length on these latter factors, since they have been covered very well in other policy texts (see, e.g., Stokey and Zeckhauser, 1978). Our attention, instead, will be focused on the importance of understanding decision processes as a basis for developing relevant policy tools.

9.3.1   *Biased information*

There is considerable evidence, as pointed out in Chapter 3, that individuals have great difficulty estimating the chances of uncertain events occurring, particularly if they are low-probability risks. For example, the public, as well as scientists, cannot easily differentiate an event whose chances of occurring is 10^{-7} from one with a probability 10^{-5}, a risk 100 times as large (Zeckhauser and Viscusi, 1990).

If consumers underestimate the probability of a disaster, then they will not purchase full insurance voluntarily unless firms commit the same error. The premium charged by insurers will be seen as too high by the homeowners in relation to their estimate of the chances of a loss. Policy questions thus arise. If there are social benefits of having homeowners protected with coverage, can data on the probability be assembled and provided to the consumer to correct this misperception? When is it more cost-effective simply to *require* individuals to purchase coverage?

Similar policy questions could be raised regarding the loss dimension. Homeowners in California overestimate the magnitude of losses to their wood-frame homes from a severe earthquake, perhaps because of media coverage and salient films such as *Earthquake*. Should experts attempt to correct this biased loss estimate if at the same time individuals underestimate the chances of such an event occurring? Or should two wrongs be left to make a right? If yes to the first question, what actions should be taken and how costly will they be? What are the likely impacts on behavior?

For many events, such as earthquakes, there is a limited statistical data base from which to determine the probability and resulting losses to property or health in a given region of the country. In this case, insurers set their premiums based on ambiguous information. The prices for these ambiguous hazards tend to be higher because of uncertainties in the data (Hogarth and Kunreuther, 1989; Kunreuther, Hogarth, and Meszaros, 1993).

For other problems, firms may have difficulty discriminating between good and bad risks. Which applicants for medical coverage are healthy, which unhealthy? If the individuals themselves know but insurers do not, then firms cannot charge differential premiums. This opens up the possibility of adverse selection where only the poorer risks purchase coverage, premiums increase to cover losses, and eventually the market becomes very thin or collapses (Akerlof, 1970).

What steps can be taken to correct this failure? Some private sector remedies are possible, such as requiring applicants to have a medical examination and using the results as a basis for the premium. Another possible solution is requiring everyone to purchase medical insurance. Then firms can charge a single premium across all classes of risks, such that the good risks subsidize the poor risks. Of course, if the consumer does not know his or her own health status relative to others, then adverse selection ceases to be a problem. In this sense, information imperfections on both the demand and supply side may lead to a more efficient market than if only firms did not know consumers' risk characteristics.

9.3.2 *Consumer decision rules*

Individuals often use simplified decision rules for making their choices. Tversky et al. (1988) propose a contingent weighting model in which individuals make biased trade-offs between dimensions such as probability and utility. The weights placed on dimensions are contingent on the way information is requested (response modes) and the problem context.

Many of the heuristics for dealing with low-probability risks seem to follow a contingent weighting process. An extreme form of such a rule is when all the weight is placed on a single dimension. For example, some individuals may decide that if the probability of an accident is below a threshold value of p^*, they will not reflect on its occurrence and hence will not consider the loss dimension.

If large groups of people at risk are unprotected against potential disasters because they use such probability threshold models, then what alternative policy options should be considered? There is no easy answer to this question since it involves issues of paternalism (i.e., forcing people to protect themselves against their will) as well as possible cross-subsidization to unprotected individuals by the rest of society (e.g., providing uninsured disaster victims with liberal federal aid). What is very clear, however, is that in many situations the private market will allocate resources differently from what would be predicted from normative models of consumer choice.

9.3.3   *Firm decision rules*

The problems faced by firms are similar to those of consumers. They use rules of thumb that reflect specific constraints. For example, a case study of a chemical company revealed that prior to the Bhopal, India, chemical explosion it was using techniques of risk assessment to determine acceptable standards for operating a plant.[4] The normal procedure was to design production processes so that the chances of an accident were at or below an acceptable probability level. Following Bhopal, instead of focusing on the probability dimension, the emphasis was placed on an analysis of *worst outcome scenarios* and ensuring that they would not occur. The company felt it needed to take this action on grounds of accountability and justification to its employees, stockholders, board of trustees, and concerned governmental groups (Bowman and Kunreuther, 1988).

This behavior is typical of many corporations. Although profit maximization may be an objective, the driving force behind many actions is satisfying a set of constraints that serve as focal reference points. March and Shapira (1992) point to a growing literature in both organizational and individual behavior suggesting that managers often make risk decisions by setting the probability of falling below the reference point at some fixed number. Events whose chances of occurrence are estimated to be below this value are put in the category "it cannot happen to me" (Mitroff and Kilmann, 1984). This approach of setting probability thresholds has been used by the Nuclear Regulatory Commission in the design of safety procedures for operating its facilities (Fischhoff, 1983) and by the insurance industry in setting premiums (Stone, 1973).

---

4 The Bhopal disaster occurred in December 1984. Methyl Isocyanate gas escaped from a Union Carbide plant, leading to more than 2,000 deaths and causing illness in countless others. For more details on the Bhopal accident, see Shrivastava (1987).

Suppose a disaster occurs whose probability was perceived to be below the threshold (such as Bhopal) and hence had been classified as "not worth worrying about." The availability bias will now lead firms to imagine how easily such a disaster could happen again. In other words, the disaster now becomes a new focal point. Firms will want to avoid any situation that resembles the disaster that just occurred. They do not rationally estimate new probabilities but will recommend steps to prevent future occurrences without making expected benefit–cost trade-offs.

Former governor of Massachusetts Michael Dukakis reacted in this way by preventing the Seabrook 1 nuclear power plant from operating in the mid 1980s. According to Dukakis, the New Hamsphire plant, two miles from the Massachusetts border, did not contain evacuation plans that would "protect the lives of the people in Massachusetts living within the 10 mile evacuation zone." The former governor also indicated that "the likelihood (of a major accident at Seabrook) is irrelevant," suggesting that he was using an outcome threshold, perhaps for political reasons (Wessel, 1986).

In other cases, firms may go through explicit benefit–cost calculations to determine whether to install safety equipment on their products. But this can backfire. The classic case of such an action was the decision by Ford not to make an $11 per car improvement that would have prevented gas tanks from breaking so easily both in rear-end collisions and in roll-over accidents. Table 9.1 depicts the relevant calculations from an internal Ford memorandum showing that the total cost of such an improvement would be $137 million and the expected benefit only $49.5 million (Dowie, 1977).

In the case of the Ford Pinto, the highly negative publicity from the discovery of the memo, as well as the large number of damage suits arising from the defect, led Ford to make these improvements on later Pinto models. The example raises difficult questions about the role of the liability system in inducing firms to adopt protective measures. Did Ford act ethically in pursuing a cost–benefit analysis? Why did they use such a low value of life ($200,000) rather than a more realistic figure (somewhere between $3 million and $6 million) in evaluating this new design? When is it appropriate to pass health and safety regulations that force product improvements that would not otherwise be made (i.e., under a free-market system)? Those questions are addressed in an interesting book by Viscusi (1991) on the role of the products liability system in dealing with those risks.

9.4 Evaluating alternative policies

In their discussion of guidelines for making social choices and designing policies, Stokey and Zeckhauser (1978) specified two fundamental principles that we subscribe to wholeheartedly in our analysis.

Table 9.1. *The cost of dying in a Pinto*

Printed below are figures from a Ford Motor Company internal memorandum on the benefits on an $11 safety improvement which would have made the Pinto less likely to burn. The memorandum purports to "prove" that the improvement is not cost effective.

Benefits
Savings: 180 burn deaths, 180 serious burn injuries, 2,100 burned vehicles.
Unit cost: $200,000 per death, $67,000 per injury; $700 per vehicle.
Total benefits: 180 × ($200,000) + 180 × ($67,000) + 2,100 × ($700) = $49.5 million

Costs
Sales: 11 million cars; 1.5 million light trucks.
Unit cost: $11 per vehicle.
Total cost: 11,000,000 × ($11) + 1,500,000 × ($11) = $137 million

---

Source: Dowie (1977). Reprinted by permission.

Principle 1: The well-being of society depends solely on the welfare of the individual members, those alive today as well as future generations. For example, if people, upon being properly informed, remain concerned about environmental issues, then the impact of a particular program on air or water quality should be taken into account as a part of the policy process; otherwise, it will not be deemed relevant.

Principle 2: Trade-offs among individuals are unavoidable. In making any policy decision, it is likely that some people will be made better off by these actions, while others will be made worse off. For example, if a regulation is passed requiring air bags in all cars, those motorists who would have preferred driving without this protection will be upset. Other car owners who want air bags in their cars will be pleased at the lower price of this feature due to the economies of mass production. Taxpayers who will not have to pay some of the medical expenses of car victims will also appreciate this regulation. Whether this policy is more desirable than a voluntary program requires making trade-offs.

9.4.1 *Efficiency and equity considerations*

A comparison of alternative policies for dealing with a specific problem requires some determination of social welfare. This, in turn, requires a definition of individual welfare and a specification of an aggregation process over people and time. Standard policy analysis assumes that individual welfare reflects a person's total well-being (i.e., the goods and services he or she consumes, the activities undertaken, etc.). Furthermore, an individual is assumed to be the best judge of her own welfare. However, there is no general agreement on how one constructs a social welfare function.[5] Should one give equal weight to the well-being of each individual? If not, how should one determine the degree of importance of one person or group over another (such as future generations)? The two criteria that normally are used to evaluate alternative policies are *efficiency* and *equity*.

A policy is considered efficient relative to the status quo if the well-being of society is improved by undertaking this policy. One criterion that satisfies efficiency is maximizing net benefits so that the gainers from a change over the status quo could, in theory, compensate the losers (Scitovsky, 1941). If this compensation were actually made, then everyone is indeed better off in the process. Scitovsky's principle only stipulates that this should be possible (i.e., that net gains exceed net losses), not that the compensation actually occurs. Standard benefit–cost analysis is an example of such a criterion, since it recommends that a particular policy be introduced if the total benefits to all parties exceed the total costs.

In reality, the implementation of a particular program may leave some individuals or groups worse off than under the status quo because it is impossible or undesirable to compensate them for their perceived loss. Not only is it difficult to measure their dissatisfaction with a particular program, but if people knew they would be receiving something in return for their discomfort, they would have a strong incentive to misrepresent their feelings.

The *equity* concerns of public policy programs have become increasingly important in cost–benefit formulation. For example, Medicare recognizes the need to aid elderly residents who cannot afford normal hospital care; younger taxpayers subsidize this group. In providing uninsured disaster victims with liberal relief, the government has determined that this special group should be aided by all U.S. taxpayers.

9.4.2 *Philosophical and ethical considerations*

The balance between efficiency and distributional considerations for specific problems is reflected in existing legislation, regulatory mechanisms, and incentive systems. Specific programs must be evaluated in the context of the existing social and cultural systems in which policy is formulated.

---

5 For more details on the challenges in constructing social welfare functions, see Stokey and Zeckhauser (1978).

Table 9.2. *Benefits and costs of dam construction*

Type of farmer	Annual irrigation benefit	Failure of dam	Per capita cost of dam construction
Safe farmer	$2,500	0	-$2,000
Farmer at risk	$2,500	-$60,000	-$2,000

Constructing a dam. The following example illustrates the impact of different philosophical systems on the choice process.

Consider the decision on whether to construct an earthen dam in a particular farming community in order to provide irrigation water. Table 9.2 depicts the relevant information regarding the proposed project. All farmers in the community are assumed to be risk neutral and identical (in terms of income, wealth, and amount of land), except for their location relative to the dam. If the dam fails, the safe farmers will face no property damage, but farmers at risk will sustain losses of $60,000 each. Hydrologic engineers have estimated that the annual probability of such a disaster occurring is .01, so that the expected annual loss to each farmer at risk is $600. The expected yearly benefit to each farmer from irrigation water provided from the dam is $2,500, whereas the per capita annual cost for constructing the dam if each farmer in the community paid an equal share is $2,000. Should the community invest funds obtained from taxes to build the dam?

The proposed project is an example of a public good. Each safe farmer would invest his own resources in the project only if he knew that other farmers would also contribute their share. Some type of coordination to raise funds will be necessary if the project is to have a chance of being approved. Suppose each farmer uses the following decision rule regarding the investment of funds in community projects:

  • *Approve* if the expected personal benefits exceed the expected costs.
  • *Disapprove* otherwise.

With this rule, the safe farmers would favor the project (net annual benefit of +$500), whereas those at risk oppose it (net annual cost of -$100). It is thus not clear what should be done if each farmer paid an equal share. Each safe farmer would obtain a net benefit of $500, whereas each farmer at risk would suffer a net expected loss of $100 (i.e., $2,500 - .01($60,000) - $2,000). Different ethical systems would suggest different types of actions for the community based on the proposed plan. Let us examine four different systems that have been proposed in the literature (see Schultze and Kneese, 1981, for more details).

A *utilitarian system,* based on the concepts of Jeremy Bentham and John Stuart Mill, implies that the criterion for action should depend on maximizing the utility of the community as a whole (J. Baron, 1988). Since all farmers are assumed to be risk neutral, the criterion of maximizing expected utility is equivalent to maximizing expected net benefits of the community.[6] The final decision then depends on the proportion of safe farmers in relation to those at risk. Since the expected benefit to the safe farmers is five times the expected costs to the risky ones, the community should build the dam if more than 20% of the farmers are in the safe category.

If there were some type of voting rule to determine whether to invest these funds, then an additional criterion would have to be satisfied. For example, if a referendum were held in the community, requiring approval by a majority of the citizens before funds could be invested, then at least 50% of the farmers voting would have to be "safe" ones.

An *egalitarian system* evaluates actions by maximizing the utility of the most deprived individuals. According to this philosophical position, which has been associated with John Rawls (1971), individuals should behave as if they were unaware of what their status would be in society. Under this "veil of ignorance," people may elect to use the following criterion: Choose the policy that achieves the highest expected welfare for the worst-off member of society. However, only extremely risk-averse people would a priori adopt this criterion under a veil of ignorance. Under the assumption that all the farmers are risk neutral, the dam should not be constructed, since those most at risk will be worse off if the project is approved than if it is not.[7]

One way for the dam to be built using Rawls's criterion would be for the safe farmers to contribute a larger per capita share through taxes than those farmers at risk. If there were an equal number in each group, then contributions of $2,300 by each safe farmer and $1,700 by each farmer at risk would produce the same net expected benefits (+$200) for each farmer and yield enough funds for constructing the dam.

An *elitist system* is exactly the opposite of an egalitarian system. Actions that further enhance the position of those who are best off are taken. Inequalities in wealth and income would thus be exacerbated by using this criterion as a guideline. In the previous example, where all farmers

6 Alternatively, one could translate the data in Table 9.2 into utilities by constructing the safe and risky farmer's utility functions using methods described in Chapter 4.
7 If farmers were risk averse, then there would be even more reason not to build the dam using Rawls's criterion, since the disutility of the $60,000 loss if the dam failed would be that much worse relative to the $2,500 irrigation benefit and $2,000 per-capita cost of the dam.

are equal prior to any decisions on the dam, approval would be given since the safe farmers would be much better off than those at risk. Any actions that would benefit this group, whether or not they harmed those at risk, would be approved. Although this system may not have much appeal to readers, it is in fact the one that has dominated for much of human history. It is captured in the oft-heard comment, "the rich get richer and the poor get poorer."

A *libertarian system* is the basis for a free-market system; it also uses the Pareto criterion as a guide to judging future actions. If the status quo is the baseline from which to judge future actions, then any project that harms a single individual would not be approved unless that person were sufficiently compensated so he or she had at least the same expected utility after a project than before.

In the case of the proposed dam, the project would be rejected unless some ways were found to provide funds for the farmers at risk so they would not sustain a net loss. This could take the form of a lower per-capita cost for the farmers at risk than for the safe farmers to finance the construction of the dam. Or some type of disaster relief fund could be disproportionately financed by the safe farmers to cover the rebuilding of damaged property if the dam failed.

It is interesting to note that by maintaining the status quo the safe farmers are worse off than had the project been approved. But this is irrelevant if the farmers at risk are worse off by building the dam. This is one reason why safe farmers may want to cross-subsidize those at risk. In any event, some farmers are damned if you construct the dam and others are damned if you don't.

9.4.3   Ex ante *and* ex post *considerations*

In designing programs that take into account efficiency and equity considerations, it is important to examine the interested parties' reactions to a specific risk before (*ex ante*) and after (*ex post*) accidents or disasters occur.

Consider automobile manufacturers' decisions about voluntarily installing passive restraints (i.e., automatic seat belts) in any of their new cars. Manufacturers will be strongly influenced by a consumer's willingness to pay for this additional feature when buying a new car. Consumers must make their own decisions on whether to demand this additional feature prior to driving the car extensively. For illustrative purposes, suppose statistical analyses reveal that the expected medical expenses following an accident are as follows:

- With seat belt on (X_1): \$20,000.
- Without seat belt on (X_2): \$70,000.

Suppose that a prototype driver, Bill, is risk neutral and does not voluntarily wear manual seat belts. He is willing to buy a car with a passive restraint if he perceives the expected benefits next year in reduced medical expenses to be greater than the cost of the automatic restraint. Automobile manufacturers currently estimate the extra cost of this feature on a car to be $100. Suppose Bill correctly estimates the probability (p) of receiving the expected savings of $50,000 from having a car with a passive restraint.

Using benefit–cost analysis, then he would be willing to pay at least $100 for the automatic seat belt if he perceived his annual probability (p) of a severe car accident to be greater than .002 if he planned on owning the car for only one year. As Bill increases the number of years he expects to keep the car, his subjective probability of a severe accident could fall considerably below .002, and still justify his purchasing a car with a passive restraint.

Suppose Bill followed a threshold model and did not consider the consequences of an accident if his estimate of p were below p^*. If he perceived $p < p^*$ (the threshold level), he would have no interest in safety measures designed to reduce a loss. If society bears some of the cost of unprotected accident victims, then it would be appropriate to consider regulations requiring passive restraints in automobiles.

How concerned should we be with consumers' *ex ante* decision rules when they may misperceive the information (e.g., underestimate probabilities of losses, or use decision rules such as threshold models that ignore possible outcomes)? There is no straightforward answer to this question. At one extreme is a position based on a libertarian philosophy: Let people make their own free choices so long as they do not harm others in the process.

If a person driving alone doesn't want to buckle up or prefers not to buy a car with an automatic seat belt, that is her choice so long as she pays for the consequences. In reality, if an individual has a severe accident, society will bear part of the medical expenses. Everyone will be affected by the loss in productivity due to absence from work, and the immediate family will bear emotional as well as out-of-pocket costs from this injury. The scenario suggests that there are ex post costs, the distribution of which must be recognized in designing *ex ante* policies. In this case, one has to understand more fully the way individuals process information and the type of decision rules they use.

Requiring passive restraints also has negative features. Consumers may find the restraints chafing and cumbersome, so that they detract from their driving pleasure.[8] Regulations do have limitations when there are con-

---

8 Motorcycle riders who are opposed to wearing helmets often make the argument that wearing this protective device is too confining.

sumers of different types. Suppose consumers fall in the class of high- and low-risk drivers and are aware of their own skills. Low-risk drivers may be *unwilling* to buy a car with an automatic restraint and might feel it is an imposition, or change their driving behavior toward more risk-taking (Peltzman, 1975). Cars may also differ in their safety features. Even if all drivers purchased the same car and were all of the same skill, some might be risk takers and others risk avoiders. Risk takers who have correct information on probabilities of an accident may still prefer to take their chances by not investing in safety devices even if they know that they would have to bear the full medical expenses from a crash. A passive restraint requirement would be opposed by this group. Similarly, there are those motorists who always wear a seat belt and would view the installation of passive restraints as an unnecessary expense.

Clearly, there are no easy answers to questions that arise because of *ex ante* and *ex post* differences between individuals. Not only will ethical and philosophical issues play a role here (e.g., libertarian vs. egalitarian positions), but so will the degree of misinformation among consumers, businesses, and policy makers. In addition, there are costs associated with implementing alternative policies that also need to be incorporated into the evaluation process.

9.5   A framework for developing public policy programs

A principal purpose of this book is to propose prescriptive strategies for improving the decision processes of individuals, organizations, and groups. We view the free-market system as a reference point for guiding the development of these programs. From a decision process perspective, we have already noted that there are systematic biases in the way individuals estimate probability and outcomes. Furthermore, the choice process by individuals when facing uncertain outcomes may not be accurately represented by assuming expected utility maximization.

In developing prescriptive recommendations for problems that involve both private and social risks, we generally favor policies that offer individuals as much choice as possible. Figure 9.1 depicts the framework that guides the development of alternative programs. The current institutional arrangements (the status quo) affect the benefits and costs of different strategies, which range from a free-market approach at one extreme to regulation at the other.

In the presentation that follows we order the different strategies by constraining individual choice as little as possible at the outset and then examining more restrictive options where these seem to be indicated. Hence, the first line of attack is simply to provide information to the relevant decision makers. Thereafter, we examine economic incentives for mod-

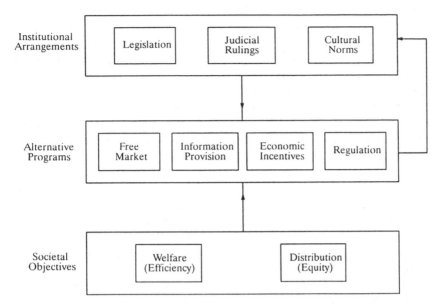

Figure 9.1. Conceptual framework for developing policy programs

ifying behavior, and lastly we consider the role of regulations and standards for meeting efficiency and distributional objectives. Certain regulatory programs may be more cost-effective than attempts to provide information and have the public freely make its decisions. Policy makers should examine all four programs before determining which course of action to adopt.

9.6   Provision of information

The principal purpose of this approach is to correct systematic biases in estimating probabilities and outcomes, while at the same time recognizing the types of decision rules that individuals use in processing such data.[9] Misperceptions of probabilities may be due to an availability bias or a failure to appreciate that the magnitude of the probability estimate is a function of the relevant time domain. Preferences between two alternatives may be greatly influenced by how the outcome from each of these decisions is presented or framed. Finally, other features of behavior, such as reluctance to make trade-offs, need to be recognized in designing programs for better handling uncertainty.

9 The material in this and the next two sections draws on Camerer and Kunreuther (1989).

9.6.1   *Correcting availability biases*

Better reporting of data by the media may be one way to correct discrepancies between actual frequency data and overestimation of probabilities due to an availability bias. A study of causes of death found that most people perceive the likelihood of deaths from highly reported disasters such as fires and homicide to be much higher than those from events such as diabetes and breast cancer that are rarely reported in the media (Combs and Slovic, 1974). The statistical fact, however, is that the latter two diseases together actually take twice as many lives as the two more dramatic events.[10]

A bias in favor of available data implies a bias against data that are hard to imagine (Slovic, Fischhoff, and Lichtenstein, 1978). In a study of fault tree judgments, for example, auto mechanics were given a variety of fault trees showing causes of a car failing to start, including a "miscellaneous" category.[11] Mechanics attached too small a probability to the miscellaneous branch, even when an important cause of failure (e.g., the "electrical system") was omitted. However, they were more accurate than students who undertook the same task but strongly suffered from the "out-of-sight–out-of-mind" bias. This finding suggests that expertise partially counteracts the availability bias. By explicitly providing data through fault trees and asking individuals to record these outcomes for future reference, one may improve an individual's ability to calibrate the probability estimation process (see Fischhoff, 1982; Dube-Rioux and Russo, 1988).

Recognizing the presence of availability biases suggests that making risks more salient should encourage people to adopt protective measures. A study by Viscusi and Magat (1987) showed that mentioning the potential hazards associated with specific products (e.g., cleaning agents) led people to take more precautionary actions (e.g., wearing rubber gloves, storing the product in a childproof location). The product labels themselves indicated the types of actions that could be taken ("Keep out of reach of children"), which surely helped the process. Some individuals overreacted to the hazard by taking more precautionary actions than deemed desirable using benefit–cost criteria while others underreacted. Another example is Jay Russo's (1977) study on unit pricing, which shows how changing the information display about prices improved shopping in supermarkets for consumers, in part by facilitating comparisons across package

10 Interestingly, the subjects underestimated the number of deaths on all four of these events. This is consistent with the availability bias, since these particular causes of death involve a single person or a small group, and hence are not usually newsworthy events.

11 A fault tree shows possible causes and subcauses (in the form of branches) of events.

sizes and brands. (For an overview of similar field studies about product information provision, see Russo and LeClerq, 1991.)

9.6.2 Changing the probability reference point

Empirical evidence suggests that individuals or firms do not pay attention to particular events because they perceive their probability of occurrence to be below a given threshold. This behavior can prove costly to both the individuals at risk as well as the rest of society should a disaster or accident occur. To encourage the adoption of protective activities, information on the probabilities of the event could be presented in a form that would lead people to pay attention.

Some individuals may not associate a time dimension with probability and hence may specify a threshold value p^* that is invariant to time. For example, suppose a homeowner on the 100-year flood plain accurately estimates the annual probability of a flood to be .01, but has a $p^* > .01$. There would be no interest on his part in purchasing flood insurance. If probabilities were aggregated over time to make them seem larger, this person might protect himself more often. For example, if this homeowner were told that the chances of experiencing at least one damaging flood in the 100-year flood plain within the next 25 years were .22, then he might pay attention to the event and buy flood insurance.

This approach has been used to increase seat belt use. The chance of a fatality on an average car trip is extremely low (about .00000025), well below the threshold many people set before paying attention to a risk. But over a lifetime of driving, the probability of a fatality is .01 (Schwalm and Slovic, 1982). In one study, 39% of respondents who were given lifetime probability figures said they would use seat belts, compared to 10% of those who were provided with the single-trip probability.[12]

Other forms of presenting probability data may also encourage protective behavior. Viscusi and Magat (1987) described the risk from a bleach as 50 gas poisonings for every 2 million homes, rather than as the equivalent probability $p = .000025$ (which equals 50/2,000,000). They then indicated that a new bleach would yield a 50% decrease in gas poisonings, rather than stating that the new probability would be $p = .0000125$. Consumers were willing to pay more for the new bleach when the benefits were stated as "percentage reduction in poisonings" rather than as a "reduction of the probability of poisoning."

There are many ways to express risk, like annual fatality rates per 100,000 persons at risk (Crouch and Wilson, 1982) or the amount of an activity

---

12 Whether individuals actually would adopt seat belts when provided with this information is still unclear.

that increases a person's chance of death by 1 in 1 million per year (Richard Wilson, 1979). The impact of providing data in these various forms has not been sufficiently examined. Furthermore, some argue (Slovic, 1986) that the standard errors and assumptions associated with these risk estimates, which are often quite large, should be explained, and that confidence intervals be presented. Otherwise, people may distrust the entire analysis.[13]

9.6.3   *Targeting information to specific groups*

One way to deal with problems of misperception is to provide individuals with more accurate data on which to base their decisions. Suppose the National Highway Traffic Safety Administration (NHTSA) is considering a campaign to tell individuals the statistical probability of an accident (p), so that decisions to buy a new car with automatic seat belts will be made with these data in mind.

If the NHTSA knew precisely those individuals who would take action on the basis of the new information, then they could perhaps single this group out for some type of special mailing. Not only is it difficult to obtain such figures on consumer willingness to process data, but most information campaigns are viewed as a public good where a message is beamed out indiscriminately to a large population through the mass media.

Assume that NHTSA is considering a television information campaign that will cost D dollars. It is only willing to undertake these expenditures if the costs exceed the expected benefits, which in this case are the reduction in injuries and fatalities due to wearing a seat belt. In order to estimate benefits, some kind of monetary value has to be placed on a human life and the savings in medical expenditures. In the case of fatalities, the dollar value would reflect future losses in productivity as measured by projected future earnings. With respect to injuries that could have been avoided by wearing a seat belt, one would again have to use a lost productivity measure. Jones-Lee (1989) and Viscusi (1992) examine how one could assign such values.

Consider the total population (N) of identical individuals who currently do not wear seat belts and hence might be candidates for purchasing an automobile with passive restraints. An analysis by the NHTSA reveals that if each person made his purchase decision on the basis of p, then he would be willing to pay for this additional safety feature. Suppose a cer-

---

13 The emerging literature on risk communication explores ways of presenting information on probabilities and outcomes of hazards. For a selected bibliography see Covello, Sandman, and Slovic (1989).

tain proportion of the population (*a*) actually revises its probability of an accident on the basis of the statistical evidence presented. The remaining fraction of the population, $1 - a$, does not receive the information from the campaign and/or does not take the time to register the information on accident probabilities. They will continue to buy an automobile without a passive restraint. For NHTSA to undertake this campaign, there must be a sufficient proportion of the affected population willing to change its behavior so that the expected gain to society in the form of reduced costs of accidents must exceed the cost of providing these data.

This example illustrates the types of comparisons that NHTSA would have to make to determine whether to undertake such a campaign. Suppose the increase in medical expenses per serious accident were $50,000 if the motorist did *not* wear a seat belt and that $10,000 of this extra cost were covered by the government through funds from general tax revenues. If $p = .002$, then the expected annual savings from taxpayer dollars for every person who buckled up would be $20 (i.e., $.002 \times \$10,000$).

Suppose 25 million people in the United States currently do not wear seat belts. If $D = \$5$ million, then 250,000 of these people would have to purchase cars with passive restraints to justify the costs of the campaign using a one-year payback period. Thus, in this example, $a > .01$ would justify the television campaign. If one computed the discounted expected benefits over a longer time horizon, then the campaign would be even more attractive and lower values of *a* could justify it.

9.6.4. *Willingness to accept and willingness to pay*

Prospect theory assumes that the magnitude of pain of losses from a reference point is larger than the amount of pleasure experienced from equivalent gains; this property is called "loss aversion" (Tversky and Kahneman, 1991). This asymmetry creates an "inertia effect": People demand a much larger price to sell a good than they would pay to buy it (Knetsch and Sinden, 1984). For instance, Thaler (1983) found that people would only pay $800 for an inoculation to reduce a hypothetical risk of death from .001 to 0 ("willingness to pay"), but they would have to be paid $100,000 to be exposed to a disease resulting in a .001 chance of death ("willingness to accept"). Economic theory predicts willingness to pay and accept should be about the same, except for a small income effect.

Viscusi and Magat (1987) found that if the risk of a product was increased by 5 injuries per 10,000, most consumers claimed they would not buy the product at *any* price. The actual magnitude of the risk was irrelevant to their decision. To illustrate, consider the case where there is a 10 in 10,000 chance of an injury from the use of a toilet bowl cleaner.

Most people would not buy the product at any price when the risk is increased to 15 in 10,000. However, when asked the *maximum* that they would pay to reduce the risk from 15 in 10,000 to 10 in 10,000, the average price increased by $.65. Related experimental results on this type of commission bias and reference point effect have been reported by Ritov, Hodes, and Baron (1989).

Dramatic differences have also been observed in the willingness to accept (WTA) a hazardous facility nearby and the willingness to pay (WTP) to locate the same facility elsewhere. In phone surveys related to the siting of a high-level nuclear waste repository, over 70% of respondents would not accept a facility in a geologically safe location within 100 miles of their homes, even if they were paid up to $5,000 per year for the next 20 years. Yet, only 40% of the respondents said they would pay an extra $100 in annual taxes over 20 years to move a repository scheduled to be built nearby to a more distant location (Easterling and Kunreuther, 1993). Issues of fairness and nontradability of conditions involving risk to life undoubtedly influence these decisions.

Asymmetries between WTA and WTP imply that measures of "contingent valuation" (the value people place on activities with voluntary, contingent risk), which are widely used in public policy analysis, reflect other factors besides probabilities and outcomes. Concerns with justification, accountability, and responsibility are important elements of individuals' decision processes (as discussed in Chapter 5). The fact that they are difficult to quantify does not diminish their importance. To date, these concerns have not been an explicit part of analytic models of choice under uncertainty, which may partially explain why psychologists have indicated that people's preferences are labile and unreliable (Fischhoff and Furby, 1988).

A comprehensive assessment of the use of the contingent valuation method (CVM) for assessing preferences for societal problems can be found in Cummings, Brookshire, and Schulze (1986) and R. Mitchell and Carson (1988). By bringing together economists and psychologists to critique this research, their study offered a set of recommendations for improving the CVM approach, while recognizing its limitations for policy purposes. More recently, a series of studies by economists and psychologists has evaluated and critiqued this approach. The recent debate between Kahneman and Knetsch (1992a,b) and V. Kerry Smith (1992) reflects the current tensions with respect to the use of this technique for policy purposes.

9.6.5   *Reluctance to make trade-offs*

Mental accounting, as discussed in Chapter 4, often simplifies decisions by segregating dollars and nonmonetary outcomes into separate categories. This makes trade-offs across different kinds of mental accounts – like dollars for lives – especially difficult. Communities will spend enormous time and energy to save "identifiable lives." For example, recall the great amount of time and energy residents of a small Texas community voluntarily spent in rescuing eight-month-old Jessica McClure, who fell into a well, and the national publicity that this one incident generated. In contrast, society has elected *not* to spend large sums of money on risk-reducing activities such as improving highway safety funds, which would, of course, be expected to save many more "statistical lives."[14] Spending freely to save an identifiable life is a public affirmation of how much we love life, a gesture that celebrates the idea that life is sacred at any cost.

Reluctance to make the trade-offs between dollars and lives leads to misguided arguments, common in public debate, that "zero risk" is the only tolerable level of risk. The desire for zero risk may have an important impact on behavior. Consider an insect spray that costs $10 per bottle and results in 15 inhalation poisonings and 15 skin poisonings for every 10,000 bottles sold. Viscusi and Magat (1987) found that, on average, survey respondents with young children were willing to pay about $2.38 more for a spray that reduced both these risks to 5 per 10,000 bottles sold, and $8.09 more for a spray with no risk at all. This finding supports the hypothesis that people are willing to pay an extra premium for zero risk. When people are asked how much they would pay to reduce the number of bullets in a game of Russian roulette, most people are willing to pay considerably more to eliminate the last bullet than to reduce the number from, say, 9 to 4 (Zeckhauser, 1973).

Budgetary constraints are sometimes a useful device for forcing regulatory agencies and individuals to prioritize their expenditures, but trade-offs between benefits and costs are generally not made explicitly. Responses from a telephone survey of households conducted by Kahneman and Knetsch (Cummings et al., 1986, pp. 191–192) on willingness to pay for hypothetical environmental changes illustrate this point. They found that Toronto residents were willing to pay approximately the same amount to clean up one lake as they would pay to clean up all the lakes in Canada. People appear to have mental budgets as to how much they would allocate for reducing an environmental risk. Spending the budget is a symbolic act that expresses their values in a qualitative way without having to pay explicitly to clean up the lakes.

14 Schelling (1968) wrote: "Let a six year old girl with brown hair need thousands of dollars for an operation that will prolong her life until Christmas, and the post office will be swamped with nickels and dimes to save her. But let it be reported that without a sales tax hospital facilities in Massachusetts will deteriorate and cause a barely perceptible increase in preventible death – not many will drop a tear or reach for their checkbook."

9.7   Economic incentives

Economic incentives may induce individuals and businesses to undertake actions they would otherwise find unattractive. An incentive can either be positive, such as a rebate or subsidy, or negative, such as a penalty or fine for not taking action.

Incentives may be useful in convincing consumers to invest in seat belts, reinforce homes to reduce potential damages from earthquakes, or purchase insurance against floods. The costs of these measures are often viewed as particularly burdensome because they are incurred up front, while the benefits are contingent on experiencing a loss. Those who invest in earthquake mitigation measures (e.g., safer construction) never see any return from this cost until an earthquake occurs and even then may not be aware as to how much more damage would have occurred if they had not adopted this measure. With respect to insurance, the premium paid for homeowners coverage only yields a return if there is damage to property or contents.

9.7.1   *Insurance incentives to consumers*

One seemingly attractive incentive for adopting loss-reduction measures is to reduce insurance premiums on coverage against a particular event. Consider the cost associated with a protective measure such as the purchase of a passive restraint or the premium paid for an insurance policy. Let p = annual probability that a loss will be experienced and b = the annual benefits of the measure. As shown in Chapter 4, mental accounting by individuals based on the concepts of prospect theory suggests that the way incentives are presented to individuals may influence their behavior.

To illustrate, consider the passive restraint example and assume that the insurance industry would save b = \$12,500 in medical expenses if there were a serious accident with probability p = .002. Then the actuarially fair annual premium reduction is \$25, somewhat less than the cost of a passive restraint. For most protective activities the benefit–cost ratio will be unattractive if a one-year horizon is used; over the life of the product the discounted benefits of premium reductions are likely to exceed this cost. In a 1987 mail survey of 331 motorists, half residing in Pennsylvania and the other half in New York, 70% indicated they would not purchase a passive restraint for \$100, even if their annual insurance premiums were reduced by \$25 (Kunreuther and Easterling, 1988). If they planned to keep the car for more than five years, then the discounted benefits of their ownership of the vehicle would have exceeded the costs of the passive restraint, assuming a discount rate of no more than 8%.[15]

---

15 The discounted benefits are derived by computing $\Sigma\, b/(1 + i)^t$ where i = annual discount rate and t is the length of time that the individual plans on owning the product.

At a more general level, one can determine the required ratio of expected annual benefits to upfront costs of protective measures as a function of the individual's discount rate and the amortization period for the particular loss-protective measure. Figure 9.2 depicts this ratio for two different discount rates (10% and 5%) for amortization periods ranging from 1 year to 10 years under the assumption that the cost is incurred at the beginning of the year and benefits are received at the end of each year. Even with a horizon as short as 3 years and a discount rate of 10%, the expected benefit only has to be 40% of the cost of the protective measure to be considered attractive by the consumer.

People may be reluctant to invest in passive restraints or other loss reduction measures because current expenses and future benefits are recorded in different mental accounts. Suppose the normal annual insurance premium was $500. Using the value function of prospect theory, Figure 9.3 shows that the annual savings of $25 from investing in a passive restraint will be extremely small (in value terms) compared with the immediate expense of $100. Mental accounting suggests that people may prefer to separate a small loss into a larger loss and a small gain, because the marginal disutility of the additional loss is less than the marginal utility of the gain (Thaler [1985] calls this the "silver lining" effect).

In the passive restraint example, the insurance industry could offer policyholders a $25 refund at the end of each year for investing in a passive restraint. By reframing the problem in this way, motorists would view the loss reduction measure as an investment in a mental savings account that yields a dividend of $25 each year. As shown in Figure 9.3, the value of such a gain, or $v(\$25)$, is considerably higher than the value of a reduction in premiums, $v(-\$475) - v(-\$500)$.

In the same spirit, insurance companies might induce more risk-averse actions on the part of their clients by charging larger premiums up front, but then providing a rebate if a person does not suffer a loss. In controlled laboratory exeriments, people prefer more expensive insurance with a possible refund over equivalent standard insurance (Slovic, Fischhoff, Lichtenstein, Corrigan, and Combs, 1977).

Companies have experimented with programs that reframe the problem so that individuals receive specific rewards for taking care. Mutual of Omaha has sold disability coverage that refunds all premiums at age 65 if no claims are made. The company earns interest on the money and creates a reverse moral hazard: People may *not* make small claims when they are near 65 because they would have to forgo the refund. A related incentive system was offered by the Mendocino County Office of Education in California, which gave a $500 deductible health insurance policy to employees. They set aside $500 to cover each employee's deductible; employees get to keep whatever remains of the $500 at the end of the year. Medical care expenses were substantially reduced during the first

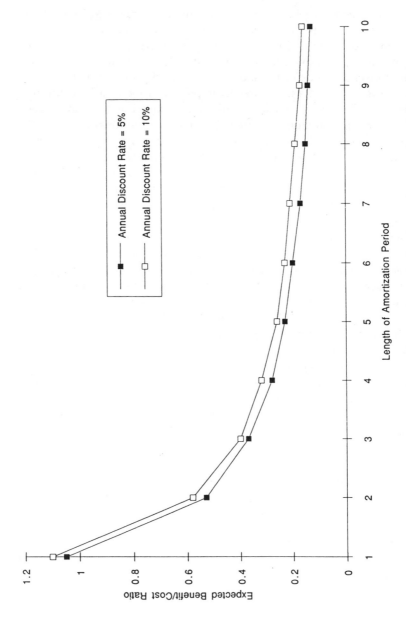

Figure 9.2. (Expected annual benefit)/cost ratio required to invest in protective measures

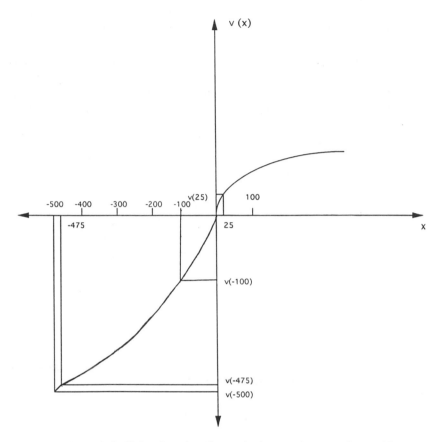

Figure 9.3. Value function for analyzing passive restraint problem

four years of the program. Besides reframing costs and benefits, such a refund reduces moral hazard by inducing employees to take better care of themselves.

Experimental evidence supports the hypothesis that rebates are attractive to individuals. E. Johnson, Hershey, Meszaros, and Kunreuther (1993) offered 100 people, mostly University of Pennsylvania hospital employees, two disability insurance policies that pay two-thirds of the employee's salary as long as he or she is unable to work. Policy 1 cost $70 and has no refund. Policy 2 costs $90 per month and offers a refund of $12,000 if the employee does not file a claim within five years. The refund is equivalent to the sum of the additional premiums.

Policy 1 should be preferred both because of the time value of money and because the rebate would not be paid if a claim were made. The rebate policy was preferred by 57% of the respondents and the average premium that people were willing to pay for it was $12.65 higher than

Policy 1. On the average, respondents felt there was a 3.6% chance of not collecting on the policy, which makes the finding that rebates make a difference even more convincing.

Another potentially effective insurance incentive is withholding payments to victims for failure to take protective action. About 60% of survey respondents who do not wear seat belts said they would buckle up if their claims payments depended on it (Kunreuther and Easterling, 1988). Withholding medical coverage appears to be a more effective policy tool than paying extra compensation. Since 1983, Nationwide Insurance Company has paid twice as much compensation to policyholders injured in car crashes while wearing seat belts, and $10,000 to the family of policyholders killed while wearing seat belts. A random sample of motorists in Connecticut indicates that these policies have not increased seat belt use. Even though Nationwide widely advertised, the study revealed only 9% of their policyholders wore seat belts, compared to 14% of those purchasing insurance from other companies (Robertson, 1984).

9.7.2   *Incentives for insurers to offer protection*

We have already pointed out in Chapter 4 that ambiguity regarding the probability associated with an event may play an important role in the decision processes of insurance managers. Few insurers offer coverage against political risk to industrial firms investing in developing countries with potentially unstable political systems. The principal argument voiced by insurers has been the difficulty in estimating the probabilities associated with losses of different magnitudes (Kunreuther and Kleindorfer, 1981).

Similar behavior has been observed regarding earthquake coverage where premiums are much higher than past loss experience would justify. Over the first 60 years (1916–1976) that this coverage was offered in California, $269 million in total premiums were collected but only $9 million in losses were experienced (Petak and Atkisson, 1982). Of course, part of the rationale for this high premium–loss ratio is the possibility of highly correlated losses should a big earthquake occur. However, a significant reason is also the uncertainty of the probability of the next severe quake.

Many of the societal problems associated with health and safety risks involve considerable ambiguity on both the probability dimension and the loss side so that the private insurance market has played a limited role in providing coverage. Consider the problem of environmental pollution damage. There is considerable ambiguity about the relationship between the exposure to a particular chemical and the possibility of contracting cancer (Anderson, Chrostowski, and Vreeland, 1990). Many years may elapse between the discovery of a leak from a hazardous waste storage facility and actual human exposure to a particular chemical, followed by a long latency period until the manifestation of the disease. In many cases it is difficult to attribute the cause of any cancer to the leak, since there are multiple pathways to this disease.

New toxic torts, new environmental legislation, and court decisions have increased the uncertainty associated with the magnitude of the losses should a suit be filed (Cheek, 1990). It is thus not surprising that insurers have all but discontinued offering environmental pollution coverage. Scenarios presented to actuaries and underwriters as part of a survey reveal that the premiums that they would charge to protect against the leak of an underground storage tank increases dramatically if the probability of a loss is ambiguous and/or the loss is uncertain in contrast to the risk being well specified (Kunreuther, Hogarth, and Meszaros, 1993).

An economic incentive system would be desirable that induces insurers to reduce their potential losses while at the same time making the situation attractive enough for them to provide coverage at affordable rates. To do this, a three-tiered system has been proposed that involves a well-specified risk-sharing arrangement among the insured party, the insurer, and the federal government (Doherty, Kleindorfer, and Kunreuther, 1990). Figure 9.4 indicates that the first layer of protection is self-insurance by industry itself. This is equivalent to a deductible on an insurance policy and is an incentive for industrial firms to use safer production techniques to reduce the loss. The second tier of coverage would be offered by private insurers, but there would be an upper limit on their potential losses so they could determine what premiums to charge. The third tier of the proposed program would require the government to provide coverage above the limit specified in Layer 2. A government agency would have to levy a fee on industrial firms to cover the potentially large losses they face. The limits on each of the layers depend on the type of coverage, total premiums written, and the number of insurers involved.

There is a close relationship between this three-tiered system and nuclear liability insurance protection in the United States. In 1957 two insurance pools were formed that made $60 million of liability coverage available to protect nuclear power plant operators. In the same year, the Price-Anderson Act was passed in which the federal government provided up to $500 million of indemnity in excess of the $60 million purchased by the pools. Congress would determine the need to provide funds for losses beyond the $560 million total.

Congress amended the Price-Anderson Act in 1975 by having the insurance pool bill each operator of a nuclear power plant up to $5 million for a pro rata share of the loss in excess of the pool's insurance. The objective was to phase out the government's indemnity by forcing the nuclear power industry and the insurance pool to cover the $560 million.

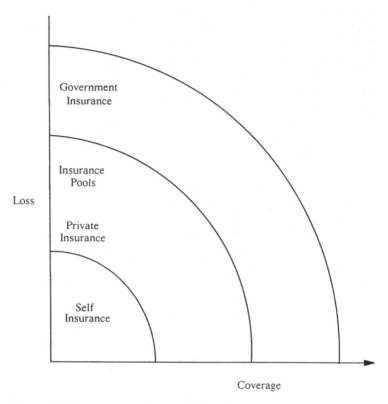

Figure 9.4. Insurance markets and tiers of coverage

This was accomplished in 1982 when insurance coverage in the pool reached $160 million and the 80th reactor was licensed to operate. In August 1988, Price-Anderson was renewed for another 15 years and each reactor operator's liability for assessments was increased from $5 million to $66.15 million. Hence, the total amount of financial protection now exceeds $5.2 billion (American Nuclear Insurers, 1989).

The three-tiered system for environmental pollution relies more heavily on a governmental role than does nuclear insurance today for several reasons. There is no natural coalition of industrial concerns, such as nuclear power plant operators, for developing an environmental pollution pool to cover losses. Furthermore, the insurance industry is reluctant to provide coverage against pollution damage today due to the ambiguity associated with the probability of a loss and potential liability. It thus appears necessary to bring the government into the picture initially to offer protection to industrial firms as well as to induce the insurance industry to offer some type of coverage (Tier 2). As loss experience increases and predictability on the nature of liability settlements improves, the government's role might be mitigated or reduced.

9.7.3 *Compensation or benefit-sharing for social risks*

At a societal level, economic incentives such as compensation have been advocated for sharing the benefits of proposed new projects with those who may be adversely affected by them (Raiffa, 1982). The obvious examples of facilities that have been searching for homes are solid waste facilities for trash disposal, low-level radioactive waste facilities for disposal of industrial, military, and medical residuals, and prisons for relieving the overcrowded jails in most states. In theory, compensation can induce people to accept facilities that benefit others more than themselves. For example, communities could be given funds for their internal needs (e.g., new hospitals, improved education system) in return for agreeing to host a prison or incinerators.

In practice, compensation has rarely been used in siting hazardous facilities because communities will only agree to host facilities if they do not create excessive health, safety, or environmental risks (Kasperson, 1986b). A number of acronyms have emerged to describe the public's and the politician's attitudes toward these facilities, such as the familiar NIMBY (not in my backyard) and the politically realistic expression NIMTOF (not in my term of office).

There are a few cases where compensation has been used successfully, but they are the exceptions rather than the rule. The town council of North Andover, Massachusetts, approved the siting of a regional resource recovery plant in exchange for a $1 per ton royalty for all waste deposited there (O'Hare, Bacow, and Sanderson, 1983). A coal-fired plant in Wyoming was approved because the utility company established a $7.5 million trust fund to preserve a stretch of the Platte River that was a migratory bird habitat (Lave and Romer, 1983). The Kodak Company agreed to compensate people in Rochester, New York, for decreases in property values that resulted from siting an industrial facility nearby ("Kodak," 1988).

A compensation agreement was negotiated by the city of Revelstoke and the British Columbia Hydro and Power Authority for building a hydroelectric dam next to the city. B.C. Hydro agreed to pay for damages caused by the dam, and gave funds to improve the city's water and sewage systems and build a recreation facility (Skaburskia, 1988).

Compensation is often rejected if it is perceived as a bribe for bearing social risk. Hence, it is essential for the community to feel that the perceived risks from the facility are acceptably low and that well-enforced monitoring and control procedures will detect any changes in this risk over time. Furthermore, the community or region hosting the facility wants to have the power to shut down the facility until the problems causing the increased risks to health and safety are remedied (Carnes et al., 1983).

If we assume there is a well-established need for a new facility and that the perceived risks are considered acceptable by the affected parties, a competitive bidding procedure between candidate sites, such as the one discussed in Chapter 7, might prove useful (Kunreuther, et al., 1987). Each community could demand funding for its own internal use in exchange for hosting the facility. The community or region selected to host the facility would receive funds from those who benefit from the facility. These include the developer, firms and organizations who will use the facility, and other communities or regions who are candidates for the host site and plan on using the facility.

A bidding procedure is most likely to be seriously considered if the default option (e.g., doing nothing) is perceived as more costly to all communities than locating the facility somewhere. In other words, the construction of a facility must satisfy the Pareto criterion that at least some are made better off than they are with preservation of the status quo, and none worse off. Compensation or benefit sharing may be an important feature of the siting process for just this reason. In addition, one needs to consider distributional issues so that all parties consider both the process and the outcome to be fair and equitable.

One procedure that addresses both equity and efficiency concerns is a lottery-auction mechanism (Kunreuther and Portney, 1991). Each of the potential host communities specifies the compensation (or benefit-sharing arrangement) that it would require to host the facility. Call the maximum amount of compensation demanded c^*. A *lottery* is then used to determine a candidate site. At the end of this stage, the winner of the lottery is the default host community and c^* dollars are earmarked for its use if the facility is hosted there.[16]

Following the lottery, an *auction* is held in which all of the candidate sites, including the lottery winner, can reduce their bid below c^* but at a level that leaves them at least as well off as not having the facility. The lowest bidder hosts the facility and gets the amount of compensation it bid. The other communities, the developer, and the beneficiaries of the facility pay compensation to the host community and/or the siting authority according to some prespecified rule. If no community bids less than c^*, the lottery winner would be the actual site and would receive c^*.

This procedure acknowledges some of the psychological principles of

---

16 Each community should be willing to participate in the lottery because whichever is chosen will be paid c^*, the maximum amount any community bid.

behavior described in previous chapters. By conducting an auction after a lottery, communities may perceive themselves as losing funds by not bidding for the facility. The initial lottery changes the reference point, so compensation may be viewed as a *benefit* rather than a bribe. The random lottery is equitable because it is equally likely for a high-income area and a low-income area to be chosen. Poor communities are not forced to accept the facility at a low price.[17]

There are challenges in implementing such a procedure. How will the beneficiaries of the facility be taxed to pay the compensation to the host community? How does one take into account differential risks between communities? Institutional procedures to address these issues can be developed, but there must be general agreement that the default option (e.g., the status quo) is unacceptable. Most important, studies show that communities will not consider compensation unless they are confident that a facility is safe and that appropriate control procedures will be used.

9.8   Regulations and standards

Regulations and standards are intended to protect our health, safety, and environment. Our interest here is in the role that mandatory insurance coverage, standards, and fines can play in dealing with the types of biases observed in individual and firm decision processes.

9.8.1   *Requiring insurance*

For some risks, it may be cheaper and more efficient to mandate insurance than to induce people to take those steps voluntarily. For example, the federal government tried to promote flood insurance by subsidizing it (instead of providing disaster relief after floods). Few people bought policies; the government provided disaster relief anyway (Kunreuther et al., 1978). Of course, a governmental commitment to eliminate disaster relief is not credible (Rodrick and Zeckhauser, 1988), since living up to the commitment creates a short-run inequity that may outweigh long-run efficiencies.

Home buyers in flood-hazard areas must now buy flood insurance to get federally insured mortgages. This regulation is appealing in several ways. It is easy to enforce. It shifts the costs of floods from taxpayers, who pay for disaster relief, to insurance companies who collect premiums to bear such costs. The regulation also creates demand for private insurance. Since the regulation forces many homeowners to be insured, neigh-

17 For a more detailed discussion of equity problems associated with siting noxious facilities see Kasperson (1986a) and MacLean (1986).

boring homeowners cannot be sure of getting generous disaster relief, which induces private lenders also to require insurance on homes for which they issue a mortgage.

It is important that the regulation was imposed only *after* economic subsidies failed to convince people to buy insurance voluntarily. Homeowners did not seem to make rational choices about insurance. They did not make trade-offs between the expected benefits of insurance and the premiums paid for protection. They rely on personal experience and discussions with friends and neighbors, often canceling their policy several years later because they did not experience any disasters and hence could not collect on their policy (Kunreuther, Sanderson, and Vetschera, 1985).

9.8.2   *Role of standards*

Judgments of riskiness are based on many dimensions other than statistical lethality. Risks that are perceived as uncontrollable or unknowable are feared even when they are statistically unlikely. A familiar example is air travel, which is uncontrollable by passengers but is much safer on a per mile basis than driving a car.[18] The technologies perceived as most risky by individuals are those that evoke dread, such as nuclear power, and those such as chemical operations where the hazards are judged to be unobservable, unknown, delayed, or new. Experts may view these hazards as less risky than the public because experts focus only on statistical measures of risk, ignoring their emotional aspects. When accidents do happen, the public may interpret accidents as signals that technology is not as safe as experts claim (Slovic, Lichtenstein, and Fischhoff, 1984). These findings underscore a more general problem with low-probability risks – because of the small sample of occurrences, experts and the public may not be able to resolve differences in beliefs.

Policy tools that reduce statistical lethality or provide insurance against risk may not be effective because of these emotional responses. People may not seek out information on specific hazards because they fear what the knowledge will imply. Homeowners may be reluctant to test their homes for radon because they do not want to know that they and their children have long been exposed to the gas. Only after the EPA suggested that people should have their homes checked for radon have people been interested in undertaking tests.[19] Testing for AIDS is similar: Because there is no cure for the disease, knowing that one has it causes misery

---

18 See, however, Evans, Frick, and Schwing (1990) for specific evidence about the types of conditions for which driving is actually safer than flying.

19 Homeowners may also prefer not to know because they might feel obliged to reveal these data to buyers if they sell their houses. See V. Smith, Desvousges, Fisher, and Johnson (1988) for a detailed analysis of the problems in communicating risks of radon.

and does not improve the chances of surviving (though it does help prevent the spread to others).

The presence of these emotional dimensions of risk suggests the need for enforceable standards that convince the public that the risks they face in their daily lives is acceptable. The presence of building codes for structures in hazard-prone areas may be due to the public's concern that they be protected by regulation rather than for them to trust a developer to follow appropriate specifications. A study of the Food and Drug Administration also revealed that regulations were deemed necessary in order to protect the public against its limited ability to determine which drugs are safe (Peltzman, 1974; Grabowski and Vernon, 1983).

When it comes to siting potentially hazardous facilities, communities will categorically oppose the project unless they are convinced that it meets rigorous safety standards and that it will be carefully monitored over time. For example, in the evaluation of a monitored retrievable storage facility in Tennessee, a local task force needed assurance that the facility was safe before even considering its operation and desirability (Peele, 1987).

9.8.3   Use of fines

Fines are a simple way of enforcing laws and regulations that require people to protect themselves against risks. The success of fines depends on the frequency of enforcement and the size of the penalty.

The framing of the regulation is likely to determine how people will react to it (Noll and Krier, 1990). Suppose there is a fine $F1$ associated with violating regulation $R1$ and a fine $F2$ associated with violating regulation $R2$. A regulatory agency is considering two types of policies regarding the enforcement of $R1$:

- Policy 1: Whenever $R1$ is violated, levy $F1$.
- Policy 2: Whenever $R1$ is violated *and* $R2$ is also violated, then levy fines $F1$ and $F2$; if $R1$ is violated alone, then *no* fine is levied.

The value function of prospect theory suggests that Policy 2 is likely to be highly ineffective relative to Policy 1 for two principal reasons. Given the convex shape of the value function in the loss domain, the addition of $F1$ will have a much smaller impact on the individual or firm's value function than if levied independently [i.e., $V(-F1) + V(-F2) < V(-F_1 - F_2)$]. Furthermore, the probability of being fined for violating $R1$ is much lower under Policy 2 than Policy 1. In fact, under Policy 2, $F1$ can be avoided entirely by making sure one always meets 2.

Recent seat belt legislation illustrates programs across states resembling these two policies. Of the 42 states that had mandatory seat belt laws at the beginning of 1993, 10 enacted a form of Policy 1 whereby the police can fine a motorist for not wearing a seat belt; the other 32 states passed legislation whereby a person can be fined for not buckling up only if the driver has violated another law such as exceeding the speed limit. The size of the seat belt fine for a first offense is relatively small (only four states have fines greater than $25, and none has a fine greater than $50) (Insurance Institute for Highway Safety, 1992). We would thus not expect high compliance under either Policy 1 or Policy 2.

Compliance with laws is influenced by other factors besides economic considerations. For example, in New York seat belt legislation has led to a usage rate of 64%, which is remarkably high given the very low chance of being fined. One explanation is that people obey laws out of social obligation, not because of anticipated fines. Most of the New Yorkers surveyed (76%) approved of their existing seat belt law and 63% of Pennsylvanians favored such a law. All of the Pennsylvania drivers surveyed who said they wore their seat belts less than half the time but still favored a mandatory seat belt law indicated that they would comply if such a law were passed.

For those individuals who do not respect the law per se, fines will be effective in encouraging certain behavior only if they have some teeth to them, either through enforcement procedures or unusually high penalties. The latter case is illustrated by the practice in many European countries (e.g., Austria, the Netherlands) of eliminating conductors on public transportation facilities with ticket machines serving this function. All riders know that there is a very low probability that they will be asked for their stamped ticket during a trip by a transit authority policeman. They also know that if they are checked and are found to be "free riding" then they face a fine that may be as much as 300 times the purchase price of the ticket (plus some public embarrassment). In this case, the perceived probability has to be very low indeed for riders not to buy a ticket unless they are gamblers at heart or penniless.

It would be interesting to know whether frequent riders comply with this regulation more than those who ride occasionally. For two individuals with identical utility functions, the number of rides per month should affect their decision even if the probability of being checked on any trip is independent of past experiences. Similarly, threshold models would predict that frequent riders would be more likely to buy a ticket than those who occasionally use public transportation.

9.8.4   *Impact of liability rules on protective behavior*

The legal system can also provide incentives for safer behavior through liability rules. A growing literature in law and economics investigates the impact of alternative liability rules designed to cover damages from accidents (i.e., harmful outcomes that neither injurers nor victims would wish to occur) (see Landes and Posner, 1987, and Shavell, 1987). Two common rules to deal with risk-related issues are strict liability and negligence.

Under strict liability, injurers must pay for all accident losses they cause. Under a negligence rule, the injurer is held liable for any accidents if his level of care is less than that specified by the courts. This so-called due care is often tied intimately to a regulation or standard set by a government agency. For example, if a firm manufactured a product that met all prescribed safety standards and a consumer suffered an injury from it, the manufacturer would not be held liable for damages. These two rules can be compared with a system of no liability where the injurer is not held responsible in any way for damages resulting from accidents to specific customers.

We wish to explore under what circumstances it is socially optimal to impose a regulation or standard on product manufacturers so that if they fail to comply they will be held liable by the courts under a negligence ruling. The analysis to follow focuses on a simple problem facing a firm manufacturing a product in which they have an opportunity to install a safety device that costs s dollars and reduces potential losses. For example, automobile manufacturers have an option to install air bags in their cars to reduce the impact of a crash; boat manufacturers can install propeller guards on their power boats to reduce the injuries to swimmers. The annual probability of an accident is denoted by p. The total discounted loss from accidents over the life of the product is given by $L(i)$, where $i = 0$ if no safety device is installed and $i = 1$ if the firm utilizes the device. By definition, $L(0) > L(1)$; otherwise, there would be no rationale for considering the device.

The firm's decision to adopt the safety device depends on its cost x relative to the reduction in loss from using the safety device. Suppose the following inequality obtains:

$$p L(0) > x + p L(1) \tag{9.4}$$

The firm will want to adopt the safety device if it is responsible for the costs of accidents, because of a regulation requiring them to install the safety device on their product. Even if the firm were not held liable, it would still want to install the safety device if customers were willing to pay for the safety feature.

If $p L(0) < x + p L(1)$, then the firm would not have a cost-based incentive to install the safety device, because the increase in the expected loss from accidents does not justify the cost of installing the device. Of course, if customers were still willing to pay the extra amount for the product with the safety feature, then the firm would install it.

If the customer has perfect information on the risk and is interested in minimizing expected losses, then the firm will want to install the safety device on its products even in the absence of liability if equation (9.4) is satisfied. The customer would know that if there were an accident, she would have to absorb the costs and hence would prefer to reduce the magnitude of the loss. As Shavell (1987) points out, if the firm did not install the safety device, its customers could go elsewhere. They would rather purchase the product from a competitor who charged a higher market price for a product with the safety feature.

One reason for introducing a regulation, and hence a negligence rule, has to do with imperfect information by customers on the risks associated with specific products. Most consumers are unaware of the design features of many products and hence are incapable of evaluating the potential benefits of different features. If this lack of knowledge translates into an underestimation of $L(0) - L(1)$, then there will be less incentive for them to want the firm to install the safety feature and charge a higher price for the product.

An additional reason for a regulation is that it may very well lower the per-unit cost of the safety feature from x to x^*. At a price of x^*, the inequality given by equation (9.4) might be satisfied, whereas it would not at a higher value of x. From a social welfare point of view, it thus makes sense to encourage firms to mass produce safety in order to lower the per-unit cost to a level where it meets benefit–cost criteria.

The case of automobile manufacturers' installing air bags illustrates both of these latter points. Customers have not demanded this feature in cars, undoubtedly because they underestimate both its potential benefits as well as the chances that they would be in a serious accident. Automobile manufacturers initially installed them selectively on cars at a price of $800. There was thus even less of a reason for car purchasers to take an interest in this feature. The U.S. Department of Transportation passed a regulation requiring all automobiles to have passive restraints either in the form of an automatic seat belt or an air bag by 1992. Once car manufacturers install air bags as part of standard equipment on some cars, the price of this safety feature is likely to drop substantially and demand for air bags will increase. Within a few years, we would expect air bags to be standard equipment on all automobiles.

9.9   Concluding remarks

We conclude this chapter with some observations regarding the linkage between decision processes and policy formulation. As a number of empirical studies have shown, individuals are often imperfectly informed about risk, so that buyers' and sellers' behaviors are not consistent with normative theories of choice, such as expected utility theory and Bayesian analysis.

Many of the societal problems involving risk entail additional difficulties for making rational choices: Experts frequently disagree with each other on the nature of the risk, and there are limited statistical data to settle these differences. Causality of uncertain outcomes (e.g., diseases) may be extraordinarily difficult to establish; hence, certain policies may be hard to justify on purely scientific ground.

Yet a set of guidelines for social policy emerges from our understanding of these impediments to the use of a free-market system. The different parties concerned with a particular problem need to appreciate their own limitations in dealing with risk and uncertainty. The consuming public needs to recognize that there is a price to pay for reducing risk, and hence trade-offs are required as society allocates its scarce resources. Business firms, when they design products and develop strategies, need to recognize nonstatistical features of risks, such as fear and dread, that affect public perception. Public sector agencies must also be cognizant of ambiguity aversion by both consumers and businesses and the need for clear guidance in their formulation of policy.

The issues facing society today require action at a number of different levels. To reduce risks, each *individual* can undertake personal loss prevention measures that may be as simple as following good health habits and investing in protective measures. At the next level, special interest *groups* can demand certain characteristics of life, such as a cleaner environment. This may require *business organizations* to develop new production methods that reduce waste and pollution, to manufacture products that meet environmental standards, and to dispose of their waste more carefully. These actions are costly and may require *governmental agencies* to play a role by promulgating regulations and standards to supplement market-based approaches, such as economic incentives.

We started the book by indicating that it was necessary to understand institutional arrangements and decision processes in order to develop meaningful prescriptions. In looking at the problems facing society today, we can see a number of opportunities to apply these principles. Better empirical data and improved theory should enable us to do a better job in designing meaningful policies at the individual, group, organization, and societal levels. This is the challenge facing decision sciences over the next decade.

Part IV

Epilogue

10

Summary and directions for the future

We have covered a vast terrain in the preceding chapters, addressing descriptive and prescriptive issues in decision making from the individual, group, organizational, and societal perspectives. Even though our examination at these four levels entails considerable complexity and scope, it hardly does justice to the real world. Decision problems are seldom just individual, group, or purely organizational. Nearly all of them are nested in a broader societal or social context and are often connected with related individual or group decisions. As such, our disembodied treatment chapter by chapter and our division of topics into eight cells (see Figure 1.1) is probably too neat and clinical.

In this epilogue, we wish to remind the reader of the broad scope and promise of decision sciences. The field has grown enormously over the last two decades. Numerous decision research groups and centers are thriving in leading business schools, social science departments such as psychology, and schools of engineering. The field is extending into medicine, law, and public policy. Several new scientific journals have been added in recent years (such as the *Journal of Risk and Uncertainty*, the *Journal of Behavioral Decision Making*, and the *Journal of Medical Decision Making*). This is not surprising, given the pervasiveness of problem solving and decision making as a human activity. It reaffirms the importance that researchers and practitioners place on analyzing decision making in a scientific manner rather than relying simply on our intuition.

Consider the challenges facing organizations in the 21st century. Most of us will be bombarded with data and information from numerous sources. New technologies such as electronic mail and facsimile machines will provide these data instantaneously with requests for fast if not immediate responses. The need for long-term visions and prioritization strategies takes on added importance in this type of environment, as does the need to couple operational and tactical decisions tightly with the strategic ends they are meant to serve. Otherwise one is likely to respond to the immediate demands without having a longer-term perspective. The challenges posed by nestedness, complexity, and legitimation will be experienced by more and more people lower in the organization. The days of armchair decision making will gradually take a back seat.

There is much we can do to prepare ourselves and others for this world. The preceding chapters have produced a long list of research issues that the field of decision sciences should consider. All of them share a common theme: the need to improve the quality of decision making in applications. This epilogue summarizes our approach to this important challenge. First, we need a general road map to guide us along the nonlinear path of high-quality decision making. Second, we need to understand key principles and concepts that support this road map. Last, we need to engage in self-audits aimed at assessing the quality of decision making in particular contexts. Individuals, teams, departments, and entire organizations need to benchmark their decision making relative to external standards. Although not all need to become world class, everyone needs a sense of where they are and how much improvement is practically feasible.

10.1   A road map for problem solving

The test of a good theory lies in its ability to predict, shape, or change the surrounding world. A key lesson of our book is that sound prescription should be based on careful description. None of the normative precepts discussed in the book are so general that they can be applied without considering specific contexts. This constitutes both the art and science of effective problem solving. To aid us in this effort, we shall use a general template that highlights the areas and issues that need attention in improving decision making. By itself, however, this template means little. It is the quality of thinking as well as our understanding of the institutional arrangements and decision processes that will determine the ultimate success or failure of any prescriptions. The following building blocks recapitulate the important elements underlying the quality of decision making discussed throughout this book.

10.1.1 *Element 1: problem finding*

What is the real problem you are trying to solve? How is the particular problem related to your goals, values, and needs? Keeping in mind that all problems can be made smaller or larger, are you examining it at the right level? Chapter 2 addresses these issues most directly by examining the sources of problem finding. Judgmental biases discussed in Chapter 3, such as anchoring and availability, may influence the type of problems one considers to be important. Past experience, salient events, and the most recent decisions regarding a course of action will focus and constrain one's attention to specific issues. Framing an issue one way may cause individuals to see it differently than posing it in another manner, as discussed in Chapter 4. Chapters 6 through 9 examine the special challenges in the problem finding process posed by group, organizational, and societal issues.

10.1.2 *Element 2: institutional arrangements*

Who are the primary and secondary stakeholders in this problem? How well do we understand and measure their goals, views, objectives, constraints, and agendas? In what ways are they similar or different from our concerns? How do they interact with each other? Chapter 5 places special emphasis on the importance of various stakeholder perspectives in choosing a solution approach. Chapters 6 through 9 then explicitly examine these issues for small groups, organizations, and society at large.

10.1.3 *Element 3: information gathering*

What information do we need to gather regarding (1) facts, (2) assumptions, and (3) personal and other stakeholders' values in order to develop a systematic approach to the problem? What biases are we likely to encounter in ourselves and others? How might we address them? What are the cost and benefits of collecting additional information? How does one relate specific solution procedures to the types of information that need to be collected? These are key questions that place information gathering at the core of the problem-finding and problem-solving processes.

Chapter 3 focuses on the judgmental biases as well as the prediction and inference tasks that impact on effective information gathering. Chapter 5 relates information needs to solution procedures. Chapter 6 explores formal models for dealing with information asymmetry between different interested parties as in principal–agent problems. And Chapters 8 and 9 consider the political and social dimensions of collecting and utilizing information.

10.1.4 *Element 4: the choice process*

What choice approaches should we consider in addressing a particular problem? Will the choice process involve other individuals and/or groups? Is it useful to use analytic techniques or rely primarily on one's intuition? What are the trade-offs between effort (cost) and accuracy (benefits) in determining which of various choice procedures to utilize? What criteria are utilized to make decisions? How are the various solution approaches impacted by nestedness, complexity, and legitimation?

Chapter 5 explores these questions from the individual decision-making perspective but recognizes that other parties are normally involved in the choice process as well. The negotiation and game settings of Chapters 6 and 7 explicitly focus on the multiparty choice situation. Chapters 8 and 9 highlight the highly textured and nested nature of social choice processes.

10.1.5 *Element 5: implementation*

Can specific approaches be successfully implemented by generating additional feedback, using legitimation criteria, and establishing control and accountability procedures? Chapter 3 speaks to the special challenges (both internal and external to the decision maker) of creating feedback that permits learning and improvement over time. Chapter 5 discusses legitimation criteria and stresses the importance of cognitive and philosophical orientations of individuals as important components in judging the appropriateness of specific problem-solving approaches. Control and monitoring issues at the group, organizational, and societal levels are addressed in Chapters 7, 8, and 9, respectively.

These building blocks interact with each other directly or indirectly through learning and feedback. Examining stakeholders (Element 2) will often change the problem perception and level of analysis (Element 1). Similarly, the choice process (Element 4) to be used may depend on and/or dictate the type of information gathered (Element 3). Implementation challenges (Element 5) will be directly related to the choice approach as well as the values, goals, and needs of the different stakeholders.

In a sense, good decision making requires a meta-analysis that sizes up the issues from a broad perspective. Effective managers or consultants strive for integration by zooming in and out of a problem and moving backward and forward across the different elements discussed here. Indeed, think back to an important decision that you have personally made. How well did you address each of the five elements? If you had to make a decision over again would you have proceeded differently? As a general rule, the more complex the decision, the greater the need to use a metastructure to guide the process.

10.2   Guiding principles and concepts

The road map for problem solving is supported by a set of key concepts and principles elaborated upon in preceding chapters. Figure 10.1 highlights five concepts that should guide the task assessment by the individual(s) concerned with specific problems and the application of solution approaches in real-world settings. Each of these concepts is briefly discussed.

Five Guiding Principles and Concepts

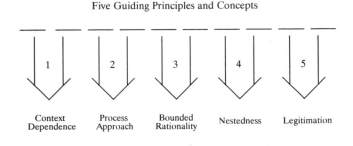

| Context Dependence | Process Approach | Bounded Rationality | Nestedness | Legitimation |

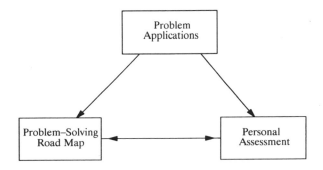

Figure 10.1. Decision quality in practice

10.2.1 *Context dependence*

Our first decision principle is that problem context can matter in subtle ways. Throughout the book we have provided examples of how changing reference points and reframing questions in terms of gains rather than losses and other presentation modes will unconsciously influence people's choices.

Of particular importance in this regard is the representation of the status quo, which often serves as a reference point, and how it relates to the alternatives open to an individual. If your car is in need of repair and the mechanic provides you with an initial estimate of $800, then you will view a bill of $500 in a much more positive light than if his preliminary figure was $200. As shown in Chapter 4, the principles of mental accounting and concepts such as loss aversion play an important role in influencing final choices among alternatives.

Credit card companies recognize the importance of problem context when they present the interest rate on unpaid bills on a monthly basis (e.g., 1.5% per month) rather than the equivalent annual figure (e.g.,

18% percent per year). Truth-in-lending laws were designed to overcome these subtle differences which may bias the decision-making process. Similarly, expressing a $200 discount on a $10,000 item in absolute dollars will be more attractive to a potential buyer than a reduction of 2%.

At a prescriptive level, when we set out to measure beliefs and values, we should vary decision contexts to see how robust or labile people's responses are. If people's choices in a given situation are highly dependent on how information is presented to them, then we need to be cautious in suggesting that a particular course of action is "optimal." Rather, we should indicate that the response depends on the form in which questions are posed to the decision maker(s).

We should also bear in mind that problem solving has an important political dimension. When combined with economic and social factors, any complex decision is amenable to negotiation and reframing. Much of decision research over the past two decades has focused on the economic and psychological dimensions. However, neither the metaphor of rational economic man nor that of adaptive or shortsighted cognitive man is sufficient for effective problem solving in the real world. Political man and social man must come more into their own as well, within the field of decision sciences, before a truly balanced decision approach is feasible.

10.2.2 *Process*

One of the key themes of this book is that process matters. Herbert Simon's distinction between procedural and substantive rationality is particularly relevant in this regard. Good decisions result from sound process, in much the same way that great golf or tennis shots result from great swings. Unlike these sports where a direct connection can be made between the process of hitting the ball and the outcome, it is often difficult to pinpoint how process affects the outcomes of complex decisions.

Consider the problem of coordinating the production and pricing decisions for a number of products offered by an industrial firm. Although there are algorithms for specifying optimal decision rules for these types of problems, there is considerable randomness from external and internal forces that influence final outcomes. The coordination process between the marketing and manufacturing managers will be important both in terms of the nature of information transmitted between the two groups and changes in the production and pricing plans. Feedback systems and a desire to keep communication channels open will enable both these groups to react to unexpected situations in ways that would be impossible if a more rigid process were followed.

Thus, in complex decisions it is often difficult to determine which option is best or to judge whether a particular outcome was primarily due to skill or chance. A sound process is a necessary condition, but even this, in our uncertain world, may not be sufficient to always guarantee a positive outcome. It just improves the odds.

A process focus means being especially sensitive to timing, sequence, and dynamics. Final outcomes do not just depend on the inputs. To use an analogy, in cooking it is not sufficient to have all the right ingredients (inputs) and just mix them in a bowl to produce an edible cake. The order of operations matters (add mix, break eggs, then stir, etc.) and feedback over time is important (via the ubiquitous teaspoon or finger). No matter how superb the ingredients, without a sound process, few of the cakes will come out right. Cookbooks are an attempt to formalize this process through sufficiently detailed descriptions to permit replication. Adherence to the template provided in the cookbook is a key to success, although there will always be some random variation. As the world's great chefs will readily attest, their skill is a masterful blend of art and science.

The process perspective has gained much in standing thanks to the quality improvement programs that are sweeping the corporate world. A key principle in this movement is that all physical and social processes exhibit irreducible variation, stemming from design limitations in equipment, variance of input materials, fluctuations in physical surroundings (e.g., temperature), human error, and so on. It is counterproductive to strive for perfect replication, either in cooking or manufacturing cars. Some degree of process uncertainty has to be expected and accepted.

The optimal amount of variation can only be determined if the process is understood in fine detail. Step one is to observe the process for a long stretch of time, without interference. Next, try to understand the sources of error or variance through careful observation and controlled experimentation. Lastly, find cost-effective ways to improve the process – both in human and physical terms – recognizing that this is a never ending pursuit, especially in the human dimension.

Producing high-quality personal decisions can follow a similar pattern. First, understand your normal (i.e., unaided or unimproved) approach with all its quirks and biases. Then determine your weak links. Is it in problem definition, information gathering, the choice process, and/or learning over time? Next, initiate decision improvements in those phases that need it most, taking stock of the impact that these changes have on final actions. Such feedback may suggest other steps that were not anticipated initially.

Returning to sports again, professional athletes dissect their past performances by studying statistics and watching slow-motion videos. Most players rely on coaches to improve their skills and develop a language or framework for self-examination. Improving the inputs to a flawed process is inherently self-limiting.

10.2.3 *Nestedness*

Successful decision making also requires that one examine complex issues from multiple perspectives. The most obvious examples of how individual actions are nested within a broader set of constituencies are societal problems such as siting a noxious facility. Not only does one have to consider the role of different stakeholders (e.g., citizens groups, industrial associations) but also the interactions between individuals and the groups they represent.

Even when one is considering an individual decision problem such as apartment selection (see Chapter 1), there are likely to be interactions that make this decision part of a broader set of issues. If the person plans to have roommates, then the final individual choice is nested in a group decision process. Once real estate agents and apartment owners have to make decisions regarding joint listings of available apartments, organizational issues become important. And, at the societal level, there are questions as to how one keeps the neighborhood safe and clean.

As a more complex example of how individual decisions are nested within other levels, consider the problem facing the director of a prestigious academic research center for automobile safety and public policy. She is approached by a group of insurance companies to conduct research on the efficacy of air bags. The issue is socially important and high on the center's agenda. Is there any harm in accepting these corporate funds as long as total academic and editorial freedom is guaranteed? If the question is viewed in isolation, there would appear to be no problem in agreeing to do this research under such conditions. However, the decision is nested within a stream of other societal currents, which may give the appearance, rightly or wrongly, of less than complete independence and integrity. Let's consider some of these nested issues.

Could acceptance of these funds lessen the integrity of the center's senior researchers or their credibility as independent scientific experts if they provide testimony at congressional hearings? Might other industries, such as automobile or seat belt manufacturers, be less likely to fund the center's activities because of its ties to the insurance industry? Are senior researchers at the center really going to produce studies in opposition to the industry, if this will seriously erode their financial support? Can they honestly advise a Ph.D. student as to which research project is best for him or her, without being unduly influenced by the center's own research agenda (especially if it funds the Ph.D. student)? Note that these questions arise with even the most dedicated and purest of scholars.

In biotechnology, it is not uncommon for scientists to hold significant stock in or receive consulting fees from the very companies whose drugs they are testing as "independent" researchers. Can any human be a consultant or investor of such a company and exercise totally independent judgments concerning the associated academic research and tests? These issues are not hypothetical but are faced by most research centers that accept private funding. They can only be justly resolved if nestedness – that is, in its larger and deeper implications – is fully recognized and divulged to outside parties.

Nestedness also means that we should think in terms of longer time horizons rather than act myopically. Today's decision may significantly influence or delimit those in the future by changing the status quo, reference points, and other people's perceptions or attitudes. In the area of negotiations it has proved especially crucial to adopt a multiperiod perspective, so as to anticipate countermoves properly, establish a reputation, build trust, learn, and so on. The experimental literature (see Chapters 6 and 7) has demonstrated that most players fail to think more than one move ahead. In general, it is these linkages over time and across broad decision problems that make nestedness challenging and important.

There is also a social aspect of nestedness that may need consideration when making decisions. When a large segment of the population is violating normative principles, it does not necessarily follow that a single rational actor can exploit this.[1] Consider the alleged shortsightedness of U.S. investors and managers. If most investors emphasize short-term earnings at the detriment of long-term capabilities and competitiveness, a rational investor or management team that pursues a longer-term course may not see any rewards in its lifetime.

The "greater fool theory" of the real-estate market in California vividly illustrates how other people's decisions impact one's own. Many people bought California homes in the 1980s feeling that the price was outrageously high but trusted that greater fools would pay even more by the time they would sell. Prices have recently declined due to a dwindling supply of greater fools.

10.2.4 *Bounded rationality*

This concept refers to people's limited information-processing abilities. In the context of decision making, bounded rationality has an impact on

---

1 Frey and Eichenberger (1989) explore this issue in more depth, developing the view that institutions, social norms, and regulation often counter or alleviate those individual biases that do not wash out or correct under aggregation (see also Chapter 9).

how people specify their values and how they make choices. With respect to values, the goals and objectives of individuals, groups, organizations, and society entail a complex web of hopes, wishes, experiences, and constraints. Trade-offs are necessary simply because of limited resources, time, and attention. Specifying a meaningful set of goals and objectives becomes difficult because of information overload.

To illustrate, consider the problem society faces in dealing with the environment. There is a broad consensus that a cleaner environment is an important societal goal. The public has a much more difficult time, however, making trade-offs between the benefits of a cleaner environment and the cost of achieving this objective. For example, the current program for cleaning up abandoned hazardous waste sites has as one of its objectives to make these areas pristine. Only recently has there been any discussion regarding the technical and economic capabilities of achieving this objective. If one forces the issue by emphasizing that there is a steep price to pay for zero risk, many individuals intuitively object to making an explicit trade-off. Focusing on a single objective, such as a "clean environment," makes life easier even though choices may have become highly skewed.

People's values and preferences evolve over time, while learning from others, from experience, and through introspection. If one possible consequence of cleaning up all hazardous waste sites is that it will bankrupt most industrial firms in the United States, we shall need to reevaluate the relative importance of the objective "pristine environment" and recognize the need to make trade-offs. However, getting to the stage where societal trade-offs are made explicitly is extremely difficult in practice. Our deepest value judgments (about health, abortion, environment, free speech, or capitalism, etc.) involve serious information gaps, biases, and anxieties.

The choices that people make reflect their limited rationality. In choosing between apartments or jobs, for instance, there are only a small number of alternatives and attributes that most of us consider. We often utilize simple decision rules, as illustrated in Chapter 4, that focus on one or two attributes and eliminate many alternatives. We should accept the need for some degree of simplification in order to deal with real world complexity. As Payne, Bettman, and Johnson (1990) emphasize, there are important trade-offs between accuracy and effort, and often such simplified models may perform quite well across a variety of problems. In more complex situations, it may be useful to develop decision support systems that in part overcome our bounded rationality.

Today there exist interactive computer systems designed to improve individual, group, and organizational decision processes. Chapters 5 and 6 discussed the use of decision support systems in the context of financial advice, portfolio analysis, and group planning. Similar support exists at the level of personal decision making, such as career planning, job selection, and even mate selection.

Our basic point is that good decision making ought to acknowledge whatever value or information complexity is present and seek to address it. The template discussed earlier with its five elements is one way to decompose complex decisions into more manageable components. As noted in Chapter 5, value complexity suggests the use of trade-off analysis; information complexity can be tackled through the use of models (e.g., Bayes' revision), diagrams, organizing frameworks, and decision support systems. The prescriptive techniques discussed throughout this book, as well as the numerous warnings and illustrations about the shortcomings of unaided, unstructured decision making, suggest how we should address the issue of complexity and bounded rationality.

10.2.5 *Legitimation*

Successful decisions require the specification of relevant criteria key stakeholders will employ to judge both the choice process and final outcome. In business as in personal life, many joint ventures fail because a partner does not appreciate the relevant criteria and yardsticks for success, fairness, and expected degrees of involvement.

A decision can only be successful if it is perceived as legitimate by all the relevant parties. In structuring a joint venture between two parties, it is not enough to specify how profits (losses) will be shared. Criteria need to be articulated regarding how policy will be set, disputes resolved, voting procedures followed, and so forth. Once evaluation criteria are agreed upon by all relevant parties, disputes and change in policy can be handled in a manner that is deemed legitimate by all concerned.

At a societal level, siting noxious facilities is complex primarily due to concerns about legitimacy of the proposed plan as perceived by one or more of the relevant stakeholders. For example, it is not feasible today simply to impose a hazardous facility on a given community. It would be viewed as unfair by the residents of the area as well as public interest groups. Indeed, a facility siting credo has been proposed by practitioners and researchers to suggest guidelines for facilitating the siting process. The credo strives to meet the "legitimacy test" by designing the siting process around such goals as instituting a broad-based participatory process, seeking consensus, and working to develop trust among the parties.

As our world becomes more interconnected and global, with strategic alliances reaching across vast cultural divides, the capacity to understand legitimation and process concerns is crucial. When people are very homogeneous, harmony is more likely. As American managers interact more with European and Asian ones, appreciating differences in values, business practices, and decision processes becomes increasingly important. Especially in these multicultural contexts, legitimation can and should be an integral part of the decision process rather than just an afterthought.

10.3   Decision process assessment

Let us now consider how an individual might evaluate the quality of his or her decision process in a particular context, that is, how to conduct decision process assessment. The five supporting principles and concepts discussed above are general in nature. As shown in Figure 10.1, they must be refined and shaped by the particular problem application. This, in turn, influences the problem-solving road map and assessment process for the relevant level(s) of decision making (i.e., individual, group, organizational, or societal).

The five elements in the road map, coupled with the supporting principles and concepts, provide benchmarks for determining how well one performs in a particular problem application. This process can be illustrated by posing a question from each of the five different elements of the road map to an individual assessing the quality of his or her personal decisions.

- Have you focused on the appropriate problem? (Element 1).
- Have you specified all the relevant stakeholders and their values and goals? (Element 2).
- Did you address the relevant biases that you are likely to encounter? (Element 3).
- Did you specify relevant criteria to evaluate the choice process? (Element 4).
- Did you establish control and accountability when implementing your decision? (Element 5).

The same procedure can be followed in evaluating other people, groups, or entities. Ideally, all decision makers should perform *personal* audits (e.g., see Russo and Schoemaker, 1989). In addition, organizations might evaluate their employees as part of periodic performance reviews. Indeed, entire groups or departments can be evaluated in terms of such criteria.

For example, the nestedness principle might translate into awareness about how a particular department's decision affects some other unit in the organization. It is likely that some departments will prove more capable at information gathering than others. We should determine why these differences exist among departments and whether there is room for improvement by adopting other approaches. In practice, benchmarking should not just be against other departments or units within the same organization but also relevant comparative groups from competitors, customers, and suppliers (to the extent that one can obtain information on their decision-making process). Such comparisons should be made with the important caveat that each decision maker, group, and organization faces its own personal constraints and challenges. The evaluation process needs to reflect these unique circumstances and aspirations.

10.4   Lessons from our students

In the fall of 1990, we conducted an informal survey with Wharton School undergraduates taking the introductory course in decision sciences that deals with decision-making processes. Draft chapters of this book were included as part of the required reading packet. At the beginning of the course, the students were asked individually to describe an important decision they had personally faced and how they had addressed or solved it. The following are some sample problems using their own language:

Student A: "I was born and raised in Los Angeles, California. I lived on the West Coast all my life. A big decision I had to make was to go to college in the East Coast or stay on the West Coast."

Student B: "Choosing a vacation site after finals."

Student C: "Newly married. Should I use birth control?"

For each of their problems, the students were privately asked to provide the following kinds of information:

1. A nutshell problem description (like the previous examples).
2. Relevant stakeholders considered.
3. Kinds of data collected.
4. Choice procedures employed.
5. Options or alternatives considered.
6. Ease of justifying the decision to others.
7. Reliance on intuition versus more analytic approaches.
8. Degree of process focus in judging the quality of their decision.
9. Perceived difficulty of the decision.
10. Time spent on making the decision.

Student A identified his parents, brother and sisters, and friends as important stakeholders. He collected data on tuition and living expenses, the academic programs, local college conditions (in terms of culture, weather, crime, housing, etc.), as well as the overall feel of the campus. He described his choice procedure as consisting of (1) rating the academic quality of each university, (2) examining pros and cons of each location, east versus west, (3) evaluation of the effect on and opinions of family and friends, and (4) his own "gut feel." This student considered only two options seriously: UCLA and the University of Pennsylvania. He rated the decision as relatively easy to justify or explain to others and characterized his approach as being on the intuitive rather than analytic side of the spectrum. He expected to judge the quality of his decision purely on grounds of results rather than process. He found this decision one of intermediate difficulty and spent about 36 hours making this decision in total.

Student C included his wife, parents, parents-in-law, siblings, a pastor, and married friends as stakeholders and collected information from such sources as books, parents, church, and other young couples.

Fifteen weeks later, at the end of the course, each student was asked to revisit his or her initial problem and analyze it prescriptively. What would they do differently (if anything at all)? The students were asked to be realistic and told that they would only be graded on seriously completing the assignment, but not on what they said or how they felt about various approaches or techniques studied.

Student B, who had to select a vacation spot for her friends and relatives after finals, drew the following lessons. "I spent so much time gathering brochures on exotic spots, trying to find a trip that would best suit me personally, that I failed to see that the key criterion was finding a trip that all or at least most of my friends could afford and enjoy." Interestingly, she also recognized afterward that travel agents (who are not disinterested parties) should have been considered in her list of stakeholders. It might have reduced the number of exotic brochures to far away and expensive places.

Student C felt that his decision was mostly an intuitive one, boiling down to "Am I mature enough to have children? Will I ever be?" Since he answered no to both questions, he decided on strict birth control. As decision consultants, we should point out that the answer to the second question was premature and unnecessary for the decision to be made at this point.

However, not all students found the book to be that useful. As one wrote: "It is my belief that nothing can fully prepare you for real-life problems and decisions. You can be warned of potential biases and taught how to better organize your thoughts, yet when it comes down to probabilities of future events, possible payoffs, values, utilities and preferences of things that can't be quantified in more than an arbitrary fashion, I, the decision maker, have to make an imperfect decision, using imperfect information, in an imperfect world."

As decision coaches, we would largely agree, except to note that there are degrees of imperfection. We shall leave the perfect decision to God and be happy if we can move people from blindly muddling through their most important decisions toward something approaching a well-considered, carefully balanced choice that recognizes the numerous pitfalls along the way of a good decision process.

Overall, however, students said they did learn some important lessons. Many would consider additional stakeholders and options, although at times also fewer (as with Student C's exotic but unrealistic places). Most students said they would collect additional data. As one put it "the data I would collect would be more exact and quantitative if possible." In addition, most would approach the problem more systematically, use analytic tools such as scoring and explicitly weighting the choice criteria. The course "has changed my approach to decision making by making me more aware of biases, more wary of relying on my intuition which can be incorrect" wrote one. Student C noted, "Lending your final decision validity and justification is very important when you need to convince others or gain their approval." Another said, "The course taught me something very important – decisions can be quantified."

Lastly, many students said they would focus more on the process than the outcomes in approaching the decision or when judging it *ex post*. "I realize how much easier decision making can be if you know methodological ways to approach decision making."

Many expected to devote more time to future decisions and some viewed their original problem as being much more difficult than they realized at the time. Clearly, ignorance has its elements of bliss. Not knowing about heuristics and biases makes decision making considerably easier, although not better. Just as with tennis or basketball, learning new techniques and approaches may initially be frustrating and temporarily lower your level of play. However, this is a price we must pay in order to improve or even just to stay with the pack as we fast approach the 21st century.

To conclude this epilogue, we should note that even though the field of decision sciences is still relatively young, a solid foundation at both the descriptive and prescriptive levels has been constructed by researchers from multiple disciplines. As the field increases its understanding of the decision-making process at the individual, group, organizational, and societal levels, there will undoubtedly be new approaches for improving the problem-finding and problem-solving process. The increasing complexity of the institutional and social context surrounding actual problems, as well as the increased quantity of information and transmission speed, will pose additional challenges in solving real-world issues. In all, it promises to be an exciting time for the field of decision sciences.

Appendix A

Expected utility theory with examples

In this appendix we prove two key theorems of the von Neumann–Morgenstern (NM) utility theory, using a numerical example along with the general case. Thereafter various illustrations are offered of how to apply expected utility (EU) theory.

A.1   EU axioms and theorems

This subsection states the von Neumann–Morgenstern (1947) axioms and proves that they imply expected utility maximization as the appropriate choice rule. Our approach follows that of Baumol (1977). Lotteries will be denoted as $[p: A, B]$, meaning a p chance of getting A and a $(1 - p)$ chance of getting B. The NM axioms are as follows:

1. *Transitivity:* If $A > B$ and $B > C$ then $A > C$, where $>$ denotes "at least as preferred as."
2. *Continuity:* For any three ordered outcomes A, B, and C, there exists a probability p such that $B \sim [p: A, C]$, where $\sim$ denotes indifference.
3. *Independence:* For any four outcomes A, B, C, and D, if $A \sim B$ and $C \sim D$ then $[p: A, C] \sim [p: B, D]$ for any p.
4. *Stochastic Dominance:* If $A > B$, then $[r: A, B] > [r': A, B]$ whenever $r > r'$.
5. *Reduction:* For any alternatives A and B and probabilities p, p_1 and p_2 $[p: [p_1: A, B], [p_2: A, B]] \sim [r: A, B]$ where $r = pp_1 + (1 - p)p_2$.

A.1.1   Theorem I

If the decision maker obeys the NM axioms, it is possible to rank order any set of (complex) lotteries on the basis of preferences among simple reference lotteries.

Proof: Say the choice is between:

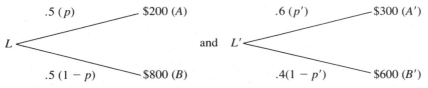

Step 1: Express the outcomes of the lotteries in terms of equivalences vis-à-vis a reference lottery. The latter should have levels that nest the possible outcomes of the lotteries of interest, say, $0 (*D*) and $1,000 (*E*). By Axiom 2, there must exist a probability p_a such that:

$$200 \sim \quad \overset{p_a}{\underset{1-p_a}{\diagdown}} \quad \overset{1,000}{\underset{0}{}} \qquad \text{or} \quad 200 \sim [p_a: 1,000, 0]$$

Note our shorthand notation for this gamble, that is, $[p_a: 1,000, 0]$. Let us assume the indifference probability p_a is .3 for this gamble. Similarly, assume the following indifference probabilities (p_b, p_a', p_b') for three other gambles (i.e., outcomes of interest).

$$800 \sim [.8: 1,000, 0] \text{ or } p_b = .8$$
$$300 \sim [.4: 1,000, 0] \text{ or } p_a' = .4$$
$$600 \sim [.7: 1,000, 0] \text{ or } p_b' = .7$$

Step 2: Substitute the equivalence lotteries into the original lotteries. This yields:

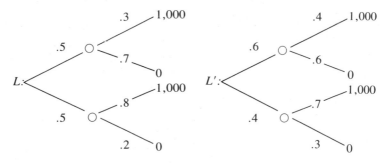

The axioms now imply that:

$$\underbrace{L \sim [.5: \quad [.3: 1,000, 0], [.8: 1,000, 0]]}_{\text{by Axiom 3}} = \underbrace{[.55: 1,000, 0]}_{\text{by Axiom 5}}$$

Hence, $L = [.55: 1,000, 0]$ by transitivity (Axiom 1) and $L' = [.52: 1,000, 0]$ (by analogy).

Step 3: Invoke Axiom 4 to conclude that (for our numerical example):

   $L > L'$ since $.55 > .52$

In sum, the trick is to first get indifference probabilities p_a, p_b, p'_a, p'_b. Then rewrite the original lottery L as follows:

   $[p: A, B] \sim [p: [p_a: E, D], [p_b: E, D]] = [r: E, D]$

where $r = pp_a + (1 - p)p_b$.

Similarly, $[p': A', B'] = [r': E, D]$; and, hence, the (relative) values of r and r' dictate the ordering of the lotteries.   Q.E.D.

A.1.2   *Theorem II*

Define $E[U[p: A, B]] = pU(A) + (1 - p)U(B)$. Assign arbitrary numbers to $U(E)$ and $U(D)$, such that $U(E) > U(D)$. It then follows that:

   $E[U[p: A, B] > E[U(p': A', B')]$ iff $L > L'$.

Proof:

   Let $E[U[p: A, B]] = pU(A) + (1 - p)U(B)$
   $= pU([p_a: E, D]) + (1 - p)U([p_b: E, D])$
   $= rU(E) + (1 - r)U(D)$

Similarly,

   $E[U[p': A', B']] = r'U(E) + (1 - r')U(D)$

Algebraically,

   $E[U(L)] > E[U(L')]$ iff $r > r'$

From Theorem I we know that $r > r'$ implies $L > L'$. Hence,

   $E[U(L)] > E[U(L')]$ implies $L > L'$ Q.E.D.

In sum, the axioms are sufficient to prove that there exists a utility index such that computing expected utilities will yield a preference ordering among lotteries in accordance with the axioms. Because the index is initialized by two arbitrary reference points, the utility function is an interval scale (i.e., unique up to positive linear transformations). However, $E[U(\tilde{x})]$ itself is only ordinal.

A.2   **Illustrations**

The following examples are meant to illustrate both the power and complexity of EU theory.

Say $U(x) = \sqrt{30 + x}$. What is the certainty equivalence (*CE*) for the following lottery L:

That is, what amount for sure is as attractive as this lottery, for the given utility function? This is the minimum price for which you would be willing to sell this lottery. Answer:

$$E[U(L)] = 1/3 \; U(6) + 2/3 \; U(19)$$
$$= 1/3 \; \sqrt{30 + 6} + 2/3 \; \sqrt{30 + 19} = 6 \; 2/3 \text{ utiles.}$$

Next find the amount for sure (*CE*) for which

$$U(CE) = 6 \; 2/3 \text{ or } \sqrt{30 + CE} = 20/3$$

Hence,

$$CE = (400/9) - 30 = 130/9 = \$14.44$$

Since the monetary expected value is

$$1/3 \; (\$6) + 2/3 \; (\$19) = \$14.67$$

this person is risk averse: That is, the lottery is valued below its expected value.

A.3 Multiple lotteries

Now suppose we played the lottery twice; what would be the *CE* of this game? Answer: There will be three possible outcomes corresponding to the following new lottery L':

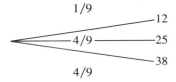

Hence,

$$E[U(L')] = 1/9U(12) + 4/9U(25) + 4/9 \; U(38)$$
$$= 1/9 \; \sqrt{42} + 4/9 \; \sqrt{55} + 4/9 \; \sqrt{68}$$
$$= .72 + 3.30 + 3.66 = 7.68 \text{ utiles}$$
$$U(30 + CE) = \sqrt{30 + CE} = 7.68$$

Thus $CE = (7.68)^2 - 30 = \$29.02$. Note that this is not twice $14.44 since new ranges of $U(x)$ come into play under repeated trials.

A.4 Buying prices

Now that we have illustrated the concept of *certainty equivalence*, let us examine the *maximum price* one should be willing to pay for the simple lottery. This is a different question, as now the money will come out of one's own pocket. Hence we must find a level of b (the maximum bid) such that not playing the lottery at all is as attractive as playing it for a cost of b dollars. In terms of utilities we must solve:

$$U(0) = 1/3 U(6 - b) + 2/3 U(19 - b)$$

or

$$\sqrt{30} = 1/3 \sqrt{36 - b} + 2/3 \sqrt{49 - b}$$

To solve this equation, let us square both sides, multiply by 9, and rearrange terms. This yields:

$$4\sqrt{(36 - b)(49 - b)} = 270 - (36 - b) - 4(49 - b)$$

or

$$4\sqrt{(36 - b)(49 - b)} = 38 + 5b$$

To solve this further, square both sides once again, which gives us:

$$16(36 - b)(49 - b) = (38 + 5b)^2$$

Multiplying these terms out then leaves us with the following quadratic equation:

$$9b^2 + 1740b - 26{,}780 = 0$$

This can now be solved with the standard formula as follows:

$$b_{1,2} = \frac{-1740 \pm \sqrt{(1740)^2 + (4) \cdot (9) \cdot (26{,}780)}}{18}$$

As we only consider the positive root, this leaves

$$b = \frac{-1740 + 1997.92}{18} = \underline{\$14.33}$$

as the answer.

A.5   Important points

The following points are important to keep in mind when applying NM utility theory.

1. The certainty equivalent (CE) of a lottery ($\tilde{x}$) offering outcomes x_i with probabilities p_i is determined from the following equation (the CE is also called the minimum selling price or reservation price):
$$U(CE) = E[U(\tilde{X})] = \Sigma\, p_i U(X_i)$$
2. Risk aversion implies that the certainty equivalent of a lottery is less than its expected value.

3. The *maximum* bid (*b*) one should offer for a lottery is determined from the following equation:

$$U(0) = \Sigma\, p_i U(X_i - b)$$

4. The certainty equivalent of playing a lottery *n* times will generally not be equal to *n* times the *CE* of playing it once.

A.6 Mean-variance analysis

Much work in finance assumes a "mean-variance world." However, only if $U(x)$ is quadratic are mean-variance choice criteria correct, that is, strictly compatible with expected utility theory for any and all distribution functions. To show this, consider a lottery (X) offering outcomes x_1 through x_n with probabilities p_1 through p_n. Let $U(x) = ax^2 + bx + c$. Then,

$$
\begin{aligned}
E[U(X)] &= \Sigma\, p_i U(x_i) = \Sigma\, p_i\, [ax_i^2 + bx_i + c] \\
&= aE(X^2) + bE(X) + c
\end{aligned}
$$

Of course, $E(X)$ is the mean (μ) of the lottery. Its variance σ^2 is $E(X^2) - \mu^2$. Thus, the preceding equation becomes:

$$
\begin{aligned}
E[U(X)] &= a[E(X^2) - \mu^2 + \mu^2] + b\mu + c \\
&= a(\sigma^2 + \mu^2) + b\mu + c
\end{aligned}
$$

If $U(x)$ is not quadratic, a Taylor series expansion around the mean provides a mean-variance approximation as follows:

$$U(x) = U(\mu) + \frac{U'(\mu)}{1!}(x - \mu) + \frac{U''(\mu)}{2!}(x - \mu)^2 + \ldots$$

If we now take the expectation of $U(x)$ for the random variable $\bar{x}$, we get

$$
\begin{aligned}
E[U(\bar{x})] &= U(\mu) + 0 + \frac{U''(\mu)}{2!}\sigma^2 + \ldots \\
&\approx f(\mu, \sigma^2)
\end{aligned}
$$

Note that mean-variance choice criteria may be strictly appropriate for other choice situations as well, for example, when $\bar{x}$ is normally distributed (see D. Baron, 1977).

A.7 Uniqueness

A further point to emphasize is that the NM utility function is unique once two initial reference points have been chosen. Since the choice of the reference points is arbitrary, it is possible to construct many different NM utility functions for the same individual. However, all such utility indexes can be obtained from each other by applying a positive linear

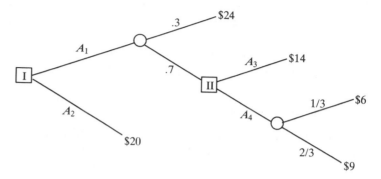

Figure A.1. Simple decision tree for a sequential choice problem

transformation and will be strategically equivalent. For example, say that for a given utility function U the following condition holds: $U(B) = pU(A) + (1 - p)U(C)$ and we wanted to see if this condition would change if we used another utility function U^*, which is a positive linear transformation of U as follows: $U^*(x) = \alpha U(x) + \beta$. We could simply use the new index and reduce it to its old form, that is:

$$U^*(B) = pU^*(A) + (1 - p)U^*(C)$$
$$= p(\alpha U(A) + \beta) + (1 - p)(\alpha U(C) + \beta)$$
$$= \alpha(pU(A) + (1 - p)U(C)) + p\beta - p\beta + \beta$$

which reduces to $\alpha U(B) + \beta$ precisely when

$$U(B) = pU(A) + (1 - p)U(C)$$

Thus, in these numerical examples, the same CE and b values would have emerged if $U(x)$ had been transformed to $\alpha U(x) + \beta$ where $a > 0$. The reader is encouraged to verify this, say for $U(x) = 10\sqrt{30 + x} - 20$.

A.8   Multistage decisions

In the example in Figure A.1 the choice is between $20 for sure ($A_2$), or a gamble ($A_1$) which either yields $24 (with a .3 chance) or a new decision between A_3 and A_4, where A_4 is itself a gamble. Such nested choice problems are commonly encountered in investment or research and development contexts, where the initial choice must incorporate future choices, depending on how the investment or technology works out. To solve such problems, one works backward. First look at Decision Node II and decide whether A_3 or A_4 is preferred. Note that the A_4 gamble corresponds to our earlier example. If we again assume that $U(x) = \sqrt{30 + x}$, this gamble's CE is $14.44 and hence A_4 is preferred. Consequently, we may substitute $14.44 in place of Decision Node II, which then leaves us with the simpler structure addressed before. Hence, decision trees are folded backward by solving each subproblem separately, until a single stage emerges. When folding backward, it is important to keep in mind at which financial position one is, as this may affect the *CEs*.[1]

A.9 Portfolio choices

A second difficulty arises if the decision alternatives are not explicitly given, or are infinite. To illustrate, consider the following simplified portfolio problem. An investor must allocate $1,000 (which is yielding no interest at the moment) among two investment opportunities *A* and *B*. Alternative *A* offers a 3/4 chance at zero return and a 1/4 chance at 30% (per month). Alternative *B* offers even chances at 0 or 5% return per month. Assuming the utility function is $U(x) = \log_{10}(x + 1)$, what is the optimal portfolio allocation for this investor?

First, let us consider the expected utilities of investing all $1,000 in either *A* or *B*.

$$E[U(A)] = 3/4\ U(0) + 1/4\ U(300)$$
$$= 3/4 \log(1) + 1/4 \log(301) = .62 \text{ utiles}$$
$$E[U(B)] = 1/2\ U(0) + 1/2\ U(50)$$
$$= 1/2 \log(1) + 1/2 \log(51) = .85 \text{ utiles}$$

Hence *B* would be preferred if it were a mutually exclusive choice. However, investing some in both options might still be better. Say $x is invested in *A* and $(1,000 - x)$ in *B*. The possible portfolio returns will then be:

A	B	Probability	Payoff
win	win	(1/4)(1/2)	$.3x + .05(1,000 - x)$
win	lose	(1/4)(1/2)	$.3x + 0$
lose	win	(3/4)(1/2)	$0 + .05(1,000 - x)$
lose	lose	(3/4)(1/2) +	0
		1.00	

The expected utility of this portfolio $\bar{P}$ is:

$$E[U(\bar{P})] = 1/8\ U(.3x + .05(1,000 - x)) + 1/8\ U(.3x)$$
$$+ 3/8\ U(.05(1,000 - x)) + 3/8\ U(0)$$
$$= 1/8 \log(.3x + 51 - .05x) + 1/8 \log(.3x + 1)$$
$$+ 3/8 \log(51 - .05x) + 3/8 \log(1)$$
$$= 1/8 \log(.25x + 51) + 1/8 \log(.3x + 1) + 3/8 \log(51 - .05x) + 0$$

---

1 This would, for instance, be the case if in Figure A.1 the .7 chance fork would furthermore yield an outright $10 profit. This amount would then have to be added to A_3 and A_4 *prior to* evaluating their expected utility levels.

To maximize $E[U(P)]$, take the derivative with respect to x and set this equal to zero. Then solve for x.

$$\frac{dE[U(x)]}{dx} = (1/8)\left(\frac{.25}{.25x + 51}\right) + 1/8\left(\frac{.3}{.3x + 1}\right)$$

$$+ 1/8\left(\frac{-.05}{51 - .05x}\right)(\log_{10}e) = 0$$

To solve this equation, first cancel out the differentiation constant $\log_{10}e$. Next put all terms under a common denominator and multiply by 8. This yields:

$$\frac{.25(.3x + 1)(51 - .05x) + .3(.25x + 51)(51 - .05x) - 3(.05x)(.25x + 51)(.3 + 1)}{(.25x + 51)(.3x + 1)(51 - .05x)} = 0$$

Of course, the denominator can now be canceled out, and the numerator multiplied through. After rearranging terms, this leaves the following quadratic equation:

$$- .01875x^2 + 4.54x + 785.4 = 0$$

Solving for the positive root yields $x = \$358.86$. Hence, the optimal allocation is to invest \$358.86 in A and the rest (\$641.14) in B. The expected utility of the portfolio in that case will be maximum, namely:

$$E\{U(\tilde{P}) \mid x = 358.86\} = 1/8 \log(108.66) + 1/8 \log(33.06)$$
$$+ 3/8 \log(140.72) = 1.093 \text{ utiles}$$

Note that this is indeed higher than investing everything in B.

This last example demonstrates the power of expected utility theory when infinitely many alternatives exist. The solution in such cases usually requires some kind of optimization procedure, such as calculus or mathematical programming techniques. In finance this problem is commonly simplified by looking only at mean and variance characteristics of the portfolios. Strictly speaking, this is only permissible if $U(x)$ is quadratic, as shown earlier. Computational complexity, however, may justify Taylor series approximations of the kind discussed earlier.

Multi-attribute value functions:
the case of certainty

Most decisions require trade-offs among competing objectives. For example, in a personnel decision, there is usually a trade-off between the capabilities of the candidate and the cost of employing the person. Viewed abstractly, such decisions can be modeled as choosing from a given set of n-dimensional vectors $\mathbf{x} = (x_1, \ldots, x_n)$. The coordinate of each vector indicates how well the particular alternative scores along that dimension or attribute. For instance, if ten candidates were considered for a particular job, and if the only criteria of interest were the persons' qualifications on the one hand and the required salary to have them join the firm on the other hand, then the choice set would consist of 10 vectors, each having two dimensions, namely x_1 and x_2, representing qualifications and salary respectively for each candidate.

Usually some kind of ordering of these ten applicants is required, either just a ranking or a positioning on a scale from 0 to say 100, so that in addition to rank order it is also indicated *how much more* desirable a particular candidate might be. To do so, let us state the problem more formally as follows. If we are given a set of alternatives X, with each $x \in X$ of the form $x = (x_1, \ldots, x_n)$, and assuming that preferences for a decision maker can be represented in the additive form:

$$U(x) = \Sigma \ w_i u_i(x_i), \qquad x = (x_1, \ldots, x_n) \in X$$

what is the form of the component value functions u_i and what are the best estimates of the weights w_i to reflect the decision maker's preferences? Thus, there are two distinct problems here: identifying the form of the u_i functions and finding the weights w_i. We shall assume that the decision maker's preferences can be, at least approximately, represented by a value function of the additive form. The next two sections briefly review the type of approaches one can use to find the component value function on the one hand and the weights on the other.

B.1   **Value functions**

How can we construct a component value function? Several approaches exist, ranging from formal to informal. We shall use a college admissions example to illustrate the various approaches. The candidates are to be judged on the basis of just their Scholastic Aptitude Test (SAT), high school grades (adjusted for the quality of school), and time spent on extracurricular activities. Let

X_1 = Verbal SAT (with scores ranging from 200 to 800)
X_2 = Adjusted average high-school grade (on a four-point scale)
X_3 = Extracurricular activity (in average hours per week)
X_4 = Quantitative SAT (with scores ranging from 200 to 800)

Based on this kind of information, how might one construct value functions (and then weights) to rank the various applicants?

B.1.1   *Introspection*

One approach is to rely on the decision makers' ability to introspect about how much equal increments in an attribute are valued. For example, how would an increase from 3.0 to 3.2 in someone's grade point average compare with an increase say from 3.5 to 3.7? If about the same, the value function for grade point average is likely linear. However, if the latter increase (from 3.5 to 3.7) is deemed to be much more impressive than the former (from 3.0 to 3.2) then the value function is likely convex. By asking the decision maker to rank and compare various fixed intervals from different locations of the scale, one may be able to plot whether the utility function is primarily linear, convex, concave, or some combination thereof.

A simple way is to start with 2.0 and judge each increment of .1 or .2 in terms of added value. This way a plot is created, which arbitrarily assigns a value of say 0 to a grade point average of 0 and 100 to a 4.0 average. All other grade point increments are now expressed relative to these extremes, after which a curve can be fitted (by hand or statistically) to the plotted points (as in Chapter 4). Alternatively, one could ask the admissions officer to draw his or her own curve directly. The same procedure can then be applied to the SAT scores and the extracurricular measure, resulting in four value functions $V_i(x_i)$, each scaled from 0 to 100.

B.1.2   *Trade-off analysis*

An alternative approach is to price out increases or decreases in the attribute under consideration relative to another attribute, such as money.

For example, how much would the school be willing to pay from a hypothetical budget fixed at say $1,000 per attribute to increase verbal SAT in a candidate (other things equal). Would each increase of, say, 10 SAT points be valued equally, resulting in a flat $(800 - 200)/1,000 = \$0.60$ per verbal SAT point, or might increases near the bottom of the scale be valued more. If the latter, a dollar value will have to be put on each increment of 10 verbal SAT points, without exceeding the $1,000 limit.

Due to our assumption of additivity, we should be able to make these judgments independent of knowing anything about the other attribute levels or values. Also, we are implicitly assuming that the value function obtained by distributing $1,000 per attribute is shaped the same as when assuming $10,000 or $100,000 per attribute. This is plausible as long as the money pool is hypothetical; but with real money, the issue becomes more complex.

Although the trade-off or pricing-out method may seem very natural, in that we commonly have to judge how much an improvement in something is worth, it suffers from one important weakness. The curve one gets by using real money as the yardstick need not be the same as the curve one gets by relying on direct drawings or comparisons of intervals, because the money scale itself may not be linear in utility. Hence, a further translation would be needed from the utility of money (for that particular person) to another scale that is linear in the underlying attribute. Thus, we must ultimately rely on introspection, that is, some comparison of intervals, in order to construct a component utility function in isolation.

B.1.3 *Other approaches*

There do exist more sophisticated techniques, such as the lottery method discussed in Chapter 4 (as well as in Appendixes A and C). However, this approach confounds the measurement of value under certainty with attitudes toward risk. Such techniques are commonly used in marketing, as well as psychology. Other sophisticated techniques employ simultaneous estimations of both weights and component value functions, as for example in conjoint measurement (see Green and Tull, 1978).

B.2 **Estimating weights**

Several approaches exist to estimate weights once component utility functions are known. A key point to remember is that the weights one obtains are dependent on the range over which the attributes can vary. We shall review the major approaches in increasing order of complexity, again using numerical illustrations where appropriate.

B.2.1 *Point allocation*

One of the simplest methods is to ask the decision maker to allocate a hundred points across the attributes of interest. The more points an attribute receives, the greater its relative importance. For example, an admissions officer might assign a weight of 20 points to VSAT (verbal SAT), 30 points to high school grade point average, 10 points to extracurricular, and 40 points to QSAT (quantitative SAT). The relative worth of two candidates *A* and *B* can now be assessed by calculating:

$$V(A) = .2V_1(a_1) + .3V_2(a_2) + .1V_3(a_3) + .4V_4(a_4)$$
$$V(B) = .2V_1(b_1) + .3V_2(b_2) + .1V_3(b_3) + .4V_4(b_4)$$

Since all value functions V_i were scored to range from 0 to 100, $V(A)$ and $V(B)$ will fall somewhere along the 0–100 scale, with the higher score representing the preferred candidate. Sensitivity analysis can now be conducted to see how robust this calculated preference is to changes in weights or value functions (being both approximations).

The direct assessment method has the virtue of great simplicity but lacks a formal or theoretical foundation. A skeptic might ask, What does it mean to give this many points to one criterion and another number of points to the next criterion? Indeed, the question of how much weight to give to each attribute is not really meaningful unless the attributes are clearly defined as well as clearly bounded in terms of an interval. For example, when shopping for a car, the question of how much weight to give to such criteria as the price of the car, driving comfort, safety, and style would depend on how much variability exists in the set of cars under consideration. If all cars are between say $10 thousand and $12 thousand in price, the price dimension would be much less important than in a case where the cars range from $8 thousand to $20 thousand.

B.2.2 *Paired comparisons*

An alternative to point allocation is to consider the attributes on a pairwise basis. In the admissions example, one might ask the decision maker how much more important verbal SAT is than high school grades. To do so, some ratio scale would have to be defined on which this judgment could be scored. Saaty (1980) recommends a 9-point scale, where the gradations range from equally important (1) to very much more important (9). For example, the admissions officer might consider QSAT to be eight times as important as extracurricular, four times as important as high-school Cum, and twice as important as VSAT. These judgments imply the following weight ratios: $w_4/w_3 = 8$; $w_4/w_2 = 4$ and $w_4/w_1 = 2$. Taking reciprocals, setting $w_4 = 1$, and then multiplying each ratio by w_4

leaves $w_3 = 1/8$; $w_2 = 1/4$; and $w_1 = 1/2$. Since we want the weights to sum to 1, we should divide each weight by the following sum: $1/8 + 1/4 + 1/2 + 1 = 1.875$. This results in the following weight estimates: $w_1 = .267$; $w_2 = .133$; $w_3 = .067$; and $w_4 = .533$.

One advantage of the paired-comparison method is that only two attributes have to be considered at a time. A negative of this is that inconsistencies may occur when testing other pairings, such as w_1 versus w_2. According to the earlier weightings, this ratio should be 2 (i.e., VSAT being twice as important as high school Cum). However, few humans will be perfectly consistent and indeed the admissions officer might well rank it as 3 (or 1.5) times as important. In that case, we need to sort out the inconsistencies. One approach is to confront the officer with the inconsistency and ask for a revision in the weights. Another approach is to do it statistically.

A variety of statistical techniques exist to average out the inconsistencies (under the assumption that they represent random noise). First, one must obtain an entire matrix of paired comparisons, with the diagonal elements equal to one and with full symmetry (meaning that $w_{ij} = 1/w_{ji}$). A simple averaging procedure is to calculate for each row its geometric mean. In other words, multiply all entries in a given row and then take the nth root (where n denotes the dimension of the matrix). In the preceding example, the first row of the matrix (which compares $w1$ against all four weights) would read: [1, 2, 4, .5]. The cross-product of these four entries equals 4, from which we can calculate the fourth-root to be 1.41. If the other rows are similarly analyzed, four roots will be obtained (one per row), whose ratios will accurately reflect the relative weights of the attributes.[1]

If many attributes exist, the paired comparison matrix may get very large. With n dimensions, $n(n + 1)/2$ separate judgments will be needed. One way around this is to arrange the attributes in hierarchical fashion. For example, in considering which apartment to rent, numerous attributes may come into play, which are difficult to keep all in mind simultaneously. One possibility is to break down the overall attractiveness of an apartment into two major categories, for example the apartment itself (i.e., the interior and layout) and its location. Nested within each of these categories we can have other breakdowns of the type shown in Figure B.1. As illustrated in this figure, at each level of the hierarchy, the paired comparison method can be separately applied so that the ratio judgments do not have to take into account the entire structure of the hierarchy. By

---

1 It has been proved, using reasonable assumptions, that this geometric mean procedure is in fact the least square estimate of the true underlying weight ratios. Other methods have been proposed, such as Saaty's eigen-vector method, but these usually do not enjoy the same solid statistical foundation.

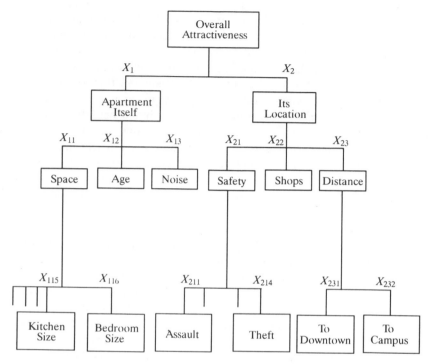

Figure B.1. Hierarchy of decision criteria for apartment selection

simply multiplying through all the weights across the various levels of the hierarchy, a final set of weights can be obtained at the bottom of the tree to indicate how important each attribute is relative to the others.

B.2.3   *Trade-off analysis*

For those who find the methods discussed so far too ad hoc, more sophisticated techniques exist that rely on careful trade-offs. The general procedure is to give the decision maker two alternatives and ask her to supply the missing entry in one of the two choice vectors so as to make them equally attractive. By asking for many such indifference judgments, the decision scientist can deduce how much weight the person must have given to the various attributes. This particular approach, which derives from a set of axioms about rational choice, is theoretically the most preferred one. Appendix C discusses some of these axioms and calculations for the more general case of risk. Here we shall just offer a simple example to explain the general idea.

To illustrate, let's focus on the trade-offs between VSAT (X_1) and QSAT (X_4). If we assume additivity, we need not worry about the levels at which the other attributes $(X_2$ and $X_3)$ are fixed. Thus, we may present the admissions officer with just [VSAT, QSAT] profiles, as follows: $A = [200, 800]$ versus $B = [800, 200]$. If A is preferred to candidate B, we know that QSAT is more important to this officer than VSAT. To be specific, we could ask how far the 800 QSAT score in A could drop before B would be preferred. Suppose the officer is exactly indifferent when A's QSAT score is dropped to 600. This implies, under additivity, the following value equation:

$$w_1 V_1(200) + w_4 V_4(600) = w_1 V_1(800) + w_4 V_4(200)$$

As noted earlier, we set the endpoints of the V_i scales equal to 0 and 100 respectively, which reduces the preceding equation to $w_4 V_4(600) = 100 w_1$, since $V_i(200) = 0$ and $V_i(800) = 100$ for $i = 1,4$. If we know the shape of V_4, we can now read off or calculate the value associated with QSAT = 600 and compute the ratio w_1/w_4.

The same approach can be followed for the other pairs of attributes, assuming known $V_i(X)$. For a detailed review of the direct trade-off approach, see Keeney and Raiffa (1976) or Keeney (1992). One weakness is that the decision maker is presumed to obey the axioms and can make fine-grained indifference judgments. As we discussed in Chapters 3 and 4, however, subjects often exhibit random inconsistencies in their responses, as well as systematic biases. As such, the direct trade-off method must be applied with care.

B.2.4 *Regression estimates*

Lastly, the weights may be estimated by simply constructing a multiple-regression model. This procedure would require the decision maker to rank-order on a scale from 0 to 100 a large number of college applicants, so that a regression can then be run between the rankings (as the dependent variable) and the attributes at which each alternative is fixed (as the independent variables). This method could verify whether the value function is indeed additive, by checking whether cross-product terms explain any significant additional variance. It could also be used to test if some of the attributes are nonlinear, or have other functional shapes than those assumed in running the regression equation. The disadvantage of the regression model is that the decision maker must simultaneously evaluate many alternatives, each of which is characterized along various attributes. The multi-attribute value approach was in part developed on the assumption that decision makers would not be able to do this very easily.

B.2.5   *Comparing the methods*

The methods differ in several important ways, as summarized in Table B.1. The direct-point-allocation method, the paired-comparison method, and the multi-attribute value method all require decomposed judgments involving subsets of the attributes. The multiple-regression on the other hand, requires holistic judgments. The measurement scales of the attributes need not be explicitly defined in the paired-comparison methods and the direct-point-allocation method. Both of these involve ratio judgments, whereas the multiple-regression method requires only interval responses. The multi-attribute value method usually requires no more than ordinal judgments. In terms of the number of judgments required, the multiple-regression method probably requires the most, followed by paired comparisons. In terms of cognitive complexity, the multiple-regression and the multi-attribute value method are probably the most difficult. Obviously, the direct-point-allocation is the simplest of all. Which method to choose would depend on the trade-offs one is willing to make between ease of use, degree of understanding on the part of the subject, and the theoretical foundation underlying a given method.

The last three rows of the table are based on a study by Schoemaker and Waid (1982) that compared the various methods. The decision task involved precisely the kind of admissions decisions we have used as illustrations. That is, subjects were asked to evaluate college applicants on the basis of VSAT, high school grade point average, a measure of extracurricular activities, and QSAT. Linear as well as nonlinear attribute value functions were used in constructing the additive value model. Hence, the methods were only compared with respect to the weights they came up with for each subject but not the component value functions. To test the predictive ability of the various methods, each subject made twenty additional pairwise comparisons of alternatives, indicating both which alternative was preferred as well as by how much. The four methods were then tested by constructing for each an additive model, using the preference information provided earlier.

The row labeled "accuracy" indicates how well the models predicted subjects' pairwise preferences (on a scale of 0 to 100% accuracy). The last two rows indicate how easy the methods are to apply and how trustworthy subjects find them. The entries marked with an asterisk are based on subjects' own perceptions (see Schoemaker and Waid, 1982); the others reflect the authors' rankings.

In conclusion, a number of approaches exist to construct and represent the preferences of a decision maker under certainty, when faced with multiple attributes. If the underlying preference structure is complex and it matters greatly that all of this complexity is reflected in the represen-

Table B.1. *Differences among methods for assessing weights*

Features	Direct point allocation	Paired comparison (e.g., Saaty)	Multiple regression model	Explicit trade-offs (Keeney–Raiffa)	Equal or unit weighting
Response scale	Interval	Ratio	Ordinal/interval	Interval	None
Judgment type	Decomposed	Decomposed	Holistic	Decomposed	Direction of signs only
Number of judgments	n	$n(n-1)/2$	$>>n$	$>>n$	n
Hierarchical	Possible	Yes	No	Yes	Not relevant
Underlying theory	None	Statistical/heuristic	Statistical/inferential	Axiomatic/deductive	Heuristic/statistical
Accuracy[a]	83%	82%	86%	85%	77%
Ease of use	Very easy	Easy[a]	Difficult[a]	Moderate[a]	Very easy
Trustworthiness	High	High[a]	Low[a]	Medium[a]	Very low

[a] Based on Schoemaker and Waid (1982). Scores for the last two features reflect either subjects' perceptions (denoted with asterisks) or the authors' perceptions.

tation, then the multi-attribute value approach is called for. If, on the other hand, the assumption of additivity is a reasonable one, and the construction of the component value functions can be arrived at independently of knowing the weights, then the representation task is significantly simplified.

Multi-attribute expected utility theory

This appendix illustrates how multi-attribute utility (MAU) theory can be applied to risky or uncertain alternatives. Since the process involved is somewhat intricate, we shall lay the problem out in discrete steps and stages as follows.

1. Determine a reasonable family (or class) of utility functions (using explicit assumptions about the person's preferences or just proceeding purely pragmatically).
2. Using a set of historical revealed preferences or hypothetical preferences questions, determine a number of equations and inequalities.
3. Using eyeball techniques, regression analysis, algebraic manipulations, and so forth, interpret these revealed preferences in terms of the parameters of a particular utility function within the assumed class.

In our experience, the richer the set of revealed preferences in (2), the better the chances are of understanding the decision maker's preference structure.

The remainder of this appendix offers a numerical illustration of the steps involved and concludes with the general case.

C.1 ·Numerical illustration

Problem: How to choose consistently among two job offers (Job $\bar{A}$, Job $\bar{B}$) characterized as risk profiles along three dimensions.

Dimensions: x_1 = job satisfaction (on a scale from 0 to 100)

              x_2 = average present value of annual salary over first three years (ranging from \$20,000 to \$40,000)

              x_3 = quality of living in job location (on a scale from 0 to 10)

Objective: Construct a utility function $U(x_1, x_2, x_3)$ such that

$$E[U\{x_1(\bar{A}), x_2(\bar{A}), x_3(\bar{A})\}] > E[U(x_1(\bar{B}), x_2(\bar{B}), x_3(\bar{B})\}]$$

if and only if Job $\bar{A}$ is preferred to Job $\bar{B}$.

The decision maker (DM) is interested in understanding her preferences for and comparing the expected utility of job offers such as the following:

Job Offer X has a job satisfaction of 80%, an average annual salary of $30,000 or $40,000 with .8 and .2 probability respectively; and living quality of 9 or 4 points with equal chances.

Job Offer Y has a job satisfaction of 40% or 80% with equal probability, a guaranteed salary of $35,000, and a known living quality of 7 points.

Suppose, for example, that the DM's multi-attribute utility function $U(x_1, x_2, x_3)$ is of the additive form

$$U(x_1, x_2, x_3) = u_1(x_1) + u_2(x_2) + u_3(x_3).$$

Then the expected utility of Job Y would be computed to be

$$E\{U(x_1(Y), x_2(Y), x_3(Y))\} = .5[u_1(40) + u_1(80)] + u_2(35) + u_3(7)$$

We can see two basic problems from this illustration: (1) how to determine the form of the overall utility function U (e.g., is it additive?) and (2) how to determine the components of the utility function so identified (in the additive case, what is the precise form of the functions $u_i(x_i)$?).

Next, we shall examine to what extent the person's preferences obey special conditions. It is assumed throughout that the person's basic preferences satisfy the standard EU axioms. However, we wish to test for more restrictive conditions because if they apply (and of course they need not), the construction of the MAU function will be much simplified. Although many types of independence tests exist, we limit ourselves here to the two most important.

C.1.1   *Conditions*

Test if the preferences of the decision maker satisfy:

1. That the pair of attributes x_i and x_j is *preferentially independent* of x_k, meaning that conditional preferences in (x_i, x_j) space given x_k do not depend on the particular level of x_k.
2. That x_i is *utility independent* of x_j, meaning that conditional preferences for lotteries on x_i given x_j do not depend on the particular level of x_j.

Key theorem: If for some x_i, the trade-offs between x_i and x_j are independent of the other variables (for all $j \neq i$); AND if for that x_i utility independence holds, THEN $U(\mathbf{x})$ is either additive or multiplicative. This theorem assumes that there are at least three attributes involved.

Algebraically: If the above conditions hold, then either U is of the additive form:

$$U(\mathbf{x}) = k_1 u_1(x_1) + k_2 u_2(x_2) + k_3 u_3(x_3)$$

where $\Sigma\, k_i = 1$, or the multiplicative form:

$$\begin{aligned} U(\mathbf{x}) = {} &k_1 u_1(x_1) + k_2 u_2(x_2) + k_3 u_3(x_3) + k\, k_1 k_2 u_1(x_1) u_2(x_2) \\ &+ k\, k_1 k_3 u_1(x_1) u_3(x_3) + k\, k_2 k_3 u_2(x_2) u_3(x_3) \\ &+ k^2 k_1 k_2 k_3 u_1(x_1) u_2(x_2) u_3(x_3) \end{aligned}$$

with $\Sigma\, k_i \neq 1$.

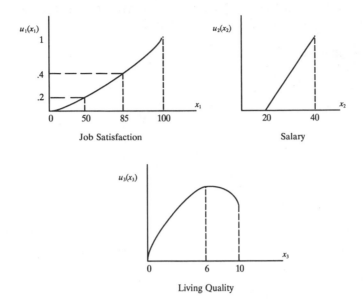

Figure C.1. Multi-attribute utility example

Multiplying by k, and adding 1 to both sides, the multiplicative form can be condensed to:

$$[1 + kU(x)] = \prod_{i=1}^{3} [kk_i u_i(x_i) + 1] \quad \text{or} \quad U(x) = \frac{\prod_{i=1}^{3} [kk_i u_i(x_i) + 1] - 1}{k}$$

(A positive k means the attributes are complementary; a negative k means they are substitutes.)

Let's assume that either the additive or multiplicative form offers a reasonable approximation. The next challenge is to estimate the component utility functions and the various weights or scaling coefficients k_i. What is nice about utility independence is that each component utility function can be scaled one-dimensionally, without needing to worry about other attributes.

C.1.2   *Utility assessment*

Using traditional lottery questions and certainty equivalents, construct the individual attribute utility functions $u_i(x_i)$. For example, consider Figure C.1.

Scale each $u_i(x_i)$ such that $u_i(x_i^w) = 0$ and $u_i(x_i^b) = 1$, where w = worst and b = best. Furthermore, set $U(100, 40, 6) = 1$, and $U(0, 20, 0) = 0$, which now defines the range form best to worst.

Rank order of k_i. Ask the decision maker to rank order the following hypothetical job offers:

$$A = [100, 20, 0]$$
$$B = [0, 40, 0]$$
$$C = [0, 20, 6]$$

Say $A > B > C \rightarrow k_1 > k_2 > k_3$ under either the additive or multiplicative form. For example, $A > B$ implies under the additive form that

$$k_1 u_1(100) + k_2 u_2(20) + k_3 u_3(0) > k_1 u_1(0) + k_2 u_2(40) + k_3 u_3(0)$$
$$\text{or} \quad k_1(1) + k_2(0) + k_3(0) > k_1(0) + k_2(1) + k_3(0)$$
$$\text{or} \quad k_1 > k_2$$

Similarly, under the multiplicative form, $A > B$ implies

$$U(A) = \frac{[kk_1 u_1(100) + 1][kk_1 u_2(20) + 1][kk_3 u_3(0) + 1] - 1}{k}$$

$$= \frac{[kk_1 + 1] - 1}{k} = k_1$$

The same logic yields $U(B) = k_2$, and hence $A > B \rightarrow k_1 > k_2$.

C.1.3   *Relative k_i values*

Fill in the missing entry (?) such that the DM is indifferent between the following two profiles.

$$\begin{array}{cc} \text{worst} & \text{worst best} \\ \downarrow & \downarrow \quad \downarrow \\ [?, 20, 0] \text{ versus } & [0, 40, 0] \end{array}$$

Say ? = 85; read from the first curve in Figure C.1 that $u_1(85) = .4$. Under the additive form:

$$k_1 u_1(85) = k_2 \rightarrow .4k_1 = k_2$$

Under the multiplicative form:

$$\frac{[kk_1 u_1(85)]}{k} = \frac{kk_2}{k} \rightarrow .4k_1 = k_2$$

Do the same for k_1 and k_3.

$$\begin{array}{cc} \text{worst} & \text{best} \\ \downarrow & \downarrow \\ [?, 20, 0] \quad \text{versus} & [0, 20, 6] \end{array}$$

Say ? = 50% and $u_1(50) = .2$; then $.2k_1 = k_3$. So now we know that

$$k_1 > k_2 > k_3; \qquad .4k_1 = k_2 \quad \text{and} \quad .2k_1 = k_3$$

Exact k_i values: Ask for a probability level p such that the DM is indifferent between Job A for sure, and a lottery offering Jobs B and C with probabilities p and $(1 - p)$ respectively, where the job profiles are:

$$A = [100, 20, 0]$$

$\tilde{L}$:
p ——— $B = [100, 40, 6]$ (ideal job)
$1 - p$ ——— $C = [0, 20, 0]$ (worst job)

Under the *additive* form, this implies that

$$U(A) = k_1u_1(100) + k_2u_2(20) + k_3u_3(0) = k_1 = E[U(\tilde{L})]$$

where $E[U(\tilde{L})] = pU(B) + (1 - p)U(C) = p(1) + (1 - p)(0) = p$.

Hence, $k_1 = p$, and thus k_2 and k_3 can now be determined further. Say $p = .6$, then $k_1 = .6$; $k_2 = .4(.6) = .24$, and $k_3 = .2(.6) = .12$.

Since $\Sigma k_i = .96$, $U(\bar{x})$ is approximately additive (i.e., $\Sigma k_i \approx 1$).

Estimating k. Suppose that $\Sigma k_i \neq 1$ and that utility independence holds as in the Key theorem, then the *multiplicative* form must be used. The preceding lottery question implies:

$$U(A) = \frac{(kk_1u_1(100) + 1)(kk_2u_2(2) + 1)(kk_3u_3(0) + 1) - 1}{k}$$

$$= \frac{(kk_1 + 1)(1)(1) - 1}{k} = k_1 \quad \text{(same as under the additive form)}$$

$$E[U(\tilde{L})] = pU(B) + (1 - p)U(C) = p$$

Hence, again $k_1 = p$. So far we have three equations with four unknowns. The fourth equation follows from the scaling convention that $U(B) = U[100, 40, 6] = 1$. Namely,

$$U(B) = \frac{(kk_1u_1(100) + 1)(kk_2u_2(40) + 1)(kk_3u_3(6) + 1) - 1}{k} = 1$$

$$= \frac{(kk_1 + 1)(kk_2 + 1)(kk_3 + 1) - 1}{k} = 1$$

or

$$k + 1 = \prod_{i=1}^{3} [kk_i + 1]$$

So we have four equations to solve, namely:

1. $.4k_1 = k_2$ $k_1 = .6$
2. $.2k_1 = k_3$ $k_2 = .24$

3. $k_1 = p = .6$ $k_3 = .12$
4. $k + 1 = \Pi \, [kk_i + 1]$ $k = .15*$

$*(1.09)(1.036)(1.018) = 1.149566 \approx 1.15$

Conclusion: In this example $U(\mathbf{x})$ is multiplicative; that is,

$$U(\mathbf{x}) = .6u_1(x_1) + .24u_2(x_2) + .12u_3(x_3) + .0216u_1(x_1)u_2(x_2)$$
$$+ .0108u_1(x_1)u_3(x_3) + .00432u_2(x_2)u_3(x_3)$$
$$+ .0003888u_1(x_1)u_2(x_2)u_3(x_3)$$

Application. Once the utility function and scaling coefficients have been estimated, we are ready to apply the function to actual options. The next section starts with a simple numerical example (to illustrate the calculations involved) and concludes with the general case for both discrete and continuous probability distributions. For additional details and proofs, the reader is advised to consult the excellent compendium by Keeney and Raiffa (1976).

Illustration: What is the expected utility of the earlier job offer with a job satisfaction of 80%, an average annual salary of \$30,000 or \$40,000 with .8 and .2 probability respectively; and living quality of 9 or 4 points with equal chances. That is,

$$\tilde{\mathbf{Y}} = \left[80, \begin{array}{c} \overset{.8}{\diagup} 30 \\ \diagdown 40 \\ {}_{.2} \end{array}, \begin{array}{c} \overset{.5}{\diagup} 9 \\ \diagdown 4 \\ {}_{.5} \end{array} \right]$$

First reformulate $\tilde{\mathbf{Y}}$ in terms of the possible outcome vectors and their associated probabilities.

$$\tilde{\mathbf{Y}}: \begin{array}{ll} [80, 30, 9] & \text{with prob.} = (.8)(.5) = .4 \\ [80, 30, 4] & \text{with prob.} = (.8)(.5) = .4 \\ [80, 40, 9] & \text{with prob.} = (.2)(.5) = .1 \\ [80, 40, 4] & \text{with prob.} = (.2)(.5) = .1 \end{array}$$

$E[U(\tilde{\mathbf{Y}})] = .4U(80, 30, 9) + .4U(80, 30, 3) + .1U(80, 40, 9) + .1U(80, 40, 3)$

with $U(x_1, x_2, x_3)$ as calculated above. Whenever $U(Y)$ is additive, the above reformulation into outcome vectors is unnecessary, provided the $\tilde{x}_i$ are statistically independent. That is:

$E[U(\tilde{\mathbf{Y}})] = k_1u_1(80) + k_2[.8u_2(30) + .2u_2(40)] + k_3[.5u_3(9) + .5u_3(4)]$

C.2   The general case

Discrete case

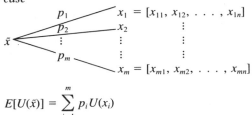

$$E[U(\bar{x})] = \sum_{i=1}^{m} p_i U(x_i)$$

If $U(x_1, \ldots, x_n) = \Sigma\, k_i u_i(x_i)$ and statistical independence holds, this simplifies to

$$\sum_{i=1}^{m} p_i U(x_i) = \Sigma\, p_i[k_1 u_1(x_{i1}) + k_2 u_2(x_{i2}) + \ldots + k_n u_n(x_{in})]$$

$$= k_1\, \Sigma\, p_i u_i(x_{i1}) + k_2\, \Sigma\, p_i u_2(x_{i2}) + \ldots + k_n\, \Sigma\, p_i u_n(x_{in})]$$

$$= k_1 E[U(\bar{x}_1)] + k_2 E[U(\bar{x}_2)] \ldots + k_n E[U(\bar{x}_n)]$$

(weighted expected utilities of attribute lotteries)

Continuous case

$$\mathbf{\bar{x}} = [\bar{x}_1, \bar{x}_2, \ldots, \bar{x}_n]$$

where $\bar{x}_i$ are random variables, and $f(x_1, x_2, \ldots, x_n)$ is their joint density function.

$$E[U(\bar{x})] = \int_{x_i^l}^{x_i^h} \ldots \int_{x_n^l}^{x_n^h} \ldots U(x_1, x_2, \ldots, x_n) f(x_1, \ldots, x_n) dx_1 dx_2, \ldots, dx_n$$

$$x_i^h = \text{highest } x_i \text{ value}$$
$$x_i^l = \text{lowest } x_i \text{ value}$$

Sources

Abel, E. *The Missile Crisis*. New York: Bantam, 1966.

Ackoff, Russell L. "Management Misinformation Systems." *Management Science*, 14, Series B, 1967, pp. 147–156.

Ackoff, Russell L. *Redesigning the Future*. New York: John Wiley, 1978.

Ackoff, Russell L., and Emery, Fred. *On Purposeful Systems*. Chicago: Aldine-Atherton, 1972.

Adams, James L. *Conceptual Blockbusting*. San Francisco: W. H. Freeman, 1974.

Adelman, Leonard. "Real-Time Computer Support for Decision Analysis in a Group Setting: Another Class of Decision Support Systems." *Interfaces*, 14 (2), March–April 1984, pp. 75–83.

Adelman, Leonard. "Supporting Option Generation." *Large Scale Systems*, 13, 1988, pp. 83–91.

Akerlof, George A. "The Market for 'Lemons': Qualitative Uncertainty and the Market Mechanism." *Quarterly Journal of Economics*, 84, Aug. 1970, pp. 488–500.

Alchian, Armen A. "Rent," in J. Eatwell, M. Milgate, and P. Newman (eds.), *The New Palgrave: A Dictionary of Economics*. London: Macmillan, 1988, pp. 141–143.

Alchian, Armen A., and Demsetz, Harold. "Production, Information Costs, and Economic Organizations." *American Economic Review*, 62 (5), Dec. 1972, pp. 777–795.

Allais, Maurice. "Le comportement de l'homme rationnel devant le risque: Critique des postulates et axioms de l'école americaine." *Econometrica* 21, 1953, pp. 503–546.

Allison, Graham T. "Conceptual Models and the Cuban Missile Crisis." *American Political Science Review*, 63 (3), 1969, pp. 689–718.

Allison, Graham T. *Essence of Decisions: Explaining the Cuban Missile Crisis*. Boston: Little, Brown, 1971.

Alter, Stephen A. *Decision Support System: Current Practice and Continuing Challenge*. Reading, Mass.: Addison-Wesley, 1980.

American Nuclear Insurers. "Nuclear Liability Insurance: Protection for the Public." Report No. 2. Mimeograph Paper, March 1989.

Amit, Raphael, and Schoemaker, Paul J. H. "Strategic Assets and Organizational Rent." *Strategic Management Journal*, 14, 1993, pp. 33–46.

Anderson, Elizabeth, Chrostowski, Paul, and Vreeland, Judy. "Risk Assessment Issues Associated with Cleaning Up Inactive Hazardous Waste Sites," in

Howard Kunreuther and Rajeev Gowda (eds.), *Integrating Insurance and Risk Management for Hazardous Wastes*. Boston: Kluwer, 1990.

Andrews, Kenneth R. *The Concept of Corporate Strategy*. New York: Dow-Jones-Irwin, 1971.

Ansoff, H. Igor. *Corporate Strategy*. New York: McGraw-Hill, 1965.

Argyris, Chris. *Strategy, Change and Defensive Routines*. Cambridge, Mass.: Harvard University, 1985.

Argyris, Chris, and Schon, Donald A. *Theory in Practice*. San Francisco: Jossey-Bass, 1974.

Argyris, Chris, and Schon, Donald A. *Organizational Learning*. Reading, Mass.: Addison-Wesley, 1981.

Arkes, H. R., and Blumer, C. "The Psychology of Sunk Cost." *Organizational Behavior and Human Decision Processes*, 35, 1985, pp. 124–140.

Armour, H. O., and Teece, David J. "Organizational Structure and Economic Performance: A Test of the Multidivisional Hypothesis." *Bell Journal of Economics*, 9 (1), 1978, pp. 106–122.

Armstrong, J. Scott. *Long-range Forecasting: From Crystal Ball to Computer*. New York: John Wiley, 1985.

Arrow, Kenneth J. *Social Choice and Individual Values*. New Haven: Yale University Press, 1963a.

Arrow, Kenneth J. "Uncertainty and the Welfare Economics of Medical Care." *American Economic Review*, 53, 1963b, pp. 941–973.

Arrow, Kenneth J. *Essays in the Theory of Risk-Bearing*. Chicago: Markham, 1971.

Arrow, Kenneth J. *The Limits of Organization*. New York: Norton, 1974.

Arrow, Kenneth J. "Risk Perception in Psychology and Economics." *Economic Inquiry*, January 20, 1982, pp. 1–9.

Asch, Solomon E. "Studies of Independence and Submission to Group Pressure." *Psychological Monographs*, 70, 1956.

Ashby, W. R. *Introduction to Cybernetics*. New York: John Wiley, 1956.

Axelrod, Robert M. *The Structure of Decision: The Cognitive Maps of Political Elites*. Princeton, N.J.: Princeton University Press, 1976.

Axelrod, Robert M. *The Evolution of Cooperation*. New York: Basic Books, 1984.

Bacharach, Michael. "Group Decisions in the Face of Differences of Opinion." *Management Science*, 22, 1975, pp. 182–191.

Bar-Hillel, Maya. "On the Subjective Probability of Compounded Events." *Organizational Behavior and Human Performance*, 9, 1973, pp. 396–406.

Bar-Hillel, Maya. "The Base-rate Fallacy in Probability Judgments." *Acta Psychologica*, 44, 1980, pp. 211–233.

Barnard, Chester I. *The Functions of the Executive*. Cambridge, Mass.: Harvard University Press, 1938.

Barnea, Amir, Haugen, Robert A., and Senbet, Lemma W. *Agency Problems and Financial Contracting*. Englewood Cliffs, N.J.: Prentice-Hall, 1985.

Barney, Jay B. "Asset Stocks and Sustained Competitive Advantage: A Comment." *Management Science*, 35, 1989, pp. 1511–1513.

Barney, Jay B., and Ouchi, William. *Organizational Economics*. San Francisco: Jossey-Bass, 1986.

Baron, D. P. "On the Utility Theoretic Foundations of Mean-Variance Analysis." *Journal of Finance*, 23 (5), Dec. 1977, pp. 1683–1697.

Baron, Jonathan. *Thinking and Deciding*. Cambridge: Cambridge University Press, 1988.

Bartlett, F. C. *Thinking*. New York: Basic Books, 1958.

Basu, Shankar, and Schroeder, Roger G. "Incorporating Judgments in Sales Forecasts." *Interfaces*, 7 (3), 1977, pp. 18–25.

Baumol, William J. *Business Behavior, Value and Growth*. New York: Macmillan, 1959.

Baumol, William J. *Economic Theory and Operations Analysis*. 4th ed. Englewood Cliffs, N.J.: Prentice-Hall, 1977.

Baumol, William J., Panzar, John C., and Willig, Robert P. *Contestable Markets and the Theory of Industry Structure*. San Diego, Calif.: Harcourt Brace Jovanovich, 1982.

Bawa, V. "Stochastic Dominance: A Research Bibliography." *Management Science* 28(6) (January 1982), 698–712.

Bazerman, Max H. *Judgment in Managerial Decision Making*. New York: John Wiley, 1986.

Bazerman, Max H., Magliozzi, T., and Neale, Margaret A. "The Acquisition of an Integrative Response in a Competitive Market." *Journal of Organizational Behavior and Human Performance*, 34, 1985, pp. 294–313.

Bazerman, Max H., and Neale, Margaret A. *Negotiating Rationally*. New York: Free Press, Macmillan, 1992.

Becker, Selwyn, and Brownson, Fred. "What Price Ambiguity? Or the Role of Ambiguity in Decision Making." *Journal of Political Economy*, 72, 1964, pp. 62–73.

Bell, David E. "Regret in Decision Making under Uncertainty." *Operations Research*, 30, 1982, pp. 961–981.

Bell, David E. "Disappointment in Decision Making under Uncertainty." *Operations Research*, 33 (1), 1985, pp. 1–27.

Bell, David E., and Raiffa, H. "Marginal Value and Intrinsic Risk Aversion," in H. Kunreuther (ed.), *Risk: A Seminar Series*. Laxenburg, Austria: International Institute for Applied Systems Analysis, 1982, pp. 325–350.

Berg, Joyce E., and Dickhaut, J. W. "Preference Reversals: Incentives Do Matter." Working Paper, Graduate School of Business, University of Chigago, Nov. 1990.

Berkowitz, L., and Walster E. *Equity Theory: Toward a General Theory of Social Interaction*. Advances in Experimental Social Psychology, Volume 9. New York: Academic Press, 1976.

Berliner, Hans. "Computer Backgammon." *Scientific American*, 242, 1980, pp. 64–72.

Bernoulli, Daniel. "Specimen Theoriae Novae de Mensura Sortis." *Commentarri Academiae Scientiarum Imperialis Petropolitanae*, 5, 1738, pp. 175–192. Translated by L. Sommer, as "Expositions of a New Theory on the Measurement of Risk," *Econometrica*, 22, 1954, pp. 23–26.

Bernoulli, Jacob. "Ars Conjectandi." 1713. Translated in Ostwald's *Klassiker der Exakten Wissenschaften*, Nos. 107 and 108. Leipzig: W. Engleman, 1899.

Bettman, James R. *An Information Processing Theory of Consumer Choice*. Reading, Mass.: Addison-Wesley, 1979.

Bettman, James R., Johnson, Eric J., and Payne, J. W. "Consumer Decision Making," in H. H. Kassarjian and T. S. Robertson (eds.), *Handbook of Consumer Behavior*. Englewood Cliffs, N.J.: Prentice-Hall, 1991, pp. 50–84.

Binmore, Kenneth, and Dasgupta, Partha (eds.). *The Economics of Bargaining*. Oxford: Blackwell, 1987.

Black, Duncan. *The Theory of Committees and Elections*. Cambridge: Cambridge University Press, 1958.

Blair, Douglas H., and Pollak, Robert A. "Acyclic Collective Choice Rules." *Econometrica*, 50 (2), 1982, pp. 931–944.

Blattberg, Robert C., and Hoch, Steve J. "Database Models and Managerial Intuition: 50% Model + 50% Manager." *Management Science*, 36 (8), Aug. 1990, pp. 887–899.

Bostic, R., Herrnstein, R. J., and Luce, R. Duncan. "The Effect on the Preference-Reversal Phenomenon of Using Choice Indifferences." *Journal of Economic Behavior and Organization*, 13 1990, pp. 193–212.

Boston Consulting Group Staff. *Perspectives on Experience*. Boston: Boston Consulting Group, 1968.

Bottger, Preston C., and Yetton, Philip W. "An Integration of Process and Decision Scheme Explanations of Group Problem Solving Performance." *Organizational Behavior and Human Decision Processes*, 42, 1988, pp. 234–249.

Bower, Joseph L., *Managing the Resource Allocation Process*. Cambridge, Mass.: Harvard University Press, 1970.

Bowman, Edward H., and Kunreuther, Howard. "Post-Bhopal Behavior at a Chemical Company." *Journal of Management Studies*, 25, 1988, pp. 387–402.

Brandstätter, H., Davis, J. H., and Stocker-Kreichgauer, G. (eds.), *Group Decision Making*. London: Academic Press, 1982.

Braybrooke, David, and Lindblom, Charles E. *A Strategy of Decision*. New York: Free Press, 1963; 2nd ed. 1970.

Brehmer, Berndt. "Cognitive Dependence on Additive and Configural Cue-criterion Relations." *American Journal of Psychology*, 82, 1969, pp. 490–503.

Brehmer, Berndt. "Social Judgment Theory and the Analysis of Interpersonal Conflict." *Psychological Bulletin*, 83, Nov. 1976, pp. 985–1003.

Brehmer, Annica, and Brehmer, Brendt. "What Have We Learned About Human Judgment from Thirty Years of Policy Capturing," in Brehmer and Joyce (1988), chap. 3, pp. 75–114.

Brehmer, Berndt, and Joyce, C. R. B. *Human Judgment: The SJT View*. Amsterdam: North-Holland, 1988.

Brunswik, Egon. "Organismic Achievement and Environmental Probability." *Psychological Review*, 50, 1943, pp. 255–272.

Brunswik, Egon. "Representative Design and Probabilistic Theory." *Psychological Review*, 62, 1955, pp. 193–217.

Burns, Tom, and Stalker, G. M. *The Management of Innovation*. London: Tavistock, 1961.

Camerer, Colin, F. "General Conditions for the Success of Bootstrapping Models." *Organizational Behavior and Human Performance*, 27, 1981, pp. 411–422.

Camerer, Colin F. "Does the Basketball Market Believe in the 'Hot Hand'?" *American Economic Review*, 79 (5), Dec. 1989a, pp. 1257–1260.

Camerer, Colin F. "An Experimental Test of Several Generalized Utility Theories." *Journal of Risk and Uncertainty*, 1989b, pp. 61–104.

Camerer, Colin F. "Recent Tests of Generalizations of Expected Utility Theory," in W. Edwards (ed.), *Utility: Theories, Measures and Applications*. Boston: Kluwer Academic Publishers, 1992, pp. 207–251.

Camerer, Colin, and Kunreuther, Howard. "Decision Processes for Low Probability Events: Policy Implications." *Journal of Policy Analysis and Management*, 8 (4), 1989, pp. 565–592.

Camerer, Colin, and Weber, Martin. "Recent Developments in Modelling Preferences: Uncertainty and Ambiguity." *Journal of Risk and Uncertainty*, 5, 1992, pp. 325–370.

Carnes, S. A., Copenhaver, E. D., Sorensen, J. H., Soderstrom, E. J., Reed, J. H., Bjornstad, D. J., and Peelle, E. "Incentives and Nuclear Waste Siting: Prospects and Constraints." *Energy Systems and Policy*, 7 (4), 1983, pp. 324–351.

Castellan, N. John. "The Analysis of Multiple Criteria in Multiple-Cue Judgment Tasks." *Organizational Behavior and Human Performance*, Oct. 1972, pp. 242–261.

Castellan, N. John. "Comments on the 'Lens Model' Equation and the Analysis of Multiple-Cue Judgment Tasks." *Psychometrika*, 38 (1), March 1973, pp. 87–100.

Castellan, N. John. "The Effect of Different Types of Feedback in Multiple-Cue Probability Learning." *Organizational Behavior and Human Performance*, Feb. 1974, pp. 44–64.

Caves, Richard E. "Industrial Organization, Corporate Strategy and Structure." *Journal of Economic Literature*, 18 (1), March 1980, pp. 64–92.

Chakravarthy, Bala S. "Adaptation: A Promising Metaphor for Strategic Management." *Academy of Management Review*, 7 (1), 1982, pp. 35–44.

Chakravarthy, Balaji S., and Lorange, Peter. *Managing the Strategy Process*. Englewood Cliffs, N.J.: Prentice-Hall, 1991.

Chamberlin, E. H. *The Theory of Monopolistic Competition*. Cambridge, Mass.: MIT Press, 1962.

Chandler, Alfred D. *Strategy and Structure: Chapters in the History of the American Industrial Enterprise*. Cambridge, Mass.: MIT Press, 1962.

Chandler, Alfred D. *The Visible Hand*. New York: McGraw-Hill, 1977.

Chandler, Alfred D. *Scale and Scope: The Dynamics of Industrial Capitalism*. Cambridge, Mass.: Belknap Press of Harvard University, 1990.

Chatterjee, Kalyan, Kersten, Gregory, and Shakun, Melvin P. (eds.). "Group

Decision and Negotiation." Focused Issue of *Management Science*, 37 (10), Oct. 1991.

Cheek, Leslie, III. "Insurability Issues Associated with Cleaning Up Inactive Hazardous Waste Sites," in Howard Kunreuther and Rajeev Gowda, (eds.), *Integrating Insurance and Risk Management for Hazardous Wastes*. Boston: Kluwer, 1990.

Chew, S. H., and MacCrimmon, Kenneth. "Alpha-Nu Choice Theory: A Generalization of Expected Utility Theory." Unpublished Manuscript, Faculty of Commerce and Business Administration, University of British Columbia, Vancouver, 1979.

Child, J., and Mansfield, R. "Technology, Size and Organization Structure." *Sociology*, 6, 1972, pp. 369–393.

Churchman, C. West. *Prediction and Optimal Decision: Philosophical Issues of a Science of Values*. Englewood Cliffs, N.J.: Prentice-Hall, 1961.

Churchman, C. West. *The Design of Inquiring Systems*. New York: Basic Books, 1971.

Clarkeson, John S. *Beyond Portfolios*. Boston: Boston Consulting Group, 1984.

Coase, Ronald. "The Nature of the Firm." *Econometrica*, 4, 1937, pp. 386–405.

Cohen, L. Jonathan. "Can Human Irrationality Be Experimentally Demonstrated?" *Behavioral and Brain Sciences*, 4, 1981, pp. 317–370.

Cohen, Michael D., March, James G., and Olsen, J. P. "A Garbage Can Model of Organizational Choice." *Administrative Science Quarterly*, 17, 1972, pp. 1–25.

Combs, Barbara, and Slovic, Paul. "Causes of Death: Biased Newspaper Coverage and Biased Judgements." *Journalism Quarterly*, 56, 1974, pp. 837–843, 849.

Condorcet, Marquis de. *Essai sur l'application de l'analyse à la probabilité des decisions rendues à la pluralité des vois*. Paris, 1785.

Cooper, Cary L. (ed.). *Theories of Group Processes*. New York: John Wiley, 1975.

Corbin Ruth. "Decisions That Might Not Get Made," in Thomas S. Wallsten (ed.), *Cognitive Processes in Choice and Decision Behavior*. Hillsdale, N.J.: Erlbaum, 1980, pp. 47–68.

Coursey, Don L., Hovis, J. L., and Schulze, William D. "The Disparity between Willingness to Accept and Willingness to Pay Measures of Value." *Quarterly Journal of Economics*, 102, Aug. 1987, pp. 679–690.

Covello, Vincent, Sandman Peter, and Slovic, Paul. "Risk Communication, Risk Statistics and Risk Comparisons: A Manual for Plant Managers," in V. T. Covello, D. B. McCallum, and M. T. Pavlova, (eds.), *Effective Risk Communication: The Role and Responsibility of Government and Nongovernment Organizations*. New York: Plenum Press, 1989, pp. 297–359.

Crouch, E. A. C., and Wilson, Richard. *Risk/Benefit Analysis*. Cambridge: Ballinger, 1982.

Cummings, Ronald G., Brookshire, David S., and Schulze, William D. *Valuing Public Goods*. Totowa, N.J.: Rowman and Littlefield, 1986.

Curley, Shawn, Yates, Frank, and Abrams, R. A. "Psychological Sources of

Ambiguity Avoidance." *Organizational Behavior and Human Decision Processes*, 38, 1986, pp. 230–56.

Cyert, Richard, and March, James. *A Behavioral Theory of the Firm*. Englewood Cliffs, N.J.: Prentice-Hall, 1963.

Dalton, D., Tudor, W., Spendolini, M., Fielding, G., and Porter, L. "Organization Structure and Performance: A Critical Review." *Academy of Management Review*, 5, 1980, pp. 49–64.

Davis, James H. "Group Decision and Social Interaction: A Theory of Social Decision Schemes." *Psychological Review*, 80, (2), March 1973, 97–125.

Dawes, Robin M., and Corrigan, B. "Linear Models in Decision Making." *Psychological Bulletin*, 81, 1974, pp. 95–106.

Dawes, Robin M. "The Robust Beauty of Improper Linear Models." *American Psychologist*, 34, 1979, pp. 571–582.

Dawes, Robin M. "Social Dilemmas." *Annual Review of Psychology*, 31, 1980, pp. 169–193.

Dawes, Robin M. *Rational Choice in an Uncertain World*. 2nd ed. San Diego: Harcourt Brace Jovanovich, 1988.

Dawes, Robin M., Faust, D., and Meehl, P. "Clinical vs. Actuarial Judgment." *Science*, 243, 1989, pp. 1668–1673.

de Bono, Edward. *Lateral Thinking*. New York: Harper and Row, 1973.

de Dombal, F. T. "Computer Aided Diagnosis of Acute Abdominal Pain: The British Experience," in J. Dowie and A. Elstein (eds.), *Professional Judgment*. Cambridge: Cambridge University Press, 1988, pp. 190–199.

DeFinetti, Bruno. "La prévision: Ses lois logiques, ses sources subjectives." *Annales de l'Institut Henri Poincaré*, 7, 1937, pp. 1–68.

DeFinetti, Bruno. *Theory of Probability: a Critical Introduction*. Vol. 1. London: John Wiley, 1974.

deGroot, Adriaan D. *Thought and Choice in Chess*. The Hague: Mouton, 1965.

De La Place, Pierre S. *A Philosophical Essay on Probabilities*. Translated by F. W. Truscott and F. L. Emory, New York: Dover, 1951.

Devinney, Timothy M. *Issues in Pricing: Theory and Research*. Lexington, Mass.: Lexington Books, D. C. Heath, 1988.

Dierickx, Ingemar, and Cool, Karel. "Asset Stock Accumulation and Sustainability of Competitive Advantage." *Management Science* 35, 1989, pp. 1504–1511.

Doherty, Michael E., and Balzer, William K. "Cognitive Feedback," in Brehmer and Joyce (1988), chap. 5, pp. 163–198.

Doherty, Neil, Kleindorfer, Paul, and Kunreuther, Howard. "An Insurance Perspective on an Integrated Waste Management Strategy," in Howard Kunreuther and Rajeev Gowda (eds.), *Integrating Insurance and Risk Management for Hazardous Wastes*. Boston: Kluwer, 1990.

Doise, W. "Intergroup Relations and Polarization in Individual and Collective Judgments." *Journal of Personality and Social Psychology*, 12, 1969, pp. 136–143.

Dowie, Mark. "Pinto Madness." *Mother Jones*, 18, Sept.-Oct. 1977, pp. 46–52.

Dorfman, Robert, Samuelson, Paul A., and Solow, Robert M. *Linear Programming and Economic Analysis.* New York: McGraw-Hill, 1958.

Douglas, Mary, and Wildavsky, Aaron. *Risk and Culture.* Berkeley, Calif.: University of California Press, 1982.

Downs, Anthony. *Inside Bureaucracy.* Boston: Little, Brown, 1967.

Driver, Michael J., and Streufert, Siegfried. "Noxity and Eucity of Information and Group Performance." *Journal of Experimental Social Psychology,* 5, 1969.

Drucker, Peter. *The Practice of Management.* New York: Harper, 1954.

Dube-Rioux, L., and Russo, J. Edward. "An Availability Bias in Professional Judgement." *Journal of Behavioral Decision Making,* 1 (4), Oct.–Dec. 1988, pp. 223–237.

Dyer, James S., and Sarin, Rakesh K. "Relative Risk Aversion." *Management Science,* 28 (8), 1982, pp. 875–886.

Easterling, Douglas, and Howard Kunreuther. *The Dilemma of Siting a Nuclear Waste Repository.* Boston: Kluwer, 1993 (in press).

Ebbesen, Ebbe B., and Konecni, V. J. "Decision Making and Information Integration in the Courts: The Setting of Bail." *Journal of Personality and Social Psychology,* 32, 1975, pp. 805–821.

Ebert, R. J., and Mitchell, T. R. "Judgement Inferences," in *Organizational Decision Processes: Concepts and Analysis.* New York: Crane, Russak, 1975, chap. 6.

Edwards, Ward. "The Theory of Decision Making." *Psychological Bulletin,* 51, 1954, pp. 380–397.

Edwards, Ward. "Conservatism in Human Information Processing," in B. Kleinmuntz (ed.), *Formal Representation of Human Judgement.* New York: John Wiley, 1968, pp. 17–52.

Einhorn, Hillel J., and Hogarth, Robin M. "Confidence in Judgment: Persistence of the Illusion of Validity." *Psychological Review,* 85, 1978, pp. 395–476.

Einhorn, Hillel J., and Hogarth, Robin M. "Behavioral Decision Theory: Processes of Judgment and Choice." *Annual Review of Psychology,* 32, 1981, pp. 53–88.

Einhorn, Hillel J., and Hogarth, Robin M. "Ambiguity and Uncertainty in Probabilistic Inference." *Psychological Review,* 92, 1985, pp. 433–461.

Einhorn, Hillel J., and Hogarth, Robin M. "Decision Making under Ambiguity." *Journal of Business* 59 (4, 2), 1986a, pp. 5225–5255.

Einhorn, Hillel J., and Hogarth, Robin M. "Judging Probable Cause." *Psychological Bulletin,* 99, 1986b, pp. 3–19.

Einhorn, Hillel J., Hogarth, Robin M., and Klemper, E. "Quality of Group Judgment." *Psychological Bulletin,* 84, 1977, pp. 158–172.

Einhorn, Hillel J., Kleinmuntz, Donald, and Kleinmuntz, Benjamin. "Linear Regression and Process-tracing Models of Judgment." *Psychological Review,* 86, 1979, pp. 465–485.

Eliashberg, Joshua, and Hauser, John. "A Measurement Error Approach for Modeling Consumer Risk Preference." *Management Science,* 31, 1985, pp. 1–25.

Ellsberg, Daniel. "Risk, Ambiguity, and the Savage Axioms." *Quarterly Journal of Economics*, 75, 1961, pp. 643–669.

Elster, Jon. *Ulysses and the Sirens*, Cambridge: Cambridge University Press, 1979.

Elster, Jon, *The Multiple Self*. Cambridge: Cambridge University Press, 1986.

Emery, Fred., and Trist, Eric L. "The Causal Texture of Organizational Environments." *Human Relations*, 18, 1965, pp. 21–32.

Eom, Hyun B., and Lee, Sang M. "A Survey of Decision Support Systems Applications (1971–1988)." *Interfaces*, 20 (3), May–June 1990, pp. 65–79.

Ericsson, K. A., and Simon, Herbert A. "Verbal Reports as Data." *Psychological Review*, 87, 1980, pp. 215–251.

Ericsson, K. A., and Simon, Herbert A. *Protocol Analysis: Verbal Reports as Data*. Cambridge, Mass.: MIT Press, 1984.

Esser, James K., and Lindoerfer, Joanne S. "Group-Think and the Space Shuttle Challenger Accident: Toward a Quantitative Case Analysis." *Journal of Behavioral Decision Making*, 2 (3), 1989, pp. 167–178.

Evans, James R. "A Review and Synthesis of OR/MS and Creative Problem Solving." *Omega International Journal of Management Science*, 17 (6), 1989, pp. 499–524.

Evans, James R., and Lindsay, William M. *The Management and Control of Quality*. St. Paul: West Publishing Company, 1989.

Evans, Leonard, Frick, Michael, and Schwing, Richard. "Is It Safer to Fly or Drive?" *Risk Analysis*, 10, 1990, pp. 239–246.

Fama, Eugene F. *Foundations of Finance*. New York: Basic Books, 1976.

Fayol, Henry. *General Industrial Management*. London: Pitman, 1949.

Feldman, M. S., and March, James G. "Information in Organizations as Signal and Symbol." *Administrative Science Quarterly*, 26, 1981, pp. 171–186.

Ferejohn, John, Forsythe, Robert, and Noll, Roger G. "Practical Aspects of the Construction of Decentralized Decision-making Systems for Public Goods," in Clifford S. Russell (ed.), *Collective Decision Making*. Baltimore: Johns Hopkins University Press, 1981.

Festinger, Leon. *Conflict, Decision and Dissonance*. London: Tavistock, 1964.

Fischhoff, Baruch. "Hindsight ≠ Foresight: The Effect of Outcome Knowledge on Judgment under Uncertainty." *Journal of Experimental Psychology: Human Perception and Performance*, 1, Aug. 1975, pp. 288–299.

Fischhoff, Baruch. "Acceptable Risk: The Case of Nuclear Power." *Journal of Policy Analysis and Management*, 2, 1983, pp. 559–575.

Fischhoff, Baruch, and Beyth, R. "'I knew it would happen' Remembered Probabilities of Once-future Things." *Organizational Behavior and Human Performance*, 13, 1975, pp. 1–16.

Fischhoff, Baruch, and Furby, Lita. "Measuring Values: A Conceptual Framework for Integrating Transaction with Special Reference to Contiguous Valuation of Visibility." *Journal of Risk and Uncertainty*, 1, 1988, pp. 147–184.

Fischhoff, Baruch, Watson, Stephen, and Hope, Chris. "Defining Risk." *Policy Sciences*, 17, 1984, pp. 123–139.

Fischhoff, Baruch. "Debiasing," in D. Kahneman, P. Slovic, and A. Tversky (eds.), *Judgment under Uncertainty: Heuristics and Biases*, Cambridge: Cambridge University Press, 1982, chap. 31, pp. 422–444.

Fishburn, Peter C. *Utility Theory and Decision Making*. New York: John Wiley, 1970.

Fishburn, Peter C. "A Comparative Analysis of Group Decision Methods." *Behavior Science*, 16 (6), Nov. 1971, pp. 538–544.

Fishburn, Peter C. "Lexicographic Orders, Utilities and Decision Rules: A Survey." *Management Science*, 20 (11), July 1974, pp. 1442–1471.

Fishburn, Peter C. "Mean-risk Analysis with Risk Associated with Below-target Returns." *American Economic Review*, 67 (2), March 1977, pp. 116–126.

Fishburn, Peter C. *The Foundations of Expected Utility*. Dordrecht, The Netherlands: D. Reidel, 1982.

Fishburn, Peter C. "SSB Utility Theory: An Economic Perspective." *Mathematical and Social Science*, 9, 1984, pp. 63–94.

Fishburn, Peter C. "A New Model for Decisions Under Uncertainty." *Economic Letters*, 21, 1986, pp. 127–130.

Fishburn, Peter C. "Uncertainty Aversion and Separated Effects in Decision Making under Uncertainty," in J. Kacprzyk and M. Fedrizzi (eds.), *Combining Fuzzy Imprecision with Probabilistic Uncertainty in Decision Making*. Berlin: Springer-Verlag, 1988.

Fishburn, Peter C. "On the Theory of Ambiguity." *International Journal of Information and Management Science*, 1992, forthcoming.

Fong, G. T. Krantz, David H., and Nisbett, Richard E. "The Effects of Statistical Training on Thinking about Everyday Problems." *Cognitive Psychology*, 18, 1986, pp. 253–292.

Forgionne, G. A. *Quantitative Decision Making*. Belmont, Calif.: Wadsworth, 1986.

French, J. R. P., and Raven B. "The Bases of Social Power," in D. Cartwright and Z. Zender (eds.), *Group Dynamics*. New York: Harper and Row, 1968, pp. 259–269.

Frey, Bruno, and Eichenberger, R. "Should Social Scientists Care about Choice Anomalies." *Rationality and Society*, 1 (1), July 1989, pp. 101–122.

Friedman, James. *Game Theory with Applications to Economics*, 2nd ed. London: Oxford University Press, 1990.

Friedman, Milton, and Savage, Leonard J. "The Utility Analysis of Choices Involving Risk." *Journal of Political Economy*, 56, 1948, pp. 279–304.

Frisch, Deborah, and Baron, Jonathan. "Ambiguity and Rationality." *Journal of Behavioral Decision Making*, 1, 1988, pp. 149–157.

Gaeth, G. J., and Shanteau, James. "Reducing the Influence of Irrelevant Information on Experienced Decision Makers." *Organizational Behavior and Human Performance*, 33, 1984, pp. 262–282.

Galbraith, Jay R. *Designing Complex Organizations*. Reading, Mass.: Addison-Wesley, 1973.

Galbraith, Jay R. *Organization Design*. Reading, Mass.: Addison-Wesley, 1977.

Gaynor, Martin, and Kleindorfer, Paul R. "Misperceptions, Equilibrium and Incentives in Groups and Organizations," in Guenter Bamberg and Klaus Spreman (eds.), *Principal–Agent Problems and Applications*. Berlin: Springer-Verlag, 1988.

Genest, Christian, and Zidek, James V. "Combining Probability Distributions: A Critique and an Annotated Bibliography." *Statistical Science*, 1 (1), 1986, pp. 114–148.

Gilovich, Thomas, Vallone, Robert, and Tversky, Amos. "The Hot Hand in Basketball: On the Misperception of Random Sequences." *Cognitive Psychology*, 17, July 1985, pp. 295–314.

Gladwell, M. "Consumers' Choices about Money Consistently Defy Common Sense." *Washington Post*, Feb. 12, 1990, p. A3.

Goldstein, William M., and Einhorn, Hillel. "A Theory of Preference Reversals." *Psychological Review* 94 (2), 1987, pp. 236–254.

Golembiewski, Robert T., and McConkie, Mark. "The Centrality of Interpersonal Trust in Group Processes," in Cary L. Cooper (ed.), *Theories of Group Processes*, New York: John Wiley, 1975, pp. 131–186.

Goodman, Paul, and Associates. *Designing Effective Work Groups*. San Francisco: Jossey-Bass, 1986.

Gordon, W. J. J. *Synectics*. New York: Harper and Row, 1961.

Grabowski, Henry, and Vernon, John. *The Regulation of Pharmaceuticals: Balancing the Benefits and Risks*. Washington, D.C.: American Enterprise Institute for Public Policy Research, 1983.

Green, Paul E., and Tull, D. S. *Research for Marketing Decisions*. 4th ed. Englewood Cliffs, N.J.: Prentice-Hall, 1978.

Grether, David M., and Plott, Charles R. "Economic Theory of Choice and the Preference Reversal Phenomenon." *American Economic Review*, 69 (4), Sept. 1979, pp. 623–638.

Grossman, Sanford, and Hart, Oliver. "An Analysis of the Principal-Agent Problem," *Econometrica*, 51, 1983, pp. 7–46.

Groves, Theodore. "Efficient Collective Choice When Compensation Is Possible." *Review of Economic Studies*, 1979, pp. 227–241

Hacking, Ian. *The Emergence of Probability*. Cambridge: Cambridge University Press, 1975.

Halperin, M. H. *Bureaucratic Politics and Foreign Policy*. Washington, D.C.: Brookings Institution, 1974.

Hammond, Kenneth R. "Probabilistic Functioning and the Clinical Method." *Psychological Review*, 62, 1955, pp. 255–262.

Hammond, Kenneth R., Hamm, R. M., Grassia, J., and Pearson, T. "Direct Comparison of the Efficacy of Intuitive and Analytical Cognition in Expert Judgement." *IEEE Transactions: Systems, Man, and Cybernetics*, 17, 1987, pp. 753–770.

Hammond, Kenneth R., Hursch C. J., and Todd, F. J. "Analyzing the Components of Clinical Inference." *Psychological Review*, 71, 1964, pp. 438–456.

Hammond, Kenneth R., Rohrbaugh, John, Mumpower, Jeryl, and Adelman, Leonard. "Social Judgment Theory: Applications in Policy Formation," in

Martin F. Kaplan and Steven Schwartz (eds.), *Human Judgment and Decision Processes in Applied Settings*. New York: Academic Press, 1977, pp. 1–27.

Hammond, Kenneth R., and Summers, D. "Cognitive Dependence on Linear and Nonlinear Cues." *Psychological Review*, 72, 1965, pp. 215–224.

Hannan, Michael T., and Freeman, John. *Organizational Ecology*. Cambridge, Mass.: Harvard University Press, 1989.

Hardin, Russell. *Collective Action*. Baltimore: Johns Hopkins University Press, 1982.

Harris, Milton, and Raviv, Artur. "Incentive Contracts with Applications to Education and Employment, Health Insurance and Law Enforcement." *American Economic Review*, 68 (1), 1978, pp. 20–30.

Harsanyi, John C., and Selten, Reinhardt. "A Generalized Nash Solution for Two-person Bargaining Games with Incomplete Information." *Management Science*, 1971, pp. 185–204.

Hauser, John R. "Consumer Preference Axioms: Behavioral Postulates for Describing and Predicting Stochastic Choice." *Management Science*, 24, Sept. 1978, pp. 1131–1141.

Hawkins, Scott A., and Hastie, Reid. "Hindsight: Biased Judgements of Past Events after the Outcomes are Known." *Psychological Bulletin*, 107 (3), 1990, pp. 311–327.

Hax, Arnoldo C., and Majluf, Nicolas S. "The Use of the Industry Attractiveness–Business Strength Matrix in Strategic Planning." *Interfaces*, 1983, pp. 77–94.

Hax, Arnoldo C., and Majluf, Nicolas S. *The Strategy Concept and Process*. Englewood Cliffs, N.J.: Prentice-Hall, 1991.

Hazen, Gordon, and Lee, Jia-Sheng. "Ambiguity Aversion in the Small and in the Large for Weighted Linear Utility." Technical Report 89-12, Department of Industrial Engineering and Management Sciences, Northwestern University, 1989.

Heath, Chip, and Tversky, Amos. "Preference and Belief: Ambiguity and Competence in Choice under Uncertainty." *Journal of Risk and Uncertainty*, 4, 1991, pp. 5–28.

Hedley, Barry. "Strategy and the 'Business Portfolio.'" *Long Range Planning*, Feb. 1977, p. 12.

Henderson, J. M., and Quandt, R. E. *Microeconomic Theory: A Mathematical Approach*. 2nd ed. New York: McGraw-Hill, 1971.

Henry, Jane (ed.). *Creative Management*. New York: Sage Publications, 1991.

Hershey, John C., Kunreuther, Howard C., and Schoemaker, Paul J. H. "Sources of Bias in Assessment Procedures for Utility Functions." *Management Science*, 28, 1982, pp. 936–954.

Hershey, John C., and Schoemaker, Paul J. H. "Risk Taking and Problem Context in the Domain of Losses: An Expected Utility Analysis." *Journal of Risk and Insurance*, 47, 1980, pp. 111–132.

Hershey, John C., and Schoemaker, Paul J. H. "Probability Versus Certainty Equivalence Methods in Utility Measurement: Are They Equivalent?" *Management Science*, 31, 1985, pp. 1213–1231.

Hey, John. "The Economics of Optimism and Pessimism: A Definition and Some Applications." *Kyklos*, 37 (2), 1984, pp. 181–205.

Hillier, Frederick, and Lieberman, Gerald. *Introduction to Operations Research*. San Francisco: Holden-Day, 1974.

Hirshleifer, Jack. *Investment, Interest and Capital*. Englewood Cliffs, N.J.: Prentice-Hall, 1970.

Hoffman, Paul J. "The Paramorphic Representation of Clinical Judgment." *Psychological Bulletin*, 47, 1960, pp. 116–131.

Hoffman, Paul J., Slovic, Paul, and Rorer, Leonard. "An Analysis-of-Variance Model for Assessment of Configural Cue Utilization in Clinical Judgment." *Psychological Bulletin*, 69, 1968, pp. 338–349.

Hogarth, Robin M. "Process Tracing in Clinical Judgment." *Behavioral Science*, 19, 1974, pp. 298–313.

Hogarth, Robin M. *Judgment and Choice*. New York: John Wiley, 1987.

Hogarth, Robin M., and Einhorn, Hillel. "Venture Theory: A Model of Decision Weights." *Management Science*, 36 (7), 1990, pp. 780–803.

Hogarth, Robin M. "Beyond Discrete Biases: Functional and Dysfunctional Aspects of Judgmental Heuristics." *Psychological Bulletin*, 90, 1981, pp. 197–217.

Hogarth, Robin M., and Kunreuther, Howard. "Risk, Ambiguity and Insurance." *Journal of Risk and Uncertainty*, 2, 1989, pp. 5–35.

Hogarth, Robin and Kunreuther, Howard. "Pricing Insurance and Warranties: Ambiguity and Correlated Risks." *Geneva Papers on Insurance*, 1992.

Holmstrom, Bengt. "Moral Hazard in Teams." *Bell Journal of Economics*, 13, 1982, pp. 324–340.

Holmstrom, Bengt, and Tirole, Jean. "The Theory of the Firm," in Richard Schmalensee and Robert D. Willig, (eds.), *Handbook of Industrial Organization*, New York: Elsevier Science Publishers, 1989, chap. 3.

Holt, Charles. "Preference Reversals and the Independence Axiom." *American Economic Review*, 76, June 1986, pp. 508–515.

Hursch, C. J., Hammond, K. R., and Hursch, J. L. "Some Methodological Considerations in Multiple-cue Probability Studies." *Psychological Review*, 71, 1964, pp. 42–60.

Hurwicz, Leonid. "The Design of Mechanisms for Resource Allocation." *American Economic Review*, 63 (2), 1973, pp. 1–30.

Huxham, C. S., and Dando, M. R. "Is Bounded-Vision an Adequate Explanation of Strategic Decision-Making Failures." *Omega*, 9 (4), 1981, pp. 371–379.

Insurance Institute for Highway Safety. *State Law Facts 1992*. Arlington, Va., July 1992.

Itami, Hiroyuki. *Mobilizing Invisible Assets*. Boston: Harvard University Press, 1987.

Janis, Irving L. *Victims of Group Think: A Psychological Study of Foreign Policy Decisions and Fiascos*. Boston: Houghton-Mifflin, 1972.

Jevons, W. S. *Essays on Economics*. London: Macmillan, 1905.

Johnson, D. M. *A Systematic Introduction to the Psychology of Thinking*. New York: Harper and Row, 1972.

Johnson, Eric J., Hershey, John, Meszaros, Jacqueline, and Kunreuther, Howard. "Framing, Probability Distortions and Insurance Decisions." *Journal of Risk and Uncertainty*, 1993 (forthcoming).

Johnson, Eric J., and Payne, John W. "Effort and Accuracy in Choice." *Management Science*, 31 (4), April 1985, pp. 395–414.

Johnson, Eric J., and Schkade, David. "Bias in Utility Assessments: Further Evidence and Explanation." *Management Science*, 35 (4), 1989, 406–424.

Jones-Lee, Michael. *The Economics of Safety and Physical Risk*. Oxford: Blackwell, 1989.

Jung, Carl G. *Psychological Types*, 1921. Translated by R. F. C. Hull and H. G. Baynes. Vol. 6 of *Collected Works of C. G. Jung*, Bollingen Series 20, Princeton, N.J.: Princeton University Press, 1971.

Jussim, L. "Self-fulfilling Prophecies: A Theoretical and Integrative Review." *Psychological Review*, 93 (4), 1986, pp. 429–445.

Kahneman, Daniel. *Attention and Effort*. Englewood Cliffs, N.J.: Prentice-Hall, 1973.

Kahneman, Daniel, and Knetsch, Jack L. "Valuing Public Goods: The Purchase of Moral Satisfaction." *Journal of Environmental Economics and Management*, 22, 1992a, pp. 57–70.

Kahneman, Daniel, and Knetsch, Jack L. "Contingent Valuation and the Value of Public Goods: A Reply." *Journal of Environmental Economics and Management*, 22, 1992b, pp. 90–94.

Kahneman, Daniel, Knetsch, Jack L., and Thaler, Richard. "Experimental Tests of the Endowment Effect and the Coase Theorem." *Journal of Political Economy*, 98 (61), Dec. 1990, pp. 1325–1348.

Kahneman, Daniel, and Tversky, Amos. "Subjective Probability: A Judgement of Representativeness." *Cognitive Psychology*, 3, 1972, pp. 430–454.

Kahneman, Daniel, and Tversky, Amos. "On the Psychology of Prediction." *Psychological Review*, 80, 1973, pp. 237–251.

Kahneman, Daniel, and Tversky, Amos. "Prospect Theory: An Analysis of Decision under Risk." *Econometrica*, 47, 1979, pp. 263–291.

Karni, Edi. *Decision Making Under Uncertainty: The Case of State-Dependent Preferences*. Cambridge, Mass.: Harvard University Press, 1985.

Karni, Edi, and Safra, Z. "'Preference Reversal' and the Observability of Preferences by Experimental Methods." *Econometrica*, 55 (3), May 1987, pp. 675–685.

Kasperson, Roger. "Six Propositions on Public Participation and Their Relevance to Risk Communication." *Risk Analysis*, 6, 1986a, pp. 275–283.

Kasperson, Roger. "Hazardous Waste Facility Siting: Community, Firm, and Governmental Perspectives," in National Academy of Engineering, *Hazards: Technology and Fairness*. Washington, D.C.: National Academy Press, 1986b.

Kaufman, Geir. "Problem Solving and Creativity," in Henry (1991), chap. 10, pp. 103–134.

Keen, Peter G. W., and Scott-Morton, Michael S. *Decision Support System: An Organizational Perspective*. Reading, Mass.: Addison-Wesley, 1978.

Keeney, Ralph L. *Value Focused Thinking*. Cambridge, Mass.: Harvard University Press, 1992.

Keeney, Ralph L., and Raiffa, Howard. *Decisions with Multiple Objectives: Preferences and Value Tradeoffs*. New York: John Wiley, 1976. (Republished. Cambridge: Cambridge University Press, 1993).

Kempton, Willett, and Neimann, Max (eds.). *Energy Efficiency: Perspectives on Individual Behavior*. Washington, D.C.: American Council for an Energy-Efficient Economy, 1987.

Khandwalla, Predip N. *The Design of Organizations*. New York: Harcourt Brace Jovanovich, 1977.

Klayman, Joshua. "On the How and Why (Not) of Learning from Outcomes," in Brehmer and Joyce, 1988, chap. 4, pp. 115–162.

Klayman, Joshua, and Ha, Young W. "Confirmation, Disconfirmation, and Information in Hypothesis Testing." *Psychological Review*, 94 (2), 1987, pp. 211–228.

Klayman, Joshua, and Ha, Young W. "Hypothesis Testing in Rule Discovery: Strategy, Structure and Content." *Journal of Experimental Psychology: Learning, Memory, and Cognition*, 15 (4), 1989, pp. 496–604.

Klein, Benjamin, Crawford, R. G., and Alchian, Armen A. "Vertical Integration, Appropriable Rents, and the Competitive Contracting Process." *Journal of Law and Economics*, 21, 1978, pp. 297–326.

Kleindorfer, Paul R., and Partovi, Fariborz. "Strategic Technology Planning." *European Journal of Operations Research*, 1989.

Kleindorfer, Paul R., and Sertel, Murat, R. "Profit-maximizing Design of Enterprises through Incentives." *Journal of Economic Theory*, 20 (3), June 1979, pp. 319–339.

Kleindorfer, Paul R., and Sertel, Murat R. "Characterizing Cooperative Solutions to Enterprise Design Problems," in Sertel (1982), pp. 227–232.

Kleindorfer, Paul R., Vetschera, Rudolf, and Seethaler, Dieter. "Spatial Bargaining Experiments with Risky Outcomes." Decision Sciences Working Paper, The Wharton School, University of Pennsylvania, Philadelphia, PA, 1992.

Knetsch, Jack L., and Sinden, Jack A. "Willingness to Pay and Compensation Demanded: Experimental Evidence of an Unexpected Disparity in Measures of Value." *Quarterly Journal of Economics*, 99, Aug. 1984, pp. 507–521.

Knight, Frank H. *Risk, Uncertainty and Profit*. Boston: Houghton Mifflin, 1921.

"Kodak to Support Values of Chemical-Site Homes." *New York Times*, June 5, 1988.

Koopmans, Tjalling C. "Stationary Ordinal Utility and Impatience." *Econometrica*, 28, 1960, pp. 207–309.

Koriat, Asher, Lichtenstein, Sarah, and Fischhoff, Baruch. "Reasons for Confidence." *Journal of Experimental Psychology: Human Learning and Memory*, 6, 1980, pp. 107–118.

Krantz, David H., Luce, Duncan R., Suppes, Patrick, and Tversky Amos. *Foundations of Measurement: Additive and Polynomial Representations*. Vol. 1. New York: Academic Press, 1971.

Kreps, David M. *Game Theory and Economic Modelling*. Oxford: Oxford University Press, 1990.

Kunreuther, Howard. *Recovery for Natural Disaster: Insurance or Federal Aid?*

Washington, D.C.: American Enterprise Institute for Public Policy Research, 1973.

Kunreuther, Howard, and Easterling, Douglas. "The Role of Fines and Insurance Incentives for Increasing Seat Belt Usage." Working Paper, Wharton Risk and Decision Processes Center, University of Pennsylvania, 1988.

Kunreuther, Howard, Fitzgerald, Kevin, and Aarts, Thomas. "Siting Noxious Facilities: A Test of the Facility Siting Credo." *Risk Analysis*, 1993 (forthcoming).

Kunreuther, Howard, Ginsberg, Ralph, Miller, L., Sagi, Phillip, Slovic, Paul, Borkan, B., and Katz N. *Disaster Insurance Protection: Public Policy Lessons*. New York: John Wiley, 1978.

Kunreuther, Howard, Hogarth, Robin, and Meszaros, Jacqueline. "Ambiguity and Market Failure." *Journal of Risk and Uncertainty*, 1993 (forthcoming).

Kunreuther, Howard, and Kleindorfer, Paul R. "Descriptive and Prescriptive Aspects of Health and Safety Regulation," in Allen R. Ferguson and Phillip E. LeVeen (eds.), *The Benefits of Health and Safety Regulation*. Cambridge, Mass.: Ballinger, 1981.

Kunreuther, Howard, Kleindorfer, Paul, Knez, Peter, and Yaksick, Rudy. "A Compensation Mechanism for Siting Noxious Facilities: Theory and Experimental Design." *Journal of Environmental Economics and Management*, 14, 1987, pp. 371–383.

Kunreuther, Howard, and Linnerooth, Joanne. *Risk Analysis and Decision Processes*. New York: Springer Verlag, 1983.

Kunreuther, Howard, and Portney, Paul. "Wheel of Misfortune: A Lottery Auction Mechanism for the Siting of Noxious Facilities." *Journal of Energy Engineering*, 117 (3), 1991, pp. 125–132.

Kunreuther, Howard, Sanderson, W., and Vetschera, R. "A Behavioral Model of the Adoption of Protective Activities." *Journal of Economic Behavior and Organization*, 6, 1985, pp. 1–15.

Kyburg, H. E., and Smokler, H. E. *Studies in Subjective Probability*. New York: John Wiley, 1964.

Laffont, Jean-Jacques. *The Economics of Uncertainty and Information*. Cambridge, Mass.: MIT Press, 1989.

Landes, William M., and Posner, Richard A. *The Economic Structure of Tort Law*. Cambridge, Mass.: Harvard University Press, 1987.

Langer, Ellen J. "The Illusion of Control." *Journal of Personality and Social Psychology* 32 (2), 1975, pp. 311–328.

Lave, Lester, and Romer, Thomas. "Specifying Risk Goals: Inherent Problems with Democratic Institutions." *Risk Analysis*, 3, 1983, pp. 217–227.

Liebenstein, Harvey. *Beyond Economic Man*. Cambridge, Mass.: Harvard University Press, 1976.

Lichtenstein, Sarah. "Bases for Preferences among Three-Outcome Bets." *Journal of Experimental Psychology*, 69 (2), 1965, pp. 162–169.

Lichtenstein, Sarah, Fischhoff, Baruch, and Phillips. Larry D. "Calibration of Probabilities: The State of the Art," in H. Jungerman and G. de Zeeuw (eds.), *Decision Making and Change in Human Affairs*. Amsterdam: D. Reidel, 1977.

Lichtenstein, Sarah, Fischhoff, Baruch, and Phillips, Larry D. "Calibration of Probabilities: The State of the Art to 1980," in Daniel Kahneman, Paul Slovic, and Amos Tversky (eds.), *Judgement under Uncertainty: Heuristics and Biases*. Cambridge: Cambridge University Press, 1982, chap. 22, pp. 306–334.

Lichtenstein, Sarah, and Slovic, Paul. "Reversals of Preference between Bids and Choices in Gambling Decisions." *Journal of Experimental Psychology*, 89 (1), 1971, pp. 140–151.

Lichtenstein, Sarah, and Slovic, Paul. "Response-Induced Reversals of Preference in Gambling: An Extended Replication in Las Vegas." *Journal of Experimental Psychology*, 101 (1), 1973, pp. 16–20.

Lindblom, Charles E. "The Science of Muddling Through." *Public Administration Review*, 19, 1959, pp. 79–88.

Lindblom, Charles E. *Politics and Markets: The World's Political–Economic Systems*. New York: Basic Books, 1977.

Lindman, Harold R. "Inconsistent Preferences among Gambles." *Journal of Experimental Psychology*, 89 (2), 1971, pp. 390–397.

Linstone, Harold A., and Turoff, Murray (eds.). *The Delphi Method*. Reading, Mass.: Addison-Wesley, 1975.

Loewenstein, George. "Anticipation and the Valuation of Delayed Consumption." *Economic Journal*, 97, Sept. 1987, pp. 666–684.

Loewenstein, George. "Frames of Mind in Intertemporal Choice." *Management Science*, 34, 1988, pp. 200–214.

Loewenstein, George, and Thaler, Richard H. "Anomalies: Intertemporal Choice." *Journal of Economic Perspectives*, 3 (4), 1989, pp. 181–193.

Loomes, Graham, and Sugden, Robert. "Regret Theory: An Alternative Approach to Rational Choice under Uncertainty." *Economic Journal* 92, 1982, pp. 805–824.

Lopes, Lola L. "Between Hope and Fear: The Psychology of Risk." *Advances in Experimental Social Psychology*, 20, 1987, pp. 255–295.

Lorange, Peter, and Vancil, Richard F. *Strategic Planning Systems*. Englewood Cliffs, N.J.: Prentice-Hall, 1977.

Luce, R. Duncan. *Individual Choice Behavior*. New York: John Wiley, 1959.

Luce, R. Duncan. "Rank-Dependent, Subjective Expected Utility Representations." *Journal of Risk and Uncertainty*, 1, 1988, pp. 305–332.

Luce, R. Duncan, and Raiffa, Howard. *Games and Decisions*. New York: John Wiley, 1957.

MacCrimmon, Kenneth R. "Understanding Strategic Decisions: Three Systematic Approaches," in J. M. Pennings and Associates (eds.), *Organizational Strategy and Change*. San Francisco: Jossey-Bass, 1985, pp. 76–98.

MacCrimmon, Kenneth R., and Larsson, S. "Utility Theory: Axioms versus 'Paradoxes'," in M. Allais and O. Hagen (eds.), *Expected Utility and the Allais Paradox*, Dordrecht, The Netherlands: D. Reidel, 1979, pp. 333–409.

MacCrimmon, Kenneth R., and Wehrung, Donald A. *Taking Risks: The Management of Uncertainty*. New York: Free Press, 1986.

Machina, Mark J. "'Expected Utility' Analysis without the Independence Axiom." *Econometrica*, 50 1982, pp. 277–323.

Machina, Mark J. "Choice under Uncertainty: Problems Solved and Unsolved." *Journal of Economic Perspectives*, 1, 1987, pp. 121–154.

Machina, Mark J. "Dynamic Consistency and Non-Expected Utility Models of Choice under Uncertainty." *Journal of Economic Literature*, 27, Dec. 1989, pp. 1622–1668.

Machlup, Fred. "Theories of the Firm: Marginalist, Behavioral, Managerial." *American Economic Review*, 57, 1967, pp. 1–33.

Mackie, J. L. *The Cement of the Universe: A Study of Causation*. Oxford: Oxford University Press, 1980.

MacLean, Douglas. "Social Values and the Distribution of Risk," in Douglas MacLean (ed.), *Values at Risk*. Totowa, N.J.: Rowman and Littlefield, 1986.

Makridakis, Spyros, Wheelwright, Stephen C., and McGee, V. E. *Forecasting: Methods and Applications*. 2nd ed. New York: John Wiley, 1983.

March, James G. "Bounded Rationality, Ambiguity, and the Engineering of Choice." *Bell Journal of Economics* 9, 1978, pp. 587–608.

March, James G. *Decisions and Organizations*. New York: Blackwell, 1988.

March, James G., and Simon, Herbert A. *Organizations*. New York: John Wiley, 1958.

March, James G., and Feldman, Martha S. "Information in Organizations as Signal and Symbol." *Administrative Science Quarterly*, 28 (2), June 1981, pp. 171–186.

March, James G., and Olsen, J. P. *Ambiguity and Choice in Organizations*. Bergen, Norway: Universites Forlaget, 1976.

March, James G., and Shapira, Zur. "Managerial Perspectives on Risk and Risk Taking." *Management Science*, 33 (11), 1987, pp. 1404–1418.

March, James G. "Variable Risk Preferences and the Focus of Attention." *Psychological Review*, 99, 1992, pp. 172–183.

Marcuse, Herbert. *One Dimensional Man*. Boston: Beacon Press, 1964.

Markowitz, Harry M. "Portfolio Selection." *Journal of Finance*, 1, March 1952, pp. 77–91.

Markowitz, Harry M. *Portfolio Selection: Efficient Diversification of Investments*. New York: John Wiley, 1959.

Marris, Robin L. *The Economic Theory of Managerial Capitalism*. Glencoe, Il: Free Press, 1964.

Marris, Robin L., and Mueller, Dennis. "The Corporation, Competition, and the Invisible Hand." *Journal of Economic Literature*, 18 (1), March 1980, pp. 32–63.

Marschak, Jacob, and Radner, Roy. *Economic Theory of Teams*. New Haven: Yale University Press, 1972.

Marwell, G., and Schmitt, D. R. *Cooperation: An Experimental Analysis*. New York: Academic Press, 1973.

Maslow, Abraham H. *Motivation and Personality*. New York: Harper and Row, 1954.

Mason, Richard O., and Mitroff, Ian I. "A Program for Research on Management Information Systems." *Management Science*, 19 (5), Jan. 1973.

Mason, Richard O., and Mitroff, Ian I. *Challenging Strategic Planning Assumptions*. New York: Wiley-Interscience, 1981.

McCaskey, Michael B. *The Executive Challenge: Managing Change and Ambiguity.* Boston: Pitman, 1982.

McCord, Mark, and de Neufville, Richard. "'Lottery Equivalents': Reduction of the Certainty Effect in Utility Assessment." *Management Science,* 32, 1986, pp. 56–60.

McKelvey, Richard D. "Intransitivities in Multidimensional Voting Models and Some Implications for Agenda Control." *Journal of Economic Theory,* 12, 1976, pp. 472–482.

McKenney, James L., and Keen, Peter. "How Managers' Minds Work." *Harvard Business Review,* 52 (2), 1974, pp. 79–90.

Mechanic, David. "Sources of Power of Lower Participants in Complex Organizations." *Administrative Science Quarterly,* 7, 1962, pp. 349–364.

Meyer, Richard F. "Preferences over Time," in Keeney and Raiffa (eds.) (1976), chap. 9, pp. 473–514.

Miles, Robert H. *Macro Organization Behavior.* Santa Monica, Calif.: Goodyear, 1980.

Miller, George A. "The Magical Number Seven, Plus or Minus Two." *Psychological Review,* 63 (2), 1956.

Miller, Gerald R., and Simons, Herbert W. (eds.). *Perspectives on Communication in Social Conflict.* Englewood Cliffs, N.J.: Prentice-Hall, 1974.

Mintzberg, Henry. *The Nature of Managerial Work.* New York: Harper and Row, 1973.

Mintzberg, Henry. "The Design School: Reconsidering the Basic Premises of Strategic Management." *Strategic Management Journal,* 11 (3), March–April 1990, pp. 171–196.

Mitchell, Deborah J., Russo, J. Edward, and Pennington, Nancy. "Back to the Future: Temporal Perspective in the Explanation of Events." *Journal of Behavioral Decision Making,* 2 (1), Jan.–March 1989, pp. 25–38.

Mitchell, Robert C., and Carson, Richard T. *Using Surveys to Value Public Goods: The Contingent Valuation Method.* Washington, D.C.: Resources for the Future, 1988.

Mitroff, Ian I., and Emshoff, James R. "On Strategic Assumption Making: A Dialectical Approach to Policy and Planning." *Academy of Management Review,* 4, 1979, pp. 1–12.

Mitroff, Ian I., and Kilmann, Ralph H. *Methodological Approaches to Social Science.* San Francisco: Jossey-Bass, 1978a.

Mitroff, Ian I., and Kilmann, Ralph H. "On Integrating Behavioral and Philosophical Systems: Towards a Unified Theory of Problem Solving." *Annual Series in Sociology,* 1, 1978b, pp. 207–236.

Mitroff, Ian I., and Kilmann, Ralph. *Corporate Tragedies.* New York: Praeger, 1984.

Mookherjee, D. "Optimal Incentive Schemes with Many Agents." *Review of Economic Studies* 51, 1984, pp. 433–446.

Moscovici, Serge. "Social Influence and Conformity," in Gardner Lindzey and Elliot Aronson (eds.), *Handbook of Social Psychology.* New York: Random House, 1985.

Moscovici, Serge, and Zavalloni, M. "The Group as a Polarism of Attitudes." *Journal of Personality and Social Psychology*, 12, 1969, pp. 125–135.

Moulin, Herve. *Game Theory for the Social Sciences*. 2nd ed. New York: New York University Press, 1986.

Murphy, Alan H., and Winkler, Robert L. "Probability Forecasting in Meteorology." *Journal of the American Statistical Association*, 79, Sept. 1984, pp. 489–500.

Myers, Isabel Briggs. *The Myers-Briggs Type Indicator*. Palo Alto, Calif.: Consulting Psychologists Press, 1962.

Myers, Isabel-Briggs. *Gifts Differing*. Palo Alto, Calif.: Consulting Psychologists Press, 1988.

Myers, Isabel-Briggs, and McCauley, Mary H. *Manual: A Guide to the Development and Use of the Myers-Briggs Type I Indicator*. Palo Alto, Calif.: Consulting Psychologists Press, 1985.

Myerson, Roger B. "Incentive Compatibility and the Bargaining Problem." *Econometrica*, 47, 1979, pp. 61–73.

Myerson, Roger B. "Optimal Auction Design." *Mathematics of Operations Research*, 6 (1), Feb. 1981, pp. 58–73.

Myerson, Roger B. *Game Theory: Analysis of Conflict*. Cambridge, Mass.: Harvard University Press, 1991.

Nash, John F., Jr. "The Bargaining Problem." *Econometrica*, 18, 1950, pp. 155–162.

Neale, Margaret A., and Bazerman, Max H. *Cognition and Rationality in Negotiation*. New York: Free Press, Macmillan, 1991.

Neale, Margaret A., Bazerman, Max H., Northcraft, Gregory B., and Alperson, Carol. "Choice Shift Effects in Group Decisions: A Decision Bias Perspective." *International Journal of Small Group Research*, March 1986, pp. 33–42.

Nelson, Richard R., and Winter, Sidney, G. *An Evolutionary Theory of Economic Change*. Cambridge, Mass.: Harvard University Press, 1982.

Neustadt, Richard E. *Presidential Power: The Politics of Leadership*. New York: John Wiley, 1960.

Newell, Allen, and Simon, Herbert A. *Human Problem Solving*. Englewood Cliffs, N.J.: Prentice-Hall, 1972.

Nisbett, Richard E., and Ross, Lee. *Human Inference: Strategies and Shortcomings in Social Judgment*. Englewood Cliffs, N.J.: Prentice-Hall, 1980.

Nisbett, Richard E., and Wilson, T. D. "Telling More Than We Can Know: Verbal Reports on Mental Processes." *Psychological Review*, 84, 1977, pp. 231–259.

Noll, Roger G., and Krier, J. E. "Some Implications of Cognitive Psychology for Risk Regulation." *Journal of Legal Studies*, 19, 1990, pp. 747–779.

Norman, Donald A. *Memory and Attention*. New York: John Wiley, 1969.

Nunamaker, Jay F., Jr., Dennis, Alan R., Valacich, Joseph S., and Vogel, Douglas R. "Information Technology for Negotiating Groups: Generating Options for Mutual Gain." *Management Science*, 37 (10), Oct. 1991, pp. 1325–1346.

Nutt, Paul. *Making Tough Decisions*. San Francisco: Jossey-Bass, 1989.

O'Hare, Michael, Bacow, Larry, and Sanderson, Deborah. *Facility Siting and Public Opposition*. New York: Van Nostrand–Reinhold, 1983.

Olson, Mancur. *The Logic of Collective Action*. Cambridge, Mass.: Harvard University Press, 1965.

Ordeshook, Peter C. *Game Theory and Political Theory*. Cambridge: Cambridge University Press, 1986.

Osborn, Alex F. *Applied Imagination*. 3rd ed. New York: Charles Scribner's Sons, 1963.

Oskamp, S. "Overconfidence in Case-Study Judgements." *Journal of Consulting Psychology*, 29, 1965, pp. 261–265.

Oster, Sharon M. *Modern Competitive Analysis*. Oxford: Oxford University Press, 1990.

Pall, Gabriel A. *Quality Process Management*. New York: Prentice-Hall, 1987.

Park, Won-woo. "A Review of Research on Groupthink." *Journal of Behavioral Decision Making*, 3, 1990, pp. 229–245.

Pattanaik, Prasanthe K. *Strategy and Group Choice*. Amsterdam: North-Holland, 1978.

Payne, John W. "Alternative Approaches to Decision Making under Risk: Moments vs. Risk Dimensions." *Psychological Bulletin*, 80 (6), 1973, pp. 493–553.

Payne, John W. "Task Complexity and Contingent Processing in Decision Making." *Organizational Behavior and Human Performance*. 16, 1976, pp. 366–387.

Payne, John W. "Contingent Decision Behavior." *Psychological Bulletin*, 92 (2), 1982, pp. 382–402.

Payne, John W., and Braunstein, M. L. "Preferences among Gambles with Equal Underlying Distributions." *Journal of Experimental Psychology*, 87, 1971, pp. 13–18.

Payne, John, Bettman, James, and Johnson, Eric. "The Adaptive Decision Maker: Effort and Accuracy in Chioce," in Robin Hogarth (ed.), *Insights in Decision Making*. Chicago: University of Chicago Press, 1990.

Peele, Elizabeth. "Innovation Process and Inventive Solutions: A Case Study of Local Public Acceptance of a Proposed Nuclear Waste Packaging and Storage Facility." *Symposium on Land Use Management*. New York: Praeger Press, 1987.

Peleg, Bezalel. *Game Theoretic Analysis of Voting in Committees*. Cambridge: Cambridge University Press, 1984.

Peltzman, Sam. *Regulation of Pharmaceutical Innovation*. Washington, D.C.: American Enterprise Institute for Public Policy Research, 1974.

Peltzman, Sam. *Regulation and Automobile Safety*. Washington, D.C.: American Enterprise Institute for Public Policy Research, 1975a.

Peltzman, Sam. "The Effects of Automobile Safety Regulation." *Journal of Political Economy*, 83, 1975b, pp. 677–725.

Penrose, Edith T. *The Theory of Growth of the Firm*. New York: John Wiley, 1959.

Pepper, Stephen C. *Concept and Quality: A World Hypothesis*, La Salle, Ill.: Open Court, 1967.

Perkins, D. *The Mind's Best Work*. Cambridge, Mass.: Harvard University Press, 1981.

Perlmuter, L. C., and Monty, R. A. "The Importance of Perceived Control: Fact or Fantasy?" *American Scientist*, 65, Nov.–Dec. 1977, pp. 759–765.

Perrow, Charles. "A Framework for the Comparative Analysis of Organizations." *American Sociological Review*, 32, April 1967, pp. 194–208.

Perrow, Charles. *Organizational Analysis: A Sociological View*. Belmont, Calif: Wadsworth, 1970.

Perrow, Charles. *Normal Accidents*. New York: Basic Books, 1984.

Petak, William, and Atkisson, Arthur. *Natural Hazard Risk Assessment and Public Policy*. New York: Springer-Verlag, 1982.

Peterson, C. R., Hammond, K. R., and Summers, D. A. "Multiple Probability Learning with Shifting Cue Weights." *American Journal of Psychology*, 78, 1965, pp. 660–663.

Pfeffer, Jeffrey. *Power in Organizations*. Marshfield, Mass.: Pitman, 1981.

Phelps, R. M., and Shanteau, James. "Livestock Judges: How Much Information Can an Expert Use?" *Organizational Behavior and Human Performance*, 21, 1978, pp. 209–219.

Phillips, Larry D. "Requisite Decision Modeling: A Case Study." *Journal of Operational Research Society*, 33, 1982, pp. 303–311.

Plott, Charles, and Levine, Michael. "A Model of Agenda Influence on Committee Decisions." *American Economic Review*, 68, 1978, pp. 146–160.

Popper, Karl R. *Conjectures and Refutations: The Growth of Scientific Knowledge*. New York: Harper and Row, 1968.

Porter, Michael E. *Competitive Strategy: Techniques for Analyzing Industries and Competitors*. New York: Free Press, 1980.

Porter, Michael E. *Competitive Advantage: Creating and Sustaining Superior Performance*. New York: Free Press, 1985.

Porter, Michael E. *The Competitive Advantage of Nations*. New York: Free Press, 1990.

Pounds, William F. "The Process of Problem Finding." *Industrial Management Review*, 11 (1), 1969, pp. 1–20.

Prahalad, C. K., and Hamel, Gary. "The Core Competence of the Corporation." *Harvard Business Review*, 68 (3), May–June 1990, pp. 79–91.

Pratt, John W., Raiffa, Howard, and Schlaifer, Robert. "The Foundations of Decisions under Uncertainty: An Elementary Exposition." *Journal of the American Statistical Association*, 59, 1964.

Pugh, D. S., Hickson, D. J., Hinnings, C. R., and Turner, C. "Dimensions of Organization Structure." *Administrative Science Quarterly*, 13, 1968, pp. 65–105.

Pugh, D. S., Hickson, D. J., Hinnings, C. R., and Turner, C. "The Context of Organization Structure." *Administrative Science Quarterly*, 14, 1969, pp. 91–114.

Quiggin, John. "A Theory of Anticipated Utility." *Journal of Economic Behavior and Organization*, 1982 (3), pp. 323–343.

Quiggin, John. "Subjective Utility, Anticipated Utility, and the Allais Paradox." *Organizational Behavior and Human Decision Processes*, 35, 1985, pp. 94–101.

Quinn, James B. "Strategic Change: Logical Incrementalism." *Sloan Management Review*, 20, 1978, pp. 7–21.

Quinn, James B. *Strategies for Change: Logical Incrementalism*. Homewood, Ill.: Richard D. Irwin, 1980.

Rabbie, J. M., Visser, L., and van Oostrum, J. "Conflict Behavior of Individuals, Dyads and Tryads in Mixed-motive Games," in Brandstätter, Davis, and Stocker-Kreichgauer, 1982, pp. 315–340.

Radner, Roy. "Repeated Principal—Agent Games with Discounting." *Econometrica*, 53, 1985, pp. 1173–1198.

Raiffa, Howard. *Decision Analysis: Introductory Lectures on Choices under Uncertainty*. Reading, Mass.: Addison-Wesley, 1968.

Raiffa, Howard. *The Art and Science of Negotiations*. Cambridge, Mass.: Harvard University Press, 1982.

Rao, R. S., and Jarvenpaa, S. L. "Computer Support of Groups: Theory-Based Models for GDSS Research." *Management Science*, 37 (10), Oct., 1991.

Rapoport, Anatol. *Two Person Game Theory*. Ann Arbor: University of Michigan Press, 1966.

Rasmusen, Eric. *Games and Information: An Introduction to Game Theory*. Cambridge: Cambridge University Press, 1989.

Rawls, John. *A Theory of Justice*. Cambridge, Mass.: Harvard University Press, 1971.

Riley, John G., and Samuelson, William F. "Optimal Auctions." *American Economic Review*, 71 (3), June 1981, pp. 381–392.

Ritov, Ilana, Hodes, Joel, and Baron, Jonathan. "Biases in Decisions about Compensation for Misfortune." Working Paper 89-11-02, Risk Management and Decision Processes Center, University of Pennsylvania, 1989.

Robertson, Leon. "Insurance Incentives and Seat Belt Use." *American Journal of Public Health*, 74, 1988, pp. 1157–1158.

Rodrick, Dani, and Zeckhauser, Richard. "The Dilemma of Government Responsiveness." *Journal of Policy Analysis and Management*, 7, 1988, pp. 601–620.

Rokeach, Milton. *The Nature of Human Values*. New York: Free Press, 1973.

Ross, Stephen. "The Economic Theory of Agency: The Principal's Problem." *American Economic Review*, 63, 1973, pp. 134–139.

Roth, Alvin E. *Axiomatic Models of Bargaining*. Berlin: Springer-Verlag, 1979.

Roth, Alvin E. "Towards a Theory of Bargaining: An Experimental Study in Economics." *Science*, 220, 1983, pp. 687–691.

Roth, Alvin E., Malouf, M. W. K., and Murnighan, J. Keith. "Sociological versus Strategic Factors in Bargaining." *Journal of Economic Behavior and Organization*, 2, 1979, pp. 153–177.

Rothkopf, Michael H., Teisberg, Thomas J., and Kahn, Edward P. "Why Are Vickrey Auctions Rare?" *Journal of Political Economy*, 1989.

Rowe, Alan, and Mason, Richard. *Managing with Style: A Guide to Understanding, Assessing and Improving Decision Making*. San Francisco: Jossey-Bass, 1987.

Rubinstein, Ariel. "Perfect Equilibrium in a Bargaining Model." *Econometrica*, 50, 1982, pp. 97–109.

Rumelhart, David E. "Schemata: The Building Blocks of Cognition," in Rand

J. Spiro, Bertram C. Bruce, and William F. Brewer, (eds.), *Theoretical Issues in Reading Comprehension*. Hillsdale, N.J.: Erlbaum, 1980.

Rumelt, Richard. "Towards a Strategic Theory of the Firm," in R. B. Lamb (ed.), *Competitive Strategic Management*, Engelwood Cliffs, N.J.: Prentice-Hall, 1984, pp. 556–570.

Rumelt, Richard. "How Much Does Industry Matter?" *Strategic Management Journal*, 3, 1991, pp. 167–696.

Russo, J. Edward. "The Value of Unit Price Information." *Journal of Marketing Research*, 14, 1977, pp. 193–201.

Russo, J. Edward., and Dosher, Barbara. "Strategies for Multiattribute Binary Choice." *Journal of Experimental Psychology: Learning, Memory & Cognition*, 9 (4), 1983, pp. 676–696.

Russo, J. Edward., Johnson, Eric J., and Stephens, DeGorah L. "The Validity of Verbal Protocols." *Memory and Cognition*, 17 (6), 1989, pp. 759–769.

Russo, J. Edward, and Leclerq, Francis. "Characteristics of Successful Product Information Programs." *Journal of Social Issues*, 47 (1), 1991, pp. 73–92.

Russo, J. Edward, and Schoemaker, Paul J. H. *Decision Traps: Ten Barriers to Brilliant Decision-Making and How to Overcome Them*. New York: Doubleday, 1989.

Saaty, Thomas L. *The Analytic Hierarchy Process*. New York: McGraw-Hill, 1980.

Saaty, Thomas L. *Multicriteria Decision Making: The Analytic Hierarchy Process*. Extended ed. RWS Publications, 1991.

Samuelson, William, and Zeckhauser, Richard. "Status Quo Bias in Decision Making." *Journal of Risk and Uncertainty*, 1 (1), March 1988, pp. 7–59.

Sarin, Rakesh, and Winkler, Robert. "Ambiguity and Decision Modeling: A Preference-Based Approach." *Journal of Risk and Uncertainty*, 5 (4), 1992, pp. 389–407.

Savage, Leonard J. *The Foundations of Statistics*. New York: John Wiley, 1954.

Schelling, Thomas C. *The Strategy of Conflict*. Cambridge, Mass.: Harvard University Press, 1960.

Schelling, Thomas C. "The Life You Save May Be Your Own," in Samuel B. Chase, Jr. (ed.), *Problems in Public Expenditure Analysis*. Washington, D.C.: Brookings Institution, 1968, pp. 127–162.

Schelling, Thomas C. *Micromotives and Macrobehavior*. New York: Norton, 1978.

Schelling, Thomas C. "Ethics, Law and the Exercise of Self-Command," in Sterling McMurrin (ed.), *The Tanner Lectures on Human Values IV*. Salt Lake City: University of Utah Press, 1983, pp. 43–79.

Schelling, Thomas C. "The Mind as a Consuming Organ," in David Bell, Howard Raiffa, and Amos Tversky (eds.), *Decision Making: Descriptive, Normative and Prescriptive Interactions*. Cambridge: Cambridge University Press, 1988, pp. 343–357.

Schkade, David, and Johnson, Eric. "Cognitive Processes in Preference Reversal." *Organizational Behavior and Human Decision Processes*, 44, 1989, pp. 203–231.

Schmeidler, David. "Subjective Probability and Expected Utility without Additivity." *Econometrica*, 57, 1989, pp. 571–587.

Schoemaker, Paul J. H. "The Role of Statistical Knowledge in Gambling Decisions: Moment vs. Risk Dimension Approaches." *Organizational Behavior and Human Performance*, 24, 1979, pp. 1–17.

Schoemaker, Paul J. H. "The Expected Utility Model: Its Variants, Purposes, Evidence, and Limitations." *Journal of Economic Literature*, 20, June 1982, pp. 529–563.

Schoemaker, Paul J. H. "Strategy, Complexity and Economic Rent." *Management Science*, 36 (10), Oct. 1990a, pp. 1178–1192.

Schoemaker, Paul J. H. "Are Risk-Attitudes Related across Payoff Domains and Response Modes?" *Management Science*, 36 (12), Dec. 1990b, pp. 1451–1463.

Schoemaker, Paul J. H. "The Quest for Optimality: A Positive Heuristic of Science?" *Behavioral and Brain Sciences*, 14, 1991a, pp. 205–245.

Schoemaker, Paul J. H. "Choices Involving Uncertain Probabilities: Tests of Generalized Utility Models." *Journal of Economic Behavior and Organization*, 16, 1991b, pp. 295–317.

Schoemaker, Paul J. H. "When and How to Use Scenario Planning: A Heuristic Approach with Illustration." *Journal of Forecasting*, 10, 1991c, pp. 549–564.

Schoemaker, Paul J. H. "Strategic Decisions in Organizations: Rational *and* Behavioral Views." *Journal of Management Studies*, 1992 (in press).

Schoemaker, Paul J. H. "Multiple Scenario Development." *Strategic Management Journal*, 1993 (in press).

Schoemaker, Paul J. H., and Hershey, John C. "Utility Measurement: Signal, Noise and Bias." *Organizational Behavior and Human Decision Processes*, 52, 1992, pp. 397–424.

Schoemaker, Paul J. H., and Waid, Carter C. "An Experimental Comparison of Different Approaches to Determining Weights in Additive Utility Models." *Management Science*, 28 (2), 1982, pp. 182–196.

Schoemaker, Paul J. H., and Waid, Carter C. "A Probabilistic Dominance Measure for Binary Choices: Analytical Aspects of a Multi-attribute Random Weights Model." *Journal of Mathematical Psychology*, 32, 1988, pp. 169–171.

Scholz, Roland W. *Cognitive Strategies in Stochastic Thinking*. Dordrecht, The Netherlands: D. Reidel, 1987.

Schubik, Martin. *Game Theory in the Social Sciences*. Cambridge, Mass.: MIT Press, 1982.

Schultze, William, and Kneese, Allen. "Risk in Benefit Cost Analysis." *Risk Analysis*, 1, 1981, pp. 81–88.

Schwalm, Norman, and Slovic, Paul. "Development and Test of a Motivational Approach and Materials for Increasing Use of Seatbelts." Technical Report PFTR 1100-82-3, Perceptronics Inc., Woodland Hills, Calif., March 1982.

Scitovsky, Tibor. "A Note on Welfare Propositions in Economics." *Review of Economic Studies*, 9, Nov. 1941, pp. 77–88.

Sebenius, J. K. "The Computer as Mediator: Law of the Sea and Beyond." *Journal of Policy Analysis and Management*, 1, 1981, pp. 77–95.

Selten, Reinhardt. "Reexamination of the Perfectness Concept for Equilibrium Points in Extensive Games." *International Journal of Game Theory*, 4, 1975, pp. 25–55.

Selznick, Philip. *Leadership in Administration: A Sociological Interpretation.* New York: Harper and Row, 1957.

Sertel, Murat R. *Workers and Incentives.* Amsterdam: North-Holland, 1982.

Sharpe, William. "A Simplified Model for Portfolio Analysis." *Management Science*, 9, 1963, pp. 277–293.

Shavell, Steven. *Economic Analysis of Accident Law.* Cambridge, Mass.: Harvard University Press, 1987.

Shiffrin, Richard M., and Atkinson, R. C. "Storage and Retrieval Processes in Long-term Memory." *Psychological Review* 76, 1969, pp. 179–193.

Shortliffe, E. H. *Computer-based Medical Consultation: MYCIN.* New York: American Elsevier, 1976.

Shrivastava, Paul. *Bhopal: Anatomy of a Crisis.* Cambridge, Mass.: Ballinger, 1987.

Siegel, Sidney. "Level of Aspiration and Decision Making." *Psychological Review*, 64, 1957, pp. 253–262.

Simon, Herbert A. "A Behavioral Model of Rational Choice." *Quarterly Journal of Economics*, 70, 1955, pp. 99–118.

Simon, Herbert A. *Administrative Behavior.* New York: Macmillan, 1957a.

Simon, Herbert A. *Models of Man.* New York: John Wiley, 1957b.

Simon, Herbert A. *Models of Thought.* New Haven: Yale University Press, 1979a.

Simon, Herbert A. "Information Processing Models of Cognition." *Annual Review of Psychology*, 30, 1979, pp. 363–396.

Simon, Herbert A. *The Sciences of the Artificial.* Cambridge: MIT Press, 1981.

Skaburskia, Andrejs. "Criteria for Compensating for the Impacts of Large Projects." *Journal of Policy Analysis and Management*, 7, 1988, pp. 668–686.

Skinner, B. F. *Beyond Freedom and Dignity.* New York: Knopf, 1969.

Sloan, Alfred. *My Years with General Motors.* New York: Doubleday, 1963.

Slovic, Paul. "Informing and Educating the Public about Risk." *Risk Analysis*, 6, 1986, pp. 403–415.

Slovic, Paul. "Perception of Risk." *Science*, 236, 1987, pp. 280–285.

Slovic, Paul, Fischhoff, Baruch, Lichtenstein, Sarah, Corrigan, B., and Combs, Barbara. "Preference for Insuring against Probable Small Losses: Insurance Implications." *Journal of Risk and Insurance*, 44 (2), 1977, pp. 237–258.

Slovic, Paul, Fischhoff, Baruch, and Lichtenstein, Sarah. "Accident Probabilities in Seat Belt Usage: A Psychological Perspective." *Accident Analysis and Prevention*, 10, 1978, pp. 281–285.

Slovic, Paul, and Lichtenstein, Sarah. "The Relative Importance of Probabilities and Payoffs in Risk Taking." *Journal of Experimental Psychology*, 78, 1968.

Slovic, Paul, and Lichtenstein, Sarah. "Comparison of Bayesian and Regression Approaches to the Study of Information Processing in Judgment." *Organizational Behavior and Human Performance*, 6, 1971, pp. 649–744.

Slovic, Paul, and Lichtenstein, Sarah. "Preference Reversals: A Broader Perspective." *American Economic Review*, 73, 1983, 596–605.

Slovic, Paul, Lichtenstein, Sarah, and Fischhoff, Baruch. "Modeling the Societal Impact of Fatal Accidents." *Management Science*, 30 (4), 1984, pp. 464–474.

Slovic, Paul, and Tversky, Amos. "Who Accepts Savage's Axiom?" *Behavioral Science*, 19, 1974, pp. 368–373.

Smith, Gerald F. "Towards a Heuristic Theory of Problem Structuring." *Management Science*, 34 (12), 1988a.

Smith, Gerald F. "Managerial Problem Identification." *Omega*, 17 (1), 1988b, pp. 27–36.

Smith, Gerald F. "Representational Effects on the Solving of an Unstructured Decision Problem." *IEEE Transactions: Systems, Man and Cybernetics*, 19, 1989, pp. 1083–1090.

Smith, Gerald F. "Heuristic Methods for the Analysis of Managerial Problems." *Omega International Journal of Management Science*, 18 (6), 1990, pp. 625–635.

Smith, V. Kerry. "Arbitrary Values, Good Causes, and Premature Verdicts: A Reaction to Kahneman and Knetsch." *Journal of Environmental Economics and Management*, 22, 1992, pp. 71–89.

Smith, V. Kerry, Desvousges, William M., Fisher, A., and Johnson, F. R. "Learning about Radon's Risk." *Journal of Risk and Uncertainty*, 1, June 1988, pp. 233–258.

Smith, Vernon L. "Microeconomic Systems as an Experimental Science." *American Economic Review*, 72 (5), Dec. 1982, pp. 923–955.

Sorenson, Theodore C. *Decision Making in the White House: The Olive Branch and the Arrows*. New York, 1963.

Sorenson, Theodore C. *Kennedy*. New York: Bantam, 1966.

Steinbruner, John D. *The Cybernetic Theory of Decision*. Princeton, N.J.: Princeton University Press, 1974.

Steiner, Ivan D. *Group Process and Productivity*. New York: Academic Press, 1972.

Steinfatt, Thomas M., and Miller, Gerald R. "Communication in Game Theoretic Models of Conflict," in Gerald R. Miller and Herbert W. Simons (eds.), *Perspectives on Communication in Social Conflict*. Englewood Cliffs, N.J.: Prentice-Hall, 1974, pp. 17–75.

Stokey, Edith, and Zeckhauser, Richard. *A Primer for Policy Analysis*. New York: Norton, 1978.

Stone, John. "A Theory of Capacity and the Insurance of Catastrophic Risks (Part I)." *Journal of Risk and Insurance*, 40, 1973, pp. 231–243.

Stoner, J. A. F. "Risky and Cautious Shift in Group Decision: The Influence of Widely Held Values." *Journal of Experimental Social Psychology*, 4, 1968, pp. 442–459.

Strotz, Robert H. "Myopia and Inconsistency in Dynamic Utility Maximization." *Review of Economic Studies*, 23, 1956, pp. 165–180.

Summers, D. A., and Hammond, Kenneth R. "Inference Behavior in Multiple-cue Tasks Involving Both Linear and Nonlinear Relations." *Journal of Experimental Psychology*, 71, 1966, pp. 751–757.

Svenson, Ola. "Are We All Less Risky and More Skillful Than Our Fellow Drivers Are?" *Acta Psychologica*, 47, 1981, pp. 143–148.

Taylor, Frederick W. *The Principles of Scientific Management*. New York: Harper and Row, 1947.

Taylor, Shelley E., and Brown, J. D. "Illusion and Well-Being: A Social Psychological Perspective on Mental Health." *Psychological Bulletin*, 193 (2), 1988, pp. 193–210.

Teece, David J. "Towards an Economic Theory of the Multiproduct Firm." *Journal of Economic Behavior and Organization*, 3, 1982, pp. 39–63.

Teece, David J., Pisano, G., and Shuen, A. "Firm Capabilities, Resources and the Concept of Strategy." Working Paper, University of California at Berkeley, 1990.

Teilhard de Chardin, Pierre. *The Phenomenon of Man*. New York: Harper and Brothers, 1959.

Thaler, Richard H. "Toward a Positive Theory of Consumer Choice." *Journal of Economic Behavior and Organization*, 1, 1980, pp. 39–50.

Thaler, Richard H. "Some Empirical Evidence on Dynamic Inconsistency." *Economic Letters*, 8, 1981, pp. 201–207.

Thaler, Richard H. "Illusions and Mirages in Public Policy." *The Public Interest*, 73, 1983, pp. 60–74.

Thaler, Richard H. "Mental Accounting and Consumer Choice." *Marketing Science*, 4, (3), 1985, pp. 199–214.

Thaler, Richard H. "Anomalies: Saving, Fungibility, and Mental Accounts." *Journal of Economic Perspectives*, 4 (1), 1990, pp. 193–205.

Thaler, Richard H., and Shefrin, H. M. "An Economic Theory of Self-Control." *Journal of Political Economy*, 89, 1981, pp. 392–405.

Thompson, James D. *Organizations in Action*. New York: McGraw-Hill, 1967.

Thompson, Michael. "Postscript: A Cultural Basis for Comparison," in Howard Kunreuther and Joanne Linnerooth (eds.), *Risk Analysis and Decision Processes*. New York: Springer-Verlag, 1983.

Tietz, R. (ed.). *Aspiration Levels in Bargaining and Economic Decision Making*. Lecture Notes in Economics and Mathematical Systems, 213. Berlin: Springer-Verlag, 1983b.

Tirole, Jean. *The Theory of Industrial Organization*. Cambridge, Mass.: MIT Press, 1989.

Tolman, Edward C. *Purposive Behavior in Animals and Men*. New York: Appleton-Century, 1932.

Tomer, John F. "Working Smarter the Japanese Way: The X-Efficiency of Theory Z Management," in Paul R. Kleindorfer (ed.), *The Management of Productivity and Technology in Manufacturing*. New York: Plenum Press, 1985, pp. 199–224.

Toulmin, Stephen E. *The Uses Of Argument*. Cambridge: Cambridge University Press, 1958.

Tversky, Amos. "Intransitivity of Preferences." *Psychological Review*, 76, 1969, pp. 31–48.

Tversky, Amos. "Elimination by Aspects: A Theory of Choice." *Psychological Review*, 79, 1972, pp. 281–299.

Tversky, Amos, and Kahneman, Daniel. "Availability: A Heuristic for Judging Frequency and Probability." *Cognitive Psychology*, 5 (2), 1973, pp. 207–232.

Tversky, Amos, and Kahneman, Daniel. "Judgments under Uncertainty: Heuristics and Biases." *Science*, 185, 1974, pp. 1124–1131.

Tversky, Amos, and Kahneman, Daniel. "Causal Schemas in Judgements under Uncertainty," in M. Fishbein (ed.), *Progress in Social Psychology*, Hillsdale, N.J.: Erlbaum, 1980.

Tversky, Amos, and Kahneman, Daniel. "The Framing of Decisions and the Psychology of Choice." *Science*, 211 1981, pp. 453–458.

Tverky, Amos, and Kahneman, Daniel. "Extensional versus Intuitive Reasoning: The Conjunction Fallacy in Probability Judgement." *Psychological Review*, 90, 1983, pp. 293–315.

Tversky, Amos, and Kahneman, Daniel. "Rational Choice and the Framing of Decisions." *Journal of Business* 59 (4, 2), 1986, pp. 5251–5284.

Tversky, Amos, and Kahneman, Daniel. "Loss Aversion in Riskless Choice: A Reference Dependent Model." *Quarterly Journal of Economics*, 106 (4), Nov. 1991, pp. 1039–1062.

Tversky, Amos, and Kahneman, Daniel. "Advances in Prospect Theory: Cumulative Representation of Uncertainty." *Journal of Risk and Uncertainty*, 5 (4), 1992, pp. 297–323.

Tversky, Amos, Sattath, S., and Slovic, P. "Contingent Weighting in Judgment and Choice." *Psychological Review*, 95, July 1988, pp. 371–384.

Tversky, Amos, Slovic, P., and Kahneman, D. "The Causes of Preference Reversal." *American Economic Review*, 80, March 1990, pp. 204–217.

Tversky, Amos, and Thaler, R. H. "Anomalies: Preference Reversals." *Journal of Economic Perspectives*, 4 (2), 1990, pp. 201–211.

Ullman, D. G., and Doherty, Michael E. "Two Determinants of the Diagnosis of Hyperactivity: The Child and the Clinician." *Advances in Developmental and Behavioral Pediatrics*, 5, 1984, pp. 167–219.

Underwood, Benton J. "Attributes of Memory." *Psychological Review*, 76, 1969, pp. 559–573.

Underwood, G. *Attention and Memory*. New York: Pergamon Press, 1976.

Van de Ven, Andrew, and Joyce, William. (eds.). *Assessing Organizational Design and Performance*. New York: John Wiley, 1981.

Van Gundy, Arthur B. *Creative Problem Solving, A Guide for Trainers and Managers*. New York: Quorum Books, 1987.

Vickrey, William. "Counter Speculation, Auctions and Competitive Sealed Tenders." *Journal of Finance*, 16, 1961, pp. 8–37.

Viscusi, W. Kip. *Reforming Products Liability*. Cambridge, Mass.: Harvard University Press, 1991.

Viscusi, W. Kip. *Fatal Tradeoffs*. New York: Oxford University Press, 1992.

Viscusi, W. Kip, and Magat, Wesley. *Learning about Risk*. Cambridge, Mass.: Harvard University Press, 1987.

Viscusi, W. Kip, Magat, Wesley A., and Huber, Joel. "The Effect of Risk Information on Precautionary Behavior," in W. K. Viscusi and W. A. Magat (eds.), *Learning about Risk*. Cambridge, Mass.: Harvard University Press, 1987a.

Viscusi, W. Kip, Magat, Wesley A., and Huber, Joel. "An Investigation of the Rationality of Consumer Valuations of Multiple Health Risks." *RAND Journal of Economics*, 18, 1987b, pp. 465–479.

von Mises, R. *Mathematical Theory of Probability and Statistics*. New York: Academic Press, 1964.

von Neumann, John, and Morgenstern, Oskar. *Theory of Games and Economic Behavior*. New York: John Wiley, 1944. 2nd ed., 1947.

von Winterfeldt, Detlof, and Edwards, Ward. *Decision Analysis and Behavioral Research*. Cambridge: Cambridge University Press, 1986.

Vroom, Victor H., and Yettin, P. W. *Leadership and Decision Making*. Pittsburgh: University of Pittsburgh Press, 1973.

Wack, Pierre. "Scenarios: Uncharted Waters Ahead." *Harvard Business Review*, 63 (5), Sept. 1985a, pp. 72–89.

Wack, Pierre. "Scenarios: Shooting the Rapids." *Harvard Business Review*, 63 (6), Nov. 1985, pp. 139–150.

Wakker, Peter. "Nonexpected Utility as Aversion of Information." *Journal of Behavioral Decision Making*, 1 (3), July–Sept. 1988, pp. 169–176.

Wallsten, Thomas. "The Costs and Benefits of Vague Information," in Robin Hogarth (ed.), *Insights in Decision Making*. Chicago: University of Chicago Press, 1980.

Waugh, Nancy C., and Norman, Donald A. "Primary Memory." *Psychological Review*, 2, 1965, pp. 89–104.

Weber, Martin, and Camerer, Colin. "Recent Developments in Modelling Preferences under Risk." *OR Spektrum*, 9, 1987, pp. 129–151.

Weber, Max. *The Theory of Social and Economic Organization*. Translated by A. M. Henderson and T. Parsons. Oxford: Oxford University Press, 1947.

Weinstein, Neil D. (ed.). *Taking Care: Understanding and Encouraging Self-Protective Behavior*. Cambridge: Cambridge University Press, 1987.

Wernerfelt, Birger. "A Resource-based View of the Firm." *Strategic Management Journal*, 5, 1984, pp. 171–180.

Wessel, David. "Seabrook Unit Faces Licensing Hurdle as Dukakis Rejects Evacuation Plans." *Wall Street Journal*, Sept. 22, 1986, p. 10.

Whyte, William F. "The Web of Word of Mouth." *Fortune*, Nov. 1954.

Wierzbicki, Andrjez. "Interactive Decision Analysis and Interpretative Computer Intelligence," in M. Grauer and A. P. Wierzbicki (eds.), *Interactive Decision Analysis*, Lecture Notes in Economics and Mathematical Systems No. 229, New York: Springer-Verlag, 1984, pp. 22–30.

Wildavsky, Aaron B. *The Politics of the Budgetary Process*. 3rd ed. Boston: Little, Brown, 1979.

Williams, Allan, and Lund, Adrian. "Seat Belt Use Laws and Occupant Crash Protection in the United States." *American Journal of Public Health*, 76, 1986, pp. 1438–1442.

Williamson, Oliver E. *The Economics of Discretionary Behavior: Managerial*

Objectives in a Theory of the Firm. Englewood Cliffs, N.J.: Prentice-Hall, 1964.

Williamson, Oliver E. *Markets and Hierarchies: Analysis and Anti-Trust Implications*. New York: Free Press, 1975.

Williamson, Oliver E. "The Modern Corporation: Origins, Evolution, Attributes." *Journal of Economic Literature*, 19, 1981, pp. 1537–1568.

Williamson, Oliver E. *The Economic Institutions of Capitalism*. New York: Free Press, 1985.

Williamson, Oliver E. "Transaction Cost Economics," in R. Schmalensee and R. D. Willig (eds.), *Handbook of Industrial Organization*, Vol. 1. New York: Elsevier Science Publishers, 1989.

Williamson, Oliver E. (ed.). *Organizational Theory*. Oxford: Oxford University Press, 1990.

Wilson, Richard. "Analyzing the Daily Risks of Life." *Technology Review*, 81, 1979, pp. 40–46.

Wilson, Robert. "The Theory of Syndicates." *Econometrica*, 36 (1), 1968, pp. 119–132.

Winkler, Robert L. "Combining Probability Distributions from Dependent Information Sources." *Management Science*, 27, April 1981, pp. 479–488.

Woodward, Joan. *Management and Technology*. London: H.M.S.O. Press, 1958.

Woodward, Joan. *Industrial Organization Theory and Practice*. Oxford: Oxford University Press, 1965.

Wright, George, and Phillips, Larry D. "Cultural Variation in Probabilistic Thinking: Alternative Ways of Dealing With Uncertainty." *International Journal of Psychology*, 15, 1980, pp. 239–257.

Yaari, Menachem E. "The Dual Theory of Choice under Risk." *Econometrica*, 55 (1), Jan. 1987, pp. 95–115.

Yates, Frank J. *Judgment and Decision Making*. Englewood Cliffs, N.J.: Prentice-Hall, 1990.

Zeckhauser, Richard. "Coverage for Catastrophic Illness." *Public Policy*, 21, 1973, pp. 149–172.

Zeckhauser, Richard, and Viscusi, W. Kip. "Risk within Reason." *Science*, 248, 1990, pp. 559–564.

Zeleny, Milan. "Descriptive Decision Making and Its Applications," in R. L. Schultz (ed.), *Applications of Management Science*. Greenwich, Conn.: JAI Press, 1981, vol. 1, pp. 327–388.

Zeuthen, F. *Problems of Monopoly and Economic Welfare*. London: G. Routledge, 1933.

Subject index

additive independence condition, 139
additive models, 123–127
additive value functions, 119
adjustment heuristic, 96
agency theory, 338
agenda control, group decisions, 265–267
air bag installation, 382
air travel risks, 378
alerting systems, 49
Allais paradox, 146–149, 170–171
alternative generation; *see also* creativity
  creativity in, 55–58
  descriptive aspects, 52–58
  isolation of, 53–54
  prescriptive aspects, 58–62
  self-imposed constraints, 56–58, 61–62
altruism, in game theory, 244–245
ambiguity
  aversion to, 166–167
  and insurance costs, 372–373
  and organizational structure, 342
  and risky choice, 165–167
analogies, in alternative generation, 60
analytical hierarchy process, 224
anchoring heuristic, 96
anticipated utility model, 159–160, 175
anticipation effect, 153–155
Arrow's theorem, 264–266, 264n9
aspiration levels, 41–42
asset integration, 151
Aston studies, 328
attention, 29–35
  management of, 46–49, 292
  and memory limits, 34–35
  problem-finding pitfalls, 44–45
attributes, valuation of, 116–119
auction framework, 270–276, 375–377
automobile safety, 346; *see also* seat belt use
availability heuristic, 94–95
  and bias, 94–95
  correction of, 362–363
  in managerial decisions, 322

and risk decisions, 353, 362–363
and scenario construction, 106

backings, in theory of arguments, 84–85
balance principle, 180, 198
bargaining, 253–260
  Nash model, 255–260
base rate ignorance, 87–92
Bay of Pigs fiasco, 216–217
Bayesian framework, 87, 232–233
benefit–cost calculations
  in safety estimates, 353
  and social policy, 355–356, 367
Bhopal, India disaster, 352
bias
  availability heuristic, 94–95
  and base rates ignorance, 87–92
  classification, 87
  and expected utility theory, 141–145
  in group decisions, 233–236
  in judgment under uncertainty, 83–100
  and recall, 113–114
  in risk information, 350–351, 361–367
  overweighting of concrete data in, 91–92
bootstrapping
  and cognitive orientation, 207
  in Lens model, 75–76
  prescriptive approach, 182–185, 197–201
  regression estimates, 81–82
Borda rule, 263–266
Boston Consulting Group, 310–312
bounded rationality, 221–222, 317, 395–397
brainstorming
  and creativity, 59
  electronic support, 222
bubble charts, 310–312
bureaucratic model, 323

calibration curves, 97–99
capacity planning problem, 189–192